ST. AUGUSTINE
THE LITERAL MEANING
OF GENESIS

DE GENESI AD LITTERAM

ANCIENT CHRISTIAN WRITERS

THE WORKS OF THE FATHERS IN TRANSLATION

EDITED BY

JOHANNES QUASTEN   WALTER J. BURGHARDT
THOMAS COMERFORD LAWLER

No. 41

ST. AUGUSTINE

THE LITERAL MEANING

OF GENESIS

TRANSLATED AND ANNOTATED

BY

JOHN HAMMOND TAYLOR, S.J.

Gonzaga University
Spokane, Washington

Volume I
BOOKS 1–6

PAULIST PRESS

New York / Mahwah

Library of Congress
Catalog Card Number: 82-61742

ISBN: 0-8091-0326-5

PUBLISHED BY PAULIST PRESS
997 Macarthur Blvd.
Mahwah, NJ 07430

PRINTED AND BOUND IN THE UNITED STATES OF AMERICA

CONTENTS

INTRODUCTION

AUGUSTINE'S STUDIES ON GENESIS

The interpretation of the creation narrative in the Book of Genesis was a subject that repeatedly occupied Augustine's mind throughout the years from his earliest days as a layman following his baptism in Milan in A.D. 387 until his advanced years when he was Bishop of Hippo. The reason for his preoccupation is not far to seek. As a young man in Carthage he had been an auditor in the Manichean religion, and because of this experience he had become deeply aware of the need to refute the dualism of the Manichees and to defend the reliability of the Old Testament against their attacks. In opposition to the Manichean doctrine of two ultimate principles, the principles of light and darkness, he constantly defended the teaching of Genesis that God created from nothing all that is outside of Himself and that He saw that it was good.

Augustine first attempted to expound the creation narrative in a work called *De Genesi contra Manichaeos libri duo (A Commentary on Genesis: Two Books against the Manichees)*, written immediately after his return from Italy to Africa in 388, when he established a monastery in Tagaste before his ordination to the priesthood.[1] In this work he tried to discover the literal meaning of every statement in the text of Genesis, but where he found that impossible, he resorted to allegorical interpretation. This is what he himself says of this work:

> Shortly after my conversion I wrote two books against the Manichees, who are in error not because they are mistaken in their interpretation of the Old Testament but because they completely reject it with impious scorn. I wanted without delay either to refute their aberrations or

to direct them to seek in the books which they hated the faith taught by Christ and the Gospels. At that time I did not see how all of Genesis could be taken in the proper sense, and it seemed to me more and more impossible, or at least scarcely possible or very difficult, for all of it to be so understood. But not willing to be deterred from my purpose, whenever I was unable to discover the literal meaning of a passage, I explained its figurative meaning as briefly and as clearly as I was able, so that the Manichees might not be discouraged by the length of the work or the obscurity of its contents and thus put the book aside. I was mindful, however, of the purpose which I had set before me and which I was unable to achieve, that is, to show how everything in Genesis is to be understood first of all not in the figurative but in the proper sense. . . . [2]

Dissatisfied with the results he had achieved in this work, Augustine returned to the same subject about three years later, this time attempting a literal commentary throughout. However, he found the task too much for him and gave it up before completing it. He called this work *De Genesi ad litteram inperfectus liber (The Literal Meaning of Genesis: An Unfinished Book).*[3] Years later, in his review of all his works four years before his death, he makes these remarks on this unfinished commentary:

When I wrote the two books on Genesis against the Manichees, I interpreted the words of Scripture according to the allegorical meaning, not venturing to expound the deep mysteries of nature in the literal sense, that is, to explain the text according to its proper historical meaning. However, in this book I wanted to see what I could accomplish in the laborious and difficult task of literal interpretation; and I collapsed under the weight of a burden I could not bear. Before completing even one book, I gave up a task that was too much for me.

But in the process of reviewing my writings this treatise in its unfinished state came into my hands. I had not published it and had decided to destroy it because I had subsequently written a work in twelve books entitled *The Literal Meaning of Genesis;* and although in that work one will encounter more questions raised than answers found, nevertheless the earlier work cannot be compared in any way with the later one. But after reviewing this unfinished book, I resolved to preserve it as evidence (which I believe useful) of my early efforts in examining and explaining the word of God, and I decided to call it *The Literal Meaning of Genesis: An Unfinished Book.*[4]

He then goes on to tell us that on the occasion of his writing the *Retractations,* he added a passage at the end (no more than sections 61 and 62 in Migne's edition), but that with this added he left the work unfinished. Furthermore, he observes that he feels no need to make any detailed critical comments on the work, since he can refer his readers to his large commentary in twelve books.

Once again, in Books 12 and 13 of his *Confessions* (397-401), Augustine (by now the Bishop of Hippo) turned his attention to the meaning of the first chapter of Genesis; and in his explanation of the text, he employed both the literal and the allegorical method. Thus, in explaining the words, *In the beginning God made heaven and earth*, he first takes "heaven" to mean "the heaven of heavens," that is, the angels, and "earth" to mean the whole material universe (including the firmament and heavenly bodies) in an unformed state.[5] This is the literal sense. But farther on, without rejecting the literal meaning, he suggests an allegorical meaning also and interprets "heaven" to refer to spiritual men and "earth" to refer to carnal men.[6] This is only one example of the method he follows throughout Books 12 and 13 of the *Confessions.*

Many readers have wondered about the connection of these last two books with the rest of the *Confessions,* but one must remember that that work is not simply an autobiography nor is it merely a confession of sin. It is essentially a book of devout reflections by the saint on the wonder of God's goodness to him, and it is primarily a *confessio laudis* (a confession of praise) rather than a mere *confessio peccati* (a confession of sin). In keeping with this purpose, therefore, Augustine turns to the first chapter of Genesis to meditate on creation and to proclaim the goodness of his Creator, thus bringing his *Confessions* to an end in the spirit in which he began when at the beginning of the first book he exclaimed with the Psalmist: *Great art Thou, O Lord, and greatly to be praised; great is Thy power and Thy wisdom infinite.*[7]

At last, in the year 401, Augustine began his great commentary *De Genesi ad litteram libri duodecim (The Literal Meaning of Genesis: A Commentary in Twelve Books).* Of this work he says in his *Retractations:* "The title of these book is *De Genesi ad litteram,* that is, not according to allegorical meanings but according to the proper historical sense. In this work there are more questions raised than answers found, and of the answers found not many have been established for certain. Those that are not certain have been proposed for further study."[8]

In these modest words the author refers to one of the major works of his long and productive life and one of the classics of patristic exegesis. He started this commentary a year after he had begun his work on *The Trinity* and worked on it for fourteen years, completing it in 415, one year before finishing the *De Trinitate.* It is interesting to note that in 413, before he had completed either of these treatises, he began *The City of God,* so that for a period of two years he had these three works in progress. They are, as Vernon J. Bourke has noted, the major works of the mature mind of St. Augustine, treating God and the soul *(The Trinity),* God and the created world *(The Literal Meaning of Genesis),* and God and society *(The City of God).*[9]

This commentary was not chronologically the final word Augustine was to say on creation, for two years after the completion of it[10] he recorded in the eleventh book of *The City of God* his thoughts on creation in connection with the origin and nature of the two cities.[11] But that short treatment, with its special purpose within the framework of *The City of God,* is not intended to modify what had been said in his major work on Genesis; indeed, it can be properly understood only in the light of this work.

The Literal Meaning of Genesis, then, is an exhaustive commentary on the text of Genesis from the beginning of chapter 1 to the end of chapter 3. It is explicitly and consistently a literal commentary. On those rare occasions where Augustine alludes to a possible allegorical interpretation, he soon recalls himself from his wanderings and reminds himself that he is searching for the literal meaning.

To the understanding of the text Augustine did not bring the philological learning of a commentator like Jerome, whose vast erudition he deeply admired. He knew no Hebrew, but, as van der Meer has said, "it would be difficult to point to a man who was more completely filled by Holy Scripture than was Augustine. Origen is the learned visionary, Jerome the 'three-tongued' scholar, but Augustine is, above all, the believing Bible student.... He literally lived in Holy Scripture...."[12]

Augustine's knowledge of Greek was on an elementary level, and when he was beginning his commentary on Genesis in 401 it was almost nonexistent. In his later years, however, he studied the language assiduously, and when he was an old man he had a modest ability in reading Greek.[13] The Old Latin translation of the Old Testament which Augustine had at hand and which was used in the churches of North Africa was based on the Greek of the Septuagint, not on the Hebrew text. But there was not a uniform Latin text; indeed, there were as many forms of the text as there were manuscripts, as St. Jerome observed in his preface to the Book of Joshua.[14] But as Augustine became more and more immersed in scriptural exegesis, he became ever more diligent in studying the Greek text and in revising the Latin version in the light of the Greek. In numerous passages in the later books of this commentary there is evidence to show that Augustine was carrying on this sort of revision.[15]

The universal Church in the fifth century held the Septuagint version in the highest esteem, and St. Augustine was among those who believed that it had been inspired by the Holy Spirit.[16] In his mind the fact that it had such authority in the Church was a guarantee of its unique character. No Scripture scholar today, of course, would attribute such great authority to this translation, but it is universally recognized as an important witness to the text. Augustine surely was engaged in a scholarly enterprise when, with no knowledge of Hebrew, he conscientiously tried to control an often faulty Latin translation by constant reference to the Septuagint. For the convenience of the reader, I have given in Appendix 2 the text of Genesis as Augustine quotes it in this work. In those places where he gives variants, I have put down the text as he quotes it the first time without indicating any later variants. Variants that are important are pointed out in the notes.

Whatever Augustine's ability in Greek in his old age, he was not able to read the Greek Fathers in the original at the time he was writing this commentary. But it seems almost certain that he had read in Latin translations two important Greek works on the first book of Genesis: St. Basil's *In Hexaemeron* translated by Eustathius and Origen's *In Genesim homiliae* translated by Rufinus.[17] Among the Christian Latin writers whose opinions Augustine considered in the preparation of this work, Tertullian is to be numbered for certain, and probably Cyprian, Lactantius, Marius Victorinus, Ambrose, and Tyconius. And since a thorough commentary on Genesis 1–3 demanded an enormous range of human learning, the extent of Augustine's reading in the subjects treated in his commentary must have been very great. The reader senses that Augustine has covered to some extent the learned works of the classical world (in so far as they are relevant to his investigations), whether in complete works or in florilegia, whether in the original or in translation, in such fields as philosophy, mathematics, physics, natural history, geography, medicine, anatomy, physiology, and psychology. In many of these fields Augustine's knowledge may be superficial, but his curiosity is amazing and his ability to bring so much diversified learning to bear on a text is truly extraordinary.

But, above all, this commentary is the work of a theologian and exegete whose purpose is to understand, as far as possible, what God has revealed in Holy Scripture. If he is interested in philosophical problems (and the notes will show how much Plotinus has influenced his thinking, expecially in Book 1), it is philosophy seen in the light of eternal truth taught us by the inspired word of God.

THE LITERAL MEANING OF GENESIS: A COMMENTARY IN TWELVE BOOKS

This commentary deals not with the whole of the Book of Genesis but only with the first three chapters, that is, from the beginning of creation to the expulsion of Adam and Eve from Paradise. It is divided into three parts. The first part, containing Books 1–5, covers the works of creation and God's rest on the seventh day. The second part, containing Books 6–11, covers problems concerning Adam's body and soul, the Garden of Paradise, the creation of the woman, the origin of the souls of Adam's descendants, the Fall, and the expulsion from Paradise. The third part, Book 12, deals with the meaning of Paradise in the Second Epistle to the Corinthians.

It is a thorough and conscientious study of the text, in which Augustine proceeds verse by verse examining the words of the inspired writer in an attempt to discover the literal (not the allegorical) meaning of the narrative. It is thorough because he searches out all available knowledge to illuminate the text, weighing the opinions of men of science in the ancient world as well as the inspired word of God in the Old and New Testaments. It is conscientious because he is careful to distinguish what is of the faith from what is based on human reason and to recognize the difference between what is established for certain and what is merely a hypothesis or thoery. Moreover, in suggesting some of his own cherished theories, he has the honesty to examine opposing theories fairly and dispassionately and to admit the weaknesses in his own.

In a work such as this, which incorporates so much of the scientific theories of the ancient world, there are bound to be many tedious passages of speculation which is outdated and which can appeal only to an antiquarian curiosity. But in spite of this limitation the commentary has a perennial interest, because for the most part it deals with fundamental problems of philosophy and theology which are independent of the scientific theories of any given age.

In the first five books Augustine treats such questions as adumbrations of the Trinity in the hexaemeron, the theory of simultaneous creation, the meaning of the "days" of creation, morning and evening and angelic knowledge, the didactic purpose of the narrative in terms of days, the meaning of God's rest on the seventh day, the relationship of the second creation narrative to the first, the divine governance of the world, and the theory of causal reasons.[18]

In Books 6 to 11 Augustine takes up such interesting questions as the creation of Adam's body and soul, the difference between a natural body and a spiritual body, Paradise and the command given to Adam, the tree of life and the tree of the knowledge of good and evil, the creation of Eve, the mystery of the creation of Eve and the origin of the Church, the threefold good of marriage,[19] the question of procreation on the supposition that Adam and Eve had not sinned, theories concerning the origin of human souls, the practice of infant baptism, the nature of the sin of Adam and Eve, the reason why God allows the unjust to sin, death and concupiscence as the result of original sin, and the punishment of Adam and Eve.

Book 12 at first sight seems to have a very tenuous connection with a commentary on Genesis, and it is indeed an appendix, an essay on the meaning of Paradise, or the third heaven, to which St. Paul (2 Cor. 12.2–4) says he was carried in ecstasy. Augustine's reason for appending this essay to the commentary on Genesis is his desire to search out the meaning or meanings of Paradise in Scripture. In any case it is an important treatise for any student of Augustine who is interested in his theory of knowledge, his observations on psychology and mysticism, and his description of the three types of visions. Ending, as it does, with Augustine's hope and longing for the beatific vision, it is a fitting conclusion to his long commentary which began with his thoughts in the bosom of the Trinity, when in the beginning God made heaven and earth: "Let me drink Thee in and ponder the marvels of Thy law from the very beginning in which Thou didst make heaven and earth unto the kingdom of Thy holy city where we shall be with Thee forever."[20]

LITERAL INTERPRETATION

A reader unfamiliar with Augustine's thought cannot progress very far in this work without being puzzled by the fact that he has called it a literal commentary. The days of creation, he suggests, are not periods of time but rather categories in which creatures are arranged by the author for didactic reasons to describe all the works of creation, which in reality were created simultaneously. Light is not the visible light of this world but the illumination of intellectual creatures (the angels). Morning refers to the angels' knowledge of creatures which they enjoy in the vision of God; evening refers to the angels' knowledge of creatures as they exist in their own created natures. Can this sort of exegesis be literal interpretation? If so, what is Augustine's notion of the literal meaning of Scripture, and what is he attempting in this commentary?

In the first chapter of Book 1 Augustine points out that the commentator who wishes to expound the literal meaning of Genesis attempts to interpret it as "a faithful record of what happened." Further on he reminds the reader that he intends to explain Holy Scripture "according to the plain meaning of the historical facts, not according to future events which they foreshadow."[21] He is, therefore, clearly distinguishing the literal or proper meaning from the allegorical, prophetic, or figurative meaning. The literal meaning tells what actually happened; the allegorical, prophetic, or figurative meaning tells what the events foreshadow or typify.

A book like the Canticle of Canticles, according to Augustine, is frankly allegorical and is clearly different in kind from the Book of Kings.[22] The latter is obviously a historical work, written to narrate events that happened. This is not to deny that passages in a historical book may contain events that foreshadow something to come. In that case the reader is justified in finding two meanings in one passage: the literal meaning, which tells

what happened, and the allegorical meaning, which tells what
the event foreshadows. But with regard to Genesis there is a
problem. Although from the fourth chapter on it is obviously a
historical narrative, the first three chapters seem to contain a
narrative of another sort. But this, says Augustine, is because
the events narrated in the first three chapters are unfamiliar to
us, and of course they are unfamiliar because they are unique.
But that, Augustine observes, does not justify one in concluding
that the events did not happen. If Adam is to be given only a
figurative meaning, who begot Cain, Abel, and Seth? The style
of the narrative shows that Genesis is intended to be historical.

In interpreting Genesis, therefore, Augustine is seeking the
literal meaning, that is, the meaning intended by the author:
"One may expect me to defend the literal meaning of the narrative as it is set forth by the author."[23] But, as Augustine notes,
this is sometimes hard to discover. Hence, when faced with a variety of seemingly possible interpretations, the reader should
search first for the meaning intended by the author; but if that
cannot be discovered, he should attempt to discern what the
context of Sacred Scripture requires; failing in that, he must see
what the faith demands.[24] If the words of God or of a prophet
inspired by God cannot be taken literally without absurdity,
then the exegete must resort to a figurative interpretation.[25]

One must not assume that a historical account becomes figurative or allegorical when the writer employs a figure of speech,
using a word in a transferred meaning.[26] When the author of
Genesis says, *Then the eyes of both were opened, and they perceived
that they were naked,* he is using "eyes were opened" in a figurative sense, but the statement does not suggest to us an allegorical
narrative. Similarly there are passages in Scripture where the
"hand of God" is said to have accomplished certain deeds, but
everyone knows that the "power of God' is meant.[27]

Furthermore Augustine observes that, when we seek the literal meaning of a passage narrating what God did, we must not
conceive of Him acting like a creature. When, for instance, God
is said to have brought all the beasts to Adam, the literal meaning does not compel us to picture this in a crudely materialistic
way. God's power works in the world through the natural ten-

dencies in living creatures and through the ministry of His angels.[28]

But, although Augustine in this treatise is concerned with the literal meaning, he does not deny that the deeds and words narrated can have an allegorical as well as literal sense. He illustrates his point from familiar allegories elsewhere in the Bible. Jerusalem on earth is a figure or type of the heavenly Jerusalem, but this is not to deny the existence of a real Jerusalem here below. Sarah and Hagar signify the two testaments, but there really were two women named Sarah and Hagar. Christ is the Lamb immolated on the Passover, but there actually was a lamb in the Old Testament that was slain and eaten.[29]

With regard to the reality of Paradise, Augustine says that some authors have taken it exclusively in the corporeal sense, others exclusively in the spiritual sense, and still others in both senses. He favors the third position:

> Briefly, then, I admit that the third interpretation appeals to me. According to it I have now undertaken to treat of Paradise if God will make this possible. Man was made from the slime of the earth—and that certainly means a human body—and was placed in a corporeal paradise. Adam, of course, signifies something else where St. Paul speaks of him as a type of the One who was to come. But he is understood here as a man constituted in his own proper nature, who lived a certain number of years, was the father of numerous children, and died as other men die, although he was not born of parents as other men are but made from the earth, as was proper for the first man. Consequently Paradise, in which God placed him, should be understood as simply a place, that is, a land, where an earthly man would live.[30]

If, therefore, we understand Augustine's distinction between the literal and the allegorical meaning, we should have no difficulty in seeing what he intends when he takes his special interpretation of light, day, morning, and evening in the first chapter of Genesis as literal. This interpretation, he tells us, must not be thought of as allegorical. It would be a mistake to consider material light as the only real light and the light referred to in Genesis as metaphorical light. Spiritual light, which is more excellent and unfailing, is the truer light.[31]

His purpose, then, is to explain, to the best of his ability, what the author intended to say about what God did when He made heaven and earth. But Augustine does not claim that he has found the final answer to all problems in the interpretation of the text. Far from it. Much of what he says is merely proposed as theory, subject to revision if another interpreter can find a better explanation. He urges his readers to keep an open mind when the meaning is not clear,[32] and he even suggests that certain passages of Scripture have been written obscurely for the precise purpose of stimulating our thought.[33] Whether or not that is the reason for the obscurity is a question. But certainly when a serious student encounters an obscure passage, his curiosity is aroused, and he is drawn to investigate the inspired words more thoroughly. Augustine looks upon this as a fruitful exercise that nourishes our souls, even when we do not arrive at any certain conclusion, provided always that any opinion we adopt is in harmony with the true faith.[34]

MANUSCRIPTS, EDITIONS, AND TRANSLATIONS

The interest in Augustine's *De Genesi ad litteram* in the Middle Ages is attested by the large number of extant manuscripts of the work in the libraries of centers of learning throughout Europe. The survey of manuscripts of Augustine started by Manfred Oberleitner and now being edited by Franz Römer[35] lists 121 manuscripts of this work found in the countries surveyed so far. The numbers in these countries are as follows: Italy 45, Great Britain and Ireland 43, Spain 11, Poland 3, and West Germany and West Berlin 19.

There is no known printed edition of this work prior to the first edition of the complete works of Augustine by Amerbach in 1506. Amerbach's edition was followed by two other complete editions in the sixteenth century: by Erasmus in 1528 and by the Louvain editors in 1576. J. de Ghellinck in his *Patristique et moyen âge* has written a detailed history of these editions and has given a critical estimate of their value.[36] These early editions were for the most part replaced by the appearance of the complete works of St. Augustine in eleven volumes edited by the Benedictine monks of S. Maur in Paris and published at Paris between 1679 and 1700.[37] The text of the *De Genesi ad litteram* is in Vol. 3 (published in 1680), cols. 117–324. The Maurist edition was reprinted by J. P. Migne in 11 vols. in 14 (Paris 1841), incorporated as Vols. 32–45 in the *Patrologia latina;* and the *De Genesi ad litteram* will be found in Vol. 34, cols. 245–486.

Although this edition by the monks of S. Maur does not give all the information on the manuscripts and the kind of *apparatus criticus* that we expect in a scholarly edition today, it is a monumental achievement in the editing of patristic texts, and to this day it has not been superseded by any new edition of the *opera omnia*. The Benedictine editors collated twenty-six manuscripts and the editions of Amerbach, Erasmus, and the Louvain editors in the preparation of the text of the *De Genesi ad litteram*.

The only new critical edition of the *De Genesi ad litteram* is that by Joseph Zycha published in 1894 in the *Corpus scriptorum ecclesiasticorum latinorum*.[38] Zycha based this edition on the following manuscripts:

E Sessorianus 13, Vittorio Emanuele Library, Rome, No. 2094, 6th century.[39]

P Parisinus 2706, Colbertinus 5150, late 7th century.[40]

R Parisinus 1804, Colbertinus 894, 9th century.

S Sangallensis 161, 9th century.

C Coloniensis 61, 12th century. Zycha did not collate the whole manuscript but only a few passages.

B Berolinensis 24, 9th or 10th century. Zycha was unable to examine this manuscript until after he had compiled his critical apparatus. In his preface he gives select variant readings from it, omitting those where it is in agreement with P and R.

He has also taken into account the testimony of Eugippius (c. 455–535), who has left a collection of extracts from the writings of Augustine, including some passages from the *De Genesi*.

Zycha has made a significant contribution to the study of the text of *De Genesi*, but his edition should be used with caution.[41] We are indebted to him for a collation of the manuscripts listed above, especially the Codex Sessorianus (E), but the text he has established differs frequently from the Maurist text on the sole authority of E. He considered, and rightly so, the Sessorianus to be "the oldest and best manuscript,"[42] but his constant reliance on it in spite of other evidence to the contrary is, in my opinion, based on uncritical infatuation. Furthermore, he has not established the relationship of the manuscripts, and without that it is risky to put great emphasis on the authority of any one manuscript over another. Finally, in choosing between variant readings he has frequently failed to take into consideration the thought and style of Augustine.

On the other hand, the Maurist edition seems to be the work of editors who understood well the thought and style of the writer, but they have given little information about manuscript readings. For the purpose of this translation, therefore, I have carefully collated the text of Zycha with that of the Maurists, and wherever there was any discrepancy that would in any way affect the meaning, I have examined the available manuscript evidence both in the apparatus of Zycha's edition and in certain manuscripts which I have myself consulted. These manuscripts are:

Bod Bodleianus, Laud. Misc. 141, Bodleian Library, Oxford, 8th-9th century.

Bru Bruxellensis 1051 (10791), Bibliothèque Royale de Belgique, Brussels, 11th century.

Lau Laurentianus, S. Marco 658, Laurentian Library, Florence, 9th century.

Nov Novariensis 83 (5), Biblioteca Capitolare, Novara, Italy, 9th century.

Pal Palatinus Latinus 234, Vatican Library, 9th century.

Par Parisinus, Nouv. Acq. Lat. 1572, Bibliothèque Nationale, Paris, 9th century.

Val Vaticanus 449, Vatican Library, 13th-14th century.

Vat Vaticanus 657, Vatican Library, 13th-14th century.

I have not examined all of these manuscripts in every doubtful case; but as the work on this translation was extended over many years and carried on in many places in Europe and in the United States, I have taken advantage of opportunities offered at different times to obtain variant readings which might help in the solution of textual problems as they occurred. Wherever I have discussed such a problem in the notes, the reader will find the results of these intermittent and incomplete investigations. Occasionally, I believe, this information throws light on a *locus perplexus*, and the results in general point to a need of a new critical edition.

The following translations of *De Genesi ad litteram* have been published:[43]

1. *In French:*

Oeuvres complètes de saint Augustin, traduit en français et annotées par Péronne, Vincent, Ecalle, Charpenter, et H. Barreau. 34 vols. (Paris 1872–78). This edition gives the Maurist text along with the French translation. *De Genesi ad litteram* is in Vol. 7.

Bibliothèque augustinienne: Oeuvres de saint Augustin (Paris 1947-, in progress). Latin text with French translation and notes. *De Genesi ad litteram*, edited by P. Agaësse and A. Solignac, with Latin text of Zycha (with corrections), is in Vols. 48–49 (1972).[44]

2. *In German:*

Aurelius Augustinus, Über den Wortlaut der Genesis, De Genesi ad litteram libri duodecim: Der grosse Genesiskommentar in zwölf Büchern, zum erstenmal in deutscher Sprache von Carl Johann Perl. 2 vols. (Paderborn 1961, 1964) .

Aurelius Augustinus, Psychologie und Mystik (De Genesi ad litteram 12), introduction, translation, and notes by Matthias E. Korger and Hans Urs von Balthasar (Sigillum 18; Einsiedeln 1960).

3. *In Spanish:*

Obras de San Agustin en edición bilingüe (Biblioteca de Autores Cristianos, Madrid 1946–67). *De Genesi ad litteram,* translated by Balbino Martín, O.S.A., is in Vol. 15 (1957) 576–1271.

ST. AUGUSTINE
THE LITERAL MEANING
OF GENESIS

BOOKS 1–6

BOOK ONE
THE WORK OF THE FIRST DAY

CHAPTER 1

The interpretation of Scripture. The meaning of heaven and earth.

1. Sacred Scripture, taken as a whole, is divided into two parts, as our Lord intimates when He says: *A scribe instructed in the kingdom of God is like a householder who brings forth from his storeroom things new and old.*[1] These new and old things are also called testaments.

In all the sacred books, we should consider the eternal truths that are taught, the facts that are narrated, the future events that are predicted, and the precepts or counsels that are given. In the case of a narrative of events, the question arises as to whether everything must be taken according to the figurative sense only, or whether it must be expounded and defended also as a faithful record of what happened. No Christian will dare say that the narrative must not be taken in a figurative sense. For St. Paul says: *Now all these things that happened to them were symbolic.*[2] And he explains the statement in Genesis, *And they shall be two in one flesh,*[3] as a great mystery in reference to Christ and to the Church.[4]

2. If, then, Scripture is to be explained under both aspects, what meaning other than the allegorical have the words: *In the beginning God created heaven and earth?*[5] Were heaven and earth made in the beginning of time, or first of all in creation, or in the Beginning who is the Word, the only-begotten Son of God? And how can it be demonstrated that God, without any change in Himself, produces effects subject to change and measured by time? And what is meant by the phrase "heaven and earth"?

Was this expression used to indicate spiritual and corporeal creatures? Or does it refer only to the corporeal, so that we may presume in this book that the author passed over in silence the creation of spiritual beings, and in saying "heaven and earth" wished to indicate all corporeal creation above and below? Or is the unformed matter of both the spiritual and corporeal worlds meant in the expression "heaven and earth": that is, are we to understand, on the one hand, the life of the spirit as it can exist in itself when not turned towards its Creator (it is by this turning towards its Creator that it receives its form and perfection, and if it does not thus turn, it is unformed);[6] and, on the other hand, bodily matter considered as lacking all the bodily qualities that appear in formed matter when it is endowed with bodily appearances perceptible by the sight and other senses?[7]

3. But perhaps we should take "heaven" to mean spiritual beings in a state of perfection and beatitude from the first moment of their creation and take "earth" to mean bodily matter in a state that is not yet complete and perfect. *The earth*, says Holy Scripture, *was invisible and formless, and darkness was over the abyss*.[8] These words seem to indicate the formless state of bodily substance. Or does the second statement[9] imply the formless state of both substances, so that bodily substance is referred to in the words, *The earth was invisible and formless*, but spiritual substance in the words, *Darkness was over the abyss?* In this interpretation we should understand "dark abyss" as a metaphor meaning that life which is formless unless it is turned towards its Creator. Only in this way can it be formed and cease being an abyss, and be illumined and cease being dark. And then what is the meaning of the statement, *Darkness was over the abyss?* Was there no light? If there was any light at all, there would be a great abundance of it, for that is the way it is in the case of a spiritual creature that turns to God, the changeless and incorporeal Light.

Chapter 2

How did God say, "Let there be light"?

4. And how did God say, *Let there be light?*[10] Was this in time or in the eternity of His Word? If this was spoken in time, it was certainly subject to change.[11] How then could we conceive of God saying it except by means of a creature? For He Himself is unchangeable. Now if it was by means of a creature that God said, *Let there be light,* how is light the first creature, if there was already a creature through which God spoke these words? Are we to suppose that light was not the first creature? Scripture has already said: *In the beginning God created heaven and earth,* and God might have made use of the heaven He created to produce an utterance subject to time and change when He said, *Let there be light.* But if this is so, God created material light to be seen with the eyes of the body when He said, *Let there be light,* using a spiritual creature He had already made when *in the beginning He created heaven and earth.* In this way, through the inward and hidden action of such a creature, the divine words, *Let there be light,* might have been uttered.

5. And was there the material sound of a voice when God said, *Let there be light,* as there was when He said, *Thou art my beloved Son?*[12] In this supposition did He use a material creature which He had made, when *in the beginning He created heaven and earth,* before there existed the light which was made at the sound of this voice? And, if so, what was the language of this voice when God said, *Let there be light?* There did not yet exist the variety of tongues, which arose later when the tower was built after the flood.[13] What then was that one and only language by which God said, *Let there be light?* Who was intended to hear and understand it, and to whom was it directed? But perhaps this is an absurdly material way of thinking and speculating on the matter.

6. What then shall we say? Is it the intellectual idea signified by the sound of the voice, in the words, *Let there be light,* that is meant here by the voice of God, rather than the material sound? And does this belong to the Divine Word, referred to in the

statement, *In the beginning was the Word, and the Word was with God, and the Word was God?*[14] When it is said of the Word, *All things have been made through Him,*[15] it becomes quite clear that light was made through Him when God said, *Let there be light,* and so this utterance of God is eternal. For the Word of God, true God in the bosom of God and the only Son of God, is co-eternal with the Father; and yet through this utterance of God in the eternal Word, creation has been brought about in time. It is true that the words "when" and "sometime" refer to time, but the when of something that must be created is eternal in the Word of God; and it is created when in the Word there is an exigency for its creation. But in the Word Himself there is no when and no eventually, because the Word is in every way eternal.

CHAPTER 3

What is the light which God created?

7. What is the light itself which was created? Is it something spiritual or material? If it is spiritual, it may be the first work of creation, now made perfect by this utterance, and previously called heaven in the words, *In the beginning God created heaven and earth.* In this supposition, we must understand that when God said, *Let there be light,* and light was made, the creature, called by its Creator to Himself, underwent a conversion and illumination.[16]

8. Why, moreover, is it stated, *In the beginning God created heaven and earth,* and not, "In the beginning God said, 'Let there be heaven and earth,' and heaven and earth were made"? For in the case of light, the words are: *God said: "Let there be light," and light was made.* Are we to understand that by the expression, *heaven and earth,* all that God made is to be included and brought to mind first in a general way, and that then the manner of creation is to be worked out in detail, as for each object the words *God said* occur? For whatever God made He made through His Word.

CHAPTER 4

The formation of a formless being.

9. But perhaps there is another reason why the expression, God said, *"Let there be...,* " could not be used in reference to the creation of formless matter, whether spiritual or material. God in His eternity says all through His Word, not by the sound of a voice, nor by a thinking process that measures out its speech, but by the light of Divine Wisdom, coeternal with Himself and born of Himself. Now an imperfect being which, in contrast to the Supreme Being and First Cause, tends to nothingness because of its formless state, does not imitate the exemplar in the Word, who is inseparably united to the Father. But it does imitate the exemplar in the Word, who exists forever in immutable union with the Father, when in view of its own appropriate conversion to the true and eternal Being, namely, the Creator of its own substance, it also receives its proper form and becomes a perfect creature.[17]

And so, when Scripture declares, *God said, "Let there be...,* we may understand this as an immaterial utterance of God in His eternal Word, as the Word recalls His imperfect creature to Himself, so that it may not be formless but may be formed according to the various works of creation which He produces in due order. In this conversion and formation the creature in its own way imitates the Divine Word, the Son of God, who is eternally united with the Father in the perfect likeness and equal essence by which He and the Father are one.[18] But it does not imitate this exemplar in the Word if it is turned from its Creator and remains formless and imperfect. Hence, when Scripture says, *In the beginning God created heaven and earth,* mention of the Son is made not because He is the Word, but only because He is the Beginning;[19] for here the origin of created being is indicated still in its imperfect and formless state.

But there is mention of the Son, who is also the Word, where Scripture declares: *God said, "Let there be...."* Thus, in Him who is the Beginning, Holy Scripture places the origin of created being, which exists through Him but still in an imperfect state.

But it shows that to Him as the Word belongs the perfecting of created being, which is called back to Him to be formed by a union with its Creator and by an imitation, in its own way, of the Divine Exemplar, who, eternally and unchangeably united with the Father, is of necessity identical in nature with Him.

CHAPTER 5

An intellectual creature is formed by turning to the Word of God. The Spirit of God stirring above creation.

10. The Divine Word and Son of God does not live a formless life. In His case not only is being the same thing as living, but living is the same thing as living wisely and happily.[20] But a creature, although it has a spiritual nature endowed with intellect or reason and seems to be quite close to the Word of God, can have a formless life. In the creature's case, being is the same thing as living,[21] but living is not the same as possessing a life of wisdom and happiness. For when it is turned away from changeless Wisdom, its life is full of folly and wretchedness, and so it is in an unformed state. Its formation consists in its turning to the changeless light of Wisdom, the Word of God.[22] The Word is the source of whatever being and life it has, and to the Word it must turn in order to live wisely and happily. The Beginning of an intellectual creature's life is indeed eternal Wisdom. This Beginning, remaining unchangeably in Himself, would certainly not cease to speak by interior inspirations and summons to the creature of which He is the Beginning, in order that it might turn to its First Cause. Otherwise such a creature could not be formed and perfect. Hence, asked who He was, the Divine Word replied: *I am the Beginning, for I am even speaking to you.*[23]

11. But what the Son speaks, the Father speaks, because in the speech of the Father, the Word, who is the Son, is uttered according to God's eternal way—if we can use the term "way" in describing God's utterance of His eternal Word. Now,[24] God has a benevolence that is sovereign, holy, and just; and it is not

out of any need but out of His goodness that His love is directed towards His works. Hence, before the words, *God said, "Let there be light,"*[25] Sacred Scripture first says: *And the Spirit of God was stirring above the water.*[26] We might say that by the term "water" the sacred writer wished to designate the whole of material creation.[27] In this way he would show whence all things that we can recognize in their proper kinds had been made and formed, calling them water, because we observe all things on earth being formed and growing into their various species from moisture.

Or we might say that by this term he wished to designate a certain kind of spiritual life, in a fluid state, so to speak, before receiving the form of its conversion. Certainly *the Spirit of God was stirring* above this creation. For all that He had begun and had yet to form and perfect lay subject to the good will of the Creator, so that, when God would say in His Word, *Let there be light,* the creature would be established, according to its capacity, in the good will and benevolence of God. Quite rightly, therefore, did it please God, as Scripture indicates: *And light was made; and God saw that the light was good.*[28]

Chapter 6

The Trinity manifested in the beginning of creation and in the formation of creatures.

12. Hence, in the very beginning of creation in its inchoate state, which has been called heaven and earth because of what was to be produced from it, it is the Blessed Trinity that is represented as creating. For, when Scripture says, *In the beginning God created heaven and earth,* by the name of "God" we understand the Father, and by the name of "Beginning," the Son, who is the Beginning, not for the Father, but first and foremost for the spiritual beings He has created and then also for all creatures; and when Scripture says, *And the Spirit of God was stirring above the water,* we recognize a complete enumeration of the Trinity. So in the conversion and in the perfecting of creatures by which their species are separated in due order, the Blessed

Trinity is likewise represented: the Word and the Father of the Word, as indicated in the statement, *God said;* and then the Divine Goodness, by which God finds pleasure in all the limited perfections of His creatures, which please Him, as indicated by the words, *God saw that it was good.*[29]

CHAPTER 7

Why the Spirit of God is said to be stirring above the waters.

13. But why does Scripture first mention creatures, still, of course, in their unfinished state, and then the Spirit of God? The sacred text says: *The earth was invisible and formless, and darkness was over the abyss;* and then it adds: *And the Spirit of God was stirring above the water.*

Now, love is generally needy and poor, so that its outpouring makes it subordinate to the objects that it loves. Hence, when there is mention of the Spirit of God, whereby the Divine Goodness and Love are to be understood, perhaps He is said to be stirring above creation, so that God may be thought of as loving the work to be produced not out of any need or necessity, but solely out of the largeness of His bounty. The Apostle, Saint Paul, has this in mind when he begins his discourse on charity by saying that he will point out *a superior way;*[30] and in another place he speaks of *the charity of Christ superior to knowledge.*[31] Since, then, it was necessary to represent the Spirit of God as stirring above, it was only natural to introduce a work already begun, over which He might be said to stir by the transcendent excellence of His power and not by any spatial relation.

CHAPTER 8

God's love for creatures gives them existence and makes them abide.

14. Moreover, when the works thus begun had been formed and perfected, *God saw that it was good.* For He found His works

pleasing, in keeping with the benevolence by which He was pleased to create them. There are, it should be noted, two purposes in God's love of His creation: first, that it may exist, and secondly, that it may abide. Hence, that there might exist an object to abide, *the Spirit of God was stirring above the waters.* That it might abide, *God saw that it was good.* And what is said of the light is said of all the works. For some[32] abide in the most exalted holiness next to God, transcending all the changes of time; but others abide according to the determinations of their time, while the beauty of the ages is unfolded by the coming and passing of things.

CHAPTER 9

The words, "Let there be light," refer to the illumination and formation of intellectual creatures.

15. Now when God said, *Let there be light,* and light was made, did He say this on a certain day or before the beginning of days? If He said it by the Word, who is coeternal with Himself, He certainly did not speak in time. On the other hand, if He spoke in time, He did not speak by His eternal Word but by a creature subject to time; and so light could not be the first creature, because there already existed a creature by which He said in time, *Let there be light.* Thus, we must suppose that before the beginning of days, He wrought the work referred to in the words, *In the beginning God created heaven and earth.* And then by the expression "heaven" we must understand a spiritual created work already formed and perfected, which is, as it were, the heaven of this heaven which is the loftiest in the material world.[33] On the second day God made the firmament, which He called heaven again. But by the expression, *earth without shape or form,*[34] and by the dark abyss, is meant the imperfect material substance from which temporal things would be made, of which the first would be light.

16. But it is difficult to understand how the words, *Let there be light,* could have been said in time by means of a creature

which God made before the beginning of time. We do not suppose that they were spoken by the sound of a voice; for a voice, whatever it is, is always corporeal. Was it from the unformed material substance that God made a material voice by which He might utter the sound, *Let there be light?* In this supposition, a material sound was created and formed before light. But if this is so, there already was time, in which the voice moved as it travelled through the successive localities of the sound. And if time already existed before light was made, at what time was the voice produced which sounded the words, *Let there be light?* To what day did that time belong? For there is a day on which light was made, and it is the first day in the series. Perhaps to this day belongs all the extent of time in which the material sound of the voice, *Let there be light,* was produced, and in which the light itself was made.

But every such utterance is produced by the speaker for the benefit of the sense of hearing in the ear of the hearer. This faculty has been made to perceive sound with the impact of air on the sense organ. Shall we say, then, that there was such a sense of hearing in that formless and shapeless creation, whatever it was, to which God thus uttered a sound when He said, *Let there be light?* Let such absurdities have no place in our thoughts.

17. Well, then, are we to suppose that a movement which was spiritual, but belonging to the order of time, spoke the words, *Let there be light,* a movement produced by the eternal Godhead through the eternal Word in a spiritual creature, which He had already made, as indicated by the statement, *In the beginning God created heaven and earth?* In other words, was this movement produced in that spiritual creation which is the heaven[35] of the visible heaven above us? Or shall we say that this was an utterance not only without any sound but also without any temporal motion of the spiritual creature in whose mind[36] it was placed and impressed, as it were, by the eternal Word of the Father, and that according to it the dark and imperfect corporeal world below was moved and directed towards its form[37] and thus became light?

Here is a matter that is difficult to understand. God's decree is not pronounced in time, and it is heard, but not in time, by a creature that transcends all time in the contemplation of truth. But when this creature transmits to beings of a lower rank the forms *(rationes)* which are, so to speak, intelligible utterances impressed upon its intellect by the unchangeable Wisdom of God, then there can be movements in the temporal order in beings subject to time that are to be formed and governed.[38]

But if the light spoken of first of all in the words, *"Let there be light,"* and light was made, must also be supposed to have a primacy in creation, it is nothing other than intellectual life, which must be in a formless and chaotic state unless it is turned to its Creator to be illumined. But when it is turned and illumined, the decree, *Let there be light,* spoken by the Word of God has been fulfilled.[39]

Chapter 10

How can we explain the light and darkness mentioned in v. 4?

18. Since the divine utterance was spoken without the limitations of time, because the Word, being coeternal with the Father, is not subject to time, was the work produced by the utterance also made independently of time? This is a question that might be asked. But how can such a theory be accepted? It is said that light was made and separated from the darkness, the names "Day" and "Night" being given to them, and Scripture declares, *Evening was made and morning made, one day.*[40] Hence it seems that this work of God was done in the space of a day, at the end of which evening came on, which is the beginning of night. Moreover, when the night was spent, a full day was completed, and the morning belonged to a second day, in which God then performed another work.

19. But here there is matter to give us pause. With no division of syllables, God in His eternal Word said, *Let there be light.* Why, then, was the creation of light so delayed until a day passed and evening came? One might say that light was made

immediately, but that the space of a day could have gone by while it was being separated from the darkness, and while light and darkness were being given their names. But it would be strange if this could have taken as much time to be done by God as it takes us to say it. And the separation of light and darkness was done, surely, in the very act of the creation of light. There could not have been any light unless it was separated from the darkness.

20. As for the fact that God called the light Day and the darkness Night, how much time could this have taken, even if God did it by syllables with the sound of a voice? Surely, it would not be more than it takes us to say: "Let the light be called Day and the darkness be called Night." No one certainly would be so foolish as to think that, because God is great beyond all beings, even a very few syllables uttered by His mouth could have extended over the course of a whole day. Furthermore, it was by His coeternal Word, that is, by the interior and eternal forms of unchangeable Wisdom, not by the material sound of a voice, that *God called the light Day and the darkness Night*. And further questions arise. If He called them with words such as we use, what language did He speak? And what was the need of fleeting sounds where there was no bodily sense of hearing? These difficulties are insurmountable in such a supposition.

21. But another explanation might be offered. Although this work of God was done in an instant, did the light remain, without night coming on, until the time of one day was complete; and did the night, following upon the daylight, continue while the hours of the nighttime passed by until the morning of the following day dawned, one day, the first one, being then complete? But if I make such a statement, I fear I shall be laughed at both by those who have scientific knowledge of these matters and by those who can easily recognize the facts of the case. At the time when night is with us, the sun is illuminating with its presence those parts of the world through which it returns from the place of its setting to that of its rising. Hence it is that for the whole twenty-four hours of the sun's circuit there is always day in one place and night in another. Surely, then, we are not

going to place God in a region where it will be evening for Him as the sun's light leaves that land for another.

In the Book of Ecclesiastes it is written: *The sun rises, and the sun goes down and is brought to his place;* that is, to the place where it rose. And the author continues: *At its rising it goes forth to the south and turns again to the north.*[41] When, therefore, the south has the sun, it is daytime for us; when the sun in its course has arrived in the north, it is night here. We cannot say that in the other region there is no daylight when the sun is there, unless our thinking is influenced by the fantasies of poets, so that we believe the sun dips into the sea and in the morning arises on the other side out of his bath.[42] Even if this were so, the ocean itself would be illumined by the presence of the sun, and daylight would be there. It could certainly illuminate the waters, since it could not be extinguished by them. But such a supposition is preposterous. Moreover, the sun was not yet created.

22. If, therefore, it was spiritual light that was created on the first day, did it perish in order that night might follow? But if it was corporeal, what is the nature of such a light, which we cannot see after the setting of the sun (because there was no moon in existence yet and no stars)? If it is always in that part of the heaven in which the sun is, and yet is not the light of the sun, but a sort of companion of the sun, so closely joined to the sun that it cannot be distinguished from it, we are back in the same difficulty. Such a light, if it is the companion of the sun, travels round like the sun and goes from its rising to its setting: it is in another part of the world at the time when this region of ours is in the darkness of night. This forces us to believe (Heaven forbid it!) that God was in one particular part of the world which this light would have to leave in order that evening might come to it.

But had God perhaps made light in that region in which He was going to make man? In this theory, it can be said that, when light had left that region, evening was made, even though the light, which had passed from there, still existed elsewhere and was due to rise in the morning with the completion of its circuit.

CHAPTER 11

*What is the connection between the light of v. 3
and the lights of v. 14?*

23. Why, then, was the sun made to rule the day[43] and shine upon the earth if that other light was sufficient to make the day and was even called the Day? Did that light illumine the higher regions far from the earth and out of sight from here, so that there was need for a sun by which day might shine upon the lower regions of the universe? Again, one might say that the brightness of day was increased by the addition of the sun, supposing that there had been a day illuminated by the previous light but less brilliantly than it now is.

And another theory has been proposed by a certain writer,[44] according to whom light was first brought on the scene in the work of creation, as indicated by the words, *"Let there be light,"* *and light was made;* but afterwards, when mention is made of the heavenly bodies, we are told what was made out of the light, this being done in the due course of the days on which the Creator decided to make His works. But where the original light went when evening came on, so that night might have its place, this author does not say, and I do not think any explanation can be found. It must not be supposed that it was extinguished to give place to the darkness of night, and again enkindled to provide for morning before these duties were performed by the sun, which began to function on the fourth day, according to Holy Scripture.

CHAPTER 12

*Difficulties connected with the succession of day and night and the
gathering of the waters.*

24. But before the appearance of the sun, in what sort of cycle could three days and nights have passed in succession? Even if there existed the light which was first created, and even if we

assume that it was a corporeal light, it is difficult to discover any
solution to propose for this problem. Perhaps one might say that
God gave the name "darkness" to the mass of earth and water
which were still not separated one from the other (a thing which
is said to have happened on the third day), in view of the dense
bodily mass of the earth and water, which light could not have
penetrated, or in view of the dark shade of the huge bulk. Now
there must be such a shade on one side of a body if there is light
on the other. Where part of a body cannot be reached by light,
because the mass of the body obstructs it, in that part there is
shade; for a place deprived of light which would illuminate it if
it were not for a body that obstructs the light, fulfills exactly the
definition of shade. If this shade, because of the size of the massive body, is large enough to cover a space of the earth equal to
that covered by daylight on the other side, it is then called
"night." Not all darkness is night. There is darkness also in
large caves in which light cannot penetrate the inner recesses
because of the solid mass that obstructs it. In such places there
is no light, and all the area is unlighted, but we do not call this
darkness "night." This word we reserve for the darkness that
comes to that part of the earth from which day has departed.
Similarly, not all light is called "day"; there is the light of the
moon, of the stars, of lamps, of lightning, and of all such objects
that shine. But that light is called "day" which precedes the
night and withdraws when night comes on.

25. But if the light first created enveloped the earth on all
sides, whether it was motionless or travelling round, it could not
be followed anywhere by night, because it did not vacate any
place to make room for night. But was it made on one side, so
that as it travelled it would permit the night to follow after from
the other? Although water still covered all the earth, there was
nothing to prevent the massive watery sphere from having day
on one side by the presence of light, and on the other side, night
by the absence of light. Thus, in the evening, darkness would
pass to that side from which light would be turning to the other.

26. Now, where were the waters gathered if they had originally covered the whole earth?[45] When some were pulled back
to lay bare the land, to what region were they brought? If there

was some bare portion of the earth where they could be gathered, dry land already was in evidence, and the waters were not occupying the whole. But if they had covered the whole, what place was there in which they might be gathered so that dry land might appear? It surely could not be that they were raised up, as the grain, after being threshed, is lifted up above the threshing floor to be winnowed and then, when piled in a stack, leaves bare the space that it had covered when it was spread about. Who would make such a statement, seeing that the great tracts of the ocean are spread equally everywhere? Even when mountainous waves are raised up, they are levelled off again with the passing of the storm; and if the tide retreats from certain shores, it must be admitted that there are other coasts where the moving waters come, and that then they make their way again to the land from which they have departed. But if water covered the whole wide world, where would it go in order to leave some of the land exposed? Could it be that water in a rarefied state, like a cloud, had covered the earth, and that it was brought together and became dense, thus disclosing some of the many regions of the world and making it possible for dry land to appear? On the other hand, it could be that the earth settled in vast areas and thus offered hollow places into which the flowing waters might pour; and dry land then would appear in the places from which the water had withdrawn.

27. Matter is not entirely unformed if it has the appearance of a cloud.

CHAPTER 13

When were water and earth created?

A further question, then, arises as to the time when God created these distinct forms and qualities of water and earth. No mention is made of this act in the six days. Hence let us suppose that God did this before any of the days began; for, before any mention of the first days, Scripture says, *In the beginning God created heaven and earth.* By the word "earth" we should then understand earth with its own fully developed form and the waters clearly marked by their visible form flooding over the earth. Accordingly, where Holy Scripture goes on to say, *The earth was invisible and formless, and darkness was over the abyss, and the Spirit of God was stirring above the water,*[46] we should not imagine any unformed matter, but earth and water already constituted with their familiar qualities, but without light, which had not yet been created. We should then understand that the earth is said to be invisible because, being covered by the waters, it could not be seen, even if someone were present to see it; and it would be formless inasmuch as it was not yet separated from the sea and bound by shores and adorned with its fruits and living creatures. If, therefore, this is the case, why were these forms of earth and water, which are certainly corporeal forms, made before the beginning of days? Why do we not read, "God said: 'Let there be earth,' and earth was made"; and "God said: 'Let there be water,' and water was made"? Or, if the whole lower order of creation was included in one act, the sacred text might have read: "God said: 'Let there be earth and water,' and so it was done."

CHAPTER 14

"Heaven and earth" must refer to formless matter.

Why is it not said, after this was done, that God saw that it was good?

28. Now, it is obvious that everything subject to change is fashioned out of something formless; and, furthermore, our Catholic faith declares, and right reason teaches, that there could not have existed any matter of anything whatsoever unless it came from God, the Author and Creator of all that has been formed or is to be formed. It is of this formless matter that the inspired writer speaks when he says to God: *Who hast made the world out of formless matter.*[47] We must conclude, then, that this same matter is referred to in words carefully chosen by a spiritual man in a manner that is accommodated to unlearned

readers or hearers, when before the enumeration of the days it is stated, *In the beginning God created heaven and earth*, etc., as far as the verse that begins, *And God said*. After that there follows the enumeration of creatures that have been formed.

CHAPTER 15

Unformed matter is prior in origin, not in time, to things formed.
The author refers to unformed matter in v. 2.

29. But we must not suppose that unformed matter is prior in time to things that are formed; both the thing made and the matter from which it was made were created together.[48] A voice is the matter from which words are fashioned, and words imply a voice that is formed. But the speaker does not first utter a formless sound of his voice and later gather it together and shape it into words. Similarly, God the Creator did not first make unformed matter and later, as if after further reflection, form it according to the series of works He produced. He created formed matter. It is true that the material out of which something is made, though not prior by time, is in a sense by its origin prior to the object produced. Accordingly, the sacred writer was able to separate in the time of his narrative what God did not separate in time in His creative act. If someone should ask whether we produce the voice from words or words from the voice, you would hardly find anyone so dull as to be unable to reply that words are produced from the voice. Although the speaker produces both at the same time, a moment's reflection will show which is the material of the thing produced.

Now, God created together both the matter which He formed and the objects into which He formed it. Holy Scripture had to mention both but could not mention both together. Which, then, had to be mentioned first, the matter from which the works of creation were made or the works produced from the matter? The answer is obvious. We also, when speaking of matter and form, understand that they exist together, but we must name them separately. In a moment's time, as we pronounce

these two words, we utter one before the other; and so in a detailed narration an account had to be given of one before the
other, although both, as I have said, were created by God together. Thus, what is prior only by origin in the act of creation is
prior also by time in the narration. Even in the case of two
things in which there is no priority of any kind, it is impossible
to name them together, to say nothing of giving an account of
them together. There can be no doubt, therefore, that this unformed matter, however slight its nature, was made by God
alone and created together with the works that were formed
from it.[49]

30. Now, we may suppose that this unformed matter is meant
by the following words: *But the earth was invisible and formless,
and darkness was over the abyss. And the Spirit of God was stirring
above the water.* With the exception of the mention of the Spirit
of God, we can surely presume that the whole passage refers to
the visible creation but implies its unformed state in terms that
are adapted to the unlearned. For these two elements, earth and
water, are more pliable than the others in the hands of an artisan, and so with these two words it was quite fitting to indicate
the unformed matter of things.

CHAPTER 16

The theory of diffusion and contraction of the light rejected.

If this explanation is acceptable, there was no mass formed
upon which the light could shine from one side while darkness
covered the other, where night could follow on the heels of day.

31. On the other hand, there is no solid reason for understanding day and night as a diffusion and contraction of the
light.[50] There were as yet no living creatures for whose well-
being such a succession of light and darkness would be provided, as we see it is provided now by the course of the sun for the
living beings later created. Moreover, no analogy can be offered
to prove such a diffusion and contraction of the light as would
account for the succession of day and night. The shaft of rays

from our eyes, to be sure, is a shaft of light.[51] It can be pulled in when we focus on what is near our eyes and sent forth when we fix on objects at a distance. But when it is pulled in, it does not altogether stop seeing distant objects, although, of course, it sees them more obscurely than when it focuses its gaze upon them. Nevertheless, the light which is in the eye, according to authoritative opinion, is so slight that without the help of light from outside we should be able to see nothing. Since, moreover, it cannot be distinguished from the outside light, it is difficult, as I have said, to find an analogy by which we might demonstrate a diffusion of light to make the day and a contraction to make the night.

CHAPTER 17

Light is the illumination of intellectual creatures. Darkness signifies creatures unformed.

32. If it was spiritual light that was made when God said, *Let there be light,* it must not be interpreted as the true Light which is coeternal with the Father, through which all things were made and which enlightens every man,[52] but rather as that light of which Scripture could say, *Wisdom has been created before all things.*[53] For when eternal and unchangeable Wisdom, who is not created but begotten, enters into spiritual and rational creatures, as He is wont to come into holy souls,[54] so that with His light they may shine, then in the reason which has been illuminated there is a new state introduced, and this can be understood as the light which was made when God said, *Let there be light.* This supposes, of course, that spiritual creatures already existed and were intended by the word "heaven," where Scripture says, *In the beginning God created heaven and earth,* and that this means not the material heaven but the immaterial heaven above it.[55] This heaven is exalted above every material thing not by its location but by the excellence of its nature. But how the mind illuminated and the illumination itself could be produced at the same time, although the illumination is placed later in the

narrative, is a point that I have already explained in treating about the creation of matter.[56]

33. But how are we to understand the evening and the night that follow upon the light? Is the answer to be found in the darkness from which this light could be divided, according to the sacred text: *And God separated the light from the darkness?*[57] Surely there were not sinners already existing and foolish creatures falling away from the light of truth, whom God would separate from creatures remaining in the light, as if marking them as light and darkness, calling the light "Day" and the darkness "Night," and thus showing that He is not the author of evil but the Ruler who governs according to deserts? Perhaps by this day all time is meant, and all the scrolls of the ages are included in this word; and so it is not called "the first day" but *one day*, as Scripture says: *And evening was made and morning made, one day.* This interpretation would imply that the making of evening means the sin of rational creatures; and the making of morning, their renewal.

34. But this is to give an allegorical and prophetical interpretation, a thing which I did not set out to do in this treatise. I have started here to discuss Sacred Scripture according to the plain meaning of the historical facts, not according to future events[58] which they foreshadow. How, then, in the account of the creation and formation of things can we find evening and morning in the created spiritual light? Is the separation of light from darkness a marking off of formed creatures from the unformed? And are the terms "day" and "night" used to indicate an orderly arrangement, showing that God leaves nothing in disarray, and that the unformed state through which things temporarily pass as they change from form to form is not unplanned? And does this expression imply that the wasting and growth by which creatures succeed one another in the course of time is something that contributes to the beauty of the world?[59] Night certainly consists in darkness which is well ordered.

35. Hence, after the creation of light, it is said, *God saw that the light was good.* This might have been uttered after all the works of the same day, so that, having stated, *God said, "Let there be light," and light was made. . .; and God separated the light from the*

darkness; and God called the light Day and the darkness Night, Scripture would then say, "And God saw that it was good," and after that add, "And evening was made and morning made." Such is the order followed in the other works of creation to which a name is given. The procedure, then, is different here because the unformed creation is marked off from formed creation in order that it may not find its end in an unformed state but rather be set aside to be formed later by other created beings of the corporeal world. If, therefore, after they had been marked off by that separation and given their names, Scripture then said, "God saw that it was good," we should take this to mean that they had been so made that nothing was left to be added to them to perfect them in their several kinds. But, because He had fully constituted only the light in this way, *God saw that the light was good,* and He distinguished it from darkness by real separation as well as by name. At that point Scripture does not say, "God saw that it was good." The unformed creation had been set apart precisely so that still other beings might be formed from it. Now, when the night with which we are all familiar, which is produced on earth by the motion of the sun, has once been marked off from day by the distribution of the heavenly bodies, the separation of day and night being thus accomplished, Scripture says, *God saw that it was good.*[60] This night was not an unformed substance out of which other beings would be formed. It was an empty space, filled only with air, devoid of the light of day: nothing had to be added to it for it to become more formed or distinguished in its kind. But evening, during all these three days before the creation of the heavenly bodies, can perhaps be reasonably understood as the end of each work accomplished, morning as an indication of a work to follow.

CHAPTER 18

*The Spirit stirring or brooding over the waters. In obscure matters
we should not be too tenacious of our opinions.*

36. Above all, let us remember, as I have tried in many ways
to show, that God does not work under the limits of time by motions of body and soul, as do men and angels, but by the eternal,
unchangeable, and fixed exemplars of His coeternal Word and
by a kind of brooding action of His equally coeternal Holy Spirit. The Greek and Latin translations say of the Holy Spirit that
He was stirring above the waters; but in Syriac, which is close to
Hebrew (this interpretation is said to be explained by a Christian scholar of Syria), the rendering is not *He was stirring above*
but rather *He was brooding over.*[61] This action is not like that of
a person who nurses swellings or wounds with the proper ap-
plication of cold or hot water; but it is rather like that of a bird
that broods over its eggs, the mother somehow helping in the
development of her young by the warmth from her body,
through an affection similar to that of love.[62] Hence, we must
not think of the matter in a human way, as if the utterances of
God were subject to time throughout the various days of God's
works. For Divine Wisdom Himself, taking our weak nature,
has come to gather the children of Jerusalem under His wings,
as a hen gathers her young,[63] not so that we may always be little
children but that, being infants in malice, we may cease being
children in mind.[64]

37. In matters that are obscure and far beyond our vision,
even in such as we may find treated in Holy Scripture, different
interpretations are sometimes possible without prejudice to the
faith we have received. In such a case, we should not rush in
headlong and so firmly take our stand on one side that, if further
progress in the search of truth justly undermines this position,
we too fall with it. That would be to battle not for the teaching
of Holy Scripture but for our own, wishing its teaching to conform to ours, whereas we ought to wish ours to conform to that
of Sacred Scripture.

CHAPTER 19

On interpreting the mind of the sacred writer. Christians should not talk nonsense to unbelievers.

38. Let us suppose that in explaining the words, *And God said, "Let there be light," and light was made,* one man thinks that it was material light that was made, and another that it was spiritual. As to the actual existence of spiritual light[65] in a spiritual creature, our faith leaves no doubt; as to the existence of material light, celestial or supercelestial, even existing before the heavens, a light which could have been followed by night, there will be nothing in such a supposition contrary to the faith until unerring truth gives the lie to it. And if that should happen, this teaching was never in Holy Scripture but was an opinion proposed by man in his ignorance. On the other hand, if reason should prove that this opinion is unquestionably true, it will still be uncertain whether this sense was intended by the sacred writer when he used the words quoted above, or whether he meant something else no less true. And if the general drift of the passage shows that the sacred writer did not intend this teaching, the other, which he did intend, will not thereby be false; indeed, it will be true and more worth knowing. On the other hand, if the tenor of the words of Scripture does not militate against our taking this teaching as the mind of the writer, we shall still have to enquire whether he could not have meant something else besides. And if we find that he could have meant something else also, it will not be clear which of the two meanings he intended. And there is no difficulty if he is thought to have wished both interpretations if both are supported by clear indications in the context.[66]

39. Usually, even a non-Christian knows something about the earth, the heavens, and the other elements of this world, about the motion and orbit of the stars and even their size and relative positions, about the predictable eclipses of the sun and moon, the cycles of the years and the seasons, about the kinds of animals, shrubs, stones, and so forth, and this knowledge he holds to as being certain from reason and experience. Now, it is a dis-

graceful and dangerous thing for an infidel to hear a Christian, presumably giving the meaning of Holy Scripture, talking nonsense on these topics; and we should take all means to prevent such an embarrassing situation, in which people show up vast ignorance in a Christian and laugh it to scorn. The shame is not so much that an ignorant individual is derided, but that people outside the household of the faith think our sacred writers held such opinions, and, to the great loss of those for whose salvation we toil, the writers of our Scripture are criticized and rejected as unlearned men. If they find a Christian mistaken in a field which they themselves know well and hear him maintaining his foolish opinions about our books, how are they going to believe those books in matters concerning the resurrection of the dead, the hope of eternal life, and the kingdom of heaven, when they think their pages are full of falsehoods on facts which they themselves have learnt from experience and the light of reason? Reckless and incompetent expounders of Holy Scripture bring untold trouble and sorrow on their wiser brethren when they are caught in one of their mischievous false opinions and are taken to task by those who are not bound by the authority of our sacred books. For then, to defend their utterly foolish and obviously untrue statements, they will try to call upon Holy Scripture for proof and even recite from memory many passages which they think support their position, although *they understand neither what they say nor the things about which they make assertion.* [67]

CHAPTER 20

We should remember that Scripture, even in its obscure passages, has been written to nourish our souls.

40. With these facts in mind, I have worked out and presented the statements of the Book[68] of Genesis in a variety of ways according to my ability; and, in interpreting words that have been written obscurely for the purpose of stimulating our thought, I have not rashly taken my stand on one side against

a rival interpretation which might possibly be better.[69] I have thought that each one, in keeping with his powers of under-standing, should choose the interpretation that he can grasp. Where he cannot understand Holy Scripture, let him glorify God[70] and fear for himself.[71] But since the words of Scripture that I have treated are explained in so many senses, critics full of worldly learning should restrain themselves from attacking as ignorant and uncultured these utterances that have been made to nourish all devout souls. Such critics are like wingless crea-tures that crawl upon the earth and, while soaring no higher than the leap of a frog, mock the birds in their nests above.[72]

But more dangerous is the error of certain weak brethren who faint away when they hear these irreligious critics learnedly and eloquently discoursing on the theories of astronomy or on any of the questions relating to the elements of this universe. With a sigh, they esteem these teachers as superior to themselves, looking upon them as great men; and they return with disdain to the books which were written for the good of their souls; and, although they ought to drink from these books with relish, they can scarcely bear to take them up. Turning away in disgust from the unattractive wheat field, they long for the blossoms on the thorn. For they are not free to see how sweet is the Lord,[73] and they have no hunger on the Sabbath. And thus they are idle, though they have permission from the Lord to pluck the ears of grain and to work them in their hands and grind them and win-now them until they arrive at the nourishing kernel.[74]

CHAPTER 21

The advantage of studying Scripture even when the meaning of the author cannot be found for certain.

41. Someone will say: "What have you brought out with all the threshing of this treatise? What kernel have you revealed? What have you winnowed? Why does everything seem to lie hidden under questions? Adopt one of the many interpretations which you maintained were possible." To such a one my answer

is that I have arrived at a nourishing kernel in that I have learnt
that a man is not in any difficulty in making a reply according
to his faith which he ought to make to those who try to defame
our Holy Scripture. When they are able, from reliable evidence,
to prove some fact of physical science, we shall show that it is
not contrary to our Scripture. But when they produce from any
of their books a theory contrary to Scripture, and therefore contrary to the Catholic faith, either we shall have some ability to
demonstrate that it is absolutely false, or at least we ourselves
will hold it so without any shadow of a doubt. And we will so
cling to our Mediator, *in whom are hidden all the treasures of wisdom and knowledge,*[75] that we will not be led astray by the glib
talk of false philosophy or frightened by the superstition of false
religion. When we read the inspired books in the light of this
wide variety of true doctrines which are drawn from a few
words and founded on the firm basis of Catholic belief, let us
choose that one which appears as certainly the meaning intended by the author. But if this is not clear, then at least we shou..:
choose an interpretation in keeping with the context of Scripture and in harmony with our faith. But if the meaning cannot
be studied and judged by the context of Scripture, at least we
should choose only that which our faith demands. For it is one
thing to fail to recognize the primary meaning of the writer, and
another to depart from the norms of religious belief. If both
these difficulties are avoided, the reader gets full profit from his
reading. Failing that, even though the writer's intention is uncertain, one will find it useful to extract an interpretation in
harmony with our faith.[76]

BOOK TWO
THE WORKS OF THE SECOND, THIRD, AND FOURTH DAYS

The firmament in the midst of the waters.

1. *And God said, "Let there be a firmament in the midst of the waters, and let it divide the water from the water." And so it was done. And God made the firmament, and God divided the water that was below the firmament from the water that was above the firmament. And God called the firmament heaven. And God saw that it was good. And there was evening and there was morning, the second day.*[1]
Concerning the divine utterance by which God said, *Let there be a firmanent,* and so forth, concerning the satisfaction with which He saw that it was good, and concerning the evening and the morning, there is no need here to repeat the explanations given in the first book. Hence, in what follows, whenever these words occur again, let them for the time being be weighed according to the interpretations already suggested.[2] But what is the firmament? Is it that heaven which extends beyond all the realm of air and above the air's farthest heights, where the lights and the stars are set on the fourth day? Or is the air itself called the firmament? This is the question that must concern us here.

2. Many hold that the waters mentioned in this place cannot be above the starry heaven, maintaining that they would be compelled by their weight to flow down upon the earth or would move in a vaporous state in the air near the earth. No one should argue against this theory by appealing to the power of God, to whom all is possible, and saying that all ought to believe

that water, even though it had the same weight as the water we know by experience, was poured forth over the region of the heavens in which the stars are set. For now it is our business to seek in the account of Holy Scripture how God made the universe, not what He might produce in nature or from nature by His miraculous power. If God ever wished oil to remain under water, it would do so. But we should not thereby be ignorant of the nature of oil: we should still know that it is so constituted as to tend towards its proper place and, even when poured under water, to make its way up and settle on the surface. Now we are seeking to know whether the Creator, who has *ordered all things in measure, and number, and weight*,[3] has assigned to the mass of waters not just one proper place around the earth, but another also above the heavens, a region which has been spread around and established beyond the limits of the air.

3. Those who deny this theory base their argument on the weights of the elements. Surely, they say, there is no solid heaven laid out above like a pavement to serve as a support for the mass of water. Such a solid body, they argue, cannot exist except on the earth, and whatever is so constituted is earth, not heaven. They go on to show that the elements are distinguished not by their locations only but also by their qualities, and that each is assigned its place in keeping with its particular qualities. Water is over earth; and if it rests or flows beneath the earth, as it does in recesses of grottoes and caverns, it is not held by the earth that is above it, but rather by that below. For if a piece of earth drops from above, it does not remain on the surface of the water, but, breaking through, it sinks and falls to the earth. There it comes to rest, for it is in its place: the water is above and the earth below. From this it is clear that while it was above the waters, it was not supported by the waters but was held up by the solid earth that forms the chambers of caverns.

4. Here it will not be out of place to caution the reader against the error about which I warned him in the first book.[4] Let no one think that, because the Psalmist says, *He established the earth above the water*,[5] we must use this testimony of Holy Scripture against these people who engage in learned discussions about the weights of the elements. They are not bound by

the authority of our Bible; and, ignorant of the sense of these words, they will more readily scorn our sacred books than disavow the knowledge they have acquired by unassailable arguments or proved by the evidence of experience.

The statement of the Psalmist can with good reason be understood figuratively. Since the terms "heaven" and "earth" often mean spiritual and carnal persons in the Church, he indicates that the "heavens" refer to the tranquil understanding of truth when he says, *Who made the heavens in understanding.*[6] "Earth," on the other hand, as the Psalmist shows, refers to the simple faith of children, not a doubtful and deceitful thing based on mythological speculations, but an unshakeable assent founded on the teaching of the prophets and the Gospels, the faith that is made firm by baptism; and so the Psalmist adds, *He established the earth above the water.*[7]

But if anyone insists on a literal interpretation of this verse, he might plausibly understand the earth above the water to be the promontories that tower over the water, whether on continents or on islands; or again, the roofs of caverns that rest on solid supports and overhang the waters below. Accordingly, even in a literal interpretation, one cannot take the words, *He established the earth above the water*, to mean that in nature a mass of water was placed underneath a mass of earth to support it.

CHAPTER 2

Air has its place above water.

5. Air, however, belongs above water (although, because of its wide domain, it may also cover dry land). This is clear from the fact that a jar placed upside down into water cannot fill up, thus clearly showing that air by its nature seeks a higher place. The jar seems to be empty, but it is obvious that it is full of air when it is thus placed with its mouth down into water. Then, finding no outlet in the higher part of the vessel, and being unable by nature to break through the waters below and make its way from beneath, the air fills all the vessel, withstands the water,

and does not allow it to enter. But place the jar so that the mouth is not downwards but to the side, and the water will flow in below while the air escapes above.

Again, if you stand the jar upright and pour water into it, the air rises from it by other paths than that of the stream of water, leaving room for the water to flow down and enter. But if the jar is forcibly pushed down so that water suddenly flows in from the sides or from above and completely covers the mouth of the jar, the air breaks through the water as it pushes upwards to make room for the water at the bottom. This commotion causes a gurgling in the jar as the air escapes gradually, being unable to escape en masse immediately on account of the narrow mouth. So too, if air is compelled to travel over water, it separates it, even when the water is flowing. The water, forced by the air current, rises up and with gurgling bubbles releases the air. The air then rushes forth to its own proper realm and makes room for the waters to fall to the bottom. But if you try to force air out of a jar under water, hoping that the air will withdraw and the jar will fill up with water as you hold it upside down, you will see that it will be surrounded by water on all sides, but not the smallest drop will find a way of getting in at the mouth down below.

CHAPTER 3

Fire has a higher place than air.

6. Fire, which rises aloft, has a propensity to mount even above the air, as one can easily see. If you hold a burning torch upside down, the tip of the flame still reaches up. But in its ascent it is extinguished by the overpowering force of the air, which crowds it above and on all sides; and, overwhelmed by the more abundant element, fire is then changed and takes on the quality of air. Thus it cannot endure long enough to leap over all the air in the heights above.

In view of this, they say that the heaven above the air is pure fire, from which they presume the stars and heavenly bodies have been made by a gathering and arranging of the flaming light into the shapes we observe in the heavens. Air and water yield to heavy objects composed of earth, which fall through the air and water until they reach the earth. Similarly, air in its turn yields to the weight of water, which falls through the air until it reaches the earth or the water. From this they argue that, if one might conceivably drop a particle of air in the expanse of the heaven above, it would necessarily fall by its weight until it came to the region of the air below. The upshot of this reasoning is that it would be even more impossible for water to have a place above the fiery heaven, since air, which is much lighter than water, cannot remain there.

CHAPTER 4

Water in a vaporous state can occupy a position above air.

7. Taking these theories into account, a certain commentator[8] has made a praiseworthy attempt to demonstrate that the waters are above the heavens, so as to support the word of Scripture with the visible and tangible phenomena of nature. First of all, he establishes the easiest step in his argument by showing that the air about us is also called "sky" or "heaven." This is true not only in our ordinary speech, in which we refer to "a clear sky" or "a cloudy sky," but also in the usage of Holy Scripture, in which there is mention of *the birds of heaven*[9] (it is obvious that the birds fly in this air about us); and our Lord, when He spoke of the clouds, said, *You know how to read the face of heaven.*[10] We often see the clouds gather also in the air near the earth, and in that case settle on the slopes of hills so that most of the mountain peaks tower above them.

The commentator referred to above, having proved that the atmosphere near us is called heaven, wished it also to be designated by the term "firmament," for the simple reason that he divides its space between water in a vaporous state and water in a denser state that flows to earth. The clouds, according to the testimony of those who have walked through them in the mountains, have this vaporous appearance, formed, as they are, of the most minute drops which are gathered and rolled together. And if further condensation takes place, so that one large drop is formed out of many small ones, the air, unable to support it, yields to its weight as it travels down, and this is the explanation of rain. Hence, from the existence of the air between the vapors that form the clouds above and the seas that stretch out below, our commentator proposed to show that there is a heaven between water and water. This painstaking enquiry is, in my opinion, quite praiseworthy; for the theory advanced is not contrary to the faith, and it makes it possible for one to accept the evidence at hand.

8. However, it seems rather clear that the weights of the elements do not prevent the presence of water even above the higher heaven when the water is in the form of those minute particles in which it can exist in the air above us. Granted that air is heavier than the heaven above it and belongs in a lower place, it undoubtedly is lighter than water; but water in a vaporous state is not prevented by its weight from being above air. So, too, above the higher heaven a thinner vapor can be spread out in still smaller drops so as not to be forced by its weight to fall. Subtle arguments are advanced to show that there is no particle of matter however small that is capable of only limited division, but that they are all divisible without limit; for every part of a body is a body, and there must necessarily be half of the quantity of every body. Hence, if water, as is obvious, can be divided into drops so small that it moves up in vapors above the air, which is lighter by nature than water, why could it not exist also above that purer heaven on high in still smaller drops and lighter mists?

CHAPTER 5

There is water even above the starry heaven.

9. Certain writers, even among those of our faith, attempt to refute those who say that the relative weights of the elements

make it impossible for water to exist above the starry heaven. They base their arguments on the properties and motions of the stars. They say that the star called Saturn is the coldest star, and that it takes thirty years to complete its orbit in the heavens because it is higher up and therefore travels over a wider course. The sun completes a similar orbit in a year, and the moon in a month, requiring a briefer time, they explain, because these bodies are lower in the heavens; and thus the extent of time is in proportion to the extent of space.

These writers are then asked why Saturn is cold. Its temperature should be higher in proportion to the rapid movement it has by reason of its height in the heavens. For surely when a round mass is rotated, the parts near the center move more slowly, and those near the edge more rapidly, so that the greater and lesser distances may be covered simultaneously in the same circular motion. Now, the greater the speed of an object, the greater its heat. Accordingly, this star ought to be hot rather than cold. It is true, indeed, that by its own motion, moving over a vast space, it takes thirty years to complete its orbit; yet by the motion of the heavens it is rotated rapidly in the opposite direction and must daily travel this course (and thus, they say, each revolution of the heavens accounts for a single day); and, therefore, it ought to generate greater heat by reason of its greater velocity. The conclusion is, then, that it is cooled by the waters that are near it above the heavens, although the existence of these waters is denied by those who propose the explanation of the motion of the heavens and the stars that I have briefly outlined.

With this reasoning some of our scholars attack the position of those who refuse to believe that there are waters above the heavens while maintaining that the star whose path is in the height of the heavens is cold. Thus they would compel the disbeliever to admit that water is there not in a vaporous state but in the form of ice. But whatever the nature of that water and whatever the manner of its being there, we must not doubt that it does exist in that place. The authority of Scripture in this matter is greater than all human ingenuity.

CHAPTER 6

The reason for everything to be created is in the Divine Word.

10. Certain commentators[11] have made a point which I think I ought not to pass over in silence. It is not without reason, according to them, that when God had said, *Let there be a firmament in the midst of the waters, and let there be a division between water and water,*[12] the author was not content to say, *And so it was done,* but added, *And God made the firmament, and God divided the water that was above the firmament from the water that was under the firmament.*[13] These commentators explain that the Person of the Father is indicated in the words, *And God said, "Let there be a firmament in the midst of the waters, and let there be a division between water and water." And so it was done.* Then they believe that in order to show that the Son made the work that the Father had said was to be made, the further statement is added, *And God made the firmament, and God divided . . .* and so forth.

11. But in the previous statement, *And so it was done,* by whom do we suppose the work was made? If by the Son, what need is there now to say, *And God made . . .* and so forth? But if we take the statement, *And so it was done,* as referring to the work of the Father, we no longer imply that the Father speaks and the Son produces the work; rather the Father could make a work without the Son, and thus the Son in turn could produce not the same thing but something else. But this is against our Catholic faith. If, however, the work referred to in the words, *And so it was done,* is the same as that indicated by the statement, *And God made. . .,* what is to prevent us from supposing that He who spoke the command likewise fulfilled it? Perhaps the commentators wish us to attend not to the words, *And so it was done,* but only to the twofold statement, *And God said, "Let there be a firmament,"* and *God made the firmament,* taking the first as indicating the Person of the Father and the second the Person of the Son.

12. But we may further ask whether we must suppose, from the words of Scripture, *And God said, "Let there be a firmament,"*

that the Father has, as it were, given an order to the Son. Yet why has Holy Scripture not made an effort to indicate the Person of the Holy Spirit too? Is the Trinity[14] indicated in these statements: *And God said: "Let there be a firmament"; And God made the firmament; And God saw that it was good?* But it ill becomes the Trinity that the Son should be, as it were, under orders in performing His work, whereas the Holy Spirit without any orders freely sees that the work performed is good. By what words would the Father order the Son to perform a work, since the Son is the original Word of the Father by which all things have been made?

Perhaps we should say that by the words of Scripture, *Let there be a firmament,* is indicated the utterance which is the Word of the Father, the only-begotten Son, in whom all created things have their being even before their creation. Whatever is in Him is life. For whatever has been made by Him is life in Him. This is the life, to be sure, that creates, whereas the creature is dependent upon Him. In one way, therefore, everything made by Him exists in Him, because He rules and holds all; but in a different manner those things exist in Him which are identified with Him. He is the Life, and this Life so exists in Him that it is identified with Him, for He is the Life and the Light of men.[15] Nothing could be created before the dawn of time (and such a being is not coeternal with the Creator) or with the beginning of time or in the course of time unless its reason[16] (if it is correct to call this the reason [*ratio*]) lives a life coeternal with the Divine Word, who is coeternal with the Father. Hence it is that Scripture, before introducing each work of creation, following the order in which it sets forth the production of each thing, looks to the Word of God and first states: "And God said: 'Let there be such a creature.' " For God does not find any cause for the creation of a thing unless in the Word of God He finds that it should be created.

13. God, therefore, did not say "Let this or that creature be made" as often as the sacred text repeats *And God said.* He begot one Word in whom He said all before the several works were made. But the narrative of the inspired writer brings the matter down to the capacity of children. Thus, in introducing singly

the various kinds of creatures, the author looks to the eternal reason of each kind in the Word of God. Of that eternal reason there is no repetition, even though the writer repeats *And God said.* Let us suppose that he wished first to state: "The firmament was made in the midst of the waters to be a division between water and water." If anyone then asked him how it was done, he would rightly reply, "God said, 'Let it be done.' " That is to say, the reason of its creation was in the eternal Word of God. And hence for the account of each work he takes as his starting point what he would have to answer in explaining it afterwards if someone should ask how it was made.

14. When, therefore, we hear, *And God said, "Let there be. . . ,"* we are given to understand that the reason of a thing created was in God. But on hearing the words, *And so it was done,* we see that the creature produced has not overstepped the limits set for its kind in the Divine Word. Finally, when we hear, *And God saw that it was good,* we recognize that creation was approved by the benevolence of the Spirit of God; not that the work pleased the Holy Spirit as something known after it was made, but rather that it pleased Him that it should remain in existence by that same Divine Goodness which previously was pleased that it should be created.

CHAPTER 7

Why does v. 7 repeat what is contained in v. 6?

15. A further question remains to be investigated. Why did the sacred writer, after saying, *And so it was done,* thus indicating the completion of the work, go on to add, *And God made the firmament?* By the words, *And God said, "Let there be a firmament. . . ." And so it was done,* it is clear that God gave utterance in His Word and that the work was made through the Word. Here, then, the Person of the Son as well as the Person of the Father can be seen.

If it is to reveal the Person of the Son that the repetition is made and the words *God made the firmament* are added, can it be that it was not by the Son that He gathered the water on the third day so that dry land might appear? In describing that work the writer does not say, "And God caused the water to be gathered," or "God gathered the water." But even there, after the words, *And so it was done*, there is a repetition in the words, *And the water under heaven was gathered together.*[17]

Can it be also that light was not created through the Son? Here there is no repetition at all. The writer might have put it this way: "And God said, 'Let there be light,' and so it was done. And God made the light, and He saw that it was good." Or at least he might have described it as he did the gathering of the waters, so as not to say, "God made the light," but only to repeat the statement, "And God said, 'Let there be light,' and so it was done; and the light was made; and God saw that the light was good." But there is no repetition here. Scripture declares, *God said, "Let there be light,"* adding nothing save the statement, *And light was made.* And the narrative then goes on with the fact that God was pleased with the light, that He divided it from the darkness, and that He gave them both their names, and that is all.

CHAPTER 8

The method of narrating the creation of each of the works is explained.

16. What then is the meaning of the repetition in the case of the other works? Perhaps we have here an indication that on the first day, the day on which the light was made, under the term "light" is revealed the creation of spiritual and intellectual creatures, by which we understand all the holy angels and virtues.[18] It follows, then, that the writer did not repeat the phrase about the creating of the work after once saying, *Light was made*, because these rational creatures did not first know their formation before they were formed, but rather they knew it in the very process of their being formed, that is to say, in the illumination of the Truth to which they were turned.[19] But the other works

that follow are so created that they first are produced in the minds of these rational creatures and then in their own proper order of being. Hence, created light is first in the Word of God according to the form by which it is created, that is to say, in Wisdom coeternal with the Father.[20] And then it exists in created light itself according to the nature in which it is created. In God it is not made but begotten; in the creature it is made because from unformed being it is formed. *And so God said, "Let there be light," and light was made,* so that what was there in the Word might now be here in this work.

But the creation of heaven[21] was first in the Word of God according to Wisdom that was begotten; then it was produced in spiritual creatures, that is, in the minds of the angels in virtue of created wisdom in them; then heaven was made, so that created heaven existed in its own proper order. The same may be said about the separation and appearance of water and earth, about the trees and herbs, about the lights in the heaven, and about the living creatures brought forth from the waters and the earth.[22]

17. The knowledge angels have of material things is not like that of brute beasts, which possess only the bodily senses. But if the angels employ any sense of this sort, they simply recognize what they interiorly know more perfectly in the Word of God Himself, who illumines them and imparts to them a life of wisdom. For in them there is the light which was made first of all, if we may say that spiritual light was made on that day.

The form *(ratio)*, therefore, according to which a creature is created, exists first in the Word of God before the actual creation of the work itself. So also the knowledge of this form is produced first in intellectual creatures not yet darkened by sin, and then the work is created. We in our acquisition of wisdom go forth to see and understand the invisible things of God through the things that are made;[23] but the angels from the moment of their creation enjoy the eternal Word Himself in holy and loving comtemplation. As they look down then on our world, they judge all by what they see interiorly, approving virtue and condemning sin.

18. It is no wonder that when the holy angels were formed by

the first creation of light, God first showed them that He was going to create the works to follow. And indeed they would not have known the mind of God except in so far as He Himself had revealed it to them. *For who has known the mind of the Lord, or who has been His counsellor? Or who has first given to Him that recompense should be made him? For from Him and through Him and in Him are all things.*[24] The angels, therefore, were instructed by God when a knowledge of the creation to follow was implanted in them and when they later acquired a knowledge of the created works in themselves.

19. Accordingly, light was made, and by this we understand that rational creatures were formed by eternal light. Then, for the rest of the works of creation, when we hear the words, "And God said, 'Let it be made,'" we must understand that the sacred writer would direct our thoughts to the eternal Word of God. But when we hear *And so it was done,* we should realize that in the created intellects of the angels there has been produced a knowledge of the essence (in the Word of God) of a creature to be made. Thus, the created work was in a sense first made in the angelic nature, which by a mysterious operation first saw in the Word of God Himself that the creature was to be made. Finally, then, when we hear a repetition of the words, *God made,* we should recognize that the created work itself is now produced in its own order of being. Moreover, by the words, *And God saw that it was good,* we should understand that the Divine Goodness was pleased in the work of creation; and thus the work which God was pleased to make would continue in its existence as a creature, as indicated by the words, *The Spirit of God was stirring above the water.*

CHAPTER 9

The shape of the material heaven.

20. It is also frequently asked what our belief must be about the form and shape of heaven according to Sacred Scripture.

Many scholars engage in lengthy discussions on these matters,[25] but the sacred writers with their deeper wisdom have omitted them. Such subjects are of no profit for those who seek beatitude, and, what is worse, they take up very precious time that ought to be given to what is spiritually beneficial. What concern is it of mine whether heaven is like a sphere and the earth is enclosed by it and suspended in the middle of the universe, or whether heaven like a disk[26] above the earth covers it over on one side?

But the credibility of Scripture is at stake, and as I have indicated more than once,[27] there is danger that a man uninstructed in divine revelation, discovering something in Scripture or hearing from it something that seems to be at variance with the knowledge he has acquired, may resolutely withhold his assent in other matters where Scripture presents useful admonitions, narratives, or declarations. Hence, I must say briefly that in the matter of the shape of heaven the sacred writers knew the truth, but that the Spirit of God, who spoke through them, did not wish to teach men these facts that would be of no avail for their salvation.

21. But someone may ask: "Is not Scripture opposed to those who hold that heaven is spherical, when it says, *who stretches out heaven like a skin?*"[28] Let it be opposed indeed if their statement is false. The truth is rather in what God reveals than in what groping men surmise. But if they are able to establish their doctrine with proofs that cannot be denied, we must show that this statement of Scripture about the skin is not opposed to the truth of their conclusions. If it were, it would be opposed also to Sacred Scripture itself in another passage where it says that heaven is suspended like a vault.[29] For what can be so different and contradictory as a skin stretched out flat and the curved shape of a vault? But if it is necessary, as it surely is, to interpret these two passages so that they are shown not to be contradictory but to be reconcilable, it is also necessary that both of these passages should not contradict the theories that may be supported by true evidence, by which heaven is said to be curved on all sides in the shape of a sphere, provided only that this is proved.

22. Our picture of heaven as a vault, even when taken in a literal sense, does not contradict the theory that heaven is a sphere. We may well believe that in speaking of the shape of heaven Scripture wished to describe that part which is over our heads. If, therefore, it is not a sphere, it is a vault on that side on which it covers the earth; but if it is a sphere, it is a vault all around. But the image of the skin presents a more serious difficulty: we must show that it is reconcilable not with the sphere (for that may be only a man-made theory) but with the vault of Holy Scripture. My allegorical interpretation of this passage can be found in the thirteenth book of my *Confessions*.[30] Whether the description of heaven stretched out like a skin is to be taken as I have interpreted it there or in some other way, here I must take into account the doggedly literal-minded interpreters[31] and say what I think is obvious to everyone from the testimony of the senses. Both the skin and the vault perhaps can be taken as figurative expressions; but how they are to be understood in a literal sense must be explained. If a vault can be not only curved but also flat, a skin surely can be stretched out not only on a flat plane but also in a spherical shape. Thus, for instance, a leather bottle and an inflated ball are both made of skin.

CHAPTER 10

The motion of heaven and the meaning of firmament.

23. With regard to the motion of heaven, certain Christian writers have enquired whether is it in reality stationary or moving.[32] If it is moving, they say, in what sense is it a firmament? But if it is stationary, how do the heavenly bodies that are thought to be fixed in it travel from east to west and the stars of the Wain complete their smaller orbits near the north pole? They present the picture of heaven turning either like a sphere, if we suppose another axis not visible to us extending from another pivotal point,[33] or like a disk, if there is no other axis. My reply is that there is a great deal of subtle and learned enquiry

into these questions for the purpose of arriving at a true view
of the matter; but I have no further time to go into these questions and discuss them, nor should they have time whom I wish
to see instructed for their own salvation and for what is necessary and useful in the Church. They must certainly bear in
mind that the term "firmament" does not compel us to imagine
a stationary heaven: we may understand this name as given to
indicate not that it is motionless but that it is solid and that it
constitutes an impassable boundary between the waters above
and the waters below. Furthermore, if the evidence shows that
the heavens actually are immovable, the motion of the stars will
not be a hindrance to our acceptance of this fact. The very scholars who have devoted the most exhaustive study to this subject
have concluded that if the stars alone were moved while the
heavens were motionless, all the known phenomena observed in
the motions of the stars might have taken place.

CHAPTER 11

*Why vv. 9–10 speak of the gathering of the waters and the appearance
of the land rather than of their creation.*

24. *And God said, "Let the water that is under the heaven be gathered together into one place, and let the dry land appear." And so it
was done. And the water that is under the heaven was gathered together
into one place, and dry land appeared. And God called the dry land
Earth and the assembled waters Seas. And God saw that it was good.*[34]
We have already dealt sufficiently with this divine work in
the first book in treating of another question.[35] Here we would
add only a brief note. If anyone is not prompted to ask when water and earth were created in their own proper natures, he may
assume that on this day there was nothing accomplished but the
separation of these two inferior elements. But another may be
concerned to know why on definite days light and heaven were
made, whereas water and earth were made outside of and before
all days; and why light and heaven were made according to the

Divine Word, as indicated when God says, *Let it be made (Fiat)*, whereas water and earth are obviously separated, not created, when God speaks.[36]

But this problem can be solved without prejudice to our faith. Before the enumeration of the days of creation, Scripture states, *The earth was invisible and formless*, thus explaining what kind of earth God had made. For it had previously been said, *In the beginning God created heaven and earth*. Now with these words the sacred writer wished to indicate nothing else but corporeal matter in its unformed state, and he chose to call it by a familiar term to avoid obscurity. But it still is possible for an unperceptive reader to take it into his head to try to separate matter and form in time, since Scripture separates them in its narrative, as if matter existed first, and after a lapse of time form was added to it. But God created these two at the same time and produced matter already formed. The unformed aspect of it is designated in Sacred Scripture by the words "earth" and "water." Earth and water indeed, even when they exist as we see them with their proper qualities, because of their strong tendency towards corruption, are nearer to an unformed state than the heavenly bodies are. Now the works of creation proper to the several days are described as formed from an unformed state each on its own day, and the sacred writer had already stated that the heavens had been made of corporeal matter (whose form is vastly different from that of earthly bodies).[37]

In describing, then, the thing that was yet to be formed from this matter in the lowest rank of beings, the author of Genesis did not wish to place it in the description of the universe of created beings with the same words and say, *Let it be made (Fiat)*. For this unformed matter that remained was not to receive the sort of form that the heavens had been given, but a form of a lower order, more corruptible, and near to formlessness. Hence, at the words, *Let the waters be gathered together, and let dry land appear*, these two things received their proper forms familiar to us and perceived by our senses, water being made fluid and earth solid. Of water, therefore, it is said, *Let it be gathered;* of earth, *Let it appear*. For water tends to ebb and flow, but earth remains immobile.

CHAPTER 12

*Why the creation of crops and trees is mentioned separately
from that of earth.*

25. *And God said, "Let the earth bring forth the nourishing crops,
seed-bearing according to their kind and their likeness, and the fruit
tree bearing its fruit, containing within itself its own seed according
to its likeness upon the earth." And so it was done. The earth brought
forth the nourishing crops, seed-bearing according to their kind and
their likeness, and the fruit tree bearing its fruit, containing within itself its seed according to its kind upon the earth. And God saw that it
was good. And there was evening and morning, the third day.*[38]
Here we must note the plan of the Ruler of the world. Since
the crops and trees created are different in species from earth
and water, and so cannot be counted among the elements, the
decree by which they are to proceed from the earth is given separately, and the customary phrases describing their creation are
put down separately. Thus Scripture says, *And so it was done,*
and then there is a repetition of what was done. There is separate mention also of the fact that God saw that it was good. But
since these creatures cling fast to the earth and are joined to it
by their roots, God wished them also to belong to the same day.

CHAPTER 13

*The works of the six days are placed in a rational
and symmetrical order.*

26. *And God said, "Let there be lights in the firmament of heaven
to shine upon the earth, to establish day and night, and to divide day
and night; let them serve as signs for the fixing of times, of days, and
of years; let them be an ornament in the firmament of heaven to shine
upon the earth." And so it was done. God made the two great lights,
the greater light to establish the day and the smaller light to establish
the night, and He made the stars. And God set them in the firmament
of heaven to shine upon the earth to establish day and night, and to*

divide light and darkness. God saw that it was good. And there was evening and there was morning, the fourth day.[39]

With regard to this fourth day, we must investigate the meaning of the plan by which water and earth were first made or divided and earth first brought forth its fruits before the stars were made in the heavens. We cannot say that the more excellent creatures were chosen to occupy a place of importance in the series of days and to stand out with special distinction by being placed at the end and in the middle. It is true that the fourth day is midway in a series of seven, but it cannot be considered midway in the days of creation, because on the seventh day no creature was made. But we might say that the light of the first day corresponds to the repose of the seventh day. Then, in this view, the order would be so arranged that one extreme would correspond with the other and the lights of heaven would occupy a prominent place in the middle.

But if the first day corresponds to the seventh, the second should correspond to the sixth. But what similarity is there between the firmament of heaven and man made to the image of God? Is it to be found in the fact that heaven occupies all the higher regions of the universe and man has been granted dominion over the lower? But what are we to say of the cattle and wild beasts that earth produced in their kinds also on the sixth day? What correspondence can there be between them and the heavens?

27. Perhaps we should rather say that the first mention of light is to be taken as the formation of the spiritual creation[40] and that afterwards the corporeal creation, this visible universe, was made in its turn. This universe, then, was created in two days in view of the two great parts that compose it, namely, heaven and earth. By analogy we also call the whole spiritual and corporeal creation heaven and earth.[41] Hence, even this globe of tempestuous air is considered as belonging to the earthly part of the universe; for, because of its misty vapors, it has the nature of body. But any peaceful region of air where winds and storm blasts cannot blow would belong to the celestial part of the universe. After the creation, then, of this corporeal universe, which as a whole is in the one place where the world has been

constituted, was it not to be expected next that it should be
filled throughout its whole expanse with parts that move from
place to place with motions appropriate to their natures? To this
class of beings plants and trees do not belong. By their roots
they are fixed in the earth; and, though they have a motion belonging to their growth, they are not moved from their given
positions by any power of their own. They are nourished and
grow where they are planted; hence, they belong more to the
earth than to the kinds of beings that move in the waters and
on the earth.

To the production, therefore, of the visible world, namely,
heaven and earth, two days were given, and hence it remains
that the other three days be assigned to the moving and visible
parts that are created within it.[42] And because heaven was first
to be created, it first must be furnished with its moving parts.
On the fourth day, therefore, there is the creation of the stars,
which shine upon the earth and illumine even this lowly dwelling place lest its inhabitants be consigned to a darksome abode.
The weak corporeal creatures that inhabit these lower regions
repair their forces with rest after motion, and thus, as the sun
revolves and night follows day, they measure their periods of
rest and activity accordingly. And night does not remain without its beauty, but with the light of moon and stars gives solace
to those men who frequently are compelled to toil by night, and
supplies a measure of light to certain animals that cannot bear
the rays of the sun.

CHAPTER 14

The lights in the firmament as signs to mark the seasons, the days,
and the years.

28. In the words of Scripture, *Let them serve as signs for the fix-*
ing of times, of days, and of years, there is obviously a good deal
of obscurity if we take this to mean that time began on the
fourth day, as if the preceding three days could have passed
without a lapse of time. For no one could conceive how the

three days passed by before the beginning of the time that is reported as commencing on the fourth day. Or who can say
whether those three days passed by at all?

Different explanations might be proposed. One might say
that "day" refers to the form of the created being, and "night"
to the privation of its form; and so formless matter, whence the
other things were to be formed, was called night. Similarly,
even in creatures that are formed the mind is able to grasp the
existence of an unformed matter in view of their changeable nature. But this matter cannot be separated as if remote in space
or prior in time.

Another might suggest rather that the mutability or possibility of perishing in the creature made and formed was called
night because there is in creatures, even though they may not
change, the possibility of change. Evening and morning in this
case would imply not the going and coming of time, but the existence of a fixed boundary by which the mind sees how far the
limits proper to a nature extend and thereby where the limits
of another nature begin.[43] Perhaps there may also be some other
explanation of these words to consider.

29. Who could lightly rush into this profound mystery and
tell what signs are meant when God says of the stars, *Let them
serve as signs?* He surely does not mean the signs that foolish men
observe, but those that are useful and necessary for practical
purposes, such signs as mariners watch in steering their ships,
or men in general when they provide for changes in climate
through summer and winter and autumn and spring. Obviously, the changes wrought by the stars are called "times"
(*tempora* = seasons)[44] not as periods of time but as the successions
of the seasons. For if any material or spiritual movement preceded the creation of the heavenly bodies and caused something to
move from future through present to past, this could not have
taken place without a lapse of time (*sine tempore*). And who could
prove that this did not happen until the stars were created? But
the fixed hours, days, and years with which we are familiar
could not be without the motions of the heavenly bodies.

Let us suppose, then, that the times *(tempora)*, days, and years
are to be understood in the way in which we reckon periods of

time either by the clock[45] or by familiar heavenly signs when
the sun rises from the east to the heights of heaven and then
again makes its way to the west. We can also observe the moon
or some other heavenly body rise from the east immediately
after sunset; and when it in turn reaches the heights of heaven,
we know that it is midnight, and we can see it setting when the
sun rises and day dawns. Whole days we measure by the course
of the sun from east to west. Years are of two kinds. There are
the ordinary years marked by the revolution of the sun, not
when it returns in its daily round to the east, but when it comes
again to the same position it previously occupied among the
stars. This happens only after the passing of 365 days and six
hours or the fourth part of a day. This fraction, when multiplied
by four, makes necessary the insertion of one day, called by the
Romans intercalary,[46] in order to make our reckoning of time
correspond once more with the revolution of the sun. There are
also those mysterious greater years that are said to have passed
when the other stars have completed their courses.[47] If we understand, then, times *(tempora)*, days, and years in this sense, no
one can doubt that they depend on the heavenly bodies and luminaries. But the matter has been put forth in such a way that
it is not clear whether the statement of Scripture, *Let them serve
as signs for the fixing of times, of days, and of years,* means that all
the heavenly bodies are to mark the course of time *(tempora)*, or
that the sun alone is to mark the passing of days and years and
the other heavenly bodies are to mark the signs and seasons.

CHAPTER 15

*Whether the moon was created as a full moon or as a new moon on
its first day.*

30. Concerning the shape of the moon at its origin, many
scholars engage in prolonged discussions. Would that they spoke
as seekers rather than posed as teachers! They say the moon was
made full because it would not be fitting for God to make something unfinished among the heavenly bodies on that day on

which the heavenly bodies are reported to have been created.[48] But their adversaries rejoin: "Then it ought to have been called the first day of the moon, not the fourteenth. For who begins to count in this fashion?" In this controversy I am neutral,[49] but I will say without qualification that, whether God made the moon on the first day of its waxing or whether He made it full, He made a perfect moon; for God, when He creates, makes the nature proper to each thing. Now, whenever a creature in its natural development in due course discloses and puts forth some perfection, this added something was previously hidden within that creature, if not in a visible and tangible corporeal way, at least by a natural power. Otherwise one would have to say that a tree bereft of its fruit and leaves in winter is then imperfect, or that in the early stages of growth, before bearing fruit, its nature was defective. But this could not rightly be said of the tree or even of the seed, for in the seed lies hidden all the perfection that comes forth with the passage of time. However, if one were to say that God had made something in an imperfect state to be perfected later by Himself, who could censure such an opinion? But there would be just cause for condemning anyone who would say that a work begun by God was perfected by another.

31. Hence, if interpreters make no complaint over the statement that the earth was invisible and formless, when in the beginning God created heaven and earth, and that later, on the third day, it became visible and formed, why do they treat the creation of the moon as if it were a matter shrouded in dark mystery? They understand in the account of the stages of the creation of the world not a real progression in time, since God created matter at the very moment he created the world, but a mere progression in the narrative. Why, then, in the case of the moon, which is also a visible object, do they not recognize that it has its entire mass and its proper round shape undiminished, even when it shines towards earth in the shape of a horn while waxing or waning? If, then, the light in it increases or is perfected or is diminished, it is not the heavenly body itself that changes but the illumined surface of it. Let us suppose that one part of its orb is always aglow. In this case, while it is turning this part towards the earth, until it is completely turned, that is,

from the first day of the new moon to the fourteenth, it seems
to grow; but it is always full, though it does not always appear
so to the inhabitants of earth. The same explanation holds even
if it is illumined by the rays of the sun. In this supposition,
when it is near the sun it can appear only in the shape of a horn,
because the rest of it, which is fully illumined, is not facing the
earth so as to be seen from here. It is only when it is opposite
the sun that the whole of its illuminated surface is visible to
us.[50]

32. Some say that they think God originally made the moon
in the fullness that it has on the fourteenth day not because we
must hold that it was made full, but because the inspired word
of God states that the moon was made *for beginning the night*.[51]
Now it appears at the beginning of night when it is full, but it
rises in the day when waxing and at a later hour each night
when on the wane. However, if by the phrase *inchoatio noctis* one
understands simply *dominion over the night* (for this is what the
Greek word ἀρχή more usually means, and in the Psalms it is
clearly written, *The sun to rule the day . . ., the moon and stars to
rule the night*),[52] one is not compelled to reckon from the fourteenth day of the moon and to believe that the moon when first
created was not the new moon in its first day.

CHAPTER 16

Are the sun, moon, and stars of equal brightness?

33. Certain persons are also wont to ask whether the luminaries of heaven, that is, the sun, moon, and stars, are in themselves
equally bright, on the supposition that their unequal distances
from earth may cause them to appear with greater or less bril-
liance to our eyes. Those who hold this opinion have no hesitation in saying that the brightness of the moon is less than that
of the sun, by which, they say, it is illumined. Concerning the
stars, they go so far as to maintain that many are the size of the
sun, or even larger than it, but that they appear small because
of their greater distance.[53] For us it would seem sufficient to

recognize that, whatever may be the true account of all this, God is the Creator of the heavenly bodies.

And yet we must hold to the pronouncement of St. Paul, *There is one glory of the sun, and another glory of the moon, and another of the stars; for star differs from star in glory.*[54] But, of course, one may reply, without attacking St. Paul: "They differ in glory to the eyes of men on earth." Or, again, since Paul speaks thus because of the likeness of the stars to risen bodies of men, whose appearance to the eyes will surely not belie their true nature, one may say: "Even in themselves the stars differ in glory, yet some are larger even than the sun."

Now those who hold this opinion will have to decide how they can give to the sun such power and dominion that certain stars, and indeed the greater stars that they honor especially in their prayers, are checked in their motion by the sun's rays and caused to move backwards from their normal path.[55] For it is not likely that stars that are larger or even equal in size could be controlled by the rays of the sun. And if they contend that the stars of the constellations, those of the Great Bear, for example, which are subject to no such influence of the sun, are higher and larger, why do they pay greater respect to those that move through these constellations? Why do they represent them as ruling the constellations? For although one could maintain that the retrograde motion of the stars, or perhaps we might say their slowing down, is not caused by the sun, but by other mysterious forces, it is nevertheless quite obvious from the books of these writers that, in the nonsense they propose in their erroneous theories concerning the power of fate, they give the greatest power to the sun.

34. But let those who are strangers to our Father who is in heaven say what they will about the heavens. For us it is neither necessary nor fitting to engage in subtle speculation about the distances and magnitudes of the stars or to give to such an enquiry the time needed for matters weightier and more sublime. We do better when we believe that those two luminaries are greater than the others, since Holy Scripture says of them, *And God made the two great lights.* These two, however, are not equal. For Scripture goes on to say, after designating the pre-eminence

of these above the rest, that they differ from one another: *the greater light to establish the day and the smaller light to establish the night.* They will certainly grant this at least to our eyes, that these two lights obviously shine more brightly upon earth, that day is illumined only by the light of the sun, and that night with all its stars does not shine as bright without the moon as when lighted by her rays.

CHAPTER 17

Astrologers must be avoided.

35. In what pertains to fate, let us be loyal to the true faith and wholeheartedly reject all subtleties of astrologers and their so-called scientific observations (or ἀποτελέσματα in their jargon), which they fancy established by their theories.[56] With such talk they try to undermine even the foundations of our belief in prayer, and with headstrong impiety they treat evil-doing that is justly reprehensible as if God were to blame as the Maker of the stars, and not man as the author of his own sins.[57] But the fact that our souls are by nature not subject to bodies, not even to heavenly bodies, they may learn even from their own philosophers. That heavenly bodies are not more powerful than earthly bodies, in the sense in which they speak, should be clear to them from observation. For when many bodies of different kinds, whether animals, plants, or trees, are inseminated at the same moment and at the very same time are born in countless numbers, not only in widely scattered regions, but even in the same locality, there is such a variety in their development, and in all they do and suffer, that the astrologers would let the stars be hanged, if I may use the expression, were they to give the matter a thought.

36. What more absurd and stupid than, after assenting to the foregoing argument, to say that the influence and power of the stars is only over the lives of men? Such a theory is refuted by the case of those twins that spend their lives in different circumstances, one prosperous and the other wretched, and meet death

in different manners, yet frequently have the same constella-tions.[58] Although there has been a slight difference in the time of their emerging from the womb, in some cases the difference is so small that astrologers cannot take it into account in their cal-culations. When Esau and Jacob were born, Jacob came forth with his hand gripping the heel of his brother, who preceded him.[59] Thus the two came into the world as if one baby twice the normal length were being born, and their so-called constel-lations could surely show no difference. What, therefore, could be sillier than that an astrologer should look at these constella-tions and, in spite of the same horoscope and the same moon, should say that one was loved by his mother and the other was not? If he contradicted this he would speak falsely; and if he did make this statement, he would speak the truth, but it would not be based on the senseless rules he learnt to chant from his as-trology books.

But if men are unwilling to believe this narrative because it is found in our books, how can they do away with the evidence they see in the world about them? They say they never go wrong if they once find the hour of conception. Well, then, let them look at human life as it is and agree to investigate the con-ception of twins.

37. Hence, we must admit that when astrologers speak the truth, they are speaking by a mysterious instinct that moves a man's mind without his knowing it. When this happens for the purpose of deceiving men, it is the work of evil spirits. To these spirits some knowledge of the truth about the temporal order has been granted, partly by reason of their keen and subtle senses, since they possess bodies of a much more subtle nature than ours,[60] partly because of their shrewdness due to the expe-rience they have had over the long ages they have lived, partly because the good angels reveal to them what they themselves have learnt from Almighty God, at the command of Him who distributes man's merits by the right principles of His hidden justice.[61] But sometimes these wicked spirits also feign the pow-er of divination and foretell what they themselves intend to do. Hence, a devout Christian must avoid astrologers and all impi-ous soothsayers, especially when they tell the truth, for fear of

leading his soul into error by consorting with demons and entangling himself with the bonds of such association.[62]

CHAPTER 18

Are the heavenly bodies ruled by spirits?

38. It is often asked whether the bright luminaries of heaven are bodies only or whether they have spirits within them to rule them; and whether, if they have such spirits, they are made living beings by their souls, or whether there is only the presence of spirits without a vital union.[63] This problem is not easy to solve, but I believe that in the course of commenting on the text of Scripture occasions may present themselves on which we may treat the matter according to the rules for interpreting Holy Scripture, presenting some conclusion that may be held, without perhaps demonstrating it as certain. Meanwhile we should always observe that restraint that is proper to a devout and serious person and on an obscure question entertain no rash belief. Otherwise, if the evidence later reveals the explanation, we are likely to despise it because of our attachment to our error, even though this explanation may not be in any way opposed to the sacred writings of the Old or New Testament. And now let us proceed to the third book of our treatise.

BOOK THREE
The Works of the Fifth and Sixth Days

The atmosphere near the earth is sometimes called heaven or heavens.

1. *And God said, "Let the waters bring forth creeping creatures having life, and winged creatures to fly abve the earth along the firmament of heaven." And so it was done. And God created the great sea monsters and all the living creeping creatures which the waters brought forth according to their kinds, and every winged bird according to its kind. And God saw that they were good, and God blessed them, saying, "Increase and multiply, and fill the waters of the sea, and let the birds multiply on the earth." And there was evening and morning, the fifth day.*[1]

It is at this point that the living and moving creatures in the lower regions of the universe are made, and first those that belong to the waters, the element most akin in quality to air. For air is so near the heaven in which the luminaries shine that it also is called heaven, but I do not know whether it could likewise be called a firmament.[2] However, heavens are referred to in the plural in reference to the very same thing that is called a heaven here. For, although in this book the singular "heaven" designates that which divides the waters above from those below, nevertheless the Psalmist says, *Let the waters that are above the heavens praise the name of the Lord.*[3] And if we are right in understanding *the heavens of heavens* as the heavens of the stars in the higher regions over the heavens of the air in the lower re-

gions, and if we take these two heavens as referred to in that
sense in the same Psalm where we read, *Praise Him, you heavens
of heavens,*[4] it is obvious that the atmosphere near the earth is
called not only heaven but also heavens, just as in Latin we use
"earth" in the plural, meaning nothing different from what is
meant by the singular, as happens in the phrases *orbis terrarum*
and *orbis terrae.*

CHAPTER 2

*The "heavens" perished in the flood when air changed into water.
The first living beings were produced from water.*

2. It was these skies where our air is that once perished in a
flood, as we read in an epistle included in the canon of Sacred
Scripture.[5] Now the moist element that had so condensed into
water as to rise fifteen cubits above the tops of the highest
mountains[6] could not have reached the stars; but, because it had
filled all or nearly all the regions of moist air in which birds fly,
the epistle speaks of the perishing of the heavens that had been.
This is unintelligible, in my view, unless the heavier air around
the earth was changed into water. Otherwise the heavens did
not perish but were raised up higher when water occupied their
space. We can more readily believe, therefore, on the authority
of this epistle, that those heavens perished and that others (as the
sacred writer states) *were put in their place*[7] by an increase and
extension of the watery element, than that the former heavens
had been raised up in such a way that the higher heavens yielded place to them.

3. In the creation, therefore, of the beings destined to inhabit
the lower regions of the universe, the whole of which is frequently included in the term "earth,"[8] it was fitting that living
beings should first be produced from the waters and afterwards
from the earth. For air is so akin to water that it thickens by being mixed with water in a vaporous state, it produces the storm
blasts (the wind, I mean), it condenses the clouds, and it can sup-

port birds in flight. Now the pagan poet spoke truly when he said, "Olympus rises above the clouds" and "Lofty things are at peace,"[9] for it is said that on the summit of Mount Olympus the atmosphere is so rarefied that no clouds overshadow it and no winds disturb it,[10] no birds can fly there, nor can men who have scaled it find the denser air to breathe that they are used to below. Nevertheless, that atmosphere is air, and from it there is a precipitation in a form like water; and hence it also is believed to have been changed into the moist element at the time of the flood. For we ought not to suppose that it occupied any part of the regions of the starry heaven when the water rose above all the mountains, even the highest.

CHAPTER 3

The question of change of one element into another. The element of air is not omitted from the account in Genesis.

4. Certainly the possibility of change being wrought in the elements has occupied the minds of even the most subtle and speculative students of these matters, and it is not an unimportant question. Some of them say that everything can be changed and transformed into everything; others hold that each element has something unique and proper to it which is quite incapable of being turned into the quality of another element.[11] Concerning this question there may be an occasion later on, God willing, for a more thorough discussion;[12] but for the purpose of our present study, I have thought it well to offer these observations so that we may appreciate how here the natural order has been preserved, which required the description of the creation of aquatic animals before that of terrestrial animals.

5. One must surely not think that in this passage of Holy Scripture there has been an omission of any one of the four elements that are generally supposed to make up the world just because there seems to be no mention of air in the account of sky, water, and earth. It is customary among the writers of Holy

Scripture to refer to the world either by the expression *heaven and earth* or occasionally *heaven, earth, and sea.* Air, therefore, belongs to the heavens, wherever in their upper regions there is serenity and peace; or to the earth, with its turbulent and misty atmosphere and its thick wet vapors (and, as a matter of fact, this atmosphere is also very often called heaven). Hence, Scripture does not say, "Let the waters bring forth the creeping creatures having life, and let the air bring forth winged creatures to fly above the earth"; but these two kinds of living creatures are described as produced from the waters. Some water, therefore, is in a liquid and flowing state; other water is in the rarefied form of a vapor distributed in the air. Both forms are classed under the moist element, the one being assigned to living creatures that creep on the earth and the other to creatures that fly.

CHAPTER 4

How the four elements are related to the five senses.

6. There are also writers who have subtle theories to relate the five senses of the body to the four elements.[13] The eyes, they say, are accommodated to fire; the ears, to air. Smell and taste they link to the moist element: smell to the humid vapors that fill this space in which birds fly; taste to water in a liquid and (one might say) bodily state. For anything that is tasted is mixed with saliva and thereby made capable of being tasted, even though it may have seemed dry on entering the mouth. Fire, however, penetrates all bodies to give motion to them.[14] For moisture freezes when heat is removed; and, though the other elements can be warmed, fire cannot be cooled. It can more readily be extinguished and cease to be fire than remain cold or become cool by contact with cold. Touch, the fifth of the senses, has an intimate connection with earth; hence, throughout the whole of a living body, which is made chiefly from earth, objects are perceived when touched.

It is also said that nothing can be seen without fire or touched without earth, and that therefore all elements are in everything, but that each thing has been named for that element that predominates in it.[15] And so, they say, it is through lack of heat, when the body grows extremely cold, that sensation is dulled; for then there is a slowing down of the motion that belongs to a body because of its heat, since fire acts upon air, air upon water, water upon earth, and, in general, finer matter penetrates what is grosser.

7. Now, the finer the nature of anything in the corporeal world, the closer its affinity to the spiritual; but these two realms are vastly different in kind, for the one is body and the other is not.

CHAPTER 5

The soul perceives through the senses of the body by means of the element of fire.

Now sensation belongs not to the body, but to the soul acting through the body.[16] Therefore, although one may demonstrate with subtle reasoning that the senses are distributed throughout the body to function by means of the different corporeal elements, nevertheless it is the soul that has the power of perceiving through sensation, and, since it is not corporeal, it produces this activity of sensation by some rather refined corporeal element. It starts the action of all the senses with fire, which has a volatile nature, but the result is not the same in each sense. In vision, for example, the soul checks the heat of fire and turns to its light. In hearing, it penetrates to pure air by means of the warmth of fire. In smell, it passes pure air and makes its way to the moist vapor that composes this atmosphere surrounding us. In taste, it goes beyond even this and pervades moist corporeal substance. When it proceeds yet farther and arrives at the ponderous element of earth, it finally causes the sensation of touch.[17]

CHAPTER 6

*The author of Genesis did not pass over air in his account
of the elements.*

8. The sacred writer, therefore, was not ignorant of the nature and order of the elements when he described the creation of visible things that move by nature throughout the universe in the midst of the elements, putting first the luminaries of the heavens, then the living creatures of the waters, and finally the living creatures of earth. He did not pass over air; but whatever regions there are of pure tranquil air, where they say no birds can fly, are joined to the higher heavens and, being designated as heaven in Sacred Scripture, are understood as belonging to the loftier part of the universe. The term "earth," therefore, is applied in general to all this lower region, including, in descent downwards, *fire, hail, snow, ice, stormy winds, and all the deeps,*[18] until we come to the dry element that is called earth in the strict sense. The air higher up, then, belonging, as it does, to the heavenly regions of the universe, has not been omitted because heaven has been named; or again, since it has no visible inhabitants such as are described in this part of the narrative, it is not included in the account of the creation of living beings. But the air of the lower regions, which takes up moist vapors from land and sea and is dense enough to support birds on the wing, receives its living creatures only from the waters. For the wet element in it keeps aloft the flying creatures, which use their wings in flight much as the fish their fins in swimming.

CHAPTER 7

*Earth in the broad sense includes the atmosphere around the earth, the
region sometimes called heaven.*

9. Thus it was with a knowledge truly divine that the inspired writer said that the flying creatures were produced from

the waters.[19] To these waters two places have been given: on earth in the rivers and seas, above the earth in the currents of air. The one is for fish, the other for birds. It is also clear that living creatures have been endowed with two senses adapted to the element of water: smell for detecting vapors, taste for detecting liquids. The fact that we perceive water and wind by touch is explained by the admixture of the element earth in all the other elements; but in the case of denser bodies there is a keener perception of earth, so that we can both touch and handle them.

The elements, then, as found both on the earth and in the surrounding atmosphere are included under the term "earth" in the broader sense of that word. Thus, the familiar Psalm enumerates all the creatures above after beginning, *Praise the Lord from the heavens;* and then all the creatures below are called upon after the words, *Praise the Lord from the earth.*[20] Now under this second head are included stormy winds and all the deeps and the fire that burns when touched;[21] and these are all grouped together under the term "earth," because fire comes forth from earth and water in motion and is itself in turn converted into the air.[22] And although fire reveals its natural bent by the fact that it rises, it cannot reach the peaceful regions of the heavens above, because it is overpowered by the abundance of surrounding air, into which it is changed and thus extinguished. Hence, in this gross and corruptible part of the universe here below there are violent motions that can extinguish fire when it breaks out as well as produce it to man's advantage or danger.

10. The sense of touch, then, which belongs properly to the element of earth, can perceive among other things the flow of water and the motion of the breezes; and so the living creatures that come from the waters, particularly birds, feed upon things of earth; and on earth also they rest and propagate their young. For part of the moisture that rises up in vapors is spread also over the earth. For this reason, when Holy Scripture says, *Let the waters bring forth the creeping creatures having life, and winged creatures to fly above the earth,* it adds very pointedly, *along the firmament of heaven.* Considerable light is now thrown upon this text, which seemed obscure at first. Holy Scripture does not say, "in the firmament of heaven," as in the case of the heavenly bod-

ies, but rather, *winged creatures to fly over the earth along the firmament of heaven*, that is, *near the firmanent of heaven*. The reason is that this region, with its moisture and mists, where birds fly, borders upon that other realm[23] that birds cannot reach, a realm that because of its rest and peace belongs to the firmament of heaven. Birds, therefore, fly in heaven, but in this heaven near us, which the Psalm we have cited above includes under the term "earth." It is to this region that Scripture frequently refers in speaking of the winged creatures of heaven, but they are said to fly along (or near) the firmament, not to be in the firmament.

CHAPTER 8

In what sense fish are called creeping creatures having life.

11. There are some who think that the phrase, *creeping creatures having life (reptilia animarum vivarum)*, rather than "living beings" *(anima viva)*, is used to indicate a dullness of sense.[24] However, if this were the reason, birds would be called "living beings." But, as a matter of fact, they are called winged creatures, as the others are called creeping creatures, with the phrase "having life" understood. I conclude, therefore, that we must accept this descripion as meaning "among living beings those creatures that creep and fly." In much the same way when referring to men we sometimes speak of "base creatures" *(ignobilia hominum)*, meaning those individuals among men who are base.[25]

There are, of course, certain animals inhabiting dry land that creep upon the earth; but the greater number by far move on foot, and the few that creep on earth are perhaps no more numerous than the few that walk in the waters.

12. But some have held the opinion that fish are called not "living beings" but *creeping creatures having life* precisely because they have no memory and no vital operation that resembles reason. But these writers have failed to observe the facts of experience; for there are authors who have recorded many astounding phenomena observed in fish ponds.[26] But whatever

may be said of the truth or falsity of these accounts, the fact that fish have a memory is beyond question. I myself have observed this fact, and anyone who has the occasion and the desire may do likewise. There is at Bulla Regia a large fountain abundantly stocked with fish.[27] Whenever an object is thrown into this pond by a person above, the fish carry it off as they swim by or tear it apart in their struggle to possess it. Having become used to being fed in this way, whenever people walk by the edge of the fountain, the fish will swim in schools back and forth alongside of them, waiting for a morsel from those whose presence they perceive.

It seems to me, therefore, to be quite reasonable that the living beings inhabiting the waters are called creeping creatures just as birds are called winged creatures. For if a lack of memory or dullness of sense prevented us from calling fish "living beings," we would surely give this name to birds, whose life is manifest to us in their memory and their chatter as well as in the skill they have in building their nests and training their young.

CHAPTER 9

Certain philosophers assign to each element its own living beings.

13. I know that certain philosophers[28] have assigned to each element its own living beings, saying that to the earth belong not only those that creep and walk upon the earth, but birds also, because they rest on earth when weary of flying; that the living beings of the air are demons; that those of the heavens are gods (and of these last we say that some are the lights of heaven and others are angels).[29] They also assign fish and sea monsters to the waters, so that no element may lack its proper living being, apparently forgetting that there is earth beneath the waters and that they cannot prove that the fish do not rest on it and regain their strength for swimming as birds do for flying. It is true, of course, that fish do this more rarely because water is more buoyant than air and thus supports even the creatures of earth when they swim, whether they learn this art by practice,

as do men, or possess it by nature, as do quadrupeds and serpents. And if these philosophers do not regard fish as land animals because they lack feet, it would follow that seals do not
belong to water, and serpents and snails do not belong to earth;
for seals have feet, and serpents and snails without any feet not
only rest upon earth but scarcely ever move away from it. Drag-
ons, it is said, being without feet, lurk in caves and move
through the air,[30] and although it is not easy to see them, there
is mention of such beasts in the works of pagan writers as well
as in our own sacred books.[31]

CHAPTER 10

*The theory that the fallen angels dwell in the misty atmosphere
around the earth.*

14. We may grant that demons are living beings inhabiting
the air and endowed with airy bodies, and that these bodies are
not subject to corruption and death because in them the element
that is more active than passive predominates.[32] For below there
are two elements, water and earth, and above there is the fire
of the starry heavens; and the passive elements are water and
earth, whereas the other two, air and fire, are active. If all this
is true, this separation of the elements does not conflict with the
statement of Holy Scripture that the birds were produced from
water rather than from air. For it must be admitted that the
dwelling place assigned to them is full of water in a refined and
vaporous state (but none the less real water) penetrating the atmosphere; but the air extends from the limits of the starry heavens down to the flowing waters and solid earth. Nevertheless,
water in its vaporous state does not penetrate all this region but
reaches up only to that point which is the limit of our atmosphere included in the term "earth," as the Psalmist indicates
when he says, *Praise the Lord from the earth.*[33] Up above this point
all is rest, and the air is joined in a common bond of peace with
the heavens, upon which it borders and from which it takes its
name.

If we may follow the opinion according to which the angels that sinned inhabited this highest region before their fall in company with their leader, who is now the Devil, but was once an archangel (although some Christian writers believe that they were not celestial or supercelestial angels),[34] it is not surprising that after their lapse into sin they were driven down into the misty atmosphere below.[35] Here, it is true, there is air, but it is air saturated with the vapor that produces winds when stirred, lightning and thunder when violently agitated, clouds when gathered in a mass, rain when condensed, snow when clouds are chilled, hail when thick clouds are tightly frozen, and a clear sky when rarefied, working under the inscrutable power of God, who governs the world He made from the highest creature to the lowest. Hence, after the Psalmist had said, *Fire, hail, snow, ice, stormy winds,* in order that no one might suppose that these stirrings of nature occur without God's providence, he immediately added, . . . *which fulfill His word.*[36]

15. Now, if the rebel angels before their fall had bodies of a celestial nature, there is no cause for wonder if these bodies in punishment were changed into the element of air so that they might undergo suffering from the element of fire, which is an element of a superior nature.[37] They were then permitted to occupy not the pure realm of air above but this misty air near earth, and this is a sort of prison house for them, in keeping with their nature, until the day of judgment.[38] Beyond this, if there are problems concerning the fallen angels that require more thorough investigation, there will be some other passage of Scripture more suited for that purpose. At the present time it is enough to note that if this region of violent storms, extending down to the earth and its seas and rivers, can support airy bodies by reason of its air, it can by reason of its moist vapors buoy up the birds produced from the waters. These vaporous mists penetrate that air which envelops land and sea and consequently belongs to the lower regions near the earth, and they unite with the air currents that become laden with moisture at night and fall in gentle dew; but if there is bitter cold weather, they freeze and settle in a white frost.

CHAPTER 11

A discussion of the various kinds of animals created.

16. *And God said, "Let the earth bring forth the living creature ac-cording to its kind: quadrupeds, and creeping things, and beasts of the earth according to their kinds, and the herds according to their kinds." And so it was done. And God made the beasts of the earth according to their kinds, and the herds according to their kinds, and all creeping things of earth according to their kinds. And God saw that they were good.*[39]

The narrative now turns to the earth proper, namely, to the other part of these lower regions that elsewhere in Scripture, along with all the seas and misty air,[40] are included under the general term "earth." The sacred writer now proceeds to de-scribe how God gave this earth of ours its own living beings. There is, of course, no doubt about the kinds of animals that the earth produced at God's word. But because the terms "herds" *(pecora)* and "beasts" *(bestiae)* are often used to indicate all irra-tional animals, there is reason to ask which animals are meant here by "beasts" and which by "herds." As for the crawling or creeping creatures of earth, there is no doubt that Scripture in-tends thereby all serpents, although they can also be called beasts; but the term "herds" is not ordinarily applied to them. Moreover, lions, panthers, tigers, wolves, foxes, and even dogs and apes, and the other creatures of this kind are normally called beasts. But the term "herd" is more appropriately re-stricted to domestic animals, which help man in his labors, as do oxen and horses and the rest, or which supply him with wool or with nourishment, as do sheep and hogs.

17. What, then, is meant by quadrupeds? All of the animals mentioned above, except certain reptiles, walk on four feet; but unless the author intended by this word to designate a partic-ular kind, he surely would not have added the word "quadru-peds" here, although in the second enumeration he does not refer to them.

We might perhaps say that there is question here of stags and fallow deer and of wild asses and boars, for these are not found with such wild beasts as lions but are more like farm animals, although they are not domesticated, and thus we might suppose they are given the special name of "quadruped." In this view these animals would be a separate class designated by a name which can be used in a general sense of all animals with four feet but which is given to them in a particular and restricted sense. Or we might infer that because the writer says three times *according to their kinds*, our attention is called to three classes. First, quadrupeds and creeping things according to their kinds; and here I believe he has indicated what quadrupeds he means, namely, those that belong to the class of creeping things, such as lizards, newts, and the like. Thus, in repeating the enumeration of animals, the author did not repeat the name "quadrupeds" apparently because he included them in the term "creeping things." With this in view, he did not say simply "creeping things," but rather *all creeping things of earth*. "Of earth" is added because there are also creeping things in the waters, and "all" is added to include those also that move on four feet, the class specifically intended above by the term "quadruped." Next, the beasts are another class, indicated also by the expression *according to their kinds*, and they are all those animals, excluding reptiles, that prowl about with fearsome mouths and claws. Finally, the herds make up a third class designated by the phrase *according to their kinds*. These have no such fierce and violent ways as wild beasts, although some may attack with their horns.

I have indicated above that the term "quadruped" in its broadest sense is obviously applied to four-footed animals and that the terms "herds" and "beasts" sometimes include all irrational animals. But the Latin word *ferae* is also used in this latter meaning. However, I did not think I should fail to comment on the way in which these words, which the sacred writer uses here of set purpose, have also their more special meanings, in keeping with the familiar habits of our ordinary speech.

CHAPTER 12

The meaning of the phrase "according to their kind."

18. Not without reason the reader may also be curious to know whether the phrase *according to their kind* is used in an off-hand and loose way of speaking, or for a good reason, with the implication perhaps that the animals had another existence prior to the moment at which they are said to have been first created. Or it may be that their kind is to be understood in reference to the higher reasons, the spiritual reasons, according to which things here below are created. But if this were the case, the same expression would be used of light, of the heavens, of water and earth, and of the heavenly bodies. For what one of these creatures is there whose eternal and immutable reason does not live in the Wisdom of God Himself, which *reaches from end to end mightily and governs all graciously?*[41] Now, the sacred writer first introduced this expression, *according to their kind,* in describing the creation of herbs and trees and continued using it through the creation of the animals of the earth. For although it is omitted in the first mention of the creatures produced from the waters, it is introduced in the repetition of this account in the words, *And God created the great sea monsters and all the living creeping creatures which the waters brought forth according to their kinds, and every winged bird according to its kind.*[42]

19. Can it be that, since these creatures were produced so that others might be born from them and by succeeding one another might keep the form originally given, the phrase *according to their kinds* refers to the propagation of their offspring, by which they would survive once created? But why in the case of crops and trees is there introduced not only the expression *according to their kinds,* but also the words *according to their likeness?* After all, animals too, whether of the waters or the earth, generate according to their likeness. Perhaps, because likeness follows kind, the author did not wish to repeat the word in each case. For he did not repeat the word "seed" each time either, although seed is contained in crops and trees, no less than in animals, although not in all. (For it has been noted that some are born from water

and earth in such a way as to be without sex, and accordingly there is seed not in them but in the elements from which they are born.) *According to their kinds*, therefore, refers to the power of the seed to reproduce a likeness in the offspring of a creature that must perish, because none of them has been made to exist only once either by living on always or by perishing without issue.

20. Why, therefore, in the case of man also was it not said, "Let Us make mankind in Our image and likeness according to his kind," since it is obvious that man too reproduces himself? One possible explanation might be that God had not made man to die if he would keep God's commandment, and so there was no need for one to survive after his predecessor would perish. But after his fall *he has been joined with senseless beasts and has become like them,*[43] so that now the children of this world generate and are generated in order that mortal men may succeed one another and the race may survive. What, then, is the meaning of the blessing given after the creation of man, *Be fruitful and multiply and fill the earth?*[44] That command could be carried out only by the act of generation. Perhaps we should not rush in with an explanation here but wait until we come to the passage in Scripture where these problems will demand a more thorough scrutiny and discussion. It may be enough to observe at this point that the phrase "according to his kind" was not used in the case of man because only one was created and from him woman was made. For there are not many kinds of men, as there are of crops, trees, fish, birds, reptiles, herds, and wild beasts, in the case of which we understand the words *according to their kinds* to indicate certain large classes in which the individuals being similar and having a common origin in one seed are distinct from individuals of other classes.

CHAPTER 13

Why the command to increase and multiply was spoken only to the fishes, the birds, and man.

21. The reader will want to know also why the creatures of the waters[45] were so important in the eyes of their Creator that they alone should receive the same blessing as man. For God blessed them also in these words: *Increase and multiply and fill the waters of the sea, and let the birds multiply on the earth.*[46] The explanation may be that for one kind of creature the blessing had to be expressed and thereafter understood as applying to the others that multiply by reproducing themselves. But in that case it would be expressed for the first creature made with the power of reproduction, that is, the crops and trees. To this difficulty we might reply that those beings that feel no instinct for propagating their young, and reproduce themselves without sensation, were judged unworthy of these words of benediction, *Increase and multiply;* but for those in whom such an instinct was implanted, God first spoke these words, so that they would be understood, though not expressly uttered, in the case of the animals of the earth. But it was necessary to repeat the blessing for man so that no one might say that there was any sin in the function of begetting children, as there is in lustful acts whether of fornication or of the improper use of marriage.

CHAPTER 14

The creation of small forms of animal life coming forth from decaying creatures.

22. With regard to certain very small forms of animal life, there is a question as to whether they were produced in the first creatures or were a later product of the corruption of perishable beings. For most of them come forth from the diseased parts or the excrement or vapors of living bodies or from the corruption of corpses; some also from decomposed trees and plants, others

from rotting fruit. Now we cannot rightly deny that God is the Creator of all these animals. For every creature has a special beauty proper to its nature, and when a man ponders the matter well, these creatures are a cause of intense admiration and enthusiastic praise of their all-powerful Maker. For He has wrought them all in His wisdom,[47] which, reaching from end to end, governs all graciously;[48] and He leaves not in an unformed state the very least of His creatures that are by their nature subject to corruption, whose dissolution is loathsome to us in our fallen state by reason of our own mortality; but He creates them tiny in body, keen in sense, and full of life, so that we may feel a deeper wonder at the agility of the mosquito on the wing than at the size of a beast of burden on the hoof, and may admire more intensely the works of the smallest ants than the burdens of the camels.

23. But whether, as I have said, we are to believe that these little animals were also made in the creation of things during the six days of the Scripture narrative, or afterwards at the decomposition of corruptible bodies, that is the question. Surely it can be said that the smallest of these animals that have their origin in the waters and the earth were made at the first creation. Among these it is not unreasonable to place those that come forth from the creatures born with the budding earth. For these creatures[49] preceded the creation not only of the animals but also of the luminaries of heaven, and, being rooted in the earth from which they came forth on the day on which the dry land appeared, obviously they are rather to be reckoned as an adjunct of the inhabitable earth than numbered among its inhabitants.

As for the other small creatures that come forth from the bodies of animals, particularly from corpses, it is absurd to say that they were created when the animals themselves were created, except in the sense that there was present from the beginning in all living bodies a natural power, and, I might say, there were interwoven with these bodies the seminal principles of animals later to appear,[50] which would spring forth from the decomposing bodies, each according to its kind and with its special properties, by the wonderful power of the immutable Creator who moves all His creatures.

CHAPTER 15

The question of the creation of poisonous and dangerous animals.

24. The question of poisonous and dangerous animals is also frequently proposed. Were they created after the fall of man as a punishment for sin? Or were they made as harmless creatures at first,[51] and did they only later begin to afflict sinful man?

The supposition that they were made as harmless creatures is not unreasonable. In this present life with all its troubles and afflictions, no one is so just as to dare to say that he is perfect, as St. Paul frankly admits when he says, *Not that I have already obtained this, or already have been made perfect.*[52] Moreover, virtue in this life must be practiced and *perfected in weakness,* and to this end trials and tribulations of the flesh are necessary, as St. Paul again makes clear when he says that to prevent his being puffed up by the greatness of revelations, he was given a thorn for the flesh, a messenger of Satan, to buffet him, and that when he had thrice besought the Lord that it might leave him, he heard in answer, *My grace is sufficient for you, for strength is made perfect in weakness.*[53]

Nevertheless, the saintly Daniel remained unharmed and undaunted in the midst of lions,[54] and he surely did not lie to God in his prayer when he confessed his own sins as well as those of his people;[55] and St. Paul himself held in his hand a deadly viper that did him no harm.[56] Even these creatures, therefore, could have been harmless if there had been no reason for inflicting fear or punishment on sinful man or for testing and perfecting his virtue. For by means of them examples of patience must be revealed for the benefit of others, and thus, too, individuals acquire a deeper self-knowledge in temptation, and, quite appropriately, the eternal salvation that was shamefully lost by self-indulgence[57] is bravely regained by endurance of pain.

CHAPTER 16

Why brute beasts inflict injury on one another.

25. But one might ask why brute beasts inflict injury on one
another, for there is no sin in them for which this could be a
punishment, and they cannot acquire any virtue by such a trial.
The answer, of course, is that one animal is the nourishment of
another. To wish that it were otherwise would not be reasonable. For all creatures, as long as they exist, have their own
measure, number, and order.[58] Rightly considered, they are all
praiseworthy, and all the changes that occur in them, even when
one passes into another, are governed by a hidden plan that
rules the beauty of the world and regulates each according to its
kind. Although this truth may be hidden from the foolish, it is
dimly grasped by the good and is as clear as day to the perfect.
Indeed, this struggle for life that goes on in the lower order of
creation does but admonish man for his own welfare to see how
resolutely he must struggle for that spiritual and everlasting life
by which he excels all brute beasts. For he sees them all, from
the largest elephants to the tiniest worms, doing their utmost either by aggressive action or cautious retreat to protect the material and temporal life which has been given them by their
position in the lower ranks of creatures. This is apparent when
one seeks to devour another for food: then the animal under attack will try to protect itself by active resistance, by flight, or
by hiding. Physical pain in any animal acts in a strange and
powerful manner upon the soul. For the soul by its mysterious
vital powers mingles with the whole being and holds it together,
and it strives to hold the unity that belongs to its nature when
it feels, not with indifference but almost with indignation, that
unity wasting away and disintegrating.

CHAPTER 17

What are we to think of animals consuming human corpses?

26. Someone may wonder how we can explain the animals that afflict man. If during his lifetime they punish him for his sins, exercise his virtue, try him for his own good, or without knowing it teach him some lesson, why do they consume his body for their food after his death? But really it makes little difference, so far as we are concerned, what states our dead body passes through in nature's mysterious transmutations. By the awesome power of our Creator the body will be fashioned again and called forth from the dead. And yet even in this there may be a lesson for the wise, teaching them to entrust everything to the providence of their Maker, who governs all things great and small by His hidden power, who knows the very numbers of the hairs of our head.[59] Thus, no anxious care for our lifeless bodies should make us dread any form of death, but with trust and courage we should not hesitate to prepare ourselves for whatever may await us.

CHAPTER 18

The creation of thorns and thistles.

27. With regard to thorns and thistles, and certain unfruitful trees, men often ask also why or when they were created, since God said, *Let the earth bring forth the nourishing crops bearing their seed . . . and the fruit tree bearing its fruit.*[60] But those who propose this difficulty show they are ignorant of the familiar legal concept of "usufruct," a term in which the word "fruit" *(fructus)* indicates an advantage.[61] The overwhelming advantages, whether obvious or hidden, to be derived from all the creatures rooted in the earth and nourished by it, are there for these men to behold themselves or to learn from others who have experienced them.

28. Concerning thorns and thistles, we can give a more defi-

nite answer, because after the fall of man God said to him, speaking of the earth, *Thorns and thistles shall it bring forth to you.*[62] But we should not jump to the conclusion that it was only then that these plants came forth from the earth. For it could be that, in view of the many advantages found in different kinds of seeds, these plants had a place on earth without afflicting man in any way. But since they were growing in the fields in which man was now laboring in punishment for his sin, it is reasonable to suppose that they became one of the means of punishing him. For they might have grown elsewhere, for the nourishment of birds and beasts, or even for the use of man.

Now this interpretation does not contradict what is said in the words, *Thorns and thistles shall it bring forth to you,* if we understand that earth in producing them before the fall did not do so to afflict man but rather to provide proper nourishment for certain animals, since some animals find soft dry thistles a pleasant and nourishing food. But earth began to produce these to add to man's laborious lot only when he began to labor on the earth after his sin. I do not mean that these plants once grew in other places and only afterwards in the fields where man planted and harvested his crops. They were in the same place before and after: formerly not for man, afterwards for man. And this is what is meant by the words *to you.* God does not say, "Thorns and thistles shall it bring forth," but *bring forth to you;* that is, they will now begin to come forth in such a way as to add to your labor, whereas formerly they came forth only as a food for other living creatures.

CHAPTER 19

The Blessed Trinity is implied in God's decree to create man.

29. *And God said, "Let Us make mankind to Our image and likeness; and let them have dominion over the fish of the sea, the birds of the air, all the cattle, and all the earth, and all the creatures that crawl on the earth." And God made man, to the image of God he made him: male and female He made them. And God blessed them and said, "In-*

crease and multiply and fill the earth and subdue it, and have domin-
ion over the fish of the sea, the birds of the air, all the cattle, all the
earth, and all the creatures that crawl on the earth." God also said,
"See, I have given you every seed-bearing plant bearing its seed over
all the earth, and every tree that has seed-bearing fruit. These will be
food for you, for all the wild animals of the earth, for all the birds of
the air, and for every creature that crawls on the earth and has the
breath of life; every green plant I give for food." And so it was done.
And God saw all that He had made, and, behold, it was very good.
And there was evening and morning, the sixth day.[63]

Later on there will be ample opportunity to treat more thoroughly of the nature of man. For the present, in concluding our
investigation into the works of the six days, I must briefly point
out the importance of the fact that in the case of the other works
it is written, *God said, "Let there be . . . ,"* whereas here it is written, *God said, "Let Us make mankind to Our image and likeness."*
Scripture would indicate by this the plurality of Persons, the
Father, Son, and Holy Spirit. But the sacred writer immediately
admonishes us to hold to the unity of the Godhead when he
says, *And God made man to the image of God.* He does not say that
the Father made man to the image of the Son, or the Son made
him to the image of the Father; otherwise the expression *to Our
image* would not be correct if man were made to the image of
the Father alone or the Son alone. But Scripture says, *God made
man to the image of God,* meaning that God made man to His own
image. The fact that here Holy Scripture says *to the image of God,*
whereas above it says *to Our image,* shows us that the plurality
of Persons must not lead us into saying, believing, or understanding that there are many gods, but rather that we must accept the Father, Son, and Holy Spirit as one God. Because of the
three Persons, it is said *to Our image;* because of the one God, it
is said *to the image of God.*

CHAPTER 20

Man the image of God. The narrative of his creation.

30. At this point we must also note that God, after saying *to Our image*, immediately added, *And let him have dominion over the fish of the sea and the birds of the air* and the other irrational animals. From this we are to understand that man was made to the image of God in that part of his nature wherein he surpasses the brute beasts. This is, of course, his reason or mind or intelligence, or whatever we wish to call it. Hence St. Paul says, *Be renewed in the spirit of your mind, and put on the new man, who is being renewed unto the knowledge of God, according to the image of his Creator.*[64] By these words he shows wherein man has been created to the image of God, since it is not by any features of the body but by a perfection of the intelligible order, that is, of the mind when illuminated.[65]

31. Consequently, what is said is similar to what was said in the case of the first light created, if we are justified in understanding this to be the intellectual light that participates in the eternal and changeless Wisdom of God.[66] Scripture does not say, "And so it was done" and then "God made the light," because (as I have already tried to explain) there was not produced some knowledge of the Word of God in the first creature preliminary to the actual production of the creature according to the exemplar in the Word.[67] But first that light was created in which there was produced a knowledge of the Divine Word by whom it was created, and the knowledge consisted precisely in this creature's turning from its unformed state to God who formed it and in its being created and formed. But afterwards, in the case of the other creatures, Scripture says, *And so it was done*, meaning that in that light, in other words, in the intellectual creation, first there was produced a knowledge of the Word; and then with the statement, "And God made this or that," there is indicated the creation of that very creature that had been uttered in the Word of God and predestined to be created.

This explanation is borne out in the case of the creation of man. For God said, *Let Us make mankind to Our own image and likeness* and so forth. And then the sacred writer does not go on to say, "And so it was done," but he proceeds immediately to add, *And God made man to the image of God.* For the nature of this creature is intellectual, as is the light previously mentioned, and so its creation is identified with its knowing the Divine Word through whom it was made.

32. If Holy Scripture were to say, "And so it was done," and then add, "And God made it," we should be given to understand that this being was first produced in the mind of a rational creature and then in reality as an existing irrational creature. But man, of whom the writer was speaking, is rational and is made perfect by this very knowledge of which there is question. For after original sin, man is renewed in the knowledge of God according to the image of his Creator. Similarly, before he grew old by sin, he was created in that very knowledge in which he would subsequently be renewed.

But certain creatures were made without that knowledge, either because they are bodies or irrational souls; and in their case a knowledge of them is first produced in intellectual creatures by the Divine Word, who said, "Let them be made." Because of this knowledge, Scripture declares, *And so it was done,* in order to show us that the knowledge of the being to be created was produced in that creature able to know it first in the Word of God. And then the corporeal and irrational creatures were made, and for this reason Scripture then adds, *And God made it.*

CHAPTER 21

Why was man, created immortal, given food to eat in Paradise?

33. It is difficult to explain how man was created immortal and at the same time in company with the other living creatures was given for food the seed-bearing plant, the fruit tree, and the green crops. If it was by sin that he was made mortal, surely before sinning he did not need such food, since his body could not corrupt for lack of it.

For it is written, *Increase and multiply and fill the earth.*[68] This apparently could not be realized without carnal intercourse of man and woman, and hence there is here also another indication that their bodies were mortal. But one might say that the manner of union might have been different in immortal bodies, so that there would be only the devout affection of charity, and not the concupiscence associated with our corrupt flesh, in the procreation of children. These children, not subject to death, would succeed their parents, who themselves would not be destined to die. Thus, finally, the earth would have been filled with immortal men, and when this just and holy society would be thus brought into being, as we believe it will be after the resurrection, there would be an end to the begetting of children. This theory can be proposed, although how it could all be explained is another matter. But at least no one will go so far as to say that there can be a need of food for nourishment except in the case of mortal bodies.[69]

CHAPTER 22

Woman, in so far as she has a rational mind, is made to the image and likeness of God.

34. Some have conjectured that at this point the interior man was created,[70] but that his body was created afterwards where Scripture says, *And God formed man of the slime of the earth.*[71] We should then take the expression, *God created man*, to refer to his spirit; whereas the statement, *God formed man*, would apply to his body. But they do not realize that there could have been no distinction of male and female except in relation to the body. There is, of course, the subtle theory that the mind of man, being a form of rational life and precisely the part in which he is made to the image of God, is partly occupied with the contemplation of eternal truth and partly with the administration of temporal things, and thus it is made, in a sense, masculine and feminine, the masculine part as the planner, the feminine as the one that obeys. But it is not in this double function that the image of God is found, but rather in that part which is devoted to

the contemplation of immutable truth. With this symbolism in mind, Paul the Apostle declares that only man is the image and glory of God, *But woman,* he adds, *is the glory of man.*[72]

Hence, although the physical and external differences of man and woman symbolize the double role that the mind is known to have in one man, nevertheless a woman, for all her physical qualities as a woman, is actually renewed in the spirit of her mind in the knowledge of God according to the image of her Creator, and therein there is no male or female. Now women are not excluded from this grace of renewal and this reformation of the image of God, although on the physical side their sexual characteristics may suggest otherwise, namely, that man alone is said to be the image and glory of God. By the same token, in the original creation of man, inasmuch as woman was a human being, she certainly had a mind, and a rational mind, and therefore she also was made to the image of God. But because of the intimate bond uniting man and woman, Scripture says merely, *God made man to the image of God.* And, lest anyone think that this refers only to the creation of man's spirit, although it was only according to the spirit that he was made to the image of God, Scripture adds, *Male and female He made him,* to indicate that the body also was now made.

Moreover, lest anyone suppose that this creation took place in such a way that both sexes appeared in one single human being (as happens in some births, in the case of what we call hermaphrodites), the sacred writer shows that he used the singular number because of the bond of unity between man and woman, and because woman was made from man, as will be shown shortly when the brief account of this passage will be elaborated in greater detail. Hence he immediately added the plural number when he said, *He made them . . . and He blessed them.* But, as I have already indicated, we shall later investigate more thoroughly the rest of the biblical account of the creation of man.

CHAPTER 23

*The words, "And so it was done," in v. 30 mean that man
understood God's plan just revealed.*

35. We must note at this point that after the words, *And so it
was done,* Scripture immediately adds, *And God saw all that He
had made, and behold, it was very good.* By this we are given to understand that man was authorized to take as his food the crops
of the fields and the fruits of the trees. With the statement, *And
so it was done,* the sacred writer ends the passage he had begun
with the words, *And God said: "See, I have given you the seed-bearing plant, etc."* For if we take the statement, *And so it was done,*
to refer to all that has been said above, we shall have to admit
that men increased and multiplied and filled the earth on this
one day, the sixth day of creation, but we know from the account in Sacred Scripture that this happened only after many
years.

It follows, then, that the authorization given to eat and the
knowledge of this fact acquired by man from divine revelation
are indicated by the words, *And so it was done.* That is to say, it
was accomplished in the sense that man knew it when God revealed it. For if he had proceeded to carry this out immediately,
that is, if he had taken for his food and eaten what had been giv-
en, the customary formula of the scriptural narrative would
have been employed, and after the statement, *And so it was done,*
which is used to indicate the previous knowledge of a work,
then the work itself would be described, and Scripture would
say, "And they took these things and ate them."[73] The matter
could have been described in this way, even though God would
not be named again. Thus, in the description of the work of the
third day, it is said, *Let the water that is under the heaven be gathered
together into one place, and let the dry land appear,* and then, *And
so it was done;* and after that Scripture does not say, "And God
did it," but the words are repeated, *And the water was gathered together into its places, etc.*

CHAPTER 24

Why it is not said of man in particular that God saw he was good.

36. Now concerning the creation of man, Holy Scripture does not say in particular (as in the case of the other things), "And God saw that this creature was good." But after man has been created and authorized to rule and to eat, it is said of all creation in general, *And God saw all that He had made, and behold, it was very good.* Why is this not said of man in particular? Approval might have first been given specifically to man, as it had been given specifically before to the other creatures, and then God would finally have said of all his creatures, "Behold, they are very good."

One possible explanation is that all was finished on the sixth day, and therefore it was necessary to say of all, *God saw all that He had made, and behold, it was very good,* rather than to say this specifically of the creatures He had made that day. But then why is such approval spoken of the cattle and wild beasts and creeping things, which belong to this same sixth day? Becasue they deserved to be pronounced good in particular and specifcally, as well as in the general approval given to the other creatures, whereas man, made to the image of God, merited this approval only along with the others? Certainly not! Of course, you might explain by saying that man was not yet perfect because he was not yet placed in Paradise. But after he was placed there, where is the approval given which was omitted here?

37. What then are we to say? Perhaps the explanation is that God, knowing man was going to sin and not remain in the perfection of the image of God, wished to say of him, not in particular but along with the rest, that he was good, thus hinting what would be. For when creatures remain in the state in which they have been created, possessing the perfection they have received, whether they have abstained from sin or were incapable of sin, they are good individually, and all in general are very good. The word "very" is not added without meaning; for in the case of parts of the body, if individual parts are beautiful, all together making up the organic whole are much more beautiful.

The eye, for example, is a pleasing and praiseworthy thing, but if we saw it separated from the body, we should not say it was so beautiful as it is when seen joined to the other members in its proper place in the whole body.

But creatures that lose their own proper beauty by sinning can in no way undo the fact that even they, considered as part of a world ruled by God's providence, are good when taken with the whole of creation. Man, therefore, before the fall, was good even when considered separately from the rest, but instead of declaring so, Scripture said something else foreshadowing the future. No false statement was made concerning man. For he who is good individually is certainly better when taken in conjunction with all. But it does not follow that, when he is good in conjunction with all, he is also good individually. Scripture limited itself to saying what was true at the time and yet intimated God's foreknowledge. For God is the all-good Creator of beings, but He is the all-just Ruler of creatures who sin. Hence, whenever creatures individually lose their loveliness by sin, nevertheless the whole of creation with them included always remains beautiful. But let us now deal with the matter of the next book.

BOOK FOUR
REFLECTIONS ON THE DAYS OF CREATION AND GOD'S REST

CHAPTER 1

Whether we take the "days" as periods of time or in some other sense, the number six must be considered.

1. *Thus the heavens and the earth were finished and all their array. And on the sixth day God finished the works He had made, and God rested on the seventh day from all the works He had made. And God blessed the seventh day and made it holy, because on it He rested from all the works He had begun.*[1]

It is a laborious and difficult task for the powers of our human understanding to see clearly the meaning of the sacred writer in the matter of these six days. Did these days and the seventh that was added all pass away, and now as we look back over times past are we recalling something that exists in name only and no longer in reality? For in all of time, many days come that are like days gone by, but no day returns identical with a day of the past.

Did those days, therefore, pass by in time? Or, as these days of ours, reckoned by the same names and number, daily run their course in the passage of time, do those days remain with us in fact in their reality? In other words, are we to understand the word "day," not only in the three days before the creation of the heavenly bodies, but also in the remaining three, as referring to the form of a thing created, and "night" as referring to the privation or disappearance of this form, or whatever term you prefer to describe the loss of form when a change turns and draws a thing from form to formlessness? Such change is in ev-

ery creature either as a possibility, without actually taking effect, as in the creatures of the higher heavens, or as a reality,
bringing about the beauty of the temporal order in creatures of
the lowest rank, produced by the decay and production that
goes on in an orderly cycle in mutable nature, as we observe in
all things earthly and mortal. Evening, then, in this sense would
be a kind of limit of each creature's perfection, and morning
would be the original state from which it would start, for every
created nature is confined within its fixed boundaries of origin
and limit.[2]

But it is difficult to find a solution to these problems. Still,
whether we accept one explanation or the other, or whether
some third and more probable theory can be found, which may
come to light in the course of our discussion, to explain how
night and evening and morning are to be understood in those
"days," it is not beside the point for us to consider the perfection of the number six in the intrinsic nature of numbers themselves. For it is by contemplating these numbers with the mind
that we count and arrange numerically even those objects perceived by our bodily senses.

CHAPTER 2

*The order of the six days of creation corresponds to the order of the
parts of the perfect number six.*

2. We have discovered, then, that six is the first perfect number, because it is the sum of its parts.[3] There are, of course, other numbers that are perfect on other grounds and for other
reasons. We have called the number six perfect in view of the
fact that it is the sum of its parts; in fact, these parts when multiplied produce exactly the number of which they are parts.

This kind of part of a number is called an aliquot part. Three,
of course, can be called a part not only of six, of which it is half,
but of all numbers larger than itself. For three is the greater part
of four and of five, since four can be broken up into three and
one, and five into three and two. Of seven, eight, nine, and the

numbers that follow, three is a part, neither greater nor half, but smaller. Seven can be broken up into three and four, eight into three and five, nine into three and six; but three cannot be called an aliquot part of any of these, with the sole exception of nine, of which it is a third, just as it is one half of six. Hence, of all the numbers I have mentioned, none is a multiple of three except six and nine: for six is the product of two times three, and nine the product of three times three.

3. The number six, therefore, as I pointed out at the beginning, is constituted by its parts when added together. There are other numbers whose parts when totalled make a smaller quantity, and still others, a larger. And as we progress through the higher numbers, we find occurring at determined intervals but with increasing rarity those numbers that are made up of parts whose total is neither less nor more but precisely equal to the number of which they are parts.

The first of these is six. In numbers there are no parts of one. For in the numbers used in counting, one is considered as not having a half or any part, but as being truly, purely, and simply one. Two has the number one as a part, namely, a half, but no other. Three has two parts, the number one, which is an aliquot part, for this is a third of it, and another larger part, two, which is not an aliquot part. Therefore, the parts of three cannot be reckoned among the aliquot parts that we are now considering. Four has two such parts: the number one, which is a fourth, and two, which is a half. But added together, one and two make three, not four. Therefore, four is not the total of its parts, for they add up to a smaller sum. Five has only one such part, namely, one, which is a fifth; for two, the smaller part of five, and three, the larger, cannot be called aliquot parts.

But six has three such parts: a sixth, a third, and a half: a sixth being one; a third, two; and a half, three. These parts, one, two, and three, when added together make six.

4. For seven the only such part is a seventh, or one. Eight has three of these parts: an eighth, a fourth, and a half, that is, one, two, and four. But these added up fall short, totalling seven rather than eight. Nine has two parts, a ninth, which is one, and a third, which is three; and these added up make four, which is

far short of nine. In ten there are three such parts: one (a tenth), two (a fifth), and five (a half), the sum of which is eight, not ten. Eleven has only the eleventh part, just as seven has only the seventh, five only the fifth, three only the third, and two only the half; and in each case the number is one. Twelve is not the sum of its parts but is short of that amount, for they add up to a number greater than twelve, their total being sixteen. The parts of twelve are five in all: a twelfth, a sixth, a fourth, a third, and a half. A twelfth is one, a sixth is two, a fourth is three, a third is four, a half is six; and these numbers, one, two, three, four, and six, add up to sixteen.

5. Briefly, then, if we go on indefinitely through the series of numbers, we find many that have no such parts other than one, as is the case with three, five, and the like; or many have such parts, but they add up to a quantity less than the number in question, as, for instance, eight and nine, and many others; or they exceed it, as happens with twelve and eighteen, and many similar numbers. All three of these types of numbers occur more frequently than those that are called perfect by reason of the fact that they are equal to the total of their aliquot parts.

After six, the next number that is similarly the sum of its parts is twenty-eight; for it has five parts: a twenty-eighth, a fourteenth, a seventh, a fourth, and a half, namely, one, two, four, seven, and fourteen, which added together equal twenty-eight. And the farther we proceed through the series of numbers, the greater is the distance between the numbers that are the sum of their parts and for that reason are called perfect. For numbers unequal to the sum of their parts are called deficient *(imperfecti);* when the parts exceed that amount, the numbers are called abundant *(plus quam perfecti).*

6. God, therefore, accomplished the works of His creation in six days, a perfect number of days. For thus it is written: *And on the sixth day God finished the works He had made.* And I am even more intrigued by this number when I consider the order of the works of creation.[4] For they are ordered like the number six itself, which rises in three steps from its parts. One, two, and three follow in order, without the possibility of any other number being inserted; and these are the parts of which six is com-

posed, one being a sixth, two being a third, and three being a half.

Thus, on one day light was created; on the two following days the universe was created, the higher part, or firmament, on one day, the lower part, namely, sea and earth, on the other. God did not fill the higher part with any material creatures to serve as nourishment, because He did not intend to place there any bodies needing such food. But on the lower regions, which He was to adorn with living creatures, each in its proper place, He first lavishly bestowed the things they would need for their sustenance. On the remaining three days, therefore, those things were created which, being contained within the universe, that is, this visible creation composed of all the elements, are themselves visible and are moved with their own proper motions. First, in the firmament, because it had been made first, He placed the heavenly bodies. Then in the lower regions He made the living creatures as right order demanded, on one day the creatures of the waters, on another day those of the land. No one is so foolish as to presume to say that God could not have made everything on one day if He had wished; or on two days if He had wished, making the spiritual world on one day, the material on another, or the heavens with all the heavenly creatures on one day, and earth with all that is on it the next day; no one can deny that He might have made everything when He wished, in whatever period of time He wished, and how He wished. Who would say that anything could have resisted His will?

<h2 style="text-align:center">CHAPTER 3</h2>

In what sense God is the measure, number, and weight of all creatures.

7. When we read that God finished all the works of His creation in six days, and when we reflect on the number six and find that it is a perfect number, and when we realize that the works of creation occur according to a pattern, in steps, as it

were, that match the aliquot parts of six,[5] we should call to mind what Scripture says elsewhere: *Thou hast ordered all things in measure and number and weight.*[6] And let the soul that is able reflect on this, calling on God for help, the source of its strength and inspiration, and let it consider whether these three—measure, number, and weight—in which, according to Scripture, God ordered all things, existed somewhere before the creation of every creature, or whether they too were created; and if they existed before creation, let us ask where.

Before creation nothing existed except the Creator. Therefore, these three were in Him. But how? The works of creation are, so Scripture tells us, in Him.[7] Shall we in some way identify measure, number, and weight with Him, and say that the works of creation are, as it were, in Him by whom they are ruled and governed? How can God be identified with measure, number, and weight? He is neither measure, nor number, nor weight, nor all three. He is surely not identified with these three things as we know them in creatures, the limit in things that we measure, the number in things that we count, the weight in things that we weigh. But in the sense that measure places a limit on everything, number gives everything form, and weight draws each thing to a state of repose and stability, God is identified with these three in a fundamental, true, and unique sense. He limits everything, forms everything, and orders everything. Hence, in so far as this matter can be grasped by the heart of man and expressed by his tongue, we must understand that the words, *Thou hast ordered all things in measure and number and weight,* mean nothing else than "Thou hast ordered all things in Thyself."[8]

8. It is a marvelous gift, granted to few persons, to go beyond all that can be measured and see the Measure without measure, to go beyond all that can be numbered and see the Number without number, and to go beyond all that can be weighed and see the Weight without weight.

CHAPTER 4

Measure, number, and weight in the immaterial realm.

Measure, number, and weight are not to be found or thought of only in stones and wood and other such bodies, earthly or heavenly, having mass or quantity. There is also the measure of an activity, which keeps it from going on without control or beyond bounds; there is the number of the affections of the soul and of the virtues, by which the soul is held away from the unformed state of folly and turned towards the form and beauty of wisdom;[9] and there is the weight of the will and of love, wherein appears the worth of everything to be sought, or to be avoided, to be esteemed of greater or less value.

But these are in the realm of spirit or mind, and this measure is limited by another Measure, this number is formed by another Number, and this weight is drawn by another Weight. There is a Measure without measure, and what comes from It must be squared with It, but It does not come from something else; there is a Number without number, by which all things are formed, but It receives no form; and there is a Weight without weight, to which are drawn those beings whose repose is joy undefiled, and there they find their rest, but It is not drawn to any other.

9. The man who knows the words "measure, number, and weight" only in their material sense is like a captive in his limited knowledge. Let him, then, rise up above all that he knows in this way; or, if he finds himself as yet unable to do this, let him not hold on to these words, to which he can attach only an earthly meaning. For a man will find himself more strongly attracted to these things of the spirit the less the attractions of the flesh draw him to things below. But if anyone, in using these words which he has learnt to connect with the lowest and meanest objects, does not wish to transfer them to those sublime things by which he tries to fill his mind with light in contemplation, he must not be compelled to do so. So long as he understands what ought to be understood, there is no need for concern over the name to be given it. But one ought to know

about the likeness of the lower realm to the higher. Otherwise reason will not take a right direction in its effort to rise from this world to the other.

10. But if anyone says that the measure, number, and weight by which, as Scripture testifies, God ordered everything, are created beings, and if by them He ordered everything, by what did He order these three things themselves? If it was by other things, how did He order everything by them, since they would be ordered by others? There is no doubt, then, that those things by which everything has been ordered are outside of the things so ordered.

CHAPTER 5

There exists in God the reason or form of the measure, number, and weight of every creature.

11. Or are we to suppose that the words, *Thou hast ordered all things in measure and number and weight,* mean, "Thou hast ordered all things so that they may have measure, and number, and weight"? For if it were said, "Thou hast ordered all material things in colors," it would not follow that Divine Wisdom, through whom all things have been made, would be understood to have first possessed in Himself the colors according to which He would make material things.[10] But rather we should understand the statement, "Thou hast ordered all material things in colors," as meaning, "Thou hast ordered all material things so that they may have colors." But, of course, the ordering of material things in colors by God the Creator, in other words, the arrangement of things whereby they have been made colored, would be unintelligible unless we understood that there existed in the Wisdom of the Creator some Form of the colors to be placed in the various kinds of material things, even though that Form in the Creator is not called a color. This is what I had in mind when I said that so long as the *thing* is granted, we need not trouble ourselves with the *words.*

12. Granted that the statement, *Thou hast ordered all things in*

measure and number and weight, means that creatures so ordered had their own proper measures, numbers, and weight, capable of change in accordance with the mutability of each species by increase and decrease, abundance and scarcity, lightness and gravity, according to divine ordinance, would we say that corresponding to the mutations in these creatures there is a mutability in the divine plan by which they are ordered? God forbid that we should entertain such a foolish thought!

CHAPTER 6

God knew measure, number, and weight in Himself.

Since, therefore, creatures were ordered in such a way as to have their own measures, numbers, and weights, where did God see these three things when He was ordering creatures? It was not outside of Himself, as is the case when we see material things with the eyes; indeed, such material things were not yet in existence when God was ordaining that they should come to be. Nor did God see them within Himself in the manner in which we see with the mind the images of material things that are not present to our eyes, as we recall what we have beheld or in imagination conjure up images from what we have seen. How, then, did God see these objects so as to order creation thus? How else than in the way in which only He can?

13. But we are mortals and sinners, and our corruptible bodies are a load upon our souls, and the earthly habitation presses down the mind that muses upon many things.[11] But even though our hearts were absolutely undefiled and our minds completely free from all burdens, even though we were already equal to the holy angels, the Essence of God would surely not be known to us as it is to Himself.

CHAPTER 7

Six would be a perfect number even if God had not created the universe according to the order of its parts.

Nevertheless, we do not behold the perfection of the number six outside of ourselves, as we see material things with our eyes, nor within ourselves after the manner in which we behold the forms of bodies and the images of visible objects, but in some other way far different from this. For it may be that some small corporeal images present themselves before the gaze of our minds when we think of the adding up of numbers that total six, or of the position of this number among other numbers, or of its division into parts; but reason with its superior nature and higher powers does not look down upon these images but rather contemplates within itself the nature of this number. By virtue of this contemplation it can say with confidence that the number one cannot be divided into any parts, that material things are infinitely divisible, and that heaven and earth, which have been made according to the number six, might more easily pass away than that it could be possible for the number six not to be made of its parts.[12] Let the spirit of man, then, always give thanks to the Creator, who has created man with the power of seeing what neither bird nor beast can see, although they share with us the sight of sky and earth, the heavenly bodies, the sea, the dry land, and everything contained therein.

14. We cannot, therefore, say that the number six is perfect precisely because God perfected all His works in six days, but rather we must say that God perfected His works in six days because six is a perfect number. Hence, even if these works did not exist, this number would be perfect; and if it had not been perfect, these works would not have been perfected according to it.

CHAPTER 8

God did not rest because of exhaustion.

15. We come now to the text of Scripture that says that God rested on the seventh day from all the works that He had made, and that He blessed this day and sanctified it because of the fact that He had rested on it. Now, in order to try, as far as we can with God's help, to grasp this truth with our intellect, we must first drive from our minds all anthropomorphic concepts that men might have. Can we be justified in saying or believing that God toiled in His work when He made the creatures described in Scripture and when He spoke and they were made? Even a man does not toil if he has only to say the word and an object is made. It is true, of course, that man's words when produced with the sound of the voice will weary the speaker if his speech is prolonged. But there are very few words recorded in the Scripture narrative where God said, *Let there be light, let there be a firmament,* and so forth to the end of the works which He completed on the sixth day. It is, therefore, absurd and ridiculous to suppose that such words would involve toil for man, to say nothing of God.

16. Could one say perhaps that God did not toil by uttering the decree which instantly produced the works He created, but by thinking over what ought to be made? Then, being relieved, as it were, of this burden, once the universe was complete He rested, and therefore He chose to bless and sanctify the day on which He was first released from the strain of such intellectual effort. But to think in this way is utter foolishness, for God's power to create and the ease with which He can exercise it are beyond our knowledge and our ability to describe.

CHAPTER 9

God rested in the sense that He gave rest in Himself to the intellectual beings He created.

What other interpretation is left, therefore, unless we understand that God gave rest in Himself to the rational beings He had created, among whom man is included, that is, that after their creation He gave them this rest by the gift of the Holy Spirit, by whom charity is poured forth in our hearts,[13] that we may be drawn to God by a desire and yearning for Him, and reaching Him may find rest, and want nothing besides? For as we are justified in saying that God does whatever we do by His operation within us, so we can rightly say that God rests when by His gift we rest.

17. We are right in accepting this interpretation, because it is true,[14] and it takes no great effort to see how God is said to rest when He causes us to rest, just as He is said to know when He makes us know. For God does not come to know in time what He formerly did not know; and yet He said to Abraham, *Now I know that you fear God.*[15] This we can only understand as meaning, *Now I have made it known.* By these expressions, which we use when we describe things as happening to God which did not happen to Him, we recognize that He causes them to happen to us. We limit such expressions, of course, to praiseworthy things, and we use this way of speaking only in so far as the language of Scripture sanctions it. For in speaking of God, we should not rashly use any such expression that we do not find in Scripture.

18. This manner of speaking, I believe, is used by St. Paul when he says, *Do not grieve the Holy Spirit of God, in whom you were sealed for the day of redemption.*[16] For the Holy Spirit in His own divine Essence cannot really be grieved, since He possesses eternal and immutable beatitude, or rather He is eternal and immutable beatitude itself. But He dwells in those who are sanctified, filling them with charity. By reason of this indwelling, men in this life feel compelled to rejoice in the advancement of the faithful in good works and also to grieve over the lapses and sins of those whose faith and piety were a source of joy. This

grief is praiseworthy because it proceeds from the love that the Holy Spirit infuses. Hence it is that this Spirit Himself is said to be grieved by those who act in such a way that holy men, for the very reason that they possess the Holy Spirit, are grieved by their deeds. By this gift of the Holy Spirit men are so good that they are saddened by evildoers, especially by those they knew or believed were good. Such grief is not only not blameworthy, but it even deserves the warmest praise and approval.

19. This is the manner of speaking used again by St. Paul in a striking way when he says, *Now knowing God, or rather known by God.*[17] For it was not at that moment that God came to know of these Galatians: they were foreknown, indeed, before the foundation of the world.[18] But because at that moment they came to know God by God's gift to them and not by their own merits or their own powers, St. Paul chose to speak figuratively, saying that they were known by God at the moment when He made Himself known to them, and he preferred to correct his expression, as if what he had said correctly were not well said, rather than allow men to attribute to themselves a power granted them by God.

CHAPTER 10

But in what sense can God Himself be said to have rested?

20. Some may be satisfied to say that God rested from all His works which He had made and which were exceedingly good in the sense that He gives rest to us when we have performed good works. But after opening up the question of the meaning of this scriptural text, I feel compelled to ask how precisely God Himself could have rested, even though it is clear that in revealing to us the fact of His own rest He has admonished us to hope to find our rest in Him.

God, of course, made heaven and earth and all that is in them, and He finished everything on the sixth day. But it cannot be said that, by a creative power given by Him, we have created something among these works, and that Scripture declares, *On the sixth day God finished the works He made,* in the sense that He gave us the power to finish them. Similarly, the statement, *God rested on the seventh day from all the works He had made,* ought not to be taken to mean our rest, which by His gift we shall attain, but primarily His rest, that of the seventh day when His works were completed. Thus, we must first point out the facts as reported by Holy Scripture and then, if necessary, indicate whatever figurative meaning they may have. It is, of course, correct to say that we shall rest after our good works, just as God rested after His. But for this reason it is also right to demand that, after our discussion on the works of God, which are obviously His, we now investigate the repose of God, which is clearly His own.

CHAPTER 11

The Sabbath rest, our future rest in God, and the rest of Christ in the tomb.

21. There is every reason, therefore, why we should enquire into this matter and explain, if we can, how the truth is found both in this text where Scripture says that God rested on the seventh day from all works He had made, and in the Gospel text where He through whom all things have been made says, *My Father works even until now, and I work.*[19] These words were spoken by our Lord to those who complained that He did not observe the Sabbath, which had been prescribed of old by the authority of this Scripture passage in remembrance of God's repose.

Now, there are solid grounds for the opinion that the observance of the Sabbath was imposed upon the Jews to foreshadow what was to be and to symbolize the spiritual rest that God by the mystery of this sign, using His own repose as an exemplar, promised to the faithful who perform good works. Our Lord Jesus Christ Himself, who suffered only when He wished, also confirmed the mystery of this repose by His own burial. For it was on the Sabbath day that He rested in the tomb, and He passed this whole day in a kind of holy leisure after He had finished on the sixth day or the day of the Preparation, which is called Friday,[20] all His works, fulfilling on the cross what was written of Him. He used this very word "finish" when He said, *"It is finished!" And bowing His head, He gave up His spirit.*[21] Is it a matter for wonder, therefore, if God, wishing in this way also to foreshadow the day on which Christ was to rest in the sepulchre, rested on one day from all His works, although after that He would work the unfolding of the progress of the ages? Thus the Gospel text is true that says, *My Father works even until now.*

CHAPTER 12

God "rests" in the sense of not creating any new nature, but still "works" in the sense of governing creation.

22. It could also be said that God rested from creating because He did not create henceforward any new kinds of creatures, and that even until now and beyond He works by governing the kinds that He then made. None the less, even on the seventh day His power ceased not from ruling heaven and earth and all that He had made, for otherwise they would have perished immediately. For the power and might of the Creator, who rules and embraces all, makes every creature abide; and if this power ever ceased to govern creatures, their essences would pass away and all nature would perish. When a builder puts up a house and departs, his work remains in spite of the fact that he is no longer there. But the universe will pass away in the twinkling of an eye if God withdraws His ruling hand.

23. Hence, the statement of our Lord, *My Father works even until now*, makes it clear that God continues the work by which He holds and governs all creation. Another meaning might be taken if Christ said, "He works now." In that case there would be no need for understanding the continuance of the work. But a different meaning must be given to the words, *even until now*, because they indicate that God has worked from the moment in which He created everything.

When Scripture says of Divine Wisdom that *It reaches from end to end mightily and governs all graciously,*[22] and that *Its motion is* swifter and more active than all motions,[23] it is quite clear, if we think well on the matter, that Wisdom, when It governs created things graciously, gives them a motion beyond our powers to comprehend or describe, a motion we might call stable, if we can conceive of such a thing. And if this motion is withdrawn and Wisdom ceases from this work, creatures will immediately perish.

St. Paul, when preaching God to the Athenians, said, *In Him we live and move and have our being.*[24] Now, if we penetrate into the meaning of this statement, in so far as the human mind can, we shall see that it supports our belief in the fact that God works ceaselessly in the creatures He has made. We do not exist in Him as a constituent element in the sense in which it is said that He has life in Himself.[25] But although we are distinct from Him, we are in Him precisely because He brings this about by His work, and this work is that by which He holds all things and by which His Wisdom *reaches from end to end mightily and governs all graciously.* It is by this divine governance that we live and move and have our being in Him.

From this it follows that if He withholds His work in creatures, we shall cease to live and move and be. It is clear, then, that God has not stopped for even one day from the work of ruling His creatures, lest they forthwith lose the natural motions by which their actions and vital processes go on. Thus He provides that they have their own proper natures and each remains in that state that it has according to its kind. Otherwise creatures would cease to exist altogether if the motion of Divine Wisdom, disposing all graciously, were withdrawn from them. Therefore, we understand that God rested from all the works that He made in the sense that from then on He did not produce any other new nature, not that He ceased to hold and govern what He had made. Hence it is true that God rested on the seventh day, and it is also true that He works even until now.

CHAPTER 13

How in the new order of grace the faithful keep a perpetual Sabbath.

24. The good works of God we see; His repose we shall see after our good works. To signify this repose, He commanded the Hebrew people to observe one day.[26] This they did in such an earthly way that they blamed our Lord when they saw Him working our salvation on that day, and He rightly replied to them by reminding them of the work of His Father, with whom He worked in equal measure, procuring our salvation[27] as well as the governance of all creatures.[28] And now, in the time of the revelation of His grace, the observance of the Sabbath, which was typified by the repose of one day, has been done away with for the faithful. For in the present order of grace a perpetual Sabbath is kept by the man who performs every good work in the hope of the rest that is to come, and yet he glories not in these good works of his, as if he possessed some good that he had not received. For thus, when he receives the sacrament of baptism, understanding it as the Sabbath day, that is, the day of our Lord's repose in the tomb, he rests from his former works, so that he walks in newness of life[29] and recognizes God working in him. God indeed works and rests at the same time, wisely governing His creation and retaining in Himself His eternal repose.

CHAPTER 14

God is said to have sanctified the day of His rest, but we are not told that He sanctified the preceding six days.

25. God was neither wearied by the act of creating nor refreshed when He ceased from it, but by His inspired word He wished to urge us to a longing for rest, when He revealed to us that He had sanctified the day on which He rested from all His works. At no time during the six days of creation do we read that He sanctified anything; and before the six days, where it is

written, *In the beginning God created heaven and earth,*[30] Scripture does not say that He sanctified them. But He did wish to sanctify the day on which He rested from all the works He had made, as if to indicate that even in Himself, who toils not in His work, repose is more important than activity. This truth as applied to man is taught us in the Gospel, where our Savior says that Mary has the better part because she sat at His feet and rested in His word, rather than Martha, in spite of the fact that out of devotion she served Him, busying herself about many things, and thus performed a good work.[31]

It is difficult to say how this principle is true as applied to God and in what sense we are to understand it. And yet, in some feeble way we can grasp the reason why God sanctified the day of His rest, although He had sanctified none of His works, not even the sixth day, on which He made man and finished all His works. What human intellect can penetrate first of all into the nature of this repose of God? Nevertheless, if it had not taken place, it never would have been stated in Scripture. I shall make my mind perfectly clear, laying down two points as certain: first, God did not find joy in a period of time devoted to rest as one might after toil as he comes to the long-sought end of his efforts; and, secondly, the words of Holy Scripture, which rightly possess supreme authority, are not idle or false when they say that God rested on the seventh day from all the works that He made, and because He rested upon it He made it holy.

CHAPTER 15

God always rests in Himself, having no need of creatures.

26. It is an imperfection and a weakness in a soul to delight in its works in such a way as to rest in them rather than to find rest from them in itself. For there is doubtless in the soul something by which these external things are produced which is superior to the things produced. Hence, where Holy Scripture says that God rested from all the works that He made, He is not

represented as taking delight in any work in such a way as to
imply that He needed to make it, or that He would have lacked
something if He had not made it, or that He was happier after
He had made it. For whatever comes from God is so dependent
upon Him that it owes its existence to Him, but He does not
owe His happiness to any creature He has made. He placed
Himself in His love above the works He had made, for He did
not sanctify the day on which He began to make them, nor that
on which He finished them, lest there appear to be an increase
in His joy because of the undertaking or completion of these
works. But He did sanctify that day on which He rested from
them in Himself.

God has never, of course, lacked this rest, but He has shown
it to us by means of the seventh day. Hence He has at the same
time shown us that rest in Him is not enjoyed except by the perfect, since in revealing His rest to us He chose only the day that
followed the perfecting of all creation. For God, who is always
in a state of tranquility, has rested, as far as we are concerned,
at that time when He has revealed Himself to us as resting.

CHAPTER 16

God has no need of the creatures He made. Our rest is in Him.

27. It should be pointed out also that God's rest, by which He
is happy in Himself, had to be revealed to us so that we might
understand what the meaning of rest is as applied to us. The
truth is that this term describes only that state in which God
makes us sharers in that rest which He has in Himself. God's
rest, therefore, when rightly understood, is His independence of
any need for any good outside of Himself. Hence, our unfailing
rest is in Him, because we attain happiness in the good that is
God, but God does not attain happiness in the good that we are.
We are in our measure a good coming from God, who made all
things exceedingly good, including ourselves. There is no other
good thing apart from God that He did not make, and therefore

He needs no good outside of Himself because He needs not the good He has made. This is His rest from all the good works He has wrought.

Of what good things could God fittingly feel no need if He had created none? For He also might be said to need no good outside of Himself not by resting in Himself from His creatures but simply by making no creatures at all. But if He were unable to create good things, He would have no power; if He were able but did not do so, He would be filled with envy.[32] Therefore, because He is all-powerful and good, He made everything exceedingly good; but because He is perfectly happy in His own goodness, He rested in Himself from the good things He had made, in that state of rest from which He has never departed. But if He were said to have rested from the making of creatures, this would mean nothing more than that He did not create them. On the other hand, unless it were said that He rested from the things He had made, the fact that He needed not what He made would be less cogently brought home to us.

28. If one should ask why God's rest had to be brought before us as occurring on the seventh day, he will understand if he recalls the perfection of the number six, of which we spoke above,[33] and its appropriate use in the perfecting of creation. For if creation had to be perfected in the number six, as it was, and if God's rest had to be revealed to us in such a way as to make it clear that He was not made happy by His creatures even when they were made perfect, it was obvious that in this revealed account of creation the day following the sixth had to be sanctified so that by it we might be borne up to desire this rest and thus also find our rest in Him.

CHAPTER 17

Our likeness to God is our rest in Him, not in ourselves, nor in His works.

29. Our likeness to God cannot be holy if we wish to be like Him in such a way as to rest in ourselves from our works as He

rested in Himself from His works. For we must rest in an immutable Good, that is, in Him who made us. This will be our most exalted state of rest, a truly holy state, free from all pride. Just as He rested from all His works because He Himself, and not His works, is His good and the source of His happiness, so we must hope that we shall find rest only in Him from all works, whether ours or His; and this is what we must desire after our good works, which, though taking place in us, we recognize as His.[34] Thus, He also rests after His good works, when He bestows rest in Himself upon us after the good works we have done when justified by Him.[35]

Our existence is a great gift from Him, but our rest in Him will be even greater. He Himself does not owe His happiness to that fact that He has made creatures, but rather to the fact that, having no need of what He has made, He has rested in Himself rather than in them. Therefore, it is not the day of His work but the day of His rest that He has made holy; for He has revealed that He is happy not by making creatures but by having no need of those He has made.

30. What, then, is so simple and easy to state, but so lofty and difficult to grasp, as God resting from all the works that He made? And where does He rest except in Himself, since He is happy only in Himself? And when, if not always? But in the days on which the creation was accomplished according to the scriptural narrative, with the appropriate place designated for God's rest, when did He rest except on the seventh day, the day that follows the finishing of creatures? For He rests from the finishing of His creatures who needs no finishing of creatures to increase His happiness.

CHAPTER 18

Why the seventh day had a morning but no evening.

31. As far as God Himself is concerned, His repose has neither morning nor evening, because it has no beginning or end. But with respect to the works that He has perfected, His repose

does have a morning but no evening. For a creature that is perfected has a beginning of its conversion to the repose of its Creator, but that repose does not have an end as the limit of its perfection, as creatures have. Hence, God's rest has a beginning not for God Himself but for the perfecting of His creatures, and, accordingly, what He perfects begins to rest in Him and in Him has a morning. In its own nature it is limited after the manner of evening, but in God it can have no evening, because there will be nothing more perfect than its perfect state of rest in Him.[36]

32. In interpreting the days of creation, we took evening to mean the limit of a created nature, and the following morning to mean the beginning of another to be created.[37] Consequently, the evening of the fifth day is the limit of what was created on the fifth day; the morning that was made after that evening is the beginning of what was to be created on the sixth day. Once this was created, evening was made as a kind of limit to it. And then, because nothing else remained to be created, morning was made after that evening, not to begin the creation of any further creature, but to begin the repose of all creation resting in its Creator.

Heaven and earth and all that they contain, that is, the whole spiritual and material creation, remain not in themselves but in Him of whom it is said, *For in Him we live and move and have our being.*[38] For although each part can exist in the whole of which it is part, the whole itself exists only in Him by whom it was created. Hence, it is not unreasonable to suppose that on the completion of the sixth day, after its evening, morning was made not to indicate the beginning of the creation of another creature, as on the other days, but the beginning of that state in which the whole of creation remains and rests in the repose of Him who made it. This repose has no beginning and no end in God; it has a beginning but not an end in creation. For it the seventh day begins with morning, but no evening ends it.

33. If during the other days, the six days of creation, evening and morning signify the passage of time such as it occurs now from day to day, I see nothing to prevent the seventh day from ending with evening and its night ending with morning, so that

it might be said of it also, "And there was evening and morning, the seventh day." For it is one of the days of which there are seven altogether, which keep recurring to make up the months and years and ages. On this supposition, the morning following the evening of the seventh day would be the beginning of the eighth; but there would have been no need for any mention of this eighth day, since it marks a return to the first, and from it the week begins again.

The more likely explanation, therefore, is this: these seven days of our time, although like the seven days of creation in name and in numbering, follow one another in succession and mark off the division of time, but those first six days occurred in a form unfamiliar to us as intrinsic principles within things created. Hence evening and morning, like light and darkness, that is, day and night, did not produce the changes that they do for us with the motion of the sun. This we are certainly forced to admit with regard to the first three days, which are recorded and numbered before the creation of the heavenly bodies.

34. Whatever evening and morning were in those days of creation, it is quite impossible to suppose that on the morning following the evening of the sixth day God's rest began. We cannot be so foolish or rash as to imagine that any such temporal good would accrue to the Eternal and Unchangeable. The repose of God, by which He rests in Himself and is happy in the Good which is identified with Himself, has no beginning and no end for Him; but this same repose of God did have a beginning for creation when it was finished. For the perfection of each thing according to the limits of its nature is established in a state of rest, that is, it has a fixed orientation by reason of its natural tendencies, not just in the universe of which it is a part, but more especially in Him to whom it owes its being, in whom the universe itself exists.[39]

Accordingly, the whole of creation, which was finished in six days, has a certain character in its own nature and another character in the order or orientation by which it is in God, not as God Himself is, but in such a way that there is no repose to give it its proper stability except in the repose of Him who desires nothing outside of Himself; and when it has attained this state it is at rest. God, then, remaining in Himself, draws back to Himself whatever He has made, so that every creature has within itself the limit of its nature, by which it is distinct from God, but in God it has its place of rest, by which it maintains its nature and identity. I realize that I have not used this term "place" in the literal sense, since literally it is used of spaces occupied by bodies. But bodies do not remain in place unless they arrive at that point to which they are drawn by an inclination that might be called an appetite of their weight, and when they find it, they are at rest. Hence it is not incongruous to transfer the meaning of the word from the material to the spiritual order and speak of place in this sense, although the reality itself is worlds apart.

35. The beginning, therefore, of the repose that creation has in its Creator is, in my opinion, signified by the morning that follows the evening of the sixth day, for it could not rest in Him unless it were finished. Hence, when all was completed on the sixth day and evening was made, then there was the morning on which all creation, finally finished, began to rest in Him who made it. In this beginning it found God resting in Himself, where it also would be able to rest in perfect stability precisely because it had need of Him, not He of it, for its repose. But since the whole of creation, whatever its state, in spite of all changes it undergoes, will not cease to be, it will always remain in its Creator, and so after that morning there was no evening.

36. This is the reason why the seventh day, on which God rested from all His works, had a morning after the evening of the sixth, but did not itself have an evening.

CHAPTER 19

Another reason why the seventh day had a morning but no evening.

There is another explanation of this matter which I believe is more the literal meaning and more readily grasped, although somewhat more difficult to explain, that is, how we understand that God's rest on the seventh day had a morning without an evening, or a beginning without an end, not just for creation but also for Himself. For if it were said that God rested on the seventh day, without the addition of the words, *from all the works He had made*, it would be idle to look for the beginning of this rest. God does not start to rest: His rest is eternal, without beginning or end. But since He rested from all the works He had made simply by having no need for them, it is clear that God's rest is neither begun nor ended.[40] However, His rest from all the works He had made was begun at the moment He finished them.[41] For He would not have rested by having no need of His works before they existed, since even when they were finished He did not need them. And because He never had any need for them at all, and because the beatitude in which He does not need them will not come to a state of completion by some sort of development, no evening was added to the seventh day.

CHAPTER 20

God created only one day which recurred seven times.

37. But there is another serious question that merits our attention. How can we understand that it was in Himself that God rested from all the works He had made, when Scripture says, *And God rested on the seventh day?* It does not say "in Himself" but *on the seventh day.*[42]

What, then, is the seventh day? Is it a creature or merely a period of time? But even a period of time is concreated with creatures subject to time, and hence it is also undoubtedly a creature. For there are not and could not have been and never can be any periods of time that God did not create. Therefore, if this seventh day is a period of time, who created it except the Creator of all times? But with regard to the six days of creation, the text of Scripture that we have already treated tells us with what creatures or in what creatures they were created.

Now the seven days of our week, with which we are all familiar, in reality pass by; but they hand on, as it were, their names to others that follow, so that thus the six days of creation are recalled, and we know when these first six days were created. But it is not clear when God created the seventh day, which is called the Sabbath. For on that day He made nothing; indeed, on that seventh day He rested from what He had made on the six days. How, then, did He rest on a day He did not create? Or, on the other hand, how did He create it immediately after the six days, since on the sixth day He finished all that He created, and He created nothing on the seventh day, but rather rested on it from all that He had made?

Perhaps we should say that God created only one day, so that by its recurrence many periods called days would pass by. It was not necessary, then, for Him to create the seventh day, for the seventh recurrence of the day God had created made it. For He separated from darkness the light of which it is written, *And God said, "Let there be light," and light was made, and He called the light Day and the darkness Night.*[43] So, then, God created a day, whose recurrence Scripture calls the second day, then the third, and so on to the sixth, on which God finished His works; and then the seventh recurrence of the day originally created was called the seventh day, and on it God rested. This seventh day, therefore, is not a creature except in so far as it is the same creature recurring for the seventh time, that creature, namely, which was created when God *called the light Day and the darkness Night.*

CHAPTER 21

How did God make present seven times the light He created on the first day?

38. We have once more fallen back into the problem from which we thought we had disentangled ourselves in the first book; for we must again ask how light could have travelled about to cause the passage of day and night not only before the heavenly bodies were made, but also before the making of the heaven which is called the firmament, and before any appearance of earth or sea into which the light could come, and from which with the approach of night it could pass away. Pressed by

the perplexities of this problem, we finally took a stand and brought our discussion to an end by advancing the opinion that the light which was first made was the formation of the spiritual creation, and that night was the matter still to be formed in the other works, the matter that was made when in the beginning God made heaven and earth, before He made day by His Word.[44]

But now, in view of what we have seen about the seventh day, it is easier to admit our ignorance of a thing that is beyond our experience and confess our inability to explain how the light that is called Day brought about the passage of day and night either by a circular motion or by contraction and diffusion, if it is material;[45] or how, if it is spiritual, it was made present to all creatures yet to be made, causing day by its presence and night by its absence, evening by the beginning of its absence and morning by the beginning of its presence. It is easier to confess our ignorance of these matters than to go against the obvious meaning of the words of Holy Scripture by saying that the seventh day is something else than the seventh recurrence of the day that God made. Otherwise, either God did not create the seventh day, or He created something, namely the seventh day, after the six days; and then Scripture will be wrong in saying that He finished all His works on the sixth day, and that He rested on the seventh from all His works. But since there can be no error in Scripture, we must conclude that the presence of the light that God made as day was repeated throughout all the works as often as day is mentioned, even on the seventh day itself, on which God rested from His works.

CHAPTER 22

Morning and evening as referring to the knowledge of the angels.

39. As for material light, it is not clear by what circular motion or going forth and returning [46] it could have produced the succession of day and night before the making of the heaven called firmament, in which the heavenly bodies were made.

This question, then, ought not to be dropped without some statement of our opinion. Hence, if the light originally created is not material but spiritual, then this light [namely, the company of angels] was made after the darkness in the sense that it turned from its unformed state to its Creator and was thus formed.[47] Consequently, after evening, morning is made, when after its knowledge of its own nature as something distinct from God, this light directs itself to praise the Light that is God, in the contemplation of which it is formed. And, because the other creatures below it are not made without its knowledge, the one and same day is repeated each time so that by this repetition as many days may recur as there are kinds of creatures, determined by the perfection of the number six.[48] Evening of the first day, therefore, is the knowledge spiritual beings have of themselves, inasmuch as they know they are not God. The morning following the evening that concludes the first day, the morning, that is, which begins the second day, is the conversion of spiritual beings, by which they direct to the praise of their Creator the gift of their creation, and receive from the Word of God a knowledge of the creature next made, namely, the firmament. The firmament, therefore, was first made in the knowledge of spiritual creatures, as indicated by the words, *And so it was done*, and afterwards in the actual firmament produced in nature itself, as revealed in the words that follow next, *And so it was done, And God made the firmament.*[49]

Then there is evening of the light, when created intellects know the firmament itself, not in the Word of God as before, but in its own nature. This knowledge, being of a lower order, is rightly designated by the term "evening." After this there is the morning that concludes the second day and begins the third. In this morning there is again a turning of its light (that is, the morning of this day) to praise God for making the firmament and to receive from His Word a knowledge of the work to be created after the firmament. When God, therefore, says, *Let the water that is under the heaven be gathered together into one place, and let the dry land appear*, the company of illuminated spirits know this in the Word of God by whom it is uttered. Hence Scripture says, *And so it was done,* that is, in the knowledge this light has from the Word of God. Then when it is said, *The water was gathered* and so forth, after the words, *And so it was done,* the creature itself was produced in its own kind. Finally, when this creature is again known by the light as something made in its own kind, though it had already known it in the Word of God as something to be made, evening is made for the third time. And the same procedure is followed in the production of the other creatures until the morning after the evening of the sixth day.

CHAPTER 23

The knowledge of a thing in the Word of God and in itself.

40. There is a vast difference between knowledge of a thing in the Word of God and knowledge of the same thing in itself. The first kind of knowledge can be considered as belonging to day; the second kind, to evening. In comparison with the light that is seen in the Word of God, all knowledge by which we know any creature in itself can rightly be called night. But this latter kind of knowledge in its turn is so different from the error or ignorance of those who know not even the creature, that in comparison with this darkness it deserves to be called day.

In a similar manner, the life that the faithful live in the corruptible body in this world, when compared with a life of infidelity and iniquity, is not unreasonably called light and day. For example, St. Paul says, *You were once darkness, but now you are light in the Lord.*[50] And again he writes, *Let us lay aside the works of darkness and put on the armor of light. Let us walk becomingly as in the day.*[51] Now, this day in its turn, in comparison with that day in which, made equal to the angels, we shall see God as He is, would also be a night; and that is why in this life we need the lamp of prophecy, as the Apostle Peter tells us: *We have the word of prophecy, surer still, to which you do well to attend, as to a lamp shining in a dark place, until the day dawns and the morning star rises in your hearts.*[52]

CHAPTER 24

Angelic knowledge.

41. The holy angels, whose equals we shall be after the resurrection,[53] if to the end we hold to Christ our Way, always behold the face of God and rejoice in His Word, the only-begotten Son, equal to the Father; and in them first of all wisdom was created. They, therefore, without any doubt know all creation, of which they are the creatures first made, and they have this knowledge first in the Word of God Himself, in whom are the eternal reasons of all things made in time, existing in Him through whom all things have been created. And then they have this knowledge in creation itself, as they look down upon it and refer it to the praise of Him in whose immutable truth they behold, as in the source of all creation, the reasons by which creatures have been made.

There the knowledge they have is like day, and so that blessed company, perfectly united by participation in the same Truth, is the day first created; here among creatures their knowledge is like evening. But immediately morning comes (and this happens on all six days), because the knowledge angels have does not remain fixed in a creature without their immediately referring it to the praise and love of Him in whom they know not the fact, but the reason, of its creation. They are the day as they remain firm in this Truth. For if the angels turned to themselves or took delight more in themselves than in Him in union with whom they are happy, they would fall swollen with pride. This is what happened with the Devil, of whom we shall have occasion to speak when it is necessary to discuss the serpent that seduced man.

CHAPTER 25

Why no mention is made of night in the six days.

42. The angels, then, know creatures in themselves, but their love is such that they willingly prefer to this sort of knowledge the knowledge they have of creatures in the Truth by which all things have been made. For they themselves have been made to share in that Truth. Through all six days, therefore, no mention is made of night, but after evening and morning there is one day; again after evening and morning, another day; then after evening and morning, a third day; and so on to the morning of the sixth day, and after that the seventh day of God's rest begins. These days have their nights, but it is the days, not the nights, that are described. For night belongs to day, not day to night, when the holy angels of heaven refer their knowledge of creatures in themselves to the honor and love of Him in whom they comtemplate the eternal reasons by which creatures were made. Perfectly united in this contemplation, the angels are one day that the Lord has made, to which the Church will be joined when freed from this pilgrimage, that we also may be glad and rejoice therein.[54]

CHAPTER 26

The meaning of day in the creation narrative.

43. All creation, then, was finished by the sixfold recurrence of this day whose evening and morning we may interpret as explained above.[55] And there was the morning that terminated the sixth day, at which time there was the beginning of the seventh, which would have no evening, since God's rest is not a creature. For creatures, when they were being produced on the other days, were known to the angels not only in God, the Truth by which they were to be made, but also in themselves as things actually made. This latter knowledge, being a kind of faded likeness of the other, constituted evening. Hence, we can no longer

take "day" to mean the form of the work created and "evening" its completion and "morning" the beginning of another work, in the account of creation.[56] Otherwise we might be forced to say, against the evidence of Scripture, that beyond the works of the six days a creature was made on the seventh day, or that the seventh day itself was not a creature. But that day, which God has made, recurs in connection with His works not by a material passage of time but by spiritual knowledge, when the blessed company of angels contemplate from the beginning in the Word of God the divine decree to create. And thus the work is first produced in their knowledge as indicated in the words, *And so it was made.* After that they know the creature itself in itself, and this is revealed to us where it is said that there was evening. Finally, they refer this knowledge of the creature to the praise of eternal Truth, where they had beheld the form of the work to be produced, and this is the meaning of the statement that it was morning.[57]

Thus, in all the days of creation there is one day, and it is not to be taken in the sense of our day, which we reckon by the course of the sun; but it must have another meaning, applicable to the three days mentioned before the creation of the heavenly bodies. This special meaning of "day" must not be maintained just for the first three days, with the understanding that after the third day we take the word "day" in its ordinary sense. But we must keep the same meaning even to the sixth and seventh days. Hence, "day" and "night," which God divided, must be interpreted quite differently from the familiar "day" and "night," which God decreed the lights that He created in the firmament should divide when He said, *And let them divide day and night.* For it was by this latter act that He created our day, creating the sun whose presence makes the day. But that other day which was originally made had already repeated itself three times when, at its fourth recurrence, these lights of the firmament were created.

CHAPTER 27

Days familiar to us are quite different from the days of creation.

44. That day in the account of creation, or those days that are numbered according to its recurrence, are beyond the experience and knowledge of us mortal earthbound men. And if we are able to make any effort towards an understanding of the meaning of those days, we ought not to rush forward with an ill-considered opinion, as if no other reasonable and plausible interpretation could be offered. Seven days by our reckoning, after the model of the days of creation, make up a week. By the passage of such weeks time rolls on, and in these weeks one day is constituted by the course of the sun from its rising to its setting; but we must bear in mind that these days indeed recall the days of creation, but without in any way being really similar to them.

CHAPTER 28

The interpretation given for "day" is not allegorical.

45. I have spoken about spiritual light, about the creation of day in angelic spirits, about their contemplation of the Word of God, about their knowledge of creatures in themselves, and about their referring this to the praise of immutable Truth, where from the first they beheld the forms of creatures yet to be before they knew these creatures as actually produced. Now it must not be thought that these interpretations are applicable to "day" and "evening" and "morning" not literally but only in some figurative and allegorical way. These interpretations, of course, are different from our ordinary understanding of light in the material sense. But it is not true that material light is literally "light," and light referred to in Genesis is metaphorical "light." For where light is more excellent and unfailing, there day also exists in a truer sense. Why, then, should that day not have a truer evening and a truer morning? For if in the days

with which we are familiar the light wanes as the day declines, and we call this evening, and if it rises again at daybreak, and we call this morning, why should we not say that there is also evening when angels after contemplating the Creator gaze down upon a creature, and that there is also morning when they rise from a knowledge of a creature to the praise of the Creator? Christ Himself is not called the Light in the same way as He is called a stone: He is literally the Light but metaphorically a stone.[58]

Whoever, then, does not accept the meaning that my limited powers have been able to discover or conjecture but seeks in the enumeration of the days of creation a different meaning, which might be understood not in a prophetical or figurative sense, but literally and more aptly, in interpreting the works of creation, let him search and find a solution with God's help.[59] I myself may possibly discover some other meaning more in harmony with the words of Scripture. I certainly do not advance the interpretation given above in such a way as to imply that no better one can ever be found, although I do maintain that Sacred Scripture does not tell us that God rested after feeling weariness and fatigue.

CHAPTER 29

Our interpretation does not imply intervals of time in angelic knowledge.

46. Someone may perhaps disagree with me and say that the angels in heaven do not gaze at one object and then at another, first at the forms of creatures existing immutably in the immutable truth of the Word of God, and then at creatures in their own proper existence, and after that refer this knowledge of creatures in themselves to the praise of the Creator. The angelic mind, it may be objected, is able with effortless ease to behold all this in a single glance. But surely the objector cannot say, nor should we listen to anyone who would say, that the heavenly society, composed of thousands of angels, does not contemplate

the eternity of the Creator, or is not aware of the mutability of creatures, or, recognizing its own inferior knowledge, does not praise the Creator. The angels may be able to do all this at once; they may actually do all this at once; as a matter of fact, they are able and they actually do. At one and the same time, therefore, they have day and evening and morning.[60]

CHAPTER 30

Evening and morning in angelic knowledge do not imply the passage of time.

47. There need be no fear that one who can grasp this explanation may still think it impossible for such a thing to take place in the minds of angels on the ground that it is impossible in the days of our world, which are constituted by the course of the sun.

It is true that such a thing is impossible on any one part of the earth. But who cannot see, if he is willing to reflect on the matter, that the universe as a whole at one and the same time has day where the sun is, night where it is not, evening where the sun sets, and morning where it rises? We who dwell on this earth certainly cannot experience all this at one time. But we should not on that account consider the creatures of this world and the circular movement of material light, subject as it is to time and space, as the equal of the spiritual light of our home in heaven. In heaven there is always day in the contemplation of immutable truth, always evening in the knowledge of creatures in their own existence, always morning in the fact that this knowledge is referred to the praise of the Creator. In that realm it is not the withdrawal of a higher light, but the difference distinguishing the lesser knowledge from the greater, that accounts for evening; and the knowledge of morning does not follow ignorance as our morning does the night, but it raises up the very knowledge of evening to the glory of the Creator.[61] The Psalmist, too, not mentioning night, says, *In the evening, in the morning, and at noon, I will speak and declare, and Thou wilt hear my voice.*[62] Perhaps he had in mind the passage of time as it is in this life, but I think he also wished to indicate the sort of life that exists beyond the bounds of time in our heavenly country, for which he longed in this land of exile.

CHAPTER 31

But when God was creating there seems to have been a succession in angelic knowledge.

48. It is true, therefore, that now the company of the angels, enjoying the unity of the day that God first made, possess day and evening and morning simultaneously. But was this true when God was creating? It would seem rather that on all six days, when God was making the works He was pleased to make on each day, the angels first saw the creature in the Word of God, and thus the creature was originally produced in the knowledge of the angels, as Scripture indicates by the words, *And so it was done.* Then, when the works of one day had been produced in their own proper nature and God had been pleased, seeing that they were good, the angels knew them once more, this time with an inferior sort of knowledge indicated by the name of evening. Finally, when evening had passed, morning came, when the angels praised God for His work and received further knowledge of other creatures to be created, this knowledge being given to them in the Word of God before the production of the works themselves.

Day, therefore, and evening and morning did not all occur simultaneously at the time of creation, but separately and in the order set forth in Sacred Scripture.

CHAPTER 32

At least there was a certain order in what angels knew.

49. But on the contrary, can we say that these three moments were simultaneous? They were not subject to the slow passage of time, as in the case of our days with the rising and setting of the sun and the return of the sun to the place of its rising. Day, evening, and morning at creation took place in the spiritual power of the minds of angels, who without any effort grasped at one and the same time all that they wished. But it does not follow from this that there was no order in these things, and no evidence of a causal connection in the process. Knowledge cannot come about unless the objects to be known go before; and these objects first exist in the Word, by which all things have been made, before they exist in all the things that have been made.

In the same way, the human mind first perceives through the bodily senses the things that have been created and according to its limited human powers forms a concept of them. It then seeks their causes in the hope of being able to arrive at those causes that dwell originally and immutably in the Word of God, and to see the invisible attributes of God, understanding them through the things that are made.[63] Who does not know how slow and difficult this task is and what time it takes because of the corruptible body that burdens the soul,[64] even the soul that soars with burning desire to pursue this object and cling to it?

But the minds of angels, united to the Word of God in pure charity, created before the other works of creation, first saw in the Word of God those works to be made before they were actually made; and thus those works were first made in the angels' knowledge when God decreed that they should come into being, before they were made in their own proper natures. The angels also knew those works in their own natures as things already made, with a knowledge admittedly of a lower order called evening. Prior to this knowledge the objects made already existed: whatever is knowable precedes knowledge. For unless the object known first exists, it cannot be known.

After this, if the angelic mind chose to find delight rather in itself than in its Creator, there would be no morning, that is, the angelic mind would not rise up from its own knowledge to the praise of the Creator. But when morning came, another work was to be made and to be known, as God said, "Let such-and-such a work be made"; and thus it likewise was first made in the knowledge of angels, and then God could say once more, *And so it was done*, and finally it was made in its own proper nature, where it would be known on the following evening.

50. Although there are no periods of time between the steps in this process, nevertheless the form of the creature to be made pre-existed in the Word of God when He said, *Let there be light.* Then appeared that light by which the minds of angels were formed; and it was produced in its own proper nature without first having an existence elsewhere [65] prior to its existence in its own proper nature. Hence Scripture does not say, "And so it was done," and then add, "And God made light"; but immediately after the word spoken by God, light was made, and this created light was united with the creating Light, God, beholding Him and beholding in Him itself, that is, the form according to which it was created. It also beheld itself in itself, as a creature far different from its Creator. And so God took pleasure in the creature He had made, seeing that it was good, and the light was separated from the darkness, and the light was called Day and the darkness Night.

And there was evening, because there was necessarily that knowledge by which a creature would be distinguished from the Creator, the creature being known in itself otherwise than in God. Then followed morning, introducing the knowledge of another creature to be made by the Word of God first in the minds of the angels and then in the firmament itself actually existing in nature. And thus God said, *Let there be a firmament,* and so it was made in the knowledge of spiritual creatures who knew the firmament before it was actually produced in its own existence. Then God made the firmament, that is, the firmament actually existing in nature, the knowledge of which, being inferior, would be as evening.

And thus creation proceeded to the end of all the works and

to the rest that God took, a rest that has no evening because it was not made as a creature, and thus there cannot be a twofold knowledge of it, a prior and more perfect knowledge in the Word of God as in the day, and a subsequent and inferior knowledge of this rest in itself as in the evening.

CHAPTER 33

God created all things simultaneously.

51. But if the angelic mind can grasp simultaneously all that the sacred text sets down separately in an ordered arrangement according to causal connection, were not all these things also made simultaneously, the firmament itself, the waters gathered together and the bare land that appeared, the plants and trees that sprang forth, the lights and stars that were established, the living creatures in the water and on the earth? Or were they rather created at different times on appointed days?

Perhaps we ought not to think of these creatures at the moment they were produced as subject to the processes of nature which we now observe in them, but rather as under the wonderful and unutterable power of the Wisdom of God, which *reaches from end to end mightily and governs all graciously.*[66] For this power of Divine Wisdom does not reach by stages or arrive by steps. It was just as easy, then, for God to create everything as it is for Wisdom to exercise this mighty power. For through Wisdom all things were made, and the motion we now see in creatures, measured by the lapse of time, as each one fulfills its proper function, comes to creatures from those causal reasons [67] implanted in them, which God scattered as seeds at the moment of creation when *He spoke and they were made, He commanded and they were created.*[68]

52. Creation, therefore, did not take place slowly in order that a slow development might be implanted in those things that are slow by nature; nor were the ages established at the plodding pace at which they now pass. Time brings about the development of these creatures according to the laws of their numbers,

but there was no passage of time when they received these laws at creation. Otherwise, if we think that, when they were first created by the Word of God, there were the processes of nature with the normal duration of days that we know, those creatures that shoot forth roots and clothe the earth would need not one day but many to germinate beneath the ground, and then a certain number of days, according to their natures, to come forth from the ground; and the creation of vegetation, which Scripture places on one day, namely the third, would have been a gradual process.

And then how many days were necessary for birds to fly, if they proceeded from the earliest stages through the periods of natural growth to the sprouting of feathers and wings? Or perhaps were eggs only created, when on the fifth day, according to the scriptural narrative, the waters brought forth every winged bird according to its kind? If this can be maintained on the ground that in the liquid substance of the eggs there already existed all that grows and develops in the required course of days, because there were already present the numerous reason-principles implanted in an incorporeal manner within corporeal creatures, why could not the same thing have been said before the appearance of eggs, when in the humid element these same reason-principles were produced, from which winged creatures might be born and develop in the time required for the growth of each species?

In this narrative of creation Holy Scripture has said of the Creator that He completed His works in six days; and elsewhere, without contradicting this, it has been written of the same Creator that He created all things together.[69] It follows, therefore, that He, who created all things together, simultaneously created these six days, or seven, or rather the one day six or seven times repeated. Why, then, was there any need for six distinct days to be set forth in the narrative one after the other? The reason is that those who cannot understand the meaning of the text, *He created all things together,* cannot arrive at the meaning of Scripture unless the narrative proceeds slowly step by step.

CHAPTER 34

All things were made both simultaneously and in six days.

53. How, then, can we say that the light was repeated six times in the knowledge of the angels from evening to morning? It was enough for them just once to have day and evening and morning together when, in the primordial and immutable forms by which creatures were made, they contemplated the whole of creation together, as it was made together, thus beholding day; and when, in things existing in their own proper nature, they knew creation, thus beholding evening; and when, recognizing this knowledge as inferior, they praised the Creator, thus beholding morning. How did morning come first, so that the angels would know in the Word what God was to make next, and afterwards know this very thing itself in the evening, if no "before" or "after" was made, because all things were made together?

As a matter of fact, the creatures mentioned in the narrative of creation were made according to a "before" and "after" during the six days, and they were also all made together. For this Scripture text that narrates the works of God according to the days mentioned above, and that Scripture text that says God created all things together, are both true. And the two are one, because Sacred Scripture was written under the inspiration of the one Spirit of truth.

54. In this sort of thing there is no lapse of time to show what is before and what after. We might say that the creation of things took place all at once and also that there was a "before" and "after," but it is more readily understood as happening all at once than in sequence. Thus also, when we look at the sun rising, it is certainly evident that our gaze could not reach it without passing over the whole expanse of air and sky that lies between. And who can calculate this distance? Now this gaze of ours or this ray from our eyes[70] would not be able to traverse the air above the sea unless it first passed over the air above the land as we look out from any inland site towards the seashore.

And then if our gaze, turned in the same direction, meets land again across the sea, it cannot pass through the air above that distant land unless it first travels through the air above the sea that lies between. And let us suppose that beyond this land across the sea only ocean remains. Can our gaze pass through the air spread out over the ocean unless it first penetrates the air over the land on this side of the ocean? The expanse of the ocean is said to be greater than anything we know; but however vast it may be, it is necessary for the rays of our eyes first to pass through the air above it, and afterwards to pass through whatever is beyond, and then finally to come to the sun that we behold.

In describing this experience, I have used the words "first" and "afterwards" several times, but in so speaking I am not denying that our gaze passes over all this space at once with a single glance of the eye. If we close our eyes and turn towards the sun, as soon as we open them we shall have the feeling that our gaze has touched the sun without our being aware that we have stretched it out to that point; and there will seem to be no lapse of time between the moment we open our eyes and the moment our gaze meets its object. Now this is certainly a ray of material light that shines forth from our eyes and touches objects so remote with such speed that it cannot be calculated or equalled. It is quite obvious, then, that all those measureless spaces are traversed at one time in a single glance; and at the same time it is also certain what part of these spaces is passed first and what part later.

55. It was only right that when St. Paul wished to express the speed with which we should rise from the dead, he said it would happen *in the twinkling of an eye*.[71] Surely nothing swifter can be found in the movements and impulses of bodies. Now, if vision in the eyes of the body is capable of such speed, what cannot intellectual vision do, even in the case of men, and much more in the case of angels? And what can we say of the speed of the supreme Wisdom of God Himself, which penetrates everywhere by reason of Its purity, and which no stain ever sullies?[72]

In such actions, therefore, which happen simultaneously, no

one sees what must have occurred "first" or "later," unless he beholds it in that Wisdom by which all things were made in due order simultaneously.

CHAPTER 35

There is no "before" or "after" in God but there is in creatures.

56. If, therefore, the day that God first made is the company of spiritual and rational creatures called supercelestial angels[73] and virtues, it was made present to all the works of God to see them in that order in which angelic knowledge foreknows in the Word of God creatures that are to be made and knows in themselves creatures already made. There are no intervals of time here; but one can speak of "before" and "after" in the relationships of creatures, although all is simultaneous in the creative act of God. For God made the creatures that were to be in the future in such a way that without Himself being subject to time He made them subject to time. Thus time when made by Him would run its course.

The seven days, therefore, with which we are familiar, which the light of a heavenly body unfolds and folds in its course, are like a shadow and a sign reminding us to seek those days wherein created spiritual light was able to be made present to all the works of God by the perfection of the number six. We are reminded also that the seventh day, the day on which God rested, has a morning but no evening, and that He rested on this day not because He needed the seventh day for rest, but because He rested in the sight of His angels from all the works He had made, resting only in Himself, who was not made. In other words, the angels that God created were made present to all His works, knowing them in Him and in themselves, as day along with evening; and after all the works of God, which were very good, there was nothing better for them to know than that God Himself was resting in Himself from all His works, needing none of them to add to His beatitude.[74]

BOOK FIVE
The Two Narratives and the Causal Reasons

Chapter 1

God made heaven and earth on one day six times repeated.

1. *This is the book of the creation of heaven and earth when day was made. God made heaven and earth and every green thing of the field before it appeared above the earth, and all the grass of the field before it sprang forth. For God had not rained upon the earth, and there was not a man to till the earth. But a spring rose out of the earth and watered all the face of the earth.*[1]

Now, certainly, further weight is added to the opinion that holds that God made one day, and that six or seven days could be numbered by reason of the repetition of this one. For Holy Scripture now states the matter more clearly, summing up in general terms all that it had said from the beginning up to this point, when it declares, *This is the book of the creation* (or *making*) *of heaven and earth when day was made.*

No one is going to say that the words "heaven" and "earth" are here intended in the sense that they had earlier in the narrative before day was said to have been made, *In the beginning God created heaven and earth.*[2] That text seems to mean that God made something apart from any day, before He made day. The interpretation that might be put upon this I have set forth above in its proper place, without, however, denying to others the right of proposing a better explanation.[3]

But now the sacred writer says, *This is the book of the creation of heaven and earth when day was made,* thus making it quite clear, I believe, that here he does not speak of heaven and earth in the

146

sense in which he used these words in the beginning before mentioning the creation of day, *when darkness was over the abyss.* Now he is speaking of the creation of heaven and earth when day was made, that is, when all parts of the world had been made distinct and all classes of things had been already formed, and thus the whole of creation, fittingly arranged, presented the appearance of what we call the universe.[4]

2. Here, therefore, the sacred writer speaks of that heaven (along with all that is in it) which God called the firmament when He created it, and of that earth (along with everything in it) which together with the abyss occupies[5] the lowest region. For he goes on to add, *God made heaven and earth;* and thus, by mentioning heaven and earth before mentioning the creation of day, and then repeating these words after mention of the creation of day, he makes it impossible for us to suppose that "heaven" and "earth" here have the same meaning that they have in the beginning before the creation of day. He states the matter as follows: *This is the book of the creation of heaven and earth when day was made. God made heaven and earth.* Hence, if anyone wishes to understand the words *the book of the creation of heaven and earth* in the sense in which it is said, *In the beginning God created heaven and earth,* before the creation of day, because in both places heaven and earth are mentioned before day was made, he ought to be corrected by the words that follow, because again, after it is said that day was made, the terms "heaven" and "earth" are once more used.

3. Now the word "when" and the statement that goes with it, *day was made,* should compel the most obstinate adversary to admit that no other interpretation is possible. For if the matter were stated thus: "This is the book of the creation of heaven and earth; day was made; God made heaven and earth," one might perhaps think that the book of the creation of heaven and earth was spoken of in the same sense as heaven and earth in the beginning[6] before day was created. And then it might be supposed that the sacred writer added, *Day was made,* in the sense in which he previously had said that God made the day,[7] and that he said immediately once again, *God made heaven and earth,* wishing them to be understood as they exist after the creation of day.

But since Scripture says, *when day was made*, whether you connect this clause with the words preceding, so that you read this
as one sentence, *This is the book of the creation of heaven and earth
when day was made*, or whether you connect it with the following
words, so that you have this sentence, *When day was made, God
made heaven and earth*, the sacred text surely compels us to understand heaven and earth as they exist after day had been made.
Then, after saying, *God made heaven and earth*, the sacred writer
adds, *and every green thing of the field*; and this was obviously
made on the third day. It is, therefore, abundantly clear that it
is one and the same day that God made, and that by the repetition of it the second day was made, and the third, and the rest
up to the seventh.

CHAPTER 2

The day God made is different from days that we know.

4. Since by the terms "heaven" and "earth" the sacred writer,
in conformity with the language of Scripture, wished us to understand here the whole of creation, we might ask why he added, *and every green thing of the field*. I believe that he put the
matter in this way in order to emphasize what day he spoke of
when he said, *When day was made*. One might easily think that
this day was a day made up of a material light by whose circuit
the hours of day and night are brought to us. But when we recall the order in which creatures were made, we find that *all the
grass of the field* was created on the third day, before the sun was
made (for it was made on the fourth day), and it is by the presence of the sun that the day with which we are familiar is constituted. When, therefore, we hear, *When day was made, God made
heaven and earth, and all the grass of the field*, we are admonished
to think of that day which may perhaps be a corporeal thing
consisting in some sort of light unknown to us, or a spiritual
thing made up of the united company of angels.[8] But at least we
know that it is different from the ordinary day with which we
are familiar; and we are attempting to discover its true nature.

CHAPTER 3

All things were created simultaneously on the day which was seven times repeated.

5. There is another consideration that may not be irrelevant. The sacred writer might have said, "This is the book of the creation of heaven and earth, when God made heaven and earth," giving us to understand by "heaven and earth" everything that is in them. This would be in keeping with the language of Scripture, where very frequently by the terms "heaven" and "earth" (sometimes with the addition of "sea") the sacred writer means the whole creation, occasionally adding the phrase, *and all things that are in them.*[9] In this case, if he had stated the matter in some such form as this, we should understand day to be present also, either the day God first made or our day, which is constituted by the presence of the sun. Now, the sacred writer did not put the matter thus but introduced the word "day" in the clause, *When day was made.*

Scripture, furthermore, does not say, "This is the book of the creation of day and heaven and earth," as if things were actually created in that order; nor does it say, "This is the book of the creation of heaven and earth, when day and heaven and earth were made, when God made heaven and earth and every green thing of the field." And again it does not say, "This is the book of the creation of heaven and earth, when God made day and heaven and earth and every green thing of the field." Finally, it does not say, "This is the book of the creation of heaven and earth; God made day and heaven and earth and every green thing of the field."[10]

The usual way of saying things called for these forms of expression; but actually Scripture says, *This is the book of the creation of heaven and earth. When day was made, God made heaven and earth and every green thing of the field.* Thus it indicates that after day had been made, then God made heaven and earth and every green thing of the field.

6. Furthermore, the earlier narrative reveals that day was first made, and it reckons this as one day. After this a second day

is added, and on this day the firmament was made; and then a third day, on which earth and sea were separated, and the earth brought forth trees and herbs. Now perhaps we have here a confirmation of what we tried to show in the previous book, that God created everything at one time. The earlier narrative stated that all things were created and finished on six successive days, but now to one day everything is assigned, under the terms "heaven" and "earth," with the addition also of "plants." If, therefore, as I have already said, "day" were understood in its ordinary sense, the reader would be corrected when he recalled that God had ordered the earth to produce the green things of the field before the establishment of that day that is marked by the sun. Hence, I do not now appeal to another book of Holy Scripture to prove that God *created all things together.*[11] But the very next page following the first narrative of creation testifies to this when it tells us, *When day was made, God made heaven and earth and every green thing of the field.* Hence, you must understand that this day was seven times repeated, to make up the seven days. And when you hear that all things were made after day was made, you may possibly understand this sixfold or sevenfold repetition which took place without lapse of time. If you cannot yet understand it, you should leave the matter for the consideration of those who can; and, since Scripture does not abandon you in your infirmity, but with a mother's love accompanies your slower steps, you will make progress. Holy Scripture, indeed, speaks in such a way as to mock proud readers with its heights, terrify the attentive with its depths, feed great souls with its truth, and nourish little ones with sweetness.

Chapter 4

Genesis 1:12 means that earth received the power of bringing forth crops and trees.

7. What, then, is the meaning of the words that follow? The text reads thus: *When day was made, God made heaven and earth and*

*every green thing of the field before it appeared above the earth, and
all the grass of the field before it sprang forth.*

What are we to make of this? Must we not ask where God
made these things before they appeared above the earth and before they sprang forth? One might be much more inclined to believe that God made them at the time when they sprang forth,
not before they sprang forth, were we not informed by the sacred text that it was before they sprang forth that God made
them. As a result, if the reader cannot discover where they were
made, he will nevertheless believe that they were made before
they sprang forth, if he piously believes Holy Scripture. It is impious, of course, not to believe it.

8. What, then, shall we say? Shall we follow the opinion of
those who say that it was in the Word of God that all things
were made before they sprang forth on the earth? But if this is
the way they were created, it was not when day was made but
before the making of day that they were created. Scripture says
quite plainly, *When day was made, God made heaven and earth and
every green thing of the field before it appeared above the earth, and
all the grass of the field before it sprang forth.* If, therefore, this was
when day was made, it was surely not before day was made.
Hence, it was not in the Word, who is coeternal with the Father
before day or anything else was made, but it was only when day
was made. For those things that are in the Word of God before
all creation were certainly not made; but they were made when
day was made, as the words of Scripture declare, although this
took place before they appeared above the earth and before they
sprang forth, as Scripture says concerning the green things and
the grass of the field.

9. Where, then, were they? Were they in the earth in the "reasons" or causes from which they would spring, as all things already exist in their seeds before they evolve in one form or
another and grow into their proper kinds in the course of time?
But these seeds that we see are already above the earth and have
already sprung forth. Or shall we say that they were not above
the earth but within the earth, and that, therefore, before they
sprang forth they were made, because they only sprang forth

when their seeds germinated and with the process of growth burst up above the ground? For this is what we see happening in due course of time in the case of each plant. Were the seeds, therefore, made when day was made, and in them was there every green thing of the field and all the grass, not with the appearance they have when they have sprung forth above the earth, but with the power they have in the formative principles of the seeds? Did earth, then, first produce the seeds?

But that is not the way Scripture put the matter when it said, *And the earth brought forth the nourishing crops* (or *grain*), *scattering the seeds according to their kind and their likeness, and the fruit tree bearing its fruit, containing within itself its seed according to its kind upon the earth.*[12] From these words it appears rather that the seeds sprang from the crops and the trees, and that the crops and trees themselves came forth not from seeds but from the earth. This is what the word of God itself declares. For it does not say, "Let the seeds in the earth bring forth the grain and the fruit-bearing tree"; but it says, *Let the earth bring forth the grain scattering its seed.*[13] It thus reveals that the seed is from the crops, not the crops from the seed. *And thus it was done, and the earth brought them forth.*[14] That is to say, it was thus done first in the knowledge of the Day mentioned above,[15] and earth now brought these creatures forth, so that they would now be made also in themselves in the created world.

10. How, then, was this done before they appeared above the earth and before they sprang forth? On the one hand, they were made with heaven and earth when that day transcending our knowledge and experience was made, which God first made; and on the other hand, they sprang forth above the earth, a thing that could not happen except on days marked by the course of the sun after the proper lapse of time for each kind. Are these two things, then, distinct? If this is so, and if that day is the society of supercelestial angels and powers united together, then God's creatures are undoubtedly known to angels with a knowledge far different from ours. Apart from the fact that they know creatures in the Word of God, through whom all things have been made, I believe that their knowledge of creatures in themselves is far different from ours. They have what

we might call a primordial or original knowledge of the creatures God first made before He rested from His works, not creating anything further. Our knowledge, on the other hand, is dependent upon the governance of creatures already made, as this takes place in time, inasmuch as God, in the unfolding of His creatures according to the perfection of the number six, is working still.[16]

11. It is, therefore, causally *(causaliter)* that Scripture has said that earth brought forth the crops and the trees, in the sense that it received the power of bringing them forth. In the earth from the beginning, in what I might call the roots of time, God created what was to be in times to come. For God later planted a paradise in the East, and there *from the earth He made every tree to grow, beautiful to the sight and good for food.*[17] But we must not say that He then added to creation something He had not previously made, something that was afterwards to be added to the completeness in which He had finished all that was very good on the sixth day. All the plants and trees had already been made in the first creation, and God rested from that creation, moving and governing in the course of history the things which He created before resting from His creation. It is in this sense that He planted not only Paradise but even now all that earth brings forth. For who now creates these things unless it is He who is working even now? But He now creates from what already exists, whereas in the beginning creatures were made by Him when none of them existed at all. It was then that the day was created which is not to be identified with Him but rather with the spiritual and intellectual creation.[18]

Chapter 5

Time began with creation. Unformed matter was prior not in time but in the order of causality.

12. With the motion of creatures, time began to run its course. It is idle to look for time before creation, as if time can be found before time. If there were no motion of either a spiri-

tual or corporeal creature, by which the future moving through the present would succeed the past, there would be no time at all. A creature could not move if it did not exist. We should, therefore, say that time began with creation rather than that creation began with time. But both are from God. For from Him and through Him and in Him are all things.[19]

The statement, "Time began with creation," should not be taken to mean that time is not a creature. It is, in fact, the motion of creatures from one state to another as they succeed one another according to the decree of God, who governs all that He has created. Hence, when we think of the first creation of things, that is, of the works from which God rested on the seventh day, we should not think of those days as solar days, nor of that work of God as if it were the same as His working now in time. Rather, He made that which gave time its beginning, as He made all things together,[20] disposing them in an order based not on intervals of time but on causal connections; and thus the creatures which were made all at once could be shown in their perfection by the sixfold repetition of the "day" of creation.

13. It is not in the order of time but in the order of causality that matter unformed and formable, both spiritual and corporeal, came first in creation. It was the substratum of what was to be made, although it did not exist before it was created.[21] It was created by none other than the sovereign and true God from whom are all things. This unformed matter has been called heaven and earth, which God made in the beginning before that one day which He made, and it is so designated because from it heaven and earth were made. It is also called invisible and formless earth and dark abyss. This interpretation I have explained in the first book.[22]

14. Among those beings which were formed from formlessness and are clearly said to be created, made, or established, the first made was day.[23] For it was fitting that the primacy in creation should be held by that being which could know the creature through the Creator, not the Creator through the creature. In the second place there was the firmament, with which the creation of the corporeal world begins. In the third place are sea

and earth, and in the earth potentially are plants and trees. For thus the earth at God's word produced these things before they sprang forth, receiving all the numbers[24] of those beings which it would bring forth in their kinds through the ages. Then, after this domicile, as it were, of creatures had been established, on the fourth day the lights and stars were created, so that first the higher part of the universe would be adorned with the visible bodies that move within the universe. On the fifth day the waters, being joined to sky and air, at God's command brought forth their inhabitants, all the fishes and birds; and they produced them potentially in the numbers which would come forth under appropriate influences in the course of time. On the sixth day the animals of the earth were made, the last beings from the last element of the world. They too were created potentially, for time would bring them into view in the ages to come.

15. The first day[25] created knew the whole array of creatures arranged in hierarchical order. Through this knowledge creation was revealed to it as if in six steps called days, and thus was unfolded all that was created; but in reality there was only one day. That day knew creation first in the Creator and then in the creatures themselves; yet it remained not in them, but directing this latter knowledge to the love of God, it brought about in all the works of creation an evening, a morning, and a midday, not involving any intervals of time but rather an order in creation. Finally, made aware of the repose of its Creator, who rested from all His works in rest that has no evening, the day thereby deserved to be blessed and sanctified. Scripture, therefore, as the Church has recognized, extols the number seven and presents it as consecrated in a sense to the Holy Spirit.[26]

16. This, then, is *the book of the creation of heaven and earth.* For *in the beginning God made heaven and earth* in the sense that He made what we might call formable matter, which was to be formed subsequently by His word. This formable matter, however, was prior to its formation not in time but in origin. When it received a form, that was when day was first made. *When day was made, God made heaven and earth and every green thing of the field before it appeared above the earth, and all the grass of the field before it sprang forth.* This is my explanation, unless someone can

propose an interpretation that is clearer and more in keeping with the text.

CHAPTER 6

The meaning of Genesis 2.5.

17. Scripture then says, *For God had not rained upon the earth, and there was not a man to till the earth.*[27] It is difficult to determine what these words mean and what they are intended to suggest. One might say that God made the grass of the field before it came forth from the earth because He had not yet rained upon the earth, since if He had made the grass after the rain, it would seem to have come forth because of the rain rather than to have been made by Him. But does this make sense? Could the vegetation coming forth after the rain be made by any other than God?

And why was there not a man to till the earth? On the sixth day God had already made man, and on the seventh He had rested from all His works. Perhaps this is a summary in which the author recalls that when God made every green thing of the field and all the grass, He had not yet rained upon the earth, and there was not yet any man. For on the third day He made the grass, and on the sixth day man. But when God made all the grass and every green thing of the field before it came forth from the earth, there was lacking not only man to till the earth but also the grass upon the earth, for it was said to have been made before it came forth. Did God make the grass on the third day precisely because there was not yet a man to produce it by tilling the earth? We surely cannot say that the many different trees and the many kinds of plants could come forth from the earth only by the work of man.

18. Is this, then, the reason why it is said that God had not rained upon the earth and that there was not yet a man to till the earth? Where the work of man is lacking, the rain brings forth plants and trees. But there are some that do not come forth even with rain unless the work of man is added. Hence, in our

time both aids are necessary for all things to come forth. But then both were lacking, and so it was that God made them by the power of His word without rain and without the work of man. Even now He makes them also, but through rain and the hands of men, although *neither he who plants nor he who waters is anything, but only God who gives the growth.*[28]

19. What is the meaning of the next statement: *But a spring rose out of the earth and watered all the face of the earth?*[29] That spring, flowing with the abundance of the Nile in Egypt, could take the place of rain for all the earth. Why, then, was it important to state that God, before He rained upon the earth, had made the beings that would bring forth plants and trees, since the spring watering the earth could be as effective as rain? And if it were somewhat less effective, then the crops produced would simply be less plentiful. Perhaps Sacred Scripture in its customary style is speaking with the limitations of human language in addressing men of limited understanding, while at the same time teaching a lesson to be understood by the reader who is able. By the "day" mentioned earlier, Scripture meant the "one day" made by God; and it said that God made heaven and earth when the day was made, thus helping us to understand, to the best of our ability, that God made everything together, although the subsequent framework of the six days of creation might seem to imply intervals of time. In a similar manner, when the author said that God made, along with heaven and earth, *every green thing of the field before it appeared above the earth, and all the grass of the field before it sprang forth,* he added, *For God had not rained upon the earth, and there was not a man to till the earth.* In putting it this way, he is saying that God did not then make the crops as He makes them now when it rains and when man tills the earth. For these crops now come forth in the course of time, though they were not there when God made all things together whence time began.

CHAPTER 7

The spring that watered all the face of the earth.

20. The statement, *But a spring rose out of the earth and watered all the face of the earth,*[29] tells us, I believe, about the production of things in the course of time following the creation of the world when all things were created together.[30] The author appropriately begins with that element from which all kinds of animals, plants, and trees are born to develop in time their numbers, each according to its nature. For all primordial seeds, whence all flesh and all vegetation are brought forth, are moist and grow from moisture. Present in these seeds are numbers of extraordinary power, bearing with them potencies that have their origin in the finished works of God, from which He rested on the seventh day.

21. It is only reasonable to ask what that spring of water is which is able to irrigate the face of the earth.[31] If it once existed but was later blocked off or dried up, an explanation should be sought. Today we see no spring watering all the face of the earth. Perhaps mankind's sin deserved this punishment, so that the abundant flow of this spring was checked and, when the effortless productivity of earth was gone, man's toil in tilling the fields was multiplied. Although Scripture nowhere gives such an explanation, man might conjecture it, were it not for the fact that the sin of mankind, for which the penalty of labor was imposed, was committed after a period of bliss in Paradise. Paradise, however, had its own enormous spring, which I shall discuss at length later on in its own proper place.[32] From this one source four great rivers, well known among the nations, are said to flow.[33] Where, then, was this spring and where these rivers when that other great spring rose out of the earth and watered all the face of the earth? For certainly at that time the Geon, which is called the Nile and is one of the four, did not water Egypt, since a spring rose out of the earth and supplied an abundant flow of water not only for Egypt but for all the face of the earth.

22. Are we to believe that God first wished to water all the

earth with one enormous spring so that the things He had potentially created would receive the help of this water and thus
come forth in the course of time on different days according to
their different kinds? And shall we say that later, after planting
Paradise, God stopped that spring and then filled the earth with
many springs as we now see it? And did He separate four
mighty rivers from the one spring of Paradise, so that the rest
of the earth, being filled with its various kinds of creatures producing their appropriate forms in due time, would have its own
springs and streams; and Paradise, planted on higher ground,
would send forth four rivers from the source of its spring? Or
should we say that God first watered the whole earth from the
one spring of Paradise flowing in great abundance, and that He
made fruitful the things He had created not at intervals but all
together, so that they would bring forth their kinds in due time;
and that later He checked the enormous torrent in that place at
its source, so that waters now would flow from different sources
of rivers and springs throughout the earth; and finally, in the
area of that spring, which no longer was watering the whole
earth but supplying only the four famous rivers, did God plant
the Paradise where He would place man, whom He had created?

CHAPTER 8

*The Holy Spirit did not inspire the writer to put down everything
about creation.*

23. Not everything has been written to tell us how time unfolded after the first creation of things and how there followed
the production of the creatures which had been made in their
first beginnings and completed on the sixth day. But as much
has been told as was judged necessary by the Holy Spirit as He
inspired the writer, who put down those things which would be
important not only for a knowledge of what had happened but
also for the foreshadowing of what was to be. In our ignorance
we conjecture about possible events which the writer omitted
knowingly. In our efforts according to our limited ability we try

with God's help to see that no absurity or contradiction may be thought to be present in Sacred Scripture to offend the mind of the reader; for he might think that events narrated by Scripture are impossible and then either give up his faith or not approach the faith.

CHAPTER 9

How could one spring water the whole earth?

24. In our investigation of the spring that watered the face of the earth, we must consider how that statement can be possible: *It rose out of the earth and watered all the face of the earth.* If our conclusions seem impossible to anyone, let him seek another by which he can show the truth of Scripture; for it is undoubtedly true even if it is not shown to be. If he wishes to argue in order to prove Scripture false, either he will say nothing true about the creation and governance of creatures; or if he says something true, he will think it false because of his lack of understanding. This will be the case, for instance, if he contends that all the face of the earth could not have been watered by one spring, no matter how large, because if it did not water the mountains, it did not water all the face of the earth; and if it did water the mountains, this would not bring nourishment to the crops but a flood upon the earth, and if this was the condition of the earth, it was all sea, and the dry land was not yet separated.

CHAPTER 10

The writer could have reference to one spring or many.

25. In answer to the foregoing objection, it could be said that this flooding might happen during recurring seasons, just as the Nile at a certain period overflows its banks and floods the plains of Egypt and at another period returns to its banks.[34] It is

thought to be swollen every year by the winter rains and snows of some remote and unknown region of the world.[35] The ocean, too, has its recurring tides, and some of its shores are for a time without waves and then in turn are flooded by the surge of the sea. And I need not mention the remarkable changes that regularly occur in certain springs which overflow at a fixed season of the year so as to water all the surrounding region, but at other times scarcely supply enough drinking water from the deepest wells.

Why, then, should it be unbelievable if at that time the whole earth was irrigated from one source in a great abyss, its waters alternately flooding and receding? It seems that Scripture wished to call that vast abyss a spring, not springs, because of the one nature of the waters. This term, however, does not include the sea, which with its great expanse of salt water washes the shores, but only those waters which earth holds in its hidden recesses, whence flow all the springs and streams in their different channels and courses to burst forth in their proper places. If Scripture so speaks of such a spring passing through countless channels in caverns and fissures beneath the ground before bursting forth on the earth, and if it is said to spread out everywhere like the locks of hair falling from the head as it waters all the face of the earth, not presenting the sight of a continuous expanse of water as in the case of the sea or a pond, but rather what we see in waters moving in river beds and twisting rivulets watering the surrounding region in flood time, who would not accept this except a very contentious person?

In this description it is understood that all the face of the earth was watered in the sense in which we say that all the material of a garment is colored when it is not continuously colored but only here and there. Certainly at the beginning, when the earth was new, if not all the surface at least the greater part was probably level, and consequently the waters gushing forth would be able to flow forth and spread out more widely.

26. Different theories are possible in discussing the size of the source of water and in speculating about the possibility of many springs or just one. First, there could have been somewhere a single source from which water gushed forth. Secondly, because

of a unity in the hidden caverns of the earth from which all the waters of all springs large and small well forth, the source could have been called one spring, rising from the earth through its various channels and watering all the face of the earth. Finally, and this is a more likely explanation, Scripture does not say, "One spring rose out of the earth," but, *A spring rose out of the earth*, thus using the singular for the plural. Hence, we are given to understand that there were many springs throughout the whole earth watering their own regions, in the same way that we say "the soldier," meaning "soldiers," and that Scripture says "locust" and "frog," using the singular for the plural in referring to the plagues with which the Egyptians were stricken, although there were countless locusts and frogs.[36] We need not labor this point any further.

CHAPTER 11

The two moments of creation.

27. We must very seriously consider whether we can consistently hold the opinion expressed above[37] when we said that there are two moments of creation: one in the original creation when God made all creatures before resting from all His works on the seventh day, and the other in the administration of creatures by which He works even now.[38] In the first instance God made everything together without any moments of time intervening, but now He works within the course of time, by which we see the stars move from their rising to their setting, the weather change from summer to winter, and in a fixed number of days the seeds sprout forth, grow, flourish, and wither away. Animals, also, within certain limits and periods of time are conceived, developed, and born, and then proceed through the stages of their lives to old age and death. And the same is true for all other such beings limited by time.

Who makes these creatures except God? And certainly in Him there is no motion such as is found in the works He makes, for He is not in time. Hence, between the things made by God from which He rested on the seventh day and those which He now works, Scripture has placed a division in the narrative and has told us that God has finished the first works of creation and has now begun to produce the later works. This is made clear in the words, *This is the book of the creation of heaven and earth. When day was made, God made heaven and earth and every green thing of the field before it appeared above the earth, and all the grass of the field before it sprang forth. For God had not rained upon the earth, and there was not a man to till the earth.*[39] The narration of the later works begins thus: *But a spring rose out of the earth and watered all the face of the earth.*[40] From the mention of this spring and subsequently throughout the narrative that follows, creatures are made in intervals of time, not all together.

CHAPTER 12

Three aspects of the works God made.

28. We must, therefore, make a threefold distinction in speaking of creation. First, there are the unchangeable forms in the Word of God; secondly, God's works from which He rested on the seventh day; finally, the things that He produces from those works even now.

Of these three, those that I put in the third place are known to us in some way by our senses and common experience. The first two are beyond our senses and ordinary human knowledge, and they must be first believed on divine authority. Then some knowledge of them can be attained through things known in accordance with each individual's limited capacity, when he has God's help enabling him to know.

CHAPTER 13

What has been made is life in Him.

29. The Wisdom of God, through which all things were created, knew them before they were made. The divine archetypes,[41] unchangeable and eternal, are attested by Scripture: *In the beginning was the Word, and the Word was with God, and the Word was God. He was in the beginning with God. All things were made through Him, and without Him nothing was made.*[42]

Who would be so insane as to say that God had made things that He did not know? And if He knew them, He must have had this knowledge within Himself, with whom was the Word, through whom all things were made. For if he knew them outside of Himself, who had taught Him? *For who has known the mind of the Lord? Or who has been His counsellor? Or who has first made a gift to Him to receive a gift in return? For from Him and through Him and in Him are all things.*[43]

30. The words that follow in St. John's Gospel also make this meaning abundantly clear, for the Evangelist adds the following statement: *What has been made is life in Him, and the life was the light of men.*[44] For rational minds—and here we include man, who is made in the image of God—have no true light except the Divine Word Himself, through whom all things have been made, and in whose life they will be able to share when cleansed from all evil and error.

CHAPTER 14

A further explanation of John 1.3–4.

31. We must not, therefore, interpret St. John's words in this way: *What has been made in Him, is life,* stopping after *What has been made in Him,* and then adding, *is life.*[45] There is nothing not made in Him; for the Psalmist says, after enumerating many creatures of the earth, *In Thy wisdom Thou hast created all things.*[46]

And the Apostle says, *For in Him all things were created in heaven and on earth, visible and invisible.*[47] It follows, therefore, if we punctuate the text in this way, that the earth itself and everything in it is life. Since it is absurd to say that all things are living, how much more absurd is it to say that they are life, especially since St. John makes clear what kind of life he is talking about when he adds, *And the life was the light of men.* Hence, we must punctuate the passage so as to provide a pause after *What has been made* and then add *is life in Him.*

It is not said that it is life in itself, in its own nature by which it is constituted as a creature; but it is life in Him because all things made through Him were known by Him before they were made. Consequently, they were in Him not as creatures made by Him but as the life and light of men, and this is Wisdom Itself, the Word Itself, that is, the only-begotten Son of God. Creatures, then, are life in Him in the sense in which the Gospel says, *As the Father has life in Himself, so He has granted the Son to have life in Himself.*[48]

32. We cannot pass over the fact that the better manuscripts read, *What has been made was life in Him.* It follows, therefore, that the words, "was life," are to be understood in accordance with the first verse of the Gospel: *In the beginning was the Word, and the Word was with God, and the Word was God. What,* therefore, *has been made,* already *was life in Him.* And it was not any kind of life. Cattle are said to live, and yet they cannot participate in wisdom. But the Word *was the life of men;* and rational beings, cleansed by His grace, can arrive at this kind of vision, than which there is nothing higher, nothing more blessed.

CHAPTER 15

In what sense creatures were life in God.

33. But even if we punctuate and understand the text as proposed above, *What has been made is life in Him,* our interpretation stands: what has been made through Him is understood to be

life in Him, the life in which He sees all things when He makes them. He has made them as He has seen them, not looking beyond Himself, but He has numbered within Himself all that He has made.

His vision and that of the Father are not different: there is one vision, as there is one substance. In the Book of Job, Wisdom, through which all things were made, is proclaimed in these words: *But where has Wisdom been found? Or where is the place of knowledge? Mortals do not know its way, and it is not found among men.*[49] And farther on the sacred writer says: *We have heard of its glory; the Lord has shown its way, and He knows its place. For He sees everything under heaven and knows all that He has made on earth. When He gave the wind its weight and the water its measure, He numbered them as He saw them.*[50]

These and similar texts prove that all these things before they were made were in the knowledge of God their Creator. And surely they are more excellent there where they are surpassingly true, where they are eternal and unchangeable. Although it ought to be sufficient for a man to know, or to believe without any hesitation, that God made all these things, I do not think that such a man can be so lacking in understanding as to suppose that God made what He did not know. Moreover, if He knew them before making them, it follows that before they were made they were with Him and known to Him as they live, and indeed are life, eternally and unchangeably. As things made, however, they have their existence, as every creature does, in their own nature.

CHAPTER 16

God is nearer to us than many creatures are.

34. The eternal and unchangeable nature of God, revealed to Moses as the self-existent Being in the words, *I am who am,*[51] exists in a manner far different from beings which are made. For that truly and originally exists which always exists in the same way, not only without change but incapable of change. Nothing

of what He made exists as He does or has within itself the first principles of all as He has. For God would not make creatures unless He knew them before He made them; nor would He know them unless He saw them; nor would He see them unless He possessed them; nor would He possess what had not yet been made except as uncreated being, as He is Himself. Although the Divine Being is beyond words and cannot be spoken of in any way with human language without recourse to expressions of time and place, whereas God is before all time and all place, nevertheless He who made us is nearer to us than many things which have been made. *For in Him we live and move and have our being;*[52] but most creatures are inaccessible to our mind because, being corporeal, they are of a different nature, and our mind is unable to see them in God, in the archetypes according to which they were made. If we could see them in God, then we should know their number, size, and nature, even without seeing them by means of the senses of our body. They are also inaccessible to the bodily senses because they are far removed or because they are separated from our sight and touch by reason of obstacles lying between us and them.

Hence it is that it is more toilsome to discover material creatures than the Creator who made them, since the joy a devout mind finds in the slightest knowledge of God is incomparably greater than anything it could experience in a thorough understanding of all material beings. For this reason those who search into this world are rightly rebuked in the Book of Wisdom: *For if their knowledge was so great that they could make judgments about the world, how did they not more readily find its Lord?*[53] For the foundations of the earth are beyond the range of our eyes, but He who founded it is near our minds.

CHAPTER 17

*He who is before time made the world with time
and rules it in time.*

35. Let us now consider all the works that God made together, which He completed on the sixth day and from which He rested on the seventh; later we shall discuss the things in which He works even now.

He Himself exists before time. But when we speak about the beginning of time, we think of creatures such as the world, with which time began. Creatures which are born in the world are said to be in time. When, therefore, Scripture says, *All things were made through Him, and without Him nothing was made,* it adds shortly after, *He was in this world, and the world was made through Him.*[54] Concerning this work of God, Scripture says elsewhere, *Who created the world out of formless matter.*[55] This world is generally referred to by the words "heaven and earth," as we noted when we pointed out that Scripture says God made them when day was made. In explaining this passage, we tried to show at some length[56] that the two statements about the creation of the world can be reconciled, namely, that it was finished in six days with all the creatures that are in it, and that it also was made when day was made, so that the account of creation agrees with the statement that *He made all things together.*[57]

CHAPTER 18

*Many creatures unknown to us. How they are known
to God and the angels.*

36. In this whole wide universe created by God there are many things we do not know, whether they are in the heavens and beyond what our senses can reach, or are in regions of the earth that may be uninhabitable, or lie hidden beneath us in the depths of the sea or the hidden caverns of the earth.

These things did not exist before they were made. How, then, were they known to God when they did not exist? On the other hand, how would He create what was unknown to Him? We cannot say He did not know what He was making. He made what He knew, therefore, and He knew things not yet made. It follows, then, that before they were made, creatures were both existent and nonexistent. They existed in God's knowledge; they did not exist in their own natures. Consequently, that "day" was made[58] to which creatures would be known in both ways, in God and in themselves: in God by morning or daytime knowledge, in themselves by evening knowledge.[59] As for God Himself, I dare not say that they were known to Him, once He had made them, in any other way than that in which He knew that He would make them; for *with Him there is no change or shadow of alteration.*[60]

CHAPTER 19

The knowledge of mysteries given to the angels.

37. Surely God does not need messengers to know creatures of lower rank, as if He could gain more knowledge through their service; but in a transcendent and wonderful way He knows all things with a knowledge that endures without change. He has messengers, however, for our sake and for theirs; for to obey and serve God in this way, to seek His counsel regarding creatures of lower rank and obey His divine precepts and commands, is a good for them in accordance with their own proper nature and being. Messengers are called *angeloi* in Greek, and by this name used in a wide sense we designate the whole heavenly city which we believe to be the first day created.

38. The mystery of the kingdom of heaven was not hidden from them; they knew what in the course of time was revealed for our salvation, namely, that we should be freed after our pilgrimage on earth to join their company. They would not be ignorant of this; for the offspring that came in due time was

placed through their ministry in the hands of a Mediator,[61] that is, in the power of Him who is their Lord both in the form of God and in the form of man.

St. Paul also says: *To me, the least of all the saints, has been given this grace, to preach among the Gentiles the unsearchable riches of Christ and to make clear how the mystery is dispensed which has been hidden from eternity in God, who created all things; so that to the principalities and powers in the heavens it would be made known through the Church of the manifold wisdom of God, which He fashioned in Christ Jesus our Lord according to His eternal purpose.*[62]

This mystery, therefore, was hidden from eternity in God but in such a way that it would be made known through the Church of God's manifold wisdom to the principalities and powers in the heavens; for the Church was there primordially where the Church of this earth is to be gathered together after the resurrection, so that we may be equal to the angels of God.[63] To them, therefore, it was known from the beginning of the ages; for no creature is before the ages, but only from the beginning of the ages. From their creation the ages began, and they began with the beginning of the ages. For their beginning is the beginning of the ages. The only-begotten Son, however, existed before the ages, and through Him the ages were created.[64] Hence, speaking as Wisdom identified with Himself as Second Person, He says, *Before the ages He established Me.*[65] In Wisdom, therefore, He made all things to whom it has been said, *In Wisdom Thou hast made them all.*[66]

39. It is not only in God that hidden mysteries have been made known to the angels, but He manifests Himself to them also here on earth when a mystery is accomplished and revealed. St. Paul testifies to this when he says, *Great, without any doubt, is the mystery of our religion, which has been manifested in the flesh, justified in the spirit, seen by the angels, preached among the nations, believed in the world, taken up in glory.*[67] Unless I am mistaken, when God is said to know anything in time, He must be said to do so because He makes it known either by angels or men. This manner of speaking, in which the result produced is signified by the cause, is frequent in Holy Scripture, especially when some-

thing is said about God which cannot be taken literally, as we are cautioned by the truth that rules our minds.

CHAPTER 20

The works which God makes even now.

40. We must, therefore, distinguish in the works of God those which He makes even now and those from which He rested on the seventh day. For there are some who think that only the world was made by God and that everything else is made by the world according to His ordination and command, but that God Himself makes nothing. Against this opinion we can cite the saying of our Lord, *My Father is working still.*[68] And lest anyone think that God is working only within Himself and not in this world, our Lord says: *The Father abiding in Me brings about his works.*[69] *And just as the Father raises the dead and gives them life, so also the Son gives life to whom He will.*[70] Furthermore, God does not make only great and important things but also the lowliest things of this earth. For St. Paul says: *Foolish man! What you sow does not come to life unless it dies. And what you sow is not the body that is to be but a mere kernel perhaps of wheat or of some other grain. But it is God who gives it a body as He has willed to do, and to each and every seed He gives an appropriate body.*[71]

Let us, therefore, believe and, if possible, also understand that God is working even now, so that if His action should be withdrawn from His creatures, they would perish.

41. But if we should suppose that God now makes a creature without having implanted its kind (*genus*) in His original creation, we should flatly contradict Sacred Scripture, which says that on the sixth day God finished all His works.[72] For it is obvious that in accordance with those kinds of creatures which He first made, God makes many new things which He did not make then. But we cannot believe that He establishes a new kind, since He finished all His works on the sixth day.

Hence, God moves His whole creation by a hidden power,

and all creatures are subject to this movement: the angels carry out His commands, the stars move in their courses, the winds blow now this way, now that, deep pools seethe with tumbling waterfalls and mists forming above them, meadows come to life as their seeds put forth the grass, animals are born and live their lives according to their proper instincts, the evil are permitted to try the just. It is thus that God unfolds the generations which He laid up in creation when first He founded it; and they would not be sent forth to run their course if He who made creatures ceased to exercise His provident rule over them.

CHAPTER 21

Divine Providence rules all creation.

42. Creatures shaped and born in time should teach us how we ought to regard them. For it is not without reason that Scripture says of Wisdom that *she graciously appears* to her lovers *in their paths and meets them with unfailing providence.*[73] We surely must not listen to those who think that only the higher regions of the world—that is, the regions at the outer edge of the denser atmosphere around the earth and beyond that point—are governed by Divine Providence, but that this lower part, which is earth and water, as well as the surrounding air, which receives moisture from vapors arising out of earth and water and in which the winds and clouds are formed, is rather the sport of chance and fortuitous motion.[74] Against these philosophers we have the Psalmist who voices the praise of the heavenly regions and then turns to the lower realm with the words:

> *Praise the Lord from the earth,*
> *monsters of the sea and all the deeps,*
> *fire, hail, snow, and ice,*
> *and storm winds fulfilling His command.*[75]

Nothing seems to be so much driven by chance as the turbulence and storms by which these lower regions of the heavens (rightly included also under the term "earth") are assaulted and buffeted. But when the Psalmist added the phrase, *fulfilling His command,* he made it quite clear that the plan in these phenomena subject to God's command is hidden from us rather than that it is lacking to universal nature. Our Savior with His own lips tells us that not a single sparrow falls to earth without God willing it, and that God Himself clothes the grass of the field, which soon is to be thrown into the oven.[76] In saying this, does not our Lord assure us that not only this whole region of the world which has been assigned to mortal and corruptible beings but also the least and lowliest parts of it are ruled by Divine Providence?

CHAPTER 22

Evidence of Divine Providence.

43. There are those who deny this truth and do not accept the authority of Sacred Scripture. They think that our part of the world is subject to turbulence arising from chance forces and not ruled by the Wisdom of the most high God; and to offer what passes for a proof, they appeal to two arguments, either the one I have mentioned about the changeableness of the weather or the one about the prosperity and adversity of men, which befall them without respect to their merits. Now, if they saw the extraordinary plan in the members of any living body, apparent not only to medical experts, who in the exercise of their profession are required to make incisions and identify and examine parts of the body, but to any man of average knowledge and intelligence, would they not cry out that these creatures never cease for an instant to be governed by God, from whom comes every rule of measures, every harmony of numbers, every order of weights?[77]

What more absurd or foolish opinion can be maintained, therefore, than to hold that the will of God and the ruling power of His providence are lacking in that whole region whose lowliest and smallest creatures are obviously fashioned by such a remarkable plan that a moment's serious attention to them fills the beholder with inexpressible awe and wonder? And in view of the fact that soul is superior to body, what is more mindless than to suppose that there is no judgment of God's providence on the deeds of men when there are such clear and overwhelming proofs of His intelligent design in man's body? But because these small things are before us and are perceived by our senses, and because we can easily search into them, the plan of creation shines forth in them; but the things whose plan we cannot see are judged to be unplanned by those who think that nothing exists unless they can see it; or if they think the thing exists, they suppose that it is identical in nature with what they have been accustomed to see.

CHAPTER 23

God created all simultaneously but works even until now.

44. Our steps, however, are guided by the same Divine Providence through Holy Scripture to keep us from falling into such a mischievous trap. From the works of God, with His grace, we should try to search out where He had created all of them together when He rested from the accomplishment of his works, whose visible forms He produces throughout the ages working even until now.

Let us, then, consider the beauty of any tree in its trunk, branches, leaves, and fruit. This tree surely did not spring forth suddenly in this size and form, but rather went through a process of growth with which we are familiar. For it sprouted forth from a root which a germ or bud first planted in the earth, and from that source the tree took its shape as it developed with all its parts. Furthermore, the germ was from a seed, and therefore in the seed all those parts existed primordially, not in the dimensions of bodily mass but as a force and causal power.[78] The bodily mass was built up by an accumulation of earth and moisture. But there exists in the tiny grain that power more wonderful and excellent by which moisture was mingled with earth forming a matter capable of being changed into wood, into spreading branches, into green leaves of appropriate shape, into beautiful and luxurious fruits, with all parts developed into a well-ordered whole. For what comes forth from that tree or hangs upon it that was not taken or drawn from a hidden treasure in the seed?[79] But the seed was from a tree, not this tree but another, and that tree was in turn from another seed. Sometimes, however, a tree is from a tree when a shoot is plucked and planted. Therefore, we have seed from tree, tree from seed, and tree from tree. But in no case do we have seed from seed unless a tree intervenes. On the other hand, we do have tree from tree without the intervention of a seed. One comes from the other, therefore, in succession, but both come from earth and not earth from them. Earth, then, is prior and is their source. The same is true of animals: we may doubt whether seeds are from animals or animals from seeds, but whichever one is prior, it is absolutely certain that it came from the earth.

45. In the seed, then, there was invisibly present all that would develop in time into a tree. And in this same way we must picture the world, when God made all things together, as having had all things together which were made in it and with it when day was made. This includes not only heaven with sun, moon, and stars, whose splendor remains unchanged as they move in a circular motion; and earth and the deep waters, which are in almost unceasing motion, and which, placed below the sky, make up the lower part of the world; but it includes also the beings which water and earth produced in potency and in their causes before they came forth in the course of time as they have become known to us in the works which God even now produces.

46. Hence it is said: *This is the book of the creation of heaven and earth. When day was made, God made heaven and earth and every green thing of the field before it appeared above the earth, and all the grass of the field before it sprang forth.*[80] He did this not as He works now through rain and man's cultivation of the land; and for this reason Scripture adds the words, *For God had not rained upon the earth, and there was not a man to till the earth.*[81] But in the beginning He created all things together and completed the

whole in six days, when six times He brought the "day" which He made before the things which He made, not in a succession of periods of time but in a plan made known according to causes.[82] On the seventh day He rested from those works, graciously revealing this rest also to the "day" that it might rejoice in this knowledge. Hence, it was not by any work but by His rest that He blessed and sanctified the seventh day.

God, then, creates no new creatures, but He directs and rules by His governance of the world all the things He made together, and thus He works without ceasing, resting and working at the same time, as I have already explained. The works which God produces even now as the ages unfold have their beginning in the narrative where Scripture says, *But a spring rose out of the earth and watered all the face of the earth.*[83] Since I have said as much as I thought was necessary about this spring, I think we should make a new start with the text that follows.

BOOK SIX
The Creation of the Man's Body

The creation of man, Gen. 2.7. How is this account related to that in Gen. 1.27?

1. *And God formed man of dust from the earth and breathed into his face the breath of life; and man was made a living being.*[1] Here we must see whether this is a restatement intended to describe the manner in which man was made, for we have read already that he was made on the sixth day. On the other hand, when God made all things together, did He make man among them in some hidden form, as He made the grass of the field before it sprang forth?[2] In this latter supposition, man would have been already made in another manner in the hidden recesses of nature, as were the beings which God created together when day was made; and later, with the passage of time, he would be made in a second manner according to the visible form in which he now lives his life for good or ill. He would then be like the grass of the field, which was made before it sprang forth on the earth, but in the course of time, when a spring watered the land, it came forth and appeared upon the earth.[3]

2. Let us first try to understand the text under consideration as a restatement. Perhaps man was made on the sixth day as day itself was originally made, and the firmament, and land and sea. These creatures are not said to have been first made and hidden away in some primordial causes and then with the unfolding of time to have come forth into the light with the visible features that shape the universe. But from the beginning of the ages, when day was made, the world is said to have been formed, and

in its elements at the same time there were laid away the creatures that would later spring forth with the passage of time, plants and animals, each according to its kind.

For we cannot believe that even the stars were made in primordial causes in the elements of the world so as to come forth later with the passage of time and to shine in the radiant forms which now glow in the heavens. Rather, all these beings were created at the same time according to the perfection of the number six when day was made. Was man also, therefore, made in the form and substance in which he now exists and lives his life for good or ill? Or was he made in a hidden form, like the grass of the field before it sprang forth, so that his appearance in due course of time would be accomplished when God would make him from the dust?

Chapter 2

First hypothesis: man was created on the sixth day in the visible shape familiar to us; the narrative in Gen. 2.7 is a recapitulation.

3. Let us assume, then, that man was formed on the sixth day in the clear and visible shape familiar to us, but that in the earlier narrative no mention was made of the details which are given in the recapitulation. Let us see whether Scripture agrees with this hypothesis.

This is the account in the narrative of the works on the sixth day: *And God said, "Let Us make mankind in Our image and likeness; and let them have dominion over the fish of the sea, the birds of the air, all the cattle, all the earth, and all the creatures that crawl on the earth." And God made man, to the image of God He made him: male and female He made them. And God blessed them and said: "Increase and multiply and fill the earth and subdue it, and have dominion over the fish of the sea, the birds of the air, all the cattle, all the earth, and all the creatures that crawl on the earth."*[4]

Man, therefore, had already been formed from the slime, and while he slept a woman had been made for him from his side; but in the earlier narrative no mention was made of the details now given in the recapitulation. We are not told that on the sixth day the male was made and later the female in due time. But Scripture says, *He made him; male and female He made them, and He blessed them.* How, then, was it that man was already placed in Paradise when a woman was made for him? Does the sacred writer recall this after passing it over originally? For Paradise was already planted on that sixth day and man was placed in it; and then he was put to sleep so that Eve might be formed, after which he awoke and gave her a name. But these events could happen only in successive periods of time. They could not, therefore, have come about in the manner in which all things were created together.

CHAPTER 3

Difficulties inherent in this hypothesis; Gen. 2.7-9 is more than a recapitulation.

4. However exalted man recognizes that power to be by which God made these things simultaneously with the others, we surely know that the words of man cannot be uttered by his voice except within a period of time. For we heard the words of man when he gave names to the animals and a name to the woman, and immediately after that when he said, *Therefore a man shall leave his father and mother and cleave to his wife, and they shall be two in one flesh.*[5] Whatever syllables were used in speaking these words, no two syllables of the utterance could have sounded together. It is, then, all the more impossible that all this could have happened simultaneously with the creation of those beings which were created together.

Consequently, we are faced with a dilemma. On the one hand, we might say that all those creatures were not made together at the dawn of the ages but were made in successive periods of time, and the day first made did not have morning and evening in a spiritual but in a corporeal nature, and morning and evening were made by some sort of revolving motion of light or by a diffusion and contraction of light.[6] On the other hand, if we take into account all that I have discussed earlier in this commentary, we have good reason to conclude that the spiritual day, mysteriously made in the beginning, was called day in so far as it was in a sense the light of wisdom.[7] I have argued that this day was made present to the works created by God, and that this was done in knowledge revealed according to a scheme designated by the number six.[8] The words of Scripture seem to support this interpretation, for after the six days are done it says: *When day was made, God made heaven and earth and every green thing of the field before it appeared above the earth, and all the grass of the field before it sprang forth.*[9] And there is the further testimony of Scripture where it is said, *He who lives forever created all things together.*[10] There can be no doubt, then, that the work whereby man was formed from the slime of the earth and a wife fashioned for him from his side belongs not to that creation by which all things were made together, after completing which God rested, but to that work of God which takes place with the unfolding of the ages as He works even now.

5. We must consider the exact words by which it is told how God planted Paradise, placed in it the man whom He had made, and brought before him the animals for him to name, and how He then formed a woman for him out of a rib taken from him, since no helper like man had been found. The narration of these facts makes it clear that these events do not belong to that work of God from which He rested on the seventh day, but rather to that work by which He works through the course of time even to this moment. For this is what the author says when he tells how Paradise was planted: *And God planted a garden in Eden in the East, and there He put the man whom He had formed. And again from the earth God made to grow every tree that is pleasant to the sight and good for food.*[11]

CHAPTER 4

Further reasons why the narrative in Gen. 2.7-9 goes beyond what was stated in the work of the six days.

When the author says, *Again from the earth He made to grow every tree that is pleasant to the sight,* he surely makes it clear that the statement about God now bringing forth trees from the earth refers to something different from what was said previously about the earth on the third day bringing forth the nourishing crops scattering their seed according to their kind and the fruit tree according to its kind.[12] This explains the expression, *Again He made to grow (Eiecit adhuc).*[13] This is over and above what God had already made to grow. In the first instance God had created things in potency and in their causes in that work in which He had created all things together, and from which, after they were finished, He rested on the seventh day. But in the second instance He created visible things in the work which belongs to the passage of time, even as He is at work to the present moment.

6. It might be objected that not every kind of tree was created on the third day, but that some kinds were postponed and created on the sixth day, when man was made and placed in Paradise. But Scripture clearly tells what creatures were made on the sixth day: the living creatures, each according to its kind, quadrupeds and creeping things and beasts, and man himself, male and female, made to the image of God.[14]

Accordingly, the author was able to omit saying how man was made (although he narrated the fact of his creation on the sixth day), so that restating the matter later he might also give the manner of his creation by telling how the man was made from the dust of the earth and the woman from his side. On the other hand, he could not omit any kind of creature, either at the moment when God said, *Let there be (Fiat)* or *Let Us make (Faciamus),* or when he himself says, *So it was done (Sic est factum)* or *God made (Fecit Deus).* Otherwise it would be to no avail that everything was systematically arranged with such great care throughout the different days if there could be any suggestion that the days were confused, so that after the assignment of plants and trees to the third day we should believe that on the sixth day certain trees were created which Scripture does not mention on the sixth day.

CHAPTER 5

Second hypothesis: in the first creation of the six days God created all living beings, including Adam and Eve, potentially and in their causes. From these causes God later created them in their visible forms.

7. Finally, what shall we say about the beasts of the field and the birds of heaven which God brought to Adam to see what he would call them? This is what the text says: *And the Lord God said: "It is not good that the man should be alone. Let Us make for him a helper like himself." And again God formed from the earth all the beasts of the field and all the birds of heaven and brought them to Adam to see what he would call them. And whatever Adam called a living creature, that is its name. And Adam gave names to all the cattle and to all the birds of heaven and to all the beasts of the field. But for Adam there was not found a helper like himself. And God cast Adam into a trance, and as Adam slept, God took one of his ribs and in its place put flesh, and the Lord God made the rib which He took from Adam into a woman.*[15]

Since, therefore, a helper like the man was not found among the cattle and beasts of the field and birds of heaven, God made him a helper of like nature from a rib taken from his side. Now, this was done when God had again formed these same beasts of the field and birds of heaven from the earth and had brought them to the man.[16] But how can this be understood as happening on the sixth day, since on that day the earth produced living creatures at the word of God, whereas on the fifth day the waters produced the birds also at the word of God? It would not be said here, *And again God formed from the earth all the beasts of the field and all the birds of heaven,* unless the earth had already produced all the beasts of the field on the sixth day, and the water all the birds of heaven on the fifth day.

In accordance, therefore, with the original work of creation, in which God made all things together, He created potentially and in their causes works from which He rested on the seventh day. But He works in a different manner now, as we see in those beings which He creates in the course of time, working even yet. Consequently, it was in days as we know them with their corporeal light caused by the sun moving in the sky that Eve was made from the side of her husband. For it was then that God again formed the beasts and birds from the earth, and since among them no helper was found for Adam similar to him, Eve was formed. It was, therefore, in such days as these that God also formed Adam from the slime of the earth.

8. It cannot be said that the male was made on the sixth day and the female in the course of days following. On the sixth day it is explicitly said, *Male and female He made them, and He blessed them*,[17] and so forth, and these words are said about both and to both. The original creation, therefore, of the two was different from their later creation. First they were created in potency through the word of God and inserted seminally into the world when He created all things together, after which He rested from these works on the seventh day. From these creatures all things are made, each at its own proper time throughout the course of history. Later the man and the woman were created in accordance with God's creative activity as it is at work throughout the ages and with which He works even now; and thus it was ordained that in time Adam would be made from the slime of the earth and the woman from the side of her husband.[18]

CHAPTER 6

A further explanation. The difference between material seeds and primordial reasons.

9. According to the division of the works of God described above, some works belonged to the invisible days in which He

created all things simultaneously, and others belong to the days in which He daily fashions whatever evolves in the course of time from what I might call the primordial wrappers. In this interpretation I hope I have not given a misguided or absurd explanation of the words of Scripture which have led me to assume this division. And since an understanding of these matters is somewhat difficult and beyond the grasp of an uneducated reader, I must take care that I am not thought to hold or say anything that I know I do not hold or say. For although I prepared the reader to understand my meaning as far as I was able in the foregoing commentary, nevertheless I suppose that many are not enlightened by my explanations and think that man existed in the original work of God by which He made everything simultaneously so as to have some form of life and to perceive, believe, and understand as addressed to himself the words which God spoke when He said, *See, I have given you every seed-bearing plant.*[19] Whoever thinks this should know that this is not what I have thought or what I have said.

10. But, again, if I say that in the original creation by which God created everything simultaneously man was not there as a man, neither in the maturity of adult life nor in the form of an infant, not as a fetus in a mother's womb nor even as a visible seed of man, someone will think he did not exist at all. Let such a one, then, go back to Scripture. He will find that on the sixth day man was made to the image of God and that he was made male and female. Let him see, then, when the woman was made: he will find that it was outside of the six days. For she was made when God formed from the earth again the beasts of the field and the birds of heaven, not when the waters brought forth the birds, and earth brought forth living creatures, among which were the beasts.

Then, in the first creation, man was made, male and female. This happened, therefore, both then and later. It cannot be then and not later, nor can it be later and not then. Nor were there different persons later, but there were the very same ones in one way then and in another way later. One will ask me how. I shall reply: "Later visibly, in the form of the human body familiar to us; not, however, generated by parents, but the man formed from the slime and the woman formed from his rib." One will ask how they were created originally on the sixth day. I shall reply: "Invisibly, potentially, in their causes, as things that will be in the future are made, yet not made in actuality now."[20]

11. My critic perhaps will not understand this. All that is familiar to him is taken away, including the material dimension of seeds. For man was nothing of the sort when he was made in the first creation of the six days. There is indeed in seeds some likeness to what I am describing because of the future developments stored up in them. Nevertheless, before all visible seeds there are the causes; but he does not understand. What, then, shall I do except to give him a salutary admonition, as far as I can, to believe Holy Scripture and to accept its teaching that man was made when God, at the making of day, made heaven and earth, concerning which Scripture elsewhere says, *He who lives for ever created all things together?*[21] And then creating all things not together but each in its own time, God formed the man from the slime of the earth and the woman from a bone taken out of the man. Scripture does not permit us to understand that in this manner the man and woman were made on the sixth day, and yet it does not allow us to assume that they were not made on the sixth day at all.

CHAPTER 7

It cannot be said that Gen. 1.27 refers only to the creation of the souls of man and woman.

12. One might suggest that it was the souls of the man and woman that God created on the sixth day. It is certainly in the spiritual and intellectual part of man that the image of God is understood to be. Their bodies, then, would be formed later.

But Scripture does not allow us to accept such an interpretation. First of all, we are told that God finished His work on the sixth day, and I do not see how we can understand this statement if there was lacking something then, which was not made in its causes, to be visibly formed later. Furthermore, the distinction between male and female can exist only in bodies. But if anyone suggests that in intellect and action[22] both sexes were somehow to be understood as in the one soul, what will he make of the food God gave from the fruit trees on the sixth day? Food is needed by man only when he has a body. Finally, if anyone wishes to interpret this food in a figurative sense, he will be departing from the literal interpretation of the facts which should first be established in commenting on a narrative of this kind.

CHAPTER 8

In what sense God spoke the words attributed to Him
in Gen. 1.27-29.

13. How, then, my critic asks, did God speak to those who did not yet hear or understand, since there was no one there to catch the words? I might reply that God spoke to them in the way Christ spoke to us when we were not yet born and were destined to come into being only after a long time, and as He spoke not only to us but also to all who would come to be after us. For it was to all who He knew would be His own that He said, *Behold I am with you until the end of the world.*[23] In a similar way God knew the prophet to whom He said, *Before I formed you in the womb, I knew you;*[24] and Levi paid tithes when he was in the loins of Abraham.[25] Why, then, could not Abraham have been in Adam in a similar manner, and Adam himself in the first works of the world, which God created simultaneously?

But the words of the Lord in the flesh spoken by His mouth, as well as the words of God spoken by the mouths of prophets, are uttered in time by a voice coming from a body, and such words with all their syllables require and fill out corresponding intervals of time. But when God said, *Let Us make mankind in Our image and likeness; and let him have dominion over the fish of the sea, the birds of the air, all the cattle, all the earth, and all the creatures that crawl on the earth;* and, *Increase and multiply and fill the earth and subdue it and have dominion over the fish of the sea, the birds of the air, all the cattle, all the earth, and all the creatures that crawl on the earth;* and, *See, I have given you every seed-bearing plant bearing its seed over all the earth, and every tree that has seed-bearing fruit; these will be food for you;*[26] these words of God, spoken before there were any sound vibrations in air and before any voice coming from man or from cloud existed, were uttered in His supreme Wisdom, through which all things were made. They were not like sounds that strike human ears, but they implanted in things made the causes of things yet to be made. Thus, God by His almighty power made what would appear in the future; and when He who is before the ages created the beginning of the ages, in what we might call the germ or root of time, He created man to be formed later in due time.

Some creatures, indeed, precede others either by reason of time or by reason of causality. But God precedes all that He made not only by reason of His superiority as the Author of all, even of causes, but also by reason of His eternity. But this topic should perhaps be more fully discussed in connection with other passages of Scripture relating more directly to it.

CHAPTER 9

God knows us before we are born, but no one is personally responsible for any good or evil before his birth.

14. This must conclude what I undertook to say about man. In expressing my views, I have tried to observe moderation so as to show a persevering spirit of enquiry rather than a dogged desire to maintain my opinions in exploring the profound meaning of Scripture.

Now, there is no doubt that God knew Jeremiah before He formed him in the womb, for He says quite clearly, *Before I formed you in the womb, I knew you.*[27] But it is difficult, if not impossible, for our limited understanding to know where God knew him before forming him. Was it in some proximate causes, as in the case of Levi, who paid tithes when he was in the loins of Abraham? [28] Was it in Adam himself, in whom the whole human race had its roots? And if in Adam, was it when he had been formed from the slime, or was it when he had been made in his causes in the works which God created simultaneously? Was it before all creation, inasmuch as God has elected and predestined His saints before the foundation of the world?[29] Or was it rather in all of these causes, whether those I have mentioned or those I have not mentioned, before Jeremiah was formed in the womb?

Whatever the case may be, I do not think it necessary to carry on a more searching enquiry, provided that it is evident to us that from the moment Jeremiah was brought into this world by his parents he led his own life and, as he grew in years, was able to choose to live it well or badly, whereas before that he had no such choice, whether before he was formed in the womb or after he was formed there but before he was born. We are left with no hesitation on this point by St. Paul's view concerning the twins in the womb of Rebecca, who up to that point had done no good or evil.[30]

15. Not in vain, however, does Scripture say that even an infant is not free from sin if he has spent one day of life on earth.[31] The Psalmist says, *In iniquity I was conceived, and in sin my mother nourished me in her womb.*[32] St. Paul says that all die in Adam, *in whom all have sinned.*[33] But let us hold for certain that, whatever merits go from parents to their offsrping and whatever grace of God sanctifies anyone before birth, there is no injustice in God, and no one before birth does any good or evil for which he is personally responsible. Some[34] hold that in another life souls have sinned to a greater or lesser degree and that they have been sent into different bodies in accordance with what they deserve because of their sins; but that does not agree with the teaching of St. Paul, who has said quite clearly that those not yet born have done nothing good or evil.

16. We must, therefore, ask ourselves again at the proper time what the whole human race contracted from the sin of our first parents, who were the only ones to commit the sin. There is no doubt, however, that man could have had no such guilt before he was fashioned from the dust of the earth and before he was living his own life. Esau and Jacob, who according to St. Paul did no good or evil before birth, could not be said to have re-

ceived some merit from their parents if their parents had done
no good or evil, nor could the human race be said to have sinned
in Adam if Adam himself had not sinned; and Adam would not
have sinned unless he were living his own life, in which he
could live either well or badly.

It is idle, therefore, to look for either a sin or a good deed of
Adam at the time when he was made in causes in the things simultaneously created but was not yet living his own life nor existing in parents so living. For in that first creation of the world,
when God created all things simultaneously, He created man in
the sense that He made the man who was to be, that is, the causal principle of man to be created, not the actuality of man already created.[35]

CHAPTER 10

*Under the influence of the primordial reasons the crops came forth
from the earth and then the seeds from the crops.*

17. Nevertheless, under one aspect these things are in the
Word of God, where they are not made but eternally existing;
under another aspect they are in the elements of the universe,
where all things destined to be were made simultaneously; under another aspect they are in things no longer created simultaneously but rather separately each in its own due time, made
according to their causes which were created simultaneously—
among which was Adam, formed from the slime and animated
by the breath of God, like the grass sprung from the earth;[36] under another aspect they are in seeds, in which they are found
again as quasi-primordial causes which derive from creatures
that have come forth according to the causes which God first
stored up in the world—and thus we have the crops from the
earth, and the seed from the crops.[37]

In all these things, beings already created received at their
own proper time their manner of being and of acting, which developed into visible forms and natures from the hidden and invisible reasons which are latent in creation as causes. Thus the

crops came forth on the earth, and man was made as a living being, and so of the other creatures, whether plants or animals, belonging to the work of God as He works even at this time. But
these beings have duplicates of themselves, as it were, carried invisibly within them by reason of the hidden power of reproduction that they possess. They have this power through their
primordial causes, in which they were placed in the created
world when day was made, before they came forth in the visible
shape proper to their kind.

CHAPTER 11

*Creatures were in one sense completed and in another sense just
begun: completed because they were made in their causal
reasons, just begun because God subsequently would
bring them forth in their visible form.*

18. Now, if the original works of God, when He created all
things simultaneously, were not perfect according to the limits
of their nature, no doubt there would later be added the perfections needed to complete their being; and thus the perfection of
all the world is made up of what we might call two halves. As
they are like parts of a whole, the total universe, whose parts
they are, is completed by their union. Moreover, if these creatures attained perfection in the sense that they are perfected
when they are brought forth individually, each at its own time,
in their visible form and reality,[38] it is surely true that either
nothing would come from them later as time unfolds, or God
would unceasingly produce from them the effects which in due
time have their origin in them.

But these works in a certain sense are already perfected, and
in another sense they are just begun. They were made by God
when in the beginning He made the world and created simultaneously all things to be unfolded in the ages to follow. They
are perfected because in their proper natures by which they fulfill their role in time they have nothing that was not present in
them as made in its causes. They are just begun, however, since

in them are seeds, as it were, of future perfections to be put forth from their hidden state and made manifest during the ages at the appropriate time.

The words of Scripture make this very clear to anyone who reads the text attentively. For it says that they were both perfected and just begun. Certainly, if they were not perfected, Scripture would not have said, *Thus the heavens and the earth were finished and all their array. And on the sixth day God finished the works He had made. . . . And God blessed the seventh day and made it holy.*[39] On the other hand, unless they had just begun, Scripture would not go on to say that *God rested on that day from all the works He had begun to make.*[40]

19. If someone should ask how God completed His works and at the same time just began them, the answer is clear from what I have said above. For He did not complete some and begin others, but the reference is to the same works from which He rested on the seventh day. We can see that God completed these works when He created all things simultaneously in such a finished state that nothing would have to be created by Him in the temporal order which had not been already created by Him here in the order of causes; and at the same time we understand that God began these works in the sense that what He had originally established here in causes He later fulfilled in effects.

Thus *God formed the dust of the earth* (or *the slime of the earth*) *into man;* that is, He formed man from the dust or slime of the earth. And *He breathed* (or *blew*) *into his face the breath of life; and man was made a living being.*[41] He was not predestined at that time, for that happened before the ages in the foreknowledge of the Creator. Nor was he at that time made in causes, whether begun in a completed state or completed in a beginning state, for that happened with the commencement of the ages in the primordial reasons when all things were created simultaneously. But he was created in time, visibly in the body, invisibly in the soul, being made up of soul and body.

CHAPTER 12

Man, like all other creatures, was made by the Word of God. He differs from all creatures of the visible world because he is made to God's image and likeness.

20. Let us, then, see how God made man, forming his body first from the earth; after that we shall look into the origin of his soul in so far as we are able. Now to think of God as forming man from the slime of the earth with bodily hands is childish. Indeed, if Scripture had said such a thing, we should be compelled to believe that the writer had used a metaphor rather than that God is contained in the structure of members such as we know in our bodies.

For it is said, *Thy hand hath scattered the nations;*[42] and, *Thou didst bring Thy people forth with a strong hand and outstretched arm.*[43] But anyone in his right mind understands that the name of a bodily member has been used in these passages for the power and might of God.

21. We should not pay any attention to the theory of those who think that man is the principal work of God on the ground that God spoke and the other creatures were made, whereas He Himself made man.[44] Man's pre-eminence lies rather in the fact that God made him to His own image.

For the things that God spoke He also made; and Scripture puts the matter this way because they were made by His Word. Now a man using words can say to other men what he thinks in time and utters with his voice. But it is not in this way that God speaks, except when He speaks through a corporeal creature, as He spoke to Abraham and to Moses, and as He spoke through a cloud about His own Son.[45] But before all creation, in order that creation might come about, God spoke by His Word who in the beginning was God with God. Since *all things were made through Him, and without Him nothing was made,*[46] it is obvious that man was made through Him. He certainly made heaven by His Word, because He spoke and it was made. Scripture, however, says, *And the heavens are the work of Thy hands.*[47] Again, concerning the lowest part of the world—its foundation, as it were—Scripture says, *For the sea is His, and He made it, and His hands formed the dry land.*[48]

We must not suppose, therefore, that a special dignity belongs to man for the reason that God Himself made him, whereas in the case of the other creatures God spoke and they were made; or that He made the other things by His word and man by His hands. The pre-eminence of man consists in this, that God made him to His own image by giving him an intellect by which he surpasses the beasts, as I have explained above. Given this honor, if man does not understand it and live a good life in accordance with it, he will be on a level with the same beasts over which he has been placed. For Scripture says, *Man, for all his dignity, has not understood; he has been joined with senseless beasts and has become like them.*[49] God also made the beasts, but not to His image.

22. We should not say, "God Himself made man, but the beasts He ordered to be made, and they were thus created."[50] For He made both man and cattle through His Word, through whom all things were made. God's Word and Wisdom and Might are all one and the same reality; and when His hand is spoken of, there is reference not to a visible member of a body but to His creative power. For the same Scripture that says God formed man from the slime of the earth says also that He formed the beasts of the field from the earth when He brought them with the birds of the air to Adam to see what he would call them. For Scripture says, *And again God formed from the earth all the beasts.*[51]

If, therefore, He Himself formed man from the earth and the beasts from the earth, what is the basis of man's greater dignity except that he was created in the image of God? This was not, however, in his body but in his intellect, about which we shall speak later.[52] And yet he does have in his body also a characteristic that is a sign of this dignity in so far as he has been made to stand erect. As a result, he is admonished by this fact that he must not seek earthly things as do the cattle, whose pleasure is entirely from the earth, in consequence of which they are all inclined forward on their bellies and bent downwards.[53]

Man's body, then, is appropriate for his rational soul not because of his facial features and the structure of his limbs, but rather because of the fact that he stands erect, able to look up to heaven and gaze upon the higher regions in the corporeal world. In like manner, his rational soul must be raised up to spiritual realities, which by their very nature are of far greater excellence, so that a man's thoughts may be on heavenly things, not on the things that are on the earth.[54]

CHAPTER 13

Did God create Adam as an infant or adult? The creative power of God is not limited by the ordinary laws of growth in living things.

23. But in what state did God make man from the slime of the earth?[55] Did He make him a fully developed man, that is, an adult in the vigor of young manhood,[56] or an infant, as He makes human beings today in mothers' wombs? He who performs these deeds is none other than He who said, *Before I formed you in the womb, I knew you.*[57] The one characteristic that distinguishes Adam from other men is that he was not born of parents but made from the earth. However, it would seem, he was made to grow through the stages of human development requiring the passage of years which we observe as necessary for man's growth.

Or was this required? In either case, whichever way God made Adam, He did what was in accordance with His almighty power and wisdom. God has established in the temporal order fixed laws governing the production of kinds of beings and qualities of beings and bringing them forth from a hidden state into full view, but His will is supreme over all. By His power He has given numbers to His creation, but He has not bound His power by these numbers.[58] For His Spirit "moved over"[59] the world that was to be made in such a way that He still moves over the world that is made, not by a material space relationship but by the excellence of His power.

24. Everyone knows that water mingling with earth and com-

ing into contact with the roots of a vine nourishes the wood of the vine and in that wood takes on a new quality which enters into the grape that gradually comes forth. As the grape grows, the water thus transformed becomes wine, which sweetens as it matures. When pressed and fermented, it acquires strength with age and becomes useful and pleasant to drink.

Now did the Lord need a vine or earth or this passage of time when without any such aids He changed water into wine, and such wine that even the guest who had had his fill would praise it?[60] Did the Author of time need the help of time?

All serpents require a certain number of days according to their kind to be implanted, formed, born, and developed. Did Moses and Aaron have to wait all those days before the rod could be turned into a serpent?[61] When events like this happen, they do not happen against nature except for us, who have a limited knowledge of nature, but not for God, for whom nature is what He has made.

CHAPTER 14

The causal reasons have a double potentiality: they may cause
a slow growth leading to maturity, or they may provide
for the instantaneous and miraculous production
of a fully mature living being.

25. It is only right to ask how God made the causal reasons which He placed in the world when He first created all things simultaneously.[62] Did He make them to cause the development of things through periods of time different for each creature according to its kind, as we observe in the shape and growth of all plants and animals that are generated? Or did He provide that through these reasons creatures would be fully formed instantaneously, as Adam is believed to have been made an adult man without any previous period of development?

But why can we not assume that the causal reasons had both potentialities, so that from them would come whatever would have pleased the Creator? For if we take the first hypothesis referred to above, certain facts present themselves to contradict our explanation of the causal reasons, such as the case of water made wine already mentioned, and all miracles that happen against the ordinary course of nature. But if we take the second hypothesis, our position will be even more absurd in that the forms and appearances of nature that we observe every day would be passing through periods of time in their development contrary to the original causal reasons governing the production of all organisms.

We must conclude, then, that these reasons were created to exercise their causality in either one way or the other: by providing for the ordinary development of new creatures in appropriate periods of time, or by providing for the rare occurrence of a miraculous production of a creature, in accordance with what God wills as proper for the occasion.

CHAPTER 15

Man was formed in accordance with the causal reason
as determined by God.

26. And yet man was made as those original causes required the first man to be made. He was not to be born of parents, since there were no humans beings before him, but to be formed from the slime of the earth in accordance with the causal reason in which he had been originally created. For if he was made otherwise, God had not created him in the works of the six days. But as he is said to have been made in those works, God surely had made the cause from which he would be a human being at the proper time and according to which he was to be created. For God had finished simultaneously in the perfection of the causal reasons the works He had begun, and He had begun the works that were to be finished in the course of the ages.

If the Creator, therefore, placed in those first causes which He originally inserted in the world not only the determination that He would form man from the slime of the earth but also the determination as to how He would form him, whether like an infant in a womb or in the form of a young man, He most certainly created him as He had foreordained, for He would not create him in a manner contrary to what He Himself had determined. On the other hand, if in the causal reasons God placed only the potentiality for man's creation in whatever way he would be created, in one way or the other (that is, if He determined in the causal reasons that it could be either one way or the other, and if He reserved to His own will the one way in which He would subsequently create him rather than foreordaining this in nature), it is obvious that in this supposition also man was not made in a manner contrary to what was in the first creation of causes. For in that case it was determined in the causes that man could be created in such a way, not that he must necessarily be created in such a way. This determination was not in the created world but in the decision of the Creator, whose will constitutes the necessity of things.

CHAPTER 16

The possibility of future growth of living beings can be known to us but not the actuality.

27. Within the limits of our human intelligence we can know the nature of a being we have observed by experience in so far as past time is concerned; but with regard to the future, we are ignorant. For example, when we see a young man, we know that it is in his nature to grow old; but we do not know if this is also in God's will. But it would not be in nature if it had not first been in the will of God, who created all things. It is undoubtedly true that there is a hidden principle[63] of old age in the body of a young man, as there is of young manhood in the body of a boy. This principle is not seen by the eyes as is boyhood in a boy or young manhood in a young man; but by another kind of knowledge we conclude that there is in nature some hidden force by which latent forms[64] are brought into view, such as young manhood from boyhood or old age from young manhood.

The principle, therefore, which makes this development possible is hidden to the eyes but not to the mind; but whether such a development must necessarily come about is completely unknown to us. We know that the principle which makes it possible is in the very nature of the body; but there is no clear evidence in that body that there is a principle by which it must necessarily take place.

CHAPTER 17

God's foreknowledge and its relation to secondary causes.

28. But perhaps there is a determination in the created universe that this man must live to old age. And if it is not in the world, it is in God. For what He wills is of necessity going to be, and those things are truly going to be which He foreknew. Many things are going to be by virtue of secondary causes; but if they are also in the foreknowledge of God as things that are going to be, they are truly going to be. But if they are there as determined otherwise, then they will come about as they are in the foreknowledge of Him who cannot be deceived.

Old age is said to be reserved for the future of a young man, but it will not come about if he is going to die before that time. His future will be as determined by other causes, whether they are interwoven with causes in the world or hidden away in God's foreknowledge. Hezekiah was going to die as determined by the causes of certain future events, but God added fifteen years to his life;[65] and in doing so He did what He foreknew before the foundation of the world He was going to do and what He kept stored up in His will. He did not do what was not going to be: that was more truly going to be which He knew He was going to do. Those years, however, would not be rightly said to have been added to his life unless they were added to something[66] which had been determined otherwise in other causes.

In accordance with certain secondary causes, therefore, Hezekiah had already finished his life; but in accordance with causes in the will and foreknowledge of God, who from eternity knew what He was going to do in time (and this is truly what was to be), he was going to finish his life at that moment when he actually finished it. For although the added fifteen years were given in response to his prayers, God, who cannot be deceived in His foreknowledge, also surely foreknew that Hezekiah was going to pray in such a way that his petition ought to be granted. Hence, that which God foreknew was necessarily going to come about.

CHAPTER 18

Whatever is determined in the causal reasons is in accordance with God's will.

29. Therefore, if the causes of all future things were inserted in the world when that day was made on which God created all things together, Adam was not made otherwise, when formed from the slime of the earth, than in the form he had in those causes where God made man in the works of the six days. It is most likely that God made him in those causes in the form of perfect manhood.

In those causes there was the determination not only of the possibility of Adam's being made in the form which God willed, but also of the necessity that he should be so created. For to suppose that God made him contrary to the cause which He undoubtedly had freely predetermined is as unthinkable as to say that He created him against His own divine will. If God, however, did not place all causes in the original creation but kept some in His own will, those which He kept in His own will are not dependent on the necessity of the causes He created. Nevertheless, those which He kept in His own will cannot be contrary to those which He predetermined by His own will; for God's will cannot contradict itself. He established them, therefore, in such a way that they would contain the possibility, not the necessity, of causing the effect which would proceed from them. The other causes He hid in the original creation in such a way that there would necessarily come from them the effect which was only a possibility in the first kind of cause.

CHAPTER 19

From St. Paul's testimony it seems that Adam was given a natural, not a spiritual, body.

30. It is often asked whether a natural body, such as we now have, was originally formed for man from the slime, or a spiritual body such as we shall have in the resurrection.[67] Although this body of ours will be changed into a spiritual body (for *it is sown a natural body, and it rises a spiritual body*[68]), nevertheless the original nature of man's body is a matter for discussion. For if it was made as a natural body, we shall not receive back what we lost in Adam but something much better (in so far as the spiritual is superior to the natural) when we shall enjoy equality with the angels of God.[69]

But angels can be ranked above other angels even in holiness. Can they be thus ranked also over our Lord? About Him it has been said, *Thou hast placed Him a little below the angels.*[70] And how could this be except in view of the weakness of the body which He took from the Virgin, receiving *the form of a servant*[71] to redeem us from servitude by dying in that form?

But why should we delay with this discussion? For St. Paul's thought is clear in this matter. When he wished to adduce evidence to prove that the body is natural, he did not refer to his own body or to the body of any contemporary, but rather to this very passage of Scripture. These are his words: *If there is a natural body, there is also a spiritual body. For thus it is written: "The first man, Adam, was made a living being." The last Adam was made a life-giving spirit. Not that which is spiritual but that which is natural was first; afterwards the spiritual. The first man was of the earth, earthy. The second Man is from heaven, heavenly. As was the earthy man, so are those who are earthy; as is the heavenly Man, so are those who are heavenly. And as we have borne the image of the earthy man, let us also bear the image of Him who is from heaven.*[72]

What can be added to this? Therefore, in faith we now carry the image of the heavenly Man, since in the resurrection we shall have what we believe, but we have borne the image of the earthy man from the very beginning of the human race.

Chapter 20

Some writers suggest that the natural body of Adam was transformed into a spiritual body when he was placed in Paradise.

31. Another question comes up here.[73] How are we renewed if we are not called by Christ back to that which we were originally in Adam? For although many things are renewed by being changed to something better without being restored to their original state, their renewal, however, takes place by their passing out of a state inferior to that which they had before renewal. How did the Prodigal Son *die and come to life*, how was he *lost and found*?[74] How is *the best robe*[75] brought to him if he does not receive the immortality which Adam lost? But how did Adam lose immortality if he had a natural body? For it will not be a natural body but a spiritual body when this corruptible nature will put on incorruption and this mortal nature will put on immortality.[76]

Some interpreters, pressed by these difficulties, on the one hand have wished to save the statement in which St. Paul gives an example of a natural body when he quotes the words, *The first man, Adam, was made a living being*,[77] and on the other hand have wished to show that it is not absurd to say that man will one day be renewed and recover immortality by returning to the primitive state that Adam lost. They have, therefore, reasoned that man first had a natural body but that he was changed when he was placed in Paradise, just as we also shall be changed in the resurrection. This change, to be sure, is not mentioned in Genesis. But wishing to harmonize the biblical texts on both points, namely, the fact of the natural body of Adam and the fact of the renewal of our bodies mentioned in many texts of Sacred Scripture, they are convinced that this is a necessary conclusion.

CHAPTER 21

Difficulties against this opinion.

32. If the foregoing conclusion is valid, we are attempting in vain to find a literal meaning before determining the figurative meaning for Paradise with its trees and their fruits.[78] For who would believe that nourishment from the fruit of trees could have been necessary for immortal and spiritual bodies? However, if no other solution can be found, we are better off in choosing to understand Paradise in a spiritual sense than to suppose that man is not renewed, since Scripture mentions his renewal so often, or to think that he gets back again what we cannot prove he lost.

Furthermore, there is the question of man's death. Many passages of Scripture speak of Adam as having merited death by sin, thus showing that he would have been exempt from death had he not sinned. How, then, would he be mortal without the necessity of dying? And how would he not be mortal if he had a natural body?

CHAPTER 22

Some writers hold that Adam, even if faithful, would not have been exempt from death. This is refuted by St. Paul.

33. Some commentators, therefore, believe that Adam by his sin did not merit the death of the body but the death of the soul, the fruit of his iniquity.[79] For they believe that because he had a natural body, he would have gone forth from it to the rest now enjoyed by the saints who have already found their repose, and that he would receive at the end of the world the same bodily members endowed with immortality. Thus the death of the body would seem to have happened not as a result of sin but naturally, as is the case with the lower animals.

But in reply to this opinion comes another statement of St. Paul, who says, *The body is a dead thing because of sin; the spirit, however, is life because of justification. But if the Spirit of Him who raised Christ from the dead dwells in you, He who raised Christ from the dead will give life to your mortal bodies also through His Spirit, who dwells in you.*[80]

From this it follows that the death of the body also is from sin. If Adam, therefore, had not sinned, he would not have suffered death even of the body, and therefore he would also have had an immortal body. How, therefore, could that body have been immortal if it was natural?

CHAPTER 23

The transformation to a spiritual body could have been contingent on Adam's remaining faithful.

34. Those interpreters who think that Adam's body was changed in Paradise do not see that there would be no difficulty about its being changed from a natural body to a spiritual body on the condition that Adam had not sinned.[81] As a result, after his life in Paradise, lived in holiness and obedience, in eternal life[82] his body would be changed. There he would no longer need bodily nourishment. There would be no need then to understand Paradise in a figurative rather than a literal sense in order to maintain the principle that Adam could not have died a bodily death unless he sinned. It is indeed true that he would not have died even a bodily death unless he had sinned. For St. Paul clearly says, *The body is a dead thing because of sin.*[83] But it could have been a natural body before sin and have become a spiritual body when God so willed after a holy life.

CHAPTER 24

In what sense we can be said to recover what Adam lost.

35. How then, they object, are we said to be renewed if we do not recover what was lost by the first man, in whom all die?[84]

We do recover this in a certain sense, and in another sense we do not. We do not recover the immortality of a spiritual body, which man has not yet obtained; but we do recover the justice from which man fell through sin.[85] We shall, therefore, be renewed from the old way of sin, not transformed into the original natural body in which Adam was made, but into a better one, that is, a spiritual body, when *we shall enjoy equality with the angels of God*,[86] when we are made ready to dwell in our heavenly home, where we shall feel no more need of the food that is corruptible.

We are renewed, therefore, *in the spirit of our minds*[87] according to the image of Him who created us, the image which Adam lost when he sinned. And we shall be renewed also in the flesh when this *corruptible nature will put on incorruption*[88] so as to become a spiritual body. Adam had not been changed into such a body, but he was destined to be if he had not merited by sin the death even of his natural body.

36. Finally, St. Paul does not say, "The body is mortal because of sin," but, *The body is a dead thing because of sin.*[89]

CHAPTER 25

Adam in the Garden was both mortal and immortal.

Adam's body before he sinned could be said to be mortal in one respect and immortal in another: mortal because he was able to die, immortal because he was able not to die.[90] For it is one thing to be unable to die, as is the case with certain immortal beings so created by God; but it is another thing to be able not to die in the sense in which the first man was created immortal.[91] This immortality was given to him from the tree of life,[92] not from his nature. When he sinned, he was separated from this tree, with the result that he was able to die, although if he had not sinned, he would be able not to die.

He was mortal, therefore, by the constitution of his natural body, and he was immortal by the gift of his Creator. For if it was a natural body he had, it was certainly mortal because it was able to die, although at the same time immortal by reason of the fact that it was able not to die. Only a spiritual being is immortal by virtue of the fact that it cannot possibly die; and this condition is promised to us in the resurrection. Consequently, Adam's body, a natural and therefore mortal body, which by justification would become spiritual and therefore truly immortal, in reality by sin was made not mortal (because it was that already) but rather a dead thing, which it would have been able not to be if Adam had not sinned.

CHAPTER 26

Our bodies compared with Adam's.

37. How could St. Paul refer to our body as dead, when he was talking about those still living, except in so far as the necessity of dying is inherent in our race from the sin of our first parents? This body of ours is also natural as was Adam's; but although it is in the same class as his, it is much inferior. For our body must of necessity die, and that was not true of Adam's. It is true that he had to wait for the transformation of his body when it would become spiritual and receive the gift of true immortality whereby it would have no need of corruptible food. But if he lived a holy life, and if his body were changed into a spiritual state, he would not die.

In our case, however, even for those who live a holy life, the body must die; and because of this necessity, arising from the sin of the first man, St. Paul called our body not a mortal thing but a dead thing, because in Adam we all die.[93] He also says, *As the truth is in Jesus for you to put off the old man, which belongs to your former manner of life, him who is corrupted through deceitful lusts* (that is to say, what Adam became through sin; notice then what follows), and *be renewed in the spirit of your minds and put on the new man, him who has been created according to God in justice and the holiness of truth.*[94] This makes clear what it was that Adam lost by his sin.

CHAPTER 27

How we are renewed.

It is in this way that we are renewed in respect of what Adam lost, that is, in the spirit of our minds; but in respect of the body, which *is sown a natural body and will rise a spiritual body,*[95] when we are renewed we shall be given a better state, which Adam has not yet attained.

38. St. Paul also says, *Putting off the old man with his deeds, put on the new man who is being renewed in the knowledge of God according to the image of his Creator.*[96] It was this image, impressed on the spirit of our minds, that Adam lost by his sin;[97] it is this that we regain through the grace of justice, not a spiritual and immortal body, which Adam had not yet received, but which all the saints will have at the resurrection. This spiritual body is the reward of the merit which Adam lost. Hence *the best robe*[98] is the justice from which he fell; or, if it signifies the clothing of an immortal body, Adam also lost this when his sin prevented him from attaining it. For we are accustomed to say that a man lost his wife; and also that he lost his honor when he has not received the honor he expected because he has offended the man from whom he had hoped to receive it.

CHAPTER 28

We are not restored in our bodies to what Adam had but in our souls.

39. In this interpretation, therefore, Adam had a natural body not only before being placed in Paradise but also when he was in Paradise. In the interior man, however, he was spiritual according to the image of his Creator. But this quality he lost by sin as he merited also the death of the body, whereas, if he had not sinned, he would have merited a change into a spiritual body.

If interiorly he also lived a natural life, we cannot say that we

are renewed by being restored to what he had. Those who are
told, *Be renewed in the spirit of your minds,*[99] are exhorted to be
spiritual. But if Adam was not spiritual even in his mind, how
are we renewed by being recalled to what man never was? The
apostles and all holy men without doubt also had natural bodies,
but interiorly they lived a spiritual life, renewed as they were
in the knowledge of God after the image of their Creator.[100] But
they were not thereby immune to sin if they should consent to
evil-doing. St. Paul indeed shows that spiritual persons can suc-
cumb to a temptation to sin when he says: *Brethren, if a man is
overtaken in any trespass, you who are spiritual should instruct him
in a spirit of gentleness, looking to yourselves lest you too be tempted.*[101] I have said[102] this lest anyone think it impossible that
Adam sinned if he was spiritual in mind though natural in body.
Nevertheless, as I weigh these considerations, I do not want to
make any hasty declarations but rather to wait and see whether
the text of Scripture elsewhere is not against my interpretation.

CHAPTER 29

The next question to be taken up is that of the soul.

40. The next question to be taken up, namely, the question of
the soul, is extremely difficult; many commentators have la-
bored on it and have left us questions to labor over. It has indeed
been impossible for me to read all the writings of all who have
searched for the truth on this question in the light of Sacred
Scripture in order to arrive at some clear and certain conclusion.[103] Moreover, the problem of the soul is such a profound
one that even those writers who arrive at a true solution are not
readily understood by readers like me; I confess that no one has
thus far so convinced me that I feel no need for further investigation about the soul.

Whether in the present study I shall find some certain and final answer, I know not. But what I am able to discover I shall
try to explain in the next book, if the Lord assists me in my efforts.

NOTES

LIST OF ABBREVIATIONS

Agaësse-Solignac	P. Agaësse and A. Solignac (eds.), *La Genèse au sens littéral en douze livres* (BA, *Oeuvres de s. Augustin*, 48–49, Bruges-Paris 1972)
Aug. Mag.	*Augustinus Magister*, Congrès international augustinien, Paris, 21–24 Septembre 1954 (3 vols. Paris 1954–55)
B	*Codex Berolinensis* 24 (Meerman-Phillipps Collection 1651), 9th–10th cent.
BA	Bibliothèque augustinienne, *Oeuvres de saint Augustin* (Paris 1941–)
Bod	*Codex Bodleianus*, Laud. Misc. 141, Bodleian Library, Oxford, 8th–9th cent.
Bonner	Gerald Bonner, *St. Augustine of Hippo: Life and Controversies* (London 1963)
Bourke	Vernon J. Bourke, *Augustine's Quest of Wisdom: Life and Philosophy of the Bish p of Hippo* (Milwaukee 1945)
Brooke-McLean *Octateuch*	A. E. Brooke and N. McLean (eds.), *The Old Testament in Greek*, Vol. 1, *The Octateuch* (Cambridge 1906)
Bru	*Codex Bruxellensis* 1051 (10791), Bibliothèque Royale de Belgique, Brussels, 11th cent.
C	*Codex Coloniensis* 61, 12th cent.
CCL	Corpus christianorum, series latina (Turnhout-Paris 1953–)
CSEL	Corpus scriptorum ecclesiasticorum latinorum (Vienna 1866–)
DarSag	Ch. Daremberg and E. Saglio, *Dictionnaire des antiquités grecques et romaines d'après les textes et les monuments* (Paris 1877–1919)

Dessau ILS	Hermannus Dessau (ed.), *Inscriptiones latinae selectae* (3 vols. in 5. Berlin 1892–1916, reprint 1954–55)
Dict. Bibl.	F. Vigouroux, *Dictionnaire de la Bible* (5 vols. Paris 1895–1912). Supplement, ed. Pirot (1928–)
Diels *Vorsokr.*	Hermann Diels (ed.), *Die Fragmente der Vorsokratiker* (3 vols. 6th ed. Berlin 1951–52)
DTC	*Dictionnaire de théologie catholique* (Paris 1903–72)
E	*Codex Sessorianus* 13, Biblioteca Vittorio Emanuele 2094, Rome, 6th cent.
Eug	Eugyppius, *Excerpta ex operibus s. Augustini*, ed. P. Knoell (CSEL 9.1, Vienna 1885)
Fischer VL	B. Fischer (ed.), *Genesis*, in *Vetus latina* 2 (Freiburg 1951)
FOC	The Fathers of the Church: A New Translation (New York–Washington, D.C. 1947–)
GCS	Die griechischen christlichen Schriftsteller der ersten Jahrhunderte (Leipzig 1897–)
Gilson	Etienne Gilson, *The Christian Philosophy of Saint Augustine*, tr. L. E. M. Lynch (New York 1960) from *Introduction à l'étude de saint Augustin* (Études de philosophie médiévale 11, 2nd ed. Paris 1943)
Hastings DB	James Hastings et al., *A Dictionary of the Bible* (4 vols. Edinburgh 1898–1902)
Hebr.	The Hebrew text of the Old Testament
ICC	*International Critical Commentary* (Edinburgh, London, New York 1895–)
JBC	*The Jerome Biblical Commentary*, eds. R. E. Brown, J. A. Fitzmyer, and R. E. Murphy (2 vols. in 1. Englewood Cliffs 1968)
Kälin	P. Bernard Kälin, *Die Erkenntnislehre des hl. Augustinus* (Beilage zum Jahresbericht der kantonalen Lehranstalt Sarnen, 1920–21, Sarnen 1921)

Lau	*Codex Laurentianus,* S. Marco 658, Laurentian Library, Florence, 9th cent.
LCL	The Loeb Classical Library (London, New York, and Cambridge, Mass. 1912–)
LSJ	H. G. Liddell and R. Scott, *A Greek-English Lexicon,* rev. by H. S. Jones (Oxford 1940)
LTK	*Lexikon fur Theologie und Kirche* (2nd ed. Freiburg 1957–67)
m	The text of *De Gen. ad litt.* in Vol. 3, part 1 of Augustine's works edited by the Benedictines of S. Maur, Paris 1680, reprinted in Migne, *Patrologia latina* 34, Paris 1841
MG	J. P. Migne (ed.), *Patrologia graeca* (Paris 1857–66)
Milne *Reconstruction*	C. H. Milne, *A Reconstruction of the Old-Latin Text or Texts of the Gospels Used by Saint Augustine* (Cambridge 1926)
Misc. Ag.	*Miscellanea agostiniana* (2 vols. Rome 1930–31)
ML	J. P. Migne (ed.), *Patrologia latina* (Paris 1844–55)
Nov	*Codex Novariensis* 83 (5), Biblioteca Capitolare, Novara, Italy, 9th cent.
NPNF	Philip Schaff (ed.), *A Select Library of the Nicene and Post-Nicene Fathers of the Christian Church* (New York 1886–89)
NRT	*Nouvelle revue théologique* (Tournai 1869–)
NT	The New Testament
OCD	*The Oxford Classical Dictionary,* eds. N. G. L. Hammond and H. H. Scullard (2nd ed. Oxford 1970)
ODCC	*The Oxford Dictionary of the Christian Church,* eds. F. L. Cross and E. A. Livingstone (2nd ed. London 1974)
OED	*The Oxford English Dictionary* (Oxford 1933)
OL	The Old Latin text or texts of the Bible
OT	The Old Testament
P	*Codex Parisinus* 2706 (Colbertinus 5150), Bibliothèque Nationale, Paris, 7th–8th cent.

Pal	*Codex Palatinus latinus* 234, Vatican Library, 9th cent.
Par	*Codex Parisinus,* Nouv. Acq. Lat. 1572, Bibliothèque Nationale, Paris, 9th cent.
Pauly-Wissowa-Kroll	Pauly-Wissowa-Kroll, *Realencyclopädie der classischen Altertumswissenschaft* (Stuttgart 1893–)
Portalié	Eugène Portalié, *A Guide to the Thought of Saint Augustine,* tr. Ralph J. Bastian (Chicago 1960) from art. "Augustin (Saint)," *Dictionnaire de théologie catholique* 1 (Paris 1903) 2268–2472
Quentin *Gen.*	*Biblia sacra juxta latinam vulgatam versionem* 1, *Liber Genesis,* ed. H. Quentin (Rome 1926)
R	*Codex Parisinus* 1804 (Colbertinus 894), Bibliothèque Nationale, Paris, 9th cent.
REAug	*Revue des études augustiniennes* (Paris 1955–)
RSV	*The Holy Bible,* Revised Standard Version
S	*Codex Sangallensis* 161, St. Gall, Switzerland, 9th cent.
SC	Sources chrétiennes (Paris 1940–)
LXX	The Septuagint translation of the Old Testament
SVF	H. von Arnim (ed.), *Stoicorum veterum fragmenta* (4 vols. Leipzig 1903–24; reprint Stuttgart 1964)
Taylor "Text"	John H. Taylor, "The Text of Augustine's *De Genesi ad litteram,*" *Speculum* 25 (1950) 87–93
TLL	*Thesaurus linguae latinae* (Leipzig 1900–)
TU	Texte und Untersuchungen zur Geschichte der altchristlichen Literatur (Berlin 1882–)
Val	*Codex Vaticanus* 449, Vatican Library, 13th–14th cent.
Vat	*Codex Vaticanus* 657, Vatican Library, 13th–14th cent.
VChr	*Vigiliae christianae* (Amsterdam 1947–)

VL	*Vetus latina:* see Fischer VL
Vulg.	The Latin Vulgate translation of the Bible
Waszink	J. H. Waszink (ed.), *Tertulliani De anima* (Amsterdam 1947)
z	The text of *De Gen. ad litt.*, ed. J. Zycha, CSEL 28.1 (Vienna 1894)
ZNTW	*Zeitschrift für die neutestamentliche Wissenschaft* (Berlin 1881–)

SELECT BIBLIOGRAPHY

Berthold Altaner, "Augustinus und Origenes," *Historisches Jahrbuch* 70 (1951) 15–41; reprinted in B. Altaner, *Kleine patristische Schriften* (TU 83, Berlin 1967) 224–52.

Berthold Altaner, "Eustathius, der lateinische Übersetzer der Hexaemeron-Homilien Basilius des Grossen," ZNTW 39 (1940) 161–70; reprinted in B. Altaner, *Kleine patristische Schriften* (TU 83, Berlin 1967) 437–47.

Gerald Bonner, St. *Augustine of Hippo: Life and Controversies* (London 1963).

Vernon J. Bourke, *Augustine's Quest of Wisdom: Life and Philosophy of the Bishop of Hippo* (Milwaukee 1945); especially pp. 224–47.

Charles Boyer, "La théorie augustinienne des raisons séminales," *Misc. Ag.* 2 (Rome 1931) 795–819; reprinted in C. Boyer, *Essais sur la doctrine de saint Augustin* (2nd ed. Paris 1932) 97–137.

Charles Boyer, *L'Idée de vérité dans la philosophie de saint Augustin* (2nd ed. Paris 1940); especially pp. 128–78.

Cuthbert Butler, *Western Mysticism: The Teaching of SS. Augustine, Gregory and Bernard on Contemplation and the Contemplative Life* (2nd ed. London 1926); especially pp. 50–62.

William A. Christian, "The Creation of the World," in *A Companion to the Study of St. Augustine*, ed. Roy W. Battenhouse (New York 1955) 315–42; originally published under the title, "Augustine on the Creation of the World," *Harvard Theological Review* 46 (1953) 1–25.

Etienne Gilson, *The Christian Philosophy of Saint Augustine*, tr. L. E. M. Lynch (New York 1960) from *Introduction à l'étude de saint Augustin* (Études de philosophie médiévale 11, 2nd ed. Paris 1943).

Bernard Kälin, *Die Erkenntnislehre des hl. Augustinus* (Beilage zum Jahresbericht der kantonalen Lehranstalt Sarnen, 1920–21, Sarnen 1921).

Matthias E. Korger, "Grundprobleme der augustinischen Erkenntnislehre: Erläutert am Beispiel von *de Genesi ad litteram* XII," *Recherches augustiniennes*, Supp. à la REAug 2 (Paris 1962) 33–57.

Matthias E. Korger and Hans Urs von Balthasar, *Aurelius Augustinus, Psychologie und Mystik* (*De Genesi ad Litteram* 12), introduction, translation, and notes (Sigillum 18, Einsiedeln 1960).

Joseph Maréchal, *Études sur la psychologie des mystiques* (2 vols. Bruges and Paris 1924, 1937); especially Vol. 2, pp. 165–88.

Michael J. McKeough, *The Meaning of the Rationes Seminales in St. Augustine* (Catholic University of America Dissertation, Washington, D.C. 1926).

F. van der Meer, *Augustine the Bishop: The Life and Work of a Father of the Church*, tr. Brian Battershaw and G. R. Lamb (London and New York 1961).

Ernest C. Messenger, *Evolution and Theology: The Problem of Man's Origin* (New York 1932); especially pp. 40–55, 160–78, 260–65.

W. Montgomery, *St. Augustine: Aspects of His Life and Thought* (London 1914); especially pp. 99–147.

W. Montgomery, "St. Augustine's Attitude to Psychic Phenomena," *Hibbert Journal* 25 (1926) 92–102.

Christopher J. O'Toole, *The Philosophy of Creation in the Writings of St. Augustine* (Dissertation, The Catholic University of America Philosophical Series, Washington, D.C. 1944).

Gilles Pelland, *Cinq études d'Augustin sur le début de la Genèse* (Tournai and Montreal 1972).

Jean Pépin, "Recherches sur le sens et les origines de l'expression 'Caelum caeli' dans le livre XII des Confessions de saint Augustin," *Archivum latinitatis medii aevi (Bulletin du Cange)* 23 (1953) 185–274.

Jean Pépin, "Une curieuse déclaration idéaliste du 'De Genesi ad litteram' (XII, 10, 21) de saint Augustin, et ses origines plotiniennes ('Ennéade' 5, 3, 1–9 et 5, 5, 1–2)," *Revue d'histoire et de philosophie religieuses* 34 (1954) 373–400.

Eugène Portalié, *A Guide to the Thought of Saint Augustine*, tr. Ralph J. Bastian (Chicago 1960) from art. "Augustin (Saint)," DTC 1 (Paris 1903) 2268–2472.

Athanase Sage, "Le péché originel dans la pensée de saint Augustin, de 412 à 430," REAug 15 (1969) 75–112.

Athanase Sage, "Péché originel: Naissance d'un dogme," REAug 13 (1967) 211–48.

John H. Taylor, "The Meaning of Spiritus in St. Augustine's *De Genesi*, XII," *Modern Schoolman* 26 (1949) 211–18.

John H. Taylor, "The Text of Augustine's *De Genesi ad litteram*," *Speculum* 25 (1950) 87–93.

G. Verbeke, *L'Évolution de la doctrine du pneuma du stoicisme à s. Augustin* (Bibliothèque de l'Institut Supérieur de Philosophie, Université de Louvain, Paris 1945).

Henry Woods, *Augustine and Evolution: A Study in the Saint's De Genesi ad Litteram and De Trinitate* (New York 1924).

J. Wytzes, "Bemerkungen zu dem neuplatonischen Einfluss in Augustins 'de Genesi ad litteram,' " ZNTW 39 (1940) 137–51.

NOTES

INTRODUCTION

[1]The text of *De Genesi contra Manichaeos* is in ML 34.173–220. I know of no English translation of it. Augustine's comments on it in his review of all his works are in *Retractationes* 1.9 or 1.10 (CSEL 36.47,10–51,20 Knöll; ML 32.599–600). The chapter numbers of *Retract.* in CSEL and ML do not agree. I have given both whenever citing *Retract.*: the first as found in CSEL and the second as found in ML.

[2]8.2.5 *infra.* In these notes all references to the translation of Augustine's commentary in this edition are by book, chapter, and section.

[3]He wrote this work in 393–94. The text is to be found in CSEL 28/1.459–503, ed. by J. Zycha, and in ML 34.219–46. I know of no English translation.

[4]*Retract.* 1.17 or 1.18 (CSEL 36.86,1–87,3 Knöll; ML 32.613).

[5]*Conf.* 12.8.8.

[6]*Conf.* 13.12.13.

[7]Ps. 144.3, cited by Aug. at the beginning of Book 1 of the *Conf.* In these notes where I give references to the Psalms, the numbers are cited according to the numbering in the Vulg. and LXX editions.

[8]*Retract.* 2.50 or 2.24 (CSEL 36.159,16–160,2 Knöll; ML 32.640). For the complete text, see Appendix I *infra.*

[9]See Bourke 202–3.

[10]Benoit Lacroix, "La date du XIe livre du *De civitate Dei*," VChr 5 (1951) 121–22.

[11]Gilles Pelland, *Cinq études d'Augustin sur le début de la Genèse* (Tournai and Montreal 1972) 214. William A. Christian, "The

Creation of the World," in *A Companion to the Study of St. Augustine*, ed. Roy W. Battenhouse (New York 1955) 323–24, suggests that the purpose of Book 11 of *The City of God* was to refute the Neoplatonic view of God and the world. Christian's article originally appeared in *Harvard Theological Review* 46 (1953) 1–25.

[12]F. van der Meer, *Augustine the Bishop: The Life and Work of a Father of the Church*, tr. Brian Battershaw and G. R. Lamb (London and New York 1961) 343.

[13]Augustine's improvement in his knowledge of Greek in his old age has been established by Pierre Courcelle, *Les lettres grecques en Occident: De Macrobe à Cassiodore* (Paris 1948) 137–53; English transl., *Late Latin Writers and Their Greek Sources*, tr. Harry E. Wedeck (Cambridge, Mass. 1969) 149–65.

[14]ML 28.463A.

[15]Thus in citing Gen. 2.19, in 6.5.7 Aug. has the expression *quid vocaret illa*, but in 9.1.1 he reads *quid vocabit illa*. The emendation does not improve the clarity or the Latinity; it merely makes the form of the Latin verb correspond exactly with the form of the Greek. In 8.8.15 in citing Gen. 2.15 he gives the OL version with the words *ut operaretur et custodiret*, but in 8.10.19 he suggests that it would be more faithful to the Greek to translate *operari eum et custodire*.

[16]*De civ. Dei* 18.43.

[17]See Berthold Altaner, "Eustathius, der lateinische Übersetzer der Hexaemeron-Homilien Basilius des Grossen," ZNTW 39 (1940) 161–70, reprinted in B. Altaner, *Kleine patristische Schriften* (TU 83, Berlin 1967) 437–47; and idem, "Augustinus und Origenes," *Historisches Jahrbuch* 70 (1951) 15–41, reprinted in B. Altaner, *Kleine patr. Schr.* 224–52.

[18]The causal reasons (*causales rationes* or *rationes seminales:* see n. 67 to Book 4 *infra*) were the occasion of a lively controversy over the compatibility or incompatibility of evolution and Catholic theology some fifty years ago. Henry de Dorlodot in his *Le Darwinisme au point de vue de l'orthodoxie catholique* (Collection Lovanium 2, Brussels 1921) gave an impetus to the controversy when he invoked the opinions of St. Augustine and certain Greek Fathers as favorable to evolutionary theory. Dorlodot's work attracted considerable attention in the English-

speaking world when it was published in an English translation by Ernest Messenger, *Darwinism and Catholic Thought* (London 1922). Reacting against Dorlodot's position (although he does not mention Dorlodot by name), Henry Woods, S.J., in his *Augustine and Evolution: A Study in the Saint's De Genesi ad Litteram and De Trinitate* (New York 1924) wrote a little book that remains today one of the best expositions of the *De Genesi ad litteram*. Two years later, in a Catholic University of America dissertation, Michael J. McKeough, O.Praem., *The Meaning of the Rationes Seminales in St. Augustine* (Washington, D.C. 1926), took a middle-of-the-road position and maintained that Augustine's doctrine could not be reconciled with a theory of transformation of species but that it could support an evolutionary theory in which living beings would gradually spring from the earth through the operation of natural laws and secondary causes. There followed several studies on the subject by European scholars, one of the most important being Charles Boyer, S.J., "La théorie augustinienne des raisons séminales," *Misc. Ag.* 2 (Rome 1931) 795–819. Boyer maintained that Aug. was not the precursor of transformism but that his theory did not necessarily exclude it. The most thorough treatment of the whole subject in Catholic theology from the viewpoint of theistic evolution was Ernest C. Messenger, *Evolution and Theology: The Problem of Man's Origins* (New York 1932).

[19]The threefold good is *fides, proles, sacramentum* (fidelity, offspring, sacrament): see 9.7.12 *infra*. Augustine's doctrine in this chapter was incorporated by Pius XI into his encyclical *Casti connubii (Acta apostolicae sedis* 22 [1930] 543–56).

[20]*Conf.* 11.2.3. Cf. Pelland, *op. cit.* 76.

[21]1.17.34 *infra*: ... *secundum proprietatem rerum gestarum, non secundum aenigmata futurarum.*

[22]8.1.2 *infra*.

[23]11.1.2 *infra*. He also declares that in interpreting Scripture it is possible to arrive at a truth which was not intended by the writer. Nevertheless, he maintains that the meaning intended by the writer, which is also true, is more worth knowing: see 1.19.38 *infra*.

[24]1.21.41 *infra*.

[25] 11.1.2 *infra.*

[26] 11.31.41 *infra.*

[27] 6.12.20 *infra,* and cf. Ps. 135.11–12.

[28] 9.14.24 *infra.*

[29] 8.4.8 *infra.*

[30] 8.1.1 *infra.*

[31] 4.28.45 *infra.*

[32] 1.18.37 *infra.*

[33] 1.20.40 *infra.*

[34] 1.21.41 *infra.*

[35] Manfred Oberleitner and Franz Römer, *Die handschriftliche Überlieferung der Werke des heiligen Augustinus* (Österreichische Akademie der Wissenschaften, Philosophisch-historische Klasse, Vienna 1969–, in progress).

[36] J. de Ghellinck, S.J., *Patristique et moyen age: Études d'histoire littéraire et doctrinale* 3 (Museum Lessianum, section historique 9, Brussels and Paris 1948) 371–411.

[37] *Sancti Aurelii Augustini opera* (11 vols. Paris 1679–1700). I have not had regular access to the original Paris impression, but I have frequently consulted the reprint published in 11 vols. in 14, Venice 1729–35. The *De Genesi ad litteram* is in Vol. 3, published in 1729, cols. 117–324. This Venice reprint appears to be a faithful reproduction of the original edition.

[38] CSEL 28/1.1–435.

[39] I follow E. A. Lowe, *Codices latini antiquiores* (Oxford 1947), Pt. 4, no. 418, in dating this MS in the 6th cent. Zycha assigns it to the 7th cent. Chapter titles of *De Gen. ad litt.* found in the *Codex Sessorianus* are included in Zycha's edition, pp. 436–56. They were first published by Angelo Mai in *Nova patrum bibliotheca* 1.2 (Rome 1852) 119–33. But in the *Sessorianus* the titles for Bk. 1 are missing and are therefore lacking in Mai and Zycha. Recently Dr. Michael M. Gorman has discovered the complete titles in a 10th c. Paris MS and partial lists of these titles in two other MSS, one in Mainz and the other in Florence. The chapter titles, according to Gorman, were certainly written before Eugippius (early 6th c.) and were known to him. I am indebted for this information to Gorman, who has graciously allowed me to read the manuscript of his article "Chapter

Headings for Saint Augustine's *De Genesi ad litteram*," REAug 26 (1980) 88–104.

[40]E. A. Lowe, "The Oldest Extant Manuscripts of Saint Augustine," *Misc. Ag.* 2 (Rome 1931) 241, assigns it to the late 7th cent. Zycha in his preface, p. VIII, says "saeculo VII–VIII."

[41]Some years ago, on the basis of a detailed study of Book 12, I expressed my reservations about Zycha's text in an article, "The Text of Augustine's *De Genesi ad litteram*," *Speculum* 25 (1950) 87–93. Since then Dr. Michael Gorman of LaVerne College in Naples has informed me that he has in progress a study of the text of Book 1 based on a collation of fifteen MSS prior to 1100.

[42]Preface, p. VI: *Omnes autem et vetustate et bonitate facile vincit codex Sessorianus. . . .*

[43]In addition to the translations which I have listed, all of which I have consulted from time to time, there are two other translations of Augustine's complete works which I have not seen but which are listed by Agaësse-Solignac, Vol. 48, p. 66: the complete works in French ed. by Raulx (Bar-le-Duc 1866), and the complete works in Russian, tr. by members of the Academy of Kiev (Kiev 1893–95).

[44]I cannot recommend too highly the edition by Agaësse and Solignac, to which I am deeply indebted. The *notes complémentaires*, which are essays on problems arising from the text, mostly philosophical and theological, are especially valuable. This edition also has a useful scriptural index.

BOOK ONE

[1]Matt. 13.52.
[2]1 Cor. 10.11.
[3]Gen. 2.24.
[4]Eph. 5.32.
[5]Gen. 1.1.
[6]A spiritual creature, whether an angel or a human soul, in Augustine's view is in an unformed state unless turned towards its Creator *(conversa ad Creatorem)*. In so turning it is illuminat-

ed; and this illumination from the immutable light of Divine Wisdom not only makes it able to know eternal truth but also forms and perfects its very being. See 1.3.7—1.4.9, 1.9.15–17, and 1.17.32 *infra*, and cf. Bourke 225–26. Augustine's language here has Neoplatonic overtones and is reminiscent of Plotinus, *Enn.* 2.4.5 and 6.7.17. But although Plotinus speaks of the formation and illumination of the Nous (the second Hypostasis), Aug. makes no such assertion about uncreated Wisdom (the Second Person of the Blessed Trinity). Rather he applies the Plotinian doctrine on this point to created wisdom, i.e., the company of blessed spirits. See A. H. Armstrong, "Spiritual or Intelligible Matter in Plotinus and St. Augustine," *Aug. Mag.* 1.277–83. Cf. also n. 16 *infra*.

[7]Plato, *Tim.* 48e–51b, had postulated an invisible, shapeless, undetermined matter upon which the Demiurge was said to have impressed a likeness of the eternal forms; but matter, as well as the forms themselves, in Plato's account existed independently of the Demiurge. In Aug., the Creator (in whose Divine Wisdom are the eternal forms) produces both the matter and the form of His creatures simultaneously *ex nihilo*. Aug. says of matter and form in *Conf.* 13.33.48: "For they were made out of nothing by Thee, not of Thee, nor of any matter not Thine, nor of matter previously existing, but of concreated matter, that is, of matter simultaneously created by Thee, because Thou didst form its formlessness without any intervening time." See Charles Boyer, *L'Idée de vérité dans la philosophie de saint Augustin* (2nd ed. Paris 1940) 135–38.

[8]Gen. 1.2.

[9]Namely, that darkness was over the abyss.

[10]Gen. 1.3.

[11]See Aug., *De civ. Dei* 11.6: "The distinction between time and eternity is based on the fact that time does not exist without motion or change, whereas in eternity there is no change. It is obvious, then, that there would be no time unless a creature were made whose movement would cause some change." For the importance of this principle in Augustine's thought, see Boyer, *op. cit.* (n. 7) 117–19.

[12]Mark 1.11.

[13]Gen. 11.7.

[14]John 1.1.

[15]John 1.3. The preposition "through" (Greek διά) here implies not an instrument used by the Father but rather the exemplary causes of creatures existing eternally in the Divine Word. See M.-J. Lagrange, *Évangile selon saint Jean* (Études bibliques, 8th ed. Paris 1948) 4–5. Hence Aug. points out that the words *Let there be light* refer to the eternal utterance in the Wisdom of God.

[16]Cf. Plotinus, *Enn.* 6.7.23 (tr. Stephen MacKenna [2nd ed. London 1956] 579): "That which soul must quest, that which sheds its light upon Intellectual-Principle, leaving its mark wherever it falls, surely we need not wonder that it be of power to draw to itself, calling back from every wandering to rest before it." See also Plotinus 1.2.4 (*op. cit.* 33): "The Soul's true Good is in devotion to the Intellectual-Principle, its kin; evil to the Soul lies in frequenting strangers. There is no other way for it than to purify itself and so enter into relation with its own; the new phase begins by a new orientation." The similarities of ideas and language are striking: in Aug., light *(lux)*, the summoning of the soul *(revocante Creatore)*, and the conversion or turning *(conversio)*; corresponding to light (φῶς), the calling back (ἀνακαλούμενον), and a new orientation (ἐπιστροφή) in Plotinus. See J. Wytzes, "Bemerkungen zu dem neuplatonischen Einfluss in Augustins 'de Genesi ad litteram,'" ZNTW 39 (1940) 139. See also my remarks in n. 6 *supra*.

[17]This passage also echoes the ideas and language of Plotinus. In *Enn.* 2.9.2, the Nous is said to imitate the Father; in *Enn.* 1.6.6, the soul in becoming a noble and beautiful thing is made like to God; in *Enn.* 5.3.7, the soul in turning to the Nous is likened to the source of its being. See Wytzes, *op. cit.* 139–40.

[18]Cf. John 10.30.

[19]Aug., like many early commentators, takes the expression *In the beginning* as referring to the Second Person of the Blessed Trinity, so that the text is said to mean that God created everything in or through His Word. This interpretation is also found in Theophilus of Antioch, *Ad Autolycum* 2.10 (Oxford Early Christian Texts, pp. 38–41 Grant; MG 6.1063–1065); Origen, *In*

Genesim homiliae 1.1 (GCS 29.1 Baehrens; MG 12.145–46); Marius Victorinus, *Liber de generatione divini Verbi* 27 (ML 8.1033); and others. But Jerome, *Liber hebraicarum quaestionum in Genesim,* cap. 1, vers. 1 (ML 23.985–87), pointed out that the Hebrew text could not literally mean *in Filio,* as certain of his predecessors had maintained. But he allowed the expression *in principio* to be applied to Christ.

[20]Augustine's account of the Divine Word, consubstantial with the Father, is radically different from Plotinus' theory of the Nous in its relation to the One. The Nous is inferior to the One and of itself unformed until it turns to the One to be illuminated and perfected (*Enn.* 2.4.5). See Wytzes, *op. cit.* (n. 16 *supra*) 138–39.

[21]Cf. Aug., *De immortalitate animae* 8.5 (ML 32.1029): "The soul cannot exist unless it lives," and *op. cit.* 9.16: "No living being can lack its own essence. But the soul is a certain form of life."

[22]See n. 6 *supra.*

[23]John 8.25: *Principium, quia et loquor vobis.* In his treatise *In Iohannis evangelium* 38.11 (CCL 36.345; ML 35.1681), Aug. explains these words by the following paraphrase of the dialogue of the Jews with Christ: " 'Since we have heard you say: "If you do not believe that I am He," what are we to believe that you are?' To this Christ replied: 'The Beginning,' that is to say, 'Believe that I am the Beginning.' And He added, 'For I am even speaking to you.' That is to say, 'For having humbled Myself on your behalf, I have descended to this conversation.' For if the Beginning, according to His divine nature, would remain with the Father and not take the form of a slave and as man speak to men, how would they believe, since their weak minds would be unable to hear the intelligible Word without the sound of human speech?" The exact meaning of John 8.25 in the original Greek is much disputed: see a survey of various interpretations in R. E. Brown, *The Gospel according to John* (Anchor Bible, New York 1966–70) 1.347–48.

[24]About seven or eight years after the publication of this commentary on Genesis, Aug., asked by his friend Dulcitius for an interpretation of Gen. 1.2, quoted the explanation given here,

beginning at the words "Now God has a benevolence," and continuing to the end of ch. 7. See *De octo Dulcitii quaestionibus* 8.2.3 (ML 40.166–67). For Augustine's practice of quoting passages from his earlier works, see G. Bardy, "Doublets dans les oeuvres de saint Augustin," REAug 1 (1955) 21–39.

[25]Gen. 1.3.

[26]Gen. 1.2.

[27]Aug. elsewhere suggests that water in this text may mean matter, pointing out that water is easily acted upon and moved and that it always enters into the growth of living things on earth. See *De Genesi ad litteram inperfectus liber* 4.13–14 (CSEL 28.466–68 Zycha; ML 34.225).

[28]Gen. 1.3–4.

[29]Intimations of the Trinity in the creation narrative are also discussed by Aug. in 1.39.53, 2.6.10–2.7.15, and 3.19.29 *infra*.

[30]1 Cor. 12.31 (Vulg.): *Et adhuc excellentiorem viam vobis demonstro.* Augustine's text reads *supereminentem viam.*

[31]Eph. 3.19. Cf. Aug., *De gratia et libero arbitrio* 19 (ML 44.905): "What is more stupid ... than to assert that the knowledge which puffs up without charity is from God, and that charity, which makes it impossible to puff up, is from ourselves? Moreover, since the Apostle speaks of *the charity of Christ superior to knowledge,* what is more foolish than to think that knowledge which has to be made subject to charity is from God, and that charity, which is superior to knowledge, is from men?"

[32]The angels.

[33]Aug. means that the angels, being spiritual creatures, are as exalted in perfection above the firmament as the firmament is exalted above the earth. He has in mind not only the fact that the firmament is far in distance above the earth but also the theory that it is far superior in its nature. See his statement, 12.30.58 *infra:* "... there is the heaven which we see above the earth and from which shine forth the luminous bodies and stars, which are far superior to earthly bodies." This notion is in Aristotle, *De caelo* 268b11–269b17; Plato, *Timaeus* 41a; Cicero, *De republica* 6.17; Seneca, *Nat. quaest.* 7.1.6–7. For the expression "the heaven of this heaven" *(caelum caeli huius)* see Aug., *Conf.* 12.2.2; and J. Pépin, "Recherches sur le sens et les origines de l'expres-

sion 'Caelum caeli' dans le livre XII des Confessions de saint Augustin," *Archivum latinitatis medii aevi (Bulletin du Cange)* 23 (1953) 185–274.

[34]Cf. Gen. 1.2.

[35]See n. 33 *supra.*

[36]Literally, "mind and reason" *(mente atque ratione).* Cf. Aug., *De ordine* 2.11.30 (CSEL 73.168 Knöll; ML 32.1009): "Reason is a movement of the mind which has the power of distinguishing and connecting the objects which become known."

[37]Towards its form: *ad speciem. Species* means "form" or "intelligible reality" (cf. εἶδος in Plato). See Aug., *De diversis quaestionibus LXXXIII, Quaestio 46, De ideis* (ML 40.29–31); and *De civ. Dei* 12.7: *Sic species intellegibiles mens quidem nostra conspicit.*

[38]This thought is developed at greater length in Book 8 *infra.* See especially 8.20.39, 8.24.45, and 8.26,48 to 8.27.50.

[39]See nn. 6 and 16 *supra.*

[40]Gen. 1.5.

[41]Eccle. 1.5.

[42]See, e.g., Statius, *Thebais* 3.407–16.

[43]Ps. 135.8.

[44]Aug. probably has in mind St. Basil's *Homiliae in Hexaemeron,* translated into Latin by Eustathius. The pertinent passage is *Hom.* 6.2 (TU 66.71–72 Amand de Mendieta-Rudberg; MG 30.924). There is considerable evidence to support the theory that Aug., when studying Genesis, consulted Eustathius' version of Basil's commentary. See n. 61 *infra.*

[45]Cf. Gen. 1.9.

[46]Gen. 1.2.

[47]Wisd. 11.18.

[48]Cf. Aug., *Conf.* 13.33.48: *de concreata, id est, simul a te creata materia.* See n. 7 *supra.* Plotinus, *Enn.* 4.3.9, also points out that in speaking of matter separately we are merely making a verbal and mental separation of things which must in reality be coexistent. See Wytzes (n. 16 *supra*) 144.

[49]Formed from it: *quae de illa formatae sunt,* following the reading of E, Nov, Lau, and z (and S, which reads *formate*). *Factae sunt* is the reading of P, R¹, C, Par, Pal, Bod, and m.

[50]Aug. here seems to have in mind the theory of St. Basil,

which he probably had read in the translation of Eustathius: Basil, *Homiliae in Hexaemeron* 2.8 (TU 66.38 Amand de Mendieta-Rudberg; MG 30.890B).

[51]Aug. followed certain medical writers in the theory of light rays issuing from the eyes, as he himself states, 7.13.20 *infra*. See also 4.34.54 and 12.16.32 *infra*, and *De Trinitate* 9.3.3 (CCL 50.296; ML 42.962–63).

[52]Cf. John 1.3,9.

[53]Sirach (Eccli.) 1.4.

[54]The expression *in animas sanctas se transfert* is borrowed from Wisd. 7.27.

[55]As the firmament is exalted above the earth, so the angels are exalted above the firmament, and thus they are called the heaven of heavens. See n. 33 *supra*.

[56]See 1.15.29–30 *supra*.

[57]Gen. 1.4.

[58]*Futurarum*, the reading adopted by z, is found in all of his MSS as well as in Par, Lau, Bod, Nov, and Pal. It is not clear what MSS authority m had for *figurarum*.

[59]The same thought occurs in Aug., *De nat. boni* 8 (CSEL 25.858, 22–28 Zycha; ML 42.554). It is a Neoplatonic doctrine: see Plotinus, *Enn.* 3.2.5, and Wytzes, *op. cit.* 141–42.

[60]Gen. 1.18.

[61]The OL text of Genesis used by Aug. reads: *Et spiritus Dei superferebatur super aquam.* The interpretation borrowed from the Syrian author uses *fovebat* instead of *superferebatur.* This interpretation, based on a Syriac translation, is also found in Ambrose, *Hexaem.* 1.8.29 (CSEL 1/1.28–29 Schenkl; ML 14.139). St. Basil in his homilies on Genesis also proposed this explanation based on the Syriac: see Basil, *Hexaem.* 2.6 (SC 26.168 Giet; MG 29.44A–B). Eustathius' Latin translation of Basil's work was available when Aug. was writing on Genesis, and a careful comparison of Aug. with Eustathius and Ambrose makes it highly probable that Eustathius was Augustine's source rather than Ambrose (although he probably knew Ambrose's work also). See Berthold Altaner, "Eustathius, der lateinische Übersetzer der Hexaemeron-Homilien Basilius des Grossen," in *Kleine patristische Schriften* (TU 83, Berlin 1967) 437–47, reprinted from

ZNTW 39 (1940) 161–70; and B. Altaner, "Augustinus und Basilius der Grosse: Eine quellenkritische Untersuchung," in *Kleine patristische Schriften* 269–76, reprinted from *Revue bénédictine* 60 (1950) 17–24; and Pierre Courcelle, *Late Latin Writers and Their Greek Sources* (Cambridge, Mass. 1969) 203. The text of Eustathius' translation has been newly edited by Emmanuel Amand de Mendieta and Stig Y. Rudberg, *Ancienne version latine des neuf homélies sur l'Hexaéméron de Basile de Césarée* (TU 66, Berlin 1958): see p. 26; and it can be found in MG 30.869–968: see col. 888B–C. According to Altaner in his article on Eustathius cited above (TU 83,441 n. 3), the Syrian scholar whom Basil cites is probably St. Ephraem.

⁶²It is impossible to give an adequate translation of this sentence. Aug. is discussing the use of the verb *fovere*, which in general means "to warm, cherish, love, support." In particular it can mean "to nurse" (e.g., a wound by appropriate treatment) or "to brood over" (as a hen does over her eggs); but there is no one English verb that has these two meanings.

⁶³Cf. Matt. 23.37.

⁶⁴Cf. 1 Cor. 14.20.

⁶⁵By "spiritual light" Aug. means sanctifying grace.

⁶⁶Aug. here seems to hold the opinion that a Scripture text can have more than one literal meaning intended by the author. However, in 1.21.41 *infra* he apparently assumes that there is one meaning intended by the writer *(voluntas scriptoris)*, which we should try to discover; but he holds that if we are unable to arrive at this, some profit can be drawn from extracting an interpretation *(eruisse sententiam)* which is in harmony with the faith. In *De doctrina christiana* 3.27.38 (ML 34.80) and *Conf.* 12.31.42, he says that in certain passages God (and probably the writer too) foresaw and wished that devout readers would take different interpretations that are in harmony with revealed truth. These explanations should be borne in mind in reading Augustine's words here, "There is no difficulty if he is thought to have wished both interpretations": a writer can wish that his words will be given several interpretations, even though he himself has only one literal meaning in writing them. See François Talon, "Saint Augustin a-t-il réellement enseigné la pluralité

des sens littéraux dans l'Écriture?" *Recherches de science religieuse* 12 (1921) 1–28.

[67]1 Tim. 1.7.

[68]*Libri* is the reading found in the MSS used by z and also in Par, Bod, Nov, Lau, and Pal. *Librum,* in the text of m, is based solely on Amerbach's edition (1506).

[69]In *De doctrina christiana* 2.6.7 (ML 34.38), Aug. maintains that God has wisely provided for obscurity in Scripture in order to curb our pride and to whet our appetite for revealed truth. See also *De civ. Dei* 11.19 and Maurice Pontet, *L'Exégèse de s. Augustin prédicateur* (Paris 1944) 133.

[70]I have followed the reading of z (based on E): *scripturam Deo.* But it must be conceded that the reading of m *(scripturae Dei)* has strong support in the MSS as it is found in P, R, S, Par, Bod, Nov, Lau, and Pal.

[71]This is not servile fear but a holy fear, the foundation of love and wisdom. See *Enarr. in Ps.* 149.15 (CCL 40.2188–89; ML 37.1958); *De diversis quaestionibus LXXXIII* 36.4 (ML 40.26); *In epist. Ioannis ad Parthos* 9.5 (ML 35. 2049).

[72]Birds symbolize devout souls that soar heavenward; their nest is the Church; their wings, which are charity, are nourished by sound faith: see *Conf.* 4.16.31, and cf. *Enarr. in Ps.* 83.7 (CCL 39.1151; ML 37.1060). The frog symbolizes babbling vanity: see *Enarr. in Ps.* 77.27 (CCL 39.1087; ML 36.1000). In this sentence I follow the reading of m, *volatu ranarum avium nidos,* which has the support of B, and which seems to be attested indirectly by R *(volatura * * rum)* and by Pal *(volatur ranarum).* E, P, S, Nov, and Par read *volaturarum,* thus supporting the text of z.

[73]Cf. Ps. 33.9.

[74]Cf. Matt. 12.1.

[75]Col. 2.3.

[76]See n. 66 *supra.*

BOOK TWO

[1]Gen. 1.6–8. Augustine's OL text follows the LXX. It differs from the original Hebr. in two places: (1) the words *And so it*

was done in the OL and LXX are at the end of v. 6, whereas in the Hebr. they are at the end of v. 7; and (2) the words *And God saw that it was good* (v. 8) are in the OL and LXX but not in the Hebr. In 2.6.10 *infra*, Aug. cites verses 6 and 7 in a slightly different form. But the differences are only verbal.

[2]See Book 1 *passim*, but especially chs. 2, 8, 9, 10, 11, 12, 16, 17.

[3]Wisd. 11.21.

[4]See 1.19.39 *supra*.

[5]Ps. 135.6.

[6]Ps. 135.5.

[7]Aug. would suggest that we can understand here the water of baptism. See *Enarr. in Ps.* 135.8 (CCL 40.1961–62; ML 37.1759).

[8]St. Basil, *Hom. in Hexaem.* 3.8 (SC 26.230–32 Giet; MG 29.72–73). Aug. had probably read Basil's commentary in the Latin translation of Eustathius. See nn. 44, 50, and 61 *supra* in Book 1.

[9]Matt. 6.26.

[10]Matt. 16.4.

[11]For example, St. Ambrose, *Exameron* 2.5.18 (CSEL 32.57 Schenkl; ML 14.154B).

[12]Gen. 1.6.

[13]Gen. 1.7.

[14]In 1.4.9–1.6.12 *supra*, Aug. suggests that the narrative implicitly reveals the Trinity as creating.

[15]John 1.4.

[16]"Reason" *(ratio)* here is the eternal form or exemplar in the Word of God. See n. 15 on Book 1 *supra*.

[17]Gen. 1.9. Augustine's OL text in v. 9 follows the LXX and reads thus: *And God said: "Let the water that is under the heaven be gathered together in one place, and let the dry land appear." And so it was done. And the water that is under the heaven was gathered together into one place, and the dry land appeared.* The last sentence is not in the original Hebr.

[18]The "Virtues" in Scripture are one of the angelic choirs: see Eph. 1.21. Aug. has already proposed the theory that the words *God created heaven* in Gen. 1.1 mean that God made the angels, and that the words *Let there be light* in Gen. 1.3 mean that God

illuminated the angels, their illumination taking place at the moment of their creation. See Book 1 *supra*, especially 1.4.9–1.5.10, 1.9.15–17, 1.17.32. Here, then, the phrase "creation *(conditio)* of spiritual and intellectual creatures" refers to both the creation and illumination of the angels.

[19] A spiritual creature is "formed" when turned towards its Creator by divine illumination. See n. 6 on Book 1 *supra*.

[20] Every creature imitates an eternal form or idea in the mind of God. See 1.4.9 *supra*.

[21] "Heaven" here means "firmament."

[22] Augustine's theory is that the words *And so it was done* indicate that God first infused an idea or form of each work to be created into the minds of the angels before the works were produced. He distinguishes four steps in the narrative, setting forth the several works of creation. Thus, in the case of the firmament: (1) *God said: "Let there be a firmament"* indicates that God the Father, in His eternity begetting the Word, decrees to create a work according to the pattern of the uncreated exemplar in the divine mind; (2) *And so it was done* indicates that God infused the idea of this work to be created into the minds of the angels; (3) *And God made the firmament* indicates that the actual work was created; (4) *And God saw that it was good* indicates God's complaisance in His work. For a further development of this theory, see 4.22.39 *infra*.

[23] Rom. 1.20.

[24] Rom. 11.34–36.

[25] The Greeks and Romans commonly held that the heavens were spherical, that in the center of this great sphere was the earth, and that the antipodes were inhabited by a race of men with whom we had no contact. See Plato, *Timaeus* 33b, Aristotle, *De caelo* 286a10–12 and 297a8, and Cicero, *De republica* 6.17.17 and 6.20.21. Lactantius, *Div. inst.* 3.24 (CSEL 19.254–57 Brandt-Laubmann; ML 6.425–28) challenged this view; and Aug., *De civ. Dei* 16.9, rejected the theory of men living in the antipodes because it seemed to be irreconcilable with the unity of the human race.

[26] The disk theory appears to be a popular conception. See Agaësse-Solignac 48.598.

[27]See e.g. 1.19.39 *supra*.

[28]Ps. 103.2.

[29]Isa. 40.22. Augustine's OL text here follows the LXX.

[30]*Conf.* 13.15.16. In this passage Aug. compares the text concerning the skin cited above (Ps. 103.2) with Isa. 34.4: *Heaven shall be folded up like a book;* and he also notes that God clothed fallen mortal man with skins (Gen. 3.21). "Hence," he concludes in subtle allegorical fashion, "as a skin Thou hast stretched out the firmament of Thy book, Thy harmonious words that Thou hast placed over us by the ministry of mortal men."

[31]Aug. may be thinking of St. Basil, who rejects some fanciful allegorical interpretations of the waters above and below the firmament as the stuff of dreams and old wives' tales. See Basil, *In Hexaem.* 3.9 (SC 26.236 Giet; MG 29.76A).

[32]Lactantius, *Div. inst.* 3.24 (CSEL 19.255 Brandt-Laubmann; ML 6.426–27), rejects the theory of a moving heaven.

[33]Augustine's words, *si est alius nobis occultus cardo ex alio vertice,* recall the words of Aratus, translated by Cicero, *De nat. deor.* 2.41.105:

extremusque adeo duplici de cardine vertex
dicitur esse polus.

[34]Gen. 1.9–10. The statement *And the water that is under the heaven was gathered into one place, and dry land appeared* is found in the OL text and the LXX but not in the Hebr.

[35]See Book 1, chs. 12 and 15.

[36]The problem arises from the fact that there is a detailed account of the creation of light in vv. 3–5 and a similarly detailed account of the creation of the heavens (the firmament) in vv. 6–8. Aug. has already (2.8.19 *supra*) distinguished four stages in the creation of each thing: *Fiat:* the divine decree to create it according to the exemplary cause in the Word of God. *Et sic est factum:* the revelation of this to the angelic intellects. *Fecit Deus:* the actual production of the work. *Et vidit Deus quia bonum est:* the divine complaisance in the work created. Here in v. 9, in the separation of water and earth, the first stage *(fiat)* seems to be lacking. See 2.8.19 *supra*.

[37]Aug. refers to the creation of the visible firmament, vv. 6–7.

³⁸Gen. 1.11–13. This text is cited in a slightly different form in 5.4.9 *infra*.

³⁹Augustine's OL text, based on the LXX, has *luminare maius in inchoationem diei et luminare minus in inchoationem noctis* (*the greater light to establish* [or *to begin*] *the day and the smaller light to establish* [or *to begin*] *the night*). The OL uses *inchoatio* to translate ἀρχή of the LXX, a word which can mean either beginning or dominion (rule). In the light of the Hebr. original it should be taken in the latter sense. Aug. is not unaware of the problem: see 2.15.32 *infra*.

⁴⁰See 1.17.32 and 2.8.16–19 *supra*.

⁴¹In *Conf.* 12.2.2, Aug. says that the whole visible universe, including the starry heavens, is "earth" *(terra)* when compared to the spiritual heaven, the world of angelic intellects that make up the "heaven of heavens" *(caelum caeli)*. We have, then, the following scheme of creation:

1. *Heaven:* the spiritual heaven, *caelum caeli.*
2. *Earth:* the corporeal universe, made up of:
   a) *Heaven:* the visible firmament.
   b) *Earth:* the place where we dwell, along with the surrounding atmosphere.

See 1.9.15 and 1.17.32 *supra* and n. 33 on Book 1.

⁴²Augustine's problem is to discover the logical structure in the six days of creation. The days are not periods of time, but they are parts of the whole of creation as revealed to the angels, and there must be some plan in their presentation. Aug. has already (section 26 *supra*) considered the balance between the first day (illumination) and the last day (repose) with the lights of the firmament in the middle. But he abandoned this when he failed to discover any correspondence between the second and sixth days. He now sees a structure in which the author presents the general regions of the universe, the firmament above and the waters and land below, in the second and third days. It is understandable, then, that the following three days of creation are given to the visible creatures that move in the corporeal universe God has created.

⁴³This explanation is suggested again in 4.1.1 *infra*.

⁴⁴Augustine's point cannot be brought out without reference

to the Latin word *tempus*, which may mean either "season" or "time." The ambiguity of this word is the cause of the difficulty in interpreting Gen. 1.14: *Sint in signa et in tempora et in dies et in annos.*

[45]The most common device for reckoning the hour of the day in the ancient world was the water clock. Aug. alludes to this device in *Conf.* 11.2.2, where he speaks of "the drops of time" *(stillae temporum).*

[46]*Bissextus* in Latin (literally, "the sixth twice"). This extra day of leap year was so called because it was inserted between February 23rd and 24th; and thus in a leap year there were two days designated as "the sixth day before the Calends of March." Aug. is here describing the year of the Roman calendar reformed by Julius Caesar in 46 B.C.

[47]The "great year" *(magnus annus)* of the Greek astronomers is that period of time that it takes for "the sun and moon and five planets to complete their courses and return to the same positions relative to one another" (Cicero, *De nat. deor.* 2.20.51). In *De Genesi ad litteram inperfectus liber* 13.38 (CSEL 28/1.487 Zycha; ML 34.236) Aug. remarks: "And perhaps when all the stars have returned to the same position, the great year is completed, a matter on which many writers have proposed a variety of opinions." This great year is mentioned in Plato, *Tim.* 39d; and an obscure and difficult passage in Plato, *Republic* 546b, is thought by some to fix its length at 36,000 years. A. E. Taylor, *A Commentary on Plato's Timaeus* (Oxford 1928) 216, says: "There appears to have been no definite tradition in the fifth century about the length of the *magnus annus.* Some fixed it at 8 years, others at 19, others at 59." In a fragment of Cicero's *Hortensius* (cited by Tacitus, *Dial.* 16.7), a work that had influenced the young Aug., the length of the great year is given as 12,954 years. Macrobius, *Commentary on Somnium Scipionis* 2.11.11, puts the number at 15,000. The obscurity of Plato's number for the great year was proverbial, as is evident from Cicero, *Ad Att.* 7.13.5: "I fail to understand the enigma of the Oppii of Velia; it is more obscure than Plato's number." This notorious obscurity may explain Augustine's reference to the mysterious *(occultiores)* years; and the use of the comparative in *maiores anni,* "greater years,"

rather than the familiar *magni anni,* "great years," may possibly
be intended as a hint at the widely different estimates put forth
by scholars.

[48]This opinion was held by St. Ephraem the Syrian and by
Severian, Bishop of Gabala: see quotations and comments in
Agaësse-Solignac 48.602–3. It is not suggested that Aug. had
read these authors, but rather that there was in the patristic age
a common store of learned comment and opinion on Scripture
that circulated throughout the East and the West.

[49]In *De Genesi ad litteram inperfectus liber* 13.40 (CSEL 28/1.488
Zycha; ML 34.236) Aug. had taken a stand: "The meaning of beginning of day *(initium diei)* and beginning of night *(initium noctis)* will be clear in a moment.... Some interpreters maintain
that Scripture implies that the moon was created full because it
is the full moon that rises at the beginning of night, that is,
shortly after sunset. But it is absurd to say that we begin our
count not from the first day of the new moon but from the sixteenth or fifteenth. Nor should we be disturbed by the argument that this luminary ought to have been created in a perfect
state. Every day it is perfect, but its perfection is visible to men
only when it is opposite the sun...." When Aug. cited Gen. 1.14
in 2.13.26 *supra,* he used *inchoatio* in his Latin version where he
here uses *initium.* For a comment on the OL translation of this
passage, see n. 39 on ch. 13 *supra* and see Augustine's own remarks in 2.15.32 *infra.*

[50]Literally, "... except when it is opposite the sun, so that the
whole of it which it [the sun] illuminates is visible to the earth."
The reading *inluminat* is supported by all the MSS of z and also
by Par, Bod, Nov, Lau, and Pal. The reading of m is *illuminatur.*
The explanation that Aug. gives here is designed to explain the
appearances, whether one assumes the moon to have its own
light or holds that its light is borrowed from the sun. This explanation is also to be found in Augustine's letter to Januarius,
Epist. 55.4.6–7 (CSEL 34.175–77 Goldbacher; ML 33.207–8); and
it is developed at greater length in *Enarr. in Ps.* 10.3 (CCL
38.75–76; ML 36.131–32). Agaësse-Solignac 48.604–7 have presented impressive evidence to support the view that Vitruvius,
De architectura 9.2, is the source of Augustine's speculations on

astronomy. Vitruvius cites Berosus, Babylonian astronomer, in support of the theory that the moon has its own light, and Aristarchus of Samos in support of the opinion that its light is from the sun.

[51]This is according to the OL version, based on what is apparently a misunderstanding of the LXX. See Augustine's remarks in what follows and cf. n. 39 on 2.13.26 *supra*.

[52]Ps. 135.8–9.

[53]Speculation about the size of the sun, especially in relation to the earth, was frequent among Greek and Roman writers, both pagan and Christian. See the references given by A. S. Pease (ed.), *Ciceronis De natura deorum* (Cambridge, Mass. 1958) 2.777–78 n. Aug., *Epist.* 14.3 (CSEL 34.33–34 Goldbacher; ML 33.79) notes the tendency we have to misjudge the size of things seen at a great distance.

[54]1 Cor. 15.41.

[55]Vitruvius, *De architectura* 9.12, refers to this same theory about the influence of the sun on stars.

[56]The Greek word ἀποτέλεσμα means the supposed "result of certain positions of the stars on human destiny": see LSJ 222 *s.v.* Aug. here speaks of "scientific observations" *(documentorum experimenta),* which are proofs derived from particular instances. See also *Conf.* 7.6.8, where he uses *experimenta* in the same sense.

[57]While searching for a solution to the problem of evil, Aug. himself had dabbled in astrology, as he tells us in the fourth and seventh books of his *Confessions*.

[58]In *Conf.* 7.6.8, Aug. gives an interesting example of a highborn youth and a slave, both of whom had been born at exactly the same moment in the same place and nevertheless spent totally different lives. This example helped to show him the absurdity of astrology.

[59]Gen. 25.25–26. This example is cited also in *Conf.* 7.6.10; *De doctr. christiana* 2.22.33 (ML 34.52); *De civ. Dei* 5.4.

[60]Aug. inclined to the opinion that the angels (good and bad) have bodies of a subtle and spiritual nature, and he compares the body of man as it will be after the resurrection to what he conceives to be the body of an angel. But to the end he remained somewhat hesitant in asserting that angels have bodies. See

Epist. 95.8 (CSEL 34.512–13; ML 33.355); *Enarr. in Ps.* 85.17 (CCL 39.1190; ML 37.1094); *De Trin.* 3.1.4–5 (CCL 50.130–31; ML 42.870–71); *De civ. Dei* 15.23.1 and 21.10.1.

[61]Variant readings in the MSS in the use of *partim* and *quia* in this sentence make the logic and structure of it uncertain. The form that it has in z, which I follow, is logical and (with minor variations) has the support of most MSS, including Par, Bod, Nov, and Pal.

[62]With great earnestness, Aug. in *De doctr. christiana* 2.23.35–36 (ML 34.52–53) warns his readers against the dangers of soothsayers, especially when they predict the truth.

[63]Plato held that each star is animated by a soul which is divine, so that the stars are indeed gods: see *Tim.* 41a–e (which Aug. quotes in *De civ. Dei* 13.16) and *Laws* 898c–899b. Aristotle, *Met.* 1073a34–39, taught that the stars are eternal and that each has its mover, which is eternal. The mover, however, is extrinsic to the star and does not function as a soul. Plotinus, *Enn.* 2.9.8 and 3.2.3, following Plato, says that good souls dwell in the heavens, infusing life into the stars, and that the stars are gods. Origen, according to Jerome, *Liber contra Ioannem hierosolymitanum* 17 (ML 23.369), held that "the sun and the moon and the whole choir of heavenly bodies are souls of creatures once rational and incorporeal, that they are now made subject to vanity, namely, to those fiery bodies that we in our ignorance call the lights of the world, and that they will be liberated from slavery to corruption unto the liberty of the glory of the sons of God." See also Origen, *De principiis* 1.7.4, tr. by Rufinus (GCS 22.90–91 Koetschau; MG 11.176). Aug. in *Ad Orosium contra Priscillianistas et Origenistas* 9.12 (ML 42.676–77) and *De civ. Dei* 11.23 rejects the view of Origen. But in the *Enchiridion* 58 (ML 40.260) he declares that he is not certain as to whether the sun, moon, and stars are numbered among the blessed company of angels.

Book Three

[1]Gen. 1.20–23. The LXX text, on which Augustine's OL text is based, gives the impression that the birds came forth from the

waters (although the original Hebrew, which Aug. did not know, implies no such thing). In what follows, as well as in *De Gen. ad litt. inperfectus liber* 14.44 (CSEL 28/1.489–90 Zycha; ML 34.236), Aug. attempts to solve the difficulty by pointing out that the atmosphere near the earth is full of moisture; hence, he infers, it may be included under the term "waters."

[2]In 2.4.7 *supra*, Aug. cites with approval the theory that the atmosphere where the clouds are formed may be called a "firmament." In *De Gen. ad litt. inperfectus liber* 14.45 (CSEL 28/1.490–91 Zycha; ML 34.238) he says that we may extend the word "firmament" to include all the region from clouds to the starry heavens; and he adds that the birds belong to the regions below the clouds, the moist atmosphere, which may be called water. Hence, he says, the birds are flying over the earth *under the firmament of heaven (sub firmamento caeli);* but his text in the present work reads *along the firmament of heaven (secundum firmamentum caeli).*

[3]Ps. 148.4–5.

[4]Ps. 148.4.

[5]2 Peter 3.5–6.

[6]Gen. 7.20.

[7]"Were put in their place": *repositos.* The word is taken from the passage cited from 2 Peter 3.7: *Caeli autem qui nunc sunt et terra eodem verbo repositi sunt.* But Aug. apparently did not notice that this verse does not refer to the flood (as did vv. 5–6) but to cosmic events associated with the Parousia.

[8]Aug. means earth with its surrounding atmosphere.

[9]Lucan, *De bello civili* 2.271–73.

[10]Cf. Homer's description, *Odyssey* 6.42–45, imitated by Lucretius, *De rerum nat.* 3.18–22, and quoted by Apuleius, *Liber de mundo* 33. See also Augustine's description, *De Gen. ad litt. inperf. liber* 14.44 (CSEL 28/1.490 Zycha; ML 34.238).

[11]According to Anaximenes, air was the primary substance, which could be changed under the proper conditions into other substances, such as fire, clouds, water, earth, and stones (Diels *Vorsokr.* 1.92, no. 13A7). In the theory of Heraclitus, the three world-masses are fire, water, and earth, and these three change

into each other in this order: see G. S. Kirk, *Heraclitus: The Cosmic Fragments* (Cambridge 1954) 325–44, nos. 31 and 36. Empedocles held that the four roots (elements), fire, air, earth, and water, are eternal and unchangeable, and that change and motion are explained by the mixture of these indestructible elements: see John Burnet, *Early Greek Philosophy* (4th ed. London 1948) 228–34. Plato, *Tim.* 49b–50a, explains how one element can be changed into another by condensation, melting, heating, or compression. Arist., *De gen. et corrup.* 331a–b, maintains that the elements can be changed into one another by changing into contraries or out of contraries. On the mutual transformation of the elements according to Plato and Arist., see W. K. C. Guthrie, *A History of Greek Philosophy* (Cambridge 1965) 2.143. Aug. was probably familiar with these theories from his reading of Cornelius Celsus' encyclopedic work on philosophy, to which he refers, *De haeresibus, praefatio* (ML 42.23). See H. Hagendahl, *Augustine and the Latin Classics* (Studia graeca et latina Gothoburgensia 20.1, Göteborg 1967) 1.34–35, and OCD (2nd ed. 1970) *s.v.* "Celsus (2)," 218.

[12]Aug. did not have the opportunity to take this subject up again. But he does remark in passing in 3.7.9 *infra* that it is said that fire comes forth from earth and water in motion and is in turn converted into air.

[13]See e.g. Plato, *Tim.* 65b–68d, and Arist., *De an.* 416b–424b.

[14]See Cicero, *De nat. deor.* 2.9.23.

[15]Anaxagoras was the first Greek philosopher to propose the theory that there is a portion of everything in everything. See Diels *Vorsokr.* 2.35, nos. 6 and 37, nos. 11–12.

[16]Cf. 12.24.51 *infra:* "It is not the body that perceives, but the soul by means of the body." Aug. consistently holds this active theory of sensation (in which he agrees with Plotinus, *Enn.* 3.6.1 and 1.1.6–7). The reason for his adherence to this view is that body cannot produce anything in spirit since spirit is superior to body (see 12.16.33 *infra*). He is hard pressed to describe sensation and usually has recourse to a negative statement, as in *De musica* 6.5.10 (ML 32.1169), where he says that what happens in the body is not hidden from the soul *(non eam latere)*. In *De*

quant. animae 25.48 (ML 32.1063) he defines sensation as *passio corporis non latens animam.* See Kälin 14, 31, and *passim;* Bourke 111–12.

[17]Further details of Augustine's physiology of sensation, borrowed from the theories of medical writers and from the Neoplatonic doctrine of the *pneuma,* are given below in 7.13.20, 7.15.21, 12.16.32. For a summary of the opinions of the medical writers, see Book 7 n. 32.

[18]Cf. Ps. 148.7–8.

[19]In reality, Scripture does not say that God produced the birds from the waters. See n. 1 *supra* in this book.

[20]Ps. 148.7.

[21]That is to say, the Psalmist includes air, water, and fire under the general term "earth."

[22]Aug. probably has in mind the production of sparks when metals are rubbed together, and the heat that is said to issue from the depths of the sea when the waters are violently stirred (see Cicero, *De nat. deor.* 2.9.25). The conversion of fire into air is explained by Aug. in the next sentence.

[23]The region between the clouds and the starry firmament: see n. 2 *supra* in this book.

[24]This is the opinion of Basil, whom Aug. had read in the translation of Eustathius. See Basil, *In Hex.* 8.1 (SC 430–33 Giet; tr. by Eustathius, TU 66.100,4–27 Amand de Mendieta-Rudberg).

[25]In this idiom a neuter adj. used substantively is modified by a partitive gen. But the partitive aspect in many instances became blurred, and the words came to form a unit to express an idea more normally expressed by a noun and adj. in agreement (e.g. *angusta viarum,* "narrow streets," Virgil, *Aen.* 2.332). The idiom was frequently used by Lucretius and Virgil. See Cyril Bailey (ed.), *Lucretius, De rerum natura* (Oxford 1947) 1.91–92; R. G. Austin (ed.), *P. Vergili Maronis Aeneidos liber secundus* (Oxford 1964) 149. It is also found frequently in Livy and Tacitus. See Othon Riemann, *Études sur la langue et la grammaire de Tite-Live* (2nd ed. Paris 1885) 102–4; A. G. Draeger, *Über Syntax und Stil des Tacitus* (Leipzig 1868) 25–26.

[26]Fish ponds *(vivaria)* were numerous and popular among the

Romans: see G. Lafaye, DarSag 5 (1915) *s.v.* "Vivarium," 959–62. They were first introduced by Lucius Murena (about a generation before the time of Cicero), according to Pliny, *Hist. nat.* 9.170. They were probably a common sight in North Africa in Augustine's time. See a description of an elaborate one found at the ancient site of Thamugadi (today Timgad in Algeria) described by Lafaye 960–61. In speaking of authors who described curious habits of fish, Aug. probably had in mind Pliny, *Hist. nat.*, Book 9, and Ambrose, *Exameron* 5.1.1–5.11.35 (CSEL 32.140–69 Schenkl; ML 14.205–22).

[27]Bulla Regia was a city southeast of Hippo on the road leading inland from Hippo to Carthage. See H. Dessau, Pauly-Wissowa-Kroll 3.1 (1897) *s.v.* "Bulla la," 1047.43–1048.14; S. A. Morcelli, *Africa christiana* (Brescia 1816–17) 1.108–9. An inscription belonging to the age of Diocletian indicates that it did not lack sumptuous public buildings (Dessau ILS 9358).

[28]Cf. Apuleius, *Liber de deo Socratis* 8–9.137–41. Aug., *De civ. Dei* 8.14 and 9.8, attributes this opinion to this work of Apuleius.

[29]See n. 63 on Book 2 *supra*.

[30]This popular belief is mentioned by Aug. also in *Enarr. in Ps.* 148.9 (CCL 40.2172; ML 37.1943) and by Cassiodorus, *Exp. in Ps.* 148.7 (CCL 98.1318; ML 70.1044D).

[31]The word "dragon" (δράκων) in the LXX is used to translate several different Hebr. words, all of which refer to real animals (such as jackals, serpents, and crocodiles) and not to fabulous monsters that fly through the air. See H. Lesêtre, *Dict. Bibl.* 2 (1899) *s.v.* "Dragon" (2), 1503–4; and G. E. Post, Hastings *DB* 1 (1898) *s.v.* "Dragon," 620–21.

[32]Demons, according to the followers of Plato, were intermediate beings (good or evil) between gods and men, having bodies of an airy nature and dwelling in the air or wandering about the earth. See M. P. Nilsson, *Greek Piety* (Oxford 1948) 170–73. Many of the early Christian writers identified the fallen angels with these creatures, and thus the word *daimon* came to mean an evil spirit only, no longer a good one. Some of these writers, under the influence of the apocryphal *Book of Henoch*, interpreted Gen. 6.2 as meaning that certain angels fell into sin by having carnal intercourse with women: see Lactantius, *Div. inst.* 2.14

(*al.* 15) (CSEL 19.162–63 Brandt-Laubmann; ML 6.330–31), and cf. Tertullian, *Apol.* 22.3 (CCL 1.128; ML 1.463–65). From this unholy union, Lactantius tells us, was born a race of demons of a lower order, the unclean spirits that tempt man. Origen rejected the extravagant legends of the *Book of Henoch*, and most of the Fathers after him attempted to base their theories concerning demons on the canonical books of Scripture. In *De civ. Dei* 15.23, Aug. excludes the *Book of Henoch* from the canon of Scripture and rejects the legend of a progeny born of fallen angels and the daughters of men. The opinions of the Fathers on this question are surveyed by E. Mangenot, DTC 4 (1911) *s.vv.* "Démon d'après les Pères," 339–84.

[33]Ps. 148.7.

[34]In Book 11, chs. 16–23 *infra,* Aug. treats of the angels and their condition antecedent to the revolt of the rebel angels. There he mentions a possible distinction between two classes of angels, *supercaelestes* and *mundani,* the theory being that the fallen angels belonged to the second or lower class. These angels of lower rank during a period of probation could possibly merit the *vita beata* already securely possessed by the higher order of *supercaelestes.* But Aug. can find no scriptural basis for this theory and, rather than suppose any such distinction or assume that the less privileged went through a period uncertain of their beatitude, he prefers to say that the Devil and his angels fell immediately after their creation: see 11.19.26 and 11.23.30 *infra.*

[35]Athenagoras, Clement of Alexandria, Origen, and many other early Christian writers hold that the fallen angels inhabit the air around the earth: see Mangenot, *op. cit.* (n. 32 *supra*) 344–52.

[36]Ps. 148.8.

[37]For Augustine's view on the "spiritual bodies" of angels, see Book 2 n. 60 *supra.* The point that Aug. makes here in saying that fire is superior to air is important in his thinking, because he frequently enunciates the principle that an agent acting on another object must be superior to that object: see 12.16.33 *infra* and *De musica* 6.5.8 (ML 32.1167–68).

[38]Aug. does not mean that the fallen angels will cease to suffer

at the last judgment: ".... even when the final judgment hurls them into a second death, that does not mean that even then they will be deprived of life, for they will not be deprived of feeling when they will be in pain" (*De civ. Dei* 13.24).

[39]Gen. 1.24–25.

[40]See 3.7.10 *supra.*

[41]Wisd. 8.1.

[42]Gen. 1.21.

[43]Ps. 48.13 according to the OL. The meaning of the Hebr. is: *He is like the beasts that perish* (Ps. 49.12 RSV).

[44]Gen. 1.28.

[45]*Aquarum animalia,* i.e., the birds and fishes, both of which, according to Aug., were produced from the waters. See Book 3, chs. 1 and 2 *supra.*

[46]Gen. 1.22.

[47]Cf. Ps. 103.24.

[48]Cf. Wisd. 8.1.

[49]Plants and trees, created on the third day.

[50]*Quasi praeseminata et quodammodo liciata primordia futurorum animalium.* Cf. *De civ. Dei* 22.14: *In qua ratione uniuscuiusque materiae indita corporali iam quodam modo, ut ita dicam, liciatum videtur esse, quod nondum est, immo quod latet, sed accessu temporis erit vel potius apparebit* ("In this principle, implanted in the matter of every body, there is apparently interwoven, if I may use the expression, the thing which does not yet exist, or more precisely is not yet seen, but which will come to be, or rather will appear, in the course of time"). In this passage from *De civ. Dei,* Aug. is explaining that all the full-grown members of adults are contained potentially in the causal principles of infants. This same doctrine applies to the problem here considered in the commentary on Genesis.

[51]I follow the reading of m, *cum iam creata essent,* which is attested by P, R, S, Par, Bod, Lau, Pal.

[52]Phil. 3.12.

[53]2 Cor. 12.7–9.

[54]Dan. 6.22, 14.39.

[55]Dan. 9.4–20.

[56] Acts 28.3–6.

[57] *Per voluptatem*, which is the reading of E², R², Bod, Lau, and m. *Per voluntatem* is found in E¹, R¹, P, Par, Pal, and z.

[58] This theory, which constantly recurs in Augustine's works wherever he discusses the relationship of creatures to their Creator, is developed at length in Book 4, chs. 3–6 *infra*. See n. 8 to Book 4.

[59] Luke 12.7.

[60] Gen. 1.11.

[61] Justinian, *Institutiones* 2.4: "Usufruct is the right of using another's property for one's own advantage without impairing the substance of that property."

[62] Gen. 3.18.

[63] Gen. 1.26–31.

[64] Eph. 4.23–24; Col. 3.10.

[65] See n. 6 to Book 1.

[66] See 1.3.7 *supra*, where Aug. suggested that the words *God said, "Let there be light," and light was made* refer to the creation of intellectual creatures, that is, the angels.

[67] See n. 22 to Book 2, explaining the four steps in the narrative of creation. In the creation of the angels, Aug. holds that the second and third steps are combined because God gives the angels a knowledge of themselves in His Word in the very act by which He illuminates them (see 2.8.16 *supra*).

[68] Gen. 1.28.

[69] Aug. does not go beyond his conclusion that there can be a need of food for nourishment only in the case of corruptible bodies, but he seems to suggest that incorruptible bodies might take food for some purpose other than nourishment.

[70] Thus, for instance, Origen, *In Genesim hom.* 1.13 (GCS 29.15,11–13 Baehrens; MG 12.155D), says: "He who was made to the image of God is our interior man, invisible and incorporeal, incorrupt and immortal."

[71] Gen. 2.7.

[72] 1 Cor. 11.7. Note that in the next paragraph Aug. goes on to observe (following Paul) that woman is renewed in the spirit of her mind in the knowledge of God according to the image of her Creator, and in this respect there is no male or female.

Hence it is only with reference to the body that woman is said to be the glory of man. This thought is further developed in 11.42.58 *infra*.

[73]Here Aug. is arguing from the theory he has already advanced concerning the four steps in the narrative of each of the works of creation. See n. 22 to Book 2 *supra*.

BOOK FOUR

[1]Gen. 2.1–3.

[2]After considering the possibility of taking "day" as a period of time marked by the motion of the heavenly bodies, Aug. in this paragraph suggests the possibility of taking it as designating the metaphysical structure of creatures. In this theory *dies = species rei quae creata est, nox = privatio vel defectus, vespera = terminus quidam perfectae conditionis, mane = incipientis [creaturae] exordium.* This interpretation has already been mentioned in 1.17.35 and 2.14.28 *supra*, and Aug. had proposed it in *De Gen. c. Man.* 1.14.20 (ML 34.183). He finally rejects it in 4.26.43 *infra*.

[3]By "part" here Aug. means aliquot part, i.e., a part of a number which divides the number without a remainder. A perfect number is one which is the sum of its aliquot parts. The first perfect number is 6 (the sum of 1, 2, and 3); the second is 28 (the sum of 1, 2, 4, 7, and 14). The third is 496, and the fourth is 8,128. In 1968, only 23 perfect numbers were known, three of them discovered in 1963: see Ralph G. Archibald, *An Introduction to the Theory of Numbers* (Columbus, Ohio 1970) 85 and 256 n. 11. The interest of Aug. in the theory of numbers may have been stirred up by the *Introductio arithmetica* of Nicomachus of Gerasa, which had been translated into Latin by Apuleius: see Thomas Heath, *A History of Greek Mathematics* (Oxford 1921) 1.97. Aug. sees great signficance in the fact that God accomplished the work of His creation in six days, a perfect number of days. See this notion also in *De Trin.* 4.4.7 (CCL 50.169; ML 42.892) and in *De civ. Dei* 11.30. Cf. Philo, *De opificio mundi* 3 (LCL 1.12–13 Colson-Whitaker).

[4]Aug. here suggests that there is a parallel between the aliquot

parts of 6 (1, 2, 3) and the order of the works of creation: 1 day for the creation of light, 2 days for the creation of the upper and lower regions of the universe, and 3 days for the creation of visible beings that move within these two regions.

[5] See the foregoing footnote.

[6] Wisd. 11.21.

[7] Aug. seems to have in mind Rom. 11.36: *Quoniam ex ipso et per ipsum et in ipso sunt omnia (For from Him and through Him and in Him are all things)*. *In ipso* ("in Him") is not a correct translation: the Greek reads εἰς αὐτόν ("to Him"). But Aug. consistently reads *in ipso:* see 8.25.46 *infra; De Trin.* 1.6.12 (CCL 50.41; ML 42.827); *De fide et symbolo* 9.19 (CSEL 41.25 Zycha; ML 40.192).

[8] Aug. sees a profound philosophical and theological meaning in Wisd. 11.21: *Omnia in mensura et numero et pondere disposuisti (Thou hast ordered all things in measure and number and weight)*, which he develops here in chs. 3 to 6, and to which he often refers in this treatise and elsewhere. All creatures, spiritual and material, have measure, number, and weight (4.4.8–10). Every creature has a limit *(mensura)* to its nature, for as a creature it is distinct from its Creator precisely because it is not all-perfect and necessary being but is rather contingent and finite. Secondly, every creature has a specific form or perfection *(numerus)*, imitating the eternal form or perfection in the Word of God, through whom it has been made. Finally, the perfection of each creature is established (by its *pondus*) in a state of stability or rest in God, who draws back to Himself whatever He has made (4.18.34 *infra*). These three things are in God even before He creates, for "He limits everything, forms everything, and orders everything" (4.3.7). These three things in creatures are an image of the perfection of the Trinity: see *De Trin.* 6.10.12 (CCL 50.242–43; ML 42.932). For an early reference to Wisd. 11.21, see *De Gen. c. Man.* 1.16.26 (ML 34.185–86). For "weight" as love in rational creatures, see *Conf.* 13.9.10. The same trinitarian view of reality is set forth under the more philosophical terms *modus, species, ordo* in *De natura boni* 3 (CSEL 25.856–57 Zycha; ML 42.553) and elsewhere. It is not unlikely that Aug. was influenced here by Neoplatonism. See the remarks of Plotinus on ὁρισμός (limitation), μορφή (form), and στάσις (repose) in

Enn. 5.1.7 (2.278,23–26 Henry-Schwyzer). For an exhaustive study of this theme in Augustine's early works, see Olivier du Roy, *L'Intelligence de la foi en la Trinité selon saint Augustin: Genèse de sa théologie trinitaire jusqu'en 391* (Paris 1966) 279–81 and *passim.*

⁹The notion that number is somehow identified with form is Platonic and ultimately Pythagorean. See David Ross, *Plato's Theory of Numbers* (Oxford 1951) 216–20.

¹⁰To understand the argument of this chapter, one should bear two points in mind. First, the ideas or forms which Plato described as existing separately, and which Plotinus placed in the Nous, are identified, in Augustine's doctrine, with eternal Wisdom, the Second Person of the Blessed Trinity. In the eternal Wisdom of God, therefore, is the exemplar according to which each creature is made. Secondly, there is a possible ambiguity in the Latin version of the Scripture text which Aug. is attempting to explain. When God is said to have created everything *in mensura et numero et pondere*, this may mean simply that God endowed creatures with these properties. But since *in* with the abl. can also mean "by means of" or "according to," the text can mean that God made each creature by means of (or according to) the measure, number, and weight of the exemplar in His eternal Wisdom.

¹¹Cf. Wisd. 9.15.

¹²Namely, of its aliquot parts. See ch. 2 *supra* and n. 3 *ibid.*

¹³Cf. Rom. 5.5.

¹⁴Aug. proposes this interpretation again in *De civ. Dei* 11.8. But here in *De Gen. ad litt.* it is put down only as a figurative meaning of the text. Farther on (chs. 10 and 16) Aug. enquires into the literal meaning.

¹⁵Gen. 22.12.

¹⁶Eph. 4.30.

¹⁷Gal. 4.9.

¹⁸1 Peter 1.20.

¹⁹John 5.17.

²⁰*Sexta sabbati* = Friday. See Tertullian, *De ieiunio* 10.5 (CCL 2.1268; ML 2.1017A).

²¹John 19.30.

[22]Wisd. 8.1.

[23]Wisd. 7.24. According to the original Greek, the text reads: *Wisdom is more active than all motion.*

[24]Acts 17.28.

[25]John 5.26.

[26]Exod. 20.8.

[27]I follow P, R, and m in reading *salutem nostram.*

[28]John 5.2–18.

[29]Rom. 6.4.

[30]Gen. 1.1.

[31]Luke 10.38–42.

[32]This is reminiscent of the dilemma of Epicurus quoted by Lactantius, *De ira Dei* (ML 7.121A). See also Plot., *Enn.* 5.4.1: "How could the most perfect and first Good remain in itself? Could it grudge to give of itself? Or could it, the source of all power, be powerless to do so? How, then, would it still be the beginning? It must needs be, then, that something come from it. . . ." But Aug. insists here (as he does consistently elsewhere: see *De Gen. c. Man.* 1.2.4 [ML 34.175]) that creation is a free act of God. He is not, therefore, in agreement with Plotinus, who holds that emanation is necessary. At first sight this passage is confusing, but Aug. seems to be simply stating the dilemma proposed by pagan philosophers without espousing their principles. See Christopher J. O'Toole, *The Philosophy of Creation in the Writings of St. Augustine* (Washington, D.C. 1944) 12–13; also Agaësse-Solignac 48.644.

[33]See Book 4, ch. 2 *supra.*

[34]Cf. Aug., *Enarr. in Ps.* 137.18 (CCL 40.1989; ML 37.1783–84): "Behold Thy work, not my work, in me; for if Thou seest mine, Thou dost condemn; if Thine, Thou dost reward. Whatever good works are mine, I have from Thee, and so they are Thine rather than mine."

[35]Cf. Aug., *Epist.* 55.10.19 (CSEL 34.190,15–18 Goldbacher; ML 33.213): "When we do good works, He is said to work in us by whose gift we perform them. So also when we rest, He is said to rest by whose bounty we rest."

[36]Every single creature, as well as all creation taken as a whole, according to Aug., has the foundation of its permanence

and stability in God. This means that it has a fixed orientation to God, and no repose will give it its proper stability except repose in Him. The beginning of the creature's repose in God is designated by the morning of the seventh day, and there is no evening of that day because the repose is destined to have no end. Rational creatures (men as well as angels) find their rest in God by reason of the fact that they are constituted in their proper order of being by turning to their Creator and thus being illuminated by Him (1.1.2, 1.3.7, 2.8.16, and *passim*). But Aug. goes further and says that all creatures are made to find their rest in God. In what sense can this be said of the visible works of creation other than man? Aug. does not raise this question here, but apparently he conceives of them as destined to find rest in God by reason of their final stability and permanence at the end of the world, when there will be a new heaven and a new earth (see *De civ. Dei* 20.16).

[37] See 2.14.28 and 4.1.1 *supra*.

[38] Acts 17.28.

[39] Cf. Aug., *Conf.* 13.9.10: "My weight is my love." See also Augustine's remarks on "measure, number, weight" *(mensura, numerus, pondus)* in 4.3.7–4.5.12 *supra*, where he comments on Wisd. 11.21.

[40] This is true when we consider the intrinsic perfection of God. Whatever relation exists between God and creatures is wholly extrinsic to Him.

[41] This is true when we consider God in reference to His creatures, but it does not imply any new perfection acquired by God.

[42] The full force of the difficulty is not brought out in English, because we must use two different prepositions, *in* and *on*. They are, of course, the same in Latin: *in seipso* and *in die septimo*.

[43] Gen. 1.3–5.

[44] See 1.17.32–35 *supra*.

[45] The theory of diffusion and contraction, proposed by St. Basil, is rejected by Aug. in Book 1, ch. 16 *supra*.

[46] See 1.16.31 *supra*.

[47] "Light" refers to illuminated intellectual creatures. Aug. has already suggested that the creation of light in Gen. 1.3 refers

to the illumination of the angels. In this theory their creation is indicated by Gen. 1.1, where it is said that God made heaven; but they are in an unformed state until (no lapse of time involved) God illuminates them and forms them. See 1.17.32 *supra*.

[48]See ch. 2 *supra*.

[49]See nn. 22 and 36 to Book 2 *supra*.

[50]Eph. 5.8.

[51]Rom. 13.12–13.

[52]1 Peter 1.19.

[53]Cf. Matt. 22.30.

[54]Ps. 117.24.

[55]See the four chapters immediately preceding.

[56]See n. 2 *supra* in this book.

[57]See nn. 22 and 36 to Book 2 *supra*.

[58]John 8.12: *I am the light of the world.* Mark 12.10: *The stone which the builders rejected has become the corner stone.*

[59]Aug. insists that his own interpretation is literal and that any alternative to it must also be literal, not allegorical. See Henry Woods, *Augustine and Evolution* (New York 1924) 8–9.

[60]But Aug. holds that, when God was actually creating, these three moments in the knowledge of angels succeeded one another. See 4.31.48 *infra*.

[61]For a discussion of Augustine's theory of morning and evening knowledge, see St. Thomas Aquinas, *Sum. theol.* 1, q. 58, a. 6.

[62]Ps. 54.18.

[63]Cf. Rom. 1.20.

[64]Cf. Wisd. 10.15.

[65]"Elsewhere" *(alibi)*, i.e., in the minds of spiritual creatures to whom God might reveal the decree to create the angels. But no such creatures existed before the angels themselves; and this is why, in Augustine's theory, Scripture does not say, "And so it was done," after the divine decree, *Let there be light.* See 2.8.16–19 *supra*.

[66]Wisd. 8.1.

[67]... *ex illis rationibus insitis veniat quas tamquam seminaliter sparsit Deus in ictu condendi....* According to Aug., in addition to the eternal reasons or causes which are in the Word of God as

the divine exemplars of the works He creates, there are also causal reasons implanted by God in the created world, accounting for the generation and growth of the living beings that appear throughout the ages. To designate the former, Aug. uses *rationes* (2.6.12), *aeternae rationes* (4.24.41), *superiores rationes* (3.12.18), *rationes incommutabiles* (5.12.28), *divinae incommutabiles aeternaeque rationes* (5.13.29), and other similar expressions. To designate the latter, he also uses a variety of expressions, such as *causales rationes* (6.14.25 and often elsewhere), *quasi semina futurorum* (6.11.18), *rationes primordiales* (6.11.19), *primordia causarum* (6.10.17), *rationes seminales* (10.20.35), *quasi seminales rationes* (9.17.32), and sometimes just *rationes* (as here). These causal reasons implanted by God in the original creation are not seeds in the sense of visible, tangible substances out of which organisms grow (6.6.11 and 6.10.17), but they are seed-like powers in the created world, causing the seeds to develop according to God's plan. Aug. adopts this theory in order to explain what he feels is a difficulty in the text of Genesis. Not having any inkling of the distinction between the Priestly tradition and the Yahwist tradition as seen in Genesis by modern criticism (see E. II. Maly, JBC 1 [1968] "Introduction to the Pentateuch," pp. 3–4, and "Genesis," p. 9), he is concerned about harmonizing the first account of creation (Gen. 1.1–2.4) with the second account (Gen. 2.5–25). In Gen. 2.2 God is said to have finished his works and to have rested on the seventh day. Furthermore, the second narrative says that God made the green things of the earth and the grass before they appeared above the earth or sprang forth, although Gen. 1.12 seems to imply that the earth had already brought them forth on the third day. A similar difficulty appears regarding the creation of the first pair of human beings: God is said to have created them on the sixth day, and yet an entirely new account of their creation is given in the second narrative. Aug. furthermore interprets Eccli. (Sirach) 18.1 as meaning that God created all things simultaneously *(simul)*. These considerations led him to conclude that when God created He did indeed create all things simultaneously, but that living things made in that original creative act were not made in actuality in their own proper substances but only potentially in their causal reasons placed in the earth by the Creator. Given the appropriate conditions of earth and moisture, these powers would produce the living creatures intended by God, which would come into being in time according to the plan of His providence. Thus God rests from all His works in the sense that He does not create any new kinds of creatures that were not in the original creation either actually or potentially; and at the same time He is working by reason of the fact that He governs the world He has made, according to the words of Christ, who says: *My Father works even until now, and I work* (John 5.17). Elsewhere in this treatise Aug. elaborates his theory on causal reasons, especially in Books 5 and 6.

[68]Ps. 32.9.

[69]Eccli. (Sirach) 18.1: *He who lives forever created all things together* (according to the OL and Vulg.). The word *simul* ("at one time," "all together") in the Latin version seems to be a mistranslation of the Greek κοινῇ ("commonly," "without exception"). A more accurate translation, therefore, would probably be: *He who lives forever created the whole universe* (RSV).

[70]See n. 51 to Book 1.

[71]1 Cor. 15.52.

[72]Wisd. 7.24–25.

[73]See n. 34 to Book 3.

[74]I follow the reading of P, R, Par, Bod, Nov, Pal, and m: *illum ab omnibus in se ipso requiescere nullo eorum egentem*. The reading *egente*, adopted by z, is found in Lau and apparently in E and S.

BOOK FIVE

[1]Gen. 2.4–6. Aug. is uncertain of the punctuation of v. 4: as he reads it, the clause *when day was made* can be attached either to the statement which precedes or to that which follows. He looks upon either alternative as allowable and consistent with the interpretation he has already given to Gen. 1.3. For a discus-

sion of Augustine's Latin version of this text, see Agaësse-Solignac 48.668–70.

[2]Gen. 1.1.

[3]According to Augustine's interpretation (see Book 1 *supra*), "heaven" in the first verse of Genesis means spiritual creatures, that is, the angels; and "earth" means all the visible works that God made. Both heaven and earth at this stage are thought of as in an unformed state, their unformed matter being prior in origin, though not in time, to their formation. The formation of creatures is described in the account that follows, with no lapse of time implied, for God concreated matter and form when He created all things simultaneously.

[4]*Mundus* in Latin (like κόσμος in Greek).

[5]*Obtinet* is the reading of E[2], P, R, S, Par, Bod, Nov, Lau, Pal, and m. *Obtinebat*, found in z, is based on E[1].

[6]The text of z here adds *fecit Deus*, apparently on the authority of E and S. These words are not found in P, R, Par, Bod, Nov, Lau, Pal, m.

[7]Gen. 1.4–5.

[8]See Book 2 n. 18 *supra*.

[9]Ps. 145.6.

[10]The last sentence of this paragraph is not found in P, R, S, Bod, Pal, m; but it is in the text of E and z and is retained by Agaësse-Solignac.

[11]Cf. Eccli. (Sirach) 18.1, and see n. 69 to Book 4 *supra*.

[12]Gen. 1.12. Augustine's text here reads: *Et produxit terra herbam pabuli (vel herbam feni), seminans semen secundum genus et secundum similitudinem, et lignum fructuosum faciens fructum, cuius semen suum in se secundum genus super terram.* (I have found no support for the reading of m in this place, *seminantem semen* for *seminans semen*.) Earlier (2.12.25 *supra*) Aug. quoted the text in the following form: *Et eiecit terra herbam pabuli semen habentem secundum suum genus et secundum similitudinem.* Augustine's revision of the text, changing *semen habentem* to *seminans semen*, is probably due to his desire to follow more closely the LXX, which reads σπεῖρον σπέρμα. It is difficult, however, to understand how Aug. construed the phrase. One might take the participle sub-

stantively, in apposition with *herbam;* or one might possibly understand *semen* as a second object of *produxit,* with *seminans* in agreement but taking no object. In any case, the meaning of Aug. is clear, and the grammatical difficulty with the text does not obscure his interpretation. For he argues that God, through the causal reasons in the earth, made the crops, which scattered their seeds and thus produced more crops. The original production of crops on the earth, therefore, was not caused by seeds but by God's power working in the earth through the causal reasons.

[13]Gen. 1.11. The textual problem about the form of the participle discussed in the preceding note occurs again here.

[14]Gen. 1.12.

[15]The "Day" in Augustine's interpretation refers to the angels. See 4.22.39 *supra,* and n. 18 to Book 2 *supra.*

[16]Cf. John 5.17.

[17]Gen. 2.8–9.

[18]Namely, the angels.

[19]Rom. 11.36.

[20]Eccli. (Sirach) 18.1. See n. 69 to Book 4 *supra.*

[21]Unformed matter and the formed creature were concreated *(concreata).* Matter is prior not in time *(tempore)* but in origin *(origine).* See 1.15.29 *supra* and n. 48 *ibid.*

[22]In addition to the passage referred to in the foregoing note, see also 1.1.3 and 1.5.10–11.

[23]Aug. is speaking of the angels. The word "heaven" in Gen. 1.1 is said to refer to the angels in a formless state. The command *Let there be light* in Gen. 1.3 is interpreted as the illumination and formation of the angelic creatures. See Book 1 *passim,* especially 1.9.15–17, and n. 18 to Book 2.

[24]The Neoplatonists, following the Neopythagorean tradition, tended to identify the forms or ideas with numbers. See Plotinus, *Enn.* 6.6.16.

[25]See n. 15 *supra.*

[26]The reference is to the seven gifts of the Holy Spirit enumerated in Isa. 11.2 (seven in the LXX and Vulg., but six in the Hebr. text). The number seven is thought of as symbolizing perfection and totality. For Augustine's comments on the seven

gifts of the Holy Spirit, see *Serm.* 250.3 (ML 38.1166).

[27]Gen. 2.5.

[28]1 Cor. 3.7.

[29]Gen. 2.6.

[30]The narrative of Genesis thus far has been concerned with the original creation. By that act plants and trees, according to Aug., were created potentially by the Creator, who placed in the earth the power which would produce them. With Gen. 2.6 begins the narrative of God's administration of the created world, in which His divine power brings forth in actuality what was there in potency. Modern biblical criticism has found here two narratives from two different sources: the Priestly tradition in Gen. 1.1–2.4a and the Yahwist tradition in Gen. 2.4b–25. See E. H. Maly, JBC 1 (1968) "Introduction to the Pentateuch," pp. 3–4, and "Genesis," p. 9.

[31]Philo asks the same question. He suggests that the singular "spring" is used for the plural "springs," meaning "all the veins of the earth producing potable water." See Philo, *Questions and Answers on Genesis* 1.3 (LCL, p. 3 Marcus). This is the solution that Aug. himself adopts as most probable: see 5.10.26 *infra*.

[32]8.7.13–14 *infra*.

[33]Phison (also spelled Pishon), Geon (also spelled Gehon and Gihon), Tigris, and Euphrates. See Gen. 2.11–14. Aug. and other ancient Christian writers identify the Phison with the Ganges and the Geon with the Nile. See 8.7.13 *infra* and n. 42 on that passage.

[34]The Nile overflows its banks from April to October.

[35]The cause of the swelling of the Nile during the summer months was widely disputed among the ancients. Herodotus (2.20–22) says there were three opinions in the matter: (1) the etesian winds blowing against the mouths of the river hinder the flow of the water to the sea; (2) the water flows from the River Ocean into the Nile; and (3) the swelling is caused by melting snows on mountains of Libya or Ethiopia. These opinions are attributed to Thales, Hecataeus, and Anaxagoras respectively. Among later writers discussing the problem are Diod. Sic. 1.38.1–1.41.10; Sen., *Quaest. nat.* 4.2.17–30; Pliny, *Nat. hist.* 5.10.51–56. For a thorough investigation of ancient theories

on this subject, see Albert Rehm, Pauly-Wissowa-Kroll 17.1 (1936) *s.v.* "Nilschwelle," 571–90.

[36]Ps. 77.45 and Ps. 104.34. In the OL version used by Aug. we read the singular (*rana* and *locusta*) in these verses.

[37]Book 5, *passim*, but especially ch. 4.

[38]Cf. John 5.17: *My Father is working still, and I am working.*

[39]Gen. 2.4–5.

[40]Gen. 2.6.

[41]The divine archetypes are called *rationes* ("reasons") in Latin. Identified with the divine perfection, they are models of which creatures are copies. See Aug., *De diversis quaest.* 46, *De ideis* (CCL 44A.70–73; ML 40.29–31). The influence of Plato and the Neoplatonists on Aug. is obvious.

[42]John 1.1–3.

[43]Rom. 11.34–36.

[44]John 1.3–4. There are two ways of punctuating vv. 3–4. We may translate: *Without Him there was made nothing that was made. In Him was life.* The words are understood in this sense by the translators of the *Westminster Version* and RSV. On the other hand, the words may be punctuated as Aug. does so as to read: *Without Him nothing was made. What has been made is life in Him.* This punctuation (with some differences in interpretation and wording) is followed by *The Jerusalem Bible, The New English Bible, The New American Bible,* and *The Translator's New Testament.*

[45]The interpretation which Aug. here rejects is found in *The New American Bible: Whatever came to be in him, found life.*

[46]Ps. 103.24.

[47]Col. 1.16.

[48]John 5.26.

[49]Job 28.12–13.

[50]Job 28.22–25. In translating *For He sees everything under heaven,* I am following the conjecture of Zycha, *perspicit* ("He sees"). The MSS read either *perficit* ("He makes") or *perfecit* ("He made"). But St. Jerome's translation of Origen's revision of Job reads *perspicit*: see *Liber Job, altera versio* 28.24 (ML 29.94). This translation was extensively used by Aug. and later Latin writers: see F. C. Burkitt, *The Old Latin and the Itala* (Texts and Stud-

ies 4.3, Cambridge 1896) 8. *Perspicit* is the correct translation of the Greek in this passage, ἐφορᾷ.

[51]Exod. 3.14.

[52]Acts 17.28.

[53]Wisd. 13.9.

[54]John 1.3,10.

[55]Wisd. 11.18.

[56]See Book 5, chs. 3 ff.

[57]Eccli. (Sirach) 18.1.

[58]The "day" is the first day of creation. Gen. 1.5: *God called the light Day and the darkness Night, and evening was made and morning was made, one day.* The Day, that is, the light, is understood by Aug. to be the angels, to whom God gave a knowledge of other creatures: see 4.22.39 *supra*.

[59]Morning and evening knowledge in the angels is explained in 4.22.39–4.24.41 *supra*.

[60]James 1.17.

[61]Gal. 3.19: *Why then the law? It was added because of transgressions until the offspring should come to whom the promise had been given, and it was promulgated by angels in the hands of a mediator.* This difficult passage was misunderstood by Aug. at the time he was writing his commentary on Genesis and his commentary on the Letter to the Galatians. See his *Epistolae ad Galatas expositionis liber unus* 24 (ML 35.2122), where he reads *semen . . . dispositum per angelos (the offspring placed through the angels)* instead of *lex . . . ordinata per angelos (the law promulgated by the angels).* In *Retract.* 2.50.2 or 2.24.2 (CSEL 36.160,5–10 Knöll; ML 32.640), Aug. corrected his misinterpretation, appealing to the better MSS, especially those in Greek: "In Book 5 and elsewhere in that work [*De Gen. ad litt.*], where I wrote of *the offspring to whom the promise had been given, and who had been placed through the angels in the hands of a mediator,* I was not faithful to the text of St. Paul, as I later discovered in consulting the better manuscripts, especially those in Greek. The statement made in the text about the Law has been taken as referring to the offspring by a translator's error in many Latin manuscripts." Aug. refers to Gal. 3.19 again in 9.16.30 and 9.18.35 *infra*.

⁶²Eph. 3.8–11. The text of v. 10 as quoted by Aug. is uncertain. According to the MSS (E, P, R, S, B, Bod, and Pal), Augustine's reading is: *per ecclesiam multiformis sapientiae Dei (through the Church of the manifold wisdom of God)*. The reading of z and m is: *per ecclesiam multiformis sapientia Dei (the manifold wisdom of God through the Church)*. The latter reading seems to make sense more readily, and it is in keeping with the original Greek as well as the Vulg., but no MSS authority has been cited for it here. The text is quoted again in 9.18.35 *infra* with a similar discrepancy between editors and MSS. Finally, it is cited in 12.28.56 *infra*, once again with the reading *sapientiae* (and no variant *sapientia* cited); and in that passage as given in a fragmentary form, *sapientiae* (the gen.) is the only possible reading.

⁶³Matt. 22.30.

⁶⁴Heb. 1.2.

⁶⁵Prov. 8.23.

⁶⁶Ps. 104.24.

⁶⁷1 Tim. 3.16.

⁶⁸John 5.17.

⁶⁹John 14.10.

⁷⁰John 5.21.

⁷¹1 Cor. 15.36–38.

⁷²Gen. 2.2.

⁷³Wisd. 6.17.

⁷⁴We do not know what philosophers Aug. had in mind in referring to this curious opinion about Providence. For a comment on the problem, see Agaësse-Solignac 48.678–79.

⁷⁵Ps. 148.7–8.

⁷⁶Matt. 10.29; 6.30.

⁷⁷Cf. Wisd. 11.21. For Augustine's interpretation of this text, see n. 8 and n. 10 to Book 4 *supra*.

⁷⁸Note the distinction between germ or bud *(germen)* and seed *(semen)*. The seed of which Aug. here speaks is the causal reason. It is not a material substance but rather a force in matter determining the growth of an organism. See n. 67 to Book 4.

⁷⁹Here the seed referred to is the visible and tangible seed.

⁸⁰Gen. 2.4–5.

⁸¹Gen. 2.5.

[82]The "day" according to Augustine's interpretation is the society of angelic spirits, whose minds are illuminated to see creatures before their creation. See 4.22.39 *supra* and n. 58 to Book 5.

[83]Gen. 2.6.

BOOK SIX

[1]Gen. 2.7.

[2]Cf. Gen. 2.5.

[3]According to Aug., in the original creation described in the first chapter of Genesis, God did not make the visible plants, trees, and animals on the earth but rather placed in the earth hidden causes, "seminal reasons," from which they would come forth. His theory is explained in Book 5; see especially chs. 7, 20, and 23 of Book 5 and n. 67 to Book 4.

[4]Gen. 1.26–28.

[5]Gen. 2.24. According to Augustine's interpretation, these words in v. 24 are spoken by Adam and are a continuation of Adam's utterance in v. 23. Modern interpreters generally understand that Adam's words end at the end of v. 23 and that v. 24 contains a comment by the author of Genesis. For Augustine's explanation, see 9.19.36 *infra*.

[6]These theories have been discussed earlier in 1.12.25, 1.16.31, and 4.21.38.

[7]There are difficulties in interpreting this sentence, partly because of the uncertainty as to whether the correct MSS reading is *conditum*, agreeing with *diem* ("day created"), or *conditam*, agreeing with *lucem* ("light created"). The Maurist editors read *conditum* and cite no variants. Zycha follows the Maurist edition in reading *conditum*, but he testifies that all the MSS he collated read *conditam*. *Conditum*, if we may judge from the context, seems to be the correct reading, and it has the authority of at least one MS (Bod) unknown to Zycha.

[8]The "light" of Gen. 1.3, which is the "Day" of Gen. 1.5, is the illuminated world of angelic intellects made perfect in their vision of God. This illumination, or this day, is presented in a

scheme of six days, the one day repeated six times, signifying that all the works of creation, which are in reality created together, are made present to the angels, who first see them in the Word of God (morning knowledge) and then in their own natures (evening knowledge). See Books 4 and 5 *passim*, especially 4.22.39, 4.26.43, 5.3.5–6, 5.5.14–16, 5.23.45–46.

[9]Gen. 2.4–5.

[10]Eccli. (Sirach) 18.1. See n. 69 to Book 4.

[11]Gen. 2.8–9.

[12]Gen. 1.12. For an explanation of Augustine's theory of seminal reasons, see n. 67 to Book 4. Pope Athanasius II (496–98) refers approvingly to Augustine's theory, quoting from *De Gen.* 6.4.5. (H. Denzinger, *Enchiridion symbolorum* [36th ed. Barcelona 1976] no. 360).

[13]*Adhuc* can have the meaning of "moreover, besides, also." See TLL 1.662,18. Here it is a translation of ἔτι in the LXX, for which this meaning is common. See J. F. Schleusner, *Novus Thesaurus in LXX* (Glasgow 1822) 1.923.

[14]Gen. 1.24,27.

[15]Gen. 2.18–22.

[16]God "had again formed" *(cum adhuc de terra finxisset)* the birds and beasts in the sense that after the sixth day His creative power at work in the seminal reasons brought forth the birds and beasts which He had created potentially in their causes *(potentialiter atque causaliter)* on the fifth and sixth days.

[17]Gen. 1.27–28.

[18]Earlier, in 5.12.28, Aug. distinguished these three steps in creation: (1) the unchangeable forms or exemplars in the Word of God according to which creatures are made; (2) God's creative work of the six days, in which He created all works together and from which He rested on the seventh day; and (3) the things He produces from the original creation as He works even now bringing to full development the things He had originally created potentially and in their causes. The third step in creation we know by experience; the other two we know only by divine authority.

[19]Gen. 1.29.

[20]*Quomodo fiunt futura non facta.* It is difficult to reproduce in

English this paradoxical statement with the brevity and clarity of the Latin original. Things made potentially in their causes come to be made *(fiunt)*, but they are things yet to be *(futura)* and at the present time are not made *(non facta)*.

[21]Eccli (Sirach) 18.1.

[22]Origen held that the interior man is made up of the masculine part, which is *spiritus*, and the feminine part, which is *anima*. See Orig., *In Gen.* (tr. by Rufinus) 1.15 (GCS 6.1, p. 19, 8–11 Baehrens; MG 12.158C). Aug. had probably read this work in Rufinus' translation.

[23]Matt. 28.20.

[24]Jer. 1.5.

[25]See Heb. 7.9–10.

[26]Gen. 1.26,28–29.

[27]Jer. 1.5.

[28]Heb. 7.9–10.

[29]Eph. 1.4.

[30]Rom. 9.10–11.

[31]Job 14.4. Augustine's text is based on the LXX.

[32]Ps. 50.7.

[33]Rom. 5.12. In the *Enarr. in Ps.* 50.10 (CCL 38.607,50–52; ML 36.592) Aug. cites the text in full in this form: *Through one man sin came into this world, and through sin death, and so death spread to all men, in whom all have sinned;* and this form of the text agrees substantially with the Vulg. The last clause in this Latin version reads, *in quo omnes peccaverunt (in whom all have sinned)*, and Aug. with most Latin writers took the phrase *in quo* as referring back to *one man* (Adam). Apart from the fact that the relative is far removed from its antecedent in this interpretation, there is a further difficulty in taking *in quo* as a correct translation of the Greek ἐφ' ᾧ, which more probably means "because." Most modern versions, therefore, render the clause *because all have sinned*, and this seems to be the correct interpretation: see J. Fitzmyer, JBC 2 (1968) "Romans," 307. But the fundamental meaning of Paul is correctly understood by Aug.: through Adam, sin and death; through Christ, justification and eternal life. Cf. Ambrosiaster (4th c. and known to Aug.), *Ad Romanos* 5.12 (CSEL 81.165–67 Vogels; ML 17.92–93), and see Bonner 373.

[34]Aug. is probably referring to Origen. See Origen, *De principiis* 1.8.1 and 3.3.5 (GCS 22.96,8–11, and 22.262,2–16 Koetschau). Aug. was familiar with the *De principiis* of Origen (see *De civ. Dei* 11.23) in the translation of Jerome or of Rufinus.

[35]Augustine's words are: *In illa enim prima conditione mundi, cum Deus omnia simul creavit, homo factus est qui esset futurus, ratio creandi hominis, non actio creati.* Aug. is saying that in the six "days" of creation, i.e., in the creative act by which God first made all things simultaneously, He had not yet formed man from the slime of the earth. He had rather placed in the earth the causal principle *(ratio seminalis)* by which the body of the first man would later be formed. This is the meaning of *ratio* in this passage. The use of *actio* is extraordinary. It has here approximately the same meaning as *actus* ("actuality" as opposed to *potentia*, "potency") in Aquinas, and ἐνέργεια or ἐντελέχεια ("actuality" as opposed to δύναμις, "potency") in Aristotle. Marius Victorinus also uses *actio* as a correlative of *potentia* very frequently in his work on the Trinity, *Against Arius*, but *potentia* usually signifies the almighty power of God the Father and *actio* the manifestation of that power in the Word. There is, however, one clear use of *potentia* and *actio* in the Aristotelian sense in reference to creatures: see *Adv. Arium* 4.12 (CSEL 83.243,17–25 Henry-Hadot; ML 8.1122A–B). This philosophical meaning of *actio* is not noted in TLL or Blaise-Chirat, *Dictionnaire latin-française des auteurs chrétiens*, or A. Souter, *A Glossary of Later Latin to 600 A.D.*

[36]Notice here the three modes of existence of created living beings: (1) existing eternally in God; (2) existing potentially in nature; (3) existing in their fully developed forms.

[37]It is important to note that in Augustine's view the world in which God created all things simultaneously contained potentially, by reason of the causes (or seminal reasons) which were created simultaneously with the world *(secundum causas simul creatas)*, all the living things that would spring forth in due time. In another sense, he says, all the living things that spring forth are contained in seeds *(in seminibus)* which are quasi-primordial causes *(quasiprimordiales causae)*. Seeds, therefore, are visible, tangible substances containing potentially the organisms

that will grow from them. But beyond these are the primordial causes, the *rationes seminales* or "seminal reasons," which are not tangible substances but creative forces hidden in nature and causing seeds to grow. It should be noted, however, that the *first* appearance of crops on the earth is not caused by seeds, according to Aug., but by God's creative power working through sun and water and the seminal reasons. We have, therefore, crops from the earth, then seeds from crops, then subsequently crops from seeds. Aug. is led to this theory by Gen. 1.12: *The earth brought forth the nourishing crops, seed-bearing according to their kind.* See Augustine's explanation in 5.4.9 *supra*.

[38]"In their visible form and reality," *in manifestas formas actusque. Actus* is used here in the same sense as *actio* in ch. 9 *supra:* see n. 35.

[39]Gen. 2.1–3. In quoting this passage here, Aug. omits the following from v. 2: *And God rested on the seventh day from all the works He had made.* These words are inserted in the text of the Maurist edition, but Zycha correctly removed them, as he did not find them in any MSS in this place. They do, however, belong to the complete text of Gen., and they are in Augustine's text of Gen. as he quotes it in 4.1.1 *supra*.

[40]Gen. 2.3.

[41]Gen. 2.7.

[42]Ps. 43.3. Augustine's version is according to the LXX text.

[43]Ps. 135.11–12. Aug. is not quoting verbatim here.

[44]In this chapter Aug. argues against those who would base the superiority of man on the fact that God Himself personally created him, whereas (they argue) He created the lower animals by His Word (*dixit et facta sunt*, sect. 21) or by His command (*iussit et facta sunt*, sect. 22). In reality, as Aug. explains, He created everything through His Word; and His power and wisdom are identified with His Word. The basis for the superiority of man, therefore, is that he is made in the image of God.

[45]See Matt. 17.5, Mark 9.7, Luke 9.35.

[46]John 1.3.

[47]Ps. 101.26.

[48]Ps. 94.5.

[49]Ps. 48.13. Augustine's version is according to the LXX text.

[50]Here Aug. seems to be refuting Origen, *In Gen.*, tr. by Rufinus, 1.12 (GCS 29.13,24–15,3 Baehrens; MG 12.155A–C).

[51]Gen. 2.19.

[52]See H. Somers, S.J., "Image de Dieu: Les sources de l'exégèse augustinienne," REAug 7 (1961) 105–25.

[53]The same notion is found in Basil, *In Hex.* 9.2 (SC 26.486,192A Giet; in tr. by Eustathius, TU 66.115,29–31 Amand de Mendieta-Rudberg). Cicero also calls attention to the superiority of man over other animals inasmuch as man is made to stand erect and look up to heaven (*Nat. deor.* 2.56.140 and *Leg.* 1.9.26). This was a commonplace among ancient writers: see the parallels collected by A. S. Pease (ed.), *M. Tulli Ciceronis De natura deorum, libri secundus et tertius* (Cambridge, Mass. 1958) 914–15.

[54]See Col. 3.2.

[55]This chapter starts off by asking whether Adam was created as an infant or as an adult and ends up with a discussion of miracles, which seem to be against the order that God Himself established. As for the condition of Adam when he was created, Aug. leaves the question open here, but in the next chapter and again in ch. 18 he assumes as more likely the common opinion that Adam was created as an adult. Augustine's speculation on this matter involves his theory about the "causal reasons" (*causales rationes*) governing the growth of all creatures from an inchoate state to full development. If God has provided that the growth of all creatures is regulated by the *causales rationes*, how do we explain the fact that Christ changed water into wine and that God changed the rod of Aaron into a serpent? In fact, can we justify the theory that Adam was created as an adult? The answer, to be developed in the next chapter, is that God made the *causales rationes* to direct the growth of a creature from its original inchoate state or (by exception) to form a creature in its fully mature state instantaneously, in accordance with God's will for the particular occasion. See the penetrating analysis of these speculations in Agaësse-Solignac 48.685–90.

[56]Augustine's words are: *in aetate perfecta, hoc est virili atque iuvenali.* This is the time of life between the ages of 31 and 45. See Censorinus, *De die natali* 14.2 (Teubner ed., p. 24 Hultsch).

[57]Jer. 1.5.

[58]The "numbers" of a being here refer to the laws of its development, based upon the specific perfection or form of the being. See Augustine's interpretation of Wisd. 11.21 *(Thou hast ordered all things in measure and number and weight)* proposed in Book 4, chs. 3–5 *supra*.

[59]Gen. 1.2.

[60]John 2.9–10.

[61]Exod. 7.10.

[62]Casual reasons: *causales rationes*. These are the seminal formative principles or reason-principles which God created and placed in the world in the original creation. See n. 67 to Book 4 *supra*.

[63]Principle: *ratio*.

[64]Forms: *numeri*. See n. 58 *supra*.

[65]Isa. 38.5; 2 Kings 20.6.

[66]I have followed the reading of Zycha, *nisi ad aliquid adderentur*, rather than the Maurist reading, *nisi aliquid adderetur*. Zycha's reading makes better sense and it has the support of most of the MSS he examined; to which we can add the testimony of Bod.

[67]Chs. 19–28 of this book deal with the question of Adam's body. Was it a natural, that is, physical body *(corpus animale)*, or a spiritual body *(corpus spiritale)?* A natural body (such as we have) is in need of material food for nourishment and is subject to fatigue, sickness, and death. A spiritual body (such as we shall have at the resurrection) is not in need of any material food, is not subject to fatigue and sickness, and is immortal. Aug. speculates on these problems, referring several times to the opinions of other interpreters without naming them. Origen, Gregory of Nyssa, and Philo have treated this matter, but it is difficult to identify particular passages in their works which Aug. may have had in mind. See the observations in Agaësse-Solignac 48.690–95.

[68]1 Cor. 15.44.

[69]Matt. 22.30.

[70]Ps. 8.6. Aug. here and in his *Enarr. in Ps.* 8.11 (CCL 38.54; ML 36.114) takes the pronoun "Him" in this text as referring to

Christ. In the *Enarr. in Ps.* he says that because of Christ's bodily weakness and the humiliation of His passion He was for a time *a little below the angels.*

⁷¹Phil. 2.7.

⁷²1 Cor. 15.44–49.

⁷³In the preceding chapter Aug. found evidence in Paul, 1 Cor. 15.44–49, to show that Adam had a natural body. But here he points out that other texts seem to imply that we look forward to a recovery of a gift lost by Adam; hence the theory of some interpreters that Adam originally had a natural body, which was changed into a spiritual body when he was placed in Paradise.

⁷⁴Luke 15.32.

⁷⁵Luke 15.22. For the symbolic meaning of *the best robe* (*stolam primam*, στολὴν τὴν πρώτην), see Tert. *De pud.* 9.16 (CCL 2.1298,70–74; ML 2.1051A); Cyr. Alex., *Exp. in Lucae evang.* 15 (MG 72.808B–C); Ps.-Aug., *Sermo* 27 (ML 40.1282). See 6.27.38 *infra.*

⁷⁶1 Cor. 15.53.

⁷⁷1 Cor. 15.45, quoting Gen. 2.7. The Maurist edition adds the second half of v. 45: *The last Adam was made a life-giving spirit.* Zycha puts this half verse in brackets, but he might well have removed it from the text entirely. It is not found in any of the MSS which he collated, nor is it found in Bod or Pal.

⁷⁸Aug. here argues that Adam's body could not have been changed into a spiritual body when he was placed in Paradise because Scripture makes it clear that by sin he merited death, and only a natural body can be subject to death.

⁷⁹Some commentators (e.g. Philo, *Legum allegoria* 1.105–7 [LCL 1.216 Colson-Whitaker]) hold that the death Adam merited by his sin was the death of the soul only and not of the body. But Aug. refutes this from Rom. 8.10–11. Without sin, therefore, Adam's body would have been immortal. But how could this have been if he had a natural body?

⁸⁰Rom. 8.10–11.

⁸¹Aug. concludes that there was no transformation of Adam's body on his being placed in Paradise. Given a natural (i.e., mortal) body, he was put in Paradise for a period of trial. If he had

not sinned, he would have been exempt from death by a special gift of God, and his body would have been transformed into a spiritual and glorious body.

[82]In eternal life: reading *in vita aeterna.* This is the reading of three of Zycha's MSS, to which we may add Bod and Pal. This seems to fit the thought of the sentence better than Zycha's reading, *in vitam aeternam.*

[83]Rom. 8.10.

[84]Aug. continues his explanation of the solution he has proposed by showing that we recover what Adam lost by his sin in the sense that we are renewed from the old way of sin and recover the justice which Adam lost, but that we do not recover a spiritual body which he lost because he never had such a body.

[85]Zycha reports that in the margin of *Codex Sangallensis* 161, 8th c., a scribe has written here: "The reader should read carefully and not assume that Adam had lost the image of God but rather that he had tarnished it."

[86]Matt. 22.30.

[87]Cf. Eph. 4.23: *Renovamini autem spiritu mentis vestrae (And be renewed in the spirit of your minds).* Aug. says: "We are renewed," *renovamur;* not: "We shall be renewed," *renovabimur.* I follow the reading of m in taking this verb in the present tense rather than in the future, which is the reading of z. Aug. obviously intends a contrast between the spiritual renewal of the soul that takes place in this life *(Renovamur ergo spiritu mentis nostrae)* and the change of our bodies into their glorious state at the resurrection *(Renovabimur autem etiam carne).* The reading of m is supported by two MSS cited by z and is also attested by Pal.

[88]Cf. 1 Cor. 15.53: *Oportet enim corruptibile hoc induere incorruptionem (For this corruptible nature must put on incorruption).* According to z, Aug. alludes to St. Paul's statement in the words *induet incorruptionem,* but according to m, *induetur incorruptione.* The MSS evidence is divided, but Aug. elsewhere cites the text in the form *induerit incorruptionem.* See *In Ioh. evang.* 8.2 (CCL 36.83,33; ML 35.1451) and *ibid.* 13.5 (CCL 36.133,37; ML 35.1495). Zycha's reading, therefore, seems more probable.

[89]Rom. 8.10.

[90]The conclusion of Augustine's reflections on the state of

Adam's body is that it was both mortal and immortal: mortal because it was a natural body, and immortal by a special gift of God made contingent on the condition that Adam would not sin.

[91] Aug. mentions three states with respect to mortality and immortality: (1) *non posse mori* (to be unable to die), (2) *posse mori* (to be able to die), (3) *posse non mori* (to be able not to die). The first state will belong to man at the resurrection; the second state belongs to man before and after the Fall; the third state belonged to Adam before the Fall. These categories correspond to categories Aug. uses elsewhere with respect to sin: *non posse peccare, posse peccare, posse non peccare.* See *C. adversarium legis et prophetarum* 1.14.20 (ML 42.614); *De correp. et gratia* 12.33 (ML 44.936); *Enchiridion* 105.28 (ML 40.281); and A. Solignac, S.J., "La condition de l'homme pécheur d'après saint Augustin," NRT 78 (1956) 359–87, especially 359–68.

[92] Cf. Gen. 2.9.

[93] Cf. 1 Cor. 15.22: *For as in Adam all die, so also in Christ shall all be made alive.* Cf. also Rom. 5.12.

[94] Eph. 4.21–24.

[95] 1 Cor. 15.44.

[96] Col. 3.9–10.

[97] When reviewing his works four years before his death, Aug. qualified this statement as follows: "In Book 6 my statement that Adam by his sin lost the image of God in which he was made must not be taken to mean that no trace of the image remained in him. Rather it was so disfigured that it needed renewal." See *Retract.* 2.50.3 or 2.24.2 (CSEL 36.160,10–13 Knöll; ML 32.640). It should be remarked here that in 6.24.35, as noted above, there is a marginal gloss in *Codex Sangallensis* cautioning the reader against taking Aug. to mean that the image of God was simply destroyed by Adam's sin. Zycha reports a similar gloss in the same MS in this chapter. The glossator, as Agaësse-Solignac suggest, was probably influenced by Augustine's own comment in his *Retract.*

[98] Luke 15.22. See n. 75 *supra.*

[99] Eph. 4.23.

[100] Cf. Col. 3.10.

[101]Gal. 6.1.

[102]*Dixi* (I have said) is the reading of m. Zycha reads *dixit* (he has said), although he has the support of only one MS (which a second hand corrected to read *dixi*) for that reading. All the other MSS collated by Zycha (and also Bod and Pal) read *dixi*. This reading is demanded by the context, for it is Aug., not Paul, who is concerned about reconciling the fact of Adam's sin with the spiritual state of his mind.

[103]Augustine's difficulty in reading all the commentaries is probably due not only to the quantity of these writings and the difficulty of obtaining copies, but also to his limited knowledge of Greek at the time he was writing his commentary on Genesis (A.D. 401–15). He was constantly studying Greek during the years of his episcopate in order to understand better the Greek text of Scripture and the works of the Greek Fathers, but it was not until after 415 that he had a sufficient mastery to read *in extenso* Greek patristic works in the original. See Pierre Courcelle, *Les lettres grecques en Occident de Macrobe à Cassiodore* (Paris 1948) 137–94; English tr. by Harry E. Wedeck, *Late Latin Writers and Their Greek Sources* (Cambridge, Mass. 1969) 149–208. At the time he was writing on Genesis, however, Aug. had read St. Basil's *In Hexaemeron*, probably in the Latin version of Eustathius, and Origen's *In Genesim homiliae*, probably in the Latin version of Rufinus. See Berthold Altaner, "Eustathius, der lateinische Übersetzer der Hexaemeron-Homilien Basilius des Grossen," ZNTW 39 (1940) 161–70, reprinted in *Kleine patristische Schriften* (TU 83, Berlin 1967) 437–47; and idem, "Augustinus und Origenes," *Historisches Jahrbuch* 70 (1951) 15–41, reprinted in *Kleine patr. Schr.* 224–52.

INDICES

1. OLD AND NEW TESTAMENTS

2. GENERAL INDEX

ANCIENT CHRISTIAN WRITERS

THE WORKS OF THE FATHERS IN TRANSLATION
Founded by J. QUASTEN *and* J. C. PLUMPE

Now edited by
J. QUASTEN • W. J. BURGHARDT • T. C. LAWLER

ST. AUGUSTINE
THE LITERAL MEANING
OF GENESIS

DE GENESI AD LITTERAM

ANCIENT CHRISTIAN WRITERS

THE WORKS OF THE FATHERS IN TRANSLATION

EDITED BY

JOHANNES QUASTEN   WALTER J. BURGHARDT

THOMAS COMERFORD LAWLER

No. 42

ST. AUGUSTINE

THE LITERAL MEANING

OF GENESIS

TRANSLATED AND ANNOTATED

BY

JOHN HAMMOND TAYLOR, S.J.

Gonzaga University
Spokane, Washington

Volume II
Books 7–12

THE NEWMAN PRESS

New York, N.Y./Mahwah, N.J.

Library of Congress
Catalog Card Number: 82-61742

ISBN: 0-8091-0327-3

Published by Paulist Press
997 Macarthur Boulevard
Mahwah, New Jersey 07430

PRINTED AND BOUND IN THE UNITED STATES OF AMERICA

CONTENTS

ST. AUGUSTINE
THE LITERAL MEANING
OF GENESIS

BOOKS 7–12

BOOK SEVEN
THE CREATION OF THE MAN'S SOUL

CHAPTER 1

*The creation of the man's soul must now be considered
in the light of Gen. 2.7.*

1. *And God formed man of dust from the earth and breathed into
his face the breath of life; and man was made a living being.*[1]
At the beginning of the preceding book I undertook to examine these words of Scripture; and I treated in a sufficiently thorough way, I believe, the creation of man, especially of his body,
according to what seemed to me to be the meaning of Scripture.
But since it is no simple matter to understand the soul, I
thought it wise to leave that question to this book, not knowing
how much the Lord would help me in my desire to say the right
thing. But I did know this much: that I was not going to say the
right thing unless He helped me.

To say the right thing is to say what is true and appropriate,
not arbitrarily rejecting anything or thoughtlessly affirming
anything so long as it is doubtful where the truth lies in the
light of the faith and Christian doctrine, but unhesitatingly asserting what can be taught on the basis of the obvious facts of
the case or the certain authority of Scripture.

2. First, then, let us examine the statement in Scripture
which says, *God breathed into his face the breath of life.*[2] Some
manuscripts read, *He inspired into his face.*[3] But since the Greek
codices have ἐνεφύσησεν, it is clear that the Latin should be
flavit or *sufflavit.*[4]

In the preceding book[5] I discussed the question of "the hands
of God" when man was represented as formed from the slime

3

of the earth. What, therefore, need I say now about the statement, *God breathed,* except that He did not breathe with mouth and lips any more than He formed man with bodily hands?

3. Nevertheless, by this word I think Scripture gives us considerable help in dealing with a difficult question.

CHAPTER 2

The breathing of the soul into man does not imply that God gave man something of His substance.

Some interpreters, basing their theory on the word "breathed," have thought that the soul is something from the very substance of God, that is, something of the nature which is His.[6] They hold this opinion because when man breathes he casts forth something of himself in his breath. But for this very reason we should be cautioned to reject this opinion as opposed to the Catholic faith. For we believe that the nature and substance of God, which is in the Trinity, as many believe but few understand, is absolutely unchangeable. But who doubts that the soul can be changed for better or worse? Hence, it is sacrilegious to suppose that the soul and God are of one substance. For this simply amounts to believing that He is changeable.

Hence, we must believe and understand without any shadow of a doubt what the true faith teaches, namely, that the soul is from God as a thing which He made, not as something from His own nature whether generated by Him or proceeding from Him in any way whatsoever.

CHAPTER 3

Further reasons to prove that the soul is not part of God's substance.

4. How then, our adversaries object, is it written, *God breathed into his face, and man was made a living being,* if the soul is not part of God, or in fact the substance of God? Indeed, from the

very word that is used it is quite clear that this is not the case. For when man breathes forth, his soul certainly moves the body, which is subject to it, and makes the breath from the body, not from itself. Our critics are surely not so unperceptive as to fail to see that when we wish to breathe forth, our breath is produced by the natural inhalation and exhalation of the air that surrounds us. And even on the supposition that in breathing out we breathed forth something which was not from the surrounding air which we inhale and exhale but from our own body, nevertheless body and soul are different by nature, and to this fact our opponents agree.

Hence, it is also true that the soul, which[7] governs and moves the body, is substantially different from the breath, which the soul regulates and causes when it produces it from the body subject to it and not from its own substance, to which the body is subject. If we are permitted a comparison of two things vastly different, we may say that as the soul rules the body, God rules His creatures. Why, then, can we not understand that God made the soul from a creature subject to Him, in view of the fact that He is said to have breathed it forth? For although the soul does not rule its body as God does the universe which He made, nevertheless it produces breath by its motion and does not make it out of its own substance.

5. We might say that the breath of God is not the soul of man but that God by breathing forth made the soul of man. But we must not think that the creatures He made by a word are better than what He made by a breath, in view of the fact that a word is better than a breath in us. Nevertheless, according to the account I have given above, there is no reason to hesitate to call the soul the breath of God, so long as we understand that it is not God's nature and substance, but simply that to breathe forth is to produce a breath, and that to produce a breath is to produce the soul.

What God says through Isaiah agrees with this explanation: *For My spirit goes forth from Me, and I have made every breath.* That He is not speaking of any corporeal breath is clear from the words that follow. For when He had said, *I have made every breath,* He added, *And because of sin I afflicted him for a time and smote him.*[8] What, therefore, is the meaning of breath except the soul, which because of sin has been smitten and afflicted? What, then, is the sense of *I have made every breath* except "I have made every soul"?

CHAPTER 4

Even one who holds that God is the world soul would not logically maintain that the breath of God is part of His substance.

6. If, then, we were to say that God is, so to speak, the soul of this corporeal world, and that the world itself is to Him a kind of body of one living being,[9] we should not truly say that He made the soul of man by His breath, except in so far as we should speak of a material soul made from the surrounding air which, as part of His body, would be subject to Him. But what He would have given[10] by breathing we should have to suppose He did not give from Himself but from the air subject to Him as part of His body, just as the soul produces breath not from itself but from something similarly subject to it, namely, its body.

But since we say not only that the body of the world is subject to God, but that He is above every creature, corporeal and spiritual, we cannot believe that He made the soul by breathing it forth from Himself or from the corporeal elements of the world.

CHAPTER 5

When breathing the soul into Adam, did God create it out of nothing or form it from some previously created spiritual being?

7. What, then, are we to say about the creation of the soul? Did God make it from that which was entirely nonexistent, that is, from nothing, or from something which He had already made in the spiritual order but which was not yet a soul? This is a real problem.[11]

For if we do not believe that God still creates anything from
nothing after He has created all things simultaneously, and if
we therefore believe that He rested from all the works which
He had begun to make and had finished, so that whatever He
would subsequently make He would make from these works, I
do not see how we can understand that He still creates souls
from nothing.

Perhaps we should say that in the works of the first six days
God made the hidden day[12] and (if this is what we are to believe)
the spiritual and intellectual realm, that is, the united company
of angelic spirits; and besides them, the world, namely, heaven
and earth; and then we should perhaps add that in these existing
beings God created the reason-principles of other beings to
come in the future, but not the beings themselves. Otherwise,
if these beings had already been created as they were destined
to be, they would no longer be destined to be. And if that is so,
there was not yet existing in the created world any human soul.
A human soul first began to exist when God breathed forth and
made it and put it into man.

8. But this does not solve the problem. We want to know
whether God created from nothing the being which is called the
soul and which before that moment was not existing, on the
supposition that His breath would not come from some subordinate substance as is the case with the breath which the soul ex-
hales from the body, as we have already pointed out. Was God's
breath, then, quite simply made from nothing when it pleased
Him to breathe forth and His breath became the soul of man?
Or was there already existing some spiritual entity which, whatever its nature, was not yet soul, and from this entity was there
made the breath of God, identified with the soul itself? There
is a parallel with man's body, which was nonexistent before
God formed it from the slime or dust of the earth. For dust or
slime was not human flesh; nevertheless, it was something from
which would be made a being which was not yet in existence.

CHAPTER 6

Was there some previously created spiritual material for the soul as there was earth for the body?

9. Is it believable, then, that in the works of the first six days God created not only the causal reason of the future human body but also the material from which it would be made, namely, earth from whose slime or dust the body would be formed, whereas in the case of the soul He created only the causal reason according to which it would be made and not any kind of material *sui generis* from which it would be made?

For if the soul were something immutable, we should have no need to look for its own special kind of matter; however, its mutability shows it sometimes deformed by vice and deception and formed by virtue and true doctrine, its nature as soul meanwhile remaining, just as the flesh remains by nature flesh though it is glowing with health or disfigured by disease or wounds.[13] But the flesh, before becoming flesh and having its natural beauty or deformity, also had the material, namely, earth, from which it was made into flesh. Perhaps, then, the soul, before it was made into the nature of soul, whose beauty is virtue and whose deformity is vice, could have had its own kind of spiritual material which was not yet soul, just as the earth from which the flesh was made was already something, although it was not flesh.

10. But there is a difference. For the earth filled the lowest part of the world before the body of man was made from it, and it gave to the world its whole substance so that even if no flesh of any living being were made from it, by its own form it would fill out the structure and mass of the world; and this is why the world is referred to as heaven and earth.

CHAPTER 7

Difficulties connected with supposing that there was a spiritual material out of which the soul was made.

If there was any such thing as a spiritual material from which the soul was made, or if there is any such thing from which souls are now made, what precisely is it? What is its name, what is its form, what use does it have in the works of creation? Is it living or nonliving? If it lives, what does it do? What does it produce in the world? Does it live a happy life or a wretched life or neither? Does it give life to anything? Or is it without this function also, and does it rest quietly in some inmost recess of the universe without active perception and vital motion? For if there was no life whatsoever in it, how could it be some sort of incorporeal, nonliving material for life yet to come? The supposition, then, is false, or this is a mystery beyond our comprehension.

But if it was already living neither happily nor wretchedly, how was it rational? But if it was made rational at the time when the human soul was made from this material, was irrational life the material of the rational (that is, human) soul? What, then, was the difference between this life and the life of cattle? Had it only the possibility of rational life and not yet the exercise of it? For we see that the soul of an infant, which is certainly the soul of a human being, has not yet begun to use reason, and nevertheless we call it a rational soul. Why, then, should we not believe that similarly in this material from which the soul has been made, the life of thought was dormant, just as in the infant's soul, which is certainly human, rational life is dormant?

CHAPTER 8

Was the life from which the soul of man is said to have been made a
happy life? Difficulties with this.

11. If the life from which the soul of man was made was already a happy life, then the soul has been given a life less excellent, and accordingly that other life is not the material of the soul, but the soul is rather an inferior emanation[14] from it. Now, when a material is formed, especially by God, it is certainly improved by the formation. But even if the human soul could be understood as an emanation of some form of life created in a blessed state by God, it could not be thought of as having begun to exist in a state according to its merits except from the moment it has begun to live its own life when it has been made a soul animating a body, using its senses as messengers,[15] and conscious of its own individual life with will, intellect, and memory. For if there is some creature from which God breathed this emanation into the flesh He formed, creating the soul by what might be called a breathing, and if the source of the emanation is in a blessed state, it is not in any way moved or changed nor does it lose anything when the effluence which becomes the soul flows from it.

CHAPTER 9

Difficulties in assuming an irrational soul as the material.
Transmigration rejected.

For it is not a body and therefore cannot be diminished by exhalation.

12. But if an irrational soul is somehow the material from which the rational (namely, human) soul is made, again a question arises about the source from which this irrational soul comes. For it too can be made only by the Creator of all beings.

Was it made from corporeal matter? If so, why can we not say the same about the rational soul? Surely, if it is granted that a certain effect can be produced step by step, no one will deny that God can accomplish the same result even if He abridges the process. Consequently, whatever the intermediate steps, if a body is the material of an irrational soul, and the irrational soul is the material of the rational soul, there is no doubt that the body is the material of the the rational soul. But I know of no one who has ever ventured such an opinion except a person who holds that the soul itself is nothing but a kind of body.

13. If we concede that an irrational soul is the basic matter out of which the rational soul is made, we must be on our guard against the danger of believing that there is the possibility of a transmigration of souls from beasts to men (a position which flatly contradicts the truth and the Catholic faith). For if an irrational soul is changed for the better, it will become the soul of a human being; similarly, if a human soul is changed for the worse, it will become the soul of a beast. Some philosophers who have held such ridiculous opinions have been a cause of embarrassment to their later followers, who have said that their predecessors did not take such a position but were simply misunderstood.[16] And I believe that this is so.

In somewhat the same way one might adopt such an interpretation of our Scripture where it says, *Man, for all his dignity, has not understood; he has been joined with senseless beasts and has become like them;*[17] or again where it says, *Deliver not up to beasts the soul that confesses to Thee.*[18] For there are some heretics who read the Catholic Scripture, and the only reason they are heretics is that their interpretation is wrong, and they obstinately maintain their false opinions against the truth of these books. But whatever the opinion of philosophers regarding the transmigration of souls, it is not consistent with the Catholic faith to believe that the souls of beasts enter into men or that the souls of men enter into beasts.

CHAPTER 10

Further arguments against transmigration.

14. History proclaims and Scripture teaches that men by their way of life can become like the beasts of the field. Hence it is that the Psalmist whom I have quoted says, *Man, for all his dignity, has not understood; he has been joined with senseless beasts and has become like them.*[19] But this refers to the present life, not to the life after death. Hence, when the Psalmist said, *Deliver not up to beasts the soul that confesses to Thee,*[20] he did not wish his soul to be handed over to the power of such beasts as the Lord bids us beware of when He says that they are clothed in the vesture of sheep but inwardly are ravenous wolves;[21] or he did not wish his soul to be handed over to the Devil and his angels, for he is called a lion and a dragon.[22]

15. What kind of argument do philosophers offer who think that the souls of human beings can be sent into beasts, or the souls of beasts sent into human beings after death? They argue, of course, that men's ways of acting would draw them to like creatures: misers to ants, plunderers to kites, violent and proud men to lions, voluptuaries to pigs, and so forth.[23] These are the arguments which they assert,[24] but they do not advert to the fact that by this reasoning it would be quite impossible for the soul of a beast to enter into a human being after death. For a pig will certainly not be more like a human being than a pig; and when lions are tamed, they become more like dogs or even sheep than men. Hence, beasts do not give up the ways of beasts, and those that are somewhat unlike the others are none the less more like their own kind than like humans. Their difference from human beings is far greater than their difference from beasts. These souls of beasts, then, will never be souls of men if like attracts like.

Now, if this argument of the proponents of transmigration is false, how can their theory be true, since they do not offer any other argument to establish even the probability, if not the truth, of the theory? I am inclined to agree with their later followers who say that men of old put this account in their books intending that it would be understood as referring to this life, where men become like beasts by the wickedness and shamefulness of their ways and thus in a sense are turned into beasts. By this means they hoped to show erring men their degradation and thus recall them from their wicked desires.

CHAPTER 11

The absurd theories of the Manicheans about transmigration.

16. Stories are told about persons who have had some kind of recollection of having been in the bodies of animals. Now, either these stories are false, or an illusion has been produced by demons in the minds of these persons. For if it happens in sleep that a man can be induced by a false recollection into seeming to recall that he was what he was not or that he did what he did not do, it should not seem strange that demons, by God's just judgment hidden from us, may be allowed to effect something similar in men's minds even in their waking hours.

17. The Manichees, who think they are Christians or like to be considered Christians, hold a doctrine on the transplantation or transmigration of souls that is more erroneous and repulsive than that of the Gentile philosophers or other false teachers who hold such theories. For the Gentile philosophers and others distinguish between the soul and God, whereas the Manichees say that the soul is nothing else than the substance of God and is simply identifed with God Himself. They have no scruple about saying it is subject to changes unworthy of its nature, so that, according to their incredible foolishness, there is no kind of plant or worm with which the soul has not commingled or to which it cannot be transplanted.

But let them put out of their minds these subtle questions which they ponder in materialistic patterns of thought, thereby of necessity falling into a morass of false, mischievous, and ludicrous opinions, and let them hold firmly to the fundamental principle that is by nature clearly implanted in every rational soul beyond all doubt and dispute, namely, that there exists a

God who is absolutely immutable and incorruptible. Then there will suddenly be an end to their long fable in its thousand forms, which in their foolish and impious minds they have shamefully fashioned[25] about the mutability of God. 18. The material from which the human soul is made, therefore, is not an irrational soul.[26]

CHAPTER 12

The human soul was not made of anything corporeal, not even of air or heavenly fire.

What, then, is the material out of which the soul was made by the breath of God? Was it a body of an earthly and humid nature?[27] By no means! From these elements the flesh was made. For what else is slime than humid earth? And we must not suppose that the soul was made from moisture alone, as if the flesh was from earth and the soul from water. For it is utterly absurd to think that the soul of man was made of material from which the flesh of fish and birds was made.[28]

19. Was the human soul, then, made out of air? For the breath belongs to this element—but our breath, not God's. Hence, I said above[29] that this identification could be considered appropriate if we believed that God was the soul of the world (the world being considered as one large living being), so that He would have breathed the soul forth from the air of His body, just as our soul breathes its breath forth from the air of its body. But since it is clear that God is infinitely above every bodily creature in the world and above every spirit which He created, how can this explanation be seriously proposed?

Should we say that the more God is present to the whole of His creation by His unparalleled almighty power, the more He would have been able to make from air the breath which would be the soul of man? But the soul is not corporeal, and whatever comes from the corporeal elements of the world must necessarily be corporeal. Now, among the elements of the world we must include air; but even if the soul were said to have been made from the element of pure and heavenly fire, we ought not to believe it.[30] There have been philosophers who maintained that all bodies are capable of being transformed into all other bodies.[31] But that any body, earthly or heavenly, is changed into soul and becomes an incorporeal being is not to my knowledge held by anyone and is not part of our faith.

CHAPTER 13

In the body the elements of fire and air, in addition to earth, are present according to the medical writers.

20. We should perhaps give some consideration to what the medical writers not only assert but also maintain that they can prove. They say that although all bodies obviously have the solidity proper to the element of earth, nevertheless they have in them also some air, which is in the lungs and is distributed from the heart through the veins, which they call arteries.[32] Furthermore, as these writers have shown, bodies also have the warm quality of fire, which is situated in the liver, and its bright quality, which is made to flow and rise up to the highest place, namely, the brain, which is, as it were, the heaven of the body.[33]

From this source come the rays which go forth out of the eyes,[34] and from this center slender ducts go out not only to the eyes but also to the other senses, namely, to the ears, the nose, and the palate, making the sensations of hearing, smelling, and tasting possible. Moreover, they say that the sense of touch, which is all over the body, is directed from the brain also through the medulla of the neck and that of the bones to which the backbone is connected, and that from there tiny channels making sensation possible are spread throughout all parts of the body.

CHAPTER 14

What the soul perceives by the intellect is far superior to what it perceives by the senses.

It is by these messengers, therefore, that the soul perceives whatever comes to its notice in the world of bodies.[35] But the soul itself is of a quite different nature, so that when it wishes to understand the divine or God, or simply to understand itself and consider its own virtues, it turns away from this light of the eyes in order to have true and certain knowledge, and recognizing that this light is no help for its purpose, in fact is even something of an obstacle, it raises itself up to the vision of the mind. How could it belong to that lower order of being, since the summit of that order is merely the light that shines from the eyes, which is no help to the soul except for the perception of bodily forms and colors? The soul itself has innumerable objects utterly unlike every kind of body, and it sees these objects only with intellect and reason, a realm beyond the reach of the senses of the body.

CHAPTER 15

The soul governs the body by means of light and air.

21. Hence, the human soul is not made of earth or of water or of air or of fire; but it is through the more subtle elements, namely, light and air, that it governs its material and grosser body, that is, moist earth which has been made into flesh.[36] For without the two subtle elements there is no sensation in the body or any spontaneous bodily movement under the direction of the soul. And just as knowing must come before making, so sensing must come before moving. Since the soul, therefore, is incorporeal, it first acts upon a body which is akin to the incorporeal, that is, fire, or rather light and air; then through these it acts upon the grosser elements of the body, such as moisture

and earth, which form the solid mass of the body and are more disposed to be acted upon than to act.[37]

CHAPTER 16

Sensation and spontaneous motion distinguish men and animals from plants and trees.

22. The statement, *Man was made a living being,*[38] in my opinion was made precisely because he began to have sensation in his body, a clear sign of animated and living flesh. Trees, indeed, move not only by reason of an external force striking them, as when they are shaken by the winds, but also through an internal motion by which the growth of a tree according to its kind takes place and by which moisture is drawn into the roots and is changed into that which constitutes a plant or tree. This process never takes place without internal motion. But this motion is not spontaneous as is that which is connected with sensation for the management of the body, as is the case in every kind of animal, which Scripture calls a living being.[39] Even in our own case, unless that first kind of motion were also in us, our bodies would not grow nor would they produce nails or hairs. But if it alone were in us without sensation or spontaneous motion, man would not be said to have been made a living being.

CHAPTER 17

Why God breathed the breath of life into the face of man.

23. The front part of the brain, from which all the sensory nerves are spread out, is placed near the brow, and the organs of sensation are in the face, with the exception of the sense of touch, which is diffused throughout the whole body. But even this sense is known to have its path going from the front part of the brain back through the top of the head and then to the

neck and the medulla of the spine, as I have already said.[40] Thus, the face along with the rest of the body has the sense of touch, but the senses of sight, hearing, smell, and taste are found only in the face. This, I believe, is why Scripture says that God *breathed into man's face the breath of life* when *he was made a living being.*[41] Indeed, the front part of the brain is rightly considered more excellent than the back part: the former leads and the latter follows; and sensation is from the former, whereas motion is from the latter, just as planning precedes an action.

CHAPTER 18

The three parts of the brain connected with sensation, motion, and memory of motion.

24. Since there is no bodily motion following sensation without an interval of time, and since we cannot act spontaneously after a lapse of time except with the aid of memory, the medical writers point out that there are three ventricles in the brain. One of these, which is in the front near the face, is the one from which all sensation comes; the second, which is in the back of the brain near the neck, is the one from which all motion comes; the third, which is between the first two, is where the medical writers place the seat of memory. Since movement follows sensation, a man without this seat of memory would be unable to know what he ought to do if he should forget what he has done.

Now, the medical writers say that the existence of these ventricles has been proved by clear indications in cases in which these parts of the brain have been affected by some disease or pathological condition. For when sensation, motion, or memory of motion were impaired, there was a clear indication of the function of each ventricle, and by applying remedies to these different ventricles physicians determined which parts needed healing. The soul, however, acts on these parts of the brain as on its organs. It is not the same thing as they are, but it vivifies

and rules all parts, and through them it provides for the body
and for this life in virtue of which man was made a living being.

CHAPTER 19

*Bodily disorders which impair the activity of the soul in the body
and eventually cause death.*

25. In seeking for the source of the soul, that is, the quasi material out of which God made this breath which is called the
soul, no corporeal material should be considered. As God by the
excellence of His nature surpasses every creature, so does the
soul surpass every corporeal creature. But light and air are bodies of a superior nature in this corporeal world, having a superiority in so far as they are more active than passive as
contrasted with water and earth. The soul, therefore, governs
the body by means of the two elements that have a kind of resemblance to the spirit.[42]

Corporeal light, for example, announces something, and it announces it not to a being that is of the same nature as itself: it
makes the announcement to the soul, but the light making the
announcement is not soul.[43] And when the soul is distressed because of a bodily affliction, it is discovered that its activity of
ruling the body is impeded by reason of a rupture of the balance
in the system, and this affliction is called pain. Moreoever, the
air which is diffused throughout the nerves[44] obeys the will so
as to move the members, but the air itself is not the will. Furthermore, the central part of the brain signals the motions in the
body, which the memory is to retain,[45] but it is not the memory.
Finally, when these functions fail competely because of some affliction or disturbance, the messengers of sensation and the
agents of motion cease to operate; and the soul, which seems to
have no further reason for remaining, departs. But if they do
not fail as completely as happens in death, the soul's attention[46]
is disturbed and it is like a man who tries unsuccessfully to put
back things that keep falling. In this case, from the nature of the

disturbance the physicians can know what part of the system is causing the dysfunction, so that, if possible, a remedy may be applied.

CHAPTER 20

The soul is distinct from the organs of the body.

26. We must distinguish the soul itself from its corporeal agents, whether vessels or organs or whatever else they may be called. The difference is evident from the fact that the soul is frequently concentrated in thought and turns itself away from everything, so that it is ignorant of many things which are present before the eyes when they are wide open and able to see. And if a person is intensely preoccupied with his thoughts while walking, he will suddenly stop and withdraw the command of the will which had set his feet in motion. On the other hand, if his concentration is not intense enough to bring him to a halt but is sufficient to keep him from attending to the motion of his body as brought to him in a message from the central part of the brain,[47] he sometimes forgets where he came from and where he is going, and without realizing it he passes by the villa for which he was heading, all this time enjoying health of body while his soul is off somewhere else.

There are corporeal particles of the corporeal heaven, that is, particles of light and air, which are the first to receive the commands of the soul which vivifies the body because they are closer to an incorporeal substance than water and earth are. The soul, then, uses these finer elements in administering the mass of the body.[48] Now, it is not clear whether God took the elements of light and air from the heavens which were round the earth and over it and mingled or joined them with the body of the living man, or whether He made them as He did flesh from the slime of the earth; but this question is not relevant to our enquiry. For it is believable that every bodily substance can be changed into every other bodily substance,[49] but to believe that any bodily substance can be changed into soul is absurd.

CHAPTER 21

The soul is incorporeal.

27. Therefore, no attention should be paid to the opinion of those who have said that the soul is from a fifth corporeal element, not earth or water or air or fire (whether earthly fire familiar to us, which is always in motion, or heavenly fire, which is pure and bright), but some other kind of being, without any established name, which is a body.⁵⁰ If those who follow this opinion agree with us on the definition of a body, namely, any substance occupying space with its length, breadth, and height,⁵¹ the soul is not that and must not be thought to be made of that. For whatever is of that nature, to put the matter briefly, can be divided or circumscribed by lines in any of its parts. But if the soul were capable of this, it could not know of lines that cannot be cut lengthwise, though it realizes full well that such lines cannot be found in the world of bodies.⁵²

28. The soul does not think of itself in this manner, for it cannot be ignorant of itself even when it is seeking to know itself. For when it seeks itself, it knows that it seeks itself, a fact it would not know unless it knew itself. For the source in which it seeks itself is itself. When, therefore, it knows itself as seeking, it certainly knows itself. Now, in its entire being it knows all that it knows; and therefore, when it knows itself as seeking, in its entire being it knows itself; and therefore it knows itself entirely. For it is not something else but itself that it knows in its entire being.

Why, then, is it still seeking itself if it knows itself as seeking? For if it did not know itself, it could not know itself as seeking itself. But this applies to the present. What it seeks to know about itself is what it was formerly or what it is going to be. Therefore, it should now cease suspecting that it is a body, because if it were, it would know itself as such, as it knows itself better than it knows heaven and earth, which it knows through the eyes of the body.

29. I pass over that power which the soul obviously possesses in common with the beasts of the field and the birds of the air

that make their way back to their stalls or nests, a power of the soul by which images of all corporeal things are received and which itself is not similar in any way to any corporeal substance. Now surely that wherein the likenesses of corporeal beings are contained ought to be like corporeal beings. But if this power of the soul is not corporeal, because it is undeniable that the images of bodies are not only stored there in memory but also are fashioned at will in countless numbers, how much more impossible is it for the soul to be like a body by reason of any other power it possesses?

30. Now, if certain writers say that in another sense everything that exists, namely, every nature and substance, is a body,[53] we should not accept this statement for fear that we may be unable to find any words to distinguish bodies and nonbodies; but at the same time we should not be inordinately anxious about a word.[54]

My way of putting it is this: whatever the soul is, it is not one of the four familiar elements, which are obviously bodies; and on the other hand, it is not identified with God. The best words to designate it are "soul" or "life-spirit." I add the word "life" because the air is also usually called "spirit."[55] However, men have called this same air "soul" (anima), so that it is impossible to find a word by which we can precisely distinguish this thing which is not a body, nor God, nor life without sensation (which apparently exists in trees), nor life without a rational mind (such as is found in beasts), but a life now inferior to that of the angels, but destined to be one with their life if in this world it lives according to the will of its Creator.

31. What, then, is the origin of the soul, that is, from what material was it made (if I may use the expression)? Or from what perfect and blessed substance did it emanate? Or was it simply made from nothing? Although we may have doubts about this problem and continue to search for a solution, there should be absolutely no doubt about the following: if it was something else before it became a soul, whatever it was, it was made by God; and in its present state it has been made by God to be a living soul. For either it was nothing or it was something other than what it now is.

But I have given enough attention to this part of our study about what could be called the material from which the soul was made.

CHAPTER 22

Did God create a causal reason of man's soul on the sixth day?

32. If the soul was in no sense existing, we must ask how it can be explained that its causal reason was said to have existed in the works which God made on the first six days when He made man to His image.[56] Man's creation according to the image of God, of course, can be rightly understood only in respect of his soul.

When we say that, when God created all things simultaneously, He created not the things and substances themselves that were to be, but rather the causal reasons of those things, we must be on our guard lest we seem to be talking nonsense. For what are these causal reasons according to which it could be said that God made in His image the man whose body He had not yet formed from the slime of the earth and into whom He had not yet breathed a soul? And even if the human body had a hidden causal reason by virtue of which it was one day to be formed, there existed the material out of which it would be formed, that is, the earth, in which it is clear that the causal reason lay hidden after the manner of a seed. But what causal reason was originally hidden away in the created world for the soul that was to be made, that is, the breath that was to be made which would be the soul of man, when God said, *Let Us make mankind to Our image and likeness*[57] (which cannot be rightly understood except in reference to the soul), if there was no substance in which it could be hidden away?

33. Now if this reason-principle was in God and not in creation, it was not yet created. How, then, was it said, *God made man to His image?*[58] But if it was already in creation, that is, in the things which God had made all together, in what creature was it? In a spiritual creature? A corporeal creature? If it was in

a spiritual creature, did it act in any way on bodies in the universe, whether heavenly or earthly? Or was it free of any such activity[59] as it existed in that spiritual creature before man was created in his own proper nature, just as in man himself, when he is duly constituted in his own proper life, there is present in a hidden and dormant state the causal principle of generation, which does not operate except through intercourse and conception? And what of that spiritual creature in which this causal reason lay hidden? Was it performing no function of its own? Why, then, had it been created? Was it in order to hold the causal reason of the future human soul or souls, as if they could not exist in themselves but only in some creature living its own life, just as the causal reason of generation cannot exist except in beings already existing and complete?

Some spiritual creature, therefore, was made to beget the soul, and in this creature was the causal reason of the future soul. That soul, then, does not come to be until God makes it to be breathed into man. In human procreation it is only God who creates and forms the new life, whether in the seed or in the infant already conceived, through His Wisdom that reaches everywhere because of Its purity, so that nothing defiled gains entrance into It,[60] while It reaches from end to end mightily and governs all graciously.[61] But I have difficulty understanding how for this one purpose some spiritual creature was made which was not mentioned in the works God created on the six days, although God is said to have created man on the sixth day. On that sixth day He did not yet make man in his own proper nature, but (according to our supposition) He made him in the causal reason placed in that creature which has not been mentioned in Scripture. There was a graver reason why that creature ought to have been mentioned: it was so perfected that it did not have to wait to be made according to its prior causal reason.

CHAPTER 23

*If a causal reason of man's soul was created, where was it stored
away? In the angels?*

34. If the day which God first made is rightly understood as
spiritual and intellectual being,[62] could it be that, when God
made man to His image on the sixth day, He placed in this spiritual and intellectual creation the causal reason of the soul which
was to be made later? Thus He would have created in advance
the cause and formative principle by which He would make
man after the seven days, and this would mean that He created
the causal reason of man's body in the earth and the causal reason of his soul in the creation of the first day.

But when this is said, what does it mean except that the angelic spiritual creation in a sense begets the human soul if there
is pre-existing in that spiritual creation the causal reason of the
human soul yet to be created, just as in man there is the causal
reason of his future offspring? Human beings, according to this
explanation, are parents of human bodies, and angels are parents of human souls, but God is the Creator of both souls and
bodies, creating bodies through men, and souls through angels.
Or can we say that He created the first body from the earth and
the first soul from the angelic nature, after placing the causal
reasons there when He originally made man in those beings
which He created simultaneously, and that subsequently He
created men from men, the body from the body and the soul
from the soul? This is a knotty problem, for it is hard to understand how the soul can be the child of an angel or of angels; but
it is far more difficult to understand how it could be the child
of the corporeal heaven, or, worse yet, of the sea and earth.

If it is absurd, therefore, to think that God laid away the causal reason of the soul in the realm of angelic beings, it would be
even more absurd to suppose that the causal reason was previously made in a corporeal creature when God was making man
to His image before He formed him in due time from the slime
of the earth and breathed life into him.

Chapter 24

The soul of the first man was created in its own proper being on the first day and laid away until God breathed it into the body He formed from the earth.

35. There is another interpretation which may be the true one, and certainly it seems to me more acceptable to human reason. Let us suppose that in the original works created simultaneously God also created the human soul, which in due time He would breathe into the members of the body formed from the slime of the earth. God had created, of course, the causal reason of the body in the works of the six days, which He created simultaneously, and by that causal reason He made the human body when the time came. Now the expression, *in His image*, can apply only to the soul, and the expression, *male and female*, can be properly understood as referring only to the body. If the authority of Scripture, therefore, and the light of reason do not contradict us, let us assume that man was made on the sixth day in the sense that the causal reason of his body was created in the elements of the world, but that his soul in its own proper being was already created with the making of the first day, and that thus created it lay hidden in the works of God until at the proper time He would breathe it into the body He would form from the slime of the earth.[63]

Chapter 25

If the soul was created before entering the body, did it enter the body by its own choice?

36. At this point we have a question of some importance to consider. If the soul was already created and hidden away, where could it be better off than where it was? What was the reason that a soul living an innocent life should be put into the life of our flesh, in which by sin it would offend Him who cre-

ated it, with the result that it would deserve the burden of toil and the penalty of suffering?

Should we say that the soul was inclined by its own will to govern a body and that in this life of the body, since it can be lived in a good or evil manner, it would have the object of its choice, the reward for goodness or the punishment for evil? This supposition would not contradict St. Paul's statement in which he says that those not yet born had done no good or evil.[64] The inclination of the will for a body is not a good or evil act for which an account must be rendered before God our Judge, when each one will receive his reward, whether good or bad, according to what he has done in the body.[65]

Why, then, can we not go further and suppose that the soul has come to the body by the command of God? Thus, if in the body it should choose to live its life according to God's laws, it would receive the reward of everlasting life in the company of the angels; but if it should despise His laws, it would undergo the punishment it deserved either in long-lasting pain or ever-lasting fire. Can it be that this theory is not acceptable because obeying the will of God is a good action, and therefore this explanation is contrary to the principle that the unborn have done neither good nor evil?

CHAPTER 26

If the soul willed to be united with the body, it had no knowledge of the future.

37. If this is so, we will admit also that the soul was not originally created so as to know its future works whether good or evil. For it is quite unbelievable that it could have tended of its own free will to life in the body if it foreknew that it would commit certain sins by which it would justly incur perpetual punishment. It is surely right in all things to praise the Creator, who[66] made them all very good. And He must not be praised only for those beings to which He gave foreknowledge. He is rightly praised also because He created the beasts; and yet hu-

man nature, even in sinners, is superior to the beasts. For it is
the nature of man that is from God, not the wickedness in
which he implicates himself by an evil use of free will. Nevertheless, if he did not possess free will, he would not have the
same high excellence in nature.

For we must think of a man living justly but not having any
foreknowledge of future events, and there we must observe
how, when he has good will, he is not prevented from leading
a life upright and pleasing to God, because in his ignorance of
the future he lives by faith. Whoever is unwilling to admit the
existence of such a creature in the real world denies the goodness of God. But whoever does not wish such a creature to undergo punishment for his sins is an enemy of justice.

CHAPTER 27

*The soul naturally tends to a body. The spiritual matter of the soul
was concreated with its form.*

38. If the soul is made to be sent into a body, we may ask
whether it is compelled to go though unwilling. But it is more
reasonable to suppose that it has such a will by nature, that is,
the nature with which it is created is such that it wishes a
body,[67] just as it is natural for us to wish to live, although living
an evil life is not prompted by nature but by a perverse will, for
which just punishment is given.

39. It is useless, then, for one to ask about the quasi material
from which the soul has been made, if we are right in understanding that it was made in those first works when day was
made. For just as those creatures which were not existing were
made, so the soul was made along with them. But if there was
any matter to be formed, either corporeal or spiritual,[68] it was
not made by anyone except God, from whom are all things; and
it preceded its formation by a priority not of time but of origin,[69] as the sound of a voice precedes a song.[70] What, then, is
more reasonable than to assume that the soul was made of spiritual matter?

CHAPTER 28

Summary of problems regarding creation. How God has both finished and begun His works. Summary of what is certain and uncertain about the soul.

40. If anyone is unwilling to concede that the soul was made before it was breathed into the formed body of man, let him consider what his reply will be when he is asked what it is made from.[71] On the one hand, he may say that God did make or does make something out of nothing after finishing the works of His creation. He then must see how he will explain the fact that man was made on the sixth day to the image of God, which cannot be rightly understood except in reference to the soul, and he must decide in what being God made the causal reason of the soul not yet existing. On the other hand, he may say that the soul was made not from nothing but from some being already existing. He will be hard pressed to find out what that being is, whether corporeal or spiritual, and to answer the questions I have proposed above. It will still be a problem to decide in what one of the created substances originally made in the six days God made the causal reason of the soul which He had not yet made either from nothing or from something.

41. If my critic wishes to avoid these difficulties by saying that man was made from the slime of the earth on the sixth day but that this fact is stated later simply as a recapitulation,[72] he must consider what he will say about the woman, since Scripture says, *Male and female He made them, and He blessed them.*[73] And if he replies that she also was made on the sixth day from the rib of man, he must decide in what sense he can assert that on the sixth day the birds were made which were brought to Adam, for Scripture declares that every kind of bird was created from the waters on the fifth day. And he must also explain how the trees planted in Paradise can be said to have been made on the sixth day, for Scripture has assigned the creation of trees to the third day. Let him also ponder the meaning of the words, *And again from the earth He made to grow every tree that is pleasant to the sight and good for food.*[74] He surely cannot say that what the

earth put forth on the third day was not pleasant to the sight and good for food, for it was among the works which God made, and all were very good.

He must also explain the meaning of the words, *Again God formed from the earth all the beasts of the field and all the birds of heaven,*[75] as if these had not all been made at the beginning, or rather as if none of these had been made before. For Scripture does not say, "And again God formed from the earth the other beasts of the field and the other birds of heaven," as if these were the ones that the earth did not produce on the sixth day or the water on the fifth. But Scripture plainly says, *all the beasts* and *all the birds.*

He must also give thought to how God made all things in six days: on the first day, day itself; on the second, the firmament; on the third, sea and earth, and from earth, plants and trees; on the fourth, the lights of heaven and the stars; on the fifth, the living beings of the waters; on the sixth, the living beings of the earth. And then he must explain the words, *When day was made, God made heaven and earth and every green thing of the field,*[76] for when day was made, He made only day itself. Moreover, how did God make *every green thing of the field before it appeared above the earth and all the grass before it sprang forth?*[77] For who would not say that it was made when it sprang forth, not before it sprang forth, unless the words of Scripture instructed him otherwise?

Let him remember also that Scripture says: *He who lives forever created all things together.*[78] And let him see how all things can be said to have been created together if their creation is separated by intervals not of hours only but even of days. He should take care also to show how these two statements, seemingly contradictory, can both be true: first, that on the seventh day God rested from all His works, which the Book of Genesis says; and second, that He works even until now, as our Lord says.[79] He should also explain how things said to be finished are also said to have been begun.[80]

42. Because of all these testimonies of Sacred Scripture, of which no one doubts the truth except an infidel or a scoffer, I have been let to hold that God first created all things simulta-

neously at the beginning of the ages, creating some in their own substances and others in pre-existing causes. Hence, the all-powerful God has made not only what is existing at the present but also what is to be, and from the making of these creatures He has rested in order to create subsequently, by administering and ruling these things, the order of time and of temporal things. Thus, He had finished His works in the sense that He had set limits for the kinds of creatures, and He had begun them inasmuch as they must reproduce themselves throughout the ages. In view of the works finished, then, He rests, and in view of the works begun He is working even until now. But if someone can find a better interpretation of these texts, I will not resist him, I will even support him.

43. With regard to the soul, which God breathed into the face of man, I have no firm position except to say that it is from God in such a way that it is not the substance of God; that it is incorporeal, that is, not a body but a spirit; that it is not born of God's substance and does not proceed from God's substance, but is made by God; that it is not made by the conversion of a body or an irrational soul into it; and hence it is made from nothing. And I hold that it is immortal in view of the nature of the life that it has, which it cannot possibly lose; but that in view of a kind of mutability that it has, making it possible to change for the better or the worse, it can be rightly considered also as mortal, for only He has true immortality of whom it has been justly said, *who alone has immortality.*[81]

The other interpretations that I have put forth in this book should be of some interest to the reader: either he may discover from them how one must investigate without rash assertions the questions which Scripture does not clearly answer; or if my way of investigation is not to his liking, he may see how I carried it on, and as a result I hope that if he can instruct me he will not refuse, and that if He cannot he will join me in searching for someone from whom both of us may learn.[82]

BOOK EIGHT
Paradise and the Command Given to Adam

Chapter 1

Different ways of interpreting Paradise. The account in Genesis is written in the style of history, not in that of allegory.

1. *And God planted a garden in Eden in the East, and there He put the man whom He formed.*[1] I am aware that many authors have written at great length on Paradise, but their theories on the subject in general can be reduced to three. There is, first, the opinion of those who interpret the word "paradise" in an exclusively corporeal sense. Then there are those who prefer to give an exclusively spiritual meaning to the word. Finally, there are those who accept the word "paradise" in both senses, sometimes corporeally and at other times spiritually.[2]

Briefly, then, I admit that the third interpretation appeals to me. According to it I have now undertaken to treat of Paradise, if God will make this possible. Man was made from the slime of the earth—and that certainly means a human body—and was placed in a corporeal paradise. Adam, of course, signifies something else where St. Paul speaks of him as a type of the One who was to come.[3] But he is understood here as a man constituted in his own proper nature, who lived a certain number of years, was the father of numerous children, and died as other men die, although he was not born of parents as other men are but made from the earth, as was proper for the first man. Consequently, Paradise, in which God placed him,[4] should be understood as simply a place, that is, a land,[5] where an earthly man would live.

2. The narrative in these books is not written in a literary style proper to allegory, as in the Canticle of Canticles, but from beginning to end in a style proper to history, as in the Books of Kings and the other works of that type. But since those historical books contain matters familiar to us from common human experience, they are easily and readily taken in a literal sense at the first reading, so that the meaning of the historical events in relation to the future may also be subsequently drawn from them.

But in Genesis, since there are matters beyond the ken of readers who focus their gaze on the familiar course of nature, they are unwilling to have these matters taken in the literal sense but prefer to understand them in a figurative sense. Accordingly, they assume that history, that is, the literal narrative of events that happened, begins at the point where Adam and Eve, dismissed from Paradise, were joined in sexual union and begot children. Do they think that all the subsequent events of the narrative are parallel to our human experience, such as the great number of years that Adam and Eve lived, the translation of Enoch, conception in the case of an old and sterile woman, and so forth?[6]

3. But there is a difference, they say, between a narration of wondrous deeds and a narration of the making of creatures. In the former case the very unfamiliar character of the deeds points to a distinction between the ordinary works of nature and miracles or marvels, as they are called, whereas in the latter case the creation of natures is presented.

In answer to this, I say that the creation of natures narrated here is something unfamiliar, because it is the creation of things for the first time. For what is so unique and unparalleled in the constitution of the things of the world as the world itself? Surely we are not to believe that God did not make the world because He does not make worlds today, or that He did not make the sun because He does not make suns today. And this response should be given not just to those who question the creation of Paradise but also to those who question the creation of man. But now, since they believe that the first man was made by God as no other has been made, why are they unwilling to believe that Paradise was made just as they now see forests are made?

4. I am speaking, of course, to those who accept the authority of Scripture; for some of them want Paradise to be understood not in the literal sense but figuratively. Elsewhere I have dealt in a different manner with those who are determined adversaries of the Book of Genesis.[7] Nevertheless, even in that work of mine I defended, as well as I was able, the literal meaning of the narrative. As a result, those who are moved by irrational motives, being obstinate or dull, may refuse to believe what Genesis says but cannot find any basis for proving it false.

On the other hand, some of our writers, who have faith in the inspired books of Scripture, are unwilling to accept Paradise in the literal sense, that is, a delightful place shaded with fruit-bearing trees, spacious, and irrigated by an abundant source of water.[8] Since they see that its extensive green fields, without any work of man, are flourishing by the hidden work of God, they reject the literal meaning of this account. But I wonder how they believe that man himself was made in a manner completely beyond their experience. If he is to be understood in a figurative sense, who begot Cain, Abel, and Seth? Did they exist only figuratively, and were they not men born of men?

Let them, therefore, examine the matter more closely to see where their presupposition leads, and let them try with us first to take in the proper sense all the events narrated. For who would not later applaud them when they understand what these events also point to in the figurative sense as signs of spiritual realities or affections or even future events? Of course, if it became utterly impossible to safeguard the truth of the faith while accepting in a material sense what is named as material in Genesis, what alternative would be left for us except to take these statements in a figurative sense rather than to be guilty of an impious attack on Sacred Scripture? But if accepting these statements in a material sense not only does not impede the understanding of the narrative of the inspired word but actually helps it, there will be no one, I think, so headstrong in disbelief as to see the proper sense to be in agreement with the rule of

faith and yet to prefer to remain in his original position, insisting that it can be taken only in the figurative sense.[9]

CHAPTER 2

In my book on Genesis against the Manicheans I frequently explained
the text in the figurative meaning. I now believe that the literal
meaning must be sought.

5. Shortly after my conversion I wrote two books against the
Manicheans,[10] who are in error not because they are mistaken
in their interpretation of the Old Testament but because they
completely reject it with impious scorn. I wanted without delay
either to refute their aberrations or to direct them to seek in the
books which they hated the faith taught by Christ and the Gospels. At that time I did not see how all of Genesis could be taken
in the proper sense, and it seemed to me more and more impossible, or at least scarcely possible or very difficult, for all of it
to be so understood.

But not willing to be deterred from my purpose, whenever I
was unable to discover the literal meaning of a passage, I explained its figurative meaning as briefly and as clearly as I was
able, so that the Manichees might not be discouraged by the
length of the work or the obscurity of its contents and thus put
the book aside. I was mindful, however, of the purpose which
I had set before me and which I was unable to achieve, that is,
to show how everything in Genesis is to be understood first of
all not in the figurative but in the proper sense; and since I did
not completely despair of the possibility of understanding it all
in this sense, I made the following statement in the first part of
Book Two:

If anyone wishes to interpret in a literal sense everything
written in this book, that is, to understand it only according
to the letter of the text, and if in doing this he avoids blas-
phemy and explains everything in agreement with the
Catholic faith, not only is he not to be discouraged, but he

should be considered an outstanding interpreter worthy of great praise. But if there is no way of understanding a passage in a devout sense worthy of God without assuming that it has been set forth in figures and enigmas, we should remember that we have the authority of the apostles, who solved so many enigmas in the books of the Old Testament, and we should stay with the kind of interpretation which we have adopted with the help of Him who bids us ask, seek, and knock.[11] Thus, our purpose should be to explain all these figures of things according to the Catholic faith, whether the matter belongs to history or prophecy, without prejudice to a better and more exact treatment which we or others, whom the Lord is pleased to enlighten, may subsequently undertake.[12]

This is what I said then. And now the Lord has wished that I should look at and consider the same matter more thoroughly, and I believe that according to His will I can reasonably hope that I shall be able to show how the Book of Genesis has been written with a proper rather than an allegorical meaning in view. With this in mind, let us examine the account of Paradise which follows, using the method with which we succeeded in explaining what went before.

CHAPTER 3

On the third day God had created in their causal reasons the plants and trees of Paradise.

6. God, therefore, *planted a garden* in a delightful place (this is the meaning of *in Eden*) *in the East, and there He put the man whom He had formed.*[13] Thus it is stated in Scripture because thus it was done. Then Scripture recapitulates in order to show how God did what has been mentioned very briefly, that is, how He planted Paradise and put there the man whom He had formed. For Scripture goes on to say, *And again from the earth God made to grow every tree that is pleasant to the sight and good for food.*[14]

Scripture does not say, "God made to grow from the earth another tree" or "the rest of the trees," but, *Again from the earth
He made to grow every tree that is pleasant to the sight and good for
food.* The earth had already produced on the third day every tree
pleasant to the sight and good for food. For on the sixth day God
had said, *See, I have given you every seed-bearing plant bearing its
seed over all the earth, and every fruit tree that has seed-bearing fruit.
These will be food for you.* [15] Can it be that first God gave one tree
and now He wished to give another? I do not think so. But since
the trees planted in Paradise are of the kinds which earth had
already produced on the third day, it again produced them in its
own time. For when Scripture says that on the third day earth
produced these trees, this was done in causes in the earth, that
is, earth in the hidden recesses of its being had then received the
power of producing them, and by this power even now earth
puts forth similar trees to be seen in their own time.

7. The words, therefore, which God spoke on the sixth day,
*See, I have given you every seed-bearing plant bearing its seed over all
the earth* and so forth, were not spoken by the sound of a voice
uttered in time but by the creative power, which is God's Word.
But it is only by sounds uttered in time that man can be
told what God spoke without sounds measured by time. For the
man formed from the slime of the earth and made a living being
by the breath of God and all the members of the human race descended from him were destined to eat the fruit of these plants
and trees which would spring forth over the earth from the productive power that earth had already received. God, therefore,
stored away in creatures the causal reasons of the plants and
trees that were to be, and, as if these plants and trees already existed, He spoke in that interior and transcendent truth which
eye has not seen nor ear heard, but which the Holy Spirit certainly has revealed to the writer.

CHAPTER 4

The literal and the figurative meanings in Scripture texts. The meaning of Genesis 2.9.

8. Serious consideration must be given to the words that follow: . . . *the tree of life also in the midst of the garden, and the tree of knowledge of good and evil.*[16] We should take care not to be compelled to turn to allegory and end up with these not being trees at all but something else signified by the name of tree. For it is said of wisdom, *She is a tree of life to all those who lay hold of her.*[17] Nevertheless, although there is the eternal Jerusalem in heaven, a city has been built on earth by which the heavenly Jerusalem is signified. Moreover, Sarah and Hagar signify the two testaments, yet they were two women who actually existed.[18] Finally, although Christ through the suffering on the wood of the cross bathes us with spiritual water, nevertheless He was also the rock which when struck by wood poured forth water for the thirsting people, concerning which it is said, *And the Rock was Christ.*[19]

All these events signified something other than what they were, but none the less they themselves existed in the world of material reality. And when they were narrated by the sacred historian, they were not set forth in figurative language, but rather in a narrative of events that prefigured what was to come.

Hence, there was a tree of life no less than the Rock which was Christ, and God did not want man to live in Paradise without the mysteries of spiritual things made present in material things. Man, then, had food in the other trees, but in the tree of life there was a sacrament.[20] And what did it signify except wisdom, of which it was said, *She is a tree of life to those who lay hold of her,* just as it was said of Christ that He is a Rock pouring forth water to all who thirst for Him?

He is rightly called by the name of that which signified Him before His coming. He is the Lamb immolated on the Passover; nevertheless, that immolation was represented not just by words but also by a real act. For one cannot say that that lamb was not a lamb; it was truly a lamb, and it was slain, and it was eaten.[21]

And although this was something that really happened, something else was prefigured by it. This event was different from that of the fatted calf which was killed for the feast in honor of the younger son on his return home.[22] In the latter case the narrative itself is a narrative of figures or types; it is not a matter of a figurative meaning of events that really happened.[23] The narrator was not the Evangelist but the Lord Himself, although the Evangelist did state that the Lord told the parable. Thus, what the Evangelist told did happen: the Lord did speak these words. But the narration told by our Lord was a parable, and in this kind of narrative one is never expected to demonstrate that events told in the story literally happened.

Christ is the Stone anointed by Jacob,[24] and *the Stone rejected by the builders, which has become the head of the corner.*[25] But in the first case there is reference to an event that really happened, whereas in the second case an event is foretold in figurative language. The former was an account of a past event written by a historian, but the latter was a proclamation by a prophet who was foretelling only events to come.

CHAPTER 5

The tree of life had a special nourishing power and a symbolic meaning.

9. Thus Wisdom, namely, Christ Himself, is the tree of life in the spiritual paradise to which He sent the thief from the cross.[26] But a tree of life which would signify Wisdom was also created in the earthly paradise. This is the meaning of Scripture, which in narrating the historical events that happened has told how man was made in the body and how living in the body he was placed in the earthly paradise.

Now if anyone thinks that souls on leaving the body are confined within visible corporeal places, though they are themselves without bodies, he may defend his opinion. There will be those who will support this position and even go so far as to hold that the rich man tormented by thirst was surely in a corporeal place, and they will not hesitate to declare that his soul was obviously corporeal in view of his parched tongue and the drop of water he craved from the finger of Lazarus.[27] For my part, I have no desire to rush into controversy with them on a question so perplexing; it is better to doubt about the mysterious than to dispute about the uncertain.

I have no doubt that the rich man is to be understood as being in the burning heat of punishment and the poor man in the cool refreshment of joy. But how we must interpret the flame of hell, the bosom of Abraham,[28] the tongue of the rich man, the finger of the poor man, the excruciating thirst, the refreshing drop of water, may possibly be discovered with considerable effort by those who humbly seek, whereas it will never be found by those who engage in acrimonious debate.

I must, then, immediately give my answer to the question we are considering, so that I may not be delayed by a problem which is profound and in need of lengthy discussions. If souls are contained in corporeal places even after they have left the body, the thief on the cross could have been brought to that paradise where the first man had been placed in the body. Having said this, I may add that with the help of a more appropriate passage in Scripture, if the need arises, we may hope somehow to determine what we should seek or what we should think in this matter.

10. But I have no doubt, and I do not think anyone else has doubts, that Wisdom is not a body and therefore not a tree. It was possible, however, that through a tree, that is, through a corporeal creature used as a sacrament, Wisdom could be signified in the earthly Paradise.[29] But this interpretation is not accepted by the reader who does not see in Scripture the many material sacraments of spiritual things, or maintains that the first man could not have been able to rule his life according to such a sacrament. Yet St. Paul speaks of this sort of sight when he says of the woman whom we believe to have been made from a rib of the man, *For this reason a man will leave his father and his mother and will cleave to his wife; and they will be two in one flesh. This is a great sacrament in Christ and in the Church.*[30]

It is strange and hardly tolerable to observe how men want to take "Paradise" as figuratively spoken and yet do not want the physical reality to have a figurative meaning.[31] But if in the case of narratives such as those about Hagar and Sarah and Ishmael and Isaac they admit that there is both historical fact and symbolic meaning,[32] I fail to see why they do not grant that the tree of life both existed as a real material tree and at the same time symbolized Wisdom.

11. It should be noted, moreover, that the fruit of the tree of life was material food, and yet it had the power to give lasting health and vigor to man's body, not in the manner of other foods but by a mysterious communication of vitality. In the case of bread on another occasion, although it was ordinary bread, it had something more in it; and by one piece of it God kept a man from hunger for a period of forty days.[33]

Shall we hesitate to believe that by the fruit of a tree, in view of its higher meaning, God gave to man protection against physical deterioration through sickness or age and against death itself? For we know that in another instance God gave to the food of man a property so marvelous that meal and oil in earthen vessels restored his failing strength and yet itself did not fail.[34] Let our adversary step forward and say that it was fitting for God to have worked miracles like this in our land but not in Paradise. But surely He worked a greater miracle in Paradise when He made man from the dust and woman from the rib of man than He worked in our land when He raised the dead to life.

<h2 style="text-align:center">CHAPTER 6</h2>

The tree of the knowledge of good and evil (Gen. 2.9).

12. We must now consider the tree of the knowledge of good and evil.[35] This tree was certainly visible and corporeal, as the other trees were. That it was a tree, therefore, there is no doubt; but what we must seek is the reason for its name.

For my part, after diligent study of that problem, I am strongly attached to the opinion of those who say that the tree did not produce harmful fruit (for He who had made all things very good[36] had planted nothing evil in Paradise), but the evil for man was his transgression of God's command.[37] It was proper that man, placed in a state of dependence upon the Lord God, should be given some prohibition, so that obedience would be the virtue by which he would please his Lord. I can truthfully say that this is the only virtue of every rational creature who lives his life under God's rule, and that the fundamental and greatest vice is the overweening pride by which one wishes to have independence to his own ruin, and the name of this vice is disobedience. There would not, therefore, be any way for a man to realize and feel that he was subject to the Lord unless he was given some command.

The tree, then, was not evil, but it was called the tree of the knowledge of good and evil because, on the supposition that man would eat of its fruit after the prohibition, there was within it the future violation of the command, and because of this transgression man would learn by undergoing punishment the difference between the good of obedience and the evil of disobedience. Scripture, therefore, has not spoken figuratively about this tree: we must understand that it has described a real tree. And this tree was named not from the apples or fruit that grew on it but from what had followed after it had been touched against God's command.[38]

CHAPTER 7

The four rivers of Paradise. The literal meaning (Gen. 2.10–14).

13. *And a river which watered Paradise went out of Eden, and from there it was divided into four parts. The name of the one is Phison; this is the one that flows around all the land of Evilat, where there is gold; and the gold of that land is good, and carbuncle and emerald are found there. And the name of the second river is Geon; it is the one that flows around the whole land of Ethiopia. And the name of the third river is Tigris, which flows by the land of the Assyrians. And the fourth river is the Euphrates.*[39]

In discussing these rivers, need I make any further effort to establish the fact that they are true rivers, not just figurative expressions without a corresponding reality in the literal sense, as if the names would signify something else and not rivers at all, in spite of the fact that they are well known in the lands through which they flow and are spoken of in nearly all the world?[40] As a matter of fact, it is evident that the four rivers are precisely those named. In the case of two of them, their names were changed in ancient times, as happened also to the Tiber, which was once called the Albula.[41]

The Geon is the river which is now called the Nile, and Phison was once the name of the river which they call the Ganges today.[42] The other two, the Tigris and the Euphrates, have kept their ancient names. These facts should persuade us to take the first meaning of the other details of this narrative in the literal sense and not to assume that the account is allegorical, but that the facts narrated really exist and that they also have some figurative meaning.[43]

This is not to say that a parable cannot take a detail from reality although the parable itself is obviously not intended to describe reality in the literal sense. An example is the parable told by our Lord about the man who was going down from Jerusalem to Jericho and fell among robbers.[44] One senses and clearly sees that this is a parable and that the whole account is figurative. Nevertheless, the two cities named in the parable are found even today existing in the same places. We would take the four rivers also in this way if we were under any compulsion to interpret the other details of the narrative about Paradise not literally but figuratively. But no good reason prohibits us from understanding things first in the literal sense. We can, therefore, follow with simplicity the authority of Scripture in the narration of these historical realities, taking them first as true historical realities and then searching for any further meaning they may have.

14. Are we hesitant to admit this because it is said that the source of some of these rivers is known and of others is completely unknown, and therefore we cannot take the account lit-

erally since the four rivers in Genesis flow from the one river of Paradise? But as we have no knowledge at all about the location of Paradise, we should rather assume that the river there is divided into four rivers, precisely as Scripture says, and that those rivers whose sources are said to be known have flowed somewhere under the earth and after flowing a great distance have sprung forth in other places which have been designated as their sources. For it is common knowledge that this sort of thing happens in the case of certain rivers, although it is known to us only when the underground courses are short.

A river, therefore, went out from Eden, that is, from the delightful place, and it watered Paradise, that is, all the beautiful and fruit-bearing trees which shaded all the land of that region.

CHAPTER 8

Why God wished man to cultivate the soil in Paradise (Gen. 2.15).

15. *And the Lord God took the man whom He made and placed him in Paradise to cultivate and guard it. And the Lord God commanded Adam, saying, "You may eat of every tree that is in Paradise, but of the tree of the knowledge of good and evil you shall not eat. In the day that you eat of it you shall die."*[45]

Having previously stated briefly that God had planted Paradise and placed there the man whom He had formed,[46] the sacred writer repeats this in order to tell how Paradise was established. Now, therefore, in his repetition he also has recounted under what conditions God had placed there the man whom He made. Let us, then, look into the meaning of the expression "to cultivate and guard."

What was the man to cultivate and guard? Did the Lord wish that the first man should work at tilling the soil? Surely he was not condemned to labor before he sinned. This is what we should think, did we not see certain men cultivating the land with such pleasure that it is a severe punishment for them to be called away from it to something else. Whatever delight there is, therefore, in the cultivation of the land was present then much more intensely when neither soil nor weather presented any obstacle. For there was no painful effort but only pleasure and enthusiasm when the gifts of God's creation came forth in a joyful and abundant harvest with the help of man's effort. Thus greater praise was given to the Creator Himself, who had imparted to the soul of man placed in a living body the art and ability to carry out his work in accordance with what he freely wished and not in accordance with what bodily needs might force upon him against his will.

16. What more impressive and wonderful spectacle than this? Where is human reason better able to speak, as it were, to nature than when man sows the seed, plants a tree, transplants a bush, grafts a mallet-shoot,[47] and thus asks, as it were, each root and seed what it can or cannot do, why it can or cannot do it, what is the extent of the intrinsic and invisible power of numbers[48] within it, and what can be attributed to the extrinsic factors applied by human effort? And how can man better understand, than he does in reflecting on these wonders, that *Neither he who plants nor he who waters is anything, but only God, who gives the growth?*[49] For even that part of the work of production which comes from outside comes from a man whom God has also created and whom He invisibly rules and governs.

CHAPTER 9

How man in Paradise willingly and joyfully cultivated the soil.

17. Now, at this point the mind lifts up its gaze to consider the whole world like a great tree of creation. In it is found a double activity of Providence, the natural and the voluntary. The natural working of Providence can be seen in God's hidden governance of the world, by which He gives growth to trees and plants; the voluntary working of His providence can be observed in the deeds of angels and men. In the natural working of Providence the heavenly bodies above and earthly bodies be-

low follow an established order: the stars and other heavenly bodies shine, night follows day and day follows night, earth firmly established is washed and encircled by waters, air moves above it all around, trees and animals are generated and born, develop, grow old, and die; and so it is with everything else in nature that comes about by an interior, natural movement.

Of the voluntary working of Providence there are other signs: creatures are instructed and learn, fields are cultivated, societies are governed, the arts are practiced, and other activities go on both in the heavenly society and in this mortal society on earth; and the good are provided for even with the help of the wicked, though all unwittingly. In man himself the same twofold power of Providence is at work: first, there is the natural work of Providence in respect to the body, that is, in the movement by which it comes into being, develops, and grows old; and then there is the voluntary working of Providence in so far as provision is made for his food, his clothing, and his well-being. So, too, in the case of the soul: by nature it is provided that it lives and has sensation; by voluntary action it is provided that it acquires knowledge and lives in harmony.

18. In the case of a tree, the art of the husbandman works exteriorly to assist its internal development. Similarly in the case of man, in so far as his body is concerned, medicine is an external help for the intrinsic natural forces; and in so far as his soul is concerned, instruction coming from an external source contributes to the interior happiness of nature. What negligence is in cultivating a tree, that unconcern about healing is in respect of the body, and indifference about learning is in relation to the soul. A superfluity of water for a tree is like harmful food for a body or an inducement to evil for the soul.

Over all things, therefore, is God, who established all things and rules all things, who in His goodness created all substances and in His justice guides all wills. Why, then, do we depart from the truth if we assume that man was placed in Paradise with the understanding that he would till the land not in servile labor but with a spiritual pleasure befitting his dignity? What is more innocent than this work for those who are at leisure, and what more provocative of profound reflection for those who are wise?

CHAPTER 10

The meaning of "cultivate" and "guard" in Gen. 2.15.

19. Man was to guard it. But guard what? Paradise? Against whom? There was surely no fear of an invader from the vicinity, or of one who would assail the borders; no fear of a thief or an aggressor. How, then, are we to understand that a corporeal paradise could have been guarded by man with corporeal means? But Scripture did not say "to cultivate and guard Paradise"; it said simply *to cultivate and guard.*[50] But if we take care to translate literally from the Greek, the text says, *And the Lord God took the man whom He made and placed him in Paradise to cultivate and guard it (or him).*[51]

But did God place the man there to work? This is the interpretation of the translator who wrote simply "to cultivate" or "to work" *(ut operaretur)*, without an object expressed. Or was it to cultivate Paradise, that is, that the man should cultivate Paradise? The text is ambiguous. But the words seem to demand that we say not "to cultivate Paradise" *(operaretur paradisum)* but rather "to work in Paradise" *(operaretur in paradiso)*.

20. Nevertheless, let us assume that we do not take the words "to cultivate Paradise" in the sense in which we took the previous statement, *And there was not a man to cultivate the earth*[52] (while admitting, of course, that the expression "to cultivate the earth" has exactly the same structure as "to cultivate Paradise"). The text is ambiguous, and we should explore both interpretations. For if it is not necessary to say "to guard Paradise" *(paradisum custodire)*, but if we can say "to keep guard in Paradise" *(in paradiso custodire)*, then what is being guarded in Paradise? As for the expression "to work in Paradise," we have already discussed our opinion. Perhaps we should say that what man cultivated in the earth by the art of agriculture he guarded or preserved within himself by discipline.[53] I mean that just as the soil which he tilled obeyed him, so he would dutifully render to his Lord, who had given him the command, the fruit of obedience, not the thorns of disobedience. In the end, since he did not wish to remain obedient and guard within himself the likeness

of the Paradise which he cultivated, he was condemned and received a field like himself, for God said, *Thorns and thistles it shall bring forth to you.*[54]

21. But if we understand the expression as meaning "to cultivate Paradise" and "to guard Paradise," man could indeed cultivate Paradise, as explained above, by the art of agriculture; he could not guard it, however, against evil or hostile men because there were none, but perhaps against beasts. But how would this be? And why? Beasts were surely not a threat to man until he had sinned. For it is later said that when the beasts were brought to him, he gave names to them all.[55] Moreover, on the sixth day, by the law of God's word, he received food in common with all the beasts.[56] And if there was already something to fear in the beasts, how could one man protect this Paradise? For it was no small place that was watered by such a mighty river. And he would have to guard it if he were able to fortify it on all sides with a wall of such a nature and such a size that a serpent would not be able to make its way in. But it would be an incredible feat if he could have kept all the serpents out before he had fortified the garden on all sides.

22. Hence, why do we pass over the interpretation that is right before our eyes? Man was indeed placed in Paradise to cultivate it by the art of agriculture, as I have argued above. The exercise of this art did not involve wearisome toil but was filled with delights, suggesting noble and salutary thoughts to the mind of a wise man. And he was placed there to guard this same Paradise for himself, so as not to commit any deed by which he would deserve to be expelled from it. Finally, he was also given a command by observing which he would guard Paradise for himself in the sense that if he obeyed it he would not be driven forth from the garden. For a person is rightly said to have failed to guard his possessions if he has acted in such a way as to lose them, even if they are preserved intact for another who has found them or has deserved to receive them.

23. There is another possible meaning for these words, and I think there is good reason for preferring it: that is, God was to cultivate man and guard him.[57] For just as man cultivates the earth not to make it earth but to develop it and make it fruitful,

so God in a much deeper sense cultivates man, whom He has created and made man, so that he may be made just if he does not turn away from his Creator by pride. For this is to apostatize from God, which Scripture calls the beginning of pride: *The beginning of man's pride is to depart from the Lord.*[58] God is the immutable Good, whereas man in both soul and body is a mutable being. Therefore, unless man turns towards the immutable Good, which is God, and stands firm in Him, he cannot be formed so as to be just and happy.[59]

Therefore, the same God who creates man and makes him man also cultivates man and guards him so that he may be good and happy. Hence, in the very statement wherein man is said to cultivate the earth (which was already earth) so that it may be adorned and fruitful, there also God is said to cultivate man (who was already man) so that he may be devout and wise, and to guard him, because when he takes more delight in the power he has in himself than in that of God, who is above him, and when he condemns the authority of God, man cannot be safe.

CHAPTER 11

The author of Genesis teaches us that God is our
true Lord (Gen. 2.15).

24. Here we should observe a fact which I think has a lesson for us and calls our attention to something important. From the opening line of this sacred book, starting with the words, *In the beginning God created heaven and earth,* all the way to this point in the narrative, the expression "Lord God" is never used but only "God."[60] But now, when God placed the man in Paradise in order to cultivate and guard him by His guidance, Scripture says, *And the Lord God took the man whom He made and placed him in Paradise to cultivate and guard him.*[61]

The author is not implying that God is not Lord of the creatures mentioned above. But this account was written for man, not for the angels or other creatures, and it was to remind him how important it is for him to recognize God as his Lord, that is, to be obedient under His rule rather than to live uncontrolled and abuse his freedom. Hence, the author did not want to put this expression earlier but rather to save it for that part of the narrative where God would put man in Paradise to cultivate and to guard him. Thus he did not say, as in all the preceding instances, "And God took the man whom He made," but rather he said, *And the Lord God took the man whom He made and placed him in Paradise in order to cultivate him* so that he would be just *and guard him* so that he would be safe, doing this by His rule, which is useful not for Him but for us.

For God does not need our service, but we need His rule so that He may cultivate and guard us. Accordingly, He alone is the true Lord, because we serve Him not for His advantage and welfare but for ours. For if He needed us, by that very fact He would not be our true Lord, since through our efforts He would be helped in His need, and being subject to that need He Himself would be in servitude. With good reason the Psalmist sang: *I said to the Lord, "Thou art my God, for Thou hast no need of my goods."*[62] And what I said about our serving Him for our advantage and welfare should not be taken to mean that we expect something from Him other than Himself, who is our supreme advantage and welfare. Thus, our love for Him is freely given according to the Psalmist: *But it is good for me to adhere to God.*[63]

CHAPTER 12

God works in man by His grace.

25. Man is not so constituted that he would be able, when once created, to perform any good deed by his own powers if his Creator abandoned him. All his good action consists in his being turned to Him by whom he has been made, and in his becoming, by his Creator's power, just, faithful, wise, and blessed always. He does not acquire these qualities and then depart, as is the case when a sick person is healed by a medical doctor and then goes his way. For the physician who healed the body worked as an outside agent assisting nature, which was working

internally under God, who is the cause of all health by that double operation of His providence about which I have spoken above.[64]

Man, therefore, must not turn to God in such a way that once being made just by Him he may depart, but rather that he may always be receiving justification from his Creator. When man does not depart from God, by this very fact, since God is present to him, he is justified, illuminated, and made happy, and God is cultivating and guarding him while he is obedient and subject to God's commands.

26. When man cultivates the earth so that the land is developed and made fertile, having done his work he departs, leaving the field ploughed or sown or irrigated or in whatever condition his work has placed it, and the work done remains when the worker is gone. But, as I have said, it is different when God cultivates a just man. He does not justify him in such a way that if the man should turn away, the work which God wrought would remain in him when he is gone.

A better example is that of air when light is present: the air has not been given its own luminosity, but it becomes luminous, for if it had been given its own luminosity and was not constantly receiving it, it would remain luminous when the light was gone. In a similar way, man is illuminated when God is present to him, but when God is absent, darkness is immediately upon him; and he is separated from God not by a distance in space but by a turning away of his will.

27. May God, then, who is immutably good, cultivate the good man and guard him. By Him we must be unceasingly made and unceasingly perfected, clinging to Him and remaining turned to Him of whom it is said, *But it is good for me to adhere to God,*[65] and to whom it is said, *I will keep my strength turned towards Thee.*[66]

For we are His work of art not only in so far as we are human beings but also in so far as we are good. When St. Paul spoke to the faithful, who had been converted from a life of sin, about the grace by which we have been saved, he said: *For by grace you have been saved through faith, and this is not your doing, but it is God's gift; it is not because of your works, so that no one may glory.*

For we are His work of art created in Christ Jesus in good works, which God has prepared, that we should walk in them.[67] Elsewhere Paul says, *With fear and trembling work out your own salvation.* But then, lest they think this could be attributed to themselves, as if they would make themselves just and good, he immediately added, *For it is God who works in you.*[68] Therefore, *The Lord God took the man whom He made and placed him in Paradise to cultivate him* (that is, to work in him) *and to guard him.*[69]

CHAPTER 13

Why man was forbidden to eat of the tree of knowledge of good and evil (Gen. 2.16–17).

28. *And the Lord God commanded Adam, saying, "You may eat of every tree that is in Paradise, but of the tree of the knowledge of good and evil you shall not eat. In the day that you eat of it you shall die.*"[70] If this tree from which man was forbidden by God to eat were an evil thing, it would seem that it was from the very nature of this evil thing that he received a deadly poison. But all the trees in Paradise were good, having been planted by God, who made all things very good,[71] and there was no evil substance there because there is no evil substance anywhere[72] (a point I shall discuss at greater length, God willing, when I take up the question of the serpent[73]). The man, therefore, was forbidden to touch that tree, which was not evil, so that the observance of the command in itself would be a good for him and its violation an evil.

29. There could not have been any more apt or cogent way of teaching that disobedience alone is a great evil, when man was found guilty of iniquity because he touched a thing against a prohibition, although if he had not been prohibited and had touched it he certainly would not have sinned.

For when some one says, for example, "Do not touch this plant," if it is poisonous and means death for the one who touches it, death will surely come to a man who defies the command.

But even if there had been no such prohibition and yet he had touched it, none the less he would surely die. For the plant would be a threat to his health and to his life whether it was forbidden to him or not. On the other hand, when someone forbids the touching of a thing against the interests not of him who touches but of him who forbids—as would be the case when a man puts his hand into another's money though forbidden by the owner to do so—the action of him who was prohibited would be a sin precisely because it could have done injury to the one who prohibited it. But when a thing is touched which would not harm him who touched it unless it were forbidden, nor anyone else no matter how often he touched it, why was it forbidden except to show the good of obedience in itself and the evil of disobedience in itself?

30. Finally, nothing else is sought by the sinner except to be free of the sovereignty of God when he does a deed that is sinful only in so far as God forbids it. If this alone were attended to, what else but the will of God would be attended to? What else but the will of God would be loved? What else but the will of God would be preferred to man's will? Leave the reason for the command in the Lord's hands. He who is His servant must do His bidding, and then perhaps by the merit of his obedience he will have grounds for seeing the reason of God's command.

But we need not prolong our enquiry into the reason for this command. If the service of God is a great good for man, God by His command makes useful whatever He wishes to command, and we must not fear that He could command what is not for our good.

CHAPTER 14

Must one experience evil in order to know evil?

31. It is impossible for the will of a man not to come tumbling down on him with a thunderous and devastating crash if he so exalts it as to prefer it to that of the One who is his superior.

This is what man has experienced in his contempt of God's command, and by this experience he has learned the difference between good and evil, that is, the good of obedience and the evil of disobedience, namely, of pride and contumacy, of the perverse imitation of God,[74] and of pernicious liberty. The tree which was the occasion of this experience for man received its name from what happened there, as I explained above.[75] For we would not feel evil except by experience, since there would be no evil unless we had committed it.

Evil is not a substance: the loss of the good is what we call evil. God is the unchangeable Good; man, in what belongs to the nature in which God created him, is indeed a good, but not unchangeable Good as God is. A changeable good, which is inferior to the unchangeable Good, becomes a greater good when it adheres to the unchangeable Good, loving and serving Him with a rational and free response of the will.

Hence, this nature so endowed is indeed a great good, because it has received the ability to cling to the highest Good. But if man is unwilling to do so, he deprives himself of the good, and in this he experiences evil, whence also by God's justice even torment follows. For what could be more contrary to justice than the well-being of him who deserts the Good? Such a thing cannot possibly be, but sometimes the evil condition resulting from the loss of the higher good is not perceived by a man who possesses an inferior good which he loves. It is according to divine justice, however, that one who has voluntarily lost what he ought to have loved should suffer the pain of losing the object that he did love. Thus the Creator is praised in all things. It is also a good that a man grieves over the good he has lost; for unless some good had remained in his being, he would not feel the punishment he has in his suffering over the loss of the good.

32. A person who loves the good without having any experience of evil, namely, one who before feeling the loss of the good chooses to hold on to it so as not to lose it, is of all mankind most worthy of praise.[76] But if this were not a matter of singular merit, it would not be attributed to the Child of the race of Israel who receiving the name Emmanuel, "God is with us,"[77] recon-

ciled us to God. He is the Man who is Mediator between man and God,[78] the Word with God and flesh with us,[79] the Word made flesh between God and us.[80] Concerning Him the prophet said, *Before the Child knows good or evil, He will reject evil-doing in order to choose the good.*[81] How does He reject or choose what He does not know except that these two are known in one way by the knowledge of good and in another way by the experience of evil? Through the knowledge of good, evil is known, although it is not felt. Good is held on to lest by loss[82] of it evil be experienced. Furthermore, by the experience of evil, good is known, since a person feels what he lost when he finds it is evil to have lost the good.

Hence, before the Child knew by experience a good which He would lack or an evil which He would feel in the loss of a good, He rejected evil to do good, that is, He was unwilling to lose what He had lest He feel the loss of what He ought not to lose. He gave a unique example of obedience, because He did not come to do His own will but the will of Him by whom He was sent.[83] In this He differed from him who chose to do his own will, not the will of his Creator. Hence, it is rightly said, *As by one man's disobedience many have been made sinners, so by one Man's obedience many are made just,*[84] *because as in Adam all die, so also in Christ shall all be made alive.*[85]

CHAPTER 15

How the tree of the knowledge of good and evil got its name.

33. Without good reason certain writers[86] are deeply puzzled when they seek to discover how the tree of the knowledge of good and evil could have been so called before man broke God's commandment by touching it and from experience discerned the difference between the good that he lost and the evil that he committed. Now, this tree was given such a name so that our first parents might observe the prohibition and not touch it, taking care to avoid suffering the consequences of touching it

against the prohibition. It was not because they subsequently went against the commandment and ate the fruit that the tree became the tree of the knowledge of good and evil; but even if they had remained obedient and had taken nothing against that commandment, it would be correctly called by what would happen to them there if they had taken the fruit. Thus, a tree might be called the "tree of satiety" because from its fruit men could have their fill. Now, if no one approached this tree, the name would not thereby be incongruous. For when men would approach it and be filled, then they would prove that the tree was appropriately named.

<h2 style="text-align:center">CHAPTER 16</h2>

How man could have understood the meaning of evil before he experienced it.

34. How could man, they ask, understand what was said to him about the tree of the knowledge of good and evil when he was completely ignorant of the meaning of evil?

Those who think this way do not notice how most unknown things are understood from their contraries which are known, so that even the names of nonexistent things can be used in conversation without puzzling the hearer. For instance, what is entirely nonexistent we call *nihil* (nothing); and anyone who understands and speaks Latin comprehends these two syllables. How does this happen except that when the mind sees what is, it recognizes by its privation what is not? The same thing can be said of the word "void." In gazing at the fullness of bodily substance, we understand by the privation of it the meaning of void as its contrary. As for the sense of hearing, we make judgments not only about words but also about silence. So, in perceiving the life within him, a man might take precautions against its opposite, that is, the privation of life (which we call death) and against anything that would cause him to lose what was so dear to him; I mean any deed of his own which might lose him his life. It does not matter what syllables make up its name; one uses the Latin word *peccatum* (sin) or *malum* (evil), for example, as a sign of that which he fixes upon in his mind.

For how do we understand what is meant when the resurrection is spoken of, which we have never experienced? Is it not because we are aware of what it is to live, and as we call the privation of that state death, so we designate as resurrection the return to the state which we perceive? And whatever word may be used to designate the same thing in any other language, the mind perceives a sign in the spoken word, and at the sound it recognizes what it would think even without the sign.

It is remarkable how nature, even before any experience, avoids the loss of what it possesses. Who taught the beasts of the field to avoid death except a feeling they have for life? Who taught the small child in arms to cling to the one who carries him if that person threatens to throw the child to the ground? This fear begins at a certain time in the baby's life, yet it is before he experiences any such fall.

35. To the first man and woman, therefore, life was already sweet, and undoubtedly they tried to avoid losing it. When God instructed them in this matter, whatever sounds or other means He used, they were able to understand. They could not be persuaded to sin unless they were first persuaded that they would not die as a result, that is, that they would not lose what they possessed and what they found joy in possessing. We shall discuss this in its proper place.

If there are those who are puzzled over how the first man and woman were able to understand God when He named or threatened what they had not experienced, they should take note and see how we recognize without any doubt or hesitation the names of all things outside of our experience only from their contraries which we have known, if they are the names of privations, or from similar things, if they are the names of positive ideas. Surely no one will ask how the first man and woman were able to speak or to understand another speaking since they had not learned to speak by growing up among those who do or by studying under a teacher. It is certainly no problem for God to teach men to speak whom He had made in such a way that they could learn this art from others in case there were others present from whom they might learn.

CHAPTER 17

Was the prohibition against eating the fruit of the tree
of the knowledge of good and evil given to both the
man and the woman?

36. With very good reason it is asked whether God gave his command to the man only or to the woman also. But the writer has not yet told how the woman was made. Can it be that she really was already made? On this supposition the writer has subsequently recapitulated what was previously done by telling how it was done.[87]

The words of Scripture are: *And the Lord God commanded Adam, saying....* The writer did not say, "He commanded them." Then he continues: *You may eat of every tree that is in Paradise.* He did not say, "You both may eat."[88] Then God added: *But of the tree of the knowledge of good and evil you* [plural] *shall not eat.* Here the verb is in the plural, presumably because God is addressing both of them; and then He concludes this command still using the plural form: *In the day that you eat of it you shall die.*[89]

Another explanation could be that, since God knew He was going to make the woman for the man, He thus gave His command with observance of the proper order so that the command of the Lord would come through the man to the woman. This is the rule that St. Paul urges in the church: *If they would learn anything, let them ask their husbands at home.*[90]

CHAPTER 18

How God spoke to Adam.

37. We may also ask how God now spoke in such a way to the
man whom He made, who was certainly from the beginning endowed with senses and intelligence, that this man could hear
and understand what God said. For the man could not receive
a command which it would be sinful for him to transgress[91] unless he understood what he received. How, then, did God speak
to him? Did He speak interiorly in his soul, through the understanding, so that the man would with wisdom understand the
will and command of God without any corporeal sounds or likenesses of corporeal things?

I do not think that God spoke in this way to the first man.
The Scripture narrative is such that we are led rather to assume
that God spoke to man in Paradise as He spoke later to the patriarchs, such as Abraham and Moses, namely, under some corporeal form. It is thus, indeed, that the first man and woman
heard the voice of God as He walked in Paradise towards evening, and they hid themselves.[92]

CHAPTER 19

*What we must believe about God in order to understand the
workings of His providence.*

38. We have here a good opportunity that we ought not to neglect according to our ability and the measure of help and grace
that God in His kindness gives us; I mean the opportunity to
contemplate the twofold working of Divine Providence which
I touched upon above in a passing way when I was speaking
about the cultivation of the earth.[93] My hope was that the mind
of the reader would gradually become accustomed to contemplate this working of Providence, for this is a great help in keeping us from thinking anything unworthy of the divine nature.

We say, then, that the sovereign, true, one, and only God, Father, Son, and Holy Spirit, that is, God and His Word and the Spirit of both, the Trinity without confusion and without separation, God *who alone has immortality and dwells in unapproachable light, whom no man has seen or can see,*[94] is not contained within any finite or infinite region in space and is not subject to change with any finite or infinite unfolding of time. In the substance which is God there is no part that is less than the whole, as is necessarily the case with those substances that are in space;[95] nor was there once in the divine substance anything that no longer is, nor will there be anything which is not yet, as is the case with substances that can be affected by change in time.

CHAPTER 20

Bodies are changeable in time and space; souls are changeable in time only; and God is not changeable in any way.

39. God, then, who lives in an unchangeable eternity, created simultaneously all things, from which the course of time would run and space would be filled and the ages would unfold by the movement of beings in time and space. He made some of these beings spiritual and some corporeal, forming matter which was not created by another and was not uncreated; but He and He alone made it unformed and formable, so that it would precede its formation not in time but in origin.[96] He established the spiritual creation above the corporeal, because the spiritual is changeable only in time, but the corporeal is changeable in time and place.[97] For example, a soul moves in time, remembering what it had forgotten, or learning what it did not know, or wishing what it did not wish; but a body moves in space, from earth to heaven, or from heaven to earth, or from east to west, or in some similar ways.

Now, whatever moves through space must of necessity simultaneously move through time. But it is not necessary that everything which moves through time must also move through space.

A substance, then, which moves only through time is more excellent than one that moves through time and space, but it is inferior to that which is immovable in both space and time. It follows, therefore, that just as a created spirit moves a body through time and space, although itself is moved through time only, so the Spirit who is Creator moves a created spirit through time, although He is Himself unmoved in both time and space. But a created spirit moves itself through time and moves a body through time and space. The Creator Spirit, however, moves Himself independently of time and space, moves a created spirit through time without space, and moves a body through time and space.

CHAPTER 21

God, eternal and unchangeable, can move His creatures through time and space. The soul, unmoved in space, none the less moves the body in space.

40. One might try, then, to understand how the eternal God, truly eternal and truly immortal and unchangeable, who is not moved in space or time, moves His creatures through time and space. But in my opinion he cannot succeed in understanding this unless he first understands how the soul, that is, a created spirit, being moved not through space but only through time, moves the body through time and space. For if he cannot yet grasp what takes place in himself, how much less will he comprehend what is above him!

41. The soul, affected by its habitual contact with the bodily senses, presumes that when it is moving the body through space it itself is also moving through space with the body. But if it could carefully discern what might be called the pivots of the members of its body and see how they are in the joints throughout the whole body, it would observe how the beginnings of motion are in these places. It will discover that the members that are moved through space are not moved unless the motion pro-

ceeds from a part of the body that is stationary. For example, one finger alone is not moved unless the hand is stationary and the finger moves from its joint, which serves as a motionless pivot.[98] When the whole hand, then, is moved from the elbow joint, the elbow from the humerus, and the humerus from the scapula, while the pivots from which the motion proceeds remain unmoved, the member that is moved goes through space. Thus, the joint of the foot is in the ankle, and the foot moves while the ankle joint is motionless. So, too, the joint of the shank is in the knee, and that of the whole leg is in the hip.

Now, the will causes no motion in any member whatsoever except from the pivot of some joint; and the command of the will originally directs the motion so that what is set in motion may be able to be impelled by that which does not move in space. Finally, in walking, one foot is not raised unless the other, firmly fixed, bears the weight of the whole body, while the foot in motion from the place at which it started to that where it is going is dependent upon the stationary joint which serves as a pivot.

42. The will, then, moves no member of the body through space except from a joint which remains unmoved. Furthermore, that part of the body which is moved and that part which is fixed so that the other can be moved has each its own corporeal dimensions by which it occupies space. With much greater reason, then, can we say that the soul which commands the movement remains unmoved in space. The members are subject to it, so that according to its desire the joint on which the member to be moved depends is firmly fixed. The soul is not a corporeal substance and does not fill the body in space as water does a skin bottle[99] or a sponge, but in a mysterious way by its incorporeal command it is united to the body which it vivifies, and by this command it rules the body through an influence,[100] not a corporeal mass. With all the more reason, then, the will commanding does not itself move through space in order to move the body through space when it moves the whole by means of the parts, without moving any parts in space except by means of those which it keeps immobile.

CHAPTER 22

Motion in space is impossible for a spiritual creature; motion in space and time is impossible for God.

43. Even if it is hard to understand, we should admit that a spiritual creature without local motion in itself moves a body through space, and that God without temporal motion in Himself moves a spiritual creature through time. One perhaps might not wish to admit this with regard to the soul, although without doubt he would not only admit it but also understand it if he could conceive of the soul as an incorporeal being, as it is. Indeed, is it not easily seen that a being which[101] has no extension in space cannot have local motion? Whatever is extended in space is a body, and consequently the soul should not be thought of as moving in space if it is admitted that it is not a body. But if one is unwilling to admit this with regard to the soul, we need not be adamant in insisting on the point. However, unless one believes that the substance of God is without any motion either in time or in space, he does not yet believe that God is completely unchangeable.

CHAPTER 23

God, forever unchangeable, moves creatures through time and space, subjecting the lower to the higher in a hierarchical order.

44. The nature of the Trinity is absolutely immutable and hence so perfectly eternal that nothing can be coeternal with It. Dwelling with Itself and in Itself beyond all time and space, It nevertheless moves through time and space the creatures dependent upon It.[102] It creates beings by Its goodness, and It rules wills by Its power, so that there is no being not from It, and as far as wills are concerned, there is no good will that It does not assist[103] and no evil will that It cannot use for a good purpose. But since God did not give free will to all beings, those to whom

He gave it are more powerful and more excellent, and those that do not have it are of necessity subject to those that do. All of this is by reason of the order established by the Creator, who never punishes an evil will to the extent of destroying the dignity of its nature. Since all bodies, then, and all irrational souls are without free will, they are subordinate to those beings that do have free will; not all of the former, however, to all of the latter, but according to an order established by the justice of the Creator.

Therefore, the providence of God rules and administers the whole creation, both natures and wills: natures in order to give them existence, wills so that those that are good may not be without merit, and those that are evil may not go unpunished. And that same God by His providence first of all subjects all creatures to Himself, and then corporeal creatures to the spiritual, the irrational to the rational, the earthly to the heavenly, the female to the male, the weak to the strong, and the poor to the rich.[104] As far as wills are concerned, God subjects to Himself those that are good, and He subjects the wicked to those who serve Him, so that an evil will may suffer what a good will does by God's command, whether the good will does this by itself or by an evil will, but only in that domain which is by nature subject even to an evil will, namely, bodies.[105] For evil wills have in themselves their own interior punishment, that is, their own wickedness.[106]

CHAPTER 24

The role of the angels in the governance of the universe.

45. Hence, every corporeal being, every irrational life, every weak or wayward will is subjected to the heavenly angels who enjoy God, being subject to Him, and serve God in beatitude; and the angels' purpose is to accomplish in or with these subject creatures what the order of nature demands in all according to the decree of Him to whom all are subject. The angels see in God immutable truth, and according to it they direct their wills.

Hence, they become partakers of His eternity, truth, and will forever beyond time and place. They are moved, however, by His command even in time, although He is not moved in time. They do not turn from or withdraw from the contemplation of Him, but they simultaneously contemplate Him without the limits of space and time and carry out His commands in their subjects, moving themselves through time and moving bodies through time and space in accordance with what is proper to their activity. Hence it is that God by the twofold working of His providence is over all creatures, that is, over natures that they may have existence, and over wills that they may do nothing without either His command or His permission.[107]

CHAPTER 25

How creatures receive intrinsic or extrinsic and corporeal or incorporeal help.

46. The whole corporeal creation, therefore, does not receive extrinsic assistance from any corporeal source.[108] For outside of this whole corporeal creation there is no corporeal being; otherwise it would not be the whole. But intrinsically it is helped by an incorporeal force, since it is God who makes it possible for it to exist, *For from Him and through Him and in Him are all things.*[109]

Parts of this same whole are enabled by intrinsic help (or I should say, are made) to be subsistent beings; and they are assisted extrinsically by some corporeal force in their development, for example, by food, by cultivation of the land, by medicine, and by anything that serves for adornment so that they may be not only healthy and productive but also fair to behold.

47. Spiritual creatures, if they are perfect and blessed, as is the case with the holy angels, in so far as their own well-being is concerned are assisted only intrinsically by an incorporeal force in order to exist and be happy. God speaks to them interiorly in a mysterious and indescribable manner, not by letters

put down with corporeal instruments, not by words sounding on corporeal ears, not by the likenesses of bodies produced imaginatively in the spirit,[110] as, for example, in dreams or in a transport of the spirit, which in Greek is called *ecstasis* (a word which we have been using as a Latin word). This kind of vision, it is true, is more interior than what the soul perceives when using the bodily senses as messengers; nevertheless, it is similar to corporeal vision, so that when it happens it either cannot in any way be distinguished from corporeal vision or at best can be distinguished only rarely and with difficulty. It is also more external than the kind of vision that takes place when the rational and intellectual soul beholds its object which it sees in unchangeable truth in the light of which it judges all else; and for these reasons the vision of ecstasy, in my judgment, should be classed as coming from an extrinsic source.[111]

A spiritual and intellectual creature, therefore, which is perfect and blessed, as the angels are, with respect to its own existence, wisdom, and beatitude is helped only intrinsically, as I have said, by the eternity, truth, and love of its Creator.[112] If we must say that the angels receive any extrinsic help, perhaps we should say that they are helped only by the fact that they see one another and rejoice that they are joined in one society with God, that they see all creatures in these companions,[113] and that therefore they give thanks and they praise their Creator. With respect to the activity of the angels by which God's providence looks out for the various classes of creatures in all the world, especially for the human race, they provide extrinsic help not only through visions presenting the likenesses of bodies[114] but also through bodies themselves that are subject to the power of angels.

CHAPTER 26

God, without being moved Himself, moves the creatures which He has made.

48. Therefore, almighty God, who sustains all things and is always the same in His immutable eternity, truth, and will, without moving through time or space, moves His spiritual creation through time, and also moves His material creation through time and space. Consequently, by this motion He rules the beings which by His interior action He has made, ruling them extrinsically both by wills subject to Himself which He moves through time, and by bodies subject to Himself and to those wills, moving these bodies through time and space—in that time and space whose reason-principle is life in God beyond time and space.[115] Hence, when God does this, we ought not to think that His substance by which He is God is changeable in time and space or movable through time and space, but we should recognize these actions in the work of His divine providence. They are not in that work by which He creates beings, but in that by which He extrinsically rules what He has intrinsically created. Without any distance or measure of space, by His immutable and transcendent power He is interior to all things because they are all in Him, and exterior to all things because He is above them all.[116] Moreover, without any distance or unit of time, by His immutable eternity He is more ancient than all things because He is before them all, and newer than all things because He is also after them all.[117]

CHAPTER 27

How God spoke to Adam (Gen. 2.16–17).

49. Scripture says: *And the Lord God commanded Adam, saying: "You may eat of every tree that is in Paradise, but of the tree of the knowledge of good and evil you shall not eat. In the day that you eat of it you shall die."*[118] Now when we hear these words, if we ask

how God spoke them, we cannot understand precisely how He did so. Nevertheless, we should hold it for certain that God speaks either through His own substance or through a creature subject to Him, but that He does not speak through His own substance except in two cases: first, in creating the whole universe, and, second, in not only creating but also illuminating spiritual and intellectual creatures when they are able to grasp His utterance, which is in His Word, *who was in the beginning with God, and the Word was God, and through the Word all things were made*.[119] But when God speaks to those who are unable to grasp His utterance, He speaks only through a creature. Now He may employ a spiritual creature exclusively, in a dream or ecstasy, using the likeness of material things; or He may speak through a corporeal creature, as the bodily senses are affected by a form that appears or the sound of a voice that is heard.

50. If Adam, therefore, was in such a state that he was able to grasp the utterance of God which He makes present to the minds of angels through His own substance, there should be no doubt that God moved Adam's mind in time in a mysterious and unaccountable manner, without Himself being moved in time, impressing upon Adam's mind a useful and salutary precept of Truth, and in the same Truth revealing in an indescribable way[120] the punishment awaiting the transgressor.[121] It is thus that all good precepts are heard or seen in unchangeable Wisdom, which at times enters holy souls, although Wisdom itself does not move in time.

But if the justice of Adam was such that he also needed the authority of another creature holier and wiser, through which he would come to know God's will and command, as we have needed the prophets and they have needed the angels, why do we doubt that God spoke to him through some such creature in a language which he could understand? When Scripture says later[122] that when our first parents had sinned they heard the voice of the Lord as He walked in Paradise, no one who holds to the Catholic faith has any doubt that this was not done by means of the very substance of God Himself but by means of a creature subject to Him.

On this point I have wished to comment more at length, because some heretics[123] think that the substance of the Son of God was visible in itself before He assumed a body, and therefore they think that the Son of God before He took a body from the Virgin was seen by the patriarchs, on the theory that it was said only of God the Father, *whom no man has seen or can see.*[124] According to them, the Son was seen in His own substance before He took on the form of a slave—an impious doctrine which a Catholic mind should put far from it.

I shall discuss this question more fully elsewhere, please God. For the present, I have finished this book, and in the following book I must hope[125] to discuss how the woman was created from the side of man.

BOOK NINE
The Creation of the Woman

The meaning of earth in Gen. 2.19.

1. *And the Lord God said: "It is not good that the man should be alone. Let Us make for him a helper like himself." And again God formed from the earth all the beasts of the field and all the birds of heaven and brought them to Adam to see what he would call them. And whatever Adam called a living creature, that is its name. And Adam gave names to all the cattle and to all the birds of heaven and to all the beasts of the field. But for Adam there was not found a helper like himself. And God cast Adam into an ecstasy, and as Adam slept, God took one of his ribs and in its place put flesh, and the Lord God made the rib which He took from Adam into a woman and brought her to Adam. And Adam said: "This now is bone of my bones and flesh of my flesh; she shall be called Woman, because she has been taken out of the man. For this reason a man shall leave his father and mother and shall cleave to his wife; and they shall be two in one flesh."*[1]

If my reader is helped at all by the reflections I have put down in the preceding books, I have no need to delay longer over the statement, *Again God formed from the earth all the beasts of the field and all the birds of heaven.* Earlier in this treatise I have explained to the best of my ability why the word "again" is used, that is, because of the first creation of creatures accomplished in the six days, when all were perfected in their causal principles and were begun in such a way that the causes would be brought subsequently to their effects.[2] Now, if anyone thinks that a different solution of this problem should be offered, I ask only that he give careful attention to all the points I have considered in

arriving at my opinion; and if he will then be able to set forth
a more probable theory, I must not only not oppose him but
must even congratulate him.

2. A reader may be puzzled because the sacred writer did not
say, "Again God formed from the earth all the beasts of the field
and from the waters all the birds of heaven," but as if God had
formed both kinds from the earth, he said, *And again God formed
from the earth all the beasts of the field and all the birds of heaven.*

Now, there are two ways in which this statement can be understood. First, the writer may simply have not mentioned the
material out of which God formed the birds of heaven because
the reader would assume, without any explicit mention, that
God is not supposed to have formed both kinds from the earth
but only the beasts of the field, and thus we shall understand,
even when Scripture is silent, what material it was from which
God formed the birds of heaven in so far as we know that they
have been produced from the waters in the original creation of
the causal reasons.[3] Another way to understand the text is to assume that the word "earth" has been used in its broadest sense
as including the waters, as is done in the Psalm where, after ex-
horting the heavenly beings to voice their praises, the Psalmist
turns to earth and says, *Praise the Lord from the earth, you sea monsters and all you deeps,*[4] without saying later, "Praise the Lord
from the waters." It is there[5] that all the deeps are, although
they praise the Lord from the earth. And it is there also that all
the creeping creatures and all the winged creatures are, and yet
they praise the Lord from the earth. On the basis of this very
broad meaning of the word "earth," in which it is used in reference to the whole world in the words *God who made heaven and
earth,* whatever has been created from either dry land[6] or from
the waters is rightly understood to have been created from the
earth.

CHAPTER 2

How God spoke when He said, "It is not good that the man should be alone. Let Us make for him a helper like himself."

3. Let us see now how we must understand the words of God when He said, *It is not good that the man should be alone. Let Us make for him a helper like himself.*[7] Did God speak this in words and syllables uttered in time? Or perhaps the writer is referring to the reason-principle which was primordially in the Word of God determining the nature of woman, the reason-principle to which Scripture also referred previously in the words, *And God said, "Let there be this or that,"* when all things were created in the beginning. Or perhaps God said this in the mind of the man himself, as He sometimes speaks to His servants interiorly. Such a servant of God was the one who said in one of the Psalms, *I will hear what the Lord God will speak in me.*[8] Again, it is possible that a revelation about this matter was made interiorly to the man by an angel through a resemblance of the sounds of human speech, although Scripture has not said whether this might have occurred in sleep or in ecstasy (for it is in such states that this kind of revelation is usually made). Or could it have been in some other way, like the revelations made to the prophets, regarding which one of them said, *And the angel who spoke to me said in me?*[9] Again, a real voice might have resounded through a corporeal creature, as happened when the voice came from a cloud, *This is My Son.*[10]

We cannot know for certain which one of all these possible explanations is the true one. But there are two things about which we should have no doubt: on the one hand, God said the words we are considering, and, on the other, if He spoke using a material voice or a resemblance of a material voice resounding in time, He did not speak by His own substance but by some creature subject to His power, as I have explained in the preceding book.[11]

4. God has been seen also in later days by holy men, now with His head as white as wool, now with the lower part of His body like brass,[12] and in different ways on different occasions.

But God did not give these visions to men through His own substance by which He is what He is, but through creatures which He made subject to Himself; and through resemblances of corporeal forms and voices He manifested and spoke what He desired. This is absolutely certain to those who faithfully believe or clearly understand that the Trinity is immutable and eternal—though unmoved through time and space, yet moving creatures through time and space. Therefore, our task now is not to seek how God spoke the words He uttered, but rather to understand what He said. Indeed, Eternal Truth Itself, through which all things have been created, assures us that it was necessary that there should be made for man a helper like himself; and in that Eternal Truth he understands this who is able to discover in It why a creature has been made.

CHAPTER 3

The woman as a helper. God's plan for procreation.

5. If one should ask why it was necessary that a helper be made for man, the answer that seems most probable is that it was for the procreation of children, just as the earth is a helper for the seed in the production of a plant from the union of the two. This purpose was declared in the original creation of the world: *Male and female He made them. And God blessed them and said, "Increase and multiply and fill the earth and subdue it."*[13] This reason for creation and union of male and female, as well as this blessing, was not abrogated after the sin and punishment of man. It is by virtue of this blessing that the earth is now filled with human beings who subdue it.

6. Although it was after the expulsion of the man and woman from Paradise that they came together in sexual intercourse and begot children, according to Scripture, nevertheless I do not see what could have prohibited them from honorable nuptial union and *the bed undefiled*[14] even in Paradise.[15] God could have granted them this if they had lived in a faithful and just manner in obedient and holy service to Him, so that without the tumultu-

ous ardor of passion[16] and without any labor and pain of childbirth, offspring would be born from their seed. In this case, the purpose would not be to have children succeeding parents who die. Rather those who had begotten children would remain in the prime of life[17] and would maintain their physical strength from the tree of life which had been planted in Paradise. Those who would be born would develop to the same state, and eventually, when the determined number would be complete, if all lived just and obedient lives, there would be a transformation, so that without any death[18] their natural bodies would receive a new quality[19] since they obeyed every command of the spirit that ruled them; and with the spirit alone vivifying them, without any help from corporeal nourishment, they would be called spiritual bodies. This could have been if the transgression of God's command had not merited the punishment of death.[20]

7. Those who think that this could not have been look at nothing but the ordinary course of nature as it is after man's sin and the punishment he received. But we ought not to be in the number of those who accept only what they have been accustomed to see. For one could not reasonably doubt that such a privilege as I have described could have been given to a person who lived an obedient and holy life, especially if there is no doubt that the garments of the Israelites were kept in their original condition so that through forty long years they showed no wear.[21]

CHAPTER 4

Why was there no nuptial union in Paradise?

8. Why, then, did they not have intercourse until they had left Paradise? The reason is that soon after the creation of the woman, before they had relations, they committed the sin because of which they were destined to die and because of which they went forth from the place of their blessedness. As a matter of fact, Scripture has not specified the length of time between their creation and the birth of their son Cain.

One might also say that the delay was due to the fact that God had not yet ordered them to come together in nuptial union. For why should they not await God's authorization for this, since there was no drive of concupiscence coming from rebellious flesh? God had not ordered such a union because He provided for everything in the light of His foreknowledge, in which He undoubtedly foresaw their fall, as a result of which the human race was to be generated as a mortal race.[22]

CHAPTER 5

In what sense Eve was made as a helper for Adam.

9. Now, if the woman was not made for the man to be his helper in begetting children, in what was she to help him? She was not to till the earth with him, for there was not yet any toil to make help necessary.[23] If there were any such need, a male helper would be better, and the same could be said of the comfort of another's presence if Adam were perhaps weary of solitude. How much more agreeably could two male friends, rather than a man and woman, enjoy companionship and conversation in a life shared together.[24] And if they had to make an arrangement in their common life for one to command and the other to obey in order to make sure that opposing wills would not disrupt the peace of the household, there would have been proper rank to assure this, since one would be created first and the other second, and this would be further reinforced if the second were made from the first, as was the case with the woman. Surely no one will say that God was able to make from the rib of the man only a woman and not also a man if He had wished to do so. Consequently, I do not see in what sense the woman was made as a helper for the man if not for the sake of bearing children.

Chapter 6

How Adam and Eve, if they had not sinned, might have been
transported to a better life after they had begotten
children on earth.

10. If it had been necessary for parents to depart from this life and be succeeded by their children, so that the human race by the departure and arrival of generations would reach a determined number of persons, it would have been possible for them, once they had begotten children and in a holy manner completed their human task, to be removed to a better life not by death but by a transformation. Now this transformation could have been the final one in which they will receive their bodies and become holy like the angels in heaven;[25] or, if that was not to be granted until it will be given to all men at the end of the world, it could have been something less than that, but a change none the less to a better state than this body of ours has or the original bodies had when God made the man from the slime of the earth and the woman from the body of the man.[26]

11. For we must not think that Elijah is now as the saints will be when the day's work will be done and they will all receive a denarius,[27] or, on the other hand, that his state is like that of men who have not yet gone out of this life. Elijah, indeed, departed hence not by dying but by being transported elsewhere.[28] Consequently, he now possesses something better than he could have had in this life, but he does not yet have what he is to possess on the last day as a reward for his life of faithful service. *For they foretold a better lot for us, that they might not arrive at complete perfection without us.*[29] If anyone supposes that Elijah could not have merited this blessing if he had married and begotten children (he is presumed not to have had a wife and children because Scripture does not say he had, although it also says nothing about his celibacy), what will our objector say about Enoch, who begot children and, being pleasing to God, did not die but was carried off?[30]

Why, then, if Adam and Eve had lived a holy life and in chas-

tity had brought forth children, could they not have yielded
place to their successors not by dying but by being transported
to another life? Enoch and Elijah, both dead in Adam and bearing in their flesh the seeds of death, will return to this life, as
it is believed, to pay this debt, and after so long a delay will
die.[31] But now they are in another life, where, before the resurrection of the body, and before the natural body is changed
to a spiritual one, they are not wasted by disease or old age.

If this is so, then, with how much more justice and good reason would it be granted to the first human beings, who were living without any sin of their own or of their parents, to be
brought to some better life, yielding place to their children, and
hence at the end of the world, with all the saints descended from
them, to be changed into a more blessed form like the angels',
not by the death of the body but by the power of God?

CHAPTER 7

The good of marriage.

12. I do not see, therefore, in what other way the woman was
made to be the helper of the man if procreation is eliminated,
and I do not understand why it should be eliminated. How explain the great merit and high honor that faithful and holy virginity has in God's eyes except that in this *time to refrain from
embracing,*[32] when there is a vast crowd from all nations to fill
up the number of the saints, the urge to experience base pleasure of the flesh does not demand what is not required for the
provision of offspring?[33] Finally, the weakness of both sexes,
with its inclination to depravity and ruin, is wisely saved by
honorable marriage, so that what could have been a duty for
men in a healthy state is a healing remedy for those who are
sick. For from the fact that incontinence is an evil it does not
follow that marriage is not good, even when by it an incontinent
couple are united in the flesh. As a matter of fact, the good of
marriage is not blameworthy because of the evil of inconti-

nence; but because of this good that evil becomes allowable *(veniale).*[34] For what is good in marriage and that by which marriages are good can never be a sin.

Now this good is threefold: fidelity, offspring, and sacrament.[35] *Fidelity* means that there must be no relations with any other person outside the marriage bond. *Offspring* means that children are to be lovingly received, brought up with tender care, and given a religious education. *Sacrament* means that the marriage bond is not to be broken, and that if one partner in a marriage should be abandoned by the other, neither may enter a new marriage even for the sake of having children. This is what may be called the rule of marriage: by it the fertility of nature is made honorable and the disorder of concupiscence is regulated.

Hence, since I have discussed this subject at length in the book I recently published called *The Good of Marriage,*[36] in which I distinguished the continence of widowhood and the excellence of virginity according to the honor of these two states, there is no need to treat this matter further in this book.

CHAPTER 8

In the attempt to avoid evil it is difficult not to fall into the opposite vice.

13. We now ask what help the woman could give the man if they were not allowed intercourse in Paradise for the purpose of begetting children. Those who have this problem perhaps suppose that all union of the sexes is sinful. For it is difficult for people who try to avoid certain vices not to rush quickly in a misguided way into their contraries. Thus, a person dreading avarice becomes prodigal, and dreading extravagance becomes avaricious. A man becomes restless if you blame him for indolence; or indolent if you blame him for restlessness. He who has been reprehended for his boldness and has come to detest it takes refuge in timidity; he who tries not to be too timid rids himself of restraint and becomes rash, and thus evil deeds are

judged not by reason but by opinion. So it is that people who do not know what is condemned by God's law respecting adultery and fornication come to denounce conjugal union even when it is for the sake of procreation.

CHAPTER 9

The woman would have been the man's helper in procreation even if they had not become subject to death by their sin.

14. There are those who do not misunderstand the nature of marriage, but none the less suppose that the power of reproduction has been given by God to provide for the succession of generations of mortal men.[37] They do not think that the first man and woman could have had carnal union except for the fact that because of their sin they were destined to die and would thus beget children to take their places. But those who think thus do not reflect on the fact that, if successors could have been sought by those destined to die, with greater reason companions could have been sought by those destined to remain living. If the earth indeed were filled with the human race, it would be true that offspring would be sought only to succeed those who would die. But if the earth was to be filled by two human beings, how could they carry out this obligation to society except by procreation?

Who is so blind as not to see that the human race is a distinguished ornament for the earth even when only a few men live good and praiseworthy lives, and that public order is of great importance when it keeps even sinners within the limits set by a certain kind of earthly peace? In spite of the fact that mankind has fallen, even sinners are superior to the beasts and birds. And yet, who does not find pleasure in contemplating this lower part of the universe, which is adorned with all these kinds of animals in keeping with its place in the whole? But no one is so lacking in understanding as to think that the world would have been less adorned if it were filled with human beings in the state of original justice who would not die.

15. The vast number of angels in the heavenly city cannot be adduced as proof that man and woman would not be joined in conjugal union if they were not to die. Indeed, the perfect number of saints destined to rise and join the angels was foreseen by the Lord when He said, *In the resurrection they will neither be married nor take wives; for they will not be subject to death, but will enjoy equality with the angels of God.*[38] Here, indeed, the earth was to be filled with men, and in view of the close ties of relationship and the bond of unity so earnestly desired, it was to be populated by men from one common ancestor. For what other purpose, then, was a female helper similar to the man sought unless it was to have the female sex assist in the sowing of the human race, as the fertility of the earth does in the sowing of crops?

CHAPTER 10

If Adam had not sinned, procreation would have taken place in Paradise without the ardor of passion.

16. Nevertheless, it may be better and more fitting to assume that the natural bodies of the couple put in Paradise were of such a nature that, before they were condemned to die, they did not have an appetite for carnal pleasure such as our bodies, sprung from mortal stock, today possess. One cannot say that nothing happened in Adam and Eve when they ate the fruit of the forbidden tree. God had not said to them, "If you eat of it, you shall die," but, *In the day that you eat of it you shall die.*[39] The result was that that very day wrought in them what St. Paul laments when he says: *I delight in the law of God according to the inner man, but I see in my members another law at war with the law of my mind and making me captive to the law of sin which dwells in my members. Unhappy man that I am! Who will deliver me from this body of death? The grace of God, through Jesus Christ our Lord.*[40] It would not be sufficient if he said, "Who will deliver me from this mortal body?" But he said, *from this body of death.* In a similar way he says elsewhere, *The body indeed is dead because of sin.*[41] He did not say, "The body is mortal," but, *The body is dead,* al-

though it was certainly also mortal because it was destined to die. Therefore, although the bodies of our first parents were natural bodies, not spiritual bodies,[42] we should not suppose that they were "dead" before they sinned—I mean necessarily destined for death: that is what happened to them on the day on which they touched[43] the tree against the prohibition.

17. Our bodies have a normal healthy state proper to them. If this condition so deteriorates that a deadly disease consumes the internal organs, and the physicians, after examining the patient, decide that death is imminent, the body is then said to be dying, but not in the same sense as when it was healthy, although then too it was destined to die some day.

Hence, the first human pair had natural bodies indeed, but bodies destined to die only if they sinned, bodies that would have received an angelic form and heavenly quality.[44] But when they disobeyed God's command, their bodies contracted, as it were, the deadly disease of death, and this changed the gift by which they had ruled the body so perfectly that they would not say, *I see in my members another law at war with the law of my mind.* For although the body before the fall was not yet spiritual, but rather natural, nevertheless it was not *this body of death* from which and with which we have been born. What, indeed, is this life from our birth, even from our conception, but the beginning of a sickness by which we must die? Death is no more inevitable for the man with dropsy or consumption[45] or elephantiasis than for the infant whose life has just begun in this body in which all men are by nature *children of wrath,*[46] a condition which is a punishment for sin.

18. Why, therefore, may we not assume that the first couple before they sinned could have given a command to their genital organs for the purpose of procreation as they did to the other members which the soul is accustomed to move to perform various tasks without any trouble and without any craving for pleasure? For the almighty Creator, worthy of praise beyond all words, who is great even in the least of His works, has given to the bees the power of reproducing their young just as they produce wax and honey.[47]

Why, then, should it seem beyond belief that He made the

bodies of the first human beings in such a way that, if they had not sinned and had not immediately thereupon contracted a disease which would bring death, they would move the members by which offspring are generated in the same way that one commands his feet when he walks, so that conception would take place without passion and birth without pain? But as it is, by disobeying God's command they deserved to experience in their members, where death now reigned, the movement of a law at war with the law of the mind,[48] a movement that marriage regulates and continence controls and restrains, so that where punishment has followed sin, there merit will come from punishment.

CHAPTER 11

The woman was created for procreation, which would have taken place in Paradise without any uncontrolled desire.

19. The woman, then, with the appearance and distinctive physical characteristics of her sex, was made for the man from the man. She brought forth Cain and Abel and all their brothers, from whom all men were to be born; and among them she brought forth Seth, through whom the line descended to Abraham and the people of Israel, the nation long well known among all men; and it was through the sons of Noah that all nations sprang.

Whoever calls these facts into question undermines all that we believe, and his opinions should be resolutely cast out of the minds of the faithful. Consequently, when someone asks what help the woman was intended to give the man, as I carefully consider to the best of my ability all that we are told, I can think of no other purpose than the procreation of children in order to fill the earth with their descendants. But the begetting of children by the first man and woman was not to have been as it is today, when there is the law of sin in the members *at war with the law of the mind*,[49] even though virtue overcomes it by the grace of God. For we must believe that this condition could not

have existed except *in this body of death,*[50] a body that is dead because of sin. What punishment could have been more deserved
than that the body, made to serve the soul, should not be willing
to obey every command of the soul, just as the soul herself refused to serve her Lord?

It is possible that God creates both body and soul from the
parents: the body from their bodies, the soul from their souls.
Or could it be that He creates souls some other way?[51] But
whatever is the case, it is not for some impossible task nor for
any trifling reward that He creates the soul. And when it is devout and faithful to God, it conquers with the help of His grace
the law of sin in the members of this body of death, which the
first man received as a punishment; and thus it gains a heavenly
reward with greater glory, showing how praiseworthy is that
obedience which by virtue was able to triumph over the punishment deserved by another's disobedience.

CHAPTER 12

*The animals were brought to Adam, and he
named them (Gen. 2.19–20). There must be
a figurative meaning in this event.*

20. I think I have sufficiently searched for God's purpose in
making the woman as the man's helper. Now we must try to understand why all the beasts of the field and all the birds of the
air were brought to Adam to be named by him, and why thereafter there seemed to be a need to create for him a woman made
from his side since no helper had been found for him like himself among the animals.[52]

There seems to me to be a prophetic meaning in what took
place; but none the less it did take place, so that with the occurrence of the event established we are free to seek its figurative
meaning. How are we to interpret the fact that Adam gave
names to the birds and to the animals on the earth but not to
the fish and all the creatures of the waters? If we examine the
various languages of mankind, we see that these living beings

are called by names men have given them in their ordinary speech. And this is true not only of creatures in the water and on the earth but also of the earth itself, the water, the sky, what appears in the sky, and what does not appear but is believed to be there; all are called by different names in the different languages of the world. We know, of course, that there was originally just one language before man in his pride built the tower after the flood and caused human society to be divided according to different languages.[53] And whatever the original language was, what point is there in trying to discover it? It was certainly the language Adam spoke; and in that language, if it has survived to our time, there are those words that were uttered when the first man named the beasts and the birds.

It is hardly believable, then, that the names of fishes in that language were determined not by man but by God and that man subsequently learnt them from God who taught him. But even if this did happen, the reason for it would certainly contain some mystical meaning. We must assume, however, that names were gradually given to various kinds of fish as they became known. But originally the herds, the beasts, and the birds were brought to the man, and when they had gathered before him and he had distinguished them according to their kinds, he gave them their names, although he could have given these names gradually also, but much more quickly than in the case of the fishes (if they were not named with the rest). Now, what is the reason for all this if there was not a plan to signify something which would be able to foreshadow the future? The order of the narrative provides for this purpose very effectively.

21. God was surely not ignorant of the fact that He had created nothing among the animals that was like the man and able to be his helper. Was it necessary that the man also should recognize his need and thereby receive his wife as a more precious gift because, in all flesh created under heaven and living in this atmosphere in which he was placed, he found nothing else like her? But it would be strange if he could not have known this unless all the animals had been brought to him and placed before his eyes. For if he had faith in God, God could have told him this in the same way in which He gave a command and ques-

tioned him when he sinned and passed judgment on him. On the other hand, if he did not have faith in God, he surely would not have known whether God, in whom he had no faith, had brought all animals to him, or whether He could have hidden in some remote corners of the world other animals like the man which He did not disclose. Hence I have no doubt that this all happened for the sake of some prophetic meaning, but none the less it really happened.

22. But in this treatise I have not attempted to examine prophetic mysteries but to interpret the narrative as a faithful history of events that happened. Thus I hope that what could seem impossible to the shallow reader and the unbeliever or at variance with the authority of Sacred Scripture itself by reason of what is alleged to be contradictory evidence, I may show by my discussion, as far as I can with God's help, to be neither impossible nor contradictory. With respect to what can appear to some readers as possible and free of any obvious contradiction, but nevertheless somewhat unnecessary or even foolish, I hope to show by my investigation that the event has not happened in the natural and customary order of things. I hope the result will be that our minds will esteem as trustworthy the authority of Sacred Scripture and assume that since it cannot be foolish it must have a mystical meaning. Indeed, I may have already considered and proposed such a figurative interpretation elsewhere or may decide to postpone it to another time.[54]

CHAPTER 13

The narrative of the formation of the woman suggests some prophetic meaning.

23. What, then, is the meaning of the statement that the woman was made from the side of the man? Let us assume that it was fitting for it to be done that way in order to emphasize the union of the man and woman. But did reason or necessity also demand that this be done while Adam slept? And that a rib be removed and flesh supplied to fill the empty space? Could not

rather flesh have been removed more appropriately for the formation of the woman, who belongs to the weaker sex? Since God was able to add so many other parts and build the rib into a woman, we cannot say He was unable to do the same with flesh after He had made man himself from the dust. And if a rib had to be removed, why was not another rib made to replace it? Furthermore, why was it not said "He formed" or "He made," as it was said with respect to all the preceding works? But the text says, *The Lord God built the rib*, as if there was question of a house rather than a human body.[55]

Since these events took place, therefore, and cannot be senseless happenings, there can be no doubt that they occurred to signify something and that God, who knows the future, mercifully foreshadowed in His works from the very beginning of the human race the fruit of ages to come; and He has willed that certain things written down should be revealed in due time to His servants by tradition handed down through succeeding generations, or by His Holy Spirit, or by the ministry of angels, in order to give testimony about promises to be fulfilled in the future and signs by which men may recognize those that have come to pass. This will become clearer and clearer in what follows.

CHAPTER 14

God brought the animals to Adam by the ministry of angels.

24. In this treatise I have attempted to find not the foreshadowing of future events but the events which actually happened, understood in their proper rather than allegorical meaning.[56] With this in mind, then, let us see how these words of Scripture can be taken: *And again God formed from the earth all the beasts of the field and all the birds of heaven* (this much I have already interpreted in the sense in which I understood it and discussed it to the extent I thought necessary), *and brought them all to Adam to see what he would call them.*[57]

Now, we should not imagine God bringing the animals to Adam in a crudely material way. What I have said in the preceding book about the twofold working of Divine Providence should be a help here.[58] We must not suppose that the animals were brought to Adam as when hunters and fowlers seek them out and drive them into their nets when they engage in the chase. Nor was there a command spoken by a voice from a cloud in words which rational creatures on hearing would understand and obey. Beasts and birds have not received such power. But according to their nature they obey God, not by a rational free choice of the will but according to the plan by which God moves all creatures at the appropriate times. Although He is Himself unmoved in time, the angels who minister to Him understand in His Word what things are to be done at appointed times. And hence, without any temporal motion in God, the angels are moved in time to accomplish His will in the creatures that are subject to them.[59]

25. All living souls, not only rational souls as in men, but also irrational souls as in beasts, birds, and fishes, are moved by what they see. But a rational soul by a free choice of the will either assents to what it sees or withholds its assent. An irrational soul, however, is not able to make such a decision: according to its nature and character it is set in motion at the sight of an object. Furthermore, no soul has control over the objects that meet its vision, whether it is a question of the exterior vision of the eyes or the interior vision of the imagination,[60] and the appetite of every living being is moved by what it sees. Thus, when these visions are brought about through the ministry of angels obeying God's will, a divine command comes not only to men and not only to birds and beasts but also to creatures hidden beneath the waters, like the sea monster that swallowed Jonah;[61] and not only to these larger creatures, but even to worms. For it is written that God's command was given to a worm to eat the root of the gourd in whose shade the prophet had rested.[62]

Now, God gave to man when He created him a power over the lower animals which he did not lose when he sinned, so that he is able to capture and tame not only cattle and beasts of burden, training them for his needs, and not only birds that he domesticates, but also those that fly at liberty as well as all sorts of wild beasts, and thus he is able to dominate these creatures by the power of reason and not just by physical force. Gaining control over them, therefore, through their appetites and sense of pain, and gradually alluring them, restraining them, and giving them some freedom, he rules them, and ridding them of their fierce ways, he develops in them habits that are almost human. How much more readily, then, can this be done by the angels, who by the command of God, which they see in His immutable Truth, which they never cease to behold, move through time and with marvelous ease move bodies subject to them through time and space,[63] producing in all living souls objects of vision to move them and appetites for bodily needs, so that unwittingly they are drawn where they should go.

CHAPTER 15

The making of the first woman. How the angels can minister to God in creation, although they cannot create.

26. Now let us see how the woman was formed, or how she was "built,"[64] to use the mysterious language of Scripture. The substance[65] of the woman was created not by any activity of substances already existing, although it was created from the substance of the man, which was already in existence. Angels cannot create any substances whatsoever.[66] The one and only Creator of every substance, whether great or small, is God, that is, the Trinity, Father, Son, and Holy Spirit. It is one thing to ask how Adam was put to sleep and a rib taken from his body without his feeling any pain. We perhaps might say that angels could have done this. But to form or build a rib into a woman, this could not have been done except by God, on whom every substance depends. Indeed, even the supplying of the flesh in the body of Adam to fill the place of the rib could not have been done, in my opinion, by the angels any more than the creation of man himself from the dust of the earth. I am not saying that the angels have no place in assisting God in creation, but they are not creators any more than farmers are creators of the crops

and the trees. *For neither he who plants is anything nor he who waters, but only God who gives the growth.*[67] This growth includes filling in with flesh part of the human body where a bone has been
removed. Such a thing is done by the work of God, that work
by which He gives being to substances that He makes, including
the angels, who are also His creation.

27. The work of the farmer is to channel the water when he
irrigates. But it is not his work to make water flow down; that
is rather the work of Him who has ordered *all things in measure
and number and weight.*[68] It is also the farmer's work to take a
shoot from a tree and plant it in the ground. But it is not his
work to take in moisture and to put forth buds, or to turn part
of the new tree down into the ground to build up the roots, and
to direct another part up above the ground in order to build up
its strength and spread its branches: all this is done by Him who
gives the increase. A physician, similarly, gives nourishment to
a sick body and applies medicine to a wound. Now, two points
should be observed in this: first, he does not create the food and
medicine, but finds them made by the work of the Creator; and
secondly, he is able to prepare food or drink and administer it,
and to make a plaster and smear it with ointment and then apply it to the right place; but from these means he employs he is
not able to produce or create energy or flesh. Nature does this
by an interior force hidden from us. But if God withdraws the
intimate activity by which He creates this substance and keeps
it in being, it will in effect be destroyed immediately and nothing will remain.

28. God, then, governs all His creation by a kind of twofold
working of His providence, about which I have spoken in the
preceding book,[69] and He rules all creatures by natural and voluntary forces. But an angel can no more create a substance than
he can create himself. The will of an angel, however, which
gives obedient service to God and carries out His commands, is
able to work on things subject to him, using them as a kind of
matter and employing forces of nature, so that something is created in time in accordance with the uncreated formative principles in the Word of God or in accordance with the formative

principles causally created in the works of the first six days.[70]
The angel's function in such a case is like that of the farmer or
the physician.

Who, then, can dare to say what ministry the angels performed for God in the making of the first woman? I would say
without hesitation that the flesh formed in place of the rib, the
body and soul of the woman, the shaping of the bodily members, all the inner organs, all the senses, and whatever there was
by which she was a creature, a human being, a woman—all this
was done by the work of God, which God did not do by the angels but by Himself, not creating His work and then leaving it,
but unceasingly creating it, so that no creature would continue
to exist, not even the angels, were He not working by His creative act.

CHAPTER 16

The difficulty of understanding the ways in which life is created.

29. In so far as our powers of observation and our human intelligence can understand nature, we have no evidence that any
flesh with life and sensation is born unless it is from one of four
sources:[71] either from water and earth, which serve as its material elements, or from the shoots or the fruits of trees, or from
the flesh of animals (as happens in the case of countless kinds of
worms and reptiles), or from the copulation of parents. We
know of no flesh born of the flesh of any living being, like it in
everything except sex. Hence, we are seeking in nature for a
similar occurrence of this creation by which a woman has been
made from the side of a man, and we can find none. The reason
for our ignorance is that although we know how men work in
this world, we do not know how angels cultivate the earth, if I
may use the expression.

If the ordinary processes of nature were to produce a certain
kind of bush without human labor, we should know nothing
else than that trees and plants were born from the earth and also
from their seeds falling again to the earth. But we should know

nothing about grafting, by which a tree of a given kind with its own roots could bear two kinds of fruits, the one proper to its own nature and the other proper to the branch that has been grafted on, both nourished from the same trunk. We have learnt this from the work of farmers. They are not, of course, the creators of trees, but to God, the Creator of the processes of nature, they offer their aid and service. For nothing would come about by their labors unless a hidden causal reason contained the product in God's work of creation.

Why is it strange, therefore, if we do not know of a human being, a woman, made from the bone of a man, since we are ignorant of the ways in which angels minister to God the Creator? We should have been unable to know that a branch from one tree could have been grafted on to another tree so as to become part of it if we were ignorant of the way farmers minister to God who creates these wonders.

30. We have no doubt, however, that God alone is the Creator of men and trees, and we firmly believe that the woman was made from the man without the aid of human procreation, even though the rib of the man may have been obtained by angels for the work of the Creator. In a similar manner, we firmly believe that a Man was also made from a woman without any nuptial embrace when the offspring of Abraham was placed through the angels in the hands of a Mediator.[72] Unbelievers consider both of these events beyond belief. But for believers, why should the account of the conception of Christ be accepted in the literal sense and the account of the creation of Eve be accepted only in a figurative sense? Are we to say that without any sexual embrace a man could have been made from a woman but not a woman from a man? Did the womb of the Virgin have the power to produce a Man, whereas the side of the man had no power to produce the woman, although in the former case the Lord would be born of His handmaid, and in the latter a handmaid would be born of a servant?

The Lord would have been able to create His flesh from a rib or from any member of the Virgin; but He who could have demonstrated that He had done again in the case of His own body what had been done before, deemed it more salutary to show that in the body of His Mother there was no cause for shame, where all was chaste.

CHAPTER 17

Was the manner of the creation of Eve determined in the reason-principle as a necessity or possibility?

31. One may ask in what way God created the woman in causal reasons when He created the first man to His image and likeness, for Scripture says at that point in the narrative, *Male and female He made them.*[73] Did the reason-principle which God concreated and mingled with the works that He made in the world have the determination by which the woman would necessarily come from the rib of the man? Or did it have only the potency from which this development could come, so that the actual determination would have been hidden in God's plans and not necessarily determined in the reason-principle?[74]

If this is the question, I will give my opinion without holding it tenaciously; but when I have proposed it, perhaps believers who are well grounded in the faith, upon thoughtfully weighing my suggestions, will accept them without doubt even though this is the first time they have considered them.

32. The ordinary course of nature in the whole of creation has certain natural laws in accordance with which even the spirit of life,[75] which is a creature, has its own appetites, determined in a sense, which even a bad will cannot elude. The elements of the physical world also have a fixed power and quality determining for each thing what it can do or not do and what can be done or not done with it. From these elements all things which come to be in due time have their origin and development as well as their end and dissolution according to their kind. Thus, a bean does not come from a grain of wheat nor wheat from a bean, and a man does not come from a beast nor a beast from a man.

Over this whole movement and course of nature there is the power of the Creator, who is able to do in all creatures something other than what the seminal reasons would bring about, but not something that He Himself had not originally made possible to be done by Him in them. For He is all-powerful not by arbitrary power but by the strength of wisdom, and in the course of time He does with each thing what He originally has made possible in it. There is, then, the mode of being by which this plant grows one way and that another way; by which one time of life is fertile, another is not; by which a human being can speak, a beast cannot. The formative principles[76] of these and similar modes of being are not only in God but have also been inserted by Him into creatures and joined to them.[77] But that a tree which has been cut down, dried out, polished, without any root or earth or water, should suddenly flower and bring forth fruit,[78] that a woman sterile in her youth should bear a child in her old age,[79] that an ass should speak,[80] and so on with other examples—God gave to the substances which He created the possibility that these actions could happen in them (for not even He would do in them what He Himself predetermined was impossible to be done in them, since He Himself is not more powerful than Himself); nevertheless, according to another mode of being He gave to these creatures the determination that these occurrences would not happen by virtue of natural forces but by virtue of the fact that they had been created so that their nature would be under the influence of a more powerful will.

CHAPTER 18

The mystery of the creation of Eve and the origin of the Church. The ministry of the angels.

33. God, therefore, has in Himself the hidden causes of certain things which He has not placed in creatures, and He makes them operative not in the work of His ordinary providence by which He brings things into being, but in that work by which He administers according to His will the things that He has created as He has willed. In this sphere of God's action is the grace

by which sinners are saved. For nature corrupted by its own evil will is unable to return to God through its own efforts, but it can do so through the grace of God, by which it is helped and renewed. We must not give up hope for men because of what Scripture says: *None who walk with her* [the strange woman] *will return*.[81] For this was said of man in view of the weight of his sinfulness, so that he who will return[82] may not attribute his return to himself but to the grace of God, not because of his works, so that he may not glory.[83]

34. Hence, St. Paul has said that the mystery of this grace was hidden, not in the world, in which the causal reasons of all things destined to come forth in the processes of nature have been hidden, as Levi was hidden in the loins of Abraham when he paid tithes,[84] but in God who created all.[85] Therefore, all things that have been made not in the natural development of things, but in a miraculous way to signify this grace, have had[86] their causes also hidden in God.

An example of such a thing might be seen in the fact that the woman was made from the side of the man—indeed, while he was asleep—and she was made strong through him, being strengthened by his bone, but he was made weak for her sake because in place of his rib it was flesh, not another rib, that was substituted. But it was not determined in the original creation that the woman was to be created in precisely that way, when on the sixth day, according to Scripture, *Male and female He made them*.[87] This act of creation determined only the possibility that it could be done thus, so that God would do[88] nothing by a changeable will contrary to the causes which His will created. How it came to pass that there was to be no other outcome, this was hidden in God, the Creator of all things.

35. St. Paul says that it was hidden *so that to the principalities and powers in the heavens it would be made known through the Church of the manifold wisdom of God*.[89] Now, the offspring to whom the promise was made was placed through the angels in the hands of a Mediator;[90] hence, we may assume with some probability that everything done miraculously beyond the ordinary course of nature to foretell or proclaim in the world the coming of the offspring was done through the ministry of angels; and yet,

there is no other who creates or restores creatures anywhere than He who alone gives the increase no matter who plants or waters.[91]

CHAPTER 19

The prophetic vision seen by Adam in his ecstasy.

36. Hence, we are justified in concluding that the ecstasy[92] in which Adam was caught up when God cast him into a sleep was given to him so that his mind in that state might participate with the host of angels and, entering into the sanctuary of God, understand what was finally to come.[93] When he awoke, he was like one filled with the spirit of prophecy, and seeing his wife brought before him,[94] he immediately opened his mouth and proclaimed the great mystery which St. Paul teaches: *This now is bone of my bones and flesh of my flesh; she shall be called Woman, because she has been taken out of man. And for this reason a man shall leave his father and his mother and shall cleave to his wife; and they shall be two in one flesh.*[95]

These were the words of the first man according to the testimony of Scripture, but in the Gospel our Lord declared that God spoke them. For He says, *Have you not read that He who made them from the beginning made them male and female and said, "For this reason a man shall leave his father and mother and shall cleave to his wife, and they shall be two in one flesh"?*[96] From this we should understand, therefore, that because[97] of the esctasy which Adam had just experienced he was able to say this as a prophet under divine guidance.

But it seems advisable to bring this book to an end at this point, so that in what follows we may revive the attention of the reader with a fresh start.

BOOK TEN
THE ORIGIN OF THE HUMAN SOUL

CHAPTER 1

A consideration of the theory that the soul of Eve was made from the soul of Adam.

1. The natural order of this treatise seems to demand now that I discuss the sin of the first man. But since Scripture has given an account of the making of the body of the woman without saying anything about her soul, I am more eager to look thoroughly into this question and ask how those writers can be refuted or not refuted who think that soul comes from human soul just as body comes from body, the seeds in both cases being passed on from parents to children.[1]

Their position is that God made just one soul, which He breathed into the face of the man whom He had formed from the dust, so that all other human souls would be created from it, just as all other human bodies are created from the body of the first man. Their fundamental reason for holding this position is that Adam was made first, and then Eve. And Scripture tells us about the source of his body and the source of his soul; that is, his body is from the dust of the earth, and his soul is from the breath of God. But when it is said that Eve was made from Adam's rib, it is not said that God gave her life in a similar fashion by His breath, and the conclusion might be drawn that both her soul and body came from him who had already been given life. For, they say, either there should have been no mention of the soul of man, so that we would understand, or at least believe, according to our ability, that it was given by God; or, if Scripture was not silent for fear that we might suppose that the soul of the man as well as his body had been made from the earth, it ought not to have been silent with regard to the soul of the woman for fear it would be thought to be transmitted as an offshoot of Adam's, if that theory is not true. Therefore, they say, there is no mention of God's breathing into her face because as a matter of fact the soul of the woman came from the man.

2. It is easy to refute this opinion. For if they assume that the soul of the woman was made from the soul of the man on the ground that Scripture has not said that God breathed into the face of the woman, why do they think that the woman received life from the man, since that also is not mentioned in Scripture? Hence, if God makes all the souls of human beings coming into this world as He made the first one, Scripture was silent about the others because what is stated as having occurred in the first case could have been reasonably understood as applicable also to the others. Accordingly, if Scripture ought to have given us any instruction at all on this point, with much greater reason it should have done so if anything happened in the case of the woman that did not happen in the case of the man; which would certainly be true if her soul came from his animated flesh, and if she did not, like Adam, receive her body from one source and her soul from another.

Scripture, then, should have informed us of this difference so that we might not think that Eve's soul was made in the way that Adam's was made according to the scriptural narrative. Consequently, since it does not say that the soul of the woman was made from the soul of the man, it is reasonable to assume that the writer by this fact wished to admonish us to suppose nothing different in her case with regard to the soul than what we had learnt about the man, that is, that the woman received her soul in the same way. Had that not been true, there would have been an obvious occasion to state the fact, if not at the formation of Eve, at least later when Adam says, *This now is bone of my bone and flesh of my flesh.*[2] How much more tender and loving it would have been if he had said, "and soul of my soul."

Nevertheless, these considerations have not solved this complicated question so as to bring me to adhere to one of these opinions as obvious and certain.

Chapter 2

A summary of previous investigations into the origin of Adam's soul.

3. Hence, we must first see whether this book of Sacred Scripture, which we have commented on from the opening verse, permits us to doubt about this matter. Then perhaps we shall be able to ask legitimately either what opinion we should choose to adopt or what restrictions we ought to observe in a matter that is uncertain.

Without doubt, on the sixth day *God made man in His image;* and in the same place in Scripture it is also said, *Male and female He made them.*[3] In the foregoing discussions, where the image of God was mentioned, I took this as referring to the soul; but where the difference of sex was mentioned, I took this as referring to the body.[4] Furthermore, the abundant and compelling evidence of Scripture in the texts which have been examined and discussed above would not allow me to understand that the man was formed from the slime of the earth and the woman from his side on the sixth day of creation; but it was clear that this was done later, after the original works of God in which *He created all things together.*[5]

I sought, therefore, to discover what we should believe about the soul of the first man, and after I had examined every aspect of the question, the explanation that seemed probable and reasonable to me was that the soul of the man was made in the original works of creation but that the seminal reason of his body was placed in the corporeal world. Otherwise we should be forced to accept, against the testimony of Scripture, the conclusion that on the sixth day the whole work was done, that is, the man made from the slime of the earth and the woman from his side, or that in the works of the six days man was not made at all; or that it was the causal reason of the body only that was made and not any reason of the soul, although it is in his soul that man is the image of God; or again (and this position is not patently opposed to the words of Scripture, but it is strange and unacceptable) that it was in a spiritual creature created for this purpose alone that the reason-principle of the human soul was

made, although the creature in which the reason-principle was
alleged to have been made was not mentioned in the works of
creation; or that it was in some creature mentioned in the works
of creation that the reason-principle of the soul was made (as in
men who are already in existence there is hidden the reason-
principle of children to be procreated); and thus we should assume the soul to be the offspring of angels or (a still more
intolerable hypothesis) the offspring of some corporeal element.[6]

CHAPTER 3

Three hypotheses considered concerning the origin of human souls.

4. But if it is now asserted that the first woman received her
soul not from the man but like him from God who made it, on
the ground that God creates an individual soul for each individual human being, then the soul of the woman was not made in
the original works of creation. On the other hand, if a universal
reason-principle of all souls had been created, as there is in men
the reason-principle of procreation, we return to the strange
and troublesome necessity of saying that human souls are the
children either of angels or (worse yet!) of the corporeal heaven
or even of some inferior element.

As a result, although the truth is hidden from us, we must
consider what could be at least the most reasonable hypothesis
to solve this problem. Is the origin of the soul to be explained
as I have just now explained it?[7] Or was there in the original
works of creation only one soul created, that of the first man,
so that all human souls would be created as the progeny of it?
Or are new souls subsequently made without even a created
causal principle preceding them in God's works of the six days?
Of these three hypotheses, the first two do not contradict what
Scripture says about the original works of creation, in which
God created everything simultaneously. In one case (the second
hypothesis) there was created in a creature, as in a parent, the
reason-principle of soul so that all souls would be reproduced by

it and be created by God when given to individual human beings, just as bodies come from parents. In the other case (the
first hypothesis) it was not the reason-principle of the soul, like
the reason-principle of offspring in the parent, but when day
was made, the soul itself was created as was the day and heaven
and earth and the lights of heaven. On either hypothesis, therefore, it is appropriate for Scripture to say, *God made man to His
image.*

5. But it is not easy to see how the third hypothesis does not
contradict the interpretation in which man is understood to
have been made on the sixth day to the image of God and to
have been visibly created after the seventh day. There is a difficulty in saying that new souls are made when neither they nor
their reason-principle (like the reason-principle of the offspring
in the parent) were made on the sixth day along with the works,
both finished and begun,[8] from which God rested on the seventh day. If we hold such an opinion, we should take care that
the lesson of Scripture be not lost when it carefully teaches us
that God finished all His works in six days and made them very
good, if He was to create further beings which He had not made
in their own substances or causally in their reason-principles.

In this case we should understand that God has in Himself (although He has not placed it in any creature) the reason of all individual souls which are to be made and given to infants coming into the world. But since souls are not creatures of a different kind from that according to which man was made to the
image of God on the sixth day, it is not correct to say that God
makes a creature now which He did not then finish. For He
made a soul then of the same nature as the souls He makes now,
and it follows, therefore, that He does not now make some new
kind of creature which He did not then create in the works He
finished. This activity of God is not contrary to the causal reasons of future things which He originally laid away in the universe, but rather it is according to them. For in human bodies,
whose continued propagation was provided from those first
works down through the ages, it was fitting that there should
be infused souls such as God now makes and infuses.

6. Consequently, no matter which one of the three interpre-

tations[9] will impress us as the most probable, we should remove all fear of seeming to hold an opinion inconsistent with the words of the Book of Genesis concerning the original creation of the six days. Let us, then, undertake a more thorough investigation of this question with God's help, and let us see if it is possible to find some solution—if not a luminously clear explanation beyond all doubt, at least an acceptable theory concerning the matter, which it will not be absurd to hold until further light will bring us to something certain. But if it is impossible to attain this goal because the weight of evidence is balanced on all sides, at least I shall not appear in my doubt to have avoided the labor of enquiry but only the excess of overconfident affirmation. In this way, I hope, he who has good reason to be certain of his position will be kind enough to instruct me. On the other hand, if anyone is tenacious of his opinion, not because of the authority of God's word or the force of manifest reason, but because of his presumption, I hope he will not refuse to share my uncertainty.

CHAPTER 4

What is known about the soul. The need to follow the testimony of Scripture in considering the origin of the soul.

7. First of all, let us hold it for certain that the substance of a soul cannot be turned into a bodily substance, so that what was soul becomes body; nor into an irrational soul, so that what was a human soul becomes the soul of a beast; nor into the Divine Substance, so that what was a soul becomes identified with God. So also, on the other hand, let us hold that neither body nor irrational soul nor the Divine Substance can be changed into a human soul. It must also be no less certain that the soul is a creature of God. Hence, if God made the human soul not from a body nor from an irrational soul nor from Himself, it follows that He makes it either from nothing or from some spiritual and, of course, rational creature.

But it is quite unreasonable to hope to demonstrate that something is made from nothing once the works were finished in which God created all things simultaneously, and I do not know if that theory can be proved with any clear evidence from the texts.[10] Furthermore, we should not be asked to explain what a man cannot even understand; or if one can understand it, I doubt if he could persuade anyone else except the sort of man who, without any other person attempting to instruct him, is himself able to understand this sort of thing. It is safer, therefore, not to treat these problems with human conjectures but to examine diligently the word of God.

CHAPTER 5

The soul is not created from the angels or the elements or the substance of God.

8. I can think of no text in the canonical books of Scripture to support the theory that God creates souls from angels functioning as parents, much less from the elements of the corporeal world. However, one might cite the passage in the book of the prophet Ezekiel where the resurrection of the dead is described with the restoration of their bodies, when the breath from the four winds of heaven is summoned, and as it blows they are brought to life and rise up: *And the Lord said to me, "Prophesy to the breath; prophesy, son of man, and say to the breath, 'Thus says the Lord, From the four winds of heaven come and breathe upon these dead and let them live.'" So I prophesied as the Lord commanded me, and the breath of life entered into them, and they came back to life and stood upon their feet, an exceedingly great host.*[11]

Here, it seems to me, these words foretold in prophetic language that men would rise up not only from the field where this action was portrayed but from all over the earth, and I think this was symbolized through the wind blowing from the four parts of the world.[12] For the breath from the body of our Lord was not the substance of the Holy Spirit when He breathed and said, *Receive the Holy Spirit,*[13] but by doing this He signified that the Holy Spirit proceeds from Him as this breath proceeded from His body. But since the world is not united to God in the unity of a person as the body of Christ is united to the Word, the only-begotten Son of God, we cannot say that the soul is from the substance of God as the breath is made from the four winds of the world.[14] But I believe that the breath was one thing and that it signified another; and this can be clearly understood in the example of the breath proceeding from the body of our Lord. This interpretation is true even though the prophet Ezekiel in the passage cited foresaw, in a revelation given under figures, not the resurrection of the body as it will be one day, but the unexpected restoration of a people without hope through the Spirit of the Lord who *has filled the whole world.*[15]

CHAPTER 6

Two theories on the origin of the soul examined in the light of Scripture.

9. Let us, then, see which opinion is supported by the testimony of Scripture. Is it the one which asserts that God made one soul and gave it to the first man, later making the others from it, as He makes the other human bodies from the body of the first man? Or is it the one which asserts that He makes an individual soul for each individual man just as He did for Adam, not making the other souls from Adam's?[16]

What God says through the mouth of Isaiah, *I have made every breath*[17] (and the words that follow show that He is speaking of the soul), can be explained according to either theory. For whether God makes souls from the one soul of the first man or from some origin beyond our knowledge, there is no doubt that He makes all souls.

10. In the Psalms it is written, *Who formed their hearts one by one.*[18] Now, if by "hearts" we wish to understand "souls," this text does not contradict either of the two theories about which we are perplexed. For, on the one hand, if God forms souls from the one soul which He breathed into the face of the first man, He Himself certainly forms all individual souls just as He forms

bodies. On the other hand, the same thing is true if He forms individual souls and sends them into bodies or if He forms them in the bodies into which He has sent them.

However, the text cited above from the Psalm, I believe, refers only to the fact that our souls are renewed and formed by grace to the image of God. Hence St. Paul says, *For by grace you have been saved through faith, and this is not your own doing, but it is God's gift; it is not because of your works, so that no one may glory. For we are His work of art, created in Christ Jesus in good works.*[19] We cannot, indeed, understand these words in the sense that our bodies have been created or formed through this grace of faith, but in the sense in which the Psalmist says, *Create in me a clean heart, O God.*[20]

11. In the same sense, I believe, we must understand the text which says, *Who formed the spirit of man within him,*[21] recognizing that it is one thing to send into a body a soul already made, and another thing to make it in man himself, that is, to remake and renew it. But even if we understand this not as referring to grace, in which we are renewed, but to nature, in which we are born, the text can be interpreted in accordance with either opinion. For in one interpretation God forms in man from the one soul of the first man that which is drawn like a seed of the soul to vivify the body; and in the other interpretation God forms the spirit of life not as the offspring of Adam's soul but infused into the body from elsewhere, and He likewise fashions it in the senses of the mortal body so that man may become a living being.

CHAPTER 7

What theory on the origin of the soul is supported by Wisdom 8.19–20?

12. A more thorough consideration is needed of the text of the Book of Wisdom which says, *A good soul fell to my lot; and being good above the common, I came to a body undefiled.*[22] This does, indeed, seem to support the theory which holds that souls

are not generated from one soul but come from above into bodies.

However, what is the meaning of the statement, *A good soul fell to my lot*? Are we to imagine that in the fountainhead of souls, if there is such a thing, there are some souls that are good and some that are not, and that they go out by lot, each lot determining what soul is to be assigned to each man? Or does God make some good and others not good at the moment of conception or birth, so that each person has the kind of soul determined by his lot? It is strange if this text simply supports those who think that souls made elsewhere are sent individually by God into individual human bodies, and does not rather support those who say that souls are sent into bodies in accordance with the merits of the deeds they performed before entering bodies.[23] Indeed, by what criterion can some good souls and some souls not good be thought to enter bodies unless it is by their deeds? It is not by their nature, for in it they are made by Him who makes all natures good. But far be it from us to contradict St. Paul, who says that those not yet born had done no good or evil,[24] thus confirming the fact that it could not have been because of deeds but because of the One calling that it was said, *The elder shall serve the younger*, when there was question of the twins still in the womb of Rebecca.[25]

Let us, then, put aside for a moment the text from the Book of Wisdom cited above. Indeed, we ought not to overlook, whether they are right or wrong, those who think that those words were spoken particularly and exclusively about the soul of the *Mediator between God and men, the Man Christ Jesus.*[26] But if necessary, we shall consider the meaning of the text later, so that if it cannot be applied to Christ, we may investigate to see how we ought to understand it, in order that we may not find ourselves contradicting the faith as handed down by St. Paul, thinking that souls have some merits for their deeds before they begin life in the body.

CHAPTER 8

What theory on the origin of the soul is supported by Psalm 103.29–30?

13. Now let us see in what sense Scripture has said, *Thou wilt take away their spirit, and they will fail and return to their dust. Thou wilt send forth Thy spirit, and they will be created, and Thou wilt renew the face of the earth.*[27]

This text seems to support the opinion of those who think that souls are created from parents as bodies are, since the Psalmist is understood as having said *their spirit* on the ground that it has come to man from man. When men die, this spirit cannot be restored to them by men so as to make the dead rise again, because it is not received a second time from parents as it originally was at birth; but it will be restored by God, who raises the dead.[28] Hence, the Psalmist calls the same spirit *their spirit* when they die and *the spirit of God* when they rise.

But those who hold that souls come not from parents but from God who sends them are able to interpret the text in keeping with their theory by understanding that the Psalmist has said *their spirit* when men are dying because it was in them and went forth from them, and that he has said *the spirit of God* when they rise because it is sent by Him and restored by Him. Consequently, this text does not refute either theory.

14. For my part, I think that this text is better understood as referring to the grace of God by which we are interiorly renewed. For in the case of all men who are proud, living their lives according to the earthly man and presuming on their emptiness, their own spirit is, in a sense, cast off when they divest themselves of the old man and become weak so that they may be made perfect by driving pride out, saying to the Lord in humble confession, *Remember that we are dust.*[29] Indeed, to them it had been said, *How can he who is dust and ashes be proud?*[30] For through the eye of faith, looking on the justice of God, so that they may not desire to establish their own justice,[31] they despise themselves, as Job says, and melt away and consider themselves

as dust and ashes.[32] This is what is meant by the statement, *And they will return to their dust*. But when they receive the Spirit of God, they say, *It is no longer I who live, but Christ lives in me*.[33] Thus, the face of the earth is renewed by the multitude of the saints through the grace of the New Testament.

CHAPTER 9

What theory on the origin of the soul is supported by Ecclesiastes 12.7?

15. The text in Ecclesiastes, . . . *and before the dust returns to the earth as it was, and the spirit goes back to God who gave it*,[34] does not support one theory more than the other but is compatible with either. The advocates of one theory can say that this proves that the soul is given not by the parents but by God, because when the dust, that is, the flesh which was made of dust, has returned to its earth, the spirit will return to God who gave it. Those on the other side reply: "You are certainly right. The spirit returns to God, who gave it to the first man when He breathed into his face, and the dust, that is, the human body, returns to the earth from which it was originally made."[35] For the spirit was not destined to return to the parents, even though it may have been created from the one spirit which was given to the first man, any more than the body after death returns to the parents, although it is certainly obvious that it was begotten by them.

Just as the body, therefore, does not return to the human beings by whom it was made but to the earth from which it was formed for the first man, so the spirit does not return to the parents by whom it has been transmitted but to God by whom it was given to the first human body.

16. The text cited above, then, clearly teaches us that God made from nothing the soul which He gave to the first man, and did not form it from some creature already made, as in the case of the body made from the earth. Hence, when the soul returns,

it can only return to the Author of its being who gave it, not to some creature from which it was made, as the body to the earth. For there is no creature from which it was made, because it was made from nothing; and hence, in returning it returns to its Maker, by whom it was made from nothing. Not all indeed return, since there are those of whom it is said, *a wind that goes and returns not.* [36]

CHAPTER 10

It is difficult to determine the origin of the soul on the basis of Scripture.

17. It is difficult, then, to collect all the texts of Holy Scripture touching this matter; and if it could be done, we should have to write a very long treatise in order to cite the passages and discuss them. But unless this would produce evidence as certain as the evidence which shows that God made the soul or that He gave it to the first man, I do not know how this question could be solved by the testimony of the sacred text. For if Scripture had said that God breathed into the face of the woman He made, just as He had done with the man, and that she was made a living being, this would throw considerable light on the question and would lead us to believe that the soul given to each newly-formed body is not from the parents. Nevertheless, we should still want to know what exactly would take place in the generation of offspring, for this is the ordinary way in which human beings spring from human beings. The first woman, indeed, was formed in a different way, and therefore it could still be maintained that Eve did not receive her soul from Adam for the reason that she was not born as a child from him. But if Scripture were to say that the first child born to them did not have a soul transmitted from his parents but rather given to him by God, then we should have to believe that others receive their souls in the same way even though Scripture is silent on this point.

CHAPTER 11

Is St. Paul's statement in Romans 5.12, 18–19 compatible with either theory on the origin of the soul?

18. Now let us consider another text and see if it proves neither of the two theories but is capable of being reconciled with both. St. Paul says, *Through one man sin came into this world, and through sin death, and so death spread to all men, in whom all have sinned.* And farther on, *Just as through one man's transgression all men were condemned, so also through the justice of One all men receive acquittal and life. For just as by one man's disobedience many have been made sinners, so by one Man's obedience many are made just.*[37]

On the basis of these words of St. Paul, those who hold the propagation of souls by generation attempt to prove their position in the following manner.[38] If sin and sinner can be understood solely in relation to the body (so their argument runs), we are not required by these words of St. Paul to believe that the soul is from the parents. But if it is the soul only that sins, although it is attracted by the allurements of the body, how must we understand the statement *in whom all have sinned* if the soul has not descended from Adam as the body has? Or how have men been made sinners through Adam's disobedience if they were in him with respect to the body only and not with respect to the soul?

19. We must be on our guard, indeed, against errors that may be implied in holding that the soul does not descend from Adam's soul. For instance, we must not make God seem to be the author of sin if He gives the soul to a body in which it must necessarily sin. Again, we must not believe that there can be a soul—apart from the soul of Christ—for which the grace of Christ is not necessary for it to be freed from sin on the ground that it did not sin in Adam if it is said that all sinned in him according to the body only, which comes from Adam, and not also according to the soul. This position is obviously contrary to the faith of the Church, for parents take even their small children and infants and rush with them to receive the grace of holy bap-

tism. Now, if the bond of sin which is loosed in them is a bond of the flesh only and not also of the soul, one could rightly ask what harm they would suffer if they went forth from the body at that early age without baptism. For if this sacrament is for the good of their bodies and not of their souls, they ought to be baptized even when dead. But since the universal Church holds to the custom of rushing to the sacrament with living infants to provide for them, fearing that when they die nothing can be done to help them, there is only one explanation, namely, each child is Adam in body and soul, and therefore the grace of Christ is necessary for him. At that age the infant in his own person has done no good or evil,[39] and thus his soul is perfectly innocent if it has not descended from Adam. Consequently, it will be an extraordinary achievement if the person who holds that the soul has not descended from Adam's soul is able to show how the soul of an infant can be justly condemned if it goes forth from the body without baptism![40]

CHAPTER 12

The cause of carnal desire is not in the flesh alone but also in the soul.

20. The testimony of Scripture is certainly true when it says, *The desires of the flesh are against the spirit, and those of the spirit against the flesh.*[41] Nevertheless, I am convinced that no one, learned or ignorant, questions the fact that the flesh can have no desires without the soul. Consequently, the cause of carnal concupiscence is not in the soul alone, much less in the flesh alone. It comes from both sources: from the soul, because without it no pleasure is felt; from the flesh, because without it carnal pleasure is not felt. Hence, when St. Paul speaks of the desires of the flesh against the spirit, he undoubtedly means the carnal pleasure which the spirit experiences from the flesh and with the flesh as opposed to the pleasure which the spirit alone experiences.

It is the spirit alone indeed, if I am not mistaken, that has a desire unmixed with carnal pleasure or any craving for carnal things, when it *longs and faints for the courts of the Lord.*[42] The spirit alone experiences also that desire about which it is said to it, *You have desired wisdom; keep the commandment, and the Lord will give it to you.*[43] For when the spirit commands the members of the body to be at the service of this desire with which the spirit alone is enkindled—for example, when one takes up a book, or when one writes, reads, discusses, listens, or when one feeds the hungry, and when other good deeds are done out of human kindness and pity—the flesh obeys, and it does not stir up concupiscence. When these and similar good desires, which the soul alone seeks, are opposed by something which delights the same soul according to the flesh, then it is said that *The desires of the flesh are against the spirit, and those of the spirit against the flesh.*

21. In this connection "the flesh" is spoken of when the soul acts according to it, for example, when one says, "The flesh desires." In the same way we say, "The ear hears" and "The eye sees," but everyone knows that it is the soul that hears by means of the ear and sees by means of the eye.[44] By the same usage we say that your hand helps a man when you put forth your hand and give something to help another. And it is with reference to the eye of faith, to which it belongs to believe what is not seen through the flesh, that Scripture says, *All flesh will see the salvation of God.*[45] But it is surely with reference to the soul alone, by which the flesh lives, that this was said; for even to look piously through the eyes of the flesh upon Christ, that is, upon the form which He assumed for our sake, does not belong to concupiscence (and one should guard against understanding the text, *All flesh will see the salvation of God,* in this sense) but to the ministry of the flesh.[46]

It is more properly said that the flesh desires when the soul not only gives animal life to the flesh but also desires something according to the flesh. It is not in the soul's power to be rid of these desires so long as there is sin in the members, that is, a strong allurement of the flesh in *this body of death,*[47] resulting from the punishment for the sin in which we are born, by which before grace all are *sons of wrath.*[48]

Against this sin those who are placed under grace carry on a war, not with the hope that sin will no longer be in their body as long as it is mortal—when it is rightly called dead—but with the hope that it will not reign.[49] And sin does not reign when its desires are not obeyed, that is, the cravings by which it lusts after allurements according to the flesh against the spirit. Hence, St. Paul did not say, "Let not sin be in your mortal body" (for he knew that the attraction of sin, which he calls sin, is there since our nature has been corrupted by the original transgression); but he said, *Let not sin reign in your mortal body to make you obey its lusts; do not yield your members as instruments of iniquity unto sin.*[50]

CHAPTER 13

The Manichean doctrine of two natures and two wills in man rejected. The sins of children.

22. In this interpretation I avoid saying that the flesh has desires without the soul (an absurd position), and I also avoid agreeing with the Manichees, who saw that the flesh could not have desires without the soul and hence assumed that it has another soul within it, having its origin in a nature opposed to God, whence it lusts against the spirit.[51] Moreover, I am not forced to say that there is some soul for which the grace of Christ is not necessary when someone says to me: "What blame has the soul of an infant deserved that it should be dangerous for it to depart from the body without receiving the sacrament of baptism, if on the one hand it has not committed any sin of its own and on the other has not descended from the first soul which sinned in Adam?"

23. I am not talking about children in their late childhood. There are some people, it is true, who are unwilling to impute personal sin to children before the beginning of puberty in their fourteenth year. I could see good reason to believe this if there were no sins except those that have to do with the genital organs. But who would dare assert that thefts, lies, and false oaths are not sins except one who wishes to commit such sins with im-

punity? Yet these sins are common in childhood, although it seems that they should not be punished in children as severely as in adults, because one hopes that with the passing years, as reason begins to take hold, these children will be able to understand better the precepts pertaining to salvation and to give them willing obedience.

But I am not now talking about children who summon every effort they can by word and deed to attack truth and justice when they are opposed to their carnal and childish pleasure[52] of body or soul. And what is in the minds of these children except the thought of the falsehood and sin which seems ready to aid them in obtaining what attracts them or avoiding what repels them? But I am speaking of infants—not because they are frequently born of adulterous parents,[53] for we ought not to find the gifts of nature in the child worthy of blame because of the sins of the parents.[54] Similarly, we cannot say that the grain ought not to ripen because it was sown by the hand of a thief; or that the sin of parents is going to plague their lives if they turn to God and mend their ways; and much less that it will plague their children if these children lead upright lives.

CHAPTER 14

Traducianism considered in the light of original sin and the practice of infant baptism.

But the age that poses a puzzling problem is that of infancy, when the soul has committed no sin of its own free will. How can the infant's soul be justified through the obedience of one Man if it is not guilty through the disobedience of another one man?[55] This is the objection of those who say that human souls are created by human parents, not without the action of the Creator, to be sure, but in a manner similar to that in which bodies are created.[56] For it is not the parents who create the bodies but rather He who said, *Before I formed you in the womb I knew you.*[57]

24. Others reply to this by saying that God gives new souls individually to human bodies so that, in spite of their being in

sinful flesh coming from original sin, they may live upright lives and, with the grace of God, bring carnal concupiscence under control, and thus gain merit whereby they may be transformed to a better state with these very bodies at the time of the resurrection and may live in Christ with the angels forever.

But since souls are mysteriously united to earthly and mortal members, especially members propagated by sinful flesh, they say that to be able first to give the body life and afterwards, with its coming of age, to rule it, these souls must be overcome by a state of forgetfulness.[58] If this condition were irreversible, God the Creator would be considered responsible. But the soul, gradually recovering from this listless state of forgetfulness (according to this theory), is able, first by the devout affection of its conversion and then by its perseverance in keeping the commandments, to turn to its God and to merit His mercy and truth. What harm, then, comes to it from being plunged into a kind of sleep for a short time when it can gradually awaken to the light of intelligence, for which the rational soul has been made, and through a good will choose a good life? But this it will not be able to do unless it will be aided by the grace of God conferred through the Mediator. If a man neglects this aid, he will be Adam not only according to the flesh but also according to the spirit. If he is solicitous about his state, he will be Adam according to the flesh only; but living a holy life according to the spirit, even the flesh which he inherited from Adam tainted by sin he will deserve to receive back purified from the stain of sin by that transformation which the resurrection promises to the saints.

25. But before he attains the age at which he can live according to the spirit, he must have the sacrament of the Mediator so that what he cannot yet do by his faith may be done for him by the faith of those who love him.[59] By this sacrament, indeed, the penalty of original sin is wiped out even in the age of infancy; but unless one is helped by this sacrament, one will not gain control over carnal concupiscence even as a young adult. Furthermore, when this concupiscence is mastered, he will not obtain the merit of eternal life except by the grace of Him whom he seeks to win. Hence, even an infant as long as he is alive

should be baptized so that the union with sinful flesh may not harm his soul. For by reason of this association the soul of an infant cannot be wise according to the spirit.[60] Indeed, this condition weighs the soul down even when it leaves the body, unless while in the body it is purified through the one and only Sacrifice of the true Priest.[61]

CHAPTER 15

Why is it necessary for infants to be baptized?

26. What happens, then, someone will say, if the parents or relatives out of unbelief or negligence fail to have the infant baptized? The same question, indeed, can be asked about adults. For they can die suddenly, or they can be sick in a home where no one will see that they are baptized. But the adults, they say, have also their own personal sins which need forgiveness; and if they are not forgiven, no one can rightly say that they are punished unjustly for the deeds which they wilfully committed during their lives.

But the soul of an infant is a different matter. Its contamination by contact with sinful flesh can in no way be imputed to it if it was not created from the first soul of Adam who sinned. For it was not by any sin but rather by nature that it was so made, and by God's gift that it was given to the body. Why, then, will it be excluded from eternal life if no one will be moved to see that the infant is baptized? Shall we say that the infant will suffer no harm? What, then, is the advantage for the one who is baptized if there is no harm done to the one who is not baptized?

27. I should like to hear what these have to say for their position who take Holy Scripture into account—either finding evidence in it for their opinion or finding that it does not contradict their interpretation—and who try to maintain that new souls not inherited from the parents are given to bodies. I must confess that I have not yet heard or read anywhere their explanation of the problem.

But I should not on that account desert the position of those who are absent if I find something that seems to support it. For they can also say that God foreknows how each soul would live if it were to have a longer life in the body, and thus He provides the ministration of the saving waters for each one who He knows would have lived in a holy manner when he would come to an age at which he could believe, if it were now[62] necessary for him to meet an early death by some hidden cause.

It is, then, a mystery beyond human powers of knowing, at least beyond mine, why an infant destined to die immediately or soon after birth is born. This is so mysterious that it can help neither of the two sides whose opinions we are discussing. For we have rejected the opinion which holds that souls are cast into bodies in accordance with the merits of a previous life, so that a soul which had not committed many sins would apparently deserve to be delivered the sooner. We rejected this theory so as not to contradict St. Paul, who testifies that those who are not yet born have done no good or evil.[63] Hence, neither those who maintain the transmission of the soul nor those who hold that individual new souls are given to individual bodies are able to show why some die early and others die late. The reason, therefore, is hidden, and so far as I can see it does not support or oppose either opinion.

CHAPTER 16

Further reflections on the need of baptism of infants.

28. Certain writers, when pressed on the subject of the death of infants and when asked why the sacrament of baptism is necessary for all human beings, whose souls have not come from the soul of him by whose disobedience *many have been made sinners*,[64] reply that all have been made sinners according to the flesh, but according to the soul those only who have lived an evil life during the time when they might have lived a good one. Moreover, they say that all souls, including those of infants, must receive the sacrament of baptism (without which even infants ought not

to depart this life) because the contamination of sin, coming from sinful flesh and infecting the soul when it enters the body, will be the ruin of the soul after death unless it is purified by the sacrament of the Mediator while still in the flesh. Thus, they say, this remedy is provided by Divine Providence for any soul which God foreknew would have lived a holy life if it were to live in this world to the age when it could make an act of faith, but which for reasons known to Him alone He wished to be born in a body and which He then without delay took from the body.

When this is their reply, what can be said against them except that we are made uncertain of the salvation of those who after a good life have died peacefully in the Church if each one is to be judged not only according to the life he lived but also according to that which he would have lived if he had been able to live longer? Indeed, in this theory souls are accountable before God not only for past sins but also for future sins, and death does not free them from guilt if it takes them before the sins are committed, nor is any benefit bestowed upon him *who was caught up lest evil change his understanding.*[65] For why is God, knowing this future wickedness as He does, not going to judge man according to it if He came to the aid of an infant who was going to die and provided that the taint of impurity from the sinful body would not harm it and thus decided to give it salvation through baptism because He foreknew that this infant, if it were to live, would have lived a good and faithful life?

29. Can this argument be rejected because it is mine? But perhaps those who maintain that they are certain of this opinion bring forth other texts of Scripture or proofs from reason to remove this ambiguity or at least to show that their theory is not contradicted by the statements of St. Paul, when with considerable emphasis he tells us of the grace by which we are saved, saying, *As in Adam all die, so also in Christ shall all be made alive;*[66] and, *As by one man's disobedience many have been made sinners, so by one Man's obedience many will be made just.*[67] By the *many sinners* referred to, St. Paul meant all men without exception, and hence just before this, speaking of Adam, he said, ... *in whom all have sinned.*[68] That the souls of infants cannot be separated

from these, since St. Paul says "all" and also since they are saved by baptism, this is understandably the position of those who think that souls are transmitted from the soul of Adam, unless they are refuted by some clear argument from reason that does not contradict Holy Scripture or by some positive testimony of Scripture itself.[69]

CHAPTER 17

The meaning of Wisdom 8.19–20.

30. Let us examine, then, as far as the scope of this work allows, the meaning of the text which we quoted and then put aside a short time ago.[70] The author of the Book of Wisdom has written, *As a child I was well endowed, and a good soul fell to my lot; and being good above the common, I came to a body undefiled.*[71]

This text seems to support those who hold that souls are not created from the souls of parents but come or descend to the body when God sends them. But it is also opposed to their theory in so far as it says, *A good soul fell to my lot,* since they undoubtedly believe that souls trickle, as it were, like brooks from one spring, or that the souls which God sends into bodies are made equal by nature and that there are not some good or better and others not good or less good. For on what basis are souls good or better, or on the other hand not good or less good, except by their manner of life adopted by the free choice of the will or by variations in the disposition of their bodies, since some are more weighed down, some less, by the body, which is corrupted and burdensome to the soul?[72] But there was no action of individual souls by which their manner of life could be distinguished before they came into bodies; and it could not have been because of a body less burdensome that the author declared his soul good when he said, *A good soul fell to my lot; and being good above the common, I came to a body undefiled.* For he says that he came to the goodness by which he was good, obtaining by lot a good soul, so that he also came to a body undefiled. He

was good, therefore, from another source before coming to the
body, but certainly not because of a difference in his way of life,
since there is no merit for deeds in a previous life; nor because
of a difference in his body, since he was good before entering
the body. What, then, was the source of the difference?

31. This text, in so far as it says, *I came to a body*, does not
seem favorable to those who maintain that souls are created as
offshoots of the soul that first sinned; but for the rest it fits that
theory, since after the author has said, *As a child I was well endowed*, explaining the reason why he was well endowed, he immediately adds, *And a good soul fell to my lot*, that is, from the
character or the well-balanced bodily disposition of his father.
Then he says, *Being good above the common, I came to a body undefiled*; and if this is understood as referring to his mother's
body, the statement, *I came to a body*, will not be in opposition
to that opinion when he is understood to have come from his father's soul and body to his mother's undefiled body. Defilement
in this connection would be either from menstrual blood, which
they say oppresses the natural endowment of the infant, or from
the contamination of an adulterous union. Hence, the words of
the Book of Wisdom are more favorable to those who speak of
the soul as an offshoot of Adam's soul; or if the other side can
explain them in keeping with their theory, this text leaves the
question open.

CHAPTER 18

The soul of Christ. Is it possible to apply Wisdom 8.19–20 to Christ?

32. If we wish to apply these words from the Book of Wisdom
to our Lord according to the created human nature assumed by
the Word, there are some details in the context which are inconsistent with His perfection. This is especially true of the fact
that the one who is speaking in this book, shortly before he said
these words which we are now discussing, confessed that he was
compacted with blood, from the seed of a man.[73] Now, this manner

of birth is irreconcilable with the birth from the Virgin, who did not conceive the body of Christ from the seed of man, as every Christian holds without any doubt.

But there are also the words of Christ in the Psalms where He says, *They have pierced My hands and feet; they have numbered all My bones. And they have looked and stared upon Me. They have divided My garments among them, and upon My vesture they have cast lots.*[74] These words belong properly to Christ alone. But earlier in the same Psalm He says, *O God, My God, look upon Me. Why hast Thou forsaken Me? Far from My salvation are the words of My sins.*[75] Now this does not properly belong to Christ except in so far as He transfigures in Himself the lowly condition of our body, since we are members of His body.

Furthermore, in the Gospel it is said, *The Child advanced in years and wisdom.*[76] Hence, if the words which we read preceding the text we are discussing in the Book of Wisdom[77] can be applied to the Lord Himself in view of the lowly form of servant that was His and the union of the body of the Church with its Head, who could be more richly endowed than the Child whose wisdom at the age of twelve was admired by the elders?[78] And what could be more excellent than the soul of Christ?

But even if the advocates of traducianism prevail, not by contentious argumentation but by proofs, it will not follow that we must believe that the soul of Christ has also come by generation from the soul of Adam, for we cannot suppose that our Lord Himself is made a sinner through the disobedience of the first man when through the obedience of Christ alone many are freed from guilt and made just. And what more undefiled than the womb of the Virgin, whose flesh, although it came from procreation tainted by sin, nevertheless did not conceive from that source? Consequently, not even the body of Christ was planted in the womb of Mary in accordance with that law which, placed in the members of the body of death, is at war with the law of the mind.[79] The holy patriarchs restrained with marriage this law of sin, not relaxing their restraint until intercourse was allowed; nevertheless, even when it was allowed they felt the force of this law.

Hence, although the body of Christ was taken from the flesh

of a woman who had been conceived from the flesh of a sinful race, nevertheless, since it was not conceived in her womb in the manner in which she had been conceived, it was not sinful flesh but the likeness of sinful flesh.[80] For He did not thereby contract the guilt that brings death, manifesting itself by involuntary motions of the flesh which must be conquered by the will and against which the spirit has its desires.[81] But He received a body immune to the contagion of sin, a body which would be able to pay the debt to death that He did not owe and to show forth the promised resurrection, thus taking fear from us and giving us hope.[82]

33. Finally, if I am asked from what source Jesus Christ received His soul, I should prefer to hear the opinions of better and more learned men; but as far as I can grasp the matter, I should respond that it was from the source whence Adam received his, rather than from Adam's own soul. For if dust taken from the earth on which no man had worked was worthy of being animated by the power of God, how much more fittingly did the body taken from the flesh on which no man had worked receive by lot a good soul. In the first case, he who was to fall would be raised up; and in the second, He who would lift the other up would descend to earth. And perhaps He said, *A good soul fell to my lot* (if this ought to be applied to our Lord), because what is given by lot is given by God; or perhaps, in conformity with our faith, it was to keep us from thinking that even the soul of Christ was raised to such excellence by any previous deeds meriting that the Word should become flesh with it and dwell among us, and thus the word "lot" was used to remove any suspicion of antecedent merits.

CHAPTER 19

The soul of Christ was not in the loins of Abraham, and hence it was not transmitted from the soul of Adam.

34. In the epistle which is called "To the Hebrews," there is a passage that merits our careful consideration. For through

Melchizedek, in whom there was a figure of the future reality, the author of the Epistle distinguished the priesthood of Christ from that of Levi when he said: *Consider how great this man is to whom even Abraham the patriarch gave a tenth part of the choicest of the spoils. And those who are from the sons of Levi, receiving the priestly office, have a commandment according to the law to take tithes from the people, that is, from their brothers, though these also have come from the loins of Abraham. But this man, who has not the same descent, received tithes from Abraham and blessed him who had the promises. Now it is beyond all dispute that the inferior is blessed by the superior. And here, indeed, mortal men receive tithes, but there it is one who testifies that he lives. And, as it is right to say it, Levi also, though receiving tithes, paid tithes through Abraham. For he was still in the loins of his father.* [83]

If this tribute, therefore, after so long a time can show how great was the priesthood of Christ compared to that of Levi, because Christ the Priest was prefigured by Melchizedek, who imposed a tithe on Abraham, and through Abraham also on Levi, he surely imposed no tithe on Christ. But if Levi had to pay the tithe because he was in the loins of Abraham, Christ did not have to pay a tithe precisely because he was not in the loins of Abraham. If we understand, however, that Levi was in Abraham not according to the soul but only according to the flesh, Christ was there also, because Christ too was from the seed of Abraham according to the flesh, and the tithe, therefore, was imposed on Him.

What, then, is significant about the marked distinction between the priesthood of Christ and the priesthood of Levi on the basis of the fact that Levi paid tithes to Melchidezek since he was in the loins of Abraham? Christ was there also, and hence they both paid tithes. But the point is that we must understand that Christ was not there in a certain sense. Yet who would deny that He was there according to the flesh? Therefore, it was according to the soul that He was not there. The soul of Christ, therefore, was not transmitted from the soul of Adam who sinned; otherwise it also would have been there.

CHAPTER 20

Even if traducianism is true, the soul of Christ was not transmitted from the soul of Adam.

35. At this point the defenders of traducianism come forth and say that their theory has been established if it is clear that Levi, even according to the soul, was in the loins of Abraham, in whose person he paid tithes to Melchizedek, so that the case of Christ can be distinguished from his in the matter of the tithes. For Christ did not pay tithes, and yet He was in the loins of Abraham according to the flesh, and so it follows that He was not there according to the soul. Hence, the conclusion is that Levi was there according to the soul.

This does not trouble me, for I am more willing to continue listening to arguments on both sides than to establish one of the two theories at this time. Meanwhile, it was my wish with this evidence from Scripture to show that the soul of Christ was not generated from the original human soul. Others will perhaps find what they must say about the rest of human souls. They may say—and this argument has some weight with me—that although no man's soul is in the loins of his father, nevertheless, Levi, being in the loins of Abraham according to the flesh, paid tithes; and Christ, being there according to the flesh, did not pay tithes.

Now, Levi was there according to the seminal reason by which he was destined to enter his mother on the occasion of carnal union; but not by such a reason was the flesh of Christ there, although the flesh of Mary was there according to such a reason. Therefore, neither Levi nor Christ was in the loins of Abraham according to the soul. According to the flesh, however, both Levi and Christ were there; but Levi according to carnal concupiscence, Christ solely according to His corporeal substance. Since in a seed there are both the visible corporeal germ and the invisible formative principle, both of these came from Abraham, or even from Adam, to the body of Mary, which was conceived and born in that manner. Christ, however, assumed the visible substance of the flesh from the flesh of the

Virgin; the formative principle of His conception, however, was not from the seed of a man, but it came from above in a far different way. Consequently, in respect of what He received from His mother, He was also in the loins of Abraham.

36. Levi paid tithes, therefore, in Abraham, since he was in Abraham's loins (although it was according to the flesh alone), just as Abraham himself was in his father's loins. In other words, he was born of his father Abraham as Abraham was born of his father, namely, through the law in the members *at war with the law of the mind*[84] and through an invisible concupiscence,[85] although the chaste and honorable rights of marriage do not allow that law of the members to prevail except in so far as they can provide for the continuation of the race through it.

But tithes were not paid through Abraham by Him whose flesh received from that source not a festering wound but the material that would heal. For since this tithing belonged to the foreshadowing of the remedy,[86] tithes were paid in the flesh of Abraham by him who was healed, not by Him who was the source of the healing. For the same flesh not only of Abraham but also of the first and earthly man had both the wound of sin and the remedy for that wound: the wound of sin in the law of the members at war with that of the mind, a law transmitted thence by a seminal reason to all generations of descendants; and at the same time the remedy of the wound in the body taken from the Virgin (from which source alone came the corporeal matter), without the working of concupiscence, but through a divine causal principle of conception and formation, for the purpose of sharing with men the necessity of dying without any taint of sin, and of giving them the hope of resurrection without any fear of disappointment.

Therefore, it is my opinion that even those who defend the traducianist theory agree that the soul of Christ is not an offshoot of the soul of the first man who sinned. For they hold that the seed of the soul is passed on by the seed of the father in intercourse,[87] but the manner of Christ's conception was totally different. They maintain also that if He had been in Abraham according to the soul, He also would have paid tithes. But Scrip-

ture attests that He did not pay tithes inasmuch as it distinguishes His priesthood from that of Levi on this very ground.

CHAPTER 21

Whatever theory is proposed about the origin of the soul of Christ,
there cannot be any question of a taint of original sin on His soul.

37. Someone may perhaps say: just as Christ could have been
in the loins of Abraham according to the flesh and not have paid
tithes, why could He not also have been there according to the
soul without paying tithes? The answer is: because the simple
substance of the soul does not grow larger when the body grows
larger, even in the opinion of those who suppose it to be a
body[88] (an opinion held especially by those who think that the
soul comes from the parents). Hence, in a corporeal seed there
can be an unseen power which acts in an immaterial way to regulate the development of a being.[89] This power cannot be seen
by the eyes, but only by the intellect, as distinct from the matter
perceived by sight and touch. The very size of the human body,
which is incomparably greater than the tiny seed, makes it quite
evident that some other matter can be taken into it that does not
have the seminal force but only bodily substance. It was this
bodily substance that was assumed by the power of God to form
the body of Christ without any human generation by carnal
union. But who would dare to say that the soul has both, namely, the visible matter of the seed and the hidden formative principle of the seed?[90]

But why should I labor over a theory which I suppose cannot
be made convincing by words to anyone except the person who
has the kind of penetrating mind that can quickly grasp an attempted explanation without waiting to hear it to the end?
Hence, I shall sum up the argument briefly. If the soul of Christ
could have come from another soul (and I assume that the reader
understood what I said about generation when speaking of the
body), the soul of Christ is from the original soul only on the

condition that it has not contracted the taint of sin; but if it could not be from that source without the guilt of sin, it has not come from that soul.

With regard to the origin of other souls, whether they are from their parents or directly from God, let that side prevail which can. I am still hesitant and wavering between the two theories, now on one side, now on the other. But there is one thing I cannot believe, and that is that the soul is a body or any kind of corporeal quality or arrangement[91] (if you want to use that word to designate what the Greeks call ἁρμονία); and I trust that with God's help in my speculations I shall never accept such a theory, no matter who chatters such nonsense.

CHAPTER 22

The doubt about the origin of the soul cannot be solved by the words of our Lord in John 3.6.

38. There is another text of some importance which can be cited for their opinion by those who hold that souls come from above, namely, the text in which our Lord says, *What is born of flesh is flesh; what is born of spirit is spirit.*[92] What is more explicit, they say, than this statement to prove that the soul cannot be born of the flesh? For what else is the soul than the spirit of life—a created spirit, to be sure, not the Creator?

But in answer the advocates of the other opinion reply: "What else do we hold when we say that the flesh is from the flesh and the soul from the soul?" For man is made of both, and we hold that both come from him: the flesh from the flesh that acts, the spirit from the spirit that desires. Moreover, it should be noted that the Lord was speaking not of carnal generation but of spiritual regeneration.

CHAPTER 23

It is difficult to decide on the correct explanation of the origin of the
soul. The practice of infant baptism.

39. After pursuing this investigation as thoroughly as time
has allowed, I should judge the weight of reason and of scriptural texts to be equal or nearly equal on both sides, were it not
for the fact that the practice of infant baptism gives greater
weight to the opinion of those who hold that souls are generated
by parents. What can be said of these arguments is not yet clear
to me. If at a later date God gives me some solution and the opportunity to write something for the benefit of those interested,
I shall not be reluctant to do so.

Now, however, I want to state in advance that the argument
from the baptism of infants is not to be so despised that we
should neglect to refute it if the truth is against it. We have two
alternatives. On the one hand, we can say that no investigation
must be made into this matter, so that we shall be satisfied to
know by our faith where we are destined to go if we live a holy
life, although we may not know where we have come from. On
the other hand, if the rational soul is not arrogant in its search
for this knowledge about itself, let it put aside obstinate debate
and give itself to diligent enquiry, humble seeking, and perseverance in knocking at the door.[93] Thus, if He knows that this
is good for us who certainly knows better than we what is for
our good, let Him grant this also, for He gives good gifts to His
children.[94]

But the custom of our mother the Church in the matter of infant baptism is by no means to be scorned, nor to be considered
at all superfluous, nor to be believed except on the ground that
it is a tradition from the apostles.[95] The age of infancy, indeed,
in spite of its smallness, bears witness of great weight, for it was
the first to have merited to shed its blood for Christ.[96]

CHAPTER 24

Those who hold the traducianist theory must be careful not to think of the soul as corporeal.

40. I earnestly beg those who have accepted the traducianist theory and hold that souls are generated by parents, to make every effort to reflect on themselves and to understand that their souls are not bodies. If we but consider the soul seriously, there is no other being that can so help us to think of God, who remains immutable above all His creation, and to recognize Him as immaterial, as the soul, which has been made to His image. On the contrary, there is nothing more likely, or perhaps nothing more logical, than that God should be thought of as a body once the soul is thought of as a body. Thus, constantly immersed in the corporeal and living the life of the senses, people are unwilling to think that the soul is anything other than a body, for they fear that if it is not a body it may be nothing. Consequently, they are all the more afraid to think that God is not a body in proportion as they fear to think that God is nothing.[97]

Thus they are taken up with images or phantasms of images[98] which the cogitative power[99] forms from familiarity with bodies, and as a result without these images and phantasms they fear they must perish in a void. Hence, it is necessary for them to paint, as it were, a picture of justice and wisdom in their minds with shapes and colors, for they cannot think of them as incorporeal. But when they are moved by justice or wisdom to praise these virtues or to do some deed in accordance with them, they cannot say what color or size, what features or shapes they have seen.

I have spoken of this matter at length elsewhere; and, God willing, I shall speak of it again when necessary.[100] But as I said above, if some persons have no doubt that souls are generated by parents, or if some are doubtful as to whether or not this is so, let them not dare to think or to say that the soul is a body. It is important to avoid this, as I have said, so that they may not think that God Himself is nothing else than a body, a body of the utmost perfection, having His own proper nature surpassing all other bodies—but a body none the less.

CHAPTER 25

*Tertullian's view of the soul. Visual images representing
immaterial reality.*

41. Tertullian thought the soul was corporeal simply because he was unable to think of it as incorporeal, and hence he feared that it would be nothing if it were not a body.[101] He also was unable to think of God in any but material terms.[102] But since he was intelligent, he sometimes saw the truth and rose above his ordinary way of thinking. For what could have been truer than what he says in one of his works, "Every corporeal being is capable of suffering"?[103] Consequently, he had to change the opinion that he had previously adopted when he said that even God was a body. Indeed, I do not think that he was so out of his mind as to believe that God was capable of suffering, so that Christ not in body only, or in body and soul, but in the Word through whom all things were made would be thought of as capable of suffering and subject to change. May such thoughts be far from the mind of a Christian!

Furthermore, when Tertullian gave the soul a color like air and light,[104] he turned to the senses and tried to furnish the soul with the various sense organs as if it were a body. He said: "This [the soul molded into the shape of the body] is the interior man, the other is exterior. They are two, but they form one being. The interior man also has his eyes and ears by which the people must have heard and seen the Lord. He also has the other members which he uses in his thoughts and employs in his dreams."[105]

42. Notice the kind of ears and eyes with which the people had to hear and see God and which the soul employs in dreams. And yet, if anyone were to see Tertullian himself in a dream, he would never say that Tertullian had seen him and that they

had conversed together, since Tertullian in his dreams had not seen him. Finally, if the soul sees itself in dreams while the body lies in one place and the soul wanders through various images seen by it, who has ever seen it with color like air and light in his dreams, except perhaps along with the other objects seen with an equally false appearance? For the soul can see images like this, but God forbid that when it awakes it should believe that it is like what it saw in the dream. Otherwise, when it sees itself as different, which is more often the case, either the soul will have been changed or what is seen then in the dream is not the soul but an incorporeal image of the soul which is formed in a mysterious way, as when it gathers images in the imagination.[106]

What Ethiopian does not normally see himself as black in dreams? Or if he sees himself in another color, has he not wondered if he has an accurate memory of the dream? But I do not know if anyone ever saw himself with color like air and light if he had never read Tertullian or heard about his opinion.

43. What are we to say about those who have been influenced by such visions and want to teach us from Scripture not about the soul but about God, saying that He is a being such as has been made present graphically to the imagination of the saints and has been described in allegorical language? These visions certainly are similar to the descriptions in allegorical passages. Hence, these interpreters are in error when they set up in their hearts the empty idols of their thoughts, not understanding that the saints judged their own visions as they would judge if they read or heard such things described by divine inspiration in figurative language. Thus, the seven ears and the seven cows are seven years;[107] and the object like a linen cloth held by four strings, looking like a dish full of different animals, is the whole world with all the nations;[108] and so of the rest, especially the immaterial things that are represented not by corporeal things but by images of them.

CHAPTER 26

Tertullian's views on the growth of the soul with the growth of the body.

44. Tertullian was unwilling to say that the substance of the soul grows with the body. He feared to say this "lest its substance be said to decrease also and so be thought capable of annihilation."[109] However, since he imagined the soul to be extended in space throughout the body, he did not fix a limit to its increase, and he held that from a small seed it became equal in size to the body. "But the power of the soul that contains the natural endowment implanted in it is gradually developed along with the body without any change in the limit of the substance which it received when breathed into the man at the beginning."[110]

We probably would not understand this had Tertullian not made his meaning clear by a comparison.[111] This is what he says:

Take a certain quantity of gold or silver, a rough mass as yet. It is in a compressed condition, and at the moment it is smaller than it will be, but within the limits of the mass there is nothing but gold or silver. Afterwards, when it is beaten out into a sheet, it becomes larger than it was before through the flattening out of the original mass, not by any increment to it, for it is stretched out but not increased. And yet there is also an increase when it is extended. For it can be increased in its dimensions, though not in its substance. Then the sheen of the gold or silver, which was there in the mass, is now brought out. It was obscure in the original state, but it was not entirely lacking. Then different shapes are given to the metal according to its malleability as the artisan shapes it, adding nothing to the mass except its form. Thus the increase in the soul is to be thought of not as adding to its bulk but as calling forth its potentialities.[112]

45. Who would believe that this writer could have been so eloquent in expressing such an opinion? But his words are more likely to make us shudder than laugh. Indeed, he would not be forced into this position if he could think of anything that exists and is not a body. What is more absurd than to think of a mass of metal being capable of increasing in one dimension, when it is pounded, without decreasing in another; or of being expanded in length and breadth without being contracted in thickness? Or can one think it possible that the mass of a body remains unchanged while all its dimensions increase unless its density is diminished? How, then, will the soul from the tiny seed fill the large body which it animates if it also is a body, but a body whose substance is not increased by any addition of matter? How will it fill the body to which it gives life unless it loses its density in proportion to the increase in size of the body which it animates? It is obvious that Tertullian feared that if the soul were to grow, it might also perish by diminishing, and yet he did not fear that it might perish by losing its density when growing in size.

But why should I delay any further on this matter? My treatment of it is going beyond what is needed to support my conclusions, and I have already made clear the positions I hold for certain and those that I consider doubtful, as well as the reasons for my doubts. With this I conclude the present book and turn to the matter that follows in the next.

BOOK ELEVEN
The Sin of Adam and Eve and Their Expulsion from Paradise

Chapter 1

The text of Genesis 2.25–3.24.

1. *Adam and his wife were both naked, and they were not ashamed. Now the serpent was the most subtle of all the wild creatures which the Lord God had made on the earth. And the serpent said to the woman: "Why did God say, 'You shall not eat of every tree in Paradise'?" And the woman said to the serpent: "We may eat of the fruit of trees that are in Paradise, but regarding the fruit of the tree in the middle of Paradise, God said: 'You shall not eat of it nor shall you touch it, lest you die.'" And the serpent said to the woman: "You will not die the death. For God knew that on the day on which you would eat of it your eyes would be open, and you would be like gods, knowing good and evil." And the woman, seeing that the tree was good for food and pleasing to the eyes and a delight to behold, took of its fruit and ate; and she gave some to her husband, and they ate. Then the eyes of both of them were opened, and they perceived that they were naked; and they sewed fig leaves together and made themselves loincloths.*

And they heard the voice of the Lord God as He walked in Paradise in the late afternoon, and then Adam and his wife hid themselves from the face of the Lord God amidst the trees of Paradise. And the Lord God called Adam and said to him: "Adam, where are you?" Adam replied: "I heard Thy voice as Thou went walking in Paradise, and I was afraid because I am naked, and I hid myself." The Lord God said to him: "Who told you that you were naked but that you have eaten of the one tree whereof I had commanded you not to eat?" And Adam re-

plied: *"The woman whom Thou gavest to be my companion gave me fruit of the tree, and I ate."* Then the Lord God said to the woman: *"What is this that you have done?"* And she replied: *"The serpent beguiled me, and I ate."*

The Lord God said to the serpent: *"Because you have done this, cursed are you above all cattle and above all beasts upon the earth. Upon your breast and your belly shall you go, and earth shall you eat all the days of your life. And I will put enmity between you and the woman and between your seed and her seed. She will lie in wait for your head, and you will lie in wait for her heel."* To the woman He said: *"I will greatly multiply your sorrows and your anguish. With sorrows you shall bring forth children, and you shall be subject to your husband, and he shall rule over you."* And to Adam he said: *"Because you have listened to the voice of your wife and have eaten of the one tree whereof I commanded you not to eat, cursed is the earth in your works. In sorrow you shall eat of it all the days of your life: thorns and thistles it shall bring forth for you, and you shall eat the crops of the field. In the sweat of your face you shall eat your bread until you return to the earth from which you have been taken, for you are earth and unto earth you shall return."*

Adam called his wife's name *"Life,"* for she is the mother of all the living. And the Lord God made garments of skin for Adam and his wife and clothed them. And the Lord God said: *"Behold, Adam has become like one of Us, knowing good and evil. And now let him not put forth his hand and take of the fruit of the tree of life and eat and live forever."* And the Lord God sent him forth from the Paradise of pleasure to till the earth from which he was taken. He drove Adam out and placed him over against the Paradise of pleasure, and He placed the cherubim and a flaming sword turning every way to guard the path to the tree of life.[1]

2. Before commenting on this Scripture text verse by verse, I think I should make here an observation which I remember having made earlier on in this treatise.[2] One may expect me to defend the literal meaning of the narrative as it is set forth by the author. But if in the words of God, or in the words of someone called to play the role of a prophet, something is said which cannot be understood literally without absurdity, there is no doubt that it must be taken as spoken figuratively in order to

point to something else.[3] It must not be doubted that the statement was made, a fact which the reliability of the writer and the promise of the commentator demand.

3. Hence, *They were both naked.* It is, then, true that the bodies of the two human beings living in Paradise were completely naked. *And they were not ashamed.* Why would they be ashamed, since they did not perceive *in their members any law at war with the law of their mind?*[4] That law was rather the penalty for sin, inflicted on them after their transgression, when disobedience violated the command and justice punished the deed. But before this happened they were naked, as has been said, and they were not embarrassed. They experienced no motion of the flesh of which they would be ashamed. They did not think that anything had to be covered, because they did not feel that anything had to be restrained. How they would have begotten children has already been discussed.[5] It must not be thought that the manner of begetting would have been the same as after the punishment which followed their sin; for before they would die, death entering the body of disobedient men by a just retribution would stir up the revolt of their disobedient members.[6] This was not the state of Adam and Eve when they were naked and were not ashamed.

CHAPTER 2

How was the serpent the most subtle of beasts?

4. The serpent was there, *the most subtle of all the wild creatures which the Lord God had made on the earth.*[7] Now, it is in a figurative sense that the serpent is called "the most subtle" *(prudentissimus)* or, according to many Latin manuscripts, "the wisest" *(sapientissimus).*[8] In the proper meaning of the word, "wisdom" *(sapientia)* is normally taken in a good sense referring to God or the angels or the rational soul; but we speak of wise bees or ants because their works suggest an imitation of wisdom.

This serpent, however, could be called the wisest of all the beasts not by reason of its irrational soul but rather because of another spirit—that of the Devil—dwelling in it. For, however great was the fall of the sinful angels from their heavenly home when they were cast out because of their rebellion and pride, they are nevertheless by nature superior to all the beasts because of the excellence of reason in them. If the Devil, therefore, entered the serpent and possessed it, communicating his spirit to it in the manner in which the prophets of demons are usually possessed,[9] it would be no wonder if he made it wiser than all beasts, which have a living but irrational soul.

But it is really a misuse of words to speak of wisdom *(sapientia)* in an evil creature, and of cunning *(astutia)* in a good one. In the proper sense and in ordinary usage, at least in Latin, men are called wise *(sapientes)* in a good sense, whereas cunning men *(astuti)* are understood to have evil in their hearts. Hence, some translators, as we can see in a large number of manuscripts, have translated the idea rather than the word into Latin, and thus have chosen to call this serpent more cunning *(astutiorem)* than all the beasts rather than wiser *(sapientiorem)* than all. I leave it to experts in Hebrew to say what the proper meaning of the word is in that language and whether in that language men may be called wise and be understood to be wise in a bad sense not by a misuse, but by the proper use, of the word.[10] We can clearly read in another passage of Sacred Scripture about men who are wise in evil and not in good.[11] And our Lord says that *the children of the world are wiser than the children of light*[12] in providing for their own future—by means, however, that are fraudulent, not just.

Chapter 3

For some reason, hidden from us, God allowed the Devil to use the serpent.

5. We certainly must not imagine that the Devil independently chose the serpent to use it in tempting our first parents and persuading them to sin. In him, it is true, there was a desire to deceive rooted in his evil and envious will; but he could not have

accomplished his end except by using an animal over which he was allowed control. The will to do harm can come from any perverse spirit, but the power to do it can come only from God, and this must be because of some hidden and sublime principle of justice, because there is no iniquity in God.

CHAPTER 4

Why did God, foreknowing the result, allow Adam to be tempted?

6. If someone asks, therefore, why God allowed man to be tempted when He foreknew that man would yield to the tempter, I cannot sound the depths of divine wisdom, and I confess that the solution to this problem is far beyond my powers. There may be a hidden reason, made known only to those who are better and holier than I am, not because of their merits but simply by the grace of God. But in so far as God gives me the ability to understand or allows me to speak, I do not think that a man would have deserved great praise if he had been able to live a good life for the simple reason that nobody tempted him to live a bad one. For by nature he would have it in his power to will not to yield to the tempter, with the help of Him, of course, who *resists the proud and gives His grace to the humble.*[13] Why, then, would God not allow a man to be tempted, although He foreknew he would yield? For the man would do the deed by his own free will and thus incur guilt, and he would have to undergo punishment according to God's justice to be restored to right order. Thus God would make known to a proud soul, for the instruction of the saints in ages to come, how wisely He uses even bad wills of souls when they perversely use their natures, which are good.

CHAPTER 5

Man fell because of his pride.

7. We must not imagine that the tempter would have caused the man to fall unless there had arisen in the man's soul a proud spirit that needed to be checked, so that the humiliation of his sin would teach him how wrong he was in relying on himself. It is truly said, *Before ruin the heart is lifted up, and before glory it is humbled.*[14] This is perhaps the voice of the man who says in the Psalm, *In my prosperity I said, "I shall never be moved."*[15] And then, when he had learned by experience what an evil is the proud reliance on one's own powers and what a good is the help of God's grace, he said, *O Lord, by Thy favor Thou hast given strength to my beauty; and then Thou hast turned Thy face away, and I have been dismayed.*[16] But whether these words were said about the first man or about another, a lesson had to be taught to a soul that exalted itself and trusted too much in its own strength, even if the lesson involved experiencing punishment; for it must learn how wretched is the state of a creature if it withdraws from its Creator.

Here also there is an important lesson about the goodness of God, since no man who turns away from Him prospers. On the one hand, those who rejoice in the pleasures that bring death cannot be free of the fear of suffering; on the other hand, those who have become insensible through an excess of pride, and fail completely to realize the disaster of their desertion, are seen to be much more unfortunate by others who have been able to recognize such an evil. The result is that if the former refuse to take the remedy which would help them to avoid such ills, their example will help others to avoid them. For the Apostle James says, *Each one is tempted when he is attracted and enticed by his own concupiscence. Then concupiscence, when it has conceived, gives birth to sin; and sin, when it is full-grown, brings forth death.*[17]

Hence, when the swelling of pride is healed, a man rises up if before the trial there was no will to remain with God, but at least after the trial there is the will to return to Him.

CHAPTER 6

Why God continually allows men to be tempted.

8. Some people are puzzled by this temptation of the first man, wondering why God allowed it to happen, as if they do not see that in our days the whole human race is unceasingly tempted by the snares of the Devil. Why does God allow this also? Perhaps we could say that by these temptations virtue is proved and exercised and that it is a more glorious victory not to have yielded when under temptation than to have been unable to be tempted. Even those who abandon their Creator and follow after their tempter continually tempt those who remain faithful to the word of God and who offer to their tempters an example of how to avoid yielding as a remedy for inordinate desires and arouse in them a holy fear as a remedy for pride. Hence St. Paul says, . . . *considering yourself, lest you also be tempted.*[18] It is remarkable how Sacred Scripture everywhere shows a continual concern about recommending that humility by which we are subject to our Creator, lest we should presume on our own strength as if we did not need His help.

Hence, since the saints make progress by means of sinners, and the faithful by means of the unfaithful, it is idle to say that God would not create those who He foreknew would be wicked. For why should He not create those who He foreknew would be a help to the good, so that they would be born to exercise and instruct men of good will in a useful way, and that they themselves would be justly punished for their own bad will?

CHAPTER 7

A creature made so as to be able not to sin is good.

9. God, they say, should have made man of such a nature that he would simply not wish to sin. Now I grant that a nature that has no desire at all to sin is a better nature. But let them grant

for their part that, on the one hand, a nature is not evil if it is so made that it would be able not to sin if it were unwilling, and that, on the other hand, the decree by which it has been punished is just, since it has sinned by its free will and not by compulsion. If right reason tells us that that creature[19] is better which finds absolutely no pleasure in what is forbidden, it also tells us that that creature is good which has it in its power to control a forbidden pleasure that may arise, so that it rejoices not only in lawful and just actions but also in the control of sinful pleasure. Hence, since the latter nature is good and the former better, why should God make only the former and not both? Therefore, those who were ready to praise God only for the first class of creatures ought to praise Him all the more for both classes. The former class is found in the holy angels, the latter in holy men.[20]

But those who have chosen evil have willingly and culpably corrupted a praiseworthy nature. However, the fact that this was foreknown is certainly no reason why they should not have been created. For they also have a place to fill in creation for the good of the saints. God, indeed, does not need the justice of any good man. How much less does He need the iniquity of a sinner!

CHAPTER 8

Why God created those who He foreknew would be wicked.

10. Who could say after serious thought, "It would be better for God not to create a man who He foreknew could be corrected by another's sin than to create that other who He foreknew must be condemned for his sin"? This would be to say that it is better that a man should not exist who by God's mercy would receive a crown of glory for using wisely the sin of another, than for that sinner also to exist who would be justly punished according to his deserts. For when reason shows beyond any doubt that there are two good things not equally good, but one superior to the other, simple people do not understand and say, "The two should be equal," which is equivalent to saying,

"Only the greater good should exist." And thus, in wishing to establish equality among the kinds of goods, they reduce the number; and senselessly increasing one kind, they destroy the other.

Who would listen to these people if they were to say, "Since sight is more excellent than hearing, there ought to be four eyes and no ears"? Hence, if that rational creature is more excellent which without any fear of punishment serves God without pride, and if among men another has been created who is so constituted that he is unable to recognize God's gifts in himself except in seeing another's punishment, so that he does not become proud but fears,[21] that is, he does not presume on himself but relies on God—who in his right mind will say, "This creature ought to be like the other"? The man who makes such an objection should see that he is really saying nothing else than, "This creature ought not to be, but only the other." This attitude reveals a simple and ignorant mind. Why would God not create also those who He foreknew would be wicked, *wishing to show His anger and manifest His power, and thus enduring with much patience the vessels of wrath prepared for destruction, in order to make known the riches of His glory for the vessels of mercy, which He has prepared beforehand for glory?*[22] *For thus let him who boasts, boast only in the Lord,*[23] when he sees that not only his existence depends on God, and not on himself, but also that his well-being depends on none other than Him from whom he has his existence.

11. Consequently, it is inappropriate to say, "There ought not to be any men on whom God would bestow such a gift of His mercy if it could not take place unless there were those also in whom He showed the justice of His punishment."

CHAPTER 9

God willed that men should be what they themselves would will to be.

Why, indeed, should there not be both kinds of men, since the goodness and justice of God are duly proclaimed in both?

12. But the objector will say: "If God had willed it, even the wicked would have been good." How much better was the will of God, namely, that men should be what they willed to be, but that the good should not go unrewarded, or the wicked unpunished, and that thereby the existence of the wicked should be useful for others! "But God foreknew that their will would be evil." He foreknew this, indeed, and because His foreknowledge cannot be wrong, it follows that the evil will was theirs, not His. "Why, then, did He create men who He foreknew would turn out in this way?" Because He not only foresaw what evil they would do but also what good He would bring about from their evil deeds. For He made them in such a way as to leave it in their power to perform some deed, even if they should deliberately choose evil, and to find that His action in their regard would be worthy of praise. Their evil will comes from themselves; their nature, which is good, and their punishment, which is just, come from God; He assigns them the place they deserve, and to others He offers a trial to profit by and an example to fear.

CHAPTER 10

Why God does not convert the wills of evil men to good.

13. But it is objected that since God is omnipotent He would be able to turn the bad wills of evil men into good wills. He would indeed. Why, then, did He not do so? Because He did not will to. Why He was unwilling is known to Him alone. We must not be wiser than we ought to be.[24] But I think I have shown above[25] that a rational creature is no small good, even a creature that is led to avoid evil by a consideration of evildoers. This class of good creatures would surely not exist if God[26] had converted all evil wills to good, if He did not mete out just punishment for any wrongdoing, and if there were only that one class of men who would advance in His service without any thought of sin or punishment of evil deeds. As a result, under

the pretext of increasing the number of more perfect men, the
number of the good would be diminished.[27]

CHAPTER 11

*God allows the unjust to sin and be punished for the instruction of
the just.*

14. They ask, therefore, if there is anything in the works of
God that needs the evil of another creature so that it may advance towards the good.

But are there men who have become so deaf and blind with
controversy that they do not hear or see that when some are
punished many are corrected? What pagan, what Jew, what her-
etic does not prove this by his daily life at home? But when
there is an argument about the truth or a search for it, these people are unwilling to look at the work of Divine Providence from
which there comes a misfortune that makes them reflect, so that
if those who are punished are not corrected, at least the others
will fear their example,[28] and the ruin of the wicked will con-
tribute to the salvation of the good.

For surely God is not the author of the malice or wickedness
of the sinners through whose just punishment He has provided
for those who were to be given such a warning in accordance
with His decrees. But although He foreknew that they were going to be wicked by their own perverse will, He did not refrain
from creating them, looking to the advantage of those creatures
who would not be able to advance to the good except by considering the lot of the wicked. Indeed, if the wicked did not exist, they would certainly serve no useful purpose. Is not a
sufficient good accomplished in the fact that they exist, since
they are surely useful for those who are good? When a man
wants them not to exist, he really desires only that he himself
may not be among their number.

15. *Great are the works of the Lord, excellent in all that He wills!*[29]
He foresees the good and He creates them; He foresees the wick-

ed and He creates them. He gives Himself to the good that they may find their delight in Him; and He graciously bestows many of His gifts on the wicked also, mercifully forgiving them, justly punishing them, and at the same time mercifully punishing them, justly forgiving them, fearing nothing from anyone's malice, needing nothing from anyone's justice, looking not to His own interests from the works of the good, and looking to the interests of the good even in the punishments of the wicked. Why, then, would He not permit a man to be tempted and thereby to be revealed,[30] convicted, and punished when his proud desire to be his own master would bring forth what it had conceived and would be confounded by its own offspring,[31] and when his just punishment would deter from the sin of pride and disobedience generations yet to come, for whose sake this event was written down and proclaimed?

CHAPTER 12

The Devil could not have used the serpent except with God's permission.

16. If someone should ask why the Devil was allowed to carry out the temptation through a serpent particularly, the authority of Scripture should be enough to suggest that it happened with some meaning intended. After all, in speaking divinely Scripture deals with a whole universe of things revealed by God corresponding in a way to this natural universe of ours which is full of the works of His hands. Not that the Devil wished to symbolize something for our instruction, but since he could not have approached man to tempt him without God's permission, he surely could not have used any other creature in this act than the one allowed him.

Consequently, whatever meaning the serpent had is to be attributed to that disposition of Providence by which the Devil indeed had his desire to harm, but permission to do so only as given him by God, either to overturn and destroy the vessels of wrath or to humble and prove the vessels of mercy.[32] We know the origin of the serpent: earth at the word of God produced all the cattle, beasts, and serpents. And all this world of creatures possessing irrational life was made subject, by the order established by God, to all the world of rational creatures having either good or bad will. What wonder, then, if the Devil is allowed to act through the serpent, since Christ Himself permitted demons to enter into pigs?[33]

CHAPTER 13

The Manichees refuse to recognize the Devil as a creature of God.

17. Commentators are accustomed to consider very carefully the nature of the Devil, since certain heretics, scandalized by his evil will, want to remove him entirely from the creatures made by the true sovereign God and to attribute him to another principle which in their account is opposed to God.[34] They cannot understand that everything that exists, in so far as it is a substance, is good, and that it could not exist except in dependence upon the true God from whom every good comes.[35] They also fail to see that an evil will is a disordered movement in which goods of a lower rank are preferred to higher goods, with the result that if the spirit of a rational creature should delight in its own power and excellence, it would be swollen with that pride by which it would fall from the beatitude of the spiritual paradise and waste away with envy. But in the case of such a spirit, it is a good that it lives and gives life to a body, whether a body composed of air, as in the case of the spirit of the Devil himself and of demons,[36] or an earthly body, as in the case of the soul of man, even a man who is wicked and perverse. Consequently, while they refuse to admit that anything made by God sins of its own free will, they say that the substance of God Himself has been corrupted and perverted, first by necessity and then irremediably by free choice! But I have already written at length about this insane error.[37]

CHAPTER 14

Envy, caused by pride, brought the Devil to ruin.

18. In this treatise we must investigate what is to be said according to Scripture about the Devil.

Did he from the very beginning of the world take delight in his own power and separate himself from that society and that charity by which the angels are blessed in their enjoyment of God? Or was he for a while in the holy company of the angels, himself just and blessed as they were? Some say that he fell from the heavenly abode because he envied man made to the image of God.[38] Envy, indeed, does not precede pride but follows it: envy is not the cause of pride, but pride is the cause of envy. Since, therefore, pride is the love of one's own excellence, and envy is the hatred of another's happiness, it is easy to see which vice begets the other. For a person who loves his own excellence envies his peers because they are equal to him, his inferiors because he fears that they may become his equals, and his superiors because he is not their equal. It is by pride, therefore, that one becomes envious, not by envy that one becomes proud.

CHAPTER 15

Pride is the beginning of all sin. The two loves in the two cities.

19. With good reason Scripture has said, *Pride is the beginning of all sin.*[39] This testimony is supported also by the statement of St. Paul, *Avarice is the root of all evils,*[40] if we understand "avarice" in the general sense of the word, that is, the attitude by which a person desires more than what is due by reason of his excellence, and a certain love of one's own interest, his private interest, to which the Latin word *privatus* was wisely given, a term which obviously expresses loss rather than gain.[41] For every privation *(privatio)* diminishes. Where pride, then, seeks to excel, there it is cast down into want and destitution, turning

from the pursuit of the common good to one's own individual good out of a destructive self-love.

In the stricter meaning of the word, avarice is what is more commonly called love of money. But St. Paul in using the word intended to go from the special to the general meaning and wished avarice to be understood in the broad sense of the word when he said, *Avarice is the root of all evils.* For it was by this vice that the Devil fell, and yet he certainly did not love money but rather his own power. Hence, it is perverse love of self that deprives *(privat)* this puffed-up spirit of the company of the holy angels, and his wretched state oppresses him as he yearns to have his fill of iniquity. In another place, then, where St. Paul said, *For men will be lovers of self,* he immediately added *lovers of money,*[42] going from the general notion of avarice, of which pride is the source, to this special sense, which is applied properly only to men. For men would not be lovers of money unless they thought that their excellence depended on their wealth. Opposed to this disease is charity, who *seeks not her own,*[43] that is, does not rejoice in her own *(privata)* excellence; it is right to say, therefore, that *she is not puffed up.*[44]

20. There are, then, two loves,[45] of which one is holy, the other unclean; one turned towards the neighbor, the other centered on self; one looking to the common good, keeping in view the society of saints in heaven, the other bringing the common good under its own power, arrogantly looking to domination; one subject to God, the other rivaling Him; one tranquil, the other tempestuous; one peaceful, the other seditious; one preferring truth to false praise, the other eager for praise of any sort; one friendly, the other envious; one wishing for its neighbor what it wishes for itself, the other seeking to subject its neighbor to itself; one looking for its neighbor's advantage in ruling its neighbor, the other looking for its own advantage. These two loves started among the angels, one love in the good angels, the other in the bad; and they have marked the limits of the two cities established among men under the sublime and wonderful providence of God, who administers and orders all that He creates; and one city is the city of the just, and the other city is the city of the wicked.

With these two cities intermingled to a certain extent in time, the world[46] moves on until they will be separated at the last judgment. The one will be joined to the holy angels and, being united with its King, will attain eternal life; the other will be joined to the wicked angels and, being united with its king, will be sent into eternal fire. Concerning these two cities I shall perhaps write more at length in another book, if the Lord is willing.[47]

CHAPTER 16

Satan fell at the very beginning of creation.

21. Scripture does not state when pride cast the Devil down, perverting his good nature with an evil will. But reason clearly tells us that this happened first; it was because of his pride that he envied man. Indeed, it is obvious to all who reflect on the matter that pride is not born of envy but rather envy of pride. One can with good reason suppose that at the beginning of time the Devil fell by pride, and that there had not been any previous time when he lived in peace and beatitude with the holy angels. On this supposition he apostatized from his Creator at the very beginning of creation. The words of our Lord, therefore, *He was a murderer from the beginning, and he stood not in the truth,*[48] should be understood in both parts of the statement as referring to what was from the beginning, namely, not only that he was a murderer but also that he stood not in the truth.

He was indeed a murderer beginning at that point at which man could be killed; but of course man could not be killed before there existed a man to be killed! From the beginning, therefore, the Devil was a murderer because he killed the first man, before whom there were no other men. And he stood not in the truth, and this from the beginning when he was created, although he would be standing now if he had wanted to stand.

CHAPTER 17

Did the Devil know from the beginning that he would sin and be condemned?

22. How, indeed, can the Devil be thought to have lived a blessed life among the blessed angels? If he had no foreknowledge of the sin he would commit and of its punishment, that is, his abandonment of God and the subsequent eternal fire, one can rightly ask why he had no such knowledge.[49] The holy angels are not uncertain of their eternal life and beatitude. For how would they be blessed if uncertain? Shall we say that God did not wish to reveal to the Devil, while he was still a good angel, what he would do or what he would suffer, while at the same time He revealed to the other angels that they would remain forever in His Truth? If this is so, the Devil before his fall was not equally blessed, indeed was not fully blessed, since those who are fully blessed are certain of their beatitude so that no fear troubles them. But what demerit did he have to be thus distinguished from the others so that God would not reveal the future to him, not even the future that pertained to him? Surely God did not punish him before he sinned, for God does not condemn the innocent.

Was he perhaps from another category of angels, to whom God did not give a foreknowledge of the future even in what pertained to them? I do not see how those creatures can be blessed who are uncertain of their own beatitude. Thus, some have thought that the Devil was not numbered among those angels whose sublime nature placed them above the heavens, but was numbered among those who were made somewhat lower in the world and assigned to different offices.[50] Such angels could perhaps have found pleasure even in something forbidden; but they would be able by their own free choice to reject that pleasure if they did not wish to sin. Their condition would be similar to that of man, especially the first man, who did not yet have in his members the penalty of sin; for even at a later time holy men obedient to God are able to be faithful and to overcome such temptations by the grace of God.

CHAPTER 18

The beatitude of man before the fall.

23. Should anyone be said to possess happiness when he is uncertain whether that state will remain or eventually be followed by a state of misery? This is a question that can be asked even about the first man. For if he foreknew his future sin and the divine chastisement, how could he have been happy? Therefore, he was not happy in Paradise. But this cannot be true, since he did not know he was going to sin. Given such ignorance, then, one of two alternatives is possible: either he was uncertain of his beatitude (and how was he truly happy?); or he had certitude based on false hope, not on knowledge (and how was he not a fool?).

24. Nevertheless, when the first man was still in a natural body,[51] if as a reward for a life of obedience he was to be given companionship with the angels and a change of body from natural to spiritual, we can understand how he had a measure of happiness even if he had no foreknowledge of his future sin. Those also were ignorant of the future to whom St. Paul said, *You who are spiritual should instruct such a man* [one who has fallen into sin] *in a spirit of gentleness, looking to yourself, lest you too be tempted.*[52] But it is not unreasonable or wrong for us to say that these spiritual persons were already happy for the very reason that they were spiritual, not in their bodies but in the justice of their faith, rejoicing in hope, patient in tribulation.[53]

With greater reason, then, and in a fuller sense, man was happy in Paradise before he sinned, although he was uncertain about his future fall. He was happy in this hope of reward, the promised transformation of the body; and his hope was such that there was no tribulation for patience to endure in combat. He was not filled with vain presumption, like a fool being certain about the uncertain, but he was strong in faith and hope. Before possessing that life where he would be unquestionably certain of his own eternal life, he could *rejoice,* as Scripture says, with *trembling;*[54] and with this rejoicing he could be happy much more abundantly in Paradise than are the saints here on earth, and less completely than the saints and the angels beyond the heavens in life eternal, but none the less enjoying a happiness that is real.

CHAPTER 19

The creation of the angels.

25. One might propose the theory that some angels could be happy in their own fashion while uncertain of their future sin and condemnation, or at least of their eternal salvation, without the hope that eventually by some change for the better they would become certain of their future lot. But this theory is unfounded and can hardly be admitted.

Of course, one might say that these angels have been created for tasks in the world and assigned to be subject to other angels more sublime and blessed,[55] so that for the faithful performance of their offices they may receive the blessed and more sublime life, in the hope of which they can rejoice and even now be rightly called blessed. If it was from this class of angels that the Devil and his companions in sin fell, their lot is like that of men who fall from the justice of faith,[56] sinning because of a similar pride, either deceiving themselves or giving assent to their seducer.

26. Let those who are able maintain this theory of two classes of good angels: the supercelestial angels, among whom the angel who fell and became the Devil was never numbered, and the mundane angels, among whom he was numbered. For my part, I confess that at the present time I can think of no basis in Scripture for this theory. But I have felt constrained to ask if the Devil had any foreknowledge of his fall before it happened, lest I should say that the angels were uncertain, or at one time had been uncertain, about their own beatitude. Hence, it is not without reason that I expressed the opinion that from the beginning of creation, that is, from the beginning of time or of the creation of the Devil himself, he fell and never stood in the truth.

CHAPTER 20

The opinion of those who say that God created the Devil in an evil state.

27. Hence, certain writers[57] hold that the Devil did not turn towards evil by the free choice of his will, but that he simply was created in evil, although created by the Lord God, the supreme and true Creator of all beings. For their opinion they cite a passage from the Book of Job referring to the Devil, where it is written, *This is the beginning of the work fashioned by the Lord, which He made to be mocked by His angels.*[58] In harmony with this is that verse from the Psalms which says, *This dragon, which Thou hast made to mock him.*[59] But there is a difference between the two texts: in the Psalm it says, *which Thou hast made,* but in Job it says, *This is the beginning of the work fashioned by the Lord.* Thus, in Job the text seems to say that in the beginning God fashioned the Devil to be evil and envious, a seducer and plainly a Devil, not corrupted by his own will but created thus.

CHAPTER 21

This opinion is refuted.

28. Certain writers attempt to show that this opinion (in which it is said that the Devil was not corrupted by his own will but was created as an evil creature by the Lord God Himself)[60] does not contradict the statement of Scripture which says, *God made all things, and behold, they were very good.*[61] With eloquence and learning they maintain that not only in the beginning but also now there are many corrupt wills, and that in spite of this the sum of all that was made, that is, all creation considered as a whole, is very good. They do not say that the wicked are good, but that by their wickedness they do not cause the glory and order of the whole creation under the rule and power and wisdom of God's providence to be disfigured or disturbed in any part. For the wills of individuals, even those that are bad, have defi-

nite and appropriate limits to their powers, and there is a balance of good and evil, with the result that the whole is beautiful when these parts are appropriately and justly ordered within it.[62]

However, it is manifestly true, as anyone can see, that it is unjust for God, without any fault on a creature's part, to condemn in it what He Himself has created in it. It is also evident and certain from the Gospel text that the Devil and his angels were condemned, for the Lord foretold that He would say to those on His left, *Go into everlasting fire, which has been prepared for the Devil and his angels.*[63] Hence, we cannot possibly believe that it was the nature created by God that merited punishment by eternal fire; rather, it was the Devil's own free will.

CHAPTER 22

Why God created angels and men who He knew would turn from Him.

29. It is not the *nature* of the Devil that is meant when Scripture says, *This is the beginning of the work fashioned by the Lord, which He made to be mocked by His angels.*[64] But this statement could refer to a body formed of air that God gave him in keeping with his evil will; or to the role assigned to him whereby God made him, in spite of his will, useful for the good; or to the fact that God, knowing this creature would be evil by his own free choice, none the less made him, not holding back His goodness but giving life and being to a will that would be depraved; for God foresaw the many good effects He would bring about from him by His divine goodness and power. But the Devil is said to be *the beginning of the work fashioned by the Lord, which He made to be mocked by His angels,* not because he was the first creature to be made, nor because he was made from the beginning as an evil creature; but God, knowing that he would have an evil will bent on harming the good, created him to be a benefit for the good.

This is the meaning of the words, *to be mocked by His angels;*

for the Devil is mocked when the temptations by which he tries
to corrupt the saints turn to their advantage, and the malice that
he has willingly chosen becomes useful, in spite of his inten-
tions, for the servants of God. Indeed, God foresaw this in creating him.

He is, then, the beginning of mocking because wicked men
are vessels of the same Devil, and a body, so to speak, with him
as their head.[65] God foresaw that they would be wicked, and yet
He created them for the benefit of the saints. Like the Devil,
they are mocked when, in spite of their will to do harm, their
example moves the saints to vigilance, to a devout humility in
submission to God, and to an understanding of grace, and when
it offers them an opportunity to suffer the wicked and to put to
the test their love of their enemies.

But the Devil is the beginning of the creation that is mocked
because he precedes it in time and in the primacy of his malice.
God accomplishes His purpose regarding the Devil through His
holy angels in the working of His providence by which He governs creatures, subjecting wicked angels to good angels so that
the sinfulness of the wicked may have the power to do not all
that it strives for but only what is allowed. And this restriction
is put on wicked men as well as wicked angels, until that justice
in which the just live by faith[66]—a faith tested now as they pa-
tiently live among men—will be turned into judgment,[67] so that
they may be able to judge not only the twelve tribes of Israel[68]
but even the angels.[69]

CHAPTER 23

In what sense the Devil was never grounded in the truth.

30. When it is said that the Devil had never *been grounded in
the truth*[70] and that he had never led a blessed life with the angels, but that he had fallen at the very beginning of his creation,
it must not be thought that he did not sin by his own free will
but was created evil by God who is good. Otherwise he would
not be said to have fallen from the beginning; indeed, he did not

fall if that is the condition in which he was created. But when he was created, he immediately turned away from the light of Truth, being swollen with pride and corrupted by delight in his own powers. It follows, then, that he did not taste the sweetness of the blessed life of the angels. He did not receive it and then scorn it; rather, being unwilling to receive it, he forsook it and lost it. Hence, he could not have had foreknowledge of his fall, since wisdom is the fruit of piety.

He was impious, then, from the beginning, and his mind was consequently blind. He fell not from what he had received but from what he would have received if he had chosen to obey God. But since he refused, he fell from what he was going to receive, and yet he did not elude the power of Him whom he would not serve. According to his just deserts, therefore, he would find no joy in the light of justice nor any pardon from its condemnation.

CHAPTER 24

The wicked are the body of the Devil, and he is their head.

31. The Prophet Isaiah, referring to the Devil, says:

> *How has he fallen from heaven,*
> *Lucifer, who rises at the dawn?*
> *He has been trampled into the earth*
> *Who sent messages to all the nations.*
> *You said in your heart:*
> *"I will ascend into heaven,*
> *Above the stars of heaven*
> *I will set my throne;*
> *I will sit on the lofty mountain,*
> *Above the lofty mountains of the north;*
> *I will ascend above the clouds,*
> *I will be like the Most High."*
> *But now you will go down to hell,*[71]

and so forth. These words are understood as addressed to the Devil under the figure of the king of Babylon.[72] But for the most part they apply to the body of the Devil, which he recruits even from the human race, especially to those who attach themselves to him through pride by rejecting the commandments of God.[73] Thus, one who was a devil was called a man in the Gospel, where it is said, *A man who is an enemy has done this.*[74] And one who was a man was in turn called a devil in the Gospel, in the words, *Did I not choose you, the twelve, and one of you is a devil?*[75]

Now, the body of Christ, which is the Church, is called Christ, as when St. Paul says, *You are Abraham's offspring,*[76] after he had said shortly before this, *The promises were made to Abraham and to his offspring. It does not say, "And to offsprings," as if to many, but as to one, "And to your offspring," which is Christ.*[77] Again, St. Paul says, *For just as the body is one and has many members, and all the members of the body, although they are many, are one body, so it is with Christ.*[78] In a similar manner, the body of the Devil is called the Devil, for he is the head of the body, that is, of the multitude of the wicked, especially of those who fall from heaven, inasmuch as they fall away from Christ and the Church. Hence it is that many statements are made figuratively, referring to the body, statements which are applicable not so much to the head as to the body and its members. Lucifer, then, who rose at dawn and fell, can be understood as the brood of apostates from Christ and the Church, a race that turned towards darkness on losing the light which it bore, just as those who turn towards God pass from darkness to light, that is, those who were darkness become light.

CHAPTER 25

The words of Ezekiel, 28.12–15, taken as referring to the body of the Devil.

32. Under the figure of the prince of Tyre these words in Ezekiel are taken as spoken to the Devil: *You are the seal of likeness*

and the crown of beauty. You were in the delights of the Paradise of God, you were adorned with every precious stone,[79] and so forth. Now these words are applicable not so much to the spirit who is the prince of evil as to his body.

The Church is called paradise according to the words of the Canticle of Canticles, *A garden enclosed, a fountain sealed up, a well of living water, a paradise of pomegranates.*[80] From here have fallen all heretics, either by public and physical separation, or by a hidden and spiritual separation in which they appear to be united with the body of the Church. All those who are separated have returned to their vomit,[81] although after the remission of all their sins they had walked for a short time in the way of justice. *It would have been better for them not to have known the way of justice than knowing it to have turned back from the holy commandment delivered to them.*[82] This is the wicked generation that the Lord describes when He says that the evil spirit goes out of a man and returns with seven other spirits, and that finding the house cleaned he dwells there, so that the last state of that man becomes worse than the first.[83] It is to this class of men, who are already constituted as the body of the Devil, that these words can be applied: *From the day when you were created with the cherubim*[84] (that is, with the throne of God, which is translated "the fullness of knowledge"),[85] and *He placed you on the holy mountain of God* (that is, in the Church, as in the Psalms, *He heard me from His holy mountain*);[86] *you were in the midst of sparkling stones* (that is, saints fervent in spirit, living stones); *you went blameless in your days, from the day you were created until iniquity was found in you.* These words could be more thoroughly examined, and perhaps it could be shown not only that this is a possible meaning but that really there is no other.

CHAPTER 26

Conclusion regarding the fall of the Devil and his angels.

33. But that would be a major undertaking and would require a treatise devoted to that subject alone. For the present, it should

be sufficient to conclude with the following possible alternatives: either (1) from the moment of his creation the Devil by his unholy pride fell from the beatitude he would have received if he had willed it; or (2) there are certain angels assigned to inferior tasks in this world, in whose company he had lived, sharing their special kind of beatitude without knowledge of the future, and from whose company he fell through pride and impiety, a kind of archangel along with angels under his leadership (if this hypothesis can be advanced—and it would be strange if it could); or (3) certainly a reason should be sought to explain how all the holy angels, if the Devil lived with them for a period of beatitude with his angels, did not themselves yet possess with certitude a foreknowledge of their unending happiness but acquired it after his downfall; or (4) a reason must be given to show how the Devil with his companions before their sin deserved to be marked off from the other angels, so that he would be ignorant of his impending fall, while they would be certain of their perseverance.[87]

Nevertheless, let us not entertain any doubt that the angels who sinned were driven into the prison house of the misty air that surrounds our earth, according to the teaching of the apostles,[88] to be detained there for punishment on the day of judgment; and that in the celestial beatitude of the holy angels, eternal life is not uncertain, nor will it be uncertain for us, according to God's mercy and grace and faithful promise, when we shall be joined to them with these bodies of ours transformed after the resurrection. In this hope we live, and in the grace of this promise we are re-created.

There are other questions about the Devil: why God created him knowing what he would become, and why the Almighty does not turn the Devil's will to good. We discussed these problems when we were treating the same question in relation to sinful men,[89] and we leave the reader to seek what may be understood or believed or even newly discovered as a better explanation.

CHAPTER 27

How the Devil used the serpent.

34. God, who has supreme power over all that He has created and who uses the ministry of His holy angels to mock the Devil—for the Devil's evil will is used to serve the Church of God—did not permit him to tempt the woman except by the serpent, nor the man except by the woman. In the serpent it was the Devil who spoke, using that creature as an instrument, moving it as he was able to move it and as it was capable of being moved, to produce the sounds of words and the bodily signs by which the woman would understand the will of the tempter. But in the woman, who was a rational creature and able by her own powers to speak, it was not the Devil who spoke, but it was the woman herself who uttered words and persuaded the man, although the Devil in a hidden way interiorly prompted within her what he had exteriorly accomplished when he used the serpent as an instrument. But if he acted solely by an interior influence, as he did in the case of Judas, whom he prompted to betray Christ,[90] he could accomplish his purpose in a soul led[91] by its pride and the love of its own power.

However, as I have already said, the Devil has the will to tempt man, but the power to do so and the manner of doing it do not depend on him.[92] Since, therefore, he was permitted to do so, he tempted; and he tempted in the manner allowed him. But he had no knowledge of the fact that this temptation would profit certain members of the human race, nor did he will that result; and in this he was mocked by the angels.

CHAPTER 28

Did the serpent understand the words of the Devil? Other uses of serpents by the Devil.

35. The serpent did not understand the meaning of the words which were spoken through him to the woman, for we cannot

suppose that its soul was changed into a rational soul. As a matter of fact, not even human beings, whose nature is rational, know what they are saying when a devil speaks through them in that state of possession which requires an exorcist. It is much less credible, then, that this serpent would understand the meaning of words which the Devil uttered through it and by it, since it would not understand a man speaking even if it were free from diabolical possession.

Many people think that serpents hear and understand the words of the Marsi, at whose incantations snakes are wont to dart forth from their hiding places.[93] But in this also a diabolical power is at work to make us recognize[94] how God's providence everywhere subjects one being to another in keeping with a natural order, and how His wisdom and power allow something to evil wills so that snakes rather than any other kind of animals become accustomed to be moved by human incantations. This indeed gives some indication that human nature was originally seduced by the words of a serpent. Demons rejoice at this power given to them, allowing them to move snakes through human incantations so as to deceive anyone they can. This is permitted to them in order[95] to show a certain affinity they have with this kind of animal, thus calling to mind what happened in the beginning. Furthermore, what happened in the beginning was permitted so that a picture of every diabolical temptation might be shown through the serpent to the human race, for these events were to be recorded for the instruction of men. This will be evident when God pronounces His sentence upon the serpent.

CHAPTER 29

In what sense the serpent is the most subtle of all the wild creatures.

36. Hence, the serpent is called *the most subtle of all the wild creatures,*[96] that is, the most astute, because of the astuteness of the Devil, who spread his wiles in it and by it. Thus we speak of a subtle or astute tongue which a subtle or acute person

moves to persuade subtly or acutely. For this power or facility certainly does not belong to the bodily member which we call the tongue but rather to the spirit which uses it. Similarly, we also say that the pens of certain writers lie, whereas in reality the ability to lie belongs only to living and thinking agents. But a pen is said to be lying when a liar tells his lies with it; and this would be the case if the serpent were called a liar because the Devil used it like a pen for his deceitful purpose.

37. I have thought it well to insist on this point lest anyone think that irrational beings have human intellects or that they are suddenly turned into rational animals. I should not like to see anyone seduced by that ridiculous and mischievous opinion about the transmigration of human souls into beasts or of bestial souls into humans.[97] The serpent, therefore, spoke to the woman just as the ass spoke to Balaam as he sat on it,[98] the difference being that in the former case it was the work of the Devil, in the latter case the work of an angel. Good and bad angels perform certain actions that are similar, just as did Moses and the magicians of Pharaoh.[99] But in these wondrous works the good angels are more powerful, and the bad angels are unable to do any of even these acts except for what God permits through the good angels, so that He may give to everyone according to the disposition of the heart or according to the grace of God. In both cases He acts with justice and goodness through the depths of the riches of the wisdom and knowledge of God.[100]

CHAPTER 30

The exchange between the serpent and the woman.

38. Therefore, *The serpent said to the woman: "Why did God say, 'You shall not eat of every tree in Paradise'?" And the woman said to the serpent: "We may eat of the fruit of trees that are in Paradise, but regarding the fruit of the tree in the middle of Paradise, God said: 'You shall not eat of it nor shall you touch it, lest you die.'"*[101]

The serpent, then, first asked the question, and the woman replied, so that her transgression would be inexcusable, and no one would be able to say that the woman had forgotten the command of God. Of course, forgetting a command, especially this unique command which was so necessary, would involve culpable negligence and serious sin. But the sin is more evident when the command is retained in memory and God as present in His command is despised. Thus, when the Psalmist said, *Those who are mindful of His commandments*, it was necessary for him to add, *in order to keep them*.[102] For many people hold them in memory to despise them, and their transgression is the more serious in so far as forgetfulness does not excuse them.

39. Then *The serpent said to the woman: "You will not die the death. For God knew that on the day on which you would eat of it your eyes would be open, and you would be like gods, knowing good and evil."*[103] How could these words persuade the woman that it was a good and useful thing that had been forbidden by God if there was not already in her heart a love of her own independence and a proud presumption on self which through that temptation was destined to be found out and cast down? Finally, not content with the words of the serpent, she also gazed on the tree and saw that it *was good for food and a delight to behold;* and since she did not believe that eating it could bring about her death, I think she assumed that God was using figurative language when He said, *If you eat of it, you shall die.* And so she took some of the fruit and ate and gave some also to her husband, who was with her, using perhaps some persuasive words which Scripture does not record but leaves to our intelligence to supply. Or perhaps there was no need to persuade her husband, since he saw that she was not dead from eating the fruit.

CHAPTER 31

In what sense the eyes of Adam and Eve were opened.

40. Therefore, *they ate, and the eyes of both were opened.*[104] Opened to what except to concupiscence for one another in punishment for sin, born of the death of the flesh?[105] Their bod-

ies, then, were no longer just natural bodies capable of being transformed into a better and spiritual condition without dying, as would have been the case if they had remained obedient, but bodies of death in which the law in the members *was at war with the law of the mind.*[106]

When they were created, of course, their eyes were not closed. Nor were they going about blind in the garden of delights, feeling their way about, in danger of unwittingly touching the forbidden tree and of picking in their ignorance the forbidden fruit. Indeed, how were the beasts and the birds brought to Adam for him to see what he would call them if he had no sight?[107] And how did it happen that the woman was brought to the man when she was made so that without seeing her he would say, *This now is bone of my bones and flesh of my flesh?*[108] Finally, how did the woman see *that the tree was good for food and that it was pleasing to the eyes and a delight to behold,*[109] if their eyes were closed?

41. Nevertheless, one should not take the whole passage in a figurative sense on the basis of one word used with a transferred meaning. Consider what was meant by the serpent's words, *Your eyes will be open.* The author states that this is what the serpent said; the meaning or thought behind what was said is left to the discernment of the reader. But the statement, *Then the eyes of both were opened, and they perceived that they were naked,*[110] is put forth in the way in which the other facts are narrated, and they cannot suggest to us an allegorical narrative.

St. Luke—to cite a parallel case—did not quote figurative language spoken by another person: it was on his own authority that he narrated what had happened when he told about the two disciples, of whom one was Cleophas, and said that when the Lord had broken bread, *their eyes were opened, and they recognized Him* whom they had not recognized on the road.[111] St. Luke does not mean that they were walking with their eyes closed, but simply that they were unable to recognize Him. In the Gospel text as well as in our passage in Genesis there is no question of a narrative with a figurative meaning, although Scripture has used a word in a transferred sense in speaking of "opened eyes" which were already literally open, meaning that they were opened to see and recognize what they had not formerly noticed.

When curiosity was stirred up and made bold to transgress a commandment, it was eager to experience the unknown, to see what would follow from touching what was forbidden, finding delight in taking a dangerous sort of liberty by bursting the bonds of the prohibition, thinking it likely that death, which had been feared, would not follow. We must assume that the fruit on that tree was similar to the fruit of other trees, which our first parents had tasted and found harmless. Hence, they supposed that God could more easily forgive sinners than they themselves could bear with patience their ignorance as to what the fruit was or why God had forbidden them to eat of it. As soon, then, as they had violated the precept, they were completely naked, interiorly deserted by the grace which they had offended by pride and arrogant love of their own independence. Casting their eyes on their bodies, they felt a movement of concupiscence which they had not known. It was in this respect, then, that their eyes were opened to that to which they had not been open before, although they were open to other things.

CHAPTER 32

Death and concupiscence the result of original sin.

42. This death occurred on the day when our first parents did what God had forbidden. Their bodies lost the privileged condition they had had, a condition mysteriously maintained by nourishment from the tree of life, which would have been able to preserve them from sickness and from the aging process. For although they had natural bodies which were to be transformed subsequently, yet even there in Paradise, in the food from the tree of life, there was a symbol of what happens through the spiritual nourishment given by Wisdom.[112] The tree of life was indeed a sacrament[113] of that nourishment which feeds the an-

gels and by their participation in eternity preserves them from corruption.

When Adam and Eve, therefore, lost their privileged state, their bodies became subject to disease and death, like the bodies of animals, and consequently subject to the same drive by which there is in animals a desire to copulate and thus provide for offspring to take the place of those that die. Nevertheless, even in its punishment the rational soul gave evidence of its innate nobility when it blushed because of the animal movement of the members of its body and when it imparted to it a sense of shame, not only because it began to experience something where there had been no such feeling before, but also because this movement of which it was ashamed came from the violation of the divine command. In this, man realized with what grace he had previously been clothed when he experienced nothing indecent in his nakedness. Then was accomplished the saying of the Psalmist, *O Lord, by Thy favor Thou hast given strength to my beauty; but Thou hast turned away Thy face, and I have become troubled.*[114]

Finally, in this troubled state they hastened to get fig leaves, they sewed aprons together, and, because they had abandoned what was to their glory, they hid what was to their shame. But I do not think they had anything particular in mind in using fig leaves as if they were especially appropriate for covering the parts of the body affected by lust; but rather I believe that in their troubled state it was by an instinct deep within them that they were impelled to do this, with the result that in spite of their ignorance they would emphasize this aspect of their punishment, and thus this action would reveal the sinner and the narrative of it would instruct the reader.[115]

CHAPTER 33

The voice of the Lord God as He walked in Paradise.

43. *And they heard the voice of the Lord God as He walked in Paradise in the late afternoon.*[116] This had been the hour when God

would visit the pair who fell away from the light of truth. Perhaps He had been accustomed to speak to them in a special interior manner (and how could it be described in human words?), just as He also speaks with the angels, enlightening their minds with His unchangeable truth, wherein their intellects know simultaneously all that happens in time but not simultaneously.

I suggest that God may have spoken thus with them, although not granting them the same degree of participation in divine wisdom that the angels have. But in a human way and in a manner less perfect, they may have had this kind of visit and conversation with God. Or perhaps it took place with the aid of a creature, either in an ecstasy of the spirit[117] with corporeal images, or in the bodily senses with some object made present to be seen or heard, just as God is accustomed to be seen or heard in a cloud through the ministry of His angels.

But their experience of hearing the voice of God as He walked in Paradise in the late afternoon could have been brought about in a visible way only by means of a creature. We cannot suppose that the substance of the Father, the Son, and the Holy Spirit, which is invisible and everywhere present in its totality, appeared to the senses of the body, moving through space and time.

44. *And then Adam and his wife hid themselves from the face of the Lord amidst the trees of Paradise.*[118] When God interiorly turns His face away and man becomes confused, small wonder that his actions, on account of his great shame and fear, are like those of a madman. And deep within Adam and Eve there was also an instinct at work by which, even in their ignorance, they performed actions which would have some meaning for their descendants, who would one day understand and for whom these actions have been recorded.

CHAPTER 34

Adam, hiding himself in shame, is called forth by God.

45. *And the Lord God called Adam and said to him: "Where are you?"*[119] This question is uttered by One who is admonishing, not by one who is ignorant. And there is surely some special meaning in the fact that just as the command was given to the man, and through him transmitted to the woman, so the man is questioned first. For the command came from the Lord through the man to the woman, but sin came from the Devil through the woman to the man. This is full of mystical meanings, not intended by the persons in whom these actions took place, but intended by the all-powerful Wisdom of God.[120] Our purpose now, however, is not to unfold hidden meanings but to establish what actually happened.

46. Adam, then, replied, *I heard Thy voice in Paradise, and I was afraid because I am naked, and I hid myself.*[121] It is quite probable that God was accustomed to appear in human form to these first two human beings, using a creature appropriate for such an action. But He raised their attention to higher things and never permitted them to notice their nakedness until after their sin, when they felt a movement in their members of which they were ashamed, in accordance with that law of the members which is punishment for sin.[122] They felt as men normally feel before the eyes of others; and, as a punishment of their sin, they had a desire to hide from Him from whom nothing can be hidden and to conceal their bodies from Him who sees the heart.

But what wonder is it if proud men, wishing to be like gods, *became vain in their thoughts, and their foolish heart was darkened?* In their prosperity *they said that they were wise,* and when God turned His face away *they became fools.*[123] If they felt shame in the presence of one another—and this is why they had made aprons for themselves—they were all the more deeply afraid, even with this covering, to be seen by God, who benevolently condescended to confront them with a visible creature having the likeness of human eyes by which they would be seen. Indeed, if God appeared to them thus in order to let them speak as human beings might speak to another human being, as Abraham did by the oak of Mamre,[124] this sort of friendship increased their shame after their sin, although it gave them confidence before their sin; and they no longer dared to show to these eyes the nakedness that offended their own.

CHAPTER 35

The excuses of Adam and Eve.

47. The Lord, therefore, wishing to interrogate the sinners in the manner followed in courts of law before imposing a greater punishment than that which already caused them to feel shame, said to them, *Who told you that you were naked but that you have eaten of the one tree whereof I had commanded you not to eat?*[125] Because of this sin, death, engendered in accordance with the judgment of God, who had threatened them with this punishment, was the cause of the concupiscence that they experienced at the sight of their bodies. This is what is meant when it is said that their eyes were opened and that a sense of shame resulted.

And Adam replied, "The woman whom Thou gavest to be my companion gave me fruit of the tree, and I ate."[126] What pride! Did he say, "I have sinned"? He has the deformity of confusion, not the humility of confession. This interrogation has been written down precisely because it took place in order to be recorded truthfully for our instruction (if it were not recorded truthfully, it would not instruct), so that we may see how men today are suffering from the disease of pride as they try to make their Creator responsible for any sin they commit, while they want attributed to themselves any good they do. Adam said, *The woman whom Thou gavest with me (mecum),* that is, *to be my companion (ut esset mecum), gave me fruit of the tree, and I ate.* As if she had been given to Adam for this purpose, and not rather that she should obey her husband and that both of them should obey God!

48. *Then the Lord God said to the woman, "What is this that you have done?" And she replied, "The serpent beguiled me, and I ate."*[127] She too fails to confess her sin. She shifts the blame to another,

and although her sex is different from Adam's, her pride is the same. Born of these first parents but not imitating them was the one who, afflicted by innumerable evils, has said and will continue to say to the end of time, *I said: "O Lord, be merciful to me; heal my soul, for I have sinned against Thee."*[128] How much better it would have been if they had said the same thing! But the Lord had not yet *cut the necks of sinners.*[129] There would be labors, sorrows, death, and all the afflictions of this world, and divine grace by which God at the opportune time comes to the aid of those whom He has taught in their affliction that they must not trust in themselves. *The serpent beguiled me,* she said, *and I ate;* as if the promptings of anyone should have been preferred to the command of God!

CHAPTER 36

God's curse on the serpent.

49. *The Lord God said to the serpent: "Because you have done this, cursed are you above all cattle and above all beasts upon the earth. Upon your breast and your belly shall you go, and earth shall you eat all the days of your life. And I will put enmity between you and the woman and between your seed and her seed. She will lie in wait for your head, and you will lie in wait for her heel."*[130] This entire statement is made in figurative language, and the reliability of the writer and the truth of his narrative demand only that we do not doubt that the words were spoken. For the words, *The Lord God said to the serpent,* are the only[131] words of the writer, and they are to be taken in the proper sense. It is true, therefore, that these words were spoken to the serpent. The rest of the words are God's words, and they leave the reader free to decide whether they are to be understood in the proper or figurative sense, in accordance with what I said in my introductory remarks at the beginning of this book.[132] And if one asks why the serpent is not questioned about his motive for acting thus, it is obvious that this animal did not act by its own nature and will, but that working by it and through it and in it

was the Devil, who had already been assigned to everlasting fire for his sin of impiety and pride.

What is said to the serpent, therefore, and is intended for him who worked through the serpent is undoubtedly to be understood in a figurative sense. For in these words the tempter is described as he will be with respect to the human race. For the human race began to be propagated only when this sentence was pronounced, apparently against the serpent but in reality against the Devil.

In the commentary I wrote entitled *Two Books on Genesis against the Manichees*, I have discussed to the best of my ability these words as they are to be understood in a figurative sense.[133] Beyond this, if I am able on another occasion to give a more thorough and appropriate interpretation of the text, may God be with me to aid me in the task. But now my attention must not be turned without necessity to a purpose other than what I have undertaken.

CHAPTER 37

The sentence pronounced on the woman.

50. *To the woman He said: "I will greatly multiply your sorrows and your anguish. With sorrows you shall bring forth children, and you shall be subject to your husband, and he shall rule over you."*[134] These words that God spoke to the woman are also more appropriately understood in a figurative and prophetic sense. The woman, of course, had not yet given birth. Furthermore, the pain and anguish of childbirth belong solely to this body of death (a death engendered by the transgression), in which the members from the beginning were those of a natural body, which, if man had not sinned, were destined not to die but to live in that other more blessed state until they would deserve to be transformed, after a life of virtue, into a better condition, as I have already stated above in several places.[135] The punishment, then, given to the woman is also understood in a literal sense; and furthermore we must give consideration to the state-

ment, *And you shall be subject to your husband, and he shall rule over you,* to see how it can be understood in the proper sense.

For we must believe that even before her sin woman had been made to be ruled by her husband and to be submissive and subject to him.[136] But we can with reason understand that the servitude meant in these words is that in which there is a condition similar to that of slavery rather than a bond of love (so that the servitude by which men later began to be slaves to other men obviously has its origin in punishment for sin). St. Paul says, *Through love serve one another.*[137] But by no means would he say, "Have dominion over one another." Hence married persons through love can serve one another, but St. Paul does not permit a woman to rule over a man.[138] The sentence pronounced by God gave this power rather to man; and it is not by her nature but rather by her sin that woman deserved to have her husband for a master. But if this order is not maintained, nature will be corrupted still more, and sin will be increased.

CHAPTER 38

The punishment of Adam and the name given to the woman.

51. *God, then, said to her husband: "Because you have listened to the voice of your wife and have eaten of the one tree whereof I commanded you not to eat, cursed is the earth in your works. In sorrow you shall eat of it all the days of your life: thorns and thistles it shall bring forth for you, and you shall eat the crops of the field. In the sweat of your face you shall eat your bread until you return to the earth from which you have been taken, for you are earth and unto earth you shall return."*[139]

Who does not know that these are the labors of man on earth? And there surely can be no doubt that they would not be if man had not lost the happiness that was his in Paradise. We must not hesitate, then, to take these words also first in their proper sense. Nevertheless we must safeguard the prophetic meaning and be open to it, as it is foremost in God's intention when He speaks these words.

It is not without reason that Adam himself by a marvelous inspiration then gave the name Life to his wife saying, *for she is the mother of all the living.*[140] These words, indeed, are not a statement or declaration of the author, but they are to be taken as the words of the first man himself. In saying *for she is the mother of all the living,* he seems to give a reason for the name he has conferred on her, explaining why he called her Life.[141]

CHAPTER 39

The garments of skin; the condemnation of man's pride.

52. *And the Lord God made garments of skin for Adam and his wife and clothed them.*[142] This was done for the sake of a symbolic meaning, but nonetheless it was done; and similarly the words which were spoken for the sake of a symbolic meaning were nonetheless spoken. I have often said, and I do not hesitate to say it again and again, that we must demand of the author of a historical narrative that his account contain the events that actually occurred and the words that were actually spoken.[143] Now in considering an event, we ask what happened and what it signifies; and in like manner, in considering words, we ask what was said and what it signifies. For we must not take as figurative the fact that something was said, whether what is said has a figurative or literal meaning.[144]

53. *And God said: "Behold Adam has become like one of Us, knowing good and evil."*[145] Now by whatever means or in whatever manner God spoke, it is certainly true that He said this; and therefore in the expression *one of Us* the plural reference must be to the Trinity, as was true in the expression *Let Us make mankind,*[146] just as the Lord also referred to Himself and the Father in the expression *We will come to him and make Our abode with him.*[147]

God, then, replied to man's proud ambition, showing the results of man's desire for what the Devil had suggested in the words *You will be like gods. Behold,* God said, *Adam has become like one of Us.* God spoke these words not so much to heap oppro-

brium on Adam as to instill in the rest of mankind, for whom
these words have been written down, a fear of being filled with
a similar pride. God said, *He has become like one of Us, knowing
good and evil.* How are we to interpret this except to say that it
is an example presented for the purpose of inspiring us with
fear because the man not only did not become what he wanted
to be but did not even retain the condition in which he had been
created?

CHAPTER 40

Adam and Eve driven from Paradise.

54. *"And now,"* God said, *"let him not put forth his hand and take
of the fruit of the tree of life and eat and live forever." And the Lord
God sent him forth from the Paradise of pleasure to till the earth from
which he was taken.*[148] The words in the first part of this text are
spoken by God; then the author records what followed as a result of what was spoken. Deprived not only of that life which
he would have received with the angels if he had observed God's
commandment, but also of that life which he had in Paradise,
where his body enjoyed a privileged state, man had to be separated entirely from the tree of life. This was necessary because
that privileged state of the body was kept in existence by an invisible power from the visible tree of life, and also because in
that tree there was a visible sacrament of invisible wisdom. He
had to be removed from the tree, then, because he was now destined to die, and because he was also excommunicated, as it
were, just as in this paradise, which is the Church, people are
sometimes excluded from the visible sacraments of the altar by
ecclesiastical discipline.

55. *He drove Adam out and placed him over against the Paradise
of pleasure.*[149] This action actually took place, but it also has a
symbolical meaning inasmuch as it prefigures a sinner living in
a wretched state over against Paradise, by which is signified the
blessed life.

And He placed the cherubim and a flaming sword turning every way to guard the path to the tree of life.[150] We must believe that this took place in the visible Paradise through the operation of the heavenly powers, so that by the ministry of angels there was placed there a kind of flaming battlement. But we must not suppose that it was done in vain, for it must also signify something about the spiritual paradise.[151]

CHAPTER 41

Theories about the nature of the sin of Adam and Eve.

56. I am aware of the fact that some exegetes have thought that the first couple were in a hurry to satisfy their desire for a knowledge of good and evil and that they wished to have before due time what was being postponed and kept for a more opportune occasion, and that the tempter induced them to offend God by anticipating what was not yet intended for them.[152] Thus by their expulsion and condemnation they were said to have been deprived of the advantage of that which they might have enjoyed to their spiritual advancement had they sought it at the proper time as God intended. Now if these writers should wish to understand the tree not in the proper sense as a real tree with real fruit but in a figurative sense, their interpretation could result in a theory apparently consistent with faith and reason.

57. There is also the opinion of those who say that the first couple anticipated marriage by a kind of theft and that they had sexual intercourse before they were united by their Creator.[153] And hence they say that sexual intercourse was signified by the word "tree," and that it had been forbidden them until they would be joined in due time.

I suppose we must assume that Adam and Eve had been created at such a young age that they were required to wait until they would reach puberty! Or perhaps the union was not allowed as soon as it was possible? If it was impossible, it certainly would not take place! Or maybe the bride had to be given away by her father, and they had to wait for the solemn pronouncing of vows, the celebration of the wedding banquet, the appraisal of the dowry, and the signing of the contract! This is ridiculous, and furthermore it is taking us away from the literal meaning of what happened, which we undertook to explain and which we have explained in so far as God has wished to help us.

CHAPTER 42

Did Adam believe the words spoken through the serpent? How was he tempted to sin?

58. There is a more serious problem to be considered. If Adam was a spiritual man, in mind though not in body,[154] how could he have believed what was said through the serpent, namely, that God forbade them to eat of the fruit of that one tree because He knew that if they did they would be gods in their knowledge of good and evil? As if the Creator would grudge so great a good to His creatures! It is surely strange if a man endowed with a spiritual mind could have believed this. Was it because the man would not have been able to believe this that the woman was employed on the supposition that she had limited understanding, and also perhaps that she was living according to the spirit of the flesh and not according to the spirit of the mind?

Is this the reason that St. Paul does not attribute the image of God to her? For he says, *A man indeed ought not to cover his head, since he is the image and glory of God, but woman is the glory of man.*[155] This is not to say that the mind of woman is unable to receive that same image, for in that grace St. Paul says we are neither male nor female.[156] But perhaps the woman had not yet received the gift of the knowledge of God, but under the direction and tutelage of her husband she was to acquire it gradually. It is not without reason that St. Paul said, *For Adam was formed first, then Eve; and Adam was not seduced, but the woman was seduced and fell into sin.*[157] In other words, it was through her that man sinned. For Paul calls him a sinner also when he says, *in the likeness of the sin of Adam, who is a type of the One to come.*[158] But he says that Adam was not seduced. In fact, Adam under interrogation did not say, "The woman whom Thou gavest to be my companion seduced me and I ate"; but, *She gave me fruit of the tree and I ate*. On the other hand, the woman said, *The serpent seduced me*.

59. Can we imagine that Solomon, a man of incredible wisdom, believed that there was any advantage in the worship of idols? But he was unable to resist the love of women drawing him into this evil, and he did what he knew should not be done lest he should inhibit the deadly delights in which he was being wasted away.[159] So it was in the case of Adam. After the woman had been seduced and had eaten of the forbidden fruit and had given Adam some to eat with her, he did not wish to make her unhappy, fearing she would waste away without his support, alienated from his affections, and that this dissension would be her death. He was not overcome by the concupiscence of the flesh, which he had not yet experienced in the law of the members at war with the law of his mind,[160] but by the sort of attachment and affection by which it often happens that we offend God while we try to keep the friendship of men.[161] That he should not have acted thus is clear from the just sentence which God pronounced on him.

60. It was, therefore, in some other way that he was deceived; but I do not think that the wiles of the serpent by which the woman was seduced could have been in any way the means of his seduction.[162] According to St. Paul, a seduction in the proper sense occurs when one is persuaded to accept as true what in reality is false; for instance, that God forbade Adam and Eve to touch the tree because He knew that if they touched it they would be like gods, as if He who made men grudged them divinity. But even if the man was moved by a spirit of pride, which could not have been hidden from God, who searches the heart, and if he was tempted by a desire to seek a new experience, when he saw that the woman after eating the fruit was not dead (as I have already suggested),[163] I do not think that Adam, if he was endowed with a spiritual mind, could have possibly believed that God had forbidden them to eat the fruit of the tree out of envy.

But enough of these speculations. Adam and Eve were induced to commit this sin in accordance with the way in which such persons can be tempted. The account was written as it must be read by all, although the content would be understood as it ought to be by only a few.

BOOK TWELVE
The Paradise or Third Heaven
Seen by St. Paul

CHAPTER 1

St. Paul's account of Paradise must be examined.

1. In writing the preceding eleven books of commentary on Genesis, I began with the opening lines of the sacred book and continued to the point where the first man was driven from Paradise. Whatever appeared to me as certain, I maintained and defended; whatever uncertain, I investigated according to my ability, sometimes venturing opinions, at other times expressing doubts. Still it was not my purpose to determine the judgment each one should form in regard to obscure questions, but rather to show the need we have of instruction in doubtful matters and to caution the reader against rash statements where we have been unable to arrive at certain knowledge.

But now, unhindered by the burden of presenting a detailed commentary on the sacred text, in this twelfth book I shall deal with the question of Paradise with greater liberty and at greater length. Otherwise I might seem to have dodged the difficulty in the passage where St. Paul apparently hints that Paradise is in the third heaven, when he says, *I know a man in Christ who fourteen years ago—whether in the body I do not know, or out of the body I do not know, God knows—such a one was caught up to the third heaven. And I know such a man—whether in the body or out of the body I do not know, God knows—that he was caught up into Paradise and heard secret words that man may not repeat.*[1]

2. In the treatment of these words it is customary to ask first

what St. Paul means by the third heaven, and then whether he
wishes us to understand that Paradise is there, or whether he
means that after he was caught up to the third heaven he was
caught up also to Paradise, wherever it may be. Thus he would
indicate that to be caught up to the third heaven is not the same
thing as to be caught up to Paradise, but that first there is the
third heaven and then Paradise.

This matter is so obscure that a solution seems to me impossible, unless one can have recourse not to the words of St. Paul
cited above but perhaps to some other passages of Scripture or
some sound reasoning to find a proof that Paradise is or is not
in the third heaven; for it is not even clear what the third heaven
is: namely, whether it is to be numbered among corporeal or
spiritual things. It might indeed be said that a man could not
have been taken with his body except to some corporeal place.
But since even St. Paul expressed himself as not knowing
whether he was caught up in the body or out of the body, who
would be so rash as to say that he knows what Paul himself says
he does not know? However, if it is impossible for the spirit to
be carried without the body to corporeal places or for the body
to be carried to spiritual places, this very doubt of his virtually
forces us to the conclusion that the region to which he was carried (for he is obviously speaking about himself)[2] was such that
it was impossible to discern clearly whether it was corporeal or
spiritual.[3]

CHAPTER 2

St. Paul could have been ignorant about how he saw Paradise
if he saw it in ecstasy.

3. When images of bodies are formed in sleep or in ecstasy,
a person does not distinguish them from bodies until he returns
to the life of the bodily senses and recognizes that he was in a
world of images which he did not derive from the senses of the
body. What man on waking from sleep is not immediately aware
that the objects he saw were mere images, although when he

saw them in his sleep he was not able to distinguish them from corporeal objects seen in his waking hours? Still I know from my own experience (and for that reason I do not doubt that others could have had or can have the same experience also) that while seeing an object in sleep I was aware that I was dreaming. I was fully convinced, even in my sleep, that the images which ordinarily deceive the imagination were not real bodies but only the phantasies of a dream. Sometimes, however, I have been misled in my attempts to persuade a friend whom I saw in a dream that the objects we were seeing were not bodies but only the images of dreamers—all the while he himself appeared among them as a mere dream image. Still I would tell him it was not true that we were even speaking to one another, and I would say that he at that moment was seeing something else in his sleep and that he had no knowledge at all of the fact that I was seeing these objects. But whenever I made an effort to persuade him that he was not real, I was partly inclined to believe that he was, since I should not be speaking to him if I really felt that he was not real. Hence my soul, which in some mysterious way was awake while I slept, was necessarily affected by the images of bodies, just as if they were real bodies.[4]

4. With regard to ecstasies, I once had the opportunity of listening to the account of a certain man, a peasant, who had been in such a state but who could not accurately describe his experience.[5] He knew that he was awake and was seeing something, though not with the eyes of the body. To use his own words, as far as I can recall them, he said: "My soul saw him, not my eyes." However, he did not know whether it was a body or the image of a body, for he was unable to make such a distinction. But he was such a simple and trustworthy man that hearing him was for me just as convincing as seeing for myself the vision he narrated.

5. Hence, if Paul saw Paradise as Peter saw the dish sent from heaven; as John, what he described in the Apocalypse; as Ezekiel, the plain with the bones of the dead and their resurrection; as Isaiah, God seated and before Him the seraphim and the altar from which the live coal was taken to cleanse the lips of the

prophet;[6] it is obvious that he could have been unable to determine whether he saw Paradise in the body or out of the body.

CHAPTER 3

*St. Paul was certain that he saw the third heaven
but uncertain as to how he saw it.*

6. But if the vision took place out of the body, and the objects of the vision were not bodies, it may still be asked whether they were images of bodies or whether they were a substance[7] that bears no resemblance to body: as, for example, God; or the mind, intelligence, or reason of man; or the virtues, such as prudence, justice, chastity, charity, piety, and so forth. These are objects that we perceive with intellectual knowledge, when we enumerate, distinguish, and define them, not by a perception of their outlines, colors, sounds, odors, or tastes, their degrees of heat or cold, their hardness or softness, or their smoothness or roughness, but by another vision, another light,[8] and another evidence far more excellent and certain than any other.

7. Again, then, let us return to the words of St. Paul himself and examine them more carefully, agreeing first of all without any hesitation that his understanding of corporeal and incorporeal nature was immeasurably more perfect than what we have been able to arrive at in our feeble attempts. Hence, if he knew that it was utterly impossible for spiritual things to be seen through the body, or bodily things to be seen out of the body, why did he not determine, through the objects that he saw, the manner in which he was able to see them? For if he was certain that they were spiritual things, why was he not equally sure that he saw them out of the body? But if he knew they were corporeal, why did he not also know that they could have been seen only through the body?

Why, then, does he doubt whether he saw them in the body or out of the body, unless perhaps he also doubts whether they were bodies or likenesses of bodies? Hence let us first see what there is in the whole tenor of the passage that gives no cause for doubt, and then perhaps from an examination of Paul's unqualified assertions the nature of his doubt will be clarified.

8. *I know*, he says, *a man in Christ, who fourteen years ago—whether in the body I do not know, or out of the body I do not know, God knows—such a one was caught up to the third heaven*. He knows, therefore, that fourteen years ago a man was caught up in Christ to the third heaven. Of this he entertains no doubt; and we, accordingly, should entertain none. But he does doubt whether it was in the body or out of the body. Hence, when he is in doubt, who of us can dare be certain? But surely we cannot, as a consequence of this, doubt the existence of the third heaven to which he says a man was carried. If objective reality was shown him, it is the third heaven that was shown. On the other hand, if an image like corporeal substances was produced, it was not the third heaven that he saw; but the vision[9] was produced in such a way that he seemed to rise above the first heaven, and then to see another one above it, and then to see still another higher up, so that, when he had come to this last one, he could say that he had been caught up to the third heaven. But that it was the third heaven to which he was caught up he did not doubt, nor did he wish us to doubt. He prefaces his account with the statement, "I know," and continues in such a manner that only the man who does not believe the Apostle himself can refuse to accept as true what the Apostle says he knows.

Chapter 4

*Difficulties about the vision St. Paul saw
and the way in which he saw it.*

9. He knows, then, that a man was caught up to the third heaven. Therefore it was actually the third heaven to which he was carried, and not some material symbol. Such a symbol was shown to Moses,[10] but he was well aware of the difference between the essence of God Himself and a visible creature in which God was wont to manifest Himself to man. Hence he

said, *Show me Thyself.*[11] Moreover, it was not an image of a material substance such as that which John saw in spirit. He asked what it was, and he received the reply, *It is a city,* or *They are peoples,* or something else, when he saw the beast or the woman or the waters or anything.[12] But St. Paul declares, *I know a man who was caught up to the third heaven.*

10. But if Paul wished to give the name "heaven" to a spiritual[13] image resembling a corporeal substance, it would also be an image of his body in which he was caught up and entered that heaven.[14] And thus he would refer to his body, although it would be only an image of his body, just as he would speak of heaven, although it would be but an image of heaven. But he would take no pains to distinguish what he knew and what he did not know. He would not say: "I know a man, who was caught up to the third heaven, but I do not know whether it was in the body or out of the body." He would simply narrate his vision and call the objects which he saw by the names of other objects which they resembled. When we speak of our dreams or of a revelation in them, we say: "I saw a mountain," or "I saw a river," or "I saw three men," and so forth. We give each image the name of the object it resembles. But the Apostle says: "This I know; that I do not know."

11. However, if both things appeared in the form of an image, both were equally known or not known. But if heaven itself was actually seen and therefore known, how could the body of the man appear only in an image?

12. For if he saw a corporeal heaven, why was he unable to recognize whether he saw it with the eyes of the body? And if by saying, *Whether in the body I do not know, or out of the body I do not know,* he wished to indicate that he was uncertain whether he saw with the eyes of the body or those of the spirit, why was he not also uncertain whether he truly saw a corporeal heaven or only an image of it? Moreover, if he saw an incorporeal substance, not under some material image but as justice, wisdom, and the like are seen, and if this was the heaven, it is evident that nothing of such a nature can be seen with the eyes of the body. Hence, if he knew that he had seen something of this sort, he could not doubt that he saw otherwise than with the

eyes of the body. *I know*, he says, *a man in Christ, who fourteen years ago....* "This I know, and let no one who believes me doubt my word." *But whether in the body or out of the body, I do not know; God knows.*

CHAPTER 5

How is Paul certain about the vision seen but uncertain about the manner in which he saw it?

13. What, then, does he know and distinguish from what he does not know, so that he may not deceive those who believe him? *This same man*, he says, *was caught up to the third heaven.* Now that heaven was either body or spirit. If it was a body and was seen with the eyes of the body, how does he know that it is that heaven and not know that he saw it in the body? But if it was spirit,[15] either it was represented under the image of a body (and in this case it is just as doubtful whether it was a body as it is whether it was seen in the body) or it was seen as wisdom is seen in the mind without any bodily images. And yet in this supposition it is certain that it could not have been seen by the body. Hence either both things[16] are certain or both uncertain. How can he be certain about what he saw and uncertain about the manner in which he saw it? Obviously he could not have seen an incorporeal nature by means of the body. But bodies, even if they can be seen[17] without their visible corporeal qualities, are certainly not in this case seen by means of the body but in a manner altogether different (if there is any vision of this sort). Hence it would be strange if this kind of vision could resemble ocular vision so closely as to deceive St. Paul or force him into a state of doubt, so that, having seen a corporeal heaven otherwise than with the eyes of the body, he would say he was uncertain whether he saw it in the body or out of the body.

14. But the Apostle, who took such pains to distinguish what he knew from what he did not know, could not be guilty of a lie. Hence perhaps[18] we should interpret him to mean that, when he was caught up to the third heaven, he could not tell

whether he was in the body (as a man's soul is in his body[19] but withdrawn from the bodily senses while he is awake or asleep or in ecstasy, though his body is said to be alive) or whether he actually went out of the body, so that his body would lie in death until, the vision over, his soul would be reunited with his dead members. In the latter case he would not awaken as if from sleep nor return to his senses as one coming from an ecstasy, but from death he would truly come to life again. Hence what he saw when caught up to the third heaven, and what he affirms with certain knowledge, he saw in reality and not under an image. But since it was doubtful whether the withdrawal from his body left his body truly dead, or whether his soul was still somehow present as it is in a living body, while his mind was carried away to see and hear the secrets of the vision—perhaps because of this doubt he said, *Whether in the body I do not know, or out of the body I do not know, God knows.*

CHAPTER 6

Three kinds of vision.

15. To see an object not in an image but in itself, yet not through the body, is to see with a vision surpassing all other visions. There are various ways of seeing, and with God's help I shall try to explain them and show how they differ.[20] When we read this one commandment, *You shall love your neighbor as yourself,* we experience three kinds of vision: one through the eyes, by which we see the letters; a second through the spirit, by which we think of our neighbor even when he is absent; and a third through an intuition of the mind, by which we see and understand love itself. Of these three kinds of vision the first is clear to everyone: through it we see heaven and earth and in them everything that meets the eye. The second, by which we think of corporeal things[21] that are absent,[22] is not difficult to explain; for we think of heaven and earth and the visible things in them even when we are in the dark. In this case we see nothing with the eyes of the body but in the soul behold corporeal

images: whether true images, representing the bodies that we have seen and still hold in memory, or fictitious images, fashioned by the power of thought. My manner of thinking about Carthage, which I know, is different from my manner of thinking about Alexandria, which I do not know.[23] The third kind of vision, by which we see and understand love, embraces those objects which have no images resembling them which are not identical with them.[24] A man, a tree, the sun, or any other bodies in heaven or on earth are seen in their own proper form when present, and are thought of, when absent, in images impressed upon the soul. There are two ways of seeing them: one through the bodily senses, the other through the spirit, in which images are contained. But in the case of love, is it seen in one manner when present, in the form in which it exists, and in another manner when absent, in an image resembling it? Certainly not. But in proportion to the clarity of our intellectual vision, love itself is seen by one more clearly, by another less so. If, however, we think of some corporeal image, it is not love that we behold.

CHAPTER 7

Three kinds of vision further explained.

16. These are the three kinds of visions about which we had something to say in the preceding books as occasion arose, though we did not there specify their number.[25] Now that we have briefly explained them, since the question under consideration demands a somewhat fuller discussion of them, we must give them definite and appropriate names, in order to avoid the encumbrance of constant circumlocution. Hence let us call the first kind of vision corporeal, because it is perceived through the body and presented to the senses of the body. The second will be spiritual, for whatever is not a body, and yet is something, is rightly called spirit; and certainly the image of an absent body, though it resembles a body, is not itself a body any more than is the act of vision by which it is perceived.[26] The third kind will be intellectual, from the word "intellect." *Mentale*

(mental) from *mens* (mind), because it is just a newly-coined word, is too ridiculous for us to employ.

17. If I should give a more detailed account of the meanings of these words, my explanation would be rather diffuse and obscure, whereas there is little or no need for such a thing. Accordingly it is sufficient to know that a thing is called corporeal either in the proper sense, when it refers to bodies, or in a metaphorical sense, as in the statement, *For in Him dwells all the fullness of the Godhead corporeally.*[27] Now the Godhead is not a body, but because St. Paul calls the religious observances of the Old Testament[28] shadows of what is to come (using the analogy of shadows in the physical world), he says that the fullness of the Godhead dwells in Christ corporeally; for in Him was fulfilled all that was prefigured by those shadows, and thus in a certain sense He is the embodiment of the shadows; that is, He is the truth of those figures and symbols. The figures, therefore, are called shadows in a metaphorical rather than proper sense of the word; and similarly, in saying that the fullness of the Godhead dwells corporeally, Paul is using a metaphor.

18. The word "spiritual" is used in different ways. Even our body, in the state in which it will be in the resurrection of the saints, is called spiritual by St. Paul when he says, *What is sown a natural body shall rise a spiritual body,*[29] meaning that it will be subject to the spirit in a wonderful way and possess every facility and incorruption, and without any need of bodily nourishment will be vivified by the spirit alone, but not that it will have an incorporeal substance. Moreover, the body as we have it in this life does not have the essence of a soul, and it cannot be identified with soul *(anima)* on the ground that it is called a living thing *(animale)*. Furthermore, the air or a wind (which is the motion of the air) is called spirit, as in the following words: *Fire, hail, snow, ice, and the spirit of the storm.*[30] The soul of man or beast also is called a spirit, as in the following passage: *And who knows whether the spirit of the children of man ascends upward, and the spirit of the beast descends downward into the earth?*[31] The word "spirit" is also used to designate the rational mind itself, in which there is, so to speak, an eye of the soul to which the image and knowledge of God pertain.[32] Hence St. Paul urges, *Be re-*

newed in the spirit of your mind, and put on the new man, which has been created according to God;[33] and elsewhere he speaks of the interior man, . . . *which is being renewed unto the knowledge of God according to the image of its Creator.*[34] So, too, after he had said, *Therefore I myself with my mind serve the law of God, but with my flesh the law of sin,*[35] he returned to the same thought in another place and added, *The desires of the flesh are against the spirit and those of the spirit against the flesh, so that you do not do what you would;*[36] and thus he indifferently gave to the same thing the name "mind" or "spirit." God also is called a spirit, as our Lord declares in the Gospel, *God is spirit, and they who worship Him must worship in spirit and in truth.*[37]

CHAPTER 8

The basis for calling the second kind of vision spiritual.

19. It is not from any of these meanings we have mentioned, in which "spirit" is used, that we take the word "spiritual" to designate the kind of vision we are now treating. It is rather from that singular use of the word, found in the Epistle to the Corinthians, in which spirit is obviously distinguished from mind. For, says St. Paul, *if I pray in a tongue, my spirit prays but my understanding is unfruitful.*[38] By the word "tongue" in this passage he is to be understood to refer to obscure and mystical signs, which profit no man if the understanding of his mind is removed from them, for he hears what he does not understand. Hence he also says, *For he who speaks in a tongue does not speak to men but to God; for no one understands, though the spirit is speaking mysteries.*[39] Thus he makes it clear enough that in this passage he is speaking of the sort of tongue in which there are signs, such as the images and likenesses of things,[40] which demand an intuition of the mind to be understood; and when they are not understood he says they are in the spirit, not in the mind. And so he declares more plainly, *If you give praise with the spirit, how shall he who fills the place of the uninstructed say "Amen" to your thanksgiving? For he does not know what you are saying.*[41]

Hence, in view of the fact that signs of things and not the things themselves are given forth by the tongue, the member of the body which is moved in the mouth in speech, St. Paul, using a metaphor, designated as tongue any production of signs before they are understood. But once the understanding has grasped the sign (and this activity is proper to the mind), then there is revelation or knowledge or prophecy or teaching. Accordingly he says, *If I come to you speaking in tongues, what shall I profit you, unless I speak to you either in revelation, or in knowledge, or in prophecy, or in teaching?*[42] And he means to say that this happens when the intellect grasps the signs, or, in other words, the tongue, so that what is done is done not by the spirit alone but also by the mind.

CHAPTER 9

The meaning of spirit.

20. Hence those to whom signs were manifested in the spirit by means of certain likenesses of corporeal objects had not yet the gift of prophecy, unless the mind had performed its function, in order that the signs might be understood; and the man who interpreted what another had seen was more a prophet than the man who had seen. Thus it is obvious that prophecy belongs more to the mind than to the spirit, in the rather special sense in which the word spirit is taken, namely, in the sense of a power of the soul inferior to the mind, wherein likenesses of corporeal objects are produced. And so Joseph, who understood the meaning of the seven ears of corn and the seven kine, was more a prophet than Pharaoh, who saw them in a dream; for Pharaoh saw only a form impressed upon his spirit, whereas Joseph understood through a light given to his mind.[43] And for this reason the former had the gift of tongues; the latter, the gift of prophecy. In the one there was the production of the images of things; in the other, the interpretation of the images produced.

Less a prophet, therefore, is he who, by means of the images of corporeal objects, sees in spirit only the signs of the things signified, and a greater prophet is he who is granted only an understanding of the images. But the greatest prophet is he who is endowed with both gifts, namely, that of seeing in spirit the symbolic likenesses of corporeal objects and that of understanding them with the vital power of the mind. Such a one was Daniel. His pre-eminence was tested and established when he not only told the king the dream he had had but also explained the meaning of it.[44] For the corporeal images themselves were produced in his spirit, and an understanding of them was revealed in his mind. I am using the word "spirit," therefore, in the sense in which Paul uses it, where he distinguishes it from the mind: *I will pray with the spirit, but I will pray with the mind also.*[45] Here he implies that signs of things are formed in the spirit and that an understanding of the signs shines forth in the mind. According to this distinction, then, I have designated as spiritual the kind of vision by which we represent in thought the images of bodies even in their absence.

CHAPTER 10

The meaning of intellectual and intelligible.

21. But the intellectual type of vision, which is proper to the mind, is on a higher plane.[46] The word "intellect," so far as I know, cannot be used in a wide variety of meanings, such as we found in the case of the word "spirit." But whether we say "intellectual" or "intelligible," we mean one and the same thing, though some[47] have wished to make a distinction between the two, designating as intelligible that reality which can be perceived by the intellect alone, and as intellectual the mind which understands. But whether there exists any being perceivable by the intellect alone but not itself endowed with intellect—this is a large and difficult question. On the other hand, I do not believe there is anyone who either thinks or says that there exists a thing which perceives with the intellect and is at the same time incapable of being perceived by the intellect. For mind is

not seen except by mind. Therefore, since it can be seen, it is intelligible, and since it can also see, it is intellectual, according to the distinction just mentioned. Putting aside, then, the extremely difficult question about a thing which would only be understood but not possess understanding, we here use "intellectual" and "intelligible" in the same sense.[48]

CHAPTER 11

Corporeal vision is ordered to the spiritual,
and the spiritual to the intellectual.

22. These three kinds of vision, therefore, namely, corporeal, spiritual, and intellectual, must be considered separately, so that reason may ascend from the lower to the higher. We have already proposed above an example by which all three kinds are illustrated in one sentence. For when we read, *You shall love your neighbor as yourself,*[49] the letters are seen corporeally, the neighbor is thought of spiritually, and love is beheld intellectually. But the letters when absent can also be thought of spiritually, and the neighbor when present can be seen corporeally. But love can neither be seen in its own essence with the eyes of the body nor be thought of in the spirit by means of an image like a body; but only in the mind, that is, in the intellect, can it be known and perceived. Corporeal vision, indeed, does not oversee any operations of the other two kinds of vision; rather, the object perceived by it is announced[50] to the spiritual vision, which acts as an overseer. For when an object is seen by the eyes, an image of it is immediately produced in the spirit.[51] But this representation is not perceived unless we remove our eyes from the object that we were gazing at through the eyes and find an image of it within our soul. And if indeed the spirit is irrational, as in the beasts, the announcement made by the eyes goes just as far as the spirit. But if the soul is rational, the announcement is made also to the intellect, which presides over the spirit. And so, after the eyes have taken their object in and announced it to the spirit, in order that an image of it may be

produced there, then, if it is symbolic of something, its meaning is either immediately understood by the intellect or sought out; for there can be neither understanding nor searching except by the functioning of the mind.

23. Baltassar the King saw the fingers of a hand writing on the wall,[52] and immediately the image of a corporeal object was impressed on his spirit by means of a bodily sensation;[53] and when the vision was gone, the image remained in his thoughts. It was seen in spirit but not understood. At the time when the sign was produced in a corporeal manner and was presented to his bodily eyes, Baltassar did not understand it, though even then he understood that it was a sign and knew this from the exercise of his mind. For since he was seeking out its meaning, it was his mind certainly that was conducting the search.

When he failed to discover the meaning, Daniel came forward; and, his mind illuminated by the spirit of prophecy, he unfolded to the troubled king the prophetic meaning of the sign.[54] For Daniel, by reason of the sort of vision that is proper to the mind, was more a prophet than the king, who had seen with the eyes of the body a corporeal sign and in thought had beheld within his spirit the image of the object after its disappearance. But the king could do no more than recognize with his intellect that it was a sign and enquire into its meaning.

24. Peter, carried out of himself, saw a vessel, held by four strings and filled with various animals, being let down from heaven; and he also heard a voice which said, *Kill and eat.*[55] When, on returning to his senses, he was reflecting on the vision, the Spirit announced to him the arrival of those whom Cornelius had sent, saying, *Behold, some men are looking for you; arise, go down, and depart with them, for I have sent them.* And when he came to Cornelius he revealed what he understood by the vision in which he had heard the words, *What God has cleansed, you must not call common.* But *God,* he said, *has shown me that I should not call any man common or unclean.*[56] Therefore, because he was carried out of the bodily senses at the time when he saw the dish, it was in the spirit that he also heard the words *Kill and eat,* and *What God has cleansed, you must not call common.* His memory retained all that he had seen and heard; and on his re-

turn to his bodily senses, he beheld the images within the same
spiritual power that had seen the vision and he pondered over
them in thought. These objects were not bodily things but images of bodily things, both at the time when he first was carried
away and beheld them, and later when he recalled them and
thought of them. When, however, he deliberated and sought for
an understanding of these signs, it was his mind that was making the effort—but all in vain until he received word of the arrival of the men from Cornelius. Now with this supplementary
vision of the bodily eyes, and with the Holy Spirit saying to
him, *Depart with them* (speaking to him within that same spirit
in which He had shown the sign and impressed the words), Peter's mind with God's help understood what was meant by all
these signs. A careful consideration of these and other similar
facts makes it abundantly clear that corporeal vision is ordered
to the spiritual, and the spiritual to the intellectual.

CHAPTER 12

Corporeal and spiritual vision.

25. But when, during our waking hours, in full possession of
our bodily senses, we experience a corporeal vision, we distinguish between this vision[57] and the spiritual vision by which we
think of absent bodies in imagination—whether recalling in
memory objects that we know, or somehow forming unknown
objects which are in the power of thought possessed by the spirit, or arbitrarily and fancifully fashioning objects which have no
real existence. From all such objects we distinguish the bodies
which we see and which are present to our senses, so that we
have no doubt that these are bodies and that the others are images of bodies. But it may sometimes be that by an excessive ap-
plication of thought, or by the influence of some disorder (as
happens to those who are delirious with fever), or by the agency
of some other spirit, whether good or evil, the images of bodies
are produced in the spirit just as if bodies were present to the
senses of the body, though the attention[58] of the soul may mean-

while remain alert even in the bodily senses. In this case images of bodies are seen appearing in the spirit, and real bodies are perceived through the eyes. The result is that at the same time one man who is present will be seen with the eyes and another who is absent will be seen in the spirit as if with the eyes. I have known people affected thus, who conversed not only with those truly present but also with others who were absent, addressing them as if they were present. Returning to their normal state, some related what they saw but others were unable to do so. In the same way also some people forget their dreams while others remember theirs.

But when the attention of the mind is completely carried off and turned away from the senses of the body, then there is rather the state called ecstasy. Then any bodies that are present are not seen at all, though the eyes may be wide open; and no sounds at all are heard. The whole soul is intent upon images of bodies present to spiritual vision or upon incorporeal realities present to intellectual vision without benefit of bodily images.

26. But when the mind is completely drawn away from the senses of the body, and the spiritual vision is occupied with the images of bodily things (whether it be in sleep or in ecstasy), if the objects seen have no special meaning, they are the imaginings of the soul itself. In such a way, even people who possess normal mental health and are unmoved by any extraordinary state of mind contemplate in thought during their waking hours the images of many bodies that are not present to the bodily senses.

But these people differ from those in an abnormal state, in that they distinguish with a sure instinct these images from bodies that are really present. Now it may be that images have some special meaning, whether they come to people who are asleep, or to those who are awake and see with their eyes bodies present before them and behold in the spirit images of bodies absent as if present before the eyes, or to those whose minds are withdrawn from the senses of the body in the state called ecstasy. But it is a remarkable thing if another spirit can so mingle with the spirit of a man as to manifest its knowledge through images presented to the mind with which it mingles, whether this mind itself understands them or whether they are understood by the other spirit and by it unfolded to the mind. But if this knowledge is revealed to the mind (and it cannot surely be revealed by a body), it follows of necessity that the revelation must come only from some spirit.

CHAPTER 13

The power of divination.

27. There are some who hold that the human soul has within itself a power of divination.[59] But if this is so, why is it not always able to exercise this power, since it always wishes to do so? Is it because it has not always the aid needed for the exercise of the power? Well then, any aid that is given to assist the soul in divination[60] could not come from nothing or from a body.[61] Hence the soul would have to receive aid from a spirit. Then how is it aided? Does something happen in the body whereby the attention of the soul is somehow disengaged and illuminated to such an extent that it sees within itself symbolic likenesses which were already there but which it did not see (just as we also have in memory many objects which we do not behold)?[62] Or are images produced in the soul which were not previously there? Or are they in some spirit into which the soul rushes and enters to see them? But if the soul already possessed them as its very own, why did the soul not also understand them? For it often happens, indeed most frequently, that it does not understand them. Should we say that, just as the spirit is assisted in order to see images within itself, the mind also, unless it receives similar aid, cannot understand the objects contained in the spirit? Or should it be said perhaps that there is no question of a removal of bodily impediments or disengagement of the soul from them in order that it may by its own power go out to the objects to be seen, but that it is carried directly to these objects, whether just to see them in the spirit or to know them also in the intellect? Or does the soul see the objects sometimes in itself and at other times by means of mingling with another spirit?

Whichever of these opinions is the right one, we ought not to be careless in our assertions. But of one thing there should be no doubt: corporeal images seen in the spirit are not always signs of other things, whether they are seen in waking hours, in sleep, or in sickness; but it would be a strange thing if an ecstasy could ever take place without the likenesses of bodily things in it having a meaning.

28. There is, of course, no cause for wonder if even those possessed by a devil occasionally speak the truth about objects beyond the reach of their senses at the time. This, to be sure, happens by some mysterious union with the evil spirit, so that the tormenter and his victim seem to be one and the same spirit. But when a good spirit seizes or ravishes the spirit of a man to direct it to an extraordinary vision, there can be no doubt that the images are signs of other things which it is useful to know, for this is a gift of God. The discernment of these experiences is certainly a most difficult task when the evil spirit acts in a seemingly peaceful manner and, without tormenting the body, possesses a man's spirit and says what he is able, sometimes even speaking the truth and disclosing useful knowledge of the future. In this case he transforms himself, according to Scripture, as if into an angel of light,[63] in order that, once having gained his victim's confidence in matters that are manifestly good, he may then lure his victim into his snares. This spirit, so far as I know, cannot be recognized except by that gift mentioned by St. Paul, where he speaks of the different gifts of God: . . . *to another the distinguishing of spirits.*

CHAPTER 14

Intellectual vision is not deceived; in the other kinds of vision deception is not always harmful.

But when the evil spirit has achieved his purpose and led someone on to what is contrary to good morals or the rule of faith, it is no great achievement to discern his presence—for in that case there are many who discern him. But the gift of discernment enables one in the very beginning (when the spirit appears as a good spirit to the majority) to judge immediately whether he is evil.

29. By means of corporeal vision as well as by means of the images of corporeal objects revealed in the spirit, good spirits instruct men and evil spirits deceive them.[64] But there is no deception in intellectual vision; for either a person does not understand, and this is the case of one who judges something to be other than it is, or he does understand, and then his vision is necessarily true.[65] The eyes are helpless when they see a body which resembles another body and which they cannot distinguish from the other; and the attention of the mind is helpless when in the spirit there is produced a likeness of a body which it cannot distinguish from the body itself. But the intellect is employed to seek out the meaning that these things have or the useful lessons that they teach; and either it finds its object and enjoys the fruit of its search, or it fails to find it and continues to reflect for fear of falling into some deadly error through a mischievous spirit of intellectual pride.

30. And with God's help the intellect prudently judges the nature and importance of those matters in which even erroneous thinking may take place without harm to the soul.[66] When, for instance, a man who is secretly evil has a good name among good men, it cannot be said that this judgment involves more danger for those who think him so than harm for the man himself—provided no error is made in the true realities, that is to say, in Goodness itself by which a person becomes good.[67] Again, men in general do not suffer any harm from the fact that in their dreams they mistake the likenesses of bodies for real bodies. Moreover, Peter suffered no harm when, upon being released from his chains and led forth by an angel, he was induced by this sudden miracle to believe that he was seeing a vision;[68] or when in his ecstasy he replied, *Nay, Lord, for never did I eat anything common or unclean,*[69] thinking that the very objects shown him in the dish were real animals. When we discover that all these things are other than we thought they were at the time we saw them, we experience no regrets that they have appeared to us in this way, provided we do not have to reproach

ourselves with an obstinate denial of the faith or with vain and sacrilegious opinions. So also when the Devil deceives us with corporeal visions, no harm is done by the fact that he has played tricks with our eyes, so long as we do not deviate from the true faith or lose the integrity of intelligence, by which[70] God instructs those who are obedient to Him. Or if the Devil should cozen the soul with a spiritual vision by means of the images of bodies, leading it to think there is a body where there is none, no harm is done the soul if it does not consent to an evil suggestion.

CHAPTER 15

Impure dreams not culpable.

31. And hence a question sometimes arises about consent given in sleep when people dream even of having carnal intercourse contrary to their previous good resolutions as well as against what is lawful. This does not happen except when there come into our dreams objects of which we also thought in our waking hours (not consenting to pleasure in them but thinking of them, as when for some reason we speak of such things), and in our sleep there appear images which naturally move the flesh. Then what nature has gathered together it discharges through the organs of generation—a fact that I could not mention without also thinking of it.

Now if the images of these corporeal things, which I have necessarily thought of in order to say what I have said, were to appear in sleep as vividly as do real bodies to those who are awake, there would follow that which in waking hours could not happen without sin. For who, at least when speaking of this matter and by the necessity of the subject saying something about carnal intercourse he has had, is able to refrain from thinking about the subject of which he is speaking? Moreover, when the image[71] that arises in the thoughts of the speaker becomes so vivid in the dream of the sleeper that it is indistinguishable from actual intercourse, it immediately moves the flesh and the natural result follows. Yet this happens without sin, just as the matter is spoken of without sin by a man wide awake, who doubtless thinks about it in order to speak of it.

But a right disposition of soul, purified by a desire for what is more perfect, kills many desires that have no connection with the natural motions of the flesh. Chaste people while awake curb and restrain these motions, though in their sleep they are unable to do so because they cannot control the appearance of those corporeal images that are indistinguishable from bodies. But because of this right disposition, the soul's merits are sometimes manifest even in sleep. Solomon even while asleep preferred wisdom to all else and begged it of the Lord without a thought for the rest; and, as Scripture attests, this was pleasing to the Lord, and He did not leave this good desire long without a fitting reward.

CHAPTER 16

Bodies perceived do not produce images in the spirit; the spirit produces them in itself.

32. Bodily sensation, therefore, belongs to the visible corporeal world and flows through the channels of the five senses, which are capable of perceiving objects even at a distance.[72] Light, the finest element in bodies and hence more akin to soul than the others, is first of all diffused in a pure state through the eyes and shines forth in rays from the eyes to behold visible objects.[73] Moreover, it intermingles in some way with pure air, with misty and vaporous air, with a crasser sort of liquid, and with solid matter; and in these four states, as well as in its pure state in ocular vision, in which it is most perfect, it brings about the five kinds of sensation.[74] This matter, I recall, I have discussed in Book Four[75] as well as in Book Seven.

Now this heaven which meets the eyes, and from which the stars and other luminous bodies shine forth, is far more perfect than all corporeal elements,[76] just as ocular vision is the most perfect of the bodily senses. But, since every spirit is unquestionably superior to every body, it follows that a spiritual nature is superior to this corporeal heaven, not because of its place but because of the excellence of its nature;[77] and the same superiority is enjoyed also by that spiritual nature in which the images of bodily things are produced.[78]

33. In this connection there is a remarkable thing to be noted. Spirit takes precedence over body, and the image of a body comes after the real body. But, since that which is second in time is produced in that which is prior in nature, the image of a body in a spirit is more excellent than the body itself in its own substance.

It must not, of course, be thought that a body produces something in the spirit, as if the spirit were subjected as matter to the action of a body. For he who produces something is in every respect more excellent than the thing from which he produces it. Now body is in no way more excellent than spirit; indeed, spirit is obviously superior to body. Hence, though we first see a body that we had not seen before and thereupon an image of it arises in our spirit, and in this same spirit we recall it when it is absent, nevertheless the body does not produce this image in the spirit, but the spirit produces it within itself.[79] It does this with a wonderful speed that far surpasses the sluggish actions of the body. As soon as the eyes have seen their object,[80] an image of it is formed without a moment's delay in the spirit of the one who sees.

And it is the same in the case of hearing. Unless the spirit immediately formed within itself and retained in memory an image of the word perceived by the ears, one could not tell whether the second syllable was actually the second one, since the first would no longer exist once it had impinged upon the ear and passed away. And so all habits of speech, all sweetness of song, all motion in the acts of our body would break down and come to nought, if the spirit did not retain a memory of past bodily motions with which to join further operations. And the spirit surely does not retain these motions except in so far as it has formed them in imagination within itself. Furthermore, there are within us images of our future actions before the actions themselves begin. For what act do we perform through the body that the spirit has not previously fashioned in thought, first seeing within itself the likenesses of all visible operations and in some way ordering them?

CHAPTER 17

Three extraordinary cases: a man possessed, a man in delirium, and a boy in great physical pain.

34. It is difficult to determine and explain how even evil spirits know these spiritual likenesses of bodies in our minds[81] or how this earthly body of ours impedes our soul and hinders it from seeing the images that are in the spirit of our fellow man. But we have abundant proof that thoughts arise in men at the suggestion of demons. And yet, if these spirits could discern the virtues within men, they would not try them. Surely if the Devil could see the remarkable and heroic patience of Job, he would not wish to suffer defeat in his efforts to tempt him. Besides, the power of evil spirits to declare from a considerable distance the occurrence of an event which some days later will be confirmed by the fact should not cause surprise. This they can do by their keenness of perception, which even with regard to corporeal objects is more perfect in them than it is in us, as well as by the remarkable speed of their bodies, which are far more subtle than ours.[82]

35. I once discovered a man possessed by an unclean spirit.[83] Though confined within his home, he would tell when a priest twelve miles away had started out to visit him. He would also declare where the priest was at each stage of his journey, how near he was, when he was entering the grounds, the house, and the bedroom, until finally he stood before him. Although the possessed man did not see all this with his eyes, still, unless he saw it some way or other, he could not declare it all so accurately.

But the man had a fever and spoke as if in delirium. And perhaps he really was delirious, but he was considered possessed because of what he said. He would accept no food from his family, but only from the priest. To the attentions of his own relatives he offered violent resistance as far as he was able. He would be quiet only when the priest came, and to him alone would he show docility and answer with submission. But his madness or possession did not yield even to the priest until he was cured of his fever, as delirious people are normally cured. After that he suffered no recurrence of the malady.

36. I know of another case of a man undoubtedly delirious, who predicted the death of a certain woman. He did this not as one foretelling the future but as if recalling a past event. "She is dead," he said when her name was mentioned in his presence; "I saw her carried out; they followed this route with her body." This he said while she was alive and well. But a few days later she died suddenly and she was carried forth along the route that he had predicted.

37. There was also among us[84] a boy who was in the early stages of puberty and suffering from a severe pain in the genital organs. The doctors were unable to diagnose the case. All they knew was that the affected nerve was hidden inside, so that even if they would remove the foreskin, which was unusually long, the nerve would not be visible but would be found only with great difficulty. The distillation of a viscous and stinging liquid inflamed the testicles and groin. The acute pain would not last long; but when the boy suffered from it, he would shout violently and toss about like a madman, as often happens when people are in great physical pain. And then in the midst of his cries he would lose all sensation and lie with his eyes open, seeing no one and remaining motionless even when someone would pinch him. After a time he would awake as if from sleep and, no longer feeling any pain, would reveal what he had seen. Then after a few days he would go through the same experience. He said that in all or in most of his visions he saw two persons, an old man and a boy, and that they told and showed him what he heard and saw.

38. One day he saw a choir of the faithful bathed in a wonderful light as they sang hymns of joy, and at the same time a company of the wicked surrounded with darkness and suffering various kinds of bitter torments. The old man and the boy were

his guides, pointing out and explaining what the one group had
done to merit their happiness and the other to merit their misery. He had this vision on Easter Sunday, after spending the
whole of Lent without feeling any of the pain from which he
had before enjoyed scarcely even a respite of three days at a
time. At the beginning of Lent he had had a vision of these two,
who had promised him that for forty days he would feel no pain.
Then they gave him a kind of medical prescription, advising
that his foreskin be removed. He followed the advice and for a
long time experienced no pain. But when his old trouble returned and he began to see the same visions, he was further ad-
vised by them to wade into the sea up to his thighs and, after
remaining there for a time, to come out. They assured him that
from then on he would never again experience the bitter pain
he had been suffering but only the annoyance of the viscous liquid that we have mentioned above.

And that is the way it turned out. Never again was he carried
out of his senses as before, nor did he have any of the visions he
used to have[85] when, in the midst of his pains and terrifying
cries, he would suddenly become silent and senseless. Later on,
however, he regained his health under the doctor's care, but he
did not remain steadfast in his pursuit of sanctity.

CHAPTER 18

The production of images in the soul is mysterious.

39. If anyone is able to discover the causes of these visions
and divinations, and the methods followed in them, and to grasp
these matters with certainty, I should prefer to listen to him
than to have other people look for a dissertation from me. Nevertheless, I shall not withhold my opinion; and thus the learned
will not be able to mock me for being assertive, nor the unlearned look to me as a teacher, but both may regard me rather
as one who discusses and investigates than as one who knows.

I consider all these phenomena similar to dreams. Now
dreams are sometimes false and sometimes true, sometimes trou-

bled and sometimes calm; and true dreams are sometimes quite similar to future events or even clear forecasts, while at other times they are predictions given with dark meanings and, as it were, in figurative expressions. And the same is to be said of all these visions. But men like to gaze in wonder at what is strange and seek the causes of the unusual, while they generally do not care to know about daily occurrences of this sort, even though their origin may often be more obscure.[86] In the case of words, namely, the signs that we use in speech, when an unusual one is heard, men ask first what it is (that is, what it means), and after learning this, they enquire about its origin; and yet there are many words in use in our daily speech about whose origin they are content to be ignorant. Similarly, when an unusual event occurs, whether in the material or spiritual order, they anxiously enquire about its causes and its nature and demand an explanation from the savants.

40. When, for example, someone asks me the meaning of *catus*,[87] and I say that it means "wise" or "sharp," and when he, not satisfied, goes on to enquire about the origin of *catus*, I usually rejoin and ask about the origin of *acutus* ("sharp"). On this point he would be equally uninformed, but because of the familiarity of the word he would willingly bear his ignorance about its origin. But when a word has a sound which is strange to his ears, he does not think he knows its meaning unless he traces out its derivation.

And so, when anyone asks me about the origin of the images of bodies that appear in ecstasy, an experience that happens but rarely to the soul, I, in turn, ask about the origin of the images that appear daily to the soul in sleep—an enquiry which men care little or nothing about. One would think that the nature of these visions was less remarkable because they are daily occurrences, or less interesting because they are a common experience. Or, if men do well in not investigating them, they will do better in restraining their curiosity about extraordinary visions; but I am much more impressed and profoundly amazed when I consider the rapidity and ease with which the soul fashions within itself images of bodies seen through the eyes of the body than when I consider the visions of dreams and even of ecstasies.

But whatever the nature of these images may be, it is certainly not corporeal. Whoever is not satisfied with this knowledge may enquire about their origin from others. I confess my ignorance.

CHAPTER 19

The causes of visions.

41. The point I wish to make can easily be established from an examination of examples.[88] Such bodily states as pallor, blushing, trembling, and even sickness are caused sometimes by the body, sometimes by the soul. They are caused by the body when a humor or some food or other matter entering the body from without diffuses itself. But they are caused by the soul when it is disturbed by fear or confused by shame or moved by anger or love or any other emotion; and this is natural inasmuch as the animating and ruling force in man even stirs him rather deeply at times when it itself is deeply moved.

And similarly, when the soul directs its gaze to objects which are presented to it, not through the bodily senses but through an incorporeal substance, and when on these occasions it cannot decide whether it beholds bodies or the likenesses of bodies, its state is attributable sometimes to the body[89] and sometimes to a spirit. It can be ascribed to the body either because of a natural phenomenon such as the dreams that come in sleep, for sleep is a function of the body, or because of ill-health. Now in the latter state the senses are sometimes afflicted with a disorder, as when delirious people see bodies as well as visions that appear like bodies and seem present before their eyes; and sometimes the senses cease operating altogether, as often has happened in the case of people suffering from a serious and prolonged illness,[90] who were without sensation for some time, though present in their bodies, and who later, returning, have stated that they saw many objects.

But these visions can be attributed to the action of a spirit when sound and healthy people are transported, whether through the senses of the body they see real bodies, and in the spirit, likenesses indistinguishable from bodies, or completely carried out of their senses and perceiving nothing at all through them, they dwell by this spiritual vision amidst the likenesses of bodies. But when an evil spirit transports men thus, he either possesses them or makes them frenzied or false prophets. When, on the contrary, a good spirit transports them, he inspires them to give a reliable account of mysteries; or if understanding is also imparted,[91] he either makes them true prophets or for the moment aids them in seeing and narrating the vision that must be revealed through them.[92]

CHAPTER 20

Impediments to sense perception.

42. But when the body is the cause of these visions, it does not present the object, for it has not the power to fashion anything spiritual. Rather, when the pathway of attention,[93] which proceeds from the brain and regulates sensation, is dormant or disturbed or blocked, the soul itself (which cannot of itself give up this function), being entirely or partially hindered by the body from sensing corporeal objects or directing the force of its attention to such objects, gathers together in the spirit the likenesses of bodies or gazes upon those that are presented to it. If it gathers them together itself, they are simply images of objects once seen; whereas, if it gazes upon images presented to it, they are the images of a vision.

Finally, when the eyes are suffering from some ailment or have ceased to function altogether (because there no longer exists in the brain the cause that co-operates in directing the attention of sensation), ocular vision ceases; but it is the body that hinders corporeal vision. Blind people see objects while asleep rather than while awake. In the brain of the sleeper the path of sensation that leads the attention to the eyes is dormant; and so the attention, turning elsewhere, beholds dream images as if they were the forms of bodies present to the eyes. The upshot is that the sleeper, thinking he is awake, fancies that he beholds not likenesses of bodies but bodies themselves; but when blind people are awake, the attention of vision is led along its customary way until it arrives at the eyes; and then it is not sent forth[94] but remains there. Hence the blind realize that they are awake and watching in darkness even through the day rather than sleeping by day or by night.

Those who are not blind usually see nothing with their eyes when they sleep with them open, but this does not mean that they see nothing at all, since in spirit they see the images of dreams; if, however, they are awake and have their eyes closed, they enjoy neither the sights of dreams nor those of waking hours. Still the path of sensation is not dormant or disturbed or blocked, but goes forth from the brain to the eyes and leads the attention of the soul to the very gates of the body, though they are barred. And the result is simply that images of bodies are conjured up, though they are never mistaken for bodies that are perceived through the eyes.

43. It is rather important, then, to determine the location of an impediment to sense perception, when such an impediment exists in the body. If there is no obstacle except at the entrances and doors of the senses (in the eyes, or the ears, or the other sense organs), the perception of bodies is simply shut off; but the attention of the soul is not turned elsewhere so as to induce it to mistake bodily images for bodies themselves.

But if the cause is in the brain, from which there are pathways for sensation leading to external objects, the channels that carry the attention are dormant or disturbed or blocked. Now the soul in this condition does not lose the tendency to direct its energies through these channels, through which it normally sees or perceives external objects. Hence it fashions similar objects so vividly that it is unable to distinguish images of bodies from real bodies, and it knows not whether it is dealing with the one or the other. When it does know, its knowledge is far different from the knowledge it has when in conscious thought it ponders over or chances upon the likenesses of bodies. This phenomenon cannot be understood at all except by those who have experienced it. I, for one, have realized while asleep that I was seeing something in my sleep;[95] but the distinction I made between the likenesses of bodies which I saw and real bodies was lacking in that sureness with which we usually make this distinction when we ponder over such images with closed eyes or when we are placed in darkness. The attention of the soul may be carried as far as the sense organs when they are impaired; or within the brain itself, from which the attention normally goes out to external objects, it may for some special reason be directed elsewhere. In either case, the soul may sometimes know that it is not seeing bodies but the likenesses of bodies; or, when less instructed, it may judge even these likenesses to be bodies but realize that it perceives them not with the body but with the spirit. Yet the attention of the mind is such that it operates far differently in these circumstances than it does when functioning in the organs of the body. Hence, also, the blind know they are awake when with a sure insight they distinguish between imaginative representations of bodies and the bodies themselves which they cannot see.

CHAPTER 21

In spiritual vision different causes do not mean different kinds of objects.

44. But when in spite of the good health of the body and the normal functioning of the senses, the soul is carried off by some mysterious spiritual power to a vision that contains images of bodies, a difference in the manner of the experience does not argue a difference in the nature of the objects seen, since there is a difference even in those causes that have their origin in the body, and sometimes the causes are even quite contrary. In the case of those who are delirious but not asleep, it is rather in the head that the paths of sensation are disturbed. The result is that they see objects that are ordinarily seen only in dreams, when the attention is turned from the perceptions of waking hours and directed to visions of this sort. Hence, although the one case occurs outside of sleep and the other in sleep, still the

objects seen do not differ in nature, for they belong to the spirit in which and from which the likenesses of bodies arise.

Similarly, when the soul of a man, sound in body and wide awake, is carried off by some mysterious spiritual force so that he sees in spirit the imaginative likenesses of bodies rather than bodies themselves, the cause of the derangement of the attention may be different in different cases, but the nature of the objects seen is the same.

And we must not suppose that when the cause is in the body, the soul always ponders over images of bodies by its own power, without any prophetic insight, as it normally does in thought; and that it is only when the soul is taken up by a spirit to gaze at such visions that they are revealed to it by God. For Scripture clearly says, *I will pour out My Spirit upon all flesh, and the young men shall see visions, and the old men shall dream dreams,*[96] thus attributing both to the work of God. And again it says, *An angel of the Lord appeared to the man in a dream, saying, "Do not be afraid to take Mary, your wife,"*[97] and on another occasion, *Take the Child and go into Egypt.*[98]

CHAPTER 22

The difficulty of explaining how certain extraordinary events are seen in the spirit.

45. I do not believe, then, that the spirit of a man is taken up by a good spirit to see these images unless they have some special meaning. But when the body causes the human spirit to direct its gaze intently upon them,[99] it must not be thought that they always have a meaning. However, they have a meaning when they are inspired by a spirit that reveals something, whether it is to a man in sleep or to one who is afflicted with some bodily ailment that takes him out of his senses. I have known instances of people, wide awake, suffering no affliction and disturbed by no madness, who were acted upon by some mysterious influence and inspired with thoughts that became

prophecies when they spoke them out. And this has happened not only to those who intended something quite different, as in the case of Caiphas, the high priest, who prophesied though he had no intention of prophesying,[100] but also to those who undertook to pronounce a divination about some future event.

46. A certain group of youths on a journey, wishing to play a hoax in a spirit of jest, pretended to be astrologers—though they knew nothing at all about the twelve signs.[101] Observing that their host listened to their talk with amazement and affirmed that it was quite true, they went on confidently with further pronouncements. Still he remained spellbound and agreed to it all. Finally, he asked them about the lot of his son, who had been away a long time. He was anxious about the boy and feared some mishap, because the delay was unforeseen. Thinking only of making the father happy for the moment, they gave no thought to the fact that he would discover the truth after their departure; and since they were soon to depart, they replied that he was safe, was on his way home, and would arrive that very day. They had no fear that after the lapse of a day the man might follow them and expose them. But to come to the point—while they were still in the house and were just getting ready to go, the son himself suddenly appeared.

47. On another occasion, while a certain pagan festival was being celebrated in a place where there were many idols, a young man was dancing to the accompaniment of a flute.[102] Though not frenzied by any spirit, he was giving a comic imitation of the frenzied devotees, and his audience understood this. At these festivals it was customary for the sacrifices to be offered and for the worshipers to go through their wild rites before the midday meal; afterwards any young men who wished to give a mock performance were allowed to do so. It was thus that the man on this day was entertaining the smiling crowd that surrounded him, when in a spirit of fun he called for silence. He then predicted that on that very night in the nearby forest a man would be killed by a lion and that at dawn the next day everyone would desert the place of the festival and gather to see the body of the dead man. And it turned out exactly that way, although from his antics it had been quite clear to the by-

standers that he had had no extraordinary or clairvoyant experience at all but had made the statement in a light and playful mood. His own amazement at what happened was all the greater because he was more keenly aware of the spirit in which he had said the words.

48. How do these things enter the spirit of man? Are they fashioned there? Or are they implanted fully formed and seen as a consequence of some sort of union, so that angels reveal to men their own thoughts and the likenesses of bodies which they fashion beforehand in their own spirit through their knowledge of future events? In such a way the angels see our thoughts;[103] not, of course, with eyes, because they see not by body but by spirit. But there is this difference: they know our thoughts whether we will it or not, whereas we cannot know theirs unless they reveal them. For they have the power, I believe, of hiding their thoughts by spiritual means, just as we can hide our bodies from the eyes of others by setting up some obstacle to obstruct their view. And what takes place in our spirit to allow a man sometimes to see only images that have a meaning, while he is unaware of the fact that they do mean something; and at other times to allow him to perceive that such images have some meaning, while he is left in ignorance of what they mean; and at still other times to allow the human soul through some sort of fuller revelation to see these images with the spirit and understand their meaning with the mind? It is extremely difficult to find an answer to these questions; and even if I had the knowledge, it would be a great task to discuss and explain the matter.

CHAPTER 23

Summary of the ways in which the likenesses of bodies are seen in the spirit.

49. But I think it is sufficient now to demonstrate this one fact, namely, that there exists in us a spiritual nature in which the likenesses of bodily things are formed. This spiritual nature

functions when we come into contact with a body by means of our bodily senses, and the image of it is immediately formed in our spirit and stored in our memory; or when we think of bodies previously known but now absent, in order to form from them a spiritual vision of those things that were already in our spirit even before we began to think of them;[104] or when we behold likenesses of bodies which we do not know but whose existence we do not doubt, not as they are in themselves but as they happen to present themselves to us; or when we arbitrarily and fancifully think of other objects that do not exist or whose existence is unknown to us; or when various forms of the likenesses of bodies come into our minds from any source whatever without our concurrence and against our will.

Again, it is the spiritual nature in us that operates when we are about to perform some bodily action and we order beforehand the stages of it, first going through it all in thought; or when in an act itself, whether we are speaking or going through some bodily motion, all the movements of the body are anticipated through their likenesses in our spirit in order that they may be executed (for no syllable, however short, could be pronounced in its proper place unless previously planned in thought). It is the spiritual nature of the soul also that is affected when dreams come in sleep, either with or without a meaning; or when, because of ill-health, the inner pathways of sensation are disturbed and the spirit so confuses images of bodies with real bodies that it is impossible or nearly impossible to distinguish between them (and this may happen whether the images have a meaning or not); or when, under the impact of some serious illness or bodily suffering that obstructs the interior paths by which the attention of the soul is sent forth and goes out to perceive its object through the sense organs, images of bodies having some meaning, or appearing without any meaning, arise or are presented while the spirit is in a state of unconsciousness more profound than sleep.

Finally, it is the spiritual nature of the soul that is acted upon when, without any bodily cause, the soul is seized by a spirit and is raised up to view such likenesses of bodies, using meanwhile the senses of the body also and confusing the images with the objects of the senses; or when the soul is taken hold of by a spirit and is so completely removed from the bodily senses that it is engaged by nothing but the likenesses of bodies in spiritual vision—in which state I am inclined to doubt whether there can be a vision of something that has no meaning.

CHAPTER 24

Spiritual vision is more excellent than corporeal vision, intellectual more excellent than spiritual.

50. Hence this spiritual nature, in which are produced not bodies but the likenesses of bodies, enjoys visions of a kind inferior to those which the mind or intelligence[105] with its light beholds. For it is by this latter power that objects of a lower order are judged and those realities are beheld which are not bodies and have no forms similar to bodies: such as the mind itself and every good affection of the soul (to which are opposed its vices, which are rightly censured and condemned in men). How else can the intellect itself be seen except by intellection? In this way also we see *charity, joy, peace, longanimity, kindness, goodness, faith, meekness, continency,*[106] and the rest, by which we draw near to God, and finally God Himself,[107] from whom are all things, through whom are all things, and in whom are all things.[108]

51. In one and the same soul, then, there are different visions: by means of the body it perceives objects such as the corporeal heaven and earth and everything that can be known in them in the degree that they are capable of being known; with the spirit it sees likenesses of bodies—a matter that I have already discussed at length;[109] and with the mind it understands those realities that are neither bodies nor the likenesses of bodies. But there is, of course, a hierarchy in these visions, one being superior to another. For spiritual vision is more excellent than corporeal, and intellectual vision more excellent than spiritual.

Corporeal vision cannot take place without spiritual, since at the very moment when we encounter a body by means of bodily sensation, there appears in the soul something not identical with the object perceived but resembling it. If this did not happen, there would be no sensation by which exterior objects are perceived.

For it is not the body that perceives, but the soul by means of the body;[110] and the soul uses the body as a sort of messenger in order to form within itself the object that is called to its attention from the outside world.[111] Hence corporeal vision cannot take place unless there is a concomitant spiritual vision; but no distinction is made between the two until the bodily sensation has passed and the object perceived by means of the body is found in the spirit. On the other hand, there can be spiritual vision without corporeal vision, namely, when the likenesses of absent bodies appear in the spirit, and when many such images are fashioned by the free activity of the soul or are presented to it in spite of itself. Moreover, spiritual vision needs intellectual vision if a judgment is to be made upon its contents, but intellectual vision does not need spiritual, which is of a lower order.[112]

And so corporeal vision is inferior to the spiritual, and both are inferior to the intellectual. When, therefore, we read, *The spiritual man judges all things, but he himself is judged by no man,*[113] we should not take "spiritual" as pertaining to the spirit which is distinguished from the mind (as in the text, *I will pray with the spirit, and I will pray with the mind also*),[114] but we must understand it as deriving from that other sense, as in the following: *But be renewed in the spirit of your mind.*[115] For I have already shown above[116] that the name "spirit" in another sense of the word is given also to the mind itself, to that power, namely, by which the spiritual man judges all things. Hence I believe that spiritual vision can be reasonably and naturally said to occupy a kind of middle ground between intellectual and corporeal vision. For I suppose that a thing which is not really a body, but like a body, can be appropriately said to be in the middle between that which is truly a body and that which is neither a body nor like a body.

CHAPTER 25

Corporeal and spiritual vision can err, but not intellectual vision.

52. But the soul is deceived by the images of things, not because of any fault of these images but because of its own erroneous opinion when through lack of understanding it confuses different objects because of their similarity. It is deceived, therefore, in corporeal vision when it fancies that what happens in the senses of the body takes place in bodies outside,[117] as when people on a moving ship seem to see stationary objects on shore in motion, or when those who gaze at the heavens think they see stars at rest which are actually moving. Such is the case, too, when the rays coming from the eyes are not focused, and two lamps seem to shine where there is only one,[118] or when an oar in the water appears to be broken. Many other similar appearances might be mentioned. The same may be said when the soul takes one object for another that has a similar color, sound, odor, taste, or touch. Thus a salve mixed with wax in a cooking vessel is mistaken for a vegetable, and the rumble of a passing carriage is thought to be thunder, and, when no other sense but that of smell is employed, balm is taken for citrus; so also a dish that has a bit of sweet flavoring tastes as if it were made of honey, and a strange ring felt in the dark is taken for gold, when it is actually copper or silver. The same may be said, too, when the eyes encounter objects suddenly and unexpectedly, and the soul in its confusion fancies it sees dream images or some similar spiritual vision.

Hence, in all cases of corporeal vision, recourse is had to the testimony of other senses, and above all to that of the mind and reason, so that we may discover the truth in these matters as far as it can be discovered. But in spiritual vision, namely, in the likenesses of bodies seen by the spirit, the soul is deceived when it judges the objects of its vision to be real bodies, or when it attaches some property of its own fancy and false conjecture to bodies that it has not seen but merely conjures up in imagination. But in the intuitions of the intellect it is not deceived. For either it understands, and then it possesses truth; or if it does not possess truth, it fails to understand. And so it is one thing for the soul to err in the objects which it sees and another for it to err because it does not see.

CHAPTER 26

Two kinds of rapture: spiritual and intellectual.

53. There are occasions, then, when the soul is carried off to objects of vision that are similar to corporeal things and are seen by the spirit in such a way that the soul is quite removed from the senses of the body, more than in sleep but less than in death. In such cases it is by virtue of divine guidance and assistance that it realizes it is seeing in a spiritual way not bodies but the likenesses of bodies. Similarly, it sometimes happens that a man in his sleep is aware that he is dreaming even before he awakes.[119] And in spiritual vision it may also be that future events, represented under images present to the soul, are clearly recognized as future because of the fact that divine assistance is given to the human mind or that someone in the vision explains the meaning of it, as happened to John in the Apocalypse.[120] Now the revelation given in such a case must be important, even though it may happen that the man who receives it does not know whether he went out of the body during the vision or was still in the body but with his spirit withdrawn from the bodily senses. If this information is not revealed to a man who experiences such an ecstasy, it is possible for him to remain in ignorance on this point.

54. Moreover, if a man has not only been carried out of the bodily senses to be among the likenesses of bodies seen by the spirit, but is also carried out of these latter to be conveyed, as it were, to the region of the intellectual or intelligible,[121] where transparent truth is seen without any bodily likeness, his vision is darkened by no cloud of false opinion, and there the virtues of the soul are not tedious and burdensome. For then there is no restraining of lust by the effort of temperance, no bearing of adversity by fortitude, no punishing of wicked deeds by justice, no

avoiding of evil by prudence. The one virtue and the whole of virtue there is to love what you see, and the supreme happiness is to possess what you love. For there beatitude is imbibed at its source, whence some few drops are sprinkled upon this life of ours,[122] that amid the trials of this world we may spend our days with temperance, fortitude, justice, and prudence.

It is surely in pursuit of this end, where there will be secure peace and the unutterable vision of truth, that man undertakes the labor of restraining his desires, of bearing adversities, of relieving the poor, of opposing deceivers. There the brightness of the Lord is seen,[123] not through a symbolic or corporeal vision, as it was seen on Mount Sinai,[124] nor through a spiritual vision such as Isaiah saw[125] and John in the Apocalypse, but through a direct vision[126] and not through a dark image, as far as the human mind elevated by the grace of God can receive it. In such a vision God speaks face to face to him whom He has made worthy of this communion. And here we are speaking not of the face of the body but of that of the mind.

CHAPTER 27

The vision granted to Moses.

Now I think we must understand in this sense what has been written of the vision granted to Moses.[127]

55. Moses, as we read in Exodus, had yearned to see God, not as he had seen Him on the mountain, nor as he saw Him in the tabernacle,[128] but in His divine essence without the medium of any bodily creature that might be presented to the senses of mortal flesh. It was his desire to see God, not by imaginary likenesses of bodies in the spirit but by a vision of the divine essence as far as this can be attained by a rational and intellectual creature when withdrawn from all bodily senses and from all obscure symbols of the spirit.

For, according to Holy Scripture, Moses said, *If, therefore, I have found favor in Thy sight, show me Thyself, that I may see Thee clearly.*[129] Now just before this we read, *And the Lord spoke to Mo-*

ses face to face as a man speaks to his friend.[130] He realized, therefore, what he saw, and he longed for what he did not see. For
shortly after this, God said to him, *For you have found grace in My
sight, and I have known you before all.*[131] And he replied, *Show me
Thy brightness.*[132] And then, indeed, an answer clothed in a figure, which it would be tedious now to explain, was given him
by the Lord, who said to him, *You cannot see My face and live; for
man shall not see My face and live.*[133] And then God continued, *Behold there is a place with Me and you shall stand upon the rock. As
soon as My Majesty will pass, I will place you upon an eminence of
the rock and cover you with My hand till I pass; and I will take away
My hand, and then you shall see My back parts; for My face shall not
be revealed to you.*[134]

However, the account that follows in the sacred text does not
state that this took place in a corporeal way, and this shows
clearly enough that the words are to be taken figuratively as referring to the Church. For the Church is "the place with the
Lord," because it is His temple and is built upon a rock; and the
rest of this narrative agrees with this interpretation.[135] But if
Moses had not merited to see the brightness of God, which he
ardently desired, God would not say, as He does in the Book of
Numbers, to Aaron and Mary, the brother and sister of Moses,
*Hear My words: If there be a prophet among you, in a vision, I, the
Lord, will become known to him, and I will speak to him in his sleep.
Not thus with My servant Moses: in all My house, he is the faithful
one. Mouth to mouth I will speak to him in My essence and not through
obscure signs, and he has seen the brightness of the Lord.*[136] This, indeed, is not to be understood as referring to a bodily substance
made present to the senses of the flesh. For certainly God spoke
thus to Moses face to face, the one in the presence of the other;
but on that occasion Moses said to God, *Show me Thyself.* And
now also, addressing those whom He reprimanded, and above
whom He thus exalted the merits of Moses, God spoke in this
way through a corporeal creature, present to the senses of the
body.

In that other manner, then, in His own divine essence, He
speaks in an incomparably more intimate and inward manner,
in an unutterable converse where no man beholds Him while

living this mortal life in the senses of the body. This vision is
granted only to him who in some way dies to this life,[137] whether he quits the body entirely or is turned away and carried out
of the bodily senses, so that he really knows not (to use the
words of St. Paul) whether he is in the body or out of the body
when he is carried off to this vision.[138]

CHAPTER 28

*The third heaven and Paradise may be understood as the
third kind of vision.*

56. If, then, the Apostle has given the name "third heaven" to
this third type of vision, which is superior to every corporeal vision by which bodies are perceived through the senses of the
body, and superior also to all spiritual vision by which the likenesses of bodies are beheld not by the mind but by the spirit,
in this vision the brightness of God is seen by those whose
hearts are purified for the vision.[139] Hence it is said, *Blessed are
the pure of heart, for they shall see God,*[140] not through any symbol
fashioned in a coporeal or spiritual manner, as if through a mir-
ror in a riddle,[141] but face to face or *mouth to mouth,* as it is said
of Moses, through a vision, that is, of God's own essence, according to the limited measure that it can be comprehended by a
mind distinct from God Himself, even after it has been
cleansed[142] from all earthly stain and carried away from all
body and likeness of body. From Him we are exiled, laden with
a mortal and corruptible burden, as long as we walk by faith and
not by vision,[143] even when we live justly in this world.[144]

But why should we not believe that, when the great Apostle
and teacher of the Gentiles was carried up to such an extraordinary vision, God wished to show him the life that is to be ours
forever after this life on earth? And why should not the name
"paradise" be given to this also, as well as to that place where
Adam lived in the body among the shade trees and the fruit
trees? For the Church also, who gathers us into the bosom of her
charity, is called *a paradise with the fruit of the orchard.*[145] But this

was said figuratively on the ground that the Church was signified, through a figure of what was to come,[146] by that Paradise
where Adam actually was.

And yet a more thoughtful consideration of the matter might
possibly suggest that the corporeal Paradise in which Adam
lived his corporeal life was a sign both of this life of the saints
now existing in the Church and of that eternal life which will
be when this life is done. Thus Jerusalem, which is translated
"the vision of peace,"[147] although it designates a certain earthly
city, is a sign of Jerusalem, our eternal mother in heaven.[148] In
the latter sense it can refer to those who in hope have been
saved[149] and in their hope wait with patience for what they do
not see. It is because of these that Scripture says, *Many are the
children of the desolate, more than of her that has a husband.*[150] Or
it can refer to the holy angels themselves throughout the
Church of God's manifold wisdom,[151] with whom we are to enjoy a peaceful and unending abode after this exile.

CHAPTER 29

Whether there are more than three heavens is difficult to say.

57. In explaining the third heaven to which St. Paul was carried, some may wish to conjecture the existence of a fourth
heaven also, and above this still more heavens, beneath which is
found the third heaven; and some actually do say that there are
seven, eight, nine, or even ten;[152] and in the one called the firmament they assert that there are many heavens and accordingly argue and conclude that they are corporeal. But to discuss
these arguments and theories at the present time would take too
long.

Moreover, one can hold, or demonstrate if he is able, that in
spiritual or intellectual visions there are also many grades and
that these are distinguished according to a progression of revelations under the influence of more or less illumination. Now
whatever the facts may be and whatever different opinions men

may be pleased to adopt, I have thus far been unable to recognize or maintain any objects or visions other than the three kinds perceived by the body and the spirit and the mind. But in establishing the number and degrees of difference in the various classes and in determining the relative grades of excellence in them, I admit my ignorance.

CHAPTER 30

Degrees of excellence in likenesses of bodies seen in the spirit.

58. Now in the corporeal light of this world there is the heaven which we see above the earth and from which shine forth the luminous bodies and stars, which are far superior to earthly bodies.[153] So, too, in the spiritual order, wherein the likenesses of bodies are seen in a kind of incorporeal light[154] that is proper to them, there are certain objects more excellent and truly divine, which angels reveal in wondrous ways. Whether by some sort of union or intermingling they have the facility and power to make their visions ours also, or in some way know how to fashion a vision in our spirit, this is a difficult matter to understand and still more difficult to explain. But in the ordinary course of our daily life there are other objects that arise in various ways from our spirit itself or are, after a fashion, suggested to the spirit by the body, according as we have been influenced by the flesh or by the mind. Thus men in their waking hours think of their troubles, turning over in their minds the likenesses of bodily things; and so in their sleep, too, they frequently dream of something they need. The reason for this is that greed is the motive force of their business dealings; and when they happen to go to sleep hungry and thirsty, they are often after food and drink with open mouth. Now, in my opinion, when these objects are compared with the revelations of angels, they ought to be assigned the same relative value that we give, in the corporeal order, to earthly bodies in comparison with celestial bodies.

CHAPTER 31

The soul longs to see the Light, which is God, illuminating the intellect, but cannot do so except when carried off in ecstasy.

59. So, also, among the objects of the intellect; there are some that are seen in the soul itself:[155] for example, the virtues (to which the vices are opposed), either virtues which will endure, such as piety, or virtues that are useful for this life and not destined to remain in the next, as faith, by which we believe what we do not see, and hope, by which we await with patience the life that shall be, and patience itself, by which we bear every adversity until we arrive at the goal of our desires.[156]

These virtues, of course, and other similar ones, which are quite necessary for us now in living out our exile, will have no place in the blessed life, for the attainment of which they are necessary. And yet even they are seen with the intellect; for they are not bodies, nor have they forms similar to bodies.

But distinct from these objects is the Light by which the soul is illumined, in order that it may see and truly understand everything, either in itself or in the light.[157] For the Light is God Himself,[158] whereas the soul is a creature; yet, since it is rational and intellectual, it is made in His image. And when it tries to behold the Light, it trembles in its weakness and finds itself unable to do so.[159] Yet from this source comes all the understanding it is able to attain. When, therefore, it is thus carried off and, after being withdrawn from the senses of the body, is made present to this vision in a more perfect manner (not by a spatial relation, but in a way proper to its being), it also sees above itself that Light[160] in whose illumination it is enabled to see all the objects that it sees and understands in itself.[161]

CHAPTER 32

*The soul at death is transported with a likeness of the body to a
"spiritual" place of punishment or of peace.*

60. Now it may be asked[162] whether the soul on its departure
from the body is brought to some corporeal region, or to an incorporeal one that is like the corporeal,[163] or to neither, but
rather to that which is more excellent than bodies and likenesses
of bodies. To this question I should reply without hesitation
that it is not brought to a corporeal region unless it is transported in union with a body or in a nonspatial way.

The further problem, whether the soul has some sort of body
after it departs from this body, may be explained by anyone who
can. I do not think it has.[164] But it is brought to a realm that
is spiritual in accordance with its merits.[165] This region, in one
case, is a place of punishment, whose nature is similar to that of
bodies; such a place as has often been shown to those who have
been carried out of the senses of the body and, while lying as if
in death, have seen the punishments of hell. Those who have un-
dergone this experience were accompanied by some sort of likeness of the body, and through it they were able to be
transported to those regions and to perceive them by the likenesses of their senses.[166] For the soul has a likeness of its body
when the body lies senseless though not yet really dead and the
soul is carried off to see those sights that many have told of after
being restored to life. Why, then, should it not have a likeness
of the body when death really overtakes it and it finally departs
from the body? It follows, therefore, that the soul is transported
either to a place of punishment of this kind or to another place
of bodily likenesses, not, however, of punishment but of peace
and joy.

61. Now it surely cannot be said that those punishments are
false or that that peace and joy are false; for there is falsity only
when, through an erroneous judgment, we mistake one thing
for another. Peter was certainly in error when he saw the dish
and fancied that bodies were in it rather than likenesses of bodies.[167] No less was he in error when, on another occasion, he

was released from his chains by an angel and went forth walking in the body and confronting bodily forms, yet thinking all the while that he was beholding a vision. For on the dish there were only spiritual forms resembling corporeal forms, whereas the actual sight of a man freed from his chains was made in a miraculous way to seem like a spiritual image. Now the soul was in error in these two cases only in so far as it took one thing for another.

Hence, once the soul has left the body, the objects acting upon it (for good or ill) may be like the corporeal and not real corporeal objects, since the soul appears to itself in the likeness of its own body. Yet these objects do exist, and the joy and vexation produced by a spiritual substance are real. For even in sleep there is a vast difference between being in joyful and in sad circumstances in our dreams. Hence some people have grieved on waking from dreams in which they had had their heart's desire; and on other occasions, awaking from dreams in which they had been shaken with terrors and tormented with suffering, they have feared the return of sleep and the recurrence of the same afflictions. And surely we cannot doubt that the afflictions of hell are more vivid and so felt more keenly; for even those who have been carried out of the senses of the body have said afterwards that they have been through a more vivid experience than that of a dream, though of course it was less vivid than it would have been had they died. Hell, then, indeed exists, but I am of the opinion that its nature is spiritual rather than corporeal.[168]

CHAPTER 33

Hell and the bosom of Abraham.

62. No hearing should be given to the advocates of the theory that hell is found in this life and not after death.[169] Let them devise their interpretations of the poets' fictions. We must not depart from the authority of Sacred Scripture; on this alone our faith in this matter rests. We may, however, be able to show that the wise men among the pagans had no doubt at all about the

reality of the lower world, where the souls of the dead are received after this life.[170] But why the lower world is said to be under the earth,[171] if it is not a corporeal place, or why it is called the lower world, if it is not under the earth—these are questions that are discussed, and not without reason.

But the soul is incorporeal; and this I proclaim confidently, not as my opniion but as certain knowledge. However, anyone who says that it is impossible for the soul to have a likeness of the body or of any members of the body ought also to deny that the soul in sleep sees itself walking or sitting or being borne away and returned, now this way, now that, on foot or through the air. None of this happens without some likeness of the body. Hence, if the soul in the lower world bears this likeness, which is not corporeal, but similar to a body, it seems also that it is in a place not corporeal but like the corporeal, whether at rest or in torment.

63. I admit, however, that I have not yet found the term "lower world" [or "hell"] applied to the place where the souls of the just are at rest.[172] Moreover, it is believed, and not without reason, that the soul of Christ went to that very region where sinners are tormented in order to release from their suffering those who He decreed should be released according to the inscrutable ways of His justice. For I do not see how else we can interpret the text, *God raised Him up from the dead, having loosed the pangs of hell because it was not possible that He should be held fast by them,*[173] unless we understand that He loosed the pangs of certain souls in hell in virtue of that power by which He is Lord. For to Him every knee does bend *of those in heaven, on earth, and under the earth,*[174] and because of His power He could not have been held in bonds by the pangs that He loosed.

Abraham and the poor man in his bosom, that is to say, in his peaceful retreat, were not in the midst of pain. Between their restful abode and the infernal torments we read that a great gulf was fixed, but they are not said to be in hell. For Christ said, *It came to pass that the poor man died and was borne away by the angels to Abraham's bosom; but the rich man also died and was buried. And, being in hell, in the midst of torments* ... and so forth.[175] Accordingly we see that hell is mentioned not in reference to the repose of the poor man but in reference to the punishment of the rich man.

64. As for the words of Jacob to his son, *You will bring down my old age with sorrow unto hell,*[176] he feared, it seems, that he would be so distraught because of his profound sorrow that he would go to the hell of sinners rather than to the resting place of the blessed. For sorrow is no small evil for the soul. Even St. Paul was quite fearful that a certain man might be overwhelmed by too much sorrow.[177] Hence, as I said, I have not found any passage in Scripture, at least in the canonical books, where the term "hell" is to be taken in a good sense. I am still looking for such a passage and can think of none, but I doubt whether anybody could tolerate an interpretation of Abraham's bosom and the resting place to which the angels carried the devoted poor man in anything but a good sense, and so I do not see how we may believe that that resting place is in hell.

CHAPTER 34

Paradise and the third heaven.

65. But while I seek an answer to this question, whether successfully or otherwise, I am compelled by the length of this book to bring it at last to an end. We began our discussion with the question of Paradise, basing it on the statement of St. Paul, where he says that he knows a man who was caught up to the third heaven, though he knows not whether it was in the body or out of the body, and that this man was caught up into Paradise and heard secret words that man may not repeat.[178] We do not, then, rashly determine whether Paradise is in the third heaven or whether St. Paul was caught up to the third heaven and then again to Paradise. For the word "paradise" properly means any wooded place, but figuratively it can also be used for any spiritual region, as it were, where the soul is in a happy state. The third heaven, therefore, whatever it is (and it is, indeed, something wonderfully and singularly sublime), is Paradise; and so also a certain joy springing from a good conscience

within man himself is Paradise. Hence the Church also, in the saints who live temperately and justly and devoutly, is rightly called Paradise,[179] vigorous as it is with an abundance of graces and with pure delights. Even in the midst of tribulations she glories in her very suffering, greatly rejoicing because, according to the multitude of the sorrows in her heart, the comforts of God give joy to her soul.[180]

How much more truly, then, can Abraham's bosom after this life also be called Paradise, where there is no temptation and where there is such wonderful rest after all the sufferings of this life. There, also, there is a light that belongs to that state, different from light elsewhere and quite excellent in its nature. It was this light that the rich man saw from his torments in the darkness of hell; and though he saw it from such a great distance, because there was a vast gulf between them, nevertheless he saw it clearly enough to recognize there the poor man he had once despised.

66. If all this is so, hell is said or believed[181] to be under the earth because of the way it is represented appropriately in the spirit by means of the likenesses of corporeal things. Now the souls of the dead who are deserving of hell have sinned through love of the flesh. They are affected, therefore, by the likenesses of bodies and are subjected to the same experience as the dead flesh itself buried under the earth.[182] Finally, hell is called the lower world, or *inferi* in Latin, because it is beneath the earth. In the corporeal world all the heavier bodies occupy a lower place if the natural tendency of their weight is not interfered with;[183] and so in the spiritual order the gloomier realm is in a lower position. Hence the Greek word for hell is said to get its meaning from the fact that the place contains no delight.[184]

And yet our Savior Himself, when He died for us, did not disdain to visit this part of the world. He could not have been ignorant of the fact that some were to be delivered from there in accordance with the mysteries of God's justice, and there He went to deliver them. Hence, when Christ said to the robber, *This day you shall be with Me in Paradise,*[185] He promised to the man's soul not hell, where sins are punished, but the repose of Abraham's bosom; for Christ is everywhere, since He Himself is the Wisdom of God, *reaching everywhere by reason of His purity.*[186] Or He may have referred to the paradise to which St. Paul was caught up after the third heaven, whether it is in the third heaven or anywhere else—if the abode of souls of the blessed is not one and the same thing called by different names.

67. It seems that we are right, then, in understanding the first heaven in general as this whole corporeal heaven (to use a general term), namely, all that is above the waters and the earth, and the second heaven as the object of spiritual vision seen in bodily likenesses (as, for instance, the vision seen by Peter in ecstasy when he saw the dish let down from above full of living creatures),[187] and the third heaven as the objects seen by the mind after it has been so separated and removed and completely carried out of the senses and purified that it is able through the love of the Holy Spirit in a mysterious way to see and hear the objects in that heaven, even the essence of God and the Divine Word through whom all things have been made. If all this is true, then I believe that Paul was carried off to that third heaven and that there is a paradise which is more excellent than all others and is, if we may use the term, the paradise of paradises. For, if a good soul finds joy in the good that is in every creature, what is more excellent than that joy which is found in the Word of God through whom all things have been made?

CHAPTER 35

Reunion of the soul with the glorified body necessary for perfect beatitude.

68. But why must the spirits of the departed be reunited with their bodies in the resurrection, if they can be admitted to the supreme beatitude without their bodies? This is a problem that may trouble some, but it is too difficult to be answered with complete satisfaction in this essay. There should, however, be no doubt that a man's mind, when it is carried out of the senses of the flesh in ecstasy, or when after death it has departed from the flesh, is unable to see the immutable essence of God just as

the holy angels see it, even though it has passed beyond the likenesses of corporeal things.[188] This may be because of some mysterious reason or simply because of the fact that it possesses a
kind of natural appetite for managing the body. By reason of
this appetite it is somehow hindered from going on with all its
force to the highest heaven, so long as it is not joined with the
body, for it is in managing the body that this appetite is satisfied.

Moreover, if the body is such that the management of it is difficult and burdensome, as is the case with this corruptible flesh,
which is a load upon the soul[189] (coming as it does from a fallen
race), the mind is much more readily turned away from the vision of the highest heaven. Hence it must necessarily be carried
out of the senses of the flesh in order to be granted this vision
as far as it is able. Accordingly, when the soul is made equal to
the angels and receives again this body, no longer a natural body
but a spiritual one[190] because of the transformation that is to be,
it will have the perfect measure of its being, obeying and commanding, vivified and vivifying with such a wonderful ease that
what was once its burden will be its glory.

CHAPTER 36

*The three kinds of vision will be made perfect in the
blessed after the resurrection.*

69. Then, indeed, there will be the three kinds of vision of
which we have been speaking, but no error will induce us to
mistake one thing for another, either in regard to corporeal objects or in regard to spiritual objects, or especially in regard to
intellectual objects.[191] There will be joy in the things of the intellect, and they will be far more luminously present to the soul
than the corporeal forms that now surround us, which we perceive through the senses of our body. Yet many are now so ab-
sorbed in these material forms that they judge them to be the
only ones, and they think that anything of a different order is
simply nonexistent. But, although the corporeal world is more

obvious, wise men live in the midst of it, clinging with greater surety to the world beyond bodily forms and beyond the likenesses of bodies, the world which they see with the intellect according to their measure, although they are not able to behold it in the mind so vividly as they do these other objects with the senses of the body.

But the holy angels, whose office it is to judge and administer the corporeal world, are not more intimately drawn to it, as if it were closer to them. And in the spirit they see its symbolic likenesses, and these they handle with such effectiveness that they can, by a revelation, introduce them even into the spirits of men. All the while they behold the immutable essence of the Creator with such clarity that because of this vision and the love it inspires they prefer the divine essence to all else, according to it judge everything, are directed towards it in all their impulses, and by it direct all the actions they perform.

Finally, although St. Paul was carried out of the senses of the body into the third heaven and Paradise, he was wanting in one point the full and perfect knowledge of things that the angels have: he did not know whether he was in the body or out of the body. But this knowledge will not be wanting to us when we shall be reunited to our bodies at the resurrection of the dead and when this corruptible body will put on incorruption and this mortal body will put on immortality.[192] For everything will be clear without any error and without any ignorance, all things occupying their proper place, the corporeal, the spiritual, and the intellectual, in untainted nature and perfect beatitude.

CHAPTER 37

A different terminology used by other interpreters.

70. I know, of course, that some highly esteemed Catholic interpreters of Sacred Scripture before the present time have explained St. Paul's statement about the third heaven as implying a distinction between corporeal, animal, and spiritual men;[193] and they add that Paul was carried off to contemplate in a won-

derfully clear vision the realm of the incorporeal, which spiritual men, even in this life, love beyond all else and long to enjoy.
My reasons for designating as spiritual and intellectual what
they apparently have called animal and spiritual (and I have simply used different terms for the same things), I have sufficiently
explained in the earlier part of this book.[194] If I have presented
my explanation clearly in spite of my limited ability, the reader
who is spiritual will approve it, or with the help of the Holy
Spirit he will gain some profit from reading this book in order
to become spiritual. And with this wish we at length bring our
treatise of twelve books to a close.

NOTES

LIST OF ABBREVIATIONS

Agaësse-Solignac	P. Agaësse and A. Solignac (eds.), *La Genèse au sens littéral en douze livres* (BA, *Oeuvres de s. Augustin*, 48–49, Bruges-Paris 1972)
Aug. Mag.	*Augustinus Magister*, Congrès international augustinien, Paris, 21–24 Septembre 1954 (3 vols. Paris 1954–55)
B	*Codex Berolinensis* 24 (Meerman-Phillipps Collection 1651), 9th–10th cent.
BA	Bibliothèque augustinienne, *Oeuvres de saint Augustin* (Paris 1941–)
Bod	*Codex Bodleianus*, Laud. Misc. 141, Bodleian Library, Oxford, 8th–9th cent.
Bonner	Gerald Bonner, *St. Augustine of Hippo: Life and Controversies* (London 1963)
Bourke	Vernon J. Bourke, *Augustine's Quest of Wisdom: Life and Philosophy of the Bishop of Hippo* (Milwaukee 1945)
Brooke-McLean *Octateuch*	A. E. Brooke and N. McLean (eds.), *The Old Testament in Greek*, Vol. 1, *The Octateuch* (Cambridge 1906)
Bru	*Codex Bruxellensis* 1051 (10791), Bibliothèque Royale de Belgique, Brussels, 11th cent.
C	*Codex Coloniensis* 61, 12th cent.
CCL	Corpus christianorum, series latina (Turnhout-Paris 1953–)
CSEL	Corpus scriptorum ecclesiasticorum latinorum (Vienna 1866–)
DarSag	Ch. Daremberg and E. Saglio, *Dictionnaire des antiquités grecques et romaines d'après les textes et les monuments* (Paris 1877–1919)

Dessau ILS	Hermannus Dessau (ed.), *Inscriptiones latinae selectae* (3 vols. in 5. Berlin 1892–1916, reprint 1954–55)
Dict. Bibl.	F. Vigouroux, *Dictionnaire de la Bible* (5 vols. Paris 1895–1912). Supplement, ed. Pirot (1928–)
Diels *Vorsokr.*	Hermann Diels (ed.), *Die Fragmente der Vorsokratiker* (3 vols. 6th ed. Berlin 1951–52)
DTC	*Dictionnaire de théologie catholique* (Paris 1903–72)
E	*Codex Sessorianus* 13, Biblioteca Vittorio Emanuele 2094, Rome, 6th cent.
Eug	Eugyppius, *Excerpta ex operibus s. Augustini*, ed. P. Knoell (CSEL 9.1, Vienna 1885)
Fischer VL	B. Fischer (ed.), *Genesis*, in *Vetus latina* 2 (Freiburg 1951)
FOC	The Fathers of the Church: A New Translation (New York–Washington, D.C. 1947–)
GCS	Die griechischen christlichen Schriftsteller der ersten Jahrhunderte (Leipzig 1897–)
Gilson	Etienne Gilson, *The Christian Philosophy of Saint Augustine*, tr. L. E. M. Lynch (New York 1960) from *Introduction à l'étude de saint Augustin* (Études de philosophie médiévale 11, 2nd ed. Paris 1943)
Hastings DB	James Hastings et al., *A Dictionary of the Bible* (4 vols. Edinburgh 1898–1902)
Hebr.	The Hebrew text of the Old Testament
ICC	*International Critical Commentary* (Edinburgh, London, New York 1895–)
JBC	*The Jerome Biblical Commentary*, eds. R. E. Brown, J. A. Fitzmyer, and R. E. Murphy (2 vols. in 1. Englewood Cliffs 1968)
Kälin	P. Bernard Kälin, *Die Ehrkenntnislehre des hl. Augustinus* (Beilage zum Jahresbericht der kantonalen Lehranstalt Sarnen, 1920–21, Sarnen 1921)

Lau	*Codex Laurentianus,* S. Marco 658, Laurentian Library, Florence, 9th cent.
LCL	The Loeb Classical Library (London, New York, and Cambridge, Mass. 1912–)
LSJ	H. G. Liddell and R. Scott, *A Greek-English Lexicon,* rev. by H. S. Jones (Oxford 1940)
LTK	*Lexikon fur Theologie und Kirche* (2nd ed. Freiburg 1957–67)
m	The text of *De Gen. ad litt.* in Vol. 3, part 1 of Augustine's works edited by the Benedictines of S. Maur, Paris 1680, reprinted in Migne, *Patrologia latina* 34, Paris 1841
MG	J. P. Migne (ed.), *Patrologia graeca* (Paris 1857–66)
Milne *Reconstruction*	C. H. Milne, *A Reconstruction of the Old-Latin Text or Texts of the Gospels Used by Saint Augustine* (Cambridge 1926)
Misc. Ag.	*Miscellanea agostiniana* (2 vols. Rome 1930–31)
ML	J. P. Migne (ed.), *Patrologia latina* (Paris 1844–55)
Nov	*Codex Novariensis* 83 (5), Biblioteca Capitolare, Novara, Italy, 9th cent.
NPNF	Philip Schaff (ed.), *A Select Library of the Nicene and Post-Nicene Fathers of the Christian Church* (New York 1886–89)
NRT	*Nouvelle revue théologique* (Tournai 1869–)
NT	The New Testament
OCD	*The Oxford Classical Dictionary,* eds. N. G. L. Hammond and H. H. Scullard (2nd ed. Oxford 1970)
ODCC	*The Oxford Dictionary of the Christian Church,* eds. F. L. Cross and E. A. Livingstone (2nd ed. London 1974)
OED	*The Oxford English Dictionary* (Oxford 1933)
OL	The Old Latin text or texts of the Bible
OT	The Old Testament

P	*Codex Parisinus* 2706 (Colbertinus 5150), Bibliothèque Nationale, Paris, 7th–8th cent.
Pal	*Codex Palatinus latinus* 234, Vatican Library, 9th cent.
Par	*Codex Parisinus,* Nouv. Acq. Lat. 1572, Bibliothèque Nationale, Paris, 9th cent.
Pauly-Wissowa-Kroll	Pauly-Wissowa-Kroll, *Realencyclopädie der classischen Altertumswissenschaft* (Stuttgart 1893–)
Portalié	Eugène Portalié, *A Guide to the Thought of Saint Augustine,* tr. Ralph J. Bastian (Chicago 1960) from art. "Augustin (Saint)," *Dictionnaire de théologie catholique* 1 (Paris 1903) 2268–2472
Quentin *Gen.*	*Biblia sacra juxta latinam vulgatam versionem* 1, *Liber Genesis,* ed. H. Quentin (Rome 1926)
R	*Codex Parisinus* 1804 (Colbertinus 894), Bibliothèque Nationale, Paris, 9th cent.
REAug	*Revue des études augustiniennes* (Paris 1955–)
RSV	*The Holy Bible,* Revised Standard Version
S	*Codex Sangallensis* 161, St. Gall, Switzerland, 9th cent.
SC	Sources chrétiennes (Paris 1940–)
LXX	The Septuagint translation of the Old Testament
SVF	H. von Arnim (ed.), *Stoicorum veterum fragmenta* (4 vols. Leipzig 1903–24; reprint Stuttgart 1964)
Taylor "Text"	John H. Taylor, "The Text of Augustine's *De Genesi ad litteram,*" *Speculum* 25 (1950) 87–93
TLL	*Thesaurus linguae latinae* (Leipzig 1900–)
TU	Texte und Untersuchungen zur Geschichte der altchristlichen Literatur (Berlin 1882–)
Val	*Codex Vaticanus* 449, Vatican Library, 13th–14th cent.

Vat	*Codex Vaticanus* 657, Vatican Library, 13th–14th cent.
VChr	*Vigiliae christianae* (Amsterdam 1947–)
VL	*Vetus latina:* see Fischer VL
Vulg.	The Latin Vulgate translation of the Bible
Waszink	J. H. Waszink (ed.), *Tertulliani De anima* (Amsterdam 1947)
z	The text of *De Gen. ad litt.*, ed. J. Zycha, CSEL 28.1 (Vienna 1894)
ZNTW	*Zeitschrift für die neutestamentliche Wissenschaft* (Berlin 1881–)

SELECT BIBLIOGRAPHY

Berthold Altaner, "Augustinus und Origenes," *Historisches Jahrbuch* 70 (1951) 15–41; reprinted in B. Altaner, *Kleine patristische Schriften* (TU 83, Berlin 1967) 224–52.

Berthold Altaner, "Eustathius, der lateinische Übersetzer der Hexaemeron-Homilien Basilius des Grossen," ZNTW 39 (1940) 161–70; reprinted in B. Altaner, *Kleine patristische Schriften* (TU 83, Berlin 1967) 437–47.

Gerald Bonner, *St. Augustine of Hippo: Life and Controversies* (London 1963).

Vernon J. Bourke, *Augustine's Quest of Wisdom: Life and Philosophy of the Bishop of Hippo* (Milwaukee 1945); especially pp. 224–47.

Charles Boyer, "La théorie augustinienne des raisons séminales," *Misc. Ag.* 2 (Rome 1931) 795–819; reprinted in C. Boyer, *Essais sur la doctrine de saint Augustin* (2nd ed. Paris 1932) 97–137.

Charles Boyer, *L'Idée de vérité dans la philosophie de saint Augustin* (2nd ed. Paris 1940); especially pp. 128–78.

Cuthbert Butler, *Western Mysticism: The Teaching of SS. Augustine, Gregory and Bernard on Contemplation and the Contemplative Life* (2nd ed. London 1926); especially pp. 50–62.

William A. Christian, "The Creation of the World," in *A Companion to the Study of St. Augustine*, ed. Roy W. Battenhouse (New York 1955) 315–42; originally published under the title, "Augustine on the Creation of the World," *Harvard Theological Review* 46 (1953) 1–25.

Etienne Gilson, *The Christian Philosophy of Saint Augustine*, tr. L. E. M. Lynch (New York 1960) from *Introduction à l'étude de saint Augustin* (Études de philosophie médiévale 11, 2nd ed. Paris 1943).

Bernard Kälin, *Die Erkenntnislehre des hl. Augustinus* (Beilage zum

Jahresbericht der kantonalen Lehranstalt Sarnen, 1920–21, Sarnen 1921).

Matthias E. Korger, "Grundprobleme der augustinischen Erkenntnislehre: Erläutert am Beispiel von *de Genesi ad litteram* XII," *Recherches augustiniennes*, Supp. à la REAug 2 (Paris 1962) 33–57.

Matthias E. Korger and Hans Urs von Balthasar, *Aurelius Augustinus, Psychologie und Mystik* (*De Genesi ad Litteram* 12), introduction, translation, and notes (Sigillum 18, Einsiedeln 1960).

Joseph Maréchal, *Études sur la psychologie des mystiques* (2 vols. Bruges and Paris 1924, 1937); especially Vol. 2, pp. 165–88.

Michael J. McKeough, *The Meaning of the Rationes Seminales in St. Augustine* (Catholic University of America Dissertation, Washington, D.C. 1926).

F. van der Meer, *Augustine the Bishop: The Life and Work of a Father of the Church*, tr. Brian Battershaw and G. R. Lamb (London and New York 1961).

Ernest C. Messenger, *Evolution and Theology: The Problem of Man's Origin* (New York 1932); especially pp. 40–55, 160–78, 260–65.

W. Montgomery, *St. Augustine: Aspects of His Life and Thought* (London 1914); especially pp. 99–147.

W. Montgomery, "St. Augustine's Attitude to Psychic Phenomena," *Hibbert Journal* 25 (1926) 92–102.

Christopher J. O'Toole, *The Philosophy of Creation in the Writings of St. Augustine* (Dissertation, The Catholic University of America Philosophical Series, Washington, D.C. 1944).

Gilles Pelland, *Cinq études d'Augustin sur le début de la Genèse* (Tournai and Montreal 1972).

Jean Pépin, "Recherches sur le sens et les origines de l'expression 'Caelum caeli' dans le livre XII des Confessions de saint Augustin," *Archivum latinitatis medii aevi (Bulletin du Cange)* 23 (1953) 185–274.

Jean Pépin, "Une curieuse déclaration idéaliste du 'De Genesi ad litteram' (XII, 10, 21) de saint Augustin, et ses origines plotiniennes ('Ennéade' 5, 3, 1–9 et 5, 5, 1–2)," *Revue d'histoire et de philosophie religieuses* 34 (1954) 373–400.

Eugène Portalié, *A Guide to the Thought of Saint Augustine*, tr.

Ralph J. Bastian (Chicago 1960) from art. "Augustin (Saint)," DTC 1 (Paris 1903) 2268–2472.

Athanase Sage, "Le péché originel dans la pensée de saint Augustin, de 412 à 430," REAug 15 (1969) 75–112.

Athanase Sage, "Péché originel: Naissance d'un dogme," REAug 13 (1967) 211–48.

John H. Taylor, "The Meaning of Spiritus in St. Augustine's *De Genesi,* XII," *Modern Schoolman* 26 (1949) 211–18.

John H. Taylor, "The Text of Augustine's *De Genesi ad litteram,*" *Speculum* 25 (1950) 87–93.

G. Verbeke, *L'Évolution de la doctrine du pneuma du stoicisme à s. Augustin* (Bibliothèque de l'Institut Supérieur de Philosophie, Université de Louvain, Paris 1945).

Henry Woods, *Augustine and Evolution: A Study in the Saint's De Genesi ad Litteram and De Trinitate* (New York 1924).

J. Wytzes, "Bemerkungen zu dem neuplatonischen Einfluss in Augustins 'de Genesi ad litteram,' " ZNTW 39 (1940) 137–51.

NOTES

BOOK SEVEN

[1]Gen. 2.7.

[2]*Flavit* vel *sufflavit in faciem eius flatum vitae.* The LXX reads: ἐνεφύσησεν εἰς τὸ πρόσωπον αὐτοῦ πνοὴν ζωῆς.

[3]*Spiravit* vel *inspiravit in faciem eius.*

[4]See *De civ. Dei* 13.24, where Aug. discusses at greater length his interpretation of the words in Gen. 2.7. He is of the opinion that the correct translation of the LXX text (see n. 2 *supra*) is *Insufflavit Deus in faciem eius flatum vitae,* not *Inspiravit Deus in faciem eius spiritum vitae;* and that this statement means that God by this act gave man a soul, not that He imparted the Holy Spirit to him.

[5]See 6.12.20 *supra.*

[6]Aug. has in mind the Manichees. See *De Gen. c. Man.* 2.8.11 (ML 34.201–2), where he refutes this opinion. He may also have in mind the Priscillianists, who held that angels and human souls are emanations from the divine substance: see G. Bardy, DTC 13.1 (1936) *s.v.* "Priscillien," 395.

[7]On the testimony of B, Pal, and m, I take *quae* as the more likely reading rather than *qua.*

[8]Isa. 57.16–17. Augustine's version is based on the LXX. The Hebr. text is translated differently in various ways. The RSV reads: *For from me proceeds the spirit, and I have made the breath of life. Because of the iniquity of his covetousness I was angry, I smote him....* In any case, breath=soul created by God: see T. K. Cheyne, *The Prophecies of Isaiah* (London 1880–81) 2.74; and this is Augustine's point.

[9]In *De civ. Dei* 7.6 Aug. mentions the Stoic doctrine on the world soul as propounded by Varro, and *ibid.* 10.2 the Platonic and Neoplatonic doctrine as set forth by Plotinus. He does not

make the doctrine of the world soul his own here: the first sentence of ch. 4 is contrary-to-fact.

[10]I follow the text of z and of the majority of the MSS he collated, in addition to that of Bod, in omitting *fecisset.*

[11]The dilemma which faces Aug. is a result of his understanding that God does not create any new beings after having finished His works at the end of the six days of creation. He has argued that the works created in the narrative of the six days were in reality created simultaneously, basing his position on Eccli. (Sirach) 18.1: *He who lives forever created all things together* (according to Augustine's Latin text). Moreoever, since Gen. 2.2 tells us that God *finished* His works on the sixth day and rested on the seventh, the inference seems to be that His rest from the works of creation continues through all subsequent ages and that He cannot be said to create any new beings. The statement in John 5.17, *My Father is working still,* refers therefore to God's administration of the world He created, not to any new creation. The continual appearance of new beings in the visible world is therefore explained by the unfolding of causal reasons, those seminal principles which God in the original creation placed in the womb of nature. Thus Aug. explains the genesis of plants, trees, shrubs, animals, even the body of man. His problem now is to see whether we can say that God in the original creation created spiritual causal reasons of all the human souls that would come into being in the course of the ages.

[12]Cf. Gen. 1.5: *God called the light Day.* This was the first day of creation, the day on which God created and illuminated the angels. Aug. holds that there was only one day, six times repeated (see 5.3.6 *supra*), and that each "day," without any passage of time, signifies a revelation of part of creation to the angels (5.23.46).

[13]See *Conf.* 12.6.6: "The mutability of mutable things is itself able to receive all the forms into which mutable things are changed," and *Conf.* 12.19.28, where he says that "everything mutable makes us recognize a certain formlessness by which it receives form or by which it is changed and altered." There is, then, spiritual as well as corporeal matter, as Aug. has explained above in 1.4.9 to 1.5.11. His account is a Christian adaptation of

the teaching of Plotinus: see A. H. Armstrong, "Spiritual or Intelligible Matter in Plotinus and St. Augustine," *Aug. Mag.* 1.277–83. Here, however, he is dealing with a different though related problem, namely, the possibility that God placed in the original creation some spiritual material out of which He would later form souls. The former problem dealt with formless *matter*, concreated with form and serving as the substratum of change. The problem here, however, deals with a possible *material* of the spiritual order, created as a substance with its own matter and form, from which the soul might be said to be formed just as the body was formed from the slime of the earth.

[14]Emanation: *defluxio.* Etymologically the word means an effluence, and it implies a substance decidedly inferior to the source from which it flowed.

[15]For the senses as messengers, see 7.14.21 and n. 35 *ibid.* Aug. throughout his life consistently holds an active theory of sensation. See Kälin 13–14 and 31, and Bourke 110–12.

[16]Aug. is apparently thinking of the views of Plato and Plotinus corrected by Porphyry. Plato, *Tim.* 42c and *Phaedo* 81d–82b, and Plot., *Enn.* 3.4.2, say that human souls are condemned to inhabit bodies of beasts in punishment for transgressions. Porphyry disagrees with this doctrine. See Aug., *The City of God* 10.30, tr. by Henry Bettenson (Penguin Books 1972) 417: "If it is considered improper to correct Plato on any point, why did Porphyry himself offer a number of important corrections? For it is an established fact that Plato wrote that after death the souls of men return to earth, and even enter into the bodies of beasts. The same belief was held also by Plotinus, the teacher of Porphyry. Nevertheless, Porphyry refused to accept it, quite rightly." But nowhere in the quotations from Porphyry found in Aug. or elsewhere in Porphyry's extant writings is there a reinterpretation of the meaning of Plato or Plotinus in the benign sense suggested by Aug. here in *De Gen. ad litt.* (see Agaësse-Solignac 48.707–8). Aug., however, may have had available some such text of Porphyry no longer extant.

[17]Ps. 48.13.
[18]Ps. 73.19.
[19]Ps. 48.13.

[20]Ps. 73.19.

[21]Matt. 7.15.

[22]Ps. 90.13.

[23]Cf. Plato, *Phaedo* 81d–82b.

[24]I follow the reading *adserunt* (or *asserunt*) found in z and all his MSS as well as in Bod and Pal. The reading of m, *afferunt*, seems to be an inadvertent error.

[25]"Which they have fashioned": *quam finxerunt.* I follow the reading of P, R. S, Bod, Pal, m. The reading of E, B, z is *pinxerunt. Fabulam fingere* ("to fashion a fable") is a common Latin idiom, but *fabulam pingere* ("to paint a fable") is strange Latin.

[26]This conclusion brings the reader suddenly back to ch. 9, where Aug. considered the possibility of an irrational soul being the material out of which God might make a rational soul. The discussion on transmigration was a digression.

[27]"Earthly and humid": i.e., made up of earth and water, two of the four elements. In the next paragraph Aug. considers the other two elements, air and fire.

[28]Cf. Gen. 1.20–22.

[29]See 7.4.6 *supra.*

[30]Zeno the Stoic held that the fifth substance (or element), which he identified with fire, was the source of reason and intellect. See Cic., *De fin.* 4.5.12. Aetius, *De placitis reliquiae* 4.3.3 (SVF 2.779), says: "The Stoics hold that the soul is a fiery, intellectual spirit." See 7.21.27 and n. 50 *ibid.*

[31]On the mutual transformation of the elements, see n. 11 to Book 3 *supra.*

[32]Erasistratus (3rd c. B.C.), following the tradition of Greek medicine, held that the air which is breathed into the lungs is taken by the pulmonary veins to the heart, where it becomes the vital *pneuma.* From the heart it finds its way through the carotid arteries to the brain, where it is transformed into a finer substance called the psychic *pneuma*, which is distributed throughout the body by the nerves, thus making sensation and motion possible. Galen (2nd c. A.D.) corrected this account in several details, especially by his observation that the arteries contain blood as well as the *pneuma*. See Margaret Tallmadge May in her introduction to Galen, *On the Usefulness of the Parts of the Body*

(Ithaca, N.Y. 1968) 1.46–48. Augustine's familiarity with the opinions of medical writers should not seem strange, for in the Empire there were many medical writers writing in Latin, among whom were Celsus, Scribonius Longus, Pliny, Priscianus, Vindicianus, Caelius Aurelianus. When Aug. was a young man in Carthage, he knew Vindicianus personally. He refers to V. as a "shrewd man" (*Conf.* 4.3.5) and an "intelligent old man" (*Conf.* 7.6.8). Vindicianus' writings were of some importance at the time: see Martin Schanz, *Geschichte der römischen Litteratur* (2nd ed. Munich 1914) 4.1,203–4. For further evidence of Augustine's interest in anatomy and physiology, see his *De anima et eius origine* 4.5.6 (ML 44.527–28) and H.-I. Marrou, *Saint Augustine et la fin de la culture antique* (4th ed. Paris 1958) 141–43.

[33]In 3.5.7 *supra*, Aug. explains that the element of fire in the body in one form or another, according to the nature of each of the five senses, makes sensation possible.

[34]This theory of rays going forth from the eyes occurs also in 1.16.31, 4.34.54, and 12.16.32. See n. 51 to Book 1 *supra*.

[35]In maintaining that the soul is not acted upon by material objects perceived in sensation, Aug. frequently uses the metaphor of the senses as messengers. Thus in 12.24.51 *infra* he says: "... the soul uses the body as a sort of messenger in order to form within itself the object that is called to its attention from the outside world." The metaphor is found in Cic., *De leg.* 1.9.26 and *De nat. deor.* 2.56.140, but it does not there imply an active theory of sensation.

[36]Augustine's notion that light and air mediate between soul and body is not only founded on the opinions of the medical writers (as he states in ch. 13 *supra*) but it owes much to the concept of *pneuma* as found in Aristotle, the Stoics, and the Neoplatonists. Aristotle, *De gen. animal.* 736b, holds that *pneuma* is a matter more divine that the four elements, mediating between soul and body. *Pneuma,* according to the Stoics (SVF 2.442), is a composite of air and fire. Plotinus (*Enn.* 1.6.3) says that fire is the most subtle of all bodies and is close to the incorporeal; but he says that light is incorporeal. Aug. does not look upon light as incorporeal, but in *De lib. arb.* 3.16.58 or 3.5.16 (CSEL

74.103,28 Green; ML 32.1279) he says: "In the world of bodies, light is of the highest excellence." But he has already (3.4.7 *supra*) reminded the reader that the corporeal and incorporeal are worlds apart: "Now, the finer the nature of anything in the corporeal world, the closer its affinity to the spiritual; but these two realms are vastly different in kind, for the one is body and the other is not." See W. R. Inge, *The Philosophy of Plotinus* (3rd ed. London 1929) 1.219-20; A. H. Armstrong, *The Architecture of the Intelligible Universe in the Philosophy of Plotinus* (Cambridge 1940, reprint Amsterdam 1967) 54-55; G. Verbeke, *L'Évolution de la doctrine du pneuma* (Paris 1945) 505. Cf. also 12.16.32 *infra*.

[37]The notion that air and fire are the more active elements and water and earth the more passive is found also in Cic., *Acad.* 1.7.26.

[38]Gen. 2.7.

[39]The phrase *living being* is used for the lower animals in Gen. 1.21 in the Vulg. text but not in Augustine's version.

[40]See 7.13.20 *supra*.

[41]Gen. 2.7.

[42]In 7.15.21 *supra*, Aug. speaks of "light and air" as a subtle substance mediating between soul and body, and then he refers to this substance as "fire, or rather light and air" (*ignis, vel potius lux et aer*). The concept was suggested by the Neoplatonic *pneuma*: see n. 36 on 7.15.21.

[43]For the senses as messengers, see 7.14.20 and n. 35 on that chapter and also n. 16 to Book 3.

[44]See 7.13.20 *supra*.

[45]See 7.18.24 *supra*.

[46]Attention: *intentio*. The Latin *intentio* here, as in 12.13.27 *infra*, means the attention of the soul to what is happening in the body. It is also used by Aug. in the phrase *vitalis intentio*, meaning the activity or influence by which the soul vivifies the body: see *Epist.* 166 (*De orig. animae hominis ad Hieron.*) 2.4 (CSEL 44.551,7-12 Goldbacher; ML 33.722).

[47]See 7.18.24 *supra*, and n. 35 on 7.14.20.

[48]See n. 36 on 7.15.21 *supra*, and n. 42 on 7.19.25.

[49]For a discussion of theories concerning the possibility of

one element changing into another, see 3.3.4 *supra* and the notes on that section.

[50]Cic., *Tusc. disp.* 10.22, wrongly attributes this theory of the nature of the soul to Aristotle. See the comment of Max Pohlenz (ed.), *Ciceronis Tusculanarum disputationum libri V* (5th ed., reprint, Stuttgart 1957) 53 n. 22. This theory was in reality held by the Stoics: see n. 30 on 7.12.19 *supra*.

[51]Cf. *Epist.* 166, *ibid.* (see n. 46 *supra*; CSEL 44.551,3–7): "If a body is a substance that is stationary or moving in space with a certain length, breadth, and height, in such a way that a greater part of it occupies a greater part of space, and a smaller part of it a smaller part of space, and less of it is in a part than in the whole, the soul is not a body."

[52]Cf. Aug., *De quant. an.* 6.10 (ML 32.1041).

[53]Tertullian, following the Stoics, held that all reality is corporeal: see a summary of his doctrine, with texts cited, in Ernest Evans (ed.), *Tertullian's Treatise against Praxeas* (London 1948) 234–36. The Stoic position on the corporeality of the soul is set forth by Tert., *De anima* 5 (CCL 2.786–87; ML 2.693–94), and is reaffirmed by Tert. in *De an.* 7 and 22.

[54]Cf. *Epist.* 166, *ibid.* (see n. 46 *supra*; CSEL 44.550,10–13), where the same difficulty about the meaning of *corpus* ("body") is mentioned.

[55]Seneca, *Naturales quaestiones* 5.13.4: "It is the amount of force that distinguishes spirit (*spiritum*) from wind (*a vento*): a wind is a violent spirit, and conversely a spirit is air gently blowing."

[56]Aug. has already satisfied himself, from a comparison of Gen. 1.27–29 with Gen. 2.7 and from an examination of other Scripture texts, that God created the causal reason of man's body on the sixth day and that this causal reason lay hidden in the earth until God, making use of it, formed Adam's body from the dust of the earth. It is, then, only reasonable to suppose that there was a causal reason also of man's soul (or men's souls) stored away somewhere in the works of the six days. But this causal reason, being the cause of an immaterial being, could not be laid away in the earth, as was the case with the formative principle of man's body. Was it, then, laid away in some imma-

terial substance created by God? This is the problem of this
chapter.

[57]Gen. 1.26.

[58]Gen. 1.27.

[59]"Free of any such activity": *hoc vacans* (z). The pronoun in
the abl. with *vacans* refers back to the notion contained in *age-
batne aliquid.* The reading *hoc vacans* apparently has the support
of all MSS collated by z, and it is found also in Pal. Bod reads
hoc vagans. Haec vacans is the reading of m, but no MSS authority
is cited for it.

[60]Cf. Wisd. 7.24–25.

[61]Cf. Wisd. 8.1.

[62]The word "heaven" in Gen. 1.1 refers to the angels conceived of as created in a formless state, and the creation of light
in Gen. 1.3 refers to their illumination and formation. In reality,
Aug. points out, they were created and formed at one and the
same moment. The *first day,* therefore, is taken to mean the
whole company of angelic spirits. See 1.9.15–17; 1.17.32; 2.8.16.

[63]The conclusion reached in this chapter is put forth modestly as a probable solution to the problem Aug. has been considering. He has been speculating about the creation of the human
soul and has asked where its causal reason (if any) was placed in
the days of creation. He has considered five hypotheses, finally
adopting the fifth as probable:

1. There was no causal reason (*ratio causalis*) of the soul laid
away in created works; there was only the eternal reason (*ratio
aeterna*) in God. But this does not explain the statement in Gen.
1.27 that God *created* man on the sixth day. See 7.22.33.

2. The causal reason was laid away in some undetermined
spiritual creature. But no such creature has been mentioned;
and if there were any such creature, it would have no other
function than to beget the soul. This is hard to comprehend. See
7.22.33.

3. God placed the causal reason of the soul in the spiritual
and intellectual creation (the angels) made on the first day. But
it is hard to understand how the human soul could be the child
of an angel or angels (7.23.34). Aug. does not elaborate on this
difficulty here, but in 10.5.8 he observes that this explanation is

not supported by any authority in the canonical books of Scripture.

4. God placed the causal reason of the soul in some corporeal creature. This is immediately dismissed as impossible (7.23.34).

5. God created the soul in its own proper being among the works of the six days. Aug. thinks it reasonable to suppose that God created man on the sixth day in the sense that He made the causal reason of his body and laid it away in the elements of the world, whereas He made the soul in its own proper being on the first day and stored it away in the works of creation (*et creata lateret in operibus Dei*) until He would breathe it into the body formed from the slime of the earth (7.24.35). This, then, is Augustine's opinion about the soul of Adam. The discussion about the souls of the rest of mankind is left to Book 10.

See Agaësse-Solignac 48.714–17, and Portalié, DTC 1.2359–61 (tr. Bastian 148–51).

[64]Cf. Rom. 9.11.

[65]Cf. 2 Cor. 5.10.

[66]All the MSS of z, and in addition also Bod and Pal, read *qui*. No MSS authority is cited for *quae*, the reading of m.

[67]Plotinus has a similar theory about the soul in *Enn.* 4.3.13.

[68]*Conf.* 12.6.6: "The mutability of mutable things is itself able to receive all the forms into which mutable things are changed." This is precisely what matter is.

[69]See nn. 7 and 48 to Book 1 *supra*.

[70]In 1.15.29 *supra*, Aug. explains that the voice is the matter of words, and words form the voice, but both proceed simultaneously from the vocal organs.

[71]Augustine's speculations have inclined him to the theory that the soul of Adam was made among the original works which God created simultaneously (see 7.24.35 *supra*). In this paragraph he considers the two possible positions that might be taken by an adversary of his theory: (1) God created the soul out of nothing at the moment He breathed it into Adam's body (in which case He must have created the causal reason of the soul on the sixth day); or (2) at the moment when God breathed the soul into Adam's body, He made it from some creature He had previously created in the six days. Both of these positions pre-

sent for Aug. serious problems, which he has already considered in Book 7, especially in chs. 5–9 and 22–23.

[72]See Augustine's analysis of this hypothesis in 6.2.3–6.3.5 *supra.*

[73]Gen. 1.27–28.

[74]Gen. 2.9.

[75]Gen. 2.19.

[76]Gen. 2.4–5.

[77]Gen. 2.5.

[78]Eccli. (Sirach) 18.1 (according to the Latin translation).

[79]Gen. 2.2 and John 5.17.

[80]See Gen. 2.1 and 2.3.

[81]1 Tim 6.16. See Aug., *De Trin.* 1.1.2 (CCL 50.29,54–64; ML 42.821): "Sacred Scripture rarely mentions what is said properly of God and is found in no creature. An example is the statement made to Moses: *I am who am,* and *He who is has sent me to you* (Exod. 3.14). For since both body and soul are said in a sense 'to be,' unless God wished being to be understood in a proper sense, He surely would not say this. The same is true of St. Paul's statement, *who alone has immortality* (1 Tim. 6.16). Since the soul is said to be immortal and is immortal in a certain sense, the Apostle would not say *who alone has* except for the fact that immortality is immutability, which no creature can have, for it belongs to the Creator alone." See also Aug., *Epist.* 143.7 (CSEL 44.257,15–17 Goldbacher; ML 33.588).

[82]Another interpretation of this sentence, based on the text of E and z, is given by Agaësse-Solignac 48.571. My interpretation follows the text of m, which is supported by P, R, S, Bod, Pal, and it tries to take into account what seems to be an intended parallelism in *ut aut noverit . . . aut . . . sciat,* in which both verbs are in the third person. The passage cited from *Epist.* 143.7 by Agaësse-Solignac, pp. 570–71 n. 41, is compatible with both m and z.

BOOK EIGHT

[1]Gen. 2.8.

[2]The corporeal or literal meaning is advocated by Jerome, *Epist.* 51.5.6–7 (CSEL 54.404,18–405,19 Hilberg; ML 22.522–23) and by John Chrysostom, *Hom. in Gen.* 13.3 (MG 53.108). The spiritual or allegorical meaning is espoused by Origen, *In Gen. hom.*, tr. Rufinus, 2.4 (GCS 29.32,19–33,6 Baehrens; MG 12.170A–B). Ambrose, *De paradiso* 1.5–6 (CSEL 32.267 Schenkl; ML 14.276) finds both meanings present. See Agaësse-Solignac 49.497–99.

[3]Rom. 5.14.

[4]The reading of Bod, Pal, and m (and I presume of the other MSS also) is *eum*. The reading *cum* in z appears to be a typographical error.

[5]*Terra scilicet.* This is the reading of P, R, S, C, Bod, Pal, and m. The reading *terrae scilicet* of z, based on E, seems unlikely: *scilicet* calls for *terra* in the nominative in apposition to *locus.*

[6]For the age of Adam, see Gen. 5.3–5; for the translation of Enoch, see Gen. 5.24; for conception in old age, see Gen. 5.3.

[7]Aug. here refers to *De Genesi contra Manichaeos* (ML 34.173–220), written when he was a young man on his return to Africa from Rome. In it he made extensive use of allegorical interpretation, being unable at that time to see all the possibilities of literal interpretation which he discovered later. See his remarks in the next chapter and also *Retract.* 1.9 or 1.10 (CSEL 36.47–51 Knöll; ML 32.599–600).

[8]Aug. probably had in mind Origen and writers influenced by him. For a criticism of some of the details of Origen's figurative interpretation of Paradise, see a letter by Epiphanius translated by Jerome and included among Jerome's works, *Epist.* 51.5 (CSEL 54.403–5 Hilberg; ML 22.521–23). On Origen and the typological interpretation of Scripture, see Jean Daniélou, *Origen*, tr. W. Mitchell (New York 1955) 139–73.

[9]In this context, the figurative meaning seems to be identified with the allegorical, whereas the proper meaning is the literal. Note the words and phrases which Aug. opposes in this chapter:

figurate .... *ad litteram*

figurate .... *proprie*
secundum allegoricam locutionem . . secundum propriam locutionem.
[10]See n. 7 above.
[11]See Matt. 7.7.
[12]*De Gen. c. Man.* 2.2.3 (ML 34.197).
[13]Gen. 2.8. Augustine's text as cited earlier (6.3.5) is: *Et plantavit Deus paradisum in Eden ad orientem, et posuit ibi hominem quem finxerat.* His gloss here, *in a delightful place* (*in deliciis*), is based on the reading of Gen. 2.15 according to the LXX in the Cod. Vat. and other MSS: καὶ ἔθετο αὐτὸν ἐν τῷ παραδείσῳ τῆς τρυφῆς (*And He placed him in the garden of delight*). The word τρυφή is used to translate the Hebr. *Eden,* which (according to one theory) is connected with the Hebr. verb meaning "to delight." See B. S. Childs, *The Interpreter's Dictionary of the Bible* 2 (1962) *s.v.* "Eden, Garden of," 22.
[14]Gen. 2.9. The word "again" translates the Latin *adhuc.* In Gen. 1.12 it has already been stated that the earth brought forth trees. According to Augustine's interpretation, that statement designates the original creation of trees in their causal reasons; it is later that God, working in the causal reasons, makes the trees appear above ground. It is in this sense that Aug. interprets *adhuc* ("again"). They are not different trees; they are the same trees now coming to their full perfection.
[15]Gen. 1.29.
[16]Gen. 2.9.
[17]Prov. 3.18.
[18]Gal. 4.24–26.
[19]1 Cor. 10.4. Cf. Exod. 17.6, Num. 20.11.
[20]The word *sacramentum* (used to translate μυστήριον in the NT) in Aug., as in other Latin Fathers, had a broader meaning than it came to have in the Middle Ages, when it was more strictly defined as applying exclusively to baptism, confirmation, penance, Eucharist, orders, matrimony, and extreme unction. See J. Finkenzeller, LTK 9 (1964) *s.v.* "Sakrament," 222–24. In Aug. *sacramentum* is a sign that relates to divine things; see *Epist.* 138.1.7 (CSEL 44.131 Goldbacher; ML 33.527) and *Sermo* 272 (ML 38.1247).
[21]Cf. Exod. 12.3–11.

[22]Luke 15.23.

[23]*Rerum figurata significatione gestarum*. This is the reading of z and apparently of all the MSS on which that text is based. It is also the reading of Bod and Pal. The text of m has *significatio*. The "figurative meaning of events that really happened" is what modern biblical criticism calls the typical sense. See R. Brown, JBC 2 (1968) "Hermeneutics," 618: "The typical sense is the deeper meaning that the things (persons, places, and events) of Scripture possess because, according to the intention of the divine author, they foreshadow future things."

[24]Gen. 28.18.

[25]Ps. 117.22; cf. Acts 4.11.

[26]Luke 23.43. For Augustine's later speculations about the good thief and Paradise, see 12.34.66 *infra*.

[27]Luke 16.24. Tertullian, *De anima* 7.1 (CCL 2.790; ML 2.697), refers to this passage in Luke and claims that it is evidence that the Evangelist holds the materiality of the soul.

[28]Aug. again alludes to the mysterious bosom of Abraham in 12.33.63 *infra*. See also *Conf.* 9.3.6.

[29]For Augustine's use of the word "sacrament," see n. 20 *supra*.

[30]Gen. 2.24, Eph. 5.31–32.

[31]Aug. probably has Origen in mind. Origen seeks everywhere in the narrative of creation and Paradise not the literal but the spiritual or allegorical meaning; but in *In Gen. hom.* 7.2 (GCS 29.71–73 Baehrens; MG 12.198–200) he takes the narrative concerning Hagar and Sarah and Ishmael and Isaac as historical, although he sees a symbolic meaning in the persons and events.

[32]Aug., *De civ. Dei* 15.2, commenting on Gal. 4.21–31, observes that Sarah and her son Isaac prefigure the heavenly city, whereas the slave girl Hagar and her son Ishmael prefigure the earthly Jerusalem, which in turn is a symbol of the heavenly city.

[33]1 Kings 19.5–8. The reference is to the food that nourished Elijah on his journey to Mt. Horeb.

[34]1 Kings 17.16. The reference is to the miracle God worked for Elijah and the widow of Zarephath.

[35]Aug. treats this question briefly here but at greater length in chs. 13 to 16 *infra*.

³⁶Cf. Gen. 1.31.

³⁷Theophilus of Antioch, *Ad Autolycum* 2.25 (Oxford Early Christian Texts, pp. 66–69 Grant; MG 6.1092), says that the tree did not contain death (that was the result of disobedience); that there was nothing in the fruit but knowledge (which is good if used properly); and that Adam had to grow and mature before he would be ready for it; hence God's command. See also Aug. 8.13.28–30 and 11.41.56 *infra*.

³⁸Theodoret of Cyrus, *Quaest. in Gen.* 2.26 (MG 80.124), notes that the tree was called *the tree of the knowledge of good and evil* in accordance with a Hebr. custom of naming places and things after striking events that occurred in them or at them.

³⁹Gen. 2.10–14.

⁴⁰Philo, *Questions and Answers on Genesis* 1.12 (LCL, p. 8 Marcus), suggests the possibility of an allegorical interpretation of the four rivers, in which they would represent the four cardinal virtues. This thought occurs also in Ambrose, *De paradiso* 3.14 (CSEL 32.273,12–14 Schenkl; ML 14.280C), and in Aug., *De Gen. c. Man.* 2.10.13 (ML 34.203).

⁴¹See Virgil, *Aen.* 8.330–32; Ovid, *Fasti* 2.389–90.

⁴²Josephus, *Jewish Ant.* 1.38–39 (LCL 4.18–21 Thackeray), identifies the Phison with the Ganges and the Geon with the Nile. See also Ambrose, *De paradiso* 3.14 (CSEL 32.273,6–9 Schenkl; ML 14.280B), and Jerome, *Lib. hebr. quaest. in Gen.* 2.11 (ML 23.941A).

⁴³Augustine's point is that the geographical details of the narrative suggest a historical account rather than an allegory. The narrative of Genesis is therefore intended primarily in the literal sense; but this does not rule out the possibility of finding figurative meanings in the things narrated or described.

⁴⁴Luke 10.30.

⁴⁵Gen. 2.15–17. In the first line of v. 15, the text of m and z reads *Dominus Deus,* but all MSS collated (E, P, R, B, Bod, Pal) except S omit *Dominus.* In view of what Aug. says in 8.11.24 *infra, Dominus* must belong in the text.

⁴⁶See Gen. 2.8.

⁴⁷*Malleolus:* mallet-shoot. Defined by OED 6.89, *s.v.* "mallet,"

n. 6: "a hammer-shaped slip of a tree or shrub for planting." See TLL 8.191.37–38. It is described by Columella, *De re rustica* 3.6.3.

[48]Cf. 5.5.14 *supra:* "For thus the earth at God's word produced these things before they sprang forth, receiving all the numbers of those beings which it would bring forth in their kinds through the ages." The Neoplatonists, following the Neopythagorean tradition, were accustomed to identify forms with numbers. See n. 58 to Book 6.

[49]1 Cor. 3.7.

[50]The OL text used by Aug. reads: *ut operaretur et custodiret.* Thus the two verbs have no object expressed. In my translation I have supplied the pronoun "it" (Paradise) as object.

[51]Aug. correctly notes that the LXX has a pronoun in the accusative case: ἐργάζεσθαι αὐτὸν καὶ φυλάσσειν. But he feels that this leaves an ambiguity in the text, since the pronoun could refer to Paradise and function as the object of the two infinitives, or it could refer to the man and function as the subject of the two infinitives. In the latter case the verbs would apparently be taken in an intransitive sense.

[52]Gen. 2.5: *Nec erat homo qui operaretur terram.*

[53]That is to say, man taught himself by his work, so that there was a spiritual harvest for his bodily labor. *Disciplina* implies a learning process.

[54]Gen. 3.18.

[55]Cf. Gen. 2.19.

[56]Cf. Gen. 1.29–30.

[57]As the Maurist editors have pointed out (Vol. 3/1, cols. 233–34, note; ML 34.381, note), this interpretation is inconsistent with the Hebr. text, where the pronoun object of the two verbs in the purpose clause is feminine and therefore must refer back to "Paradise." Apart from the fact that Aug. was not familiar with the Hebr. text, this interpretation seems to have struck him only as an afterthought, since the interpretation he has given in the preceding paragraph is the obvious conclusion of all that he has previously said on the subject. However, as Aug, has already said (1.19.38) in discussing two possible interpretations of an obscure passage, on the supposition that both are consistent with

the faith and the context: ". . . there is no difficulty if he [the writer] is thought to have wished both interpretations if both are supported by clear indications in the context." See n. 66 to Book 1.

⁵⁸Eccli. (Sirach) 10.12.

⁵⁹Speaking of a spiritual creature, Aug. says in 1.1.2 *supra:* ". . . it is by this turning towards its Creator that it receives its form and perfection, and if it does not thus turn, it is unformed. . . ."

⁶⁰The expression "Lord God" (*Dominus Deus*), in which "Lord" *(Dominus)* translates the Hebr. *Yahweh,* begins at verse 4b of ch. 2 in the Vulg. and occurs also in verses 5, 7, 8, and 9 (see Quentin *Gen.* 146). However, Aug. was following the OL text, and it omits *Dominus* in all these verses (see Fischer VL 37–42; but note some variants cited there). The LXX in most MSS has *Lord God* (κύριος ὁ θεός) in verses 4b and 8, but not in 5, 7, and 9 (however, there are some variants; see Brooke-McLean *Octateuch* 4). Apparently the LXX text which Aug. was using omitted κύριος in all these verses before verse 15. According to modern exegetes, the creation narrative in Gen. 1.1 to 2.4a, in which the one word "God" (*Elohim*) is consistently used, comes from the Priestly tradition (P); but the narrative in Gen. 2.4b to 3.24, where the word "Lord" (*Yahweh*) is added, comes from the Yahwist tradition (J). See Eugene H. Maly, JBC 1 (1968) "Genesis," 9. Aug., of course, was not familiar with the Hebr. text.

⁶¹This is an interpretation of Gen. 2.15 proposed by Aug. above in 8.10.23. But it is not consistent with the Hebr. text. See n. 57 *supra.*

⁶²Ps. 15.2.

⁶³Ps. 72.28.

⁶⁴In 8.9.17–18 *supra,* Aug. distinguishes the natural and the voluntary working of Providence.

⁶⁵Ps. 72.28.

⁶⁶Ps. 58.10. See Augustine's comment, *Enarr. in Ps.* 58, *Sermo* 1, n. 18 (CCL 39.742–43; ML 36.704): "There is an origin and source of strength, there is a root of wisdom, and if it needs to be said, there is what we may call a region of unchangeable

Truth. Withdrawing from this, the soul is in darkness; approaching it, the soul is illuminated. Approach and be illuminated, because withdrawing you are in darkness. Therefore *I will keep my strength turned towards Thee.* I will not withdraw from Thee, I will not rely on myself."

[67] Eph. 2.8–10.

[68] Phil. 2.13.

[69] Gen. 2.15.

[70] Gen. 2.16–17. See Augustine's comment on this text, 8.6.12 *supra.*

[71] Cf. Gen. 1.12 and 1.31.

[72] Aug. in his works against the Manichees consistently maintains that an evil substance cannot exist and that evil is simply the privation of good. For a summary of his doctrine on this point, see *De natura boni* 1–18 (CSEL 25/2.855–62 Zycha; ML 42.551–57) and *Enchiridion* 3.10–12 (CCL 46.53–54; ML 40.236–37).

[73] See Book 11, especially chs. 12–13 *infra.*

[74] Aug. frequently speaks of pride (and all the vices that flow from it) as a perverse imitation of God. See *Conf.* 2.6.13; *De civ. Dei* 19.12.2; *De vera relig.* 45.84 (CCL 32.243,21–23; ML 34.160).

[75] See 8.6.12 *supra.*

[76] Such a person has no experiential knowledge of evil; but since he must make choices to avoid losing the good which he possesses, he must have some knowledge of evil. He knows it, as Aug. goes on to say, *per prudentiam boni.* For a penetrating analysis of this problem and of this whole chapter, see Agaësse-Solignac 49.507–10.

[77] Isa. 7.14, Matt. 1.23.

[78] 1 Tim. 2.5.

[79] John 1.1 and 1.14.

[80] It is not clear why Aug. used Christ as an example of one who did not choose evil. He certainly did not mean that there was a possibility for Christ to choose evil (see the references given by Agaësse-Solignac 49.509 to show that Aug. explicitly rejects such a possibility).

[81] Isa. 7.16 (according to the LXX). The correct translation

from the Hebr. is: *For before the child knows how to refuse the evil and choose the good, the land before whose two kings you are in dread will be deserted* (RSV).

[82]I read *amissione* on the authority of Bod, Pal, and m. The reading *amissio* in Zycha (p. 254, line 4) seems to be a typographical error, since he quotes no variants.

[83]John 6.38.

[84]Rom. 5.19.

[85]1 Cor. 15.22.

[86]It is not known who these writers are. Agaësse-Solignac 49.509 suggest the possibility of a disciple of Marcion and a disciple of Porphyry.

[87]In discussing the creation of Adam, Aug. had already considered (6.2.3 *supra*) the hypothesis that Gen. 2.7 is a recapitulation of Gen. 1.27–29, but he rejected this theory.

[88]Gen. 2.16: *Ab omni ligno quod est in paradiso esca edes.* Augustine remarks: *Non dixit, edetis.* His point is that since the verb is in the singular, God is addressing Adam alone.

[89]Gen. 2.17. Augustine's version is from the OL text based on the LXX. It reads as follows (with the three finite verbs in the plural): *De ligno autem cognoscendi bonum et malum non manducabitis de illo. Qua die autem ederitis ab eo, morte moriemini.* The Vulg. correctly translates this verse from the Hebr. with these verbs in the singular: *De ligno autem scientiae boni et mali ne comedas. In quocumque enim die comederis ex eo, morte morieris.* But in both the Vulg. and the OL, as well as in the Hebr. and LXX, the singular is used in v. 16.

[90]1 Cor. 14.35.

[91]The text of this passage is perplexed: see the apparatus in z, and Agaësse-Solignac 49.66–67 n. 32. I follow the reading of P and m: *quo transgresso reus esset.* However, I have found MSS authority for the reading of z, *quo transgressor eius esset,* in Bod and Pal.

[92]Gen. 3.8. See Augustine's reconsideration of this, 8.27.50 *infra*.

[93]In 8.9.17–18 *supra*, Aug. distinguishes a twofold activity of Providence: natural and voluntary.

[94]1 Tim. 6.16.

[95]At this place in the text (as pointed out in the apparatus of z) there is a dislocated line in the Migne edition. The first line in ML 34.388, *immoto cardine moveatur: sic tota palma ab articulo,* should be the first line in col. 389. This displacement took place in the Migne reprint, not in the original Maurist edition.

[96]God concreated the matter and form of all things simultaneously, as explained in 1.15.29 *supra.* See nn. 7 and 48 to Book 1 *supra.*

[97]The doctrine of three levels of reality (God in every way unchangeable, the soul changeable in time but not in place, and body changeable in both time and place) is a frequent theme in Aug. See e.g. *De vera relig.* 10.18 (CCL 32.199; ML 34.130) and *Epist.* 18.2 (CSEL 34/1.45 Goldbacher; ML 33.85). This doctrine is fundamental in Augustine's metaphysics: see Bourke 118–19 and 226–27.

[98]At this place in the text there is a line missing in Migne's edition. See n. 95 *supra.*

[99]Skin bottle: *utrem.* By a misprint the text in Migne reads *utrum* (but not so in the original edition of m). The *uter* referred to is the skin of an animal sewn to serve as a bottle, commonly used by the ancients for transporting wine and water. See V. Chapot, DarSag 5 (1919) *s.v.* "Uter," 613–16.

[100]Influence: *intentio.* In a letter to Jerome, *Epist.* 166 (*De orig. animae hominis*) 2.4 (CSEL 44.551,7–9 Goldbacher; ML 33.722), Aug. says: "For it [the soul] reaches throughout the whole body which it animates, not by a local diffusion of parts but by a vital influence (*quadam vitali intentione*)." See n. 46 to Book 7 *supra.*

[101]*Quod* (not *quae*), on the authority of R, Pal, and m.

[102]As pointed out by Agaësse-Solignac 49.512, Aug. in this passage is concerned about a philosophical problem: the relationship of the free will of creatures to the providence of God, which rules the world. He is not here concerned with the theological problem that preoccupied him in the Pelagian controversy: whether a corrupt will could perform good deeds and how a human act could be good in the sense of meritorious. It is entirely possible that he had finished Book 8 of this work before

the outbreak of the controversy with the Pelagians. He was working on the commentary on Genesis, A.D. 401–15. The anti-Pelagian polemic began A.D. 412.

[103]*Cui non prosit,* according to the MSS collated by z, as well as Bod and Pal. There is no MSS evidence cited by z for the reading of m, *cui non praesit.*

[104]It would be unrealistic to expect in a theologian of the 5th c. the concern about the inequities in human society that one finds in theologians of the late 20th c. We might say, of course, that these inequities do not come about by God's command (*iussu*) but by His permission (*permissu*): see 8.24.45 *infra.* But commenting on Gal. 3.28, *There is neither Jew nor Greek, there is neither slave nor free, there is neither male nor female, for you are all one in Christ Jesus,* Aug., *Epist. ad Gal.* 28 (ML 35.2125), says that this ideal will find its fulfilment when we shall see God face to face, and that these differences are taken away by the unity of the faith (*ab unitate fidei*) but they remain in the life of mortal man (*in conversatione mortali*); and he goes on to say that the apostles have told us that these differences are to be observed. In Augustine's view, then, they are part of the human condition in view of the fall of man.

[105]The Devil may assail the body of man but not his soul. Satan for a time seemed to have supreme power over Job, but he could do nothing that God did not permit him to do: see Aug., *Enarr. in Ps.* 26, *Enarr.* 2, n. 5 (CCL 38.156; ML 36.201). Aug. remarks also that the Devil had no power to force our first parents to sin: he could only use the subtle art of persuasion. See *In Ioannem* 12.10 (CCL 36.126; ML 35.1489). On the other hand, as Aug. points out in 8.24.45 *infra,* God uses His angels as His ministers in carrying out the designs of His providence, and He has made subject to them the whole of corporeal nature, all irrational life, and all wills that are weak and corrupt.

[106]Commenting on Ps. 2.12, *Embrace discipline, lest at any time the Lord be angry, and you perish from the just way,* Aug. says, *Enarr. in Ps.* 2.10 (CCL 38.6; ML 36.72): "This is a severe punishment, which is feared by those who have had any taste of the sweetness of justice, for he who perishes from the way of justice will wander with utter misery through the ways of iniquity."

[107]See Augustine's comments on the twofold activity of God's providence, 8.9.17–18 *supra*.

[108]To prepare the way for a discussion of the manner in which God spoke to Adam, Aug. in this chapter distinguishes the various ways in which creatures are preserved and cared for under God's providence. They are sustained "intrinsically" (*intrinsecus*) by God Himself, who creates and illuminates them, and "extrinsically" (*extrinsecus*) by creatures according to God's will and plan. They are sustained "by an incorporeal force" (*incorporaliter*) when the help comes from God directly or from a created spirit, and "by a corporeal force" (*corporaliter*) when the help comes from a material being.

[109]Rom. 11.36. For Augustine's reading of this text, see n. 7 to Book 4 *supra*.

[110]Spirit (*spiritus*) in this commentary on Gen. has a special meaning. Aug. defines it, 12.9.20 *infra*, as "a power of the soul inferior to the mind, wherein likenesses of corporeal objects are produced." See my article, "The Meaning of *Spiritus* in St. Augustine's *De Genesi*, XII," *Modern Schoolman* 26 (1949) 211–18. See also n. 13 to Book 12 *infra*.

[111]In Book 12 Aug. explains three kinds of vision which the soul has: (1) through the eyes (*per oculos*), (2) through the spirit or imagination (*per spiritum*), and (3) through the mind (*per contuitum mentis*). See 12.6.15 *infra*.

[112]See 8.24.45 *supra*.

[113]*In eis ipsis*, which is the reading of P, R, S, Bod, Pal, and m. An angel sees all creatures in his companions because, according to Aug., God first produced in the minds of angels the works He would create before creating them in their own order of being. See 2.8.16–17 *supra*.

[114]See 12.36.69 *infra*.

[115]Reason-principle: *ratio*. The eternal reason-principles or forms (*rationes aeternae*) of all created things are in the Word of God, where they are identified with Him and His life. In this sense the *ratio* of a creature is said to be life in God. See my article, "Augustine, *Conf.*, IX, 10, 24," in *American Journal of Philology* 79 (1958) 66–70.

[116]The mystery of God's transcendence and immanence is the

subject of Augustine's reflections in *Conf.* 1.2.2–1.4.4. Confront-
ed with this mystery, he prefers to say that we are in God rather
than that God is in us (*Conf.* 1.2.2): "Therefore I should not be,
O my God, I should not be at all unless You were in me; or rather must I not say, I should not be unless I were in You, *from
whom are all things, through whom are all things, in whom are all
things?*"

[117]Cf. *Conf.* 10.27.38: "Late have I loved Thee, Beauty ever ancient, ever new, late have I loved Thee!"

[118]Gen. 2.16–17.

[119]Cf. John 1.1–3.

[120]In an indescribable way: *ineffabiliter*, according to the reading in E¹(?), P, R, S, Eug, Bod, Pal, and m.

[121]Augustine's speculation here about the way in which God
may have spoken to Adam is not in agreement with the opinion
he adopted in 8.18.37 *supra*, where he said that God must have
spoken through a creature. One is tempted to ask whether Aug.
returned to the latter part of Book 8 and revised it or expanded
it after completing Book 12. Certainly the ideas and the language of Book 8, ch. 25, where the ground is prepared for ch.
27, are remarkably similar to what is found in Book 12 about vision, dreams, ecstasy, and the "spirit." See Agaësse-Solignac
49.514.

[122]Gen. 3.8.

[123]Aug. is thinking of the Arians. In *Epist.* 148.2.10 (CSEL
44.340,8–16 Goldbacher; ML 33.626) he says: "The most blessed
Athanasius, Bishop of Alexandria, when he was arguing against
the Arians, who say that only God the Father is invisible, but
think that the Son and the Holy Spirit are visible, proved by the
authority of holy Scriptures and by his own careful reasoning
that the Trinity is equally invisible, pressing the point vigorous-
ly that God has not been seen except by taking the appearance
of a creature; that according to the essential nature of His Godhead, God is completely invisible, that is, Father and Son and
Holy Spirit, except in so far as He can be known by mind and
spirit" (tr. Sr. W. Parsons, FOC 20.231). See Berthold Altaner,
"Augustinus und Athanasius," *Kleine patristische Schriften* (TU
83, Berlin 1967) 260–68.

[124]1 Tim. 6.16.

[125]The correct reading is in doubt. The variants are:

in consequenti sperandum est: E, S, R², z
in consequentis perandum est: Bod
in consequentis parandum est: P
in consequentibus parandum est: R¹, B, m.

If we assume that E etc. have the original reading and that Bod is a corruption of that, it is easy to understand P as an unsuccessful attempt at emendation of Bod and to see in R¹ etc. an emendation of P introduced to make the text grammatical.

BOOK NINE

[1]Gen. 2.18–24.

[2]In 6.5.7 *supra,* Aug. has explained that in the works of the six days God created living beings potentially and in their causes and that now He works in a different manner as He creates these beings in their full perfection in the course of time.

[3]On the fifth day: see Gen. 1.20–23.

[4]Ps. 148.7.

[5]I read *ibi,* following P, R, S, Bod, Pal, and m; and in the next sentence *ibi* also on the authority of P, R, Bod, and m. Zycha, following E (and also S in the second sentence), reads *ubi* in both places, thus making these two sentences questions.

[6]*Arida* is the reading of P, R, S, Bod, Pal, and m.

[7]Gen. 2.18.

[8]Ps. 84.9.

[9]Zach. 1.9.

[10]Matt. 3.17.

[11]See 8.27.49–50 *supra.*

[12]Apoc. 1.14–15.

[13]Gen. 1.27–28.

[14]Heb. 13.4.

[15]Before Augustine's time it was commonly held that there would not have been any sexual intercourse for the procreation of children in Paradise if man had not fallen. John Chrys., *Hom. in Gen.* 18.4 (MG 53.153), says that our first parents in Paradise

imitated the life of the angels and that it was as a result of their disobedience that God provided that the human race should be propagated by sexual intercourse; and again in *De virginitate* 14.5–6 (SC 125.142 Musurillo-Grillet; MG 48.544) he says that marriage is the consequence of the fall of our first parents. If Adam, then, had not sinned, how would men have been multiplied? Like the angels, by the creative act of God: see *loc. cit.* Similarly, Greg. Nyss., *De hominis opificio* 17 (MG 44.188–89), holds that the desire for the union of the sexes for the purpose of procreation is the result of the Fall. There would have been no procreation if man had not fallen, and man's life would have been like that of the angels. Aug. goes against this tradition when he holds that marriage and human sexuality are not a consequence of the Fall. In this view, human procreation would have taken place in Paradise if man had not fallen, but it would have been without *libido*. Aug. looks upon human sexuality as something created by God antecedent to the Fall and independent of it. In guarding himself against the errors of the Manichees, who held that sexual desire and procreation were from the Evil Principle, he came to a balanced view of human sexuality which is remarkable in a writer of that period.

[16]In 3.21.33 *supra*, Aug. suggests that sexual union would take place in Paradise "with only the devout affection of charity, and not the concupiscence associated with our corrupt flesh" (*solo piae caritatis adfectu, nulla corruptionis concupiscentia*).

[17]In the prime of life: *in aliquo formae statu*, i.e., without suffering the decline of old age and eventually death.

[18]Without any death: *sine ulla morte*. Zycha reads *sine illa morte*, but this must be a typographical error.

[19]St. Paul, 1 Cor. 15.44, makes a distinction between the natural body (*corpus animale*) which we now have and the spiritual body (*corpus spiritale*) which we shall have in the resurrection. In 6.19.30 *supra*, Aug. argued that Adam was given a natural body. He maintains, therefore, that if man had not sinned, his natural body *sine ulla morte* would be transformed *in aliam qualitatem*, i.e., into a glorified state. The transformation would not take place by death, in which the soul leaves the body, but by a blessed change from mortality to immortality, from a natural

state to a spiritual state: see *De bono coniugali* 2.2 (CSEL 41.190,1–6 Zycha; ML 40.375).

[20]The theory expressed here about the generation of children in Paradise if man had not fallen was already proposed in 3.21.33 *supra*.

[21]Deut. 29.5: *I have led you forty years in the wilderness; your clothes have not worn out upon you, and your sandals have not worn off your feet* (RSV).

[22]I understand *mortale* as a predicate adjective referring back to *genus humanum*.

[23]Aug. has already suggested that man cultivated the soil in Paradise with delight and pleasure and without any wearisome toil. See 8.8.15 *supra*.

[24]Augustine's attitude towards women was not entirely unaffected by the social customs of his times. One should remember, however, the deep love he had for the woman who bore him a son (*Conf.* 6.15.25), the place of honor his mother Monica held in the community at Cassiciacum, where she took part in philosophical discussions with Aug. and his friends (as e.g. in *De beata vita*), and the courtesy and consideration he manifested towards women with whom he corresponded as a bishop.

[25]Cf. Matt. 22.30.

[26]In Book 6, chs. 19–23, Aug. argued that Adam was created and placed in Paradise with a natural (i.e., mortal) body. If he had not sinned, he would have been exempt from death by a special gift of God and his body would have been transformed into a spiritual and glorious body.

[27]Cf. Matt. 20.10.

[28]2 Kings 2.11.

[29]Heb. 11.40. Augustine's reading of the text is: *Pro nobis enim meliora providerunt, ne sine nobis perfecti perficerentur.* These are the exact words in which he quotes the text also in *De peccatorum meritis et remissione* 2.31.50 (CSEL 60.121,17–18 Urba-Zycha; ML 44.181). But the Greek text reads: τοῦ θεοῦ περὶ ἡμῶν κρεῖττόν τι προβλεψαμένου, ἵνα μὴ χωρὶς ἡμῶν τελειθῶσιν (*Since God had foreseen something better for us in order that they might not be made perfect apart from us*). The promises made to the OT saints would not be fulfilled until Christ had wrought our redemption,

and thus they would share in the fruits of the redemption with us (see M. M. Bourke, JBC 2 [1968] "Epistle to the Hebrews," 402). D. DeBruyne, "Saint Augustin réviseur de la Bible," in *Misc. Ag.* 2.537, holds that Aug. simply misunderstood the text. But with good reason Agaësse-Solignac 49.102-3 suggest that Aug. may have read a Greek text different from the traditional one.

[30]Cf. Gen. 5.24.

[31]Cf. Mal. 4.5-6 Vulg. = 3.23-24 Hebr. Aug., *Sermo* 299.11 (ML 38.1376), says that the two witnesses of Apoc. 11.3-13 are Enoch and Elijah.

[32]Cf. Eccle. 3.5: *A time to embrace and a time to refrain from embracing.*

[33]Cf. *De bono coniugali* 9.9 (CSEL 41.200,24-201,3 Zycha; ML 40.380): "In the early days of the human race, especially for the purpose of propagating the people of God, through whom the Prince and Saviour of all the nations was to be proclaimed and to be born, the saints had an obligation to use the good of marriage, which was not to be sought as a good in itself but as a good necessary for the sake of another good." In Augustine's view, therefore, virginity was not recommended in the early years of human history because God's will required widespread procreation of children among the chosen people to fill up the number of saints determined by the divine plan. God's will for the human race in general is still that it should increase and multiply, but when this divine command is being carried out by an abundance of births, virginity is especially pleasing to God if it is embraced for good and holy reasons. Hence the OT period was the *tempus amplexandi,* and the NT period is the *tempus continendi ab amplexu* for those called to such a state.

[34]*Sed propter hoc bonum veniale est illud malum.* It is *veniale* in the sense that it is excusable and allowable. The idea and the language are based on 1 Cor. 7.6: *I say this by way of concession* (κατὰ συγγνώμην, *secundum veniam*). Cf. *De civ. Dei* 21.26: *Hoc secundum veniam concedit Apostolus* ("The Apostle says this by way of concession"). The concupiscence, therefore, which is satisfied in the marital act is a result of original sin, and the offspring born of this union is *caro peccati*; but *coniugalis concubitus*

that takes place with procreation in view is not a sin. See Aug., *De nuptiis et concupiscentia* 1.12.13 (CSEL 42.226,1–12 Urba-Zycha; ML 44.421–22), and Charles Boyer, S.J., *Saint Augustin* (Les moralistes chrétiens, Paris 1932) 237–38. Hence Aug., *De bono coniugali* 3.3 (CSEL 41.191,14–16; ML 40.375), says: "There is a dignity associated with the ardor of passion when husband and wife think of themselves as father and mother as they are united in the marital act." And yet procreation is not the only good of marriage. Aug., *De bono con.* 3.3, speaks eloquently of the union between man and wife of advanced years who by mutual consent refrain from sexual intercourse and yet are bound together in a true companionship founded on deep love transcending the ardor of sexual desire.

35The threefold good of marriage, *fides* (fidelity), *proles* (offspring), and *sacramentum* (sacrament), is treated also in *De bono coniugali* 24.32 and *De nuptiis et concupiscentia* 1.17.19. In those works the order is *proles, fides, sacramentum*, but here it is *fides, proles, sacramentum*. *Fides* is the perfect fidelity of husband and wife, excluding relations with any other persons. *Proles* means the loving acceptance of children, tender care for their upbringing, and provision for their religious education. *Sacramentum* (see Eph. 5.32) is the "sacramental meaning, that is, the indissoluble bond between Christian spouses which is a figure of the union of Jesus Christ with His Church" (E. Portalié, DTC 1 [1909] *s.v.* "Augustin," 2431 [tr. Bastian 267]). Pius XI incorporated much of what Aug. says about these three goods in the Encyclical *Casti connubii (Acta apostolicae sedis* 22 [1930] 543–56).

36*De bono coniugali* (A.D. 400–401). See n. 33 *supra* for references to the text in CSEL and ML. There are English translations by C. L. Cornish in Library of the Fathers 22 (Oxford 1847), reprinted in NPNF 3 (1887, reprinted 1917); and C. T. Wilcox in FOC 27 (1955); and the Latin text with French tr. by G. Combès in BA 2 (1948). E. Portalié, DTC 1 (1909) *s.v.* "Augustin," 2304, says that this work is "the most complete patristic treatise on the duties of the married state" (tr. Bastian 66).

37See n. 15 *supra*.

38Matt. 22.30. The words *for they will not be subject to death (non enim incipient mori)* are not in the Greek text, or the Itala, or the

Vulg. Milne *Reconstruction* does not give a quotation with these words included but does give a variant, *neque morientur,* in their place, from *Contra Adimantum* 25 (CSEL 25.183,25 Zycha; ML 42.168). Aug. was probably quoting from memory and apparently commingling Matt. and Luke. Luke 20.35–36 has: *But those who are accounted worthy to attain to that age and to the resurrection from the dead neither marry nor are given in marriage, for they cannot die any more, because they are equal to angels* (RSV).

[39]Gen. 2.17.

[40]Rom. 7.22–25.

[41]Rom. 8.10.

[42]Aug. bases the distinction between natural and spiritual bodies on 1 Cor. 15.44: see 6.19.30 *supra.* A natural body is mortal; a spiritual body is immortal and glorious, such as the body we shall have at the resurrection. Aug. holds that Adam had a natural (i.e., mortal) body, but that he would have been exempt from death by a special gift of God if he had not sinned. His body would have eventually been transformed into a spiritual and glorious body. See Book 6, chs. 19–25.

[43]They touched: *tetigerunt* according to P, R, S, Pal, m.

[44]See n. 19 *supra.*

[45]*Syntecticus* (consumptive) is the reading of E, R (*supra lin. manu* 1), Bod, z.

[46]Eph. 2.3.

[47]See Arist., *Hist. animalium* 5.21; Verg., *Georg.* 4.197–202; Plin., *Nat. hist.* 11.16.46. For a survey of ancient theories on bees, see B. G. Whitfield, "Virgil and the Bees: A Study in Ancient Apicultural Lore," *Greece & Rome,* N.S. 3 (1956) 99–117. See also Aug., *De Trin.* 3.8.13 (CCL 50.140,52–54; ML 42.876).

[48]Cf. Rom. 7.23.

[49]Rom. 7.23.

[50]Rom. 7.24.

[51]For Augustine's speculations on the origin of the soul, see Book 7 *supra.* There, after considering the possibilities regarding the soul of Adam, he suggested, as a probable opinion, that Adam's soul was created on the first day and laid away until God breathed it into the body He formed from the slime of the earth (7.24.35). With regard to the souls of Adam's descendants, there

are greater problems because of the doctrine of the transmission of original sin. Here in Book 9, as also in 7.23.34, he suggests hesitatingly that God may create souls from the souls of parents. The problem of the origin of the soul troubled Aug. all his life. For a survey of his tentative solutions and recurring doubts, see E. Portalié, DTC 1 (1909) *s.v.* "Augustin (Saint)," 2359–61 (tr. Bastian 148–51).

[52]Cf. Gen. 2.19–20.

[53]Cf. Gen. 11.1–9.

[54]In *De Gen. c. Man.* Aug. had already proposed many figurative meanings, but he had not done so for Gen. 2.19–20.

[55]Gen. 2.22: *Et aedificavit* (ᾠκοδόμησεν) *Dominus Deus costam quam sumpsit de Adam in mulierem.* Aug. is aware of the picturesque metaphor in the Greek verb οἰκοδομέω used in the LXX, and he feels that the statement must have some figurative meaning. That meaning is brought out in 9.18.34 *infra,* where it is suggested that the formation of Eve from the side of Adam is a figure of the Church coming from the pierced side of Christ on the Cross. The figurative meaning is reinforced, according to Aug., by the verb "build" (*aedificavit*), which applies most aptly to the Church. See n. 85 *infra.*

[56]For Augustine's desire to find the literal meaning rather than prophetical allegory, see 1.17.33–34 *supra.*

[57]Gen. 2.19.

[58]See 8.9.17 *supra,* where Aug. distinguishes the natural working of God's providence from the voluntary. By the former he refers to God's providence working in the laws of nature; by the latter he refers to God's providence working through the ministry of angels and men. Cf. also 8.24.45—8.26.48 *supra.*

[59]In the preceding book, chs. 23–26, Aug. has explained how God uses the ministry of angels in governing the world. Newman from his early days was very close to Aug. in his belief in the ministry of angels in the forces of nature. See *Apologia pro Vita Sua* (new ed. London 1902) ch. 1, p. 28.

[60]Augustine's word for imagination (with Neoplatonic overtones) is *spiritus:* see 12.9.20 *infra* and n. 110 to Book 8 *supra.*

[61]Jonah 2.1.

[62]Jonah 4.6–7.

[63]See 8.26.48 *supra.*

[64]See n. 55 *supra* on Gen. 2.22.

[65]In this passage, where Aug. uses *natura* I have used "substance" in the translation. "Substance" in English, in the sense of the substratum in which accidents or properties inhere, seems to be the appropriate word. As a matter of fact, Aug. considers *natura* and *substantia* as synonyms. See e.g. *De moribus eccl. cath. et de mor. Manich.* 2.2.3 (ML 32.1346).

[66]Cf. Aug., *De Trin.* 3.8.13 (CCL 50.141,59–68; ML 42.876), where he says that parents are not creators of men nor farmers creators of crops, and so, too, angels (good or bad) are not creators even though they know the seeds of things hidden from us and can scatter them (with God's permission) to accelerate the growth of things.

[67]1 Cor. 3.7.

[68]Wisd. 11.21. For Augustine's philosophical reflections on this text, see Book 4, chs. 3–6 *supra.*

[69]See n. 58 *supra* and 8.9.17.

[70]In Books 4, 5, and 6 *passim,* Aug. has explained his views on the eternal reasons in God and the reason-principles in creation. For the eternal reasons, see especially 4.24.41 and 5.12.28; for the created reason-principles in nature, see especially 4.33.51–52 and 5.23.45.

[71]For views of the ancients on spontaneous generation, see Arist., *Hist. animalium* 5.19.

[72]Cf. Gal. 3.19. For Augustine's interpretation of this text, see n. 61 to Book 5 *supra.*

[73]Gen. 1.27. Aug. has already attempted to harmonize the two accounts of the creation of Adam by his theory that Adam's soul was created in the works of the first day (7.24.35 *supra*) and that the reason-principle of his body was created and placed in nature on the sixth day (6.5.7–8, 6.6.10, 6.8.13 *supra*). When God, therefore, formed Adam from the slime of the earth, He formed him visibly in accordance with the invisible reason-principle which He had already created (6.15.26 *supra*), and He then breathed into Adam's body the soul He had created on the first day. This chapter now takes up the question of the creation of Eve. If we assume that her soul was already created on the first

day, how was her body made in the reason-principles created on the sixth day? Was the manner of the creation of Eve from the rib of Adam provided in the reason-principle of man as a necessity or as a possibility? This is the question raised in this chapter.

74In discussing miracles, 6.13.24–6.14.25 *supra*, Aug. has already suggested that reason-principles can have different potentialities to be fulfilled in accordance with the will of God the Creator according to a plan known to Him alone.

75"The spirit of life" is the soul. Cf. Gen. 2.7, and see Aug. 7.1.1–7.2.3 *supra*; cf. also Gen. 7.15, and see Aug., *Quaest. in Hep.* 1.9 (CSEL 28.7,17–22 Zycha; ML 34.550). The soul, of course, has certain appetites (such as the desire to attain the good, real or apparent) which free will cannot escape.

76Formative principles: Augustine's word is *rationes*. In this statement it refers to both the eternal reasons (*rationes aeternae*) in God and the seminal reasons (*quasi seminales rationes*) in the created world.

77Inserted and joined: *inditae atque concretae*. *Concretae*, which is the reading of E, P, Bod, Pal, and z, is from *concerno*. The form *concrevit* from this verb is also found above in the first sentence of this chapter (290.26 in Zycha's text).

78Cf. Num. 17.8.

79Cf. Gen. 18.10–15; 21.1–2.

80Cf. Num. 22.28.

81Prov. 2.19.

82"Who will return": *revertetur* (the future) is the reading of Bod and z, and apparently of most of the MSS collated by z. P, Pal, and m read *revertitur* (the present). Agaësse-Solignac reproduce the text of z but translate according to the reading of m.

83Cf. Eph. 2.9.

84Cf. Heb. 7.9–10: *One might even say that Levi himself, who receives tithes, paid tithes through Abraham, for he was still in the loins of his ancestor when Melchizedek met him* (RSV). See 6.8.13–6.9.14 *supra*.

85The mystery of the grace that was hidden (Eph. 3.8–11) was the Church, through which the unsearchable riches of Christ were to be bestowed on mankind. This mystery and all the events and prophecies that were to prepare the way for it, according to Aug., were not hidden in the seminal reasons of the world but in the plan of God, which was made known to the angels and carried out through their ministry. The first and most striking foreshadowing of the Church is the creation of Eve. As Adam was in ecstasy (or sleep), his side was opened and from one of his ribs was created the woman who was to be the mother of the whole human race. In like manner, when Christ was dead on the Cross, His side was opened and the Church was born, the mother of us all, who would bring us forth to a new life in Christ. Aug. brings out this parallelism in very general terms here, but he is much more explicit in *Sermo* 336.5.5 (ML 38.1474–75) and *Tract. in Iohan.* 120.2 (CCL 36.661; ML 35.1953). Cf. John Chrys., *Catecheses* 3, *Sermo ad neoph.* 17 (SC 50.176 Wenger). It should be noted, however, that here in his commentary on Gen. Aug. points out two interesting aspects of the creation of Eve as foreshadowing the origin of the Church: (1) the use of the verb *aedificavit* (see n. 55 *supra*) in the narrative, and (2) the fact that God used a rib rather than flesh of Adam, the significance of which is explained by Aug. here in sect. 34.

[86]I follow the reading *fuerunt* of Bod and z, with which E and S, collated by z, apparently agree. P, R, Pal, and m read *fuerant*.

[87]Gen. 1.27.

[88]*Faceret* is the reading of Bod and z and apparently of E and S, collated by z. P, R, Pal, and m read *fieret*. If we assume that *faceret* was the original reading, we can readily understand that a scribe would have inadvertently changed *faceret* to *fieret* as his eye fell on *fieret* just three words farther on in the same line.

[89]Eph. 3.10. For the problem raised by Augustine's reading of this text, see 5.19.38 *supra* (where it is quoted in full) and n. 62 *ibid.*

[90]Cf. Gal. 3.19. See n. 72 *supra* and n. 61 to Book 5.

[91]Cf. 1 Cor. 3.7.

[92]It is important to note that Aug. refers here to Adam's state in Gen. 2.21 as an ecstasy and that in translating that passage from the LXX at the beginning of this book (9.1.1 *supra*) he also used "ecstasy." Earlier, in *De Gen. c. Man.* 2.1.1 (ML 34.195), he had used *sopor*, and in this work (6.5.7 *supra*) *mentis alienatio*. The

word "ecstasy" (ἔκστασις) is used in the LXX, and it aptly describes the state in which Adam had his prophetic vision according to Augustine's interpretation.

[93]Cf. Ps. 72.17. Augustine's expression *intellegeret in novissima* is based on the LXX: συνῶ εἰς τὰ ἔσχατα αὐτῶν.

[94]*Cum ad se adductam mulierem suam videret*, according to the text of E, S, R², Bod, and z. But P, C, R¹, Pal, and m have *costam* before *mulierem*.

[95]Gen. 2.23–24. Augustine's allusion to St. Paul is to Eph. 5.31–32, where he quotes Gen. 2.24 and then adds: *This is a great mystery, and I mean with reference to Christ and the Church.* Christ is the new Adam from whose side, opened on the Cross, the Church came forth. The great mystery of which St. Paul speaks is the bond of Christian marriage between man and wife as a symbol of the union between Christ and the Church. Aug. seems to have been influenced in his interpretation of Adam's ecstasy by Tertullian, *De anima* 11.4 (p. 15,16–22 Waszink; ML 2.665).

[96]Matt. 19.4.

[97]I accept the reading *propter* found in P, R, S, C, Bod, Pal, and m.

BOOK TEN

[1]The theory referred to by Aug. is called traducianism. A grossly materialistic form of this theory is found in Tertullian, who holds that the soul is corporeal and who says in *De anima* 19.6 (p. 27,28–31 Waszink; ML 2.681–82) that it is an offshoot of the soul of Adam; and in *op. cit.* 27.5 (p. 38,36–39,2 Waszink; ML 2.695–96) that in sexual intercourse the male seed which is implanted contains moisture from the body and heat from the soul to bring about the new being. As far as Eve is concerned, he says, *op. cit.* 36.4 (p. 52,30–34 Waszink; ML 2.713), that there was no need for God to breathe a soul into her because in the rib removed from Adam's side there was a shoot (*tradux*) of both his soul and his body. Aug. unhesitatingly rejects this materialistic traducianism of Tertullian: see *Epist.* 190.14 (CSEL 57.148,5–

149,2 Goldbacher; ML 33.861), but here he considers the possibility of a spiritual traducianism, in which the immaterial souls of parents would somehow generate the souls of their children as their bodies generate children's bodies. Jerome, *Epist.* 126.1 (CSEL 56.143,13–16 Hilberg; ML 22.1086), says that Tertullian and Apollinaris and most of the writers of the West (but here he is surely exaggerating) are traducianists. For a survey of traducianist theories, see A. Michel, DTC 15 (1946) *s.v.* "Traducianisme," 1350–65.

²Gen. 2.23.

³Gen. 1.27.

⁴See Books 6–7 *passim*, especially 6.7.12, 6.12.22, 7.22.32.

⁵Eccli. (Sirach) 18.1. For an explanation of Augustine's understanding of this text, see n. 69 to Book 4 *supra.* For Augustine's explanation of the creation of Adam and Eve, harmonizing Gen. 1.27 with Gen. 2.7 and 2.21–22, see 7.28.40–43 *supra.*

⁶These speculations about the soul of Adam are to be found in Book 7 *passim:* see especially chs. 22–24. Augustine's tentative solution to the problem of Adam's soul is stated in 7.24.35: it was created in its own proper being (not in a reason-principle) on the first day and laid away until God breathed it into the body He formed from the earth. See my observations in n. 63 to Book 7.

⁷"As I have just now explained it" (*hoc quod modo dixi*), that is, according to the theory that all human souls (not just Adam's) were created on the first day. As Agaësse-Solignac 49.154–55 n. 8 have explained, and as Augustine's argument that follows makes clear, he is not referring to what immediately precedes in ch. 3 but to the theory proposed as probable and reasonable (*credibilius vel tolerabilius*) in ch. 2, namely, that the soul was created by God on the first day. As proposed in ch. 2, this referred only to Adam's soul. Now in ch. 3 Aug. offers it as the first of three possible explanations of the origin of *all* human souls.

⁸"Finished and begun": *consummatis et inchoatis.* The words echo the statements in Gen. 2.1, *Et consummata sunt caelum et terra,* and Gen. 2.3, *In ipso requievit ab omnibus operibus suis quae inchoavit Deus facere.* The works just begun are those created in their reason-principles but not yet visibly created. The works

that are finished are those that have been created in their own substances.

⁹In this chapter Aug. has considered three possible positions: (1) all human souls were created in the original creation and are infused into their bodies at the appropriate time in history (creationism); (2) only Adam's soul was originally created, and all other souls are the offspring of it (spiritual traducianism); (3) only Adam's soul was originally created, and all other souls are directly and individually created by God throughout history (creationism).

¹⁰See 7.5.7 *supra* and n. 11 on that passage.

¹¹Ezek. 37.9–10. In Hebrew the one word *ruah* means "spirit," "breath," "wind" (*The Jerusalem Bible*, p. 1407 n.). I have translated the Latin *spiritus* with "breath."

¹²These words in Ezekiel foretell "the messianic restoration of Israel after the sufferings of the Exile. . . . But also, by the imagery chosen, he is already preparing minds for the idea of an individual resurrection of the body . . ." (*The Jerusalem Bible, loc. cit.*).

¹³John 20.22.

¹⁴Cf. 7.3.4–7.4.6 *supra*.

¹⁵Wisd. 1.7.

¹⁶In ch. 3 above (see n. 9), Aug. explained three possible theories on the origin of the soul. Here he considers only the second and third alternatives (spiritual traducianism and creationism). Aug. gives no explanation of why he suddenly changes from three alternative hypotheses to two. However, the first and third had this in common, that God directly creates souls *ex nihilo*, whereas in the second He creates souls as the offspring of Adam's soul. For a discussion of the problem, see Agaësse-Solignac 49.533–34.

¹⁷Isa. 57.16: *For from Me a spirit will go forth, and I have made every breath* (LXX).

¹⁸Ps. 32.15: *Qui finxit singillatim corda eorum.*

¹⁹Eph. 2.8–10.

²⁰Ps. 50.12.

²¹Zech. 12.1.

²²Wisd. 8.19–20: *Sortitus sum animam bonam, et cum essem magis*

bonus, veni ad corpus incoinquinatum. The word *bonus,* "good," translates the Greek ἀγαθός, which can also mean "noble" and is so rendered in some translations. In spite of the impression that this text gives when detached, the context shows that Greek ideas of pre-existence, with merit and demerit, are foreign to the author. See A. G. Wright, JBC 1 (1968) Wisdom 8.17–21, p. 562. For a further discussion of this text, see 10.17.30–31 *infra.*

23Aug. probably has Origen in mind. See Origen, *De principiis* 1.8.1 and 3.3.5 (GCS 5.96 and 261–62 Koetschau). Aug. has already rejected this theory, 6.9.15 *supra.*

24Rom. 9.11.

25Rom. 9.12. Cf. Gen. 25.23. For Augustine's views on the election of Jacob, see *De div. quaest. ad Simpl.* 1.2.1–12 (ML 40.111–18).

261 Tim. 2.5: *One Mediator between God and men, the Man Christ Jesus.* See 10.18.32–33 *infra.*

27Ps. 103.29–30. The Latin *spiritus,* which may mean either "spirit" or "breath," is used in both v. 29 and v. 30. I have translated it as "spirit," but "breath" could be used as well in rendering the text as it is discussed here.

28Cf. 2 Mac. 7.23.

29Cf. Ps. 102.14.

30Eccli. (Sirach) 10.9.

31Cf. Rom. 10.3.

32Job 42.6. The wording used by Aug. here is that of the OL, based on the LXX. He quotes the OL directly in *De civ. Dei* 22.29 (CCL 48.859,117–18; ML 41.799) as follows: *Propterea despexi memet ipsum et distabui et existimavi me terram et cinerem (I, therefore, despised myself and melted away, and I considered myself dust and ashes).*

33Gal. 2.20.

34Eccle. 12.7. See Augustine's discussion of this text in *Epist.* 143.8–9 (CSEL 44.258,10–260,10 Goldbacher; ML 33.588–89).

35Cf. Gen. 3.19: *In the sweat of your face you shall eat bread till you return to the ground, for out of it you were taken; you are dust, and to dust you shall return* (RSV).

36Ps. 77.39. See 1.4.9 *supra,* where Aug. says that a creature by turning back to God its Creator is formed and perfected. Here he takes Ps. 77.39 as a description of the formlessness of the creature who lacks that necessary conversion to its Creator (*conversio ad Creatorem*).

[37]Rom. 5.12,18–19. See n. 33 to Book 6 *supra* for a explanation of Augustine's understanding of this text.

[38]Aug. may have Tertullian in mind. See Tert., *De anima* 40.1 (p. 56,15–17 Waszink; ML 2.719), and see Waszink's note, p. 448, together with the remarks of Agaësse-Solignac 49.535 ff.

[39]Cf. Rom. 9.11.

[40]Aug. is here drawn to the traducianist theory (spiritual traducianism) in order to account for the transmission of original sin. He does not see how infant baptism can be explained except on the basis of the traducianist hypothesis. Yet he is also attracted to creationism, and to the end of his days he was unable to solve this problem. See *Retract.* 1.1.8 or 1.1.3 (CSEL 36.16,8–9 Knöll; ML 32.587), where, commenting on a passage in his *Contra academicos* (A.D. 386), he says about his thinking concerning the origin of the soul: *nec tunc sciebam, nec adhuc scio* ("I did not know then, and I still do not know"). Cf. also *Retract.* 2.71.1 or 2.45 (CSEL 36.184,1–185,6 Knöll; ML 32.649) and 2.82.1 or 2.56 (CSEL 36.195,7–196,6; ML 32.653).

[41]Gal. 5.17.

[42]Ps. 83.3.

[43]Eccli. (Sirach) 1.26(33). The reading *will give* (*praebebit*) is uncertain. The future, *praebebit*, is found in E[2], R, and z. The present, *praebet*, is the reading of E[1], P, S, B, Bod, Pal, and m. I accept *praebebit* as the more likely reading because it is the correct translation of the LXX, and also because it is found elsewhere when Aug. quotes this text: see *Enarr. in Ps.* 118, *Sermo* 22.8 (CCL 40.1740; ML 37.1566).

[44]See 12.24.51 *infra*, where Aug. says: "It is not the body that perceives, but the soul by means of the body; and the soul uses the body as a sort of messenger in order to form within itself the object that is called to its attention from the outside world."

[45]Luke 3.6.

[46]In one sense the flesh is at war with the spirit, but in an-

other it is also in the service of the spirit. With this in mind, Aug. refers to "the ministry of the flesh" (*ministerium carnis*), echoing Tert., *De anima* 40.2 (p. 56,18–26 Waszink; ML 2.719).

[47]Cf. Rom. 7.24: *Wretched man that I am! Who will deliver me from this body of death?*

[48]Eph. 2.3.

[49]Cf. Rom. 5.20–21: *Where sin increased, grace abounded all the more, so that, as sin reigned in death, grace also might reign through justice to eternal life through Jesus Christ our Lord.*

[50]Rom. 6.12–13.

[51]See Aug., *Conf.* 8.10.22–24, where he refutes the Manichean doctrine of two natures and two wills in man, one good and the other evil.

[52]*Voluptatem* ("pleasure") is the reading of E[2], P, R, S, Bod, Pal, and m. Zycha reads *voluntatem* ("desire"), following E[1].

[53]*Adulteris* ("adulterous parents") is the reading adopted by z. It has the authority (apparently) of E, R[1], and of many MSS collated by the Maurists (see their note *h.l.*). *Adulteriis* ("adulteries") is the reading of P, R[2], S, Bod, Pal, and m.

[54]Augustine's point is that the infant has not inherited any sin from his immediate parents, but only original sin from Adam. The child of a saintly father and mother is just as much in need of baptism as the child of adulterous parents.

[55]Cf. Rom. 5.19.

[56]This question was brought up by Celestius (a disciple of Pelagius), who was in Africa at the time of the conference of the Catholic and Donatist bishops, presided over by the imperial legate Marcellinus, A.D. 411. To inherit sin from Adam, Celestius said, it would be necessary that the soul, like the body, be generated by the carnal union of the parents; but most Catholics, he said, reject this explanation (traducianism). As for baptism, he held that the expression *in remissionem peccatorum* ("for the remission of sins") in relation to infant baptism was meaningless; for it implies guilt, and how can infants be guilty of anything? He admitted that infants needed baptism and should be baptized but denied that it was for the purpose of cleansing them from original sin. He was condemned by the Council of Carthage, A.D. 412. Since Aug. was working on his commentary

on Genesis A.D. 401–15, it is highly probable that Celestius was in his mind when he was writing Book 10. For Celestius see ODCC 258–59; also Georges de Plinval, *Pélage, ses écrits, sa vie, et sa réforme* (Lausanne 1943) 254–60; and Bonner 381.

⁵⁷Jer. 1.5.

⁵⁸This theory about the origin of the soul should be compared with what Aug. says in an early work (A.D. 388–95), *De libero arbitrio* 3.20.56–3.21.59 (CCL 29.307–10; ML 32.1298–1300). There he explained four different theories but confessed his inability to establish any one of them as true. Light is shed on our passage in *De Gen. ad litt.* by what he writes in *De libero arbitrio* about souls, which are said to come into bodies from a previous existence: "When they enter this life and submit to wearing mortal members these souls must also undergo forgetfulness of their former existence and the labours of their present existence, with consequent ignorance and toil which in the first man were a punishment involving mortality and completing the misery of the soul" (*op. cit.* 3.20.57, tr. John H. S. Burleigh, *Augustine: Earlier Writings*, The Library of Christian Classics 6 [London 1953] 204–5). It is important to note that although Aug. admits the possibility of the pre-existence of the soul (with subsequent forgetfulness on entering the body), he resolutely rejects the teaching of Origen and Priscillian, who held that souls were condemned to inhabit bodies in punishment for previous sins. See *Epist.* 164.7.20 (CSEL 44.539,4–8 Goldbacher; ML 33.717). Again, in *Epist.* 166.9.27, he rejects that error with the greatest emphasis: *non credo, non adquiesco, non consentio.* Origen's opinion was officially condemned in the 6th c. by Pope Vigilius, and Priscillian's opinion also in the 6th c. by the First Council of Braga. See H. Denzinger and A. Schönmetzer (eds.), *Enchiridion symbolorum* (34th ed. Barcelona 1967) nos. 403 and 456.

⁵⁹In *De baptismo contra Donatistas* 4.25.32 (CSEL 51.260 Petschenig; ML 43.176) Aug. explains that two things are necessary for salvation: *sacramentum baptismi* ("the sacrament of baptism") and *conversio cordis* ("conversion of the heart"). But in cases in which there is no bad will, God can supply for one or the other, as He supplied for the sacrament in the case of the good thief on the Cross and as He constantly supplies for conversion of the

heart in the case of infants receiving baptism. Aug., therefore, reminds us that God does not mercilessly condemn infants who, coming into the world with the stain of original sin, die in infancy without any personal guilt. See also *Epist.* 98.1–3 (CSEL 34.520–24 Goldbacher; ML 33.359–61). But unfortunately this leaves unexplained the mystery of infants who die without anyone to baptize them.

[60]The ignorance of infancy and childhood is due to the union of the soul with the flesh of fallen human nature; in other words, it is the result of original sin.

[61]*Veri sacerdotis* ("of the true Priest") according to z; but *mediatoris veri sacerdotis* ("of the Mediator who is true Priest") according to m. The word *mediatoris* is lacking in all the MSS collated by Zycha and also in Bod and Pal; and a note in m states that it is absent from most MSS.

[62]"If it were now (*nunc*) necessary" is the reading of Bod and Pal and of z and all the MSS he collated. The reading of m is: "If it were not (*non*) necessary."

[63]Cf. Rom. 9.11.

[64]Rom. 5.19.

[65]Wisd. 4.11.

[66]1 Cor. 15.22.

[67]Rom. 5.19.

[68]Rom. 5.12. For Augustine's understanding of this text, see n. 33 to Book 6 *supra*.

[69]Aug. seems to mean that the traducianist theory more obviously points to the need of baptism for infants than the creationist theory does.

[70]See 10.7.12 *supra*.

[71]Wisd. 8.19–20. For the meaning of this text, see n. 22 *supra*.

[72]Wisd. 9.15: *For a corruptible body weighs down the soul, and this earthy dwelling burdens the thoughtful mind.*

[73]Wisd. 7.2.

[74]Ps. 21.17–19.

[75]Ps. 21.2.

[76]See Luke 2.40 and 2.52.

[77]Aug. refers to Wisd. 7.1–2: *I also am mortal like all men, a descendant of the first-formed child of earth; and in the womb of a moth-*

er I was molded into flesh, within the period of ten months, compacted with blood, from the seed of a man and the pleasure of marriage (RSV). His point is that these words cannot apply to Christ personally; He can be represented as saying them only in so far as He speaks for men whose nature He has assumed.

[78]Luke 2.42–48.

[79]Rom. 7.23.

[80]*Similitudo carnis peccati.* Cf. Rom. 8.3: *Deus filium suum mittens in similitudinem carnis peccati* (*God sending His Son in the likeness of sinful flesh*).

[81]Cf. Gal. 5.17.

[82]Original sin as transmitted to the descendants of Adam can be described as inherited disease (as it was generally described in the Christian East) or inherited guilt (as it was often described by the Latin writers. The two views can also be combined, and that is the way Aug. conceives original sin here and elsewhere. See Bonner 371.

[83]Heb. 7.4–10.

[84]Rom. 7.23.

[85]"Invisible concupiscence" (*invisibilem concupiscentiam*). Aug. uses this phrase to point out the difference between the seminal reason of Levi and that of Christ in the loins of Abraham. Since both Levi and Christ are descendants of Abraham, it can be said that their bodies were potentially present in his body by reason of the appropriate seminal reasons. But the seminal reason determining the conception of Levi in the womb of his mother was to cause the creation of that new body by means of the conjugal act in which concupiscence played a role (hence the invisible concupiscence in the seminal reason). The seminal reason, however, determining the conception of Christ in the womb of His virgin mother was to cause the creation of His body from her flesh by the action of the Holy Spirit without any male seed or carnal concupiscence.

[86]Melchizedek (to whom the tithes were paid) was a figure of Christ, who by His passion and death would bring to mankind a remedy for the wounds of sin.

[87]Aug. elsewhere rejects the notion of a seed of the soul (*semen animae*) in a materialistic sense (materialistic traducianism); but

he does consider possible the theory that souls can be spiritually generated by souls (spiritual traducianism). See 10.1.1 *supra* and n. 1 *ibid.*

[88]This is Tertullian's opinion. See 10.26.44 *infra.*

[89]The Latin is *quae incorporaliter numeros agit.* In Augustine's terminology the "numbers" of a being are the laws that regulate its development. See 6.13.23 *supra* and n. 58 *ibid.*

[90]Aug. does not seem to answer here the specific question raised at the beginning of this paragraph (Could not Christ have been in the loins of Abraham according to the soul without paying tithes?), but rather he presents an argument against traducianism in general by showing that the seminal reason of the soul, if there is such a thing, cannot function like the seminal reason of the body. He comes to the point, however, in what follows.

[91]*Coaptatio* (arrangement) is the Latin word Aug. uses to translate the Greek ἁρμονία (harmony). Cic., *Tusc. disp.* 1.10.19, tells us that Aristoxenus, musician and philosopher, pupil of Aristotle, held that the soul is "a special tuning up (*intentio*) of the natural body analogous to that which is called harmony in vocal and instrumental music" (LCL, p. 24 King). *Coaptatio* is a Late Latin coinage, and Aug. was the first to use it as a translation of ἁρμονία (see TLL 3.1385,37–57).

[92]John 3.6.

[93]Matt. 7.7.

[94]Matt. 7.7–11.

[95]Aug. was firm and consistent in his conviction that the practice of infant baptism had been handed down from the apostles. See *De baptismo* 4.24.31 (CSEL 51.259,2–4 Petschenig; ML 43.174): ". . . what the universal Church holds on to, although it has not been defined by the councils but has always been kept intact, is rightly believed to have been handed down by the authority of the apostles. . . ." Also *Sermo* 176.2.2 (ML 38.950): "The Church has always had this practice, has always held on to it. It has received it from the faith of our fathers, it guards it unfailingly to the end."

[96]Cf. Matt. 2.16.

[97]In the *Conf.,* Aug. often speaks of the serious problem he

had of breaking with habits of thought he had acquired as a Manichee and of thinking of God as an immaterial being. See *Conf.* 3.6.10, 4.7.12, 5.10.19, 7.1.1.

[98]Images or phantasms of images: *phantasias vel phantasmata imaginum.* In Augustine's terminology a *phantasia* is an image evoked from the memory of a sense object once perceived; a *phantasma* is a representation of a sense object not previously perceived but conjured up by the soul within itself, See *Conf.* 3.6.10 and *De musica* 6.11.32 (ML 32.1180).

[99]*Cogitatio* is the activity by which the soul gathers together and concentrates on groups of images stored in the memory. See Bourke 214–17 and 243; and cf. *Conf.* 10.11.18.

[100]In *Conf.* 7.1.1 Aug. speaks of the difficulty he had in his youth of conceiving of any substance that could not be seen by the eyes; but in *Conf.* 10.6.8 he explains that he now knows that the God whom he loves is beyond all that the bodily senses can possibly perceive. In *De libero arbitrio* 2.3.8–2.6.14 (CSEL 74.43,11–52,13 Green; ML 32.1244–49) he explains the distinction between the senses, which perceive material things, and reason, which perceives the eternal unchangeable. Later in this work on Genesis, 12.24.50 *infra*, he points out that the objects of intellectual knowledge transcend both bodies and the images of bodies in the imagination.

[101]Tert., *De anima* 7.3 (CCL 2.790,11–15; ML 2.698A), argues that a soul that has left the body and gone to hell cannot be nothing: "For it would be nothing if it were not a body" (*Nihil enim si non corpus*).

[102]Tert., *Adversus Praxean* 7.8 (CCL 2.1166,49; ML 2.186A): "For who will deny that God is a body, although God is a spirit?" (*Quis enim negabit Deum corpus esse, etsi Deus spiritus est?*)

[103]Tert., *De an.* 7.4 (CCL 2.790,22–23; ML 2.698B).

[104]*Op. cit.* 9.5 (CCL 2.793,43–44; ML 2.701B): "What other color, therefore, will you expect the soul to have except that of air and light?" (*Quem igitur alium animae aestimabis colorem quam aerium ac lucidum?*)

[105]*Op. cit.* 9.8 (CCL 2.793,65–794,68; ML 2.702B).

[106]Literally, "as in cogitation" (*sicut in cogitatione*). See n. 99 *supra*.

[107]See Gen. 41.26.

[108]See Acts 10.11.

[109]Tert., *De an.* 37.5 (CCL 2.840,33–34; ML 2.759A).

[110]*Ibid.* (CCL 2.840,34–36; ML 2.759A).

[111]After *similitudine* the text in m reads: *eorum quae videmus.* These words, which are not found in the MSS of z, nor in Bod or Pal, are almost certainly a gloss on the text.

[112]*De an.* 37.6–7 (CCL 2.840,36–49; ML 2.759A–B). Waszink 432 comments on the statement, "For it can be increased in its dimensions" (*habitu*), as follows: "this word . . . was of course intended to conceal the weak points of the argument; but already Augustine showed how little successful Tert. has been." Waszink refers, of course, to the paragraph immediately following in Aug.

BOOK ELEVEN

[1]Gen. 2.25–3.24. The text used by Aug. is the OL, which for the most part is based on the LXX. But contrary to the LXX text, the OL text of Aug. in Gen. 3.15 has the feminine pronoun *ipsa* (referring to the woman, namely, the Virgin Mary as the second Eve): *Ipsa tibi servabit caput, et tu servabis eius calcaneum* (*She will lie in wait for your head, and you will lie in wait for her heel*). The LXX is faithful to the Hebr. here in using the masc. pronoun αὐτός referring to the seed or descendant, namely, Christ. The OL texts were not unanimous in reading *ipsa*. Thus, Cyprian, *Testim.* 2.9 (CSEL 3.74,13–14 Hartel; ML 4.733A), cites the passage as follows: *Ipse tuum calcabit* [al. *observabit*] *caput et tu observabis calcaneum eius.* See M. A. Fahey, S.J., *Cyprian and the Bible: A Study in Third-Century Exegesis* (Beiträge zur Geschichte der biblischen Hermeneutik 9, Tübingen 1971) 59.

[2]See 8.1.1–4 *supra.*

[3]For an example of this type of exegesis, see 5.19.39 *supra.*

[4]Rom. 7.23.

[5]See 9.3.5 to 9.11.19 *supra;* especially 9.3.6 and 9.10.18.

[6]Just as Adam's will had disobeyed God, so Adam's members would disobey his will. This is the meaning of *iustissimo recipro-*

catu ("by a just retribution"). This notion is also found in *De civ. Dei* 13.13.

[7]Gen. 3.1.

[8]Readings in the OL text are: *sapientior, prudentior, astutior, sapientissimus, prudentissimus.* See Fischer VL 56. The Vulg. reads *callidior.*

[9]I follow the reading of z, *impleri solent,* which is attested by E, S, and Bod. P, R, Pal, and m read *implere.* I have not seen any MS evidence for *solet,* the reading of m.

[10]The Hebr. word (*'arum*) used to describe the serpent means "crafty," "shrewd," "sensible." It is predicated of persons both good and evil. See William Gesenius, *Hebrew and English Lexicon of the Old Testament,* ed. Francis Brown *et al.* (Oxford 1907) 791, and J. Skinner, *Genesis* (ICC, New York 1910) 71.

[11]Jer. 4.22.

[12]Luke 16.8.

[13]James 4.6 (cf. Prov. 3.34).

[14]Prov. 16.18. Aug. follows the OL text: *Ante ruinam exaltatur cor, et ante gloriam humiliatur.*

[15]Ps. 29.7.

[16]*Ibid.* 8.

[17]James 1.14–15.

[18]Gal. 6.1.

[19]*Creaturam* is found in E, P, R², S, Eug, Bod, and z. The reading of R¹, Pal, and m is *naturam.*

[20]Cf. Aug., *Contra adversarium legis et prophetarum* 1.14.20 (ML 42.614): "If they think that man should have been made in such a way that he would not wish to sin, they should not be displeased that he has been made in such a way that he would not be able to sin if he were unwilling. For if a man who would be unable to sin would be better, a man who would be able not to sin is good." Hence the better nature is that of the angels and saints in heaven, who have *non posse peccare;* but the nature of man in this life, who has *posse non peccare,* is good. Only the angels and saints in heaven have true *libertas* in Augustine's terminology; in this life we have *liberum arbitrium,* which implies the possibility of choosing evil. See *De correptione et gratia* 12.33 (ML 44.936) and Gilson 323–24.

[21]Cf. Rom. 11.20.

[22]Rom. 9.22–23.

[23]2 Cor. 10.17.

[24]Cf. Rom. 12.3.

[25]See ch. 8 *supra.*

[26]Zycha's text reads *omnipotens Deus,* following E. But *omnipotens* is lacking in P, R, S, Bod, Pal, Eug, and m.

[27]Cf. Voltaire: "Le mieux est l'ennemi du bien."

[28]*Exemplum* (in the acc. case) is the reading of E, P, R, S, Bod, Pal, and z. *Exemplo* is found in Eug and m.

[29]Ps. 110.2. Augustine's understanding of this verse is clear from his comment, *Enarr. in Ps.* 110.2 (CCL 40.1622,28–30; ML 37.1464): "Thus, whatever you choose, Almighty God will not be at a loss to accomplish His will in you."

[30]To be revealed: *prodendum,* the reading of E, P, S, Eug, Bod, and z. *Providendum* is the reading of R, B, and Pal. *Probandum* is the reading of m, but the editors of m have this remark in a note: "*In Mss. probae notae,* prodendum."

[31]Cf. James 1.15: *Then desire when it has conceived gives birth to sin; and sin when it is full-grown brings forth death* (RSV).

[32]Cf. Rom. 9.22–23.

[33]Matt. 8.31–32. At the beginning of this chapter Aug. asks why the serpent was chosen rather than any other animal, but he does not answer his own question. However, in *De civ. Dei* 14.11, he points out that the Devil chose an animal suited to his purpose, inasmuch as it was "slippery and able to move with tortuous twists and turns."

[34]The "certain heretics" referred to here are the Manichees. For Mani's denial of the creation of the Devil by God, see Hegemonius, *Acta Archelai* 5 (GCS 16.7,5–7 Beeson; MG 1436A).

[35]See Aug., *De natura boni* 1–4 (CSEL 25.855–57 Zycha; ML 42.551–53).

[36]In accordance with the beliefs of his day, Aug. held that demons had *corpora aeria,* bodies composed of air. See *De divinatione daemonum* 3.7 (CSEL 41.603,15–19 Zycha; ML 40.584). For further details of his theories about demons, see *De civ. Dei,* Books 9 and 10 *passim,* and F. van der Meer, *Augustine the Bishop* (London 1961) 67–75.

[37]Augustine's works against the Manichees written prior to the completion of *De Genesi ad litteram* were: *De moribus ecclesiae catholicae et de moribus Manichaeorum* (388–89), *De Genesi contra Manichaeos* (388–90), *De duabus animabus contra Manichaeos* (391–92), *Disputatio contra Fortunatum Manichaeum* (392), *Contra Adimantum Manichaeum* (394), *Contra epistulam Manichaei* (397), *Contra Faustum Manichaeum* (400), *De actis cum Felice Manichaeo* (404), *De natura boni* (405), *Contra Secundinum Manichaeum* (405–6). For a study of Augustine's controversies with the Manichees, see Gerald Bonner, *St. Augustine of Hippo: Life and Controversies* (London 1963) 193–236.

[38]Tertullian's opinion is that the honor given by God to man stirred up in the Devil an impatience which led to envy; see Tert., *De patientia* 5.5–6 (CCL 1.303; ML 1.1256B): "Even when the Lord God subjected to His own image, that is, to man, all the works He had made, the Devil bore it with impatience. For he would not have grieved, had he endured it, nor would he have envied man, had he not grieved ..." (tr. E. J. Daly, FOC 40.200). Envy was clearly the Devil's downfall, according to Cyprian's account: Cypr., *De zelo et livore* 4 (CSEL 3.421,8–11 Hartel; ML 4.665C): "From it [jealousy] the Devil in the very beginnings of the world, did first both perish and destroy. He who long had been upheld in Angelic majesty, he the accepted and dear to God, when he beheld man made after God's likeness, did in malignant wrath break forth into envy ..." (tr. C. Thornton, Library of Fathers 3 [Oxford 1840] 268). See E. Mangenot, DTC 4 (1911) "Démon d'après les Pères," 347–49. In what follows, Aug. proceeds to give a definition of envy, *Cum igitur ... invidentia ... sit odium felicitatis alienae,* which echoes Cic., *Tusc. disp.* 3.10.21: *Invidentia aegritudo est ex alterius rebus secundis.* The word *invidentia,* coined by Cic., is a rare word but a favorite of Aug.: see H. Hagendahl, *Augustine and the Latin Classics* (Studia graeca et latina Gothoburgensia 20, Göteborg 1967) 148.

[39]Eccli. (Sirach) 10.13. See William M. Green, *Initium omnis peccati superbia: Augustine on Pride as the First Sin* (Univ. of Cal. Pub. in Class. Philology 13.13, Berkeley 1949) 407–31.

[40]1 Tim. 6.10.

[41]Aug. sees significance in the fact that in Latin the adj. *pri-*

vatus ("private") is used as a synonym for *proprius* ("personal, one's own") in referring to the object of the inordinate attachment of a heart that is filled with avarice and therefore pride. Immoderate love of one's own *private* good leads inevitably to a *privation* of one's true good; and this principle applies whether there is a question of the fall of the rebel angels or the fall of an avaricious man.

⁴²2 Tim. 3.2.

⁴³1 Cor. 13.5.

⁴⁴*Ibid.* 4.

⁴⁵Cf. *De civ. Dei* 14.28: "Two loves have built two cities: the love of self to the contempt of God has built the earthly city; and the love of God to the contempt of self, the heavenly city."

⁴⁶*Saeculum:* "the world of men and of time." See R. A. Markus, *Saeculum: History and Society in the Theology of St. Augustine* (Cambridge 1970) viii.

⁴⁷Aug. reveals here his intention to write his *City of God.* At this time that work was, in the words of E. Gilson, "still a project": see Gilson's foreword to *The City of God* in FOC 6.lviii. The *De Gen. ad litt.* was begun in 401 and finished in 415. The *De civ. Dei* was begun in 413 and finished in 426.

⁴⁸John 8.44. It should be noted that Augustine's explanation of the fall of Satan here in 11.14.18 to 11.16.21 had a deep influence on the thought of St. Ignatius Loyola as expressed in the First Exercise of his *Spiritual Exercises:* see Hugo Rahner, *Ignatius the Theologian* (New York 1968) 69–73.

⁴⁹The text of the first two sentences of ch. 17 as found in z reads as follows: *Quomodo enim duxisse vitam beatam inter beatos angelos credi potest, qui futuri sui peccati atque subplicii, id est desertionis et ignis aeterni, [praescius non fuit]? Si praescius non fuit, merito quaeritur, cur non fuerit.* The text in m is substantially the same. I have added the brackets to indicate that the bracketed words, *praescius non fuit,* found in m and z, are not in the MSS (E, P, R, S, B, Bod, and Pal). In the absence of any known MSS authority, I assume that at some late date in the transmission of the text these words were added to supply a predicate for *qui.* Agaësse-Solignac have rightly removed the interpolated words; but they have made the two sentences into one, thus leaving an

awkward and puzzling anacolouthon after *qui*. This difficulty is eliminated if the first sentence is made to end with *potest* followed by a question mark, and then by a new sentence beginning with *qui* (as a connecting relative): *Quomodo enim duxisse vitam beatam inter beatos angelos credi potest? Qui futuri sui peccati atque subplicii, id est desertionis et ignis aeterni, si praescius non fuit, merito quaeritur cur non fuerit.*

[50]Marius Victorinus, *In epist. ad Eph.* 1.21 (Teubner ed. 145,20 Locher; ML 8.1251B), speaks about two classes of angels, *potestates vel mundanae vel caelestes*. See also Victorinus, *Adv. Arium* 4.5.7–8 (SC 68.512 Henry-Hadot; ML 8.1116A). In 3.10.14 *supra*, Aug. noted that some Christian writers were of the opinion that the Devil and his followers were not *caelestes* or *supercaelestes*, but he did not espouse that opinion. See n. 34 to Book 3 *supra*.

[51]The body as it is in this life is called a "natural body" (*corpus animale*); after the resurrection it will be a "spiritual body" (*corpus spiritale*). See 1 Cor. 15.44. Aug. shows, 6.19.30 *supra*, that Adam's body, even in Paradise, was a natural body.

[52]Gal. 6.1.

[53]Cf. Rom. 12.12.

[54]Ps. 2.11.

[55]This is based on the theory that there are two categories of angels, *mundani* and *caelestes* (or *supercaelestes*): see n. 50 *supra*.

[56]For the "justice of faith," see Rom. 3.21–26.

[57]These writers attribute the creation of the Devil to God, and therefore they are not Manichees. Their identity is not known. Agaësse-Solignac 49.550 suggest Lactantius as one possibility, but the text is uncertain. Whoever they are, their position differs from that of Aug. in that they hold that God created the Devil in an evil state, whereas he holds that the Devil was created as a good angel and that he turned away from God by his own free will.

[58]Job 40.14 (or 40.19). See n. 64 *infra*, and cf. *De civ. Dei* 11.15.

[59]Ps. 103.26.

[60]The words enclosed in parentheses are found in Bod and Pal, and apparently in all the MSS collated by or for m and z; but the Maurist editors, influenced by a marginal note in the *Codex Colbertinus*, considered the passage a gloss and removed it

from the text (see note *h.l.* in m). Zycha and Agaësse-Solignac have followed the MSS (rightly, I believe) and included the passage in the text.

[61]Gen. 1.31.

[62]It is difficult to say whose opinion Aug. has summarized in this paragraph. Since these writers are concerned about harmonizing Gen. 1.31 with their theory that God created the Devil as an evil creature, they are not Manichees but apparently Christians. Apart from the untenable opinion that God created the Devil as an evil creature, the rest of the paragraph is a fair summary of the thoughts of Lactantius on the mixture of good and evil in the world under divine providence. Thus he says, *Div. inst.* 5.7.8 (CSEL 19.420,16–17 Brandt; ML 6.571B): ". . . without evil and vice there is no virtue"; and *Div. inst.* 5.22.17 (CSEL) or 5.23 (ML): "How can a general prove the valor of his soldiers unless he have an enemy?" This concept was a familiar Stoic teaching: see Cic., *Nat. deor.* 3.35.86 and 3.37–38.90; and it is taken up into his system by Plotinus in his treatise on providence (*Enn.* 3.2 and 3). Aug. had developed the same theme in *De ordine*, Bk. 1 (written at Cassiciacum, A.D. 386, when he was preparing for baptism). See Aimé Solignac, S.J., "Réminiscences plotiniennes et porphyriennes dans le début du 'De ordine' de saint Augustin," *Archives de philosophie* N.S. 20 (1957) 446–65, esp. 446–50.

[63]Matt. 25.31.

[64]Job 40.14 (40.19 in Hebr.). The OL of Aug. (based on LXX) reads:

Hoc est initium figmenti Domini,
quod fecit ut inludatur ab angelis eius.

The Vulg. text is:

Ipse est principium viarum Dei;
qui fecit eum applicabit gladium eius.

RSV reads:

He is the first of the works [Hebr. *ways*] *of God;*
let him who made him bring near his sword.

The second line of the text in Hebr. is defective, and translations are conjectural: see Marvin H. Pope, *The Anchor Bible: Job* (New York 1965) 266. In the context two enormous beasts are described: Behemoth (= the hippotamus?) and Leviathan (= the crocodile?). The words in v. 14 (v. 19) refer to Behemoth. "Behemoth and Leviathan are symbols of chaotic powers, monstrous, menacing, and incomprehensible to man; yet they, too, are of God's creation; in them he takes pleasure; through them aspects of his being are manifested" (R. A. F. MacKenzie, JBC 1 [1968] "Job," 532). It is not surprising, then, that Aug. and other commentators have taken Behemoth as representing the Devil.

[65]The concept of the wicked forming a kind of body of which the Devil is the head was familiar to Aug. from the *Liber regularum* of Tyconius, Donatist theologian of the late 4th c. (ML 18.15–66). Aug. discusses these rules in *De doctr. christ.* 3.30.42–3.37.55 (CCL 32.102–15; ML 34.81–88). The seventh rule is *de diabolo et eius corpore*. This notion is also found in Cyril of Alexandria, Hilary, Ambrose, and Ambrosiaster, as well as in certain later writers: see Sebastian Tromp, S.J., *Corpus Christi quod est ecclesia* 1 (2nd ed. Rome 1946) 160–66; and Agaësse-Solignac 49.551–52.

[66]Cf. Rom. 1.17.

[67]Cf. Ps. 93.15.

[68]Cf. Matt. 19.28.

[69]Cf. 1 Cor. 6.3.

[70]John 8.44.

[71]Isa. 14.12–15.

[72]This is the interpretation of Tyconius, *Liber regularum* 7 (ML 18.55–56). See Aug., *De doctr. christ.* 3.37.55 (CCL 32.115,15–23; ML 34.88), and cf. *De civ. Dei* 11.15.

[73]For the concept of the Devil as head of the body of all the wicked, see ch. 22 *supra* and n. 65.

[74]Matt. 13.28: *Inimicus homo hoc fecit.* See Tyconius, *Liber reg.* 7 (ML 18.61A).

[75]John 6.70.

[76]Gal. 3.29.

[77]Gal. 3.16.

[78]1 Cor. 12.12.

[79]Ezek. 28.12–13. See Tyconius, *Liber reg.* 7 (ML 18.60), and cf. Aug., *De civ. Dei* 11.15.

[80]See Cant. 4.12–13.

[81]Cf. Prov. 26.11 and 2 Peter 2.22.

[82]2 Peter 2.21.

[83]Cf. Matt. 12.43–45. The expression *he dwells there* is based on the reading *inhabitare*, found in P, R, Bod, Pal, and m; *intrare* is found in E, S, Eug, and z.

[84]Ezek. 28.13–15. Aug. is quoting according to the OL, which is based on the LXX: *A die qua creatus es tu cum cherub, et posuit te in monte sancto Dei, fuisti in medio lapidum flammeorum; ambulasti sine vitio tu in diebus tuis ex quo die creatus es tu, donec inventa sunt delicta tua in te.*

[85]Cf. Augustine's observation in *De Gen. c. Man.* 2.23.35 (ML 34.214): "According to those who have explained the Hebrew words in Scripture, cherubim is rendered *scientiae plenitudo* (the fullness of knowledge) in Latin."

[86]Ps. 3.5.

[87]With some hesitation Aug. here favors the first alternative, which he has already explained in chs. 16 and 23 above. The second alternative has been discussed in chs. 17 and 19, and the problem raised in the fourth alternative was brought up in ch. 17. In *De civ. Dei* 11.11–15 he considers the same alternatives and leaves the matter undecided. Towards the end of his life, A.D. 426–27, in *De correp. et gratia* 10.27 (ML 44.932–33), Aug. seems to have favored the third alternative, namely, that the Devil and his angels before their fall enjoyed (along with the good angels) a certain measure of happiness, but not complete beatitude since they did not know whether their happiness would be without end. When the rebel angels fell and the good angels chose to remain faithful, God revealed to the latter that they would never fall and that therefore their happiness would be unending. See Gérard Philips, *La raison d'être du mal d'après saint Augustin* (Museum Lessianum, section théologique 17, Louvain 1927) 202–4.

[88]Cf. 2 Peter 2.4. In *De civ. Dei* 15.23 Aug. quotes this text in the following form: *For if God spared not the angels that sinned, but casting them down, handed them over to the dark prison of the lower world to be kept for punishment at the judgment....* See also *De civ. Dei* 11.33 and 21.23. It should be noted that in *De civ. Dei* Aug. follows St. Peter more closely in picturing the fallen angels un-

der the earth, whereas here he pictures them in the atmosphere surrounding the earth.

[89]See chs. 6–11 and 22 *supra*.

[90]John 13.2.

[91]I accept the reading *inducta*, found in E², P, R, S, Bod, Pal, Eug, and m. *Induta*, found in E¹, is accepted by z and Agaësse-Solignac.

[92]See 11.12.16 *supra*.

[93]The Marsi, an ancient Italic people, lived in the mountains east of Rome. Their magicians were celebrated for snake-bite cures and were credited with a remarkable ability to charm snakes. Aug. may have had in mind the observation of Pliny the Elder, *Nat. hist.* 28.4.19 (LCL, p. 15, tr. Jones): "Many believe that by charms pottery can be crushed, and not a few even serpents; that these themselves can break the spell, this being the only kind of intelligence they possess; and by the charms of the Marsi they are gathered together even when asleep at night." See E. T. Salmon, OCD (2nd ed. 1970) *s.v.* "Marsi," 651–52; and Philipp, Pauly-Wissowa-Kroll 14.2 (1930) *s.v.* "Marsi," 1977–79.

[94]*Ad agnoscendam*, according to E, B, Bod, Pal, and z. Eug has *agnoscendum*. P, R, S, and m read *cognoscendam*.

[95]*Quo* in E, R, Eug, Bod, and z. P, S, Pal, and m read *quod*.

[96]Gen. 3.1.

[97]The theory of transmigration, which appears from time to time in Greek and Roman writers, is traced back to the teaching of Pythagoras: see John Burnet, *Greek Philosophy: Thales to Plato* (London 1914, rpt. 1943) 43. Aug. has already discussed and rejected the theory (7.9.13–7.11.17 *supra*). With regard to the position of Plato and the Neoplatonists in this matter, see n. 16 to Book 7 *supra*.

[98]Num. 22.28.

[99]Exod. 7.8–13.

[100]Rom. 11.33. The text of m omits *et scientiae* (*and knowledge*) inadvertently, it seems. These two words are in the passage in Romans, and they are in all of the MSS of z as well as in Bod and Pal, which I have consulted. Furthermore, Aug. himself quotes the text elsewhere with these words in it: see *Enarr. in Ps.* 7.1,35–36 (CCL 38.36; ML 36.98).

[101]Gen. 3.1–3.

[102]Ps. 102.18.

[103]Gen. 3.4–5.

[104]Gen. 3.6–7.

[105]When Adam and Eve disobeyed God's command, "their bodies contracted, as it were, the deadly disease of death" (9.10.17 *supra*); and desires according to the flesh became inevitable *in this body of death* (10.12.21 *supra*). Cf. St. Paul, Rom. 5.12 and 7.23–24.

[106]Rom. 7.23. The distinction between natural body (such as we have in this life) and spiritual body (such as we shall have at the resurrection) is based on 1 Cor. 15.44. Aug. has already explained that Adam had a natural body (6.19.30) which, if he had not sinned, would have been transformed *sine ulla morte . . . in aliam qualitatem* (9.3.6 *supra;* and cf. 9.10.17).

[107]Cf. Ambrose, *De paradiso* 13.63 (CSEL 32.323,6–7; ML 14.307B): "For how did Adam have his bodily eyes closed when he saw all the animals and gave each its name?"

[108]Gen. 2.23.

[109]Gen. 3.6.

[110]Gen. 3.7.

[111]Luke 24.31.

[112]The symbolism of the tree of life has been explained at greater length in 8.4.8 and 8.5.10 *supra.*

[113]In Aug. *sacramentum* is a sign that relates to divine things. See n. 20 on 8.4.8 *supra.*

[114]Ps. 29.8.

[115]Irenaeus, *Adv. haereses* 3.23.5 (SC 211.456–60 Rousseau-Doutreleau; MG 7.963), attributes Adam's action not merely to a feeling that he must cover parts associated with concupiscence, but to fear and confusion for having disobeyed and to a feeling that he was unworthy to appear in the sight of God.

[116]Gen. 3.8.

[117]*Spiritus* here, as in 12.9.20 *infra,* has a special meaning, namely, ". . . a certain power of the soul inferior to the mind, wherein likenesses of corporeal objects are produced."

[118]Gen. 3.8.

[119]Gen. 3.9.

[120]Aug. does not here develop the "mystical meanings" he sees in the difference between man and woman, but in *De Gen. c. Man.* 2.11.15 (ML 34.204) he says that woman typifies the sensitive or appetitive part of the soul, and man typifies the reason which rules the sensitive or appetitive part. Hence he sees in man and woman a symbol of the marriage between contemplation and action in the mind of each individual human being: see *De Trin.* 12.12.17 (CCL 50.371–73; ML 42.1007–8). Cf. Ambrose, *De par.* 15.73 (CSEL 32.331,8–9 Schenkl; ML 14.311): "Woman is a symbol of the senses, man a symbol of the mind."

[121]Gen. 3.10.

[122]Cf. Rom. 7.23.

[123]Rom. 1.21–22.

[124]Gen. 18.1.

[125]Gen. 3.11.

[126]Gen. 3.12.

[127]Gen. 3.13.

[128]Ps. 40.5.

[129]Cf. Ps. 128.4.

[130]Gen. 3.14–15.

[131]I follow the text of P, R, Pal, and m, which reads *verba sola. Sola* is omitted in E, S, Bod, and z.

[132]See 11.1.2 *supra.*

[133]See *De Gen. c. Man.* 2.17.26–2.18.28 (ML 34.209–10), where Aug. suggests that the breast and the belly of the serpent signify respectively pride and carnal desire; that earth signifies either sinners or the vice of curiosity; that the enmity is between the serpent and the woman (rather than the man) because woman is a type of the sensate part of human nature; and that the seed of the Devil is temptation to sin, whereas the seed of the woman is the fruit of good works.

[134]Gen. 3.16. In this chapter Aug suggests that the words spoken by God to the woman have a figurative meaning in addition to their obvious literal meaning. By sin man lost the liberty he had in Paradise, and as a result he is subject to human authority, a condition which was not intended by God for man in the state of original justice. The subjection, therefore, of the woman to the rule of her husband is a symbol of the beginning of an order

in which man would have dominion over man, a condition which in turn is a reminder of man's slavery to sin. Augustine's thinking on this subject is expressed in *De civ. Dei* 19.15: "This is what the natural order demands, this is how God made man. For He said: *Let him have dominion over the fish of the sea, the birds of the air, and all the creatures that crawl on the earth.* He wanted rational man, made to His image, to have dominion over irrational creatures only, not man over man, but man over beast. . . . The condition of servitude is rightly understood as placed upon man as a result of sin."

[135]See e.g. 6.25.36, 9.3.6, 9.10.17 *supra*.

[136]This statement seems to contradict the principle explained above in n. 134, but Aug. makes it clear that the service given in love in the state of original justice is worlds apart from the servitude enforced by the dominion of one human being over another human being as a result of original sin.

[137]Gal. 5.13.

[138]1 Tim. 2.12.

[139]Gen. 3.17–19.

[140]Gen. 3.20.

[141]Aug. does not propose any figurative meaning of these words here, but elsewhere (*De Gen. c. Man.* 2.21.31 [ML 34.212]) he suggests that the woman is called Life because she represents the sensate part of human nature which (as wife to husband) must be subject to reason and which through reason conceives by the Word of Life the burden of virtuous living; and that when this same sensate nature by the travail and pangs of self-denial resists evil habits and brings forth good habits, she is called the Mother of the Living.

[142]Gen. 3.21.

[143]Aug. has repeatedly insisted that he is writing a literal commentary and that he must first determine the literal interpretation of the facts narrated in the text. Once the reality of the event has been established, he feels that one is free to seek a figurative meaning, but that is not his preoccupation in this treatise. See e.g. 6.7.12 and 9.12.20 *supra*.

[144]Aug. does not here pursue the possibility of a symbolical

meaning in the garments of skin, but he has already in *De Gen. c. Man.* 2.21.32 (ML 34.212) said that they signify death (which is the result of Adam's sin). This interpretation (apparently suggested by the fact that an animal must die if his skin is to be used for clothing) is found in Gregory of Nazianzus, Gregory of Nyssa, Methodius, and Epiphanius. See passages cited by J. Pépin, "Saint Augustin et le symbolisme néoplatonicien de la vêture," *Aug. Mag.* 1.301.

[145]Gen. 3.22.

[146]Gen. 1.26.

[147]John 14.23.

[148]Gen. 3.22–23.

[149]Gen. 3.24.

[150]Gen. 3.24.

[151]In *De Gen. c. Man.* 2.23.35 (ML 34.214) Aug. has already conjectured a figurative meaning. The cherubim signify the fullness of wisdom, and the turning sword symbolizes temporal punishment. The sword is flaming because it burns away every tribulation and thus purifies the just. Hence no one can come to the tree of life except through endurance of tribulation and the fullness of wisdom.

[152]This is the opinion of Theophilus of Antioch: see n. 37 to Book 8 *supra.*

[153]Clem. Alex., *Stromata* 3.14 (GCS 52 [15].239,16–20 Stählin-Früchtel; MG 8.1193C–1196A).

[154]See 6.28.39 *supra.*

[155]1 Cor. 11.7.

[156]Gal. 3.28.

[157]1 Tim. 2.13–14.

[158]Rom. 5.14.

[159]1 Kings 11.4.

[160]Cf. Rom. 7.23.

[161]Adam's sin had its roots in a disorder of conjugal love, not in any disorder of sexual desire. See Agaësse-Solignac 49.558.

[162]At this point in the text the following clause is found in B, P², R, Pal, and m: *in illo modo quo illa* [al. *illam*] *potuit.* (The acc. *illam* occurs in R and Pal.) This clause (absent in E and Eug, the

two oldest witnesses to the text, as well as in S and Bod) appears to be a gloss, and I follow z and Agaësse-Solignac in omitting it.

[163]See 11.30.39 *supra*.

BOOK TWELVE

[1]2 Cor. 12.2–4.

[2]This is obvious from the fact that in introducing this subject Paul says that he must boast (v. 1).

[3]The third heaven is identified with Paradise and the vision of God. According to J. J. O'Rourke, JBC 2 (1968), "The Second Letter to the Corinthians," 289: "The first heaven was our earth's atmosphere; the second, the region of the stars; the third, the place where God dwells and is seen as he truly is." For a discussion of other opinions on the subject, see E.-B. Allo, *Seconde épître aux Corinthiens* (Études bibliques, Paris 1937) 306–7.

[4]In his *De cura pro mortuis gerenda* 11.13 (CSEL 41.642,12–643,4 Zycha; ML 40.602) Aug. says that during the time of his stay in Milan he appeared one night in a dream to Favonius Eulogius, a professor of rhetoric at Carthage, who was one of his former pupils. Aug. states that when he returned from Milan to Carthage, Eulogius told him of the dream and said that he had been puzzling over a passage in one of the rhetorical works of Cicero before retiring. "I explained the difficulty in the passage," Aug. says, "although in reality it was not I but my image, while I was unaware of this, for I was far across the sea either doing or dreaming something else, with not a thought in my head about the problems of Eulogius."

[5]This is a common experience of mystics. See e.g. St. Teresa's account in her *Life*, ch. 27, in *The Complete Works of St. Teresa of Jesus*, tr. E. Allison Peers (3 vols. New York 1946) 1.171.

[6]For the dish, see Acts 10.11; for John's vision, Apoc. 1.12–20; for the bones of the dead, Ezek. 37.1–10; for the seraphim and altar, Isa. 6.1–7.

[7]In Augustine's terminology "essence" and "substance" are synonyms. See *De moribus ecclesiae catholicae et de moribus Manichaeorum* 2.2.2 (ML 32.1346).

[8]Cf. Aug., *Solil.* 1.8.15 (ML 32.877): "Earth and light are visible, but earth cannot be seen unless it is illumined. Anyone, then, who understands the things that are taught in the various branches of learning admits without hesitation that they are true. But he must believe that they cannot be understood unless they are illumined by what we might call their own sun." A material object, then, is seen when a person with normal and healthy eyesight turns his gaze to the object, provided that the object is illuminated by light whose source is the sun. In intellectual vision the mind that is pure sees immaterial truth if it turns its gaze interiorly to the incorporeal world illuminated by God, the Light of the soul. This theory of illumination is based on Plotinus, *Enn.* 5.5.7, and is developed by Aug. under the influence of Scripture (especially John 1.9) in his *De magistro* and *De Trinitate*, Book 12. For a further explanation of this theory, which is essential to Augustinian philosophy, see Gilson 77–96 and Bourke 112–17 and 216–17.

[9]*Ostensio:* "vision." More precisely, the word means an image presented to the imagination in a vision. It is a postclassical word found in Tertullian, Apuleius, and the Vulg. It is used again in 12.20.42 *infra.*

[10]Exod. 33.9–11.

[11]Exod. 33.13: *Ostende mihi temet ipsum* (according to the OL, based on the LXX).

[12]Apoc. 13.1, 17.1, 17.3, 17.15, 17.18.

[13]"Spiritual" means "belonging to the spirit," but it should be noted that *spiritus* ("spirit") has a special meaning in this book, namely, ". . . a power of the soul inferior to the mind, wherein likenesses of corporeal objects are produced" (12.9.20 *infra*). It is, then, that part of the soul in which images are formed, and hence *spiritus* is often translated as "imagination." The notion of the word in this context, however, has been influenced to some extent by the Neoplatonic doctrine of the *pneuma,* and I have thought it well to translate the noun by the English "spirit" and the adjective by the English "spiritual." Aug. explains *spiritus* more fully in chs. 6–12 *infra.* See n. 164 *infra* and my article, "The Meaning of *Spiritus* in St. Augustine's *De Genesi,* XII," *Modern Schoolman* 26 (1948–49) 211–18. Cf. also Gilson 269–70 n.

1, Bourke 242–43, and G. Verbeke, *L'Evolution de la doctrine du Pneuma du stoicisme à s. Augustin* (Paris 1945) 371–72, 502, and *passim*.

[14]This theory is developed in ch. 32 *infra*.

[15]Here "spirit" does not have the special meaning it has elsewhere in this book explained in n. 13 *supra*. In this place it means an immaterial reality. The argument here is based on a disjunction which presents four possibilities:

1. *Body:*
   a) seen with the eyes of the body (in which case St. Paul would be just as certain about the manner of seeing as about the thing seen); or
   b) seen without the eyes of the body (but the possibility of this kind of vision is doubtful; and if it could occur, it probably would be so different from corporeal vision as to leave no doubt about the manner in which the object was seen).

2. *Spirit:*
   a) represented by an image of a body (in which case he would doubt just as much whether it was a body as whether it was seen in the body); or
   b) perceived immediately by the intellect (in which case it would be certain that it was not seen by the body).

The possibility of the case mentioned under 1b is so doubtful that Aug. relegated it to the end. This accounts for the curious order of the argument: the obvious possibilities are discussed first, and then a conceivable but unlikely case is taken up for the sake of completeness. The upshot of the argument is that St. Paul could not be at the same time certain about the object seen and doubtful about the manner of seeing. About what, then, does he doubt? If we suppose that the soul alone was carried away, there will remain a doubt about the relation that meanwhile existed between body and soul; and this is the doubt expressed in the words, *whether in the body or out of the body, I do not know.* Aug. explains this in the next paragraph.

[16]Both things: the object seen and the manner of seeing.

[17]*Etiam si possunt videri* is the reading of P, R, S, Bru, Val, Vat,

and m. The reading of z, *non possent*, is based on E. The reading *si possunt* seems to be demanded by the sense: see the analysis of the argument of this passage in n. 15 *supra*.

[18]Aug. modestly proposes a possible explanation of Paul's doubt, namely, that while his soul alone was carried away to the vision, the doubt centered around the relation that the soul meanwhile had to its body. Two kinds of relations are possible: (1) the soul remained united with the body as its form (and thus it was *in corpore*), while the mind was carried away in contemplation; (2) the soul was separated from the body (and thus it was *extra corpus*), so that the body during the vision lay in death.

[19]Aug. frequently uses the word *intentio* in describing the soul's activity in the body. See his *Epist.* 166 *De origine animae hominis ad Hieronymum* 2.4 (CSEL 44.551,7–9 Goldbacher; ML 33.722): "For the soul pervades the whole body that it animates not by a local distribution of parts (*non locali diffusione*) but by a vital impulse (*quadam vitali intentione*)." In addition to this vital impulse (*vitalis intentio*), the activity or influence by which the soul vivifies the body, there is the attention (*intentio*) of the soul, by which it observes the modifications of the sense organs: see 7.19.25 *supra*. In the case of a soul in ecstasy, the *vitalis intentio* continues while the other *intentio* is inoperative.

[20]The three types of vision here described are distinguished by the objects seen and the power of the soul that sees: bodies seen by the soul through the instrumentality of the body, likenesses of bodies seen by the spirit (see n. 13 *supra*), and immaterial realities seen by the intellect. For a discussion of these three types of vision, see Michael Schmaus, *Die psychologishce Trinitätslehre des hl. Augustinus* (Münsterische Beiträge zur Theologie 11, Münster 1927) 365–69; Cuthbert Butler, *Western Mysticism* (2nd ed. London 1926) 50–55; Matthias E. Korger, "Grundprobleme der augustinischen Erkenntnislehre: Erläutert am Beispiel von *de Genesi ad litteram* XII," *Recherches augustiniennes*, Supp. à la REAug 2 (Paris 1962) 33–57; Matthias E. Korger and Hans Urs von Balthasar, *Aurelius Augustinus, Psychologie und Mystik* (Sigillum 18, Einsiedeln 1960) 6–23; Bourke 242–46; Agaësse-Solignac 49.575–85.

[21]Zycha, following E, reads *corpora corporalia*, an obvious dit-

tography. All other MSS reported omit *corpora*. See Taylor "Text" 89.

[22]*Quo absentia corporalia cogitantur.* The verb *cogitare,* which comes from *co-agitare,* refers to the action by which the mind gathers together and considers images stored in the memory. See Augustine's explanation in *Conf.* 10.11.18 and again in *De Trin.* 11.3.6 (CCL 50.340; ML 42.988).

[23]A true image (e.g. Augustine's image of Carthage) is elsewhere called *phantasia;* a fictitious image (e.g. his image of Alexandria) is elsewhere called *phantasma.* See *De Trin.* 8.6.9 (CCL 50.281; ML 42.954–55); *De musica* 6.11.32 (ML 32.1180); *Epist.* 120.2.10 (CSEL 34.712,22–24 Goldbacher; ML 33.457).

[24]In intellectual vision there is no image like the object seen but not identical with it. In this respect intellectual vision differs from spiritual, for in the latter vision there is an image like the object but not identical. The imaginative representation of a man or a tree is similar to its object but not actually the real object. If I close my eyes and gaze upon these images, I am beholding images resembling their objects but not identical with them. But Aug. maintains that it is otherwise when the intellect gazes upon an immaterial object such as love (*dilectio*): one man may see it more clearly than another, but each sees the same object (*dilectio*). The man with the less perfect intuition does not see an image of *dilectio;* he sees *dilectio* itself less clearly.

[25]See especially 1.9.17, 1.16.31, 3.5.7, 4.7.13, 4.24.41, 5.16.34, 7.13.20, 7.19.25, 8.5.9, 8.16.34, 8.25.47, 8.27.49, 9.2.3–4, 9.14.25.

[26]See n. 13 *supra.*

[27]Col. 2.9.

[28]Religious observances of the Old Testament: *sacramenta veteris testamenti.* For the meaning of *sacramentum,* see n. 20 to Book 8 *supra.*

[29]1 Cor. 15.44.

[30]Ps. 148.8.

[31]Eccle. 3.21 (according to the OL).

[32]Cf. 3.20.30 *supra.*

[33]Eph. 4.23–24. The "new man" is human nature restored by grace.

[34]Col. 3.10.

[35]Rom. 7.25.

[36]Gal. 5.17.

[37]John 4.24.

[38]1 Cor. 14.14. Augustine's exegesis of πνεῦμα (spirit) in this passage is questionable. St. Paul is talking about a man with the gift of tongues, and he says that it is the man's spirit that prays (not his mind). The spirit, then, is here the soul in so far as it is under the influence of the Holy Spirit: see Max Zerwick, *Analysis philologica Novi Testamenti graeci* (Rome 1953) 384.

[39]1 Cor. 14.2.

[40]Cf. *De doctr. christ.* 2.1.1 (CSEL 80.33,23–25 Green; ML 34.35): "For a sign is a thing which, besides the impression it makes on the senses, causes something else to come into the mind as a consequence of itself."

[41]1 Cor. 14.16.

[42]1 Cor. 14.6.

[43]Gen. 41.1–32.

[44]Dan. 2.27–45; 4.16–24.

[45]1 Cor. 14.15.

[46]See 12.24.51 *infra*.

[47]It is not certain whom Aug. has in mind, but he may be thinking of Victorinus. See Pierre Hadot, *Porphyre et Victorinus* (2 vols. Paris 1968) 1.100.

[48]Jean Pépin, "Une curieuse déclaration idéaliste du 'De Genesi ad litteram' (XII, 10, 21) de saint Augustin, et ses origines plotiniennes ('Ennéade' 5,3,1–9 et 5,5,1–2)," *Revue d'histoire et de philosophie religieuses* 34 (1954) 373–400, argues that in this passage Aug. considers "intellectual" and "intelligible" as coextensive and so practically identical. But, although Aug. says that every intellectual being is intelligible, he considers dubious the proposition that every intelligible being is intellectual. For his present purpose he says that the third and highest type of vision can be called "intellectual" or "intelligible," but this does not thereby make him an idealist in the sense that he would identify being with the objects of thought. See Agaësse-Solignac 49.566–68.

[49]Matt. 22.39.

[50]For the senses as messengers, see n. 16 to Book 3 and n. 35 to Book 7 *supra*.

[51]This explanation is repeated in 12.24.51 *infra*. In describing the production of the image in the "spirit," Aug. uses a passive expression: *continuo fit imago eius in spiritu*. Thus he points out a temporal concomitance of the internal image with the modification that takes place in the eyes, and he avoids any expression that would imply that the sense object or the eyes exercise any causality on the soul.

[52]Dan. 5.5.

[53]By means of a bodily sensation: *per corporis sensum*. According to Augustine, a sensation is an impression made upon the body that of itself does not go unnoticed by the soul: *passio corporis per seipsam non latens animam* (*De quantitate animae* 25.48 [ML 32.1063]). The body does not in any way act on the soul in Augustine's theory of knowledge. Hence *per corporis sensum* denotes not the agent acting on the soul but the instrument used by the soul in acting on itself (or used by God or an angel in acting on it). It follows, then, that when Aug. says here, ". . . immediately the image of a corporeal object was impressed on his spirit," he means that it was impressed by the soul itself, the spirit acting on the spirit. See 12.16.32–33 *infra*.

[54]Dan. 5.25–28.

[55]Acts 10.11–16.

[56]Acts 10.17–28.

[57]The reading of E is *visione*, not *visiones* as z reports.

[58]See n. 19 *supra*.

[59]Belief in divination was widespread in the Roman world; it was part of the popular religion and was systematized in the official state religion. See W. Warde Fowler, *The Religious Experience of the Roman People* (London 1911) 292–313. Plato had no use for diviners (*Laws* 913b, 933d–e), and Aristotle argued that so-called prophetic dreams were not caused by God (*De divinatione per somnia*), but the Stoics upheld the popular belief in divination and incorporated it into their system: see R. D. Hicks, *Stoic and Epicurean* (New York 1910) 41. Divination is defined by Chrysippus as the power of "knowing, seeing, and explaining signs that are given by the gods to men" (Cicero, *De div.* 2.130). It was thought to take place through such means as ecstasy,

dreams, inspection of the entrails of animals, and the observation of unusual natural phenomena and other signs (*ibid.* 2.26–
27).

[60]*Ad hoc adiuvari* is the reading of all the MSS, and I believe
it should be followed. See Taylor "Text" 90.

[61]Aug. takes up every explanation that might be offered: the
aid might come from (1) nothing, or (2) a body, or (3) a spirit.
The first two explanations are too absurd to need refutation;
they are dismissed with a rhetorical question: the first (from
nothing) for obvious reasons, the second (from a body) for the
reason that body cannot act on spirit according to Aug. (see
12.16.32 *infra*). It only remains then (*proinde restat*) to take up the
third (from a spirit).

[62]When freed from the necessity of observing what takes
place in the body, the soul is able to turn its attention within
and gaze on images to which it would otherwise not attend. In
translating *quasi relaxetur et emicet eius intentio*, I have rendered
emicet by the English "is illuminated." Aug. explicitly asserts in
12.30.58 *infra* that in the spiritual order there is an incorporeal
light proper to it, illuminating the likenesses of bodies seen in
the spirit.

[63]2 Cor. 11.14.

[64]They deceive men by inducing an error in judgment. According to Aug., sensation is an appearance and as such is infal-
lible. The senses perceive what they perceive, and there is an
end of it; error with regard to sense objects is due to the judgment: see *Contra acad.* 3.11.26 (CSEL 63.66 Knöll; ML 32.947).
But it should be noted that Aug. did not deny the validity of
sense knowledge: see Charles Boyer, *L'Idée de vérité dans la philosophie de saint Augustin* (Paris 1920) 41–44.

[65]Again in 12.25.52 *infra*, Aug. insists that there can be no error in intellectual vision: "For either it [the intellect] understands, and then it possesses truth; or if it does not possess truth,
it fails to understand." The objects of intellectual vision are realities "which are not bodies and have no forms similar to bodies" (12.24.50); and Aug. immediately proceeds to give examples
of such realities, including the mind, good dispositions of the

soul, the intellect itself, the virtues, and finally God Himself. Again, in 12.31.59, he cites piety, faith, hope, and patience as examples of objects seen by the intellect under illumination. As Agaësse-Solignac 49.579 point out, when here and elsewhere Aug. gives examples of objects seen by the intellect illuminated by God, the examples are mostly of the ethical or theological order. When illumination is applied to objects known by experience involving sense knowledge, such as an arch or a man, it is not for the purpose of forming the concept but rather for the purpose of formulating the law of the object known or of defining what it must be: see Gilson 90–91.

[66]The impossibility of error in the soul's vision of eternal truth was maintained in the preceding paragraph. But the same soul can pass judgments on the changeable objects of sense, and these judgments are liable to error. But this sort of error is not harmful to the soul so long as the soul does not lose its vision of eternal truth. It is the *ratio superior* that knows eternal truth, and in this consists wisdom (*sapientia*); it is the *ratio inferior* that judges sensible things, and in this consists knowledge (*scientia*): see *De Trinitate* 12 and Gilson 115–26. The one is immune from error, the other is liable to it. But they are not two distinct faculties; they are two offices of the one mind or intellect.

[67]The imaginary objector asserts that a danger threatens good men when they are deceived into thinking that a secretly wicked man is good. Aug. denies that there is any real danger, provided that the mind falls into no error in regard to Goodness itself.

[68]Acts 12.7–9.

[69]Acts 10.14.

[70]The context seems to suggest that *qua*, which is found in Bru and m, is the correct reading. See Taylor "Text" 90.

[71]Image = *phantasia*. For the distinction between *phantasia* and *phantasma*, see n. 23 *supra*.

[72]In this chapter Aug. summarizes his theories on the psychology of sensation, which he has developed at greater length in 3.4.6–3.5.7, 7.13.20, 7.15.21, and 7.19.25–7.20.26 *supra*.

[73]See n. 51 to Book 1 *supra*.

[74]See 3.4.6 *supra*.

⁷⁵I think Aug. has nodded here. It is in Books 3 and 7 that he has treated this matter: see n. 72 *supra*. But it is true that in 4.34.54 he does mention the theory of light rays going forth from the eyes.

⁷⁶Cf. *De Gen. ad litt. inperfectus liber* 8.29 (CSEL 28/1.479,16–19 Zycha; ML 34.232), where Aug. asserts that heavenly bodies are far superior to bodies on this earth.

⁷⁷Cf. *De libero arbitrio* 3.5.16 (CSEL 74.103–4 Green; ML 32.1278–79).

⁷⁸The power that conjures up the images of bodies must be more excellent than even the starry heavens, for it is the immaterial soul itself.

⁷⁹The fundamental principle of Augustine's theory of sensation is here set down in syllogistic form. The same argument is put in a slightly different form in *De musica* 6.5.8 (ML 32.1167–68).

⁸⁰Aug. does not wish us to suppose that the eyes see, for he has already said in ch. 4 that the body does not see, but the soul through the body. Hence he means that the soul sees using the body as an instrument, but he puts the matter in popular terminology.

⁸¹From this statement and from 12.22.48 *infra*, it is evident that Aug. holds that angels, good and bad, can read our thoughts. With regard to the secrets of the heart (*secreta cordis*), i.e., our innermost thoughts that pertain to our future free acts, the Fathers of the Church generally held that angels could not read them: see G. Bareille, DTC 1 (1909) *s.v.* "Angéologie d'après les Pères," 1200–1201. Aug. here (ch. 17), in speaking of Job's temptation, and in *Enarr. in Ps.* 7.9 (CCL 38.42–43; ML 36.103–4), is in agreement with the traditional teaching. But in *Retract.* 2.56 or 2.30 (CSEL 36.167 Knöll; ML 32.643), he speaks of demons knowing the *dispositiones* of men, and he doubts whether they have this knowledge by their perception of some bodily change hidden to the human eye or by some direct spiritual means. It is not clear that by *dispositiones* he means what other theologians understand by *secreta cordis*, and in any case he is not positive in his assertions.

[82]For Augustine's opinion on the question of angels' bodies, see n. 60 to Book 2.

[83]Of this case, W. Montgomery, "St. Augustine's Attitude to Psychic Phenomena," *Hibbert Journal* 25 (1926) 101, says that there are many questions one would like to ask if it were possible to examine the witnesses. But he adds: ". . . the case makes a strong impression both of genuineness and of being accurately recorded. And once again the sobriety of the handling is remarkable."

[84]Among us: *apud nos*. When Aug. returned to Tagaste in A.D. 388, he set up a little monastery, and he moved it to Hippo when he became bishop. As the boy mentioned here was pursuing a life of sanctity at this time (see the last sentence of this chapter), it is quite likely that he was a novice in the religious community and that *apud nos* means "in our monastery."

[85]Following Val and m, I read *quale* where z reads *nisi*. See Taylor "Text" 90.

[86]Aug. argues that the continual production of images in the soul is more mysterious and marvelous than the extraordinary occurrence of an ecstasy. Seneca, *Nat. quaest.* 7.1, argues in a similar vein in considering the marvels to be observed in the daily movements of the heavens. The wonderful to be found in the ordinary is a favorite theme with Aug.: see e.g. *Sermo* 126.3.4 (ML 38.699).

[87]*Catus:* "shrewd," "wise," "sharp," a Sabine word, cognate with *acutus*, used by Cic., *De leg.* 1.16.45, with the apology, *ut ita dicam;* not common in classical prose. See TLL 3.623,18–73.

[88]In this chapter Aug. briefly explains the unusual changes that affect body and soul. He proceeds as follows:

I. Unusual changes in the body are caused by:
   A. the body, e.g. through humors or food, or
   B. the soul, e.g. through fear or shame.
II. Unusual experiences of the soul are due to:
   A. something in the body, as happens in dreams and delirium, or
   B. something in the soul, as when (though the body is normal) the mind is carried away to a vision:

1. the mind meanwhile using the senses of the body, or
2. the mind meanwhile being completely independent of the senses.

The visions described in IIB are caused by a spirit, either good or evil.

[89]This is explained in the next chapter.

[90]I read *male adfecti:* see Taylor "Text" 90–91.

[91]A man is not necessarily a prophet when he narrates a vision, even though the vision may have a prophetic meaning. But when his mind is illumined so that he can understand and explain the meaning of the vision, then he is truly a prophet.

[92]These are endowed with the gift of prophecy for the moment. Aug. distinguishes them from "true prophets" only because the gift of prophecy is not habitual in them.

[93]For the meaning of *intentio* in Aug., see n. 19 *supra.* For Augustine's physiology of sensation, see 12.16.32 *supra.*

[94]Aug. has a picturesque way of describing sensation. The attention of the soul is "sent forth" or "thrust out" (*exeritur*) by the soul to the object; or, as he says later in this chapter, it "presses on" (*nititur*) towards its object.

[95]Aug. has already described (12.2.3 *supra*) his awareness in dreams of the fact that he was dreaming. He also mentions that this awareness did not imply a full realization of the nature of the images seen in the dream.

[96]Joel 2.28 (Vulg.), 3.1 (Hebr.); Acts 2.17.

[97]Matt. 1.20.

[98]Matt. 2.13.

[99]The sense in which the body is a cause has been explained in 12.20.42–43 *supra.*

[100]John 11.50–51.

[101]*Utrum duodecim signa dicerentur:* lit. "whether the signs were called the twelve signs" or "whether the twelve signs were discussed" (among the astrologers). The *duodecim signa* are the twelve signs of the Zodiac: see Aratus, *Phaenomena,* tr. by Cicero, 317–19 (*Poetae latini minores* 1.21 Baehrens); cf. Cic., *De div.* 2.42.89.

[102]Aug. was familiar with these pagan festivals, having occa-

sionally witnessed them in his youth. See *De civ. Dei* 2.4, where he describes them and condemns them for the obscene rites performed on such occasions.

[103]On the question of angels reading our thoughts, see n. 81 *supra.*

[104]Aug. here speaks of images stored in memory from previous sense perceptions but not now the subject of thought until they are again summoned up.

[105]This includes both intellect (*intellectus*) and reason (*ratio*): "We are accustomed to reserve the word 'mind' for that which is rational and intellectual in us" (Aug., *De anima et eius origine* 4.22.36 [CSEL 60.414,13–14 Urba-Zycha; ML 44.545]).

[106]Cf. Gal. 5.22–23. There is a considerable discrepancy in the NT MSS in this enumeration. The Vulg. text of Wordsworth and White has: *caritas, gaudium, pax, longanimitas, bonitas, benignitas, fides, modestia, continentia.* The OL text of Cyprian has: *agape, gaudium, pax, magnanimitas, bonitas, fides, mansuetudo, continentia, castitas:* see H. F. von Soden, *Das lateinische Neue Testament in Afrika zur Zeit Cyprians* (TU 33, Leipzig 1909) 602.

[107]To this list of objects of intellectual vision, Aug., *De Trin.* 12.14.23 (CCL 50.376,54–58; ML 42.1010), adds the intelligible and immutable forms (*rationes*) of material bodies and even of the motions of bodies. See n. 65 *supra.* When Aug. includes God Himself among the objects of intellectual vision, he does not mean that the ordinary way of knowing God in this life is by an intuitive vision of His essence, though he holds that such a vision is possible by a special gift of God even in this life: see chs. 27 and 34 *infra.*

[108]"In whom" (*in quo*) is based on a misreading of the text; it should be "unto whom." See n. 7 to Book 4 *supra.* But Aug. gives the text a trinitarian interpretation, with *in quo* referring to the Holy Spirit: see *De fide et symbolo* 9.19 (CSEL 41.25,16–22 Zycha; ML 40.192).

[109]See chs. 6–23 of this book.

[110]For Augustine's active theory of sensation, see n. 16 to Book 3 *supra,* and n. 53 to Book 12.

[111]For the senses as messengers, see n. 35 to Book 7 *supra.*

[112]But Aug. holds that there may be a phantasm concomitant with the intuitive act of the mind: see 4.7.13 *supra*.

[113]1 Cor. 2.15.

[114]1 Cor. 14.15.

[115]Eph. 4.23.

[116]See 12.7.18.

[117]Aug. here gives some stock examples of alleged sense deception. References to examples such as these are found in pagan and Christian writers, including Aristotle, Diogenes, Laertius, Sextus Empiricus, Lucretius, Cicero, Seneca, Tertullian, Jerome, and Augustine, but some of Augustine's examples seem to be based on his own observation. See my article, "Remus Infractus," *Classical Bulletin* 28 (1951–52) 25–26.

[118]The text of z reads *duae lucernae species*. But *duae* (apparently a typographical error) should be corrected to *duas*. See Taylor "Text" 88. The supposition here is that light from the object strikes the eyes, and rays of light are sent out from the eyes towards the object (see 12.16.32 *supra*); but if these latter rays are not in focus, the object is seen double. Lucretius, 4.447–50, says that this phenomenon can be tested by pressing the finger under one eyeball.

[119]Aug. describes his own experience in 12.2.3 *supra*.

[120]Apoc. 1.10 ff.

[121]For Augustine's use of these words here, see 12.10.21 *supra*.

[122]For this use of the metaphor of a fountain, see Ps. 35.10 and Aug., *Conf.* 9.10.23.

[123]Cuthbert Butler, *Western Mysticism* (London 1922) 87, is of the opinion that Aug. is here describing a personal experience wherein he believed that he had been granted an immediate vision of "the brightness of the Lord."

[124]Exod. 19.18.

[125]Isa. 6.1.

[126]"Through a direct vision": per *speciem*. Cf. 2 Cor. 5.7 and Aug., *Sermo* 88.4 (ML 38.541): "Walk by faith (*per fidem*) so that you may come to vision (*ad speciem*). There will be no vision to give joy in the fatherland (*in patria*) unless a man is comforted by faith on the way (*in via*)."

[127]Aug. argues from Num. 12.6–8 that Moses was granted a vision of God's essence in this life.

[128]Exod. 19.18, 33.9.

[129]Exod. 33.13. *Ostende mihi temet ipsum* (*Show me Thyself*) is from the OL text, based on the LXX.

[130]Exod. 33.11.

[131]Exod. 33.17.

[132]Exod. 33.18.

[133]Exod. 33.20. According to Aug., this text implies two truths: (1) the vision of God properly belongs to the future life (*Epist.* 147 *De videndo Deo* 13.32 [CSEL 44.306,10–11 Goldbacher; ML 33.611]), and (2) God cannot be seen with the eyes of the body (*Sermo* 6.1 [ML 38.60]). But he argues below in this chapter that a man can, by a special favor of God, be granted this vision in this life, if his soul is temporarily withdrawn from the life of the senses.

[134]Exod. 33.21–23.

[135]Aug. develops his figurative interpretation of this passage in *Enarr. in Ps.* 138.8 (CCL 40.1994–96; ML 37.1789–90). Moses represents the Jewish people. The passing of God symbolizes the passing of Christ through the world. The hand of God, who was angry with the Jews, was placed over their eyes that they might not see the face of Christ, that is, His divinity. After His ascension, their eyes were opened and they saw Christ in His Church (*posteriora mea*). See also a brief reference to this exegesis in *Epist.* 147 *De videndo Deo* 13.32 (CSEL 44.306,11–17 Goldbacher; ML 33.611).

[136]Num. 12.6–8. So also in *Epist.* 147, *loc. cit.*, Aug. argues that this text proves that Moses was granted a vision of God's essence in this life.

[137]The same condition is laid down in *Epist.* 147.13.31.

[138]2 Cor. 12.2.

[139]Aug. argues that the third heaven is the vision of God face to face and that it is to be taken as identical with "paradise" in 2 Cor. 12.2–4.

[140]Matt. 5.8.

[141]Cf. 1 Cor. 13.12.

[142]The reading found in E and the other MSS which I have

examined, as well as in m, is *mundata*. *Mandata*, found in the text of z, is apparently a typographical error.

[143]Cf. 2 Cor. 5.6–7.

[144]Cf. Titus 2.12.

[145]Cf. Cant. 4.13.

[146]*Per formam futuri:* cf. Rom. 5.14.

[147]Vision of peace: see Jerome, *Liber de nominibus hebraicis* 73 (ML 23.873), and Eusebius, *Commentaria in Psalmos, In Ps. 75,* v. 3 (MG 23.880C–D). But the original meaning of the word was "foundation of Shalem": see L.-H. Vincent, *Dict. bibl., Supp.* 4 (1949) *s.v.* "Jérusalem," 898–99.

[148]Cf. Gal. 4.26.

[149]Cf. Rom. 8.24–25.

[150]Gal. 4.27. Hagar, the slave girl, as St. Paul explains, typifies the OT and the synagogue bringing forth children unto bondage. Sarah, the free woman, is a type of the NT and the Church bringing forth children that are free. *Many are the children of the desolate* (i.e., of the Church which was once sterile). The Church, says Paul, has now far more children than the woman who had a husband (the synagogue). For Augustine's explanation of this allegory, see *De civ. Dei* 15.2.3.

[151]Eph. 3.10. The MSS of Aug. read: *per ecclesiam multiformis sapientiae Dei.* For a discussion of the textual problem, see n. 62 to Book 5 *supra.*

[152]Scripture speaks of three heavens: (1) the atmosphere in which the birds and clouds move, (2) the starry firmament, (3) beyond these, the abode of God and the blessed. See J. Bellamy, *Dict. bibl.* 2 (1899) *s.v.* "Ciel," 750–51. Greek astromony, followed by Cic., *De republica* 6.17, divided the universe into nine spheres: heaven, which contains the fixed stars (and in Stoicism is identified with God), the seven spheres of the seven planets, and the sphere of the earth. Marius Victorinus, *In Epist. ad Eph.* 2.4.10 (p. 178,11–12 Locher; ML 8.1274B), says: "What heavens? Many say there are three; others say there are more; my opinion is that there are three." St. Hilary, *Tract. in Psalmum 135* 10 (ML 9.773–74), advises his readers not to be too tenacious of their opinions in the matter of the number of heavens.

[153]Aug., *De Gen. ad litt. inperfectus liber* 8.29 (CSEL

28/1.479,17–18 Zycha; ML 34.232), says: "In the realm of bodies there is nothing more excellent than a heavenly body." Arist., *De caelo* 268b–269a, arguing from the circular motion of the heavenly bodies, says that the heavens consist of a fifth substance more divine than the four elements. Cic., *De republica* 6.17, says that above the moon all things are eternal. Cf. Plato, *Tim.* 41a, a passage quoted by Aug. (in Cicero's translation), *De civ. Dei* 13.16.1. Sen., *Nat. quaest.* 7.1.6–7, notes two opinions: one that the stars are all fire, and the other that they have bodies of an earthly substance.

[154]*Luce quadam incorporali ac sua.* Cuthbert Butler, *Western Mysticism* (London 1922) 52, remarks: "This evidently is mere makeshift, and I do not know any other place where Augustine attempts to define the light wherein are seen the objects of spiritual or imaginary vision." It may be, however, that Aug. postulates this light only in the case of the supernatural manifestations that are mentioned in what immediately follows.

[155]In the preceding chapter a close parallel was shown to exist between the relative value of the objects of ocular vision and the relative value of the objects of spiritual vision. Now a similar scale of values is found in the objects of intellectual vision. Thus we have:

1. in ocular vision:
   terrestria and *caelestia;*
2. in spiritual vision:
   naturaliter visa and *demonstrata ab angelis;*
3. in intellectual vision:
   intellectualia in ipsa anima and *Deus illuminans.*

But all comparisons limp, and Aug. was not unaware of the fact that in intellectual vision there is an infinite gulf that separates the two objects, whereas in the other two kinds of vision the two classes of objects have merely a different degree of excellence in the same order.

[156]These are mentioned simply as examples of the objects of intellectual vision. For a longer list, see 12.24.50 *supra.*

[157]"Either in itself or in the light" (*vel in se vel in illo*): these words designate the two ways in which the intellect, illumined by God, who is the Light of the soul, can see the intelligible re-

ality which is the object of its vision. First, *in se:* this refers to
normal intellectual vision in this life, when divine illumination
makes the objects of the highest kind of vision present to the intellect so that it sees them "in itself." Second, *in illo [lumine]:* this
refers both (1) to the vision granted to the soul in the next life,
when it beholds the Light, which is God, face to face and in that
Light knows all else that it knows, and (2) to the extraordinary
case of the soul in this life caught up in ecstasy by a special grace
of God to see a fleeting vision of the Light and in it a vision of
the immaterial reality illumined by the Light. Gilson 93 proposes a different interpretation of this text. According to him,
in se refers to the knowledge that the just man has of the virtues
which he possesses in his own soul; *in illo [lumine]* refers to the
knowledge that the unjust man has of the virtues which he does
not possess in his own soul but can see only "in the light." Aug.,
therefore, according to Gilson, is explaining how a man who is
not just can have an intellectual knowledge of justice. But if this
statement is examined in the context of the whole chapter, I
think it is clear that the words *in se* and *in illo* are to be explained
as I have attempted to explain them above. Nevertheless, it is
true that Augustine's theory of illumination does provide for
the case of the sinner whose mind is enabled to see certain
truths under the influence of divine illumination. Although the
sinner turns away from the light, still he is touched by it. See
Aug., *De Trin.* 14.15.21 (CCL 50A.450; ML 42.1052).

[158]Aug. frequently speaks of God as the Light which illumines the intellect. But there are also passages where he is careful to distinguish between the Light that is God Himself and the
created light that God gives to the mind, as in *Contra Faustum*
20.7 (CSEL 25.541,27–29 Zycha; ML 42.372): ". . . this light is not
that Light which is God Himself. For this is a creature, and He
is the Creator; this is made, and He is the One who made it. . . ."
See also *Epist.* 147 *De videndo Deo* 17.44 (CSEL 44.318,16–319,1
Goldbacher; ML 33.616). Hence, when Aug. says that the Light
illuminating the soul is God Himself, we must understand him
to mean that the ultimate source of the light is God, who gives
a created light to the mind.

[159]From this statement it is clear that Aug. was not an ontolo-

gist. Nevertheless, the possibility of a supernatural vision of the uncreated Light (even in this life by a special gift of God) is stated in the last sentence of this chapter.

[160]"It sees above itself that Light in whose illumination ..." (*supra se videt illud quo adiuta*). The text of z is rendered obscure by the inadvertent omission of *illud*, which is in the MSS, including E (and no variants are cited by z).

[161]Aug. has just mentioned the frustration of the soul in its attempts to behold the Light which is God. In other words, there is no normal and natural vision of God in this life. Now he concludes by describing a supernatural vision or ecstasy in which the intellect *does* see the uncreated Light which is the source of all its illumination. Cf. Augustine's description of his own mystical experience at Milan before his conversion: "I entered, and I saw with the eye of my soul (such as it was), above this eye of my soul and above my mind, the unchangeable Light" (*Conf.* 7.10.16).

[162]The difficulty proposed here is briefly mentioned in 8.5.9 *supra*, but there the problem is left unsettled.

[163]"To an incorporeal one that is like the corporeal" (*ad incorporalia corporalibus similia*). These words imply that the objects of spiritual vision can have an objective, extramental, but noncorporeal existence. This is indeed puzzling. But we must bear in mind that *spiritus* in this book is described as having some of the functions of the Neoplatonic πνεῦμα, understanding, of course, that in Neoplatonism the *pneuma* is a tenuously material vehicle of the soul, whereas in Aug. the *spiritus* is the lower part of the immaterial soul in which sensible objects are represented. Plotinus, *Enn.* 4.7.4, says that there are thousands of soulless *pneumata;* and these beings, whatever they are, though they would be tenuously corporeal for Plotinus, may have suggested to Aug. the idea of an incorporeal region that is like the corporeal. In any case, Aug. makes it clear in the following paragraph that he is only proposing an opinion. See n. 13 to this book *supra*.

[164]In *Epist.* 162.3 (CSEL 44.514,7–19 Goldbacher; ML 33.706), Aug. rejects the Neoplatonic doctrine of the *pneuma*, an astral body that was said to serve as a vehicle of the soul, and denies

the theory that the soul at death takes some bodily entity from the body (*aliquod corpus ex corpore*). Porphyry, *Sententiae* 32 (29), had maintained that the *pneuma*, stamped with an image of the body, accompanies the soul at death. In Augustine's theory, there is no pneumatic body. Its function in man's cognition is taken care of by the *spiritus*, which is immaterial. But this *spiritus* has a likeness of the body (*similitudo corporis*), just as Porphyry's *pneuma* has an image (εἴδωλον) of it.

[165]"But it is brought to a realm that is spiritual in accordance with its merits" (*Ad spiritalia vero pro meritis fertur*). Aug. proposes the same theory in *De natura et origine animae* (*De anima et eius origine*) 4.18.26–27 (CSEL 60.405–7 Urba-Zycha; ML 44.539–41). However, in *De civ. Dei* 21.10.2, which is a later work (A.D. 413–26), he maintains that the fire of hell will be corporeal (*corporeus ignis erit*). But, he says, a spirit can suffer from a corporeal fire "in a mysterious but real way" (*op. cit.* 21.10.1); for just as spirit can be united with body to form a living man, so a spirit in a mysterious manner can be united with fire, not to give it life but to receive punishment from it.

[166]". . . by the likenesses of their senses" (*similibus sensibus*). The text is uncertain. The readings that I have found in the MSS and editions which I have examined are: *similibus* E[1], z; *al. similia* E[2]; *similia sensibus* P; *similis sensibus* R; *similibus sensibus* S, B, Bod, Nov, Lau[2], Pal, Bru, Agaësse-Solignac; *similitudinibus sensuum* Val, Vat, m. In an article in *Speculum* 25 (1950) 91, I defended the reading of m, *similitudinibus sensuum*. But since then the evidence I have discovered in Bod, Nov, Lau, and Pal, and the comments of Agaësse-Solignac 49.438–39 n. 17, have led me to believe that *similibus sensibus* is the more likely reading. In effect it comes to the same thing as *similitudinibus sensuum*, and the meaning of Aug. is clear. It is interesting to note that in *Epist.* 162.3 (CSEL 44.514,17–19 Goldbacher; ML 33.706) Aug. describes the soul as out of the body when it sees images in sleep (or when it is completely separated in death) and that he says it takes with it eyes that are not corporeal but like the eyes of the body (*quosdam simillimos* [*oculos*]). He says that in sleep it sees with these eyes objects that are not bodies but *similar* to bodies (*quibus visa simillima cernit in somnis, sed nec ipsa corporea*).

167Acts 12.7–9, discussed by Aug. in chs. 11 and 14 *supra*.

168In *De civ. Dei* 21.10.1 (a later work) Aug. holds the opinion that the fire of hell is material.

169Lucretius, 3.978 ff., says that the torments pictured as happening in the lower world are in reality the sufferings men undergo in this life, that Tantalus, Tityos, Sisyphus, and the daughters of Danaus are types of people tormented in this world, and that Tartarus, Cerberus, and the Furies are symbols of the punishment of crime here on earth.

170Among the wise men of whom Aug. is thinking he would surely include Plato and Vergil. See e.g. Plato, *Phaedo* 107d–108c, 113d–114b, *Phaedrus* 248e–249b, *Republic* 330d–e, 363d–e, 615a–616a, *Laws* 870d–e, 881a, and Verg., *Aen.* 6.268–901.

171See *Retract.* 2.50.4 or 2.24.2 (CSEL 36.160,13–16 Knöll; ML 32.640): "In Book 12 where I was speaking of hell, I think I should have said that it is under the earth rather than giving a reason why it is believed to be or said to be under the earth as if it were not so." See 12.34.66 *infra*.

172Aug. says the same thing in *Epist.* 187.2.6 (CSEL 57.85–86 Goldbacher; ML 33.834), but he seems to have been mistaken about the meaning of the scriptural word for hell or the lower world. It is called *sheol* in Hebr., ᾅδης (*Hades*) in Greek, and *infernus* or *inferi* in Latin. These words in Scripture designate a vast area below the earth where the departed, the just as well as the wicked, were before the resurrection of Christ, the wicked being in a special part of that area called Gehenna. See M.-J. Lagrange, *Évangile selon saint Luc* (2nd ed. Paris 1921) 445 n. 23. In *De civ. Dei* 20.15 Aug. does favor the opinion that before the redemption the souls of the just were *apud inferos* in a region completely separated from the torments of the damned, but he does not know of any scriptural support for this doctrine.

173Acts 2.24. This statement according to the commonly accepted Greek text should read: *God raised Him up, having loosed the pangs of death* (λύσας τὰς ὠδῖνας τοῦ θανάτου). The OL (followed by Aug. here) reads *solutis doloribus inferorum*, and the Vulg. substantially agrees with this, reading *solutis doloribus inferni*; and in this they follow a variant reading, ᾅδου for θανάτου, recorded among the variants in modern critical editions of the NT. Aug., therefore, was led to believe on the basis of a faulty text that the risen Christ released a certain number of sinners from the torments of hell: the original text does not bear that meaning. But it was, according to Aug., not a wholesale deliverance of the damned. Christ freed whom He willed (*quos voluit*): see *Epist.* 164.5.14 (CSEL 44.534,16 Goldbacher; ML 33.715).

[174]Cf. Phil. 2.10.

[175]Luke 16.22–23.

[176]Gen. 44.29. *Unto hell* (*ad inferos*) means "to sheol," the abode of the dead, not necessarily the place of torment. See n. 172 *supra*.

[177]2 Cor. 2.7.

[178]2 Cor. 12.2–4.

[179]Cf. Eccli. (Sirach) 40.28.

[180]Cf. Ps. 93.19.

[181]See Augustine's remark in *Retractationes* cited in n. 171 *supra*.

[182]Through the *spiritus* the soul in hell is afflicted by infernal images analogous to the material forces that act upon the dead body under the earth. The influence of Porphyry's doctrine on the *pneuma* is obvious here. See nn. 13, 163, and 164 to this book.

[183]See Arist., *De caelo* 269b, and Cic., *De nat. deor.* 2.116.

[184]This etymology assumes that "Hades" (ᾅδης) is derived from α privative and ἥδω, "I delight." The derivation of the word is uncertain: α privative with ἰδεῖν, "to see," has been suggested as a possibility (see LSJ [1940] *s.v.* Ἀιδης, a derivation that was commonly accepted in the time of Plato (see J. Burnet, *Plato's Phaedo* [Oxford 1911] 80).

[185]Luke 23.43.

[186]Wisd. 7.24.

[187]See Acts 10.10–12.

[188]With regard to the state of the soul in heaven before the resurrection of the body, Aug. is elsewhere less positive. Treating this point in *Retract.* 1.13.3 or 1.14.2 (CSEL 36.67,6–68,1 Knöll; ML 32.606), written a dozen years after *De Gen. ad litt.*, he does not definitely decide whether the souls of the just now in heaven enjoy the beatific vision in the same manner as the an-

gels do. But he has no doubt that the just are in a state of joy (*In Iohannis evang.* 49.10 [CCL 36.425; ML 35.1751]) and that they see God face to face (*Enarr. in Ps.* 119.6 [CCL 40.1783; ML 37.1602]).

[189]See Wisd. 9.15.

[190]See 1 Cor. 15.44.

[191]For Augustine's explanation of error, see 12.25.52 *supra.*

[192]See 1 Cor. 15.53.

[193]Aug. may have St. Ambrose in mind. See Ambr., *De paradiso* 11.53 (CSEL 32/1.309,21–310,6; ML 14.300).

[194]Chs. 7–10 of Book 12.

APPENDIX 1: TESTIMONIA

1. *Retractationes* 1.17 or 1.18 (CSEL 36.86,13–17 Knöll; ML 32.613): I had not published it [*De Genesi ad litteram inperfectus liber*] and had decided to destroy it because I had subsequently written a work in twelve books entitled *De Genesi ad litteram;* and although in that work one will encounter more questions raised than answers found, nevertheless the earlier work cannot be compared in any way with the later one.

2. *Retractationes* 2.50 or 2.24 (CSEL 36.159,10–160,18 Knöll; ML 32.640): At this same time [when he was writing *De bono coniugali* and *De sancta virginitate*] I wrote a commentary on Genesis in twelve books, starting at the beginning and continuing to the place where Adam was driven from Paradise and a flaming sword was set there to guard the way of the tree of life. But when I had written eleven books on the text up to this point, I added a twelfth in which I entered into a more thorough consideration of the question of Paradise. The title of these books is *De Genesi ad litteram* (*The Literal Meaning of Genesis*), that is, not according to allegorical meanings but according to the proper historical sense. In this work there are more questions raised than answers found, and of the answers found not many have been established for certain. The others that are not certain have been proposed for further study. I started these books after I had begun my work on *The Trinity*, but I finished them before I completed that treatise. In this review I have listed these treatises in the order in which I began them.

In Book 5 [5.19.38] and elsewhere in this work [9.16.30, 9.18.35], where I wrote of *the offspring to whom the promise had been given, and who had been placed through the angels in the hands of a mediator,* I was not faithful to the text of St. Paul, as I later discovered in consulting the better manuscripts, especially those in Greek. The statement made in the text about the Law has been taken as referring to the offspring by a translator's error in many Latin manuscripts. In Book 6 [6.27.38] my statement that Adam by his sin lost the image of God in which he was made must not be taken to mean that no trace of the image remained in him. Rather it was so disfigured that it needed renewal. In Book 12 [12.33.62] where I was speaking of hell, I think I should have said that it is under the earth rather than given a reason why it is believed to be or said to be under the earth as if it were not so. This treatise begins with the words: "Sacred Scripture, taken as a whole, is divided into two parts."

3. *Epistula* 159.2 (CSEL 44.499,17–500,4 Goldbacher; ML 33.699): This question [i.e., of images arising in the soul in sleep and in waking hours] is thoroughly examined in the twelfth book of the commentary which I wrote on Genesis, and my discussion there abounds in examples taken from my personal experiences and from reliable accounts of others. You yourself, when you read this essay, can judge my ability and my success in treating these matters; that is, if the Lord allows me to publish these books, after making whatever corrections are possible and appropriate, and thus to avoid more prolonged discussions which would mean a further delay for my friends who are waiting to see the treatise.

APPENDIX 2
THE OLD LATIN TEXT OF GENESIS USED BY AUGUSTINE

CHAPTER 1

1. In principio fecit Deus caelum et terram.

2. Terra erat invisibilis et incomposita, et tenebrae erant super abyssum. Et Spiritus Dei superferebatur super aquam.

3. Et dixit Deus, Fiat lux; et facta est lux.

4. Vidit Deus lucem quia bona est; et divisit Deus inter lucem et tenebras.

5. Et vocavit Deus lucem diem et tenebras noctem, et facta est vespera et factum est mane dies unus.

6. Et dixit Deus, Fiat firmamentum in medio aquarum et sit dividens inter aquam et aquam: et sic est factum.

7. Et fecit Deus firmamentum et divisit Deus inter aquam quae erat infra firmamentum, et inter aquam quae erat super firmamentum.

8. Et vocavit Deus firmamentum caelum. Et vidit Deus quia bonum est. Et facta est vespera, et factum est mane, dies secundus.

9. Et dixit Deus: Congregetur aqua quae est sub caelo in congregationem unam, et adpareat arida. Et factum est sic. Et congregata est aqua quae

1. In the beginning God created heaven and earth.

2. The earth was invisible and formless, and darkness was over the abyss. And the Spirit of God was stirring above the water.

3. And God said, "Let there be light," and light was made.

4. God saw that the light was good; and God separated the light from the darkness.

5. And God called the light Day and the darkness Night, and evening was made and morning made, one day.

6. And God said, "Let there be a firmament in the midst of the waters, and let it divide the water from the water." And so it was done.

7. And God made the firmament, and God divided the water that was below the firmament from the water that was above the firmament.

8. And God called the firmament Heaven. And God saw that it was good. And there was evening and there was morning, the second day.

9. And God said, "Let the water that is under the heaven be gathered together into one place, and let the dry land appear." And so it was

est sub caelo in congregationem
suam, et adparuit arida.

10. Et vocavit Deus aridam terram et
congregationem aquae vocavit mare.
Et vidit Deus quia bonum est.
11. Et dixit Deus: Germinet terra
herbam pabuli ferentem semen secundum genus et secundum similitudinem et lignum fructiferum faciens
fructum, cuius semen in ipso in similitudinem suam super terram. Et factum est sic.

12. Et eiecit terra herbam pabuli semen habentem secundum suum genus et secundum similitudinem, et
lignum fructiferum faciens fructum,
cuius semen eius insit secundum genus super terram. Et vidit Deus quia
bonum est.
13. Et facta est vespera, et factum est
mane, dies tertius.
14. Et dixit Deus: Fiant luminaria in
firmamento caeli, sic ut luceant super
terram in inchoationem diei et noctis
et ut dividant inter diem et noctem,
et sint in signa et in tempora et in
dies et in annos;
15. et sint in splendorem in firmamento caeli, sic ut luceant super terram. Et factum est sic.
16. Et fecit Deus duo luminaria mag-
na, luminare maius in inchoationem
diei et luminare minus in inchoationem noctis, et stellas.
17. Et posuit ea Deus in firmamento
caeli, sic ut luceant super terram,

18. et ut sint in inchoationem diei et
noctis, et ut dividant inter lucem et
tenebras. Et vidit Deus quia bonum
est.

done. And the water that is under
the heaven was gathered together
into one place, and dry land appeared.
10. And God called the dry land
Earth and the assembled waters Seas.
And God saw that it was good.
11. And God said, "Let the earth
bring forth the nourishing crops,
seed-bearing according to their kind
and their likeness, and the fruit tree
bearing its fruit, containing within itself its own seed according to its likeness upon the earth." And so it was
done.
12. And the earth brought forth the
nourishing crops, seed-bearing according to their kind and their likeness, and the fruit tree bearing its
fruit, containing within itself its seed
according to its kind upon the earth.
And God saw that it was good.
13. And there was evening and
morning, the third day.
14. And God said, "Let there be
lights in the firmament of heaven to
shine upon the earth, to establish day
and night, and to divide day and
night; let them serve as signs for the
fixing of times, of days, and of years;
15. let them be an ornament in the
firmament of heaven to shine upon
the earth." And so it was done.
16. God made the two great lights,
the greater light to establish the day
and the smaller light to establish the
night, and He made the stars.
17. And God set them in the firmament of heaven to shine upon the
earth,
18. to establish day and night, and to
divide light and darkness. God saw
that it was good.

19. Et facta est vespera, et factum est mane, dies quartus.
20. Et dixit Deus: Educant aquae reptilia animarum vivarum et volatilia super terram secundum firmamentum caeli. Et factum est sic.

21. Et fecit Deus cetos magnos et omnem animam animalium reptilium, quae eduxerunt aquae, secundum genus eorum, et omne volatile pennatum secundum genus. Et vidit Deus quia bona sunt.

22. Et benedixit ea Deus dicens: Crescite et multiplicamini et inplete aquas in mari, et volatilia multiplicentur super terram.
23. Et facta est vespera, et factum est mane, dies quintus.
24. Et dixit Deus: Educat terra animam vivam secundum genus: quadrupedia et reptilia et bestias terrae secundum genus et pecora secundum genus. Et factum est sic.

25. Et fecit Deus bestias terrae secundum genus, et pecora secundum genus, et omnia reptilia terrae secundum genus. Et vidit Deus quia bona sunt.

26. Et dixit Deus: Faciamus hominem ad imaginem et similitudinem nostram; et dominetur piscium maris et volatilium caeli, et omnium pecorum, et omnis terrae, et omnium reptilium repentium super terram.
27. Et fecit Deus hominem, ad imaginem Dei fecit eum: masculum et feminam fecit eos.
28. Et benedixit eos Deus dicens: Crescite et multiplicamini, et inplete

19. And there was evening, and there was morning, the fourth day.
20. And God said, "Let the waters bring forth the creeping creatures having life, and winged creatures to fly above the earth along the firmament of heaven." And so it was done.
21. And God created the great sea monsters and all the living creeping creatures which the waters brought forth, according to their kinds, and every winged bird according to its kind. And God saw that they were good.
22. And God blessed them, saying, "Increase and multiply and fill the waters of the sea, and let the birds multiply on the earth."
23. And there was evening and morning, the fifth day.
24. And God said, "Let the earth bring forth the living creature according to its kind: quadrupeds, and creeping things, and beasts of the earth according to their kinds, and cattle according to their kinds." And so it was done.
25. And God made the beasts of the earth according to their kinds, and cattle according to their kinds, and all creeping things of earth according to their kinds. And God saw that they were good.
26. And God said, "Let Us make mankind in Our image and likeness; and let them have dominion over the fish of the sea, the birds of the air, all the cattle, all the earth, and all the creatures that crawl on the earth."
27. And God made man, to the image of God He made him: male and female He made them.
28. And God blessed them and said, "Increase and multiply and fill the

terram, et dominamini eius, et princi-pamini piscium maris, et volatilium caeli, et omnium pecorum, et omnis terrae, et omnium reptilium repentium super terram.

earth and subdue it, and have dominion over the fish of the sea, the birds of the air, all the cattle, all the earth, and all the creatures that crawl on the earth."

29. Et dixit Deus: Ecce dedi vobis omne pabulum seminale, seminans semen quod est super omnem terram, et omne lignum quod habet in se fructum seminis seminalis. Vobis erit ad escam,

29. God also said, "See, I have given you every seed-bearing plant bearing its seed over all the earth, and every tree that has seed-bearing fruit. These will be food for you,

30. et omnibus bestiis terrae, et omnibus volatilibus caeli, et omni reptili repenti super terram quod habet in se spiritum vitae; et omne pabulum viride in escam. Et factum est sic.

30. for all the wild animals of the earth, for all the birds of the air, and for every creature that crawls on the earth and has the breath of life; every green plant I give you for food." And so it was done.

31. Et vidit Deus omnia quae fecit, et ecce bona valde. Et facta est vespera, et factum est mane, dies sextus.

31. And God saw all that He had made, and behold, it was very good. And there was evening and morning, the sixth day.

CHAPTER 2

1. Et consummata sunt caelum et terra et omnis ornatus eorum.

1. Thus the heavens and the earth were finished and all their array.

2. Et consummavit Deus in die sexto opera sua quae fecit, et requievit Deus die septimo ab omnibus operibus suis quae fecit.

2. And on the sixth day God finished the works He had made, and God rested on the seventh day from all the works He had made.

3. Et benedixit Deus diem septimum et sanctificavit eum, quia in ipso requievit ab omnibus operibus suis quae inchoavit Deus facere.

3. And God blessed the seventh day and made it holy, because on it He rested from all the works He had begun.

4. Hic est liber creaturae caeli et terrae. Cum factus est dies, fecit Deus caelum et terram

4. This is the book of the creation of heaven and earth. When day was made, God made heaven and earth

5. et omne viride agri antequam esset super terram, et omne fenum agri antequam exortum est. Non enim pluerat Deus super terram, et homo non erat qui operaretur terram.

5. and every green thing of the field before it appeared above the earth, and all the grass of the field before it sprang forth. For God had not rained upon the earth, and there was not a man to till the earth.

6. Fons autem ascendebat de terra et inrigabat omnem faciem terrae.

7. Et finxit Deus hominem pulverem de terra et insufflavit in faciem eius flatum vitae. Et factus est homo in animam viventem.

8. Et plantavit Deus paradisum in Eden ad orientem et posuit ibi hominem quem finxerat.

9. Et eiecit Deus adhuc de terra omne lignum pulchrum ad aspectum et bonum ad escam, et lignum vitae in medio paradiso, et lignum scientiae dinoscendi bonum et malum.

10. Flumen autem exiit de Eden, quod inrigabat paradisum et inde divisum est in quattuor partes.

11. Ex his uni nomen est Phison; hoc est quod circuit totam terram Evilat, ubi est aurum;

12. aurum autem terrae illius bonum, et ibi est carbunculus et lapis prasinus.

13. Et nomen flumini secundo Geon; hoc est quod circuit totam terram Aethiopiam.

14. Flumen autem tertium Tigris; hoc est quod fluit contra Assyrios. Flumen autem quartum Euphrates.

15. Et sumsit Dominus Deus hominem quem fecit et posuit eum in paradiso ut operaretur et custodiret.

16. Et praecepit Dominus Deus Adae, dicens: Ab omni ligno quod est in paradiso escae edes;

17. de ligno autem cognoscendi bonum et malum non manducabitis de illo. Qua die autem ederitis ab eo, morte moriemini.

18. Et dixit Dominus Deus: Non bonum est esse hominem solum; fa-

6. But a spring rose out of the earth and watered all the face of the earth.

7. And God formed man of dust from the earth and breathed into his face the breath of life. And man was made a living being.

8. And God planted a garden in Eden in the east, and there He put the man whom He had formed.

9. And again from the earth God made to grow every tree that is pleasant to the sight and good for food, the tree of life also in the midst of the garden, and the tree of the knowledge of good and evil.

10. And a river which watered Paradise went out of Eden, and from there it was divided into four parts.

11. The name of one is Phison; this is the one that flows around all the land of Evilat, where there is gold;

12. and the gold of that land is good, and carbuncle and emerald are found there.

13. And the name of the second river is Geon: it is the one that flows around the whole land of Ethiopia.

14. And the name of the third river is Tigris, which flows by the land of the Assyrians. And the fourth river is the Euphrates.

15. And the Lord God took the man whom He made and placed him in Paradise to cultivate and guard it (or him).

16. And the Lord God commanded Adam, saying, "You may eat of every tree that is in Paradise;

17. but of the tree of the knowledge of good and evil you shall not eat. In the day that you eat of it you shall die."

18. And the Lord God said, "It is not good that the man should be alone.

ciamus illi adiutorium secundum ipsum.

19. Et finxit Deus adhuc de terra omnes bestias agri et omnia volatilia caeli et adduxit illa ad Adam ut videret quid vocaret illa; et omne quodcumque illud vocavit Adam animam vivam, hoc est nomen illius.

20. Et vocavit Adam nomina omnibus pecoribus et omnibus volatilibus caeli et omnibus bestiis agri. Adae autem non est inventus adiutor similis ipsi.

21. Et iniecit Deus mentis alienationem super Adam, et obdormivit, et sumsit unam de costis eius et adimplevit carnem in locum eius.

22. Et aedificavit Dominus Deus costam quam accepit de Adam in mulierem, et adduxit eam ad Adam.

23. Et dixit Adam: Hoc nunc os ex ossibus meis et caro de carne mea; haec vocabitur mulier quoniam ex viro suo sumta est.

24. Et propter hoc relinquet homo patrem et matrem et conglutinabitur ad uxorem suam, et erunt duo in carne una.

25. Et erant ambo nudi Adam et mulier eius et non pudebat illos.

Let us make for him a helper like himself."

19. And again God formed from the earth all the beasts of the field and all the birds of heaven and brought them to Adam to see what he would call them. And whatever Adam called a living creature, that is its name.

20. And Adam gave names to all the cattle and to all the birds of heaven and to all the beasts of the field. But for Adam there was not found a helper like himself.

21. And God cast Adam into an ecstasy, and as Adam slept, God took one of his ribs and in its place put flesh.

22. And the Lord God made the rib which He took from Adam into a woman and brought her to Adam.

23. And Adam said, "This now is bone of my bones and flesh of my flesh; she shall be called Woman because she has been taken out of the Man.

24. For this reason a man shall leave his father and mother and shall cleave to his wife; and they shall be two in one flesh."

25. Adam and his wife were both naked, and they were not ashamed.

CHAPTER 3

1. Serpens autem erat prudentissimus omnium bestiarum quae sunt super terram quas fecit Dominus Deus. Et dixit serpens mulieri: Quid quia dixit Deus: Non edetis ab omni ligno paradisi?

2. Et dixit mulier serpenti: A fructu ligni quod est in paradiso edemus;

1. Now the serpent was the most subtle of all the wild creatures which the Lord God had made on the earth. And the serpent said to the woman, "Why did God say, 'You shall not eat of every tree in paradise'?"

2. And the woman said to the serpent, "We may eat of the fruit of trees that are in Paradise;

3. de fructu autem ligni quod est in medio paradisi dixit Deus: Non edetis ex eo neque tangetis illud ne moriamini.

4. Et dixit serpens mulieri: Non morte moriemini.

5. Sciebat enim Deus quoniam qua die manducaveritis de eo aperientur vobis oculi et eritis tamquam dii, scientes bonum et malum.

6. Et vidit mulier quia bonum lignum in escam et quia placet oculis videre et decorum est cognoscere, et sumens de fructu eius edit et dedit et viro suo secum, et ederunt.

7. Et aperti sunt oculi amborum, et agnoverunt quia nudi erant; et consuerunt folia fici et fecerunt sibi campestria.

8. Et audierunt vocem Domini Dei deambulantis in paradiso ad vesperam et absconderunt se Adam et mulier eius a facie Domini Dei in medio ligni paradisi.

9. Et vocavit Dominus Deus Adam et dixit illi: Adam, ubi es?

10. Et dixit ei: Vocem tuam audivi deambulantis in paradiso et timui, quia nudus sum, et abscondi me.

11. Et dixit illi: Quis nuntiavit tibi quia nudus es, nisi a ligno quod praeceperam tibi tantum ne ex eo manducares ab eo edisti?

12. Et dixit Adam: Mulier quam dedisti mecum haec mihi dedit a ligno, et edi.

13. Et dixit Dominus Deus mulieri: Quid hoc fecisti? Et dixit mulier: Serpens seduxit me, et manducavi.

3. but regarding the fruit of the tree in the middle of Paradise, God said, 'You shall not eat of it nor shall you touch it, lest you die.' "

4. And the serpent said to the woman, "You will not die the death.

5. For God knew that on the day on which you would eat of it your eyes would be open, and you would be like gods, knowing good and evil."

6. And the woman, seeing that the tree was good for food and pleasing to the eyes and a delight to behold, took of its fruit and ate; and she gave some to her husband, and they ate.

7. Then the eyes of both of them were opened, and they perceived that they were naked; and they sewed fig leaves together and made themselves loincloths.

8. And they heard the voice of the Lord God as He walked in Paradise in the late afternoon, and then Adam and his wife hid themselves from the face of the Lord God amidst the trees of Paradise.

9. And the Lord God called Adam and said to him, "Adam, where are you?"

10. Adam replied, "I heard Thy voice as Thou wert walking in Paradise, and I was afraid because I am naked, and I hid myself."

11. The Lord God said to him, "Who told you that you were naked but that you have eaten of the one tree whereof I had commanded you not to eat?"

12. And Adam replied, "The woman whom Thou gavest to be my companion gave me fruit of the tree, and I ate."

13. Then the Lord God said to the woman, "What is this that you have done?" And she replied, "The serpent beguiled me, and I ate."

14. Et dixit Dominus Deus serpenti:
Quia fecisti hoc, maledictus tu ab
omnibus pecoribus et ab omnibus
bestiis quae sunt super terram. Super
pectus tuum et ventrem tuum ambu-
labis et terram edes omnes dies vitae
tuae.
15. Et inimicitias ponam inter te et
inter mulierem et inter semen tuum
et inter semen eius. Ipsa tibi servabit
caput, et tu servabis eius calcaneum.

16. Et mulieri dixit: Multiplicans
multiplicabo tristitias tuas et gemi-
tum tuum. In tristitiis paries filios, et
ad virum tuum conversio tua, et ipse
tui dominabitur.

17. Adae autem dixit: Quia audisti
vocem mulieris tuae et edisti de ligno
de quo praeceperam tibi de eo solo
non edere, maledicta terra in operibus tuis; in tristitiis edes illam omnes
dies vitae tuae;

18. spinas et tribulos edet tibi, et
edes fenum agri.

19. In sudore faciei tuae edes panem
tuum, donec convertaris in terram,
ex qua sumtus es, quia terra es et in
terram ibis.

20. Et vocavit Adam nomen mulieris
suae "Vita" quoniam haec est mater
omnium viventium.
21. Et fecit Dominus Deus Adam et
mulieri eius tunicas pelliceas et in-
duit eos.
22. Et dixit Dominus Deus: Ecce
Adam factus est tamquam unus ex
nobis in cognoscendo bonum et malum. Et nunc ne aliquando extendat
manum et sumat de ligno vitae et
edat et vivat in aeternum.

14. The Lord God said to the serpent, "Because you have done this,
cursed are you above all cattle and
above all beasts upon the earth. Upon
your breast and your belly shall you
go, and earth shall you eat all the
days of your life.
15. And I will put enmity between
you and the woman and between
your seed and her seed. She will lie
in wait for your head, and you will
lie in wait for her heel."
16. To the woman He said, "I will
greatly multiply your sorrows and
your anguish. With sorrows you shall
bring forth children, and you shall be
subject to your husband, and he shall
rule over you."
17. And to Adam He said, "Because
you have listened to the voice of your
wife and have eaten of the one tree
whereof I commanded you not to eat,
cursed is the earth in your works. In
sorrow you shall eat of it all the days
of your life;
18. thorns and thistles it shall bring
forth for you, and you shall eat the
crops of the field.
19. In the sweat of your face you
shall eat your bread until you return
to the earth from which you have
been taken, for you are earth and
unto earth you shall return."
20. Adam called his wife's name
"Life," for she is the mother of all
the living.
21. And the Lord God made garments of skin for Adam and his wife
and clothed them.
22. And the Lord God said, "Behold,
Adam has become like one of Us,
knowing good and evil. And now let
him not put forth his hand and take
of the fruit of the tree of life and eat
and live forever."

23. Et dimisit illum Dominus Deus de paradiso voluptatis operari terram ex qua sumtus est.

24. Et eiecit Adam et conlocavit eum contra paradisum voluptatis, et ordinavit Cherubim et flammeam rhomphaeam quae vertitur custodire viam ligni vitae.

23. And the Lord God sent him forth from the Paradise of pleasure to till the earth from which he was taken.

24. He drove Adam out and placed him over against the Paradise of pleasure, and He placed the cherubim and a flaming sword turning every way to guard the path to the tree of life.

INDICES

1. OLD AND NEW TESTAMENTS

2. GENERAL INDEX

343

256n37; reason for name, 41–42,
55–56, 256n38; mentioned, 38, 67
Tree of Life, the: the guarding of,
134, 299n151; man separated from
173–74; the meaning of, 39–41,
296n112; the power of, 39; as a
sacrament, 164; mentioned, 38
Trinity, the: as Creator, 88; as
eternal, 63, 73; as immutable, 63,
73; and the nature of God, 4; and
the substance of God, 4; and time
and space, 73; mentioned, 172–73,
264n123
Tromp, Sebastian, 293n65
Tyconius, 293n65, 293n72, 293n74,
293n79
Tyre, 156

V
Varro, 243n9
Verbeke, G., 248n36
Victorinus, Marius, 291n50, 305n47,
315n152
Vigilius, Pope, 281n58
Vincent, L. H., 315n147
Vindicianus, 247n32
Virgil, 256n41, 320n170
Virgin, the, 69, 91–92, 120–21,
123–24, 209, 283n85, 286n1
Virginity, 77, 78, 268n33
Visions: causes of, 205–06, 211–12;
and dreams, 180, 204–05, 206–09;
meanings of, 209–11; perfection of,
229–30; types of, 185–95, 263n111,
303n20, 305n48; mentioned:
264n112, 301n8, 316n157
—corporeal: and deception, 196–97,
198; defined, 186–88; and the Devil,
198; perfection of, 229–30;
relationship to other types of
vision, 191–95, 213–16, 219
—intellectual: and deception, 196–97,
307–08n65; defined, 186, 190–91;
perfection of, 229–30; relationship

to other types of vision, 191–93,
213–16, 219; mentioned, 301n8,
304n24, 305n48, 312n107, 316n155
—spiritual: causes of, 208–09; and
deception, 196–98; defined, 186,
188–90; and the Devil, 198; and
divine guidance, 216; perfection of,
229–30; relationship to other types
of vision, 191–95, 213–16, 219,
318n163
Voltaire, 288n27
von Balthasar, Hans Urs, 303n20
von Soden, H. F., 312n106

W
Whitfield, B. G., 270n47
Wilcox, C. T., 269n36
Will, the: of the Devil, 152–53,
154–55, 159; of God, 53, 142; of
man, 63–64, 87; and the order of
nature, 64; mentioned, 19, 62
Wisdom: Christ as, 39; and cunning,
136; and the Tree of Life, 39–41,
164
Water, the element of, 19, 21–22,
246n27, 248n37
Woman: Augustine and, 267n24; as
the glory of man, 175; the soul of,
96–97, 99, 108; and submission to
man, 297n134. See also Eve
Word, the: of God, 37, 48, 101; made
flesh, 55
World Soul, the, 6, 243–44n9
Wright, A. G., 278n22

Y
Yahweh. See God
Yahwist tradition, the, 258n60

Z
Zarephath, the widow of, 255n34
Zeno the Stoic, 246n30
Zerwick, Max, 305n38
Zodiak, the, 311n101

ANCIENT CHRISTIAN WRITERS

The Works of the Fathers in Translation
Founded by J. QUASTEN and J. C. PLUMPE

Now edited by
J. QUASTEN • W. J. BURGHARDT • T. C. LAWLER